THE ART OF ASSEMBLY LANGUAGE PROGRAMMING VAX-11™

J. F. Peters III

Saint John's University
Collegeville, Minnesota

RESTON PUBLISHING COMPANY, INC.
A Prentice-Hall Company
Reston, Virginia

To my family and students

Library of Congress Cataloging in Publication Data

Peters, James F.
  The art of assembly language programming VAX-11.

  Includes bibliographies and index.
  1. VAX-11 (Computer)—Programming.   2. Assembler
language (Computer program language)   I. Title.
QA76.8.V37P48   1985   001.64′2   84-13283
ISBN 0-8359-0184-X

Copyright © 1985 by
Reston Publishing Company
A Prentice-Hall Company
Reston, Virginia 22090

10   9   8   7   6   5   4   3   2   1

Printed in the United States of America.

CONTENTS

18. RECURSION   541

19. FLOATING POINT NUMBERS   565

APPENDICES

SELECTED SOLUTIONS

ANSWER KEY

INDEX

PREFACE

The term *art* refers to the skill that comes with knowledge and practice. It also means knowing how to apply the principles of a subject. In this sense, art has something to do with *imitation*, but it also involves *design*. That is to say, skill, in part, comes from a sense of design, a sense of structure, and a perception of form, and it enables an individual to mold scattered bits and pieces into pleasing and meaningful forms.

These remarks apply to assembly language programming just as much as to other activities. Assembly language programming requires a sense of structure, of striving for a technique that will make program texts meaningful. Yet this is less likely to occur in assembly language programs than anywhere else. Why? Assembly language programs tend to be cumbersome because they consist of so many bits and pieces. It takes considerable skill to fit the pieces together so that an assembly language program will make sense and not just produce correct results.

This text was written with the idea that skill in programming on the assembly language level is derived from the imitation of model programs. With this in mind, lots of model programs—in other words, lots of examples—are given in this text. It helps a great deal in the beginning to have assembly language programs to imitate. As much as possible, this text presents sample programs with the principles of structured programming in mind.

At the same time, new assembly language programmers should be encouraged to design their own instructions. New instructions can be created, designed, and implemented using procedures like those found in VAX-11 Macro. New instructions can also be developed using macros. The combination of procedures and macros offers a powerful incentive to invent, to design, and to learn the art of assembly language programming.

Basically, this book is about learning to produce an assembly language program. The presentation, however, will not be restricted to programming, but will also include a look at the organization of a typical computer. Assembly language programming is, in fact, concerned with the way memory is organized inside a computer. As a result, an assembly language programmer needs to get very close to the pulse of a machine, its registers, its methods of managing memory, its execution cycles, and its native instruction repertoire.

Because both machine organization and assembly language programming are central topics here, this text contains two levels. One deals with machine organization, both generic concepts as well as machine-specific features. The other deals with methods of translation used by assemblers, both the generic notion of assembly in terms of the two-pass or one-pass method, and VAX-11 assembly language programming specifics. In addition, some attention is given to the generic notion of macro assembly as well as the specifics of VAX-11 Macro assembly.

The overall aim of this book is to give the reader a broad perspective of the demands of computer systems in general so that he or she will know what it takes to write an assembly program on any machine, whether it is a VAX-11 or not.

It should be pointed out, however, that assembly programming on a VAX-11 is a pleasure. Its instruction repertoire is rich, broadly conceived, workable, and useful. It is a good system to learn on.

Note to the Student

You will probably find the selected solutions to the exercises and lab projects helpful. To try out the programs in the chapters or in the selected solutions, you will want to set up a copy of the procedure library called IO.MAR and the macro library called PAS.MAR. These appear in Appendix C. To do this, use an editor to type them into a machine (a VAX-11, any model). Appendix C also contains instructions for setting up the .OLB and .MLB versions of these libraries. The .OLB and .MLB versions each take a minimum of 100 blocks disk storage. The source texts for these libraries take considerably less. Each time you finish using these libraries, delete the .OLB and .MLB files to make room for libraries in your account. You might want to consider setting up a co-op so that these libraries can be shared, rather than keeping a copy of each library in each person's account. You can write many programs without these libraries, but they will make life easier for you.

Each chapter ends with a summary and a review quiz, which you will probably find helpful in preparing for exams. References are also provided that you can follow up for further study.

Finally, I would appreciate any suggestions you might have. Please let me know if you would like to see additional or different kinds of material in the summaries, examples, or selected solutions. I sincerely hope that you will write to me if you have any questions, sample programs, corrections, or suggestions to offer. You can reach me by writing to:

> Compter Science Department
> St. John's University
> Collegeville MN 56321

Note to the Instructor

Copies of all the programs and libraries are available on 5¼, RX50 diskettes used on Rainbow-100s or on a DECMATE. These can be purchased by writing to me at the above address.

The libraries in Appendix C will be useful. Appendix C also contains instructions for setting up these libraries in a group account and using the

set protection

command, which will make it possible for users in other accounts to link their programs with these libraries and copy them into their own account. It is a good idea to allow them to be read by others, but not modified by others. In other words, leave libraries write-protected, read-unprotected.

You will probably also find the trick with ⟨CTRL⟩ ⟨Y⟩ described in chapter 3 useful. This is something we discovered in trying to determine what a VAX-11/780 was doing with our programs. Chapter 3 also describes how to set up an infinite loop, which will make it easier to get a memory dump before the processor clears memory. The great advantage of including an infinite loop inside small, beginning programs without any I/O is that it enables you to see a memory dump, to see the results of the processor operations, easily and quickly.

In using this book, you might want to try the following scheme:

Topic	Class time
1. Assign chapters 1 and 2 to be read.	0 hours
2. Start with chapter 3 (use ⟨CTRL⟩ ⟨Y⟩ to get started without the libraries).	2 hours
3. Illustrate the uses of the macros in chapter 4. (You will need both PAS.MAR and IO.MAR in Appendix C for this.)	1 hour

Note: Try creating simple macros *without* arguments to demonstrate further the idea of inventing new instructions. R. Pattis, *Karel the Robot: A Gentle*

Introduction to the Art of Programming, is helpful, here. Try

```
Begin:      .word
            drawrobot
            drawstairs
            drawarrow
            drawbeep
            $exit_s
            .end begin
```

without any reference to the macros themselves, at first, to draw a picture like the following one:

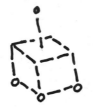

Then create the macros to *define* the instructions, using the chapter I/O macros.

4.	Control structures, chapter 5.	2 hours
5.	Stacks and queues, chapter 6 (intensive) (At this point, it is helpful to look back at the material on base conversions in chapter 2).	3 hours
6.	Closed routines, chapter 7.	1.5 hours
7.	Procedures, chapters 8 and 9 (intensive).	3 hours
8.	Assign chapter 10 to be read.	0 hours
9.	Chapter 11 (intensive; refer back to extended precision products in chapter 2).	2 hours
10.	Chapter 12.	1 hour
11.	Chapter 13 (assign to be read).	0 hours
12.	Chapter 14 (random numbers).	1.5 hours
13.	Chapter 15 (assign to be read).	0 hours
14.	Chapters 16–17.	3 hours
15.	Chapter 18.	1 hour
16.	Chapter 19 (intensive).	2 hours

Organization of the Text

Exercises are easier than lab projects. They take less time. They are more appropriate for individual work. Lab projects are designed with a team approach in mind.

Because QIO takes considerable time to master, I/O macros are used in the beginning to make it easy to develop programs that print results and that can obtain data from a keyboard. By chapter 9, it becomes possible to deal with QIO directly.

Chapters 1–8 are IO macro-dependent. The IO macros used in these chapters facilitate the use of the IO procedures in Appendix C. Chapters 9–19 rely on the use of both new and old IO procedures as well as other procedures. Chapters 15–19 demonstrate how to create macros with arguments.

Acknowledgments

I wish to thank the following persons for their help and criticisms in preparing this text: Sue Rosenberger, Mark Tinguely, Ken Hortsch, Terri Hager, Lori Kaufenberg, Geoff Brunkhorst, Paul St. Michel, Diana Messina, Patrick Holmay, all of whom are at St. John's University, Henry A. Etlinger at the Rochester Institute of Technology, and Evalyn Schoppet at Reston Publishing Company.

1.
MACHINE ORGANIZATION

Almost all conventional modern computers are based upon the "stored program computer" concept generally credited to the mathematician John von Neumann (1903–1957).

—John J. Donovan, *Systems Programming*

1.0
AIMS

- Introduce some commonly used terms and symbols.
- Explain commonly used design concepts that originated with the von Neumann machine.
- Describe the central processor, control function, memory and execution cycle on a modern computer.
- Look at some of the features of VAX-11 computer organization.
- Introduce the VAX-11 instruction set.

1.1
INTRODUCTION

This chapter gives an overview of computer structures, particularly the key features that need to be examined by anyone beginning to study an assembly language. Since an assembly language programmer is interested primarily in the design of a computer's instruction set, this chapter looks at some of the features of VAX-11 instructions: how they are stored in memory, the data types that can be used with instruction operands, available registers, the role of the processor status register in conditional branches, and so on.

The chapter opens with an explanation of some basic terms followed by a description of the design concepts for a computer proposed by J. von Neumann in 1946. These concepts have had far-reaching influence in the organization and implementation of modern computers.

Next, the discussion turns to the computer structures on what might be termed a generic computer. In other words, we will be concerned with features that are common to various computers. In addition, we will be comparing the key features found on various widely used machines.

The final topic to be discussed is the organization of a VAX-11 computer. The example used here is the VAX-11/780, which is the oldest computer in the VAX-11 family.

1.2

SOME TERMINOLOGY AND USEFUL SYMBOLS

The basic building block of a computer is a *bit*, which is an abbreviation of *bi*nary digi*t*. By extension, it may refer to the physical representation of a binary digit in different forms, such as a magnetized spot on a recording surface or a pulse in an electronic circuit. It can be compared to an ordinary light switch with two states. If a bit is in its on-state, it is taken to have a value of 1. If a bit is in its off-state, then it is taken to have a value of zero. In its physical form, a bit is commonly a two-state device (a flip-flop made possible with transistor-to-transistor logic or TTL) inside a chip such as the Schottky TTL AMD 2900 4-bit chip. Four of these chips can be combined to form a 16-bit central processor.

In some ways a computer can be considered the sum of its bits. Various configurations of its bits are used to represent information: data, locations of data, and instructions. *Data* are numeric values to be operated on by the processor. Locations of data are represented with bit strings called *addresses* (the binary "names" of memory locations). *Instructions* specify operations for the processor to perform. Any *program* is a collection of instructions executed (carried out) sequentially by a processor. On the machine level, all instructions, addresses, and data are contained in bit strings. These strings are in binary notation; that is, base two is used to construct a string of 0s and 1s like the following one:

1101 0100 0101 0110

which is the instruction that tells VAX-11 to clear register 6 (R6). *Registers* are special storage locations inside the central processor of a computer. They store bit strings representing information (numbers, characters, addresses, and status of devices inside the computer). VAX-11 registers have 32 bits.

In the above example, R6 inside the VAX-11 (VAX stands for Virtual Address Extension) is available for general use in VAX-11 assembly language programs. It can function as an *accumulator*, which means it can be used like a scratch pad to carry out arithmetic operations. R6 can also be used in addressing (pointing to or selecting) memory locations. The 6502 processor in Apple computers has one accumulator. By contrast, a PDP-11 has six and a VAX-11 has twelve registers that can be used as accumulators. The twelve VAX-11 accumulators (R0 through R11) are part of a set of sixteen general registers (R0 through R15) employed in addressing.

A *machine* program is a sequence of bit strings like the clear-R6 string mentioned above. On the machine level, bit strings represent instructions, data, and memory addresses. Each *machine instruction* contains an *operation code* (op code) to tell the processor what to do. For example, in

1101 0100   0101 0110

op code
tor CLRL   R6

the leading 8 bits tell the VAX-11 processor to perform a "clear" operation. The remaining 8 bits of the CLRL instruction specify both R6 *and* how it is to be used (its *addressing mode*). The complete VAX-11 symbolic equivalent of the above bit string is

CLRL R6

This is an example of an assembly language instruction. (Details of this and other VAX-11 instructions are discussed in chapter 3, along with addressing modes for processor registers.)

An *assembly language program* is the symbolic equivalent of a machine program. Op codes are represented by *mnemonics* such as CLRL. An *assembler* is itself a program that translates assembly language programs into bit strings that the machine can operate on. "Assembler" is a contraction of the term *Assembly* (level) programm*er*. The product of *assembling* (translating down to the machine level) a program is an *object module*. This is a sequence of bit strings, usually with incomplete addresses referenced by the assembly program.

The term *source text* refers to the symbolic input to an assembler. The source text is "fed" to the assembler for translation down to the machine level (Figure 1.1).

FIGURE 1.1
Assembly of a Source Text

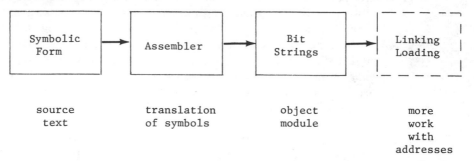

Before the translation of a source text is complete, two more programs come into play: a *linker*, which handles any other object modules referenced by the source text; and a *loader,* which assigns the final addresses (called *run-time addresses*) to the object module. The output from linking and loading the input object module is an executable *load module*.

Suppose, for example, that you want to find a member of the following sequence:

$$\ldots, \quad 0, \quad 1, \quad 1, \quad 2, \quad 3, \quad \ldots, \quad 4181, \quad 6765, \quad 10946, \ldots$$

$$F(0) \quad F(1) \quad F(2) \quad F(3) \quad F(4) \qquad F(19) \quad F(20) \quad F(21)$$

This is known as the Fibonacci sequence. Its distinctive characteristic is that each term (*after* the first two terms) is the sum of the preceding two terms. A Pascal program (called "leaves") to compute F(21) is given in Figure 1.2. The name is derived from the fact that Fibonacci number patterns can be found in the veins of tree leaves.

In Figure 1.3 a VAX-11 assembly language program is given which also computes F(21). The object module of the assembler source text in Figure 1.3 is shown in Figure 1.4.

On the VAX-11, the bit strings of the object module are written in base sixteen, or hexadecimal notation (which is explained later). Notice that

        CLRL R6

becomes

          D4   5 6
        ‾‾‾‾‾‾‾‾‾   ‾‾‾‾‾‾‾‾‾
      1101   0100   0101   0110

in the object module. When the machine equivalent of the source text (a collection of bit strings) is executed, F(21) is loaded into the VAX-11 mem-

FIGURE 1.2
A Pascal Equivalent of an Assembly Language Program

```
              program leaves(output);
              var
                      a,b,sum,count,r:integer;
              begin
              a:=0;b:=1;sum:=0;count:=20;r:=0;
              repeat
                      sum := a + b;
                       a := b;
                       b := sum;
                       r := r + 1
              until r = count;
              write(´              sum = ´,sum)
              end.


              RUN FG12

                      sum =        10946
```

ory; the location in which it is loaded has the symbolic address SUM. Notice the parallel structures in the Pascal and assembly language texts in the following example. Also note that a reverse arrow ($\leftarrow$) is used to represent the assignment of a value.

Pascal	*Assembler*	*Assignment*
sum := a+b	ADDL3 A,B,SUM	SUM $\leftarrow$ a+b

Another example of a parallel between a VAX-11 assembly language instruction and Pascal is given next. That is, a MOVL (MOVe Longword = 32 bits) in

MOVL B,A

is equivalent to

a := b

in Pascal. The AOBLSS (add and branch, if less) instruction is an example of a powerful VAX-11 branch instruction. This instruction allows us to set up the equivalent of a single-condition repeat/until loop in Pascal. That is, it allows us to set up a flow-of-control mechanism within an assembly program like the one shown in Figure 1.5. That is, the processor will transfer control back to the beginning of the COMPUTE loop and repeat the exe-

FIGURE 1.3
A VAX-11 Source Text

```
;
;Ref.:  Figure 1.3 (An assembler program)
;
;Method: set up a repeat loop to compute a Fibonacci number.
;
;Var
        a:          .long 0
        b:          .long 1
        sum:        .long 0
        count:      .long 20

        .entry  begin,0
        clrl    r6                              ;set up r6 for repeat loop
compute:
        add13   a,b,sum                         ;sum <-- a + b
        movl    b,a                             ;  a <-- b
        movl    sum,b                           ;  b <-- sum
        aoblss  count,r6,compute ;until
                                                ;      r6 = count
                                                ;note:
                                                ;
                                                ; ^aoblss^ reads ^add & branch,
                                                ;          if r6 < count (after
                                                ;          adding 1 to r6)
                                                ;result:
                                                ;    The final value from the
                                                ;above loop will be stored in
                                                ;the memory location labelled
sum.
        $exit s                                 ;terminate execution, here
        .end begin                              ;tell processor where to start
                                                ;executing program--transfer
                                                ;control to loc. begin
```

cution of the instructions inside the loop, if the condition

$$COUNT = R6$$

is *not* true. Notice, also, that the processor executes the instructions inside the repeat loop once, before it checks the condition. (A more generalized assembly language equivalent of a repeat/until loop is discussed in chapter 5.)

Memory on a computer can be explained in terms of bits. That is, a *memory location* in a computer is a set of connected bits. A *memory address* is a set of bits used to tag (identify) a memory location. The minimum number of bits that can be addressed at one time (with one instruction) provides a means of classifying computers. For example, the smallest addressable unit

FIGURE 1.4
A VAX-11 Object Module

```
;Ref.:  Figure 1.4 (An object module)
```

	Machine Instructions			Address	Line no.
				0000	1
				0000	2
		00000000		0000	3
		00000001		0004	4
		00000000		0008	5
		00000014		000C	6
				0010	7
			0000	0010	8
		56	D4	0012	9
				0014	10
				0014	11
				0014	12
ED AF	EB AF	E9 AF	C1	0014	13
	E0 AF	E6 AF	D0	001B	14
	DF AF	E5 AF	D0	0020	15
	EA 56	E4 AF	F2	0025	16
				002A	17
				002A	18
				002A	19
				0033	20

of memory on an IBM 370 or PDP-11, or a VAX-11, is 8 bits, which equals a *byte*. (PDP stands for Programmed Data Processor.) Such machines are said to be *byte-addressable machines*.

On the IBM 370 two bytes make up a half-word, four bytes a word. On a PDP-11, two bytes make up a full word. Meanwhile, on a VAX-11, two bytes make up a word and four bytes make up a long word.

The CDC Cyber 170 is an example of a machine that is not byte-addressable. Each of its addresses has 60 bits! This is also the size of a word on the CDC Cyber 170.

Digital Equipment Corporation (DEC) has suggested a useful notation to represent the content of a memory location:

A   = address of a location in memory

(A) = content of location A

((A)) = content of location with address in location A

In effect, ((A)) refers to memory content in terms of the address of a memory

FIGURE 1.5
Flow-of-Control for a Repeat Loop

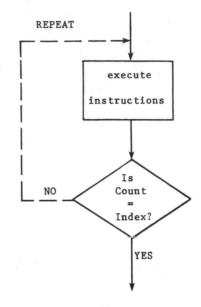

location. These notations are useful in discussing instructions that address memory.

All information (instructions, data, addresses) is *represented* numerically in base eight (octal) on PDP-11s and the CDC Cyber system. On systems like IBM 360/370s or VAX-11s, information is represented in base sixteen, or in hexadecimal notation (hex). On micros like the TRS-80 and Apple IIe, hex is also used to represent machine instructions, addresses, and data. All of these computers "think" in base two or binary.

1.2.1 Base Two Numbers: Binary

The binary or base two system of numeration is one in which the numbers are represented by two digits: 0 and 1. The meaning of a number in the base two system is determined by two factors. First, the *position* of each digit indicates a power of 2, which is to be multiplied by the digit appearing in that position. Second, the powers of 2 increase sequentially from the right, beginning with 2 raised to the power of zero (2^0). For example, the meaning of a four-digit number such as 1101 would be analyzed as follows:

$$1101 = 1 \times 2^3 + 1 \times 2^2 + 0 \times 2^1 + 1 \times 2^0$$
$$= 8 + 4 + 0 + 1$$
$$= 13 \text{ (base ten)}$$

In general, if a digit is in the nth place of a binary number, then it is multiplied by 2^{n-1}. Computers have used the base two system to represent numbers because its two digits, 0 and 1, can be interpreted as "off" and "on," relative to the flow of electrons in a circuit.

The next point to note is that in base two the result of adding 1 and 1 is not represented with a 2. Remember, base two has only two symbols! As a result,

1 + 1 = 10 (base two)

since

$$10 \text{ (base two)} = 1 \times 2^1 + 0 \times 2^0$$
$$= 2 + 0$$
$$= 2 \text{ (base ten)}$$

1.2.2 Base Eight Numbers: Octal

The base eight system uses eight digits: 0, 1, 2, 3, 4, 5, 6, and 7. Notice that the symbol 8 is *not* a base eight symbol! You can guess what is coming next. The sums (in octal)

2 + 6 = 3 + 5 = 4 + 4 = 5 + 2 + 1 = 10 (base eight)

Why?

$$10 \text{ (base eight)} = 1 \times 8^1 + 0 \times 8^0$$
$$= 8 + 0$$
$$= 8 \text{ (base ten)}$$

As in other systems, the position of a digit in a base eight number is significant. It indicates a power of 8, starting with 8^0 as the coefficient of the rightmost digit of an octal number. For example,

$$077777 = 0 \times 8^5 + 7 \times 8^4 + 7 \times 8^3 + 7 \times 8^2 + 7 \times 8^1 + 7 \times 8^0$$
$$= 0 + 7 \times 4096 + 7 \times 512 + 7 \times 64 + 7 \times 8 + 7$$
$$= 28672 + 3584 + 448 + 56 + 7$$
$$= 32767$$

which is the largest signed integer on a PDP-11. In general, an octal digit in the nth place of a number, is multiplied by 8^{n-1}.

1.2.3 Base Sixteen Numbers: Hexadecimal

Base sixteen has sixteen symbols:

Symbol	Value (in base ten)	Symbol	Value (in base ten)
0	0	8	8
1	1	9	9
2	2	A	10
3	3	B	11
4	4	C	12
5	5	D	13
6	6	E	14
7	7	F	15

The position rule is again applicable. That is, a hex digit in the nth place of a hex number is multiplied by 16^{n-1}. Arithmetic in hex will not be strange so long as the hex symbol is related to its position in the hex number. Consider, now, the reduction of hex numbers to decimal. For example,

$$A11 \text{ (hex)} = 10 \times 16^2 + 1 \times 16^1 + 1 \times 16^0$$
$$= 10 \times 256 + 16 + 1$$
$$= 2560 + 17$$
$$= 2577 \text{ (base ten)}$$

Next, consider how hex numbers are added together. For example

$$A + A = F + 5 = E + 6 = 14 \text{ (hex)}$$
$$= 20 \text{ (base ten)}$$

When the sum of two hex numbers equals 16 (base ten), we write 10 (hex). For example,

$$A + 6 = B + 5 = C + 4 = D + 3 = 10 \text{ (hex)}$$

Since

$$10 \text{ (hex)} = 1 \times 16^1 + 0 \times 16^0$$
$$= 16 + 0$$
$$= 16 \text{ (base ten)}$$

This will be useful later. In hex, the largest signed integer on a VAX-11 computer is 7FFF FFFF, the largest unsigned integer is FFFF FFFF. (A hex programmer would say this is 8 foxes.) Now try computing the decimal equivalents of these numbers as an exercise.

1.3

THE VON NEUMANN MACHINE

The first electronic computer was built by J. Presper Eckert and J. W. Mauchly during 1943–46 at the Moore School, University of Pennsylvania. It was dubbed the ENIAC (Electronic Numerical Integrator and Computer). The ENIAC used patch-panel wire connectors to set up data paths. It worked like a ''party-line telephone—many units would listen but only one would transmit'' (H. D. Huskey, 1983). It had 18,000 vacuum tubes and weighed 30 tons. By today's standards, it was slow. By the standards of 1940, it blitzed along. It had twenty accumulators. A pair of these could add or subtract a pair of ten-digit numbers in 200 microseconds (1 microsecond = 10^{-6} seconds). In contrast, two accumulators on a PDP-11/34A can perform the same function in 2.16 microseconds. Digital Equipment Corporation (DEC®) introduced its PDP-11/34A in 1978, the same year it introduced its VAX-11/780 computer.

The first electronic stored-program computer was built in 1944. It was known as the EDVAC (Electronic Discrete Variable Automatic Computer). Shortly afterward, in 1946, John von Neumann published the first paper on the stored-program concept. The machine designed by von Neumann has come to be known as the von Neumann Machine. Its design was based on the following concepts:

1. Programs (their instructions) as well as data are stored in the *same* memory. Earlier machines had used separate memories, one for data and another memory for instructions.

2. The computer uses *linear* organization of memory to store instructions and data. Memory locations are addressed (identified or labelled) with consecutive location numbers. Addresses range from 0 to some power of 2. In this scheme, instructions and data are indistinguishable in memory. J. K. Iliffe (1972, p. 3) singles out linear memory design as ''perhaps the most important characteristic of the von Neumann model.'' The linear organization of memory led von Neumann to formulate another concept—the program counter.

3. A *program counter*, or PC, is a register inside the processor that is ''dedicated'' to holding the address of the next instruction to be executed by the processor. This innovation made it possible to add a control function

to the processor. The PC is used by the processor to locate the next unit of information it needs to fetch. Each time an instruction is fetched from memory, the PC points to the next unit of information (instruction or datum) in memory.

4. von Neumann also devised a method of entering (*writing* to memory) and retrieving (*reading* from memory) instructions and data under program control.

1.4
COMPUTER ORGANIZATION IN TERMS
OF COMPUTER STRUCTURES

A *computer* is a device designed to perform operations in sequence as instructed by commands stored in memory. The organization of a typical computer is illustrated in Figure 1.6.

1.4.1 The Central Processing Unit (CPU)

The Central Processing Unit (CPU) consists of two principal subunits: the control unit (CU), and arithmetic and logic unit (ALU). The CPU is somewhat like the central nervous system of a human being. Its CU controls the flow of instructions and data to memory (the store cycle) and from memory (the "fetch" or "read" cycle).

The CU receives program instructions from memory one by one in sequence. It interprets them, and then sends appropriate control (gating) signals to the various units of the computer. The CU coordinates the operation of the machine—that is, it manages the flow of traffic to various units inside the machine. How it does this is another story.

The ALU takes its cue from the control signals it receives from the CU. It carries out the comparisons and arithmetic operations called for by instructions found in the *instruction register* (IR). On a VAX-11, the processor IR is called an instruction buffer, which is not one register. It holds 64 bits.

The IR can be compared to a bulletin board. It receives its bulletins (instructions) at the behest of the CU. The IR is linked to the main memory (the source of sequences of instructions) through two other registers associated with memory control, the *memory address register* (MAR) and *memory buffer register* (MBR). The MAR is used to hold the address of the memory location containing either instructions or data to be transferred (read

FIGURE 1.6
Organization of a Typical Computer

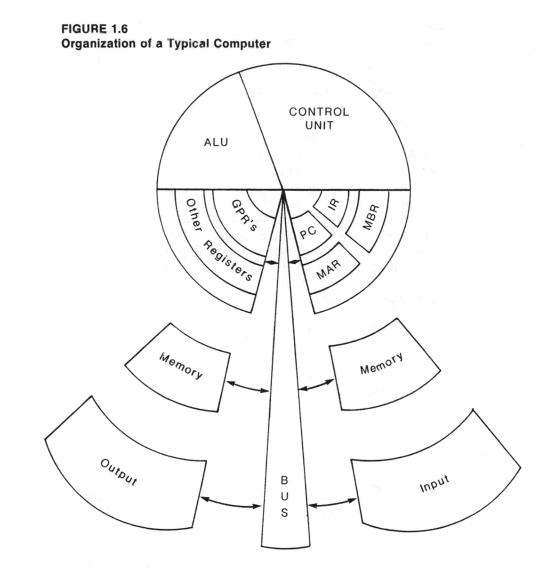

Legend:
   GPRs: General Purpose Registers
   PC   : Program Counter
   IR   : Instruction Register
   MAR : Memory Address Register
   MBR : Memory Buffer Register
   ALU : Arithmetic and Logic Unit
   BUS : Path for Information

into) to the MBR. Similarly, the CU uses the MAR to hold the address of a result to be transferred from the MBR into memory.

1.4.2 The Processor Control Function

The control unit of the processor oversees the fetching of instructions from memory, the decoding of each instruction code, and the generation of control signals that initiate execution of the fetched instruction. An *instruction* from memory specifies *that the machine is to do something, to carry out an operation.*

An instruction is in the form of an *operation code* (op code). The op code will be part of the bit string fetched from memory. On a VAX-11 computer, the op code begins with the *least significant bit* of the instruction. This will be followed by specifications for required operands (data called for by the instruction). For example, the VAX-11 instruction to add a constant to the content of register 6 and put the result in register 7 is symbolically represented as follows:

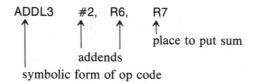

```
ADDL3    #2,  R6,   R7
```
place to put sum
addends
symbolic form of op code

The complete instruction as a bit string is given in hex by

```
57    56    02    C1
```
op code for ADDL3
operand = constant 2
operand R6
operand R7

The op code C1 (its mnemonic is ADDL3) is contained in the *leading* byte of the instruction. If the location for the byte containing C1 is 204, for example, then the following storage scheme would be used to store this instruction in memory:

C1 at 204

02 at 205

56 at 206

57 at 207

IBM 370 instructions also contain the op code for the instruction in the leading bits of the instruction bit string. This arrangement is unlike instructions used by computers in the PDP-11 family. On PDP-11s, the op code begins with the most significant bit (the trailing bit) of the instruction string.

The collection of all op codes recognizable to a machine is known as its *instruction set*. The instruction set varies in size and diversity, depending on the machine. On a VAX-11, for example, there are 240 instructions. By contrast, the basic instruction set for a PDP-11 comprises 83 instructions.

Many control units of CPUs now have their own fast memory. This memory is called the *control store*, or sometimes the *microstore*. This store is usually a safe, read-only memory (ROM). It contains a collection of permanently stored instructions called *microinstructions*.

The microinstructions of the control store are used "to implement the control functions of a computer" (M. J. Flynn, 1983, p. 978). These are put together by CPU architects to form *microprograms*, the function of which is to direct the execution of the instruction set. The collection of microprograms in the control store is known as the *firmware* of the computer.

The PDP 11/24 is an example of a smaller machine having microprograms to handle control. Its control unit has 552 16-bit words of microprogram instructions. Moving up the scale, the VAX-11/730 has 16,384 (or 16 $\times$ 1024 = 16K) 24-bit microwords. This control store permits both reading and writing (the store itself is programmable). The firmware on the VAX-11/730 makes it possible to run PDP-11 programs on the VAX-11. The control store on a VAX-11/750 is in ROM only. It contains 6K 80-bit-long microwords, which describe "the operation and sequencing of the central processing unit" (Digital Equipment Corporation, 1982, p. 107).

1.4.3 Instruction Execution Cycle

The control unit regulates the *instruction execution cycle*. This cycle utilizes the PC, IR, MAR, and MBR registers in three phases:

I-phase: Fetch *instruction* from memory location identified by the PC and put fetched information (a bit string) in the IR.

O-phase: Fetch *operand*(s) that might be required by the instruction in the IR.

E-phase: *Execute* the instruction in the IR.

The procedure used by the processor to carry out the phases of the instruction cycle is outlined in Figure 1.7.

FIGURE 1.7
Instruction Cycle

```
Procedure Execute:

Begin

    1.  (I-phase) Initialize MAR with address in PC;

        1.1  Transfer bit string in memory location identified
             by MAR to the MBR;

        1.2  Increment PC to point to the address of next
             instruction to be fetched;

        1.3  Transfer (MBR) to the IR;

        1.4  Interpret the fetched instruction;

    2.  (O-phase) The (IR) will specify if operands
        are needed:

        2.1  The operand (IR)-operand address is
             transferred to the MAR;

        2.2  The operand specified by the (MAR)
             is transferred to the MBR;

        2.3  (MBR) is transferred to a processor register;

        2.4  If additional operands are required,
             repeat step 2.1;

    3.  (E-phase) Execute the instruction in the IR

    End.
```

This cycle works thanks to the two key design concepts of the basic von Neumann machine—linear memory and the PC. Linear memory, or the sequential storage of instructions and data for a program, makes it possible to use a PC, which ensures that the next instruction for a program will *immediately* follow the one currently being executed. Such a simple idea, such a beautiful result!

The amount that the PC is incremented will vary, depending on the machine. On a PDP-11, for example, the PC is incremented by 2. On a VAX-11, the PC-increment will vary, depending on the size of the current instruction. That is, *after* an instruction is fetched, the PC is incremented by the number of bytes in the instruction.

In the example given earlier, if we assume the ADDL3 instruction is at location 204 (hex), then the next instruction will be found at location 208. We would increment the PC by 4, since the ADDL3 instruction uses 4 bytes.

A. S. Tanenbaum (1976, p. 18) singles out the PC as "the most important register" of the central processor.

1.4.4 Memory Organization

Addresses identify memory locations. *Addresses* are bit strings representing integers from 0 to $n - 1$ where n is the number of locations in memory. If the word size of the machine is n, then typically there are 2^n possible addresses and corresponding memory locations. The word size and address size are typically the same. They are on PDP-11s and VAX-11s. There are exceptions, however. For example, the word size of the CDC 6600 computer is 60 bits, but the addresses are always 18-bit quantities. Register instructions are 15 bits, while instructions including a memory address are 30 bits. On the IBM 360 and 370, the word size is 32 bits, whereas addresses are 24 bits, but no instruction may specify more than a 12-bit address.

Suppose, for example, we have a 4-bit computer (call it the PLUS-4). The word size of the PLUS-4 is 4. Its addresses are bit strings, each consisting of 4 bits. The collection of all its possible addresses is called its address space (see Figure 1.8).

FIGURE 1.8
Plus-4 Address Space

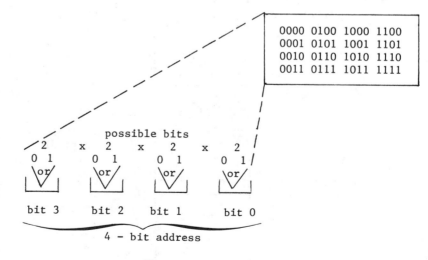

Since each bit in the bit string can be either a 0 or a 1, it is possible to compute the total number of bit strings in the address space:

$$2 \times 2 \times 2 \times 2 = 2^4 = \text{possible addresses}$$

2 possibilities for bit 0
2 possibilities for bit 1
2 possibilities for bit 2
2 possibilities for bit 3

Although it is tiny by contrast, the PLUS-4 address space is comparable to the VAX-11 address space. That is, the word size n of both machines determines an address space with 2^n units of information. Each memory location on the PLUS-4 contains 4 bits or half a byte (a nibble). On a VAX-11, each address references a byte. The word size of the VAX-11 is 32 bits. Its address space contains 2^{32} addresses or 4, 294, 967, 296 addresses of

FIGURE 1.9
VAX-11 Memory Organization

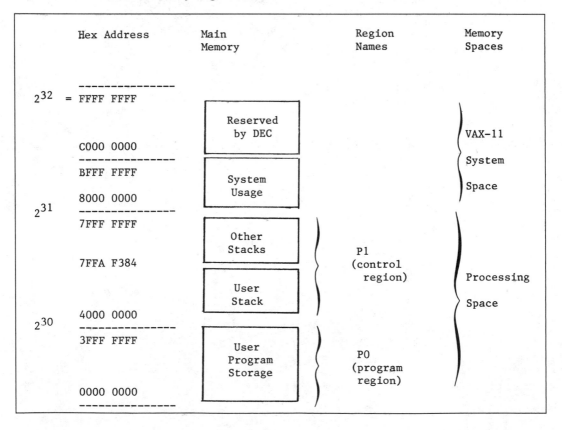

bytes that it can reference. The VAX-11 address space is subdivided into four regions, as shown in Figure 1.9. The addresses in the figure are given in hex. As an exercise, try computing the decimal equivalents of these addresses as a whole number and as a power of 2. For example,

$$4, 294, 967, 296 = 2^{32} = \text{FFFF FFFF (hex)}$$

Notice that

$$512 \text{ (decimal)} = 2^9$$

DEC subdivides VAX-11 memory addressable by programs (the PO space) into pages, *each* with 512 bytes.

1.5

VAX-11 ORGANIZATION

Digital Equipment Corporation introduced the VAX-11/780 in 1978 as a virtual address extension of computers in the PDP-11 family. Virtual addressing relies on the use of an idealized address space where the 512-byte long pages of the address space are contiguous. To the programmer working with a VAX-11, addresses generated by a program appear to lie in contiguous (side-by-side or end-to-end) pages of memory. In reality the VAX-11 uses a combination of hardware (special registers) and software to relocate program-generated addresses to available pages in physical or actual memory. The addresses in a program are segmented and parceled out to available physical pages, which are *not* necessarily contiguous. Virtual addressing allows the VAX-11 to store program segments in both physical memory and on a disk. It will manage the scattered program segments, that is, put them into the *physical address space* when they are needed. This allows many users to use the same address space at the same time and enables each to have 2^{23} virtual memory pages, even when the same memory at any one time may contain relocated segments of many programs. The space containing virtual addresses is known as the logical address space. This is part of the user-level behavior of the machine. The actual implementation of a VAX-11 program is hidden from its users.

The layout of the VAX-11/780 is shown in Figure 1.10.

The VAX-11 processor uses what is known as *cache* (pronounced "cash") *memory* to speed up processing. In the above figure, the data cache is inside the processor. It has an 8K (K = 1024) or 8192-byte capacity; this storage unit is both more costly and faster than main memory subsystems outside the processor. Each time the VAX-11 fetches one of the instructions

FIGURE 1.10
VAX-11/780 Organization

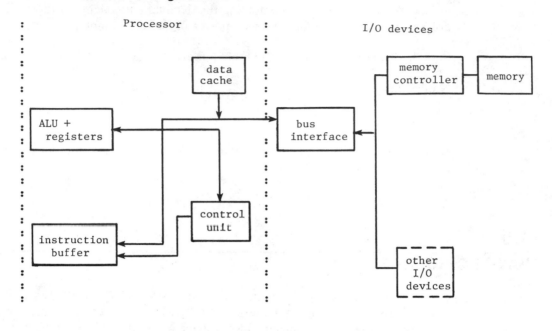

NOTE: represents a path called a bus along
             which binary information flows

of a program it first checks the cache to see if the required addresses and their contents are already there. The cache always contains a copy of the most commonly used addresses and their contents. If the addresses requested by the processor control unit are not "cached," then the VAX-11 sends a request to the appropriate memory controller. Because it is able to copy 64 bits at a time from main memory into the data cache, it does not have to make as many fetches from main memory.

A measure of success of cache memory is its hit ratio—that is, how often (what percentage of the time) data and instructions sought by the CPU are found in the cache. In 8,000 samples from an 8-hour day, D. W. Clark (1983, p. 29) found an average hit ratio of 82.8% on a VAX-11/780. The net effect of using a data cache is speedier processing. Cache memory is another feature of the VAX-11 organization that cannot be seen by the user.

1.5.1 VAX-11 General-Purpose Registers

The VAX-11 processor has 16 registers for the programmer to use. Each one holds 32 bits (see Table 1.1). R6 through R11 can be readily used either

TABLE 1.1
VAX-11 Registers, A Selection

Register	Symbol	Purpose
R15	PC	Program counter
R14	SP	Stack pointer
R13	FP	Frame pointer used in procedure calling (see chap. 9)
R12	AP	Argument pointer used in procedure calling (see chap. 9)
R6:R11	None	General purpose
R0:R5	None	Used by VAX-11 character and other instructions

as accumulators (to manipulate data) or as mechanisms to address operands. Furthermore, they are not used by the processor for any of its instructions.

The PDP-11 was the first machine to use one of its general registers as the program counter. This practice has been carried over in VAX-11 machines, which use register 15 as the program counter.

Register 14 on a VAX-11 is used to hold addresses of a dedicated area of memory, called a user stack (this is in the low end of P1, the control region of the user memory space). A *stack* is a linear list in which the last element put into the list is the first one to be taken off. In other words, a stack is a list that is managed according to the Last In, First Out (LIFO) rule. The first stack position is called the *stack bottom*. When an item is inserted into the stack, the operation is called a *push*. The *top of a stack* is the position occupied by the last element *pushed*. A stack deletion is called a *pop*.

The VAX-11 user stack is a *downward stack*, since each element pushed into it is located immediately below the preceding element pushed in. In other words, a push moves the top of the user stack *down* in memory. As noted above, register 14 is used for this operation. It is written as SP in VAX-11 assembly programs (R14 is *not* recognized!). The SP holds the address of the top of the stack, *after* the first push. Initially, when the VAX-11 user stack is empty, SP holds the address of the memory location immediately above the stack bottom. That is, initially SP = 7FFAF384 (hex), for example. The SP is called the *stack pointer*.

VAX-11 assembler includes special instructions to handle pushing and popping:

```
PUSHL   <element>        ;push element
POPL    <destination>    ;pop element into specified destination
```

Figure 1.11 shows three pushes and two pops. Notice that a

```
PUSHL   <element>
```

FIGURE 1.11
VAX-11 Push/Pop Cycles

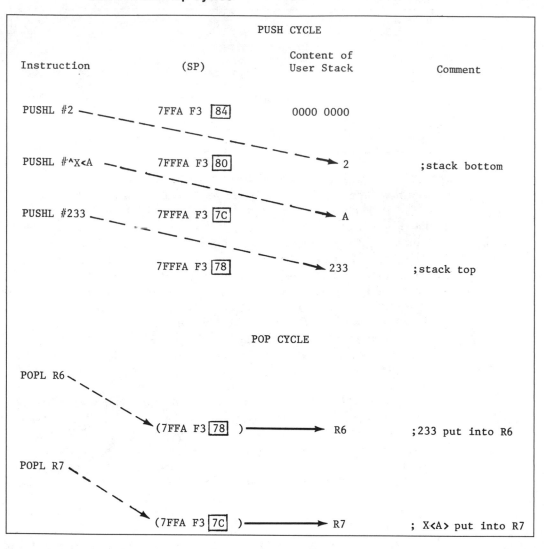

decrements the SP by 4, leaving the address of the top of the user stack in the SP after a push. Also notice that each

POPL   <destination>

increments the old (SP) by 4, leaving the address of the new stack top in the SP. (The use of stacks is examined further in chapter 8.)

The presence of a system stack on PDP-11s and VAX-11s distinguishes them from the IBM 360/370 computers, which have no stack. C. P. Pfleeger (1982, p. 131) observes that the absence of a stack on the IBM 360/370 series makes the problem of saving the contents of registers "a bit more involved."

In theory, R0 through R11 on a VAX-11 can be used for the arithmetic and addressing memory elements used in assembly programs. In practice, it is better to avoid R0 through R5 and use R6 through R11 as general registers in programming. Why? VAX-11 macro uses R0 through R5 (also written R0:R5) for many of its instructions. As a result, you cannot rely on the contents of these registers in formulating a program. The system does not use R6:R11. These are general purpose and reliable registers. (They are discussed in chapters 3 and 4.)

1.5.2 Condition Codes

One of the registers on the VAX-11 processor is used to control branching within a program; that is, it controls external events. It is called the processor status longword (PSL) (see Figure 1.12).

The low word of the PSL is called the processor status word (PSW) (bits 0 through 15, or 0:15). Bits 5:7 of the PSW are used to control the processor's response to events in the external world. Bit 4 is used in debugging. Bits 0:3 are called the *condition codes* of the PSW. They are extremely important. *Each* operation called for by a VAX-11 instruction affects

FIGURE 1.12
VAX-11 Processor Status Longword

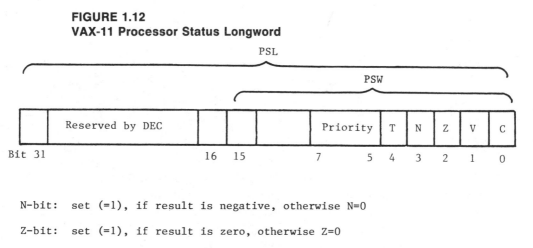

N-bit: set (=1), if result is negative, otherwise N=0

Z-bit: set (=1), if result is zero, otherwise Z=0

V-bit: set (=1), if two numbers with the same sign produce
        a result with an opposite after an operation

C-bit: set (=1), if a carry occurs. If bit 31 is 1
        before an operation, then a 1 is added to it,
        a carry occurs and C will be set.

these bits (they indicate the result of the last instruction executed). For example, suppose R6 contains FFFF FFFF (hex). This would be the twos complement of -1 (we explain complement arithmetic in the next chapter). This number *behaves* like -1, too. Keep in mind that R6 holds 32-bit long strings. Then, if we ask the VAX-11 processor to execute

$$
\begin{array}{r}
\text{ADDL2 \#1, R6 with FFFF FFFF (hex)} \\
+1 \\
\hline
\leftarrow\ \overline{0000\ \ 0000} \\
\text{last carry lost}
\end{array}
$$

the last 1 carried in this operation does not show up in the result in R6, but the *fact* that a carry occurred is recorded in bit 0 (the C-bit) of the PSW. It is set after this operation. Since a zero is left in R6 after this operation, bit 2 (the Z-bit) is also set. Since the result is not negative and no overflow occurred, then bit 3 (the N-bit) and bit 1 (the V-bit) are *not* set. That is, the PSW should contain

	N	Z	V	C
	0	1	0	1

(The overflow bit will be set if an operation produces a result that is too large for the type of data used.) If we had used

MOVL   # ^X   <FFFF FFFF>,   R6

unary operator to tell the processor that the number that follows is written in hex

immediate mode addressing explained in chapter 3 (this tells the processor the first operand immediately follows the op code)

specifies that all 32 bits of R6 will be used

a move instruction that puts a copy of the first operand into R6

the result of this operation would be taken as a negative number (^X<FFFFFFFF> is the twos complement of -1). So the N-bit (bit 3) of the PSW would be set, the remaining bits (0:2) would be zero.

If a conditional branch instruction is used in a VAX-11 assembly language program, the condition codes of the PSW are checked to determine whether a branch should occur. If the condition for a branch life

BEQL (Branch, if equal) <label>

symbolic address for instruction to be executed if the Z-bit = 1 in the PSW

is satisfied, then instead of executing the next instruction in the sequence of instructions for a program, processor control passes to the instruction with the symbolic address given by <label>. For example, assume there is an FFFFFFFE (hex) in R6 with

```
            ADDL2 #2, R6        ;Sets Z-bit of PSW, since
                                ;FFFFFFFE + 2 = 0
←────────── BEQL NEXT           ;Branch, to NEXT, if Z=1
                 ⋮
            <actions>
                 ⋮
└→ NEXT:    <instruction>       ;continue execution
```

Then flow-of-control would pass to the instruction labelled NEXT.

The VAX-11 instruction set has an instruction

```
MOVPSL      <32-bit location>
```

that moves a copy of the desired PSL to a desired location. For example,

```
MOVPSL  R6
```

puts a copy of the PSL in R6. This instruction is sometimes useful. It also distinguishes the VAX-11 from the PDP-11 instruction set, for example, which lacks such an instruction.

1.5.3 Two VAX-11 Data Types

The VAX-11 instruction set accommodates a variety of integer types as well as character and string types. The integer types are shown in Table 1.2.

The data types in Table 1.2 refer to the possible bit strings (also called *bit fields*) that VAX-11 instructions can handle. If an address in an assembler program references one of these bit strings, it is always addressing byte 0.

By default, integers in a source text are treated as base ten numbers by the VAX-11 assembler. For example, if we use

```
ADDL2   #233, R6      ;add 233 (10) to content of R6
```

the 233 is taken by the VAX-11 as 233 (base ten). A generous selection of unary operators is available to change this. A *unary* (single) operator is used

TABLE 1.2
VAX-11 Integer Types

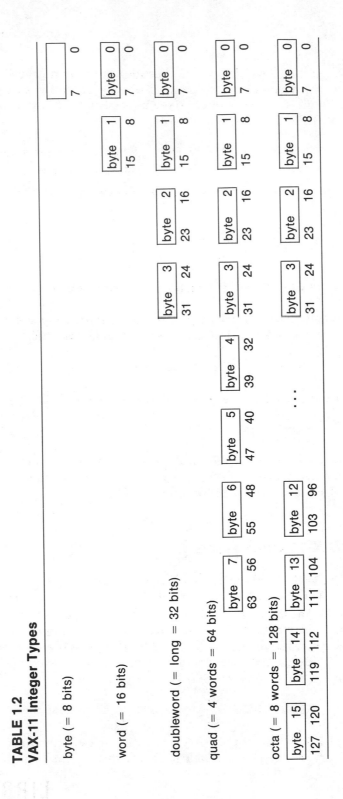

byte (= 8 bits)

word (= 16 bits)

doubleword (= long = 32 bits)

quad (= 4 words = 64 bits)

octa (= 8 words = 128 bits)

as a prefix in

> # <unary operator><constant>

to specify what data type the <constant> represents. The set of unary operators is given in Table 1.3. For example, if we use

> ADDL2 #ˆX<233>, R6   ;add 233 (16) to content of R6

the 233 is taken by the VAX-11 as 233 (hex). That is

$$ˆX<233> = 2 \times 16^2 + 2 \times 16^1 + 3 \times 16^0$$
$$= 2 \times 256 + 48 + 3$$
$$= 563 \text{ (decimal)}$$

This feature will often prove useful. The hex unary operator, for example, makes it possible to address hex locations in memory. If the VAX-11 assembler prints information about memory addresses used in a program, they will be given in hex.

Finally, string data can be used. The VAX-11 assembler includes instructions to handle what are known as ASCII codes which are used to build strings. The acronym ASCII stands for American Standard Code for Information Interchange. It has 128 codes (0:127), which are shown in Table 1.4.

Input on a VAX-11 is in ASCII. If we type an A, the ASCII code (its decimal equivalent!) is put into a keyboard buffer (temporary storage area). Each character we type requires a byte of memory (bits 0 through 7 of a byte are used to handle a single ASCII code). This means numeric input must be handled in a special way. That is, the ASCII codes need to be put

TABLE 1.3
VAX-11 Unary Operators

Unary Operator	Data Type Signified
ˆB	binary
ˆD	decimal
ˆO	octal
ˆX	hexadecimal
ˆA	ASCII (American Standard Code for Information Interchange)
ˆF	floating point
ˆC	ones complement

TABLE 1.4
ASCII Character Codes for the VAX-11

CHAR	DEC	HEX	CHAR	DEC	HEX	CHAR	DEC	HEX
NUL	0	0	+	43	2B	V	86	56
^A	1	1	,	44	2C	W	87	57
^B	2	2	-	45	2D	X	88	58
^C	3	3	.	46	2E	Y	89	59
^D	4	4	/	47	2F	Z	90	5A
^E	5	5	0	48	30	[	91	5B
^F	6	6	1	49	31	\	92	5C
BEL	7	7	2	50	32	]	93	5D
BKSP	8	8	3	51	33	^	94	5E
TAB	9	9	4	52	34	—	95	5F
LF	10	A	5	53	35	`	96	60
VT	11	B	6	54	36	a	97	61
FF	12	C	7	55	37	b	98	62
CR	13	D	8	56	38	c	99	63
SO	14	E	9	57	39	d	100	64
^O	15	F	:	58	3A	e	101	65
^P	16	10	;	59	3B	f	102	66
XON	17	11	<	60	3C	g	103	67
^R	18	12	=	61	3D	h	104	68
XOFF	19	13	>	62	3E	i	105	69
^T	20	14	?	63	3F	j	106	6A
^U	21	15	@	64	40	k	107	6B
^V	22	16	A	65	41	l	108	6C
^W	23	17	B	66	42	m	109	6D
^X	24	18	C	67	43	n	110	6E
^Y	25	19	D	68	44	o	111	6F
^Z	26	1A	E	69	45	p	112	70
ESC	27	1B	F	70	46	q	113	71
FS	28	1C	G	71	47	r	114	72
GS	29	1D	H	72	48	s	115	73
RS	30	1E	I	73	49	t	116	74
US	31	1F	J	74	4A	u	117	75
SP	32	20	K	75	4B	v	118	76
!	33	21	L	76	4C	w	119	77
"	34	22	M	77	4D	x	120	78
#	35	23	N	78	4E	y	121	79
$	36	24	O	79	4F	z	122	7A
%	37	25	P	80	50	{	123	7B
&	38	26	Q	81	51	|	124	7C
'	39	27	R	82	52	}	125	7D
(	40	28	S	83	53	~	126	7E
)	41	29	T	84	54	DEL	127	7F
*	42	2A	U	85	55			

together internally to form a single number. For example, if we type

```
2     3     3
↑     ↑     ↑
|     |     ASCII 50
|     ASCII 51
ASCII 51
```

what goes into the keyboard buffer is not a *single* number—in this case 233—but *three* ASCII codes. Later we show how to deal with the problem of feeding the machine numbers.

1.6

SUMMARY

The design concepts introduced by von Neumann underpin the organization of a typical contemporary computer. Chief among these design concepts is linear memory, which stores instructions and data in sequential order. The instruction that immediately follows the current one being executed by the processor begins with the byte *immediately following the last byte of the current instruction*. This arrangement makes the PC possible. It also provides the basis for what we call the instruction execution cycle.

The degree to which the PC is incremented to find the next instruction will depend on the organization of the instruction set for a particular machine. On PDP-11s, for example, all instructions occupy two bytes and all instructions begin with an even address. In this case the PC is incremented by 2 *each* time an instruction is fetched from memory. On a VAX-11, some instructions like EDIV (Extended DIVide) have as many as four operands. Each operand specifier can use one or more bytes. The op code for each instruction uses one or, at most, two bytes. The EDIV instruction, for example, typically uses as many as 11 bytes. This means the VAX-11 PC will be incremented by a varying amount after each instruction is fetched from memory. The PC increment on a VAX-11 is computed in terms of the number of bytes used by the current instruction.

The distinction made between a logical address space and a physical address space is important on virtual address machines like the VAX-11. VAX-11 Macro (what DEC calls its assembler) will represent the addresses of an assembly program as consecutive, virtual addresses. They belong to an *apparent* set of contiguous memory pages. During program translation, these beginning addresses will be relocated to the physical address space, where they will be segmented into memory pages. Each time the binary version of an assembly program is run, the segments of a program are parceled out differently, depending on the availability of pages in physical memory at the time. The user is not aware that a dynamic is at work here. An understanding of this dynamic will be helpful later in debugging a program and in examining what has happened to our program in memory.

Finally, it is important to understand the design principles underpinning the machine organization of contemporary computers. To do so, we need to look at the computer as a logical machine, and see it in terms of its user-level behavior. *Before* we can consider how a machine carries out an operation, however, we first need to know what a machine will do. For example, we can examine the framework for an instruction execution cycle on a VAX-11 without concerning ourselves initially, for example, with the use of data cache by the processor. On a VAX-11, the use of cache memory makes the basic idea of the instruction execution cycle more efficient, not different. That is, the use of a data cache allows the VAX-11 to reduce the number of times it fetches information from main memory. It brings a quadword at a time from main memory, even if only one two-byte instruction is called for.

1.7

EXERCISES

1. Make a table like Table 1.1 giving a complete list of registers discussed in this chapter.

2. The PLUS-4 Computer Company is located in Bertha's Kitty Boutique in Lake Woebegone, Minnesota. It has just introduced the PLUS-4/784 with 8-bit data and addresses. Show the entire address space of this computer. Assume PLUS-4/784 memory is loaded (locations 0:E) with Fibonacci numbers F(0) through F(13). All addresses and data on the PLUS-4/780 are written in hex. Assume the remaining locations are filled with zeros.

3. Assume the PLUS-4/784 has twelve accumulators as well as a separate PC and each of the other registers needed in the instruction execution cycle. Assume it needs to fetch an add-instruction

     250   ADDL2 @#^X<300>, R6

from memory location 250. Assume @#^X<300> is used by the processor in fetching an operand from location 300 (hex). That is, PC ← ^X<300> to obtain an operand at location 300. Write out the steps of I-, O-, and E-phases of the instruction-execution cycle on the PLUS-4/784.

4. Make a list of locally available computers and their addressing capabilities as well as the maximum number of bits allowed for either an instruction or a datum. Put this in table form.

5. Make a table showing the types of storage available on each of the computers given in the table in the preceding exercise.

6. Suppose a machine has 26-bit virtual addressing. How many possible addresses are in its virtual address space?

7. Suppose the VAX-11 SP is pointing to location 1000 (hex). Then, as is done in Figure 1.11, portray what happens when we PUSHL #2, then PUSHL #^X<C>, then PUSHL #5, then PUSHL #9, then PUSHL #^C<1>, followed by three successive POPs. Show the content of the SP at each step of the way. (All addresses and memory contents are in hex.)

8. VAX-11 memory is subdivided into 512-byte pages:

```
Address       page
00000000  ⎫
   ⋮      ⎬  page 0
000001FF  ⎭
00000200  ⎫
   ⋮      ⎬  page 1
000003FF  ⎭
```

Give the beginning and ending addresses for the first 10 pages in VAX-11 memory.

9. Give the decimal equivalent of

(a) 200 (hex)

(b) 400 (hex)

(c) FFFFFFFF (hex)

(d) 1A (hex)

(e) A1 (hex)

(f) 1111 1111 (binary)

(g) 0111 1010 1100 1111 1110 1000 (binary)

10. The term *bit* is a contraction of what two words?

11. If 210 is the first of 20 longword addresses on a VAX-11, give the remaining 19 longword addresses.

1.8

LAB PROJECTS

1. Using the arrangement for the VAX-11 system stack shown in Figure 1.11 as a guide, use the natural numbers (positive integers 1, 2, 3, . . .) to do the following:

   (a) Push the *hex* equivalent of the first 20 natural numbers, showing

Assembler Instruction	Stack Address	Stack Content	Comment

   in each case. Be careful to identify the stack bottom and stack top.

   (b) Pop six stack elements into registers R6:R11, showing

Assembler Instruction	Stack Address	Destination Content	Comment

2. Using Figures 1.6 and 1.10 as a guide, sketch the organization of a local computer. Be sure to indicate

   (a) Available general registers, the size of the bit string each contains.

   (b) The size of an address bit string and the size of the physical address space.

   (c) The presence or absence of a system user stack and stack pointer.

   (d) The presence or absence of cache memory.

   (e) The number of instructions in the processor instruction set.

   (f) The base used in representing information in the computer (in hex? in octal?). If characters are represented in hex, is ASCII used?

   (g) The number of bits in a
   - (i) byte
   - (ii) word

1.9

REVIEW QUIZ

1. Indicate whether the following statements are true or false:

   (a) An assembler is a translator.

(b) An object module is executable.

(c) Object module code is machine code.

(d) CLRL is VAX-11 assembler mnemonic for CLcaRLy.

(e) VAX-11 registers have 31 bits.

(f) Bit zero of the PSL is bit zero of the PSW.

(g) Bit 3 of the PSW is the N bit.

(h) The highest hex address in the P0 (user program region) is 4FFF FFFF.

(i) The system stack is located above the user program region on a VAX-11.

(j) The processor execution cycle begins with the O-phase.

(k) On a von Neumann machine, memory is organized nonlinearly.

(l) The IR holds the address of the next instruction to be executed.

(m) The PC holds the next instruction to be executed by the processor.

(n) The most significant bit of a long word is bit 31.

(o) A double- or longword has 31 bits.

(p) A word has 15 bits.

(q) A quadword has 64 bits.

2. Compute the following:

(a) $X<15>$

(b) $C<0>$

(c) 512 bytes $\times$ 2 = ? bits   Hint: each 0 is replaced by 1.

1.10

REFERENCES

Clark, D. W. ''Cache Performance in the VAX 11/780.'' *ACM Transactions on Computer Systems,* vol. 1, no. 1 (February 1983), 24–37. See Especially pp. 27–29.

Digital Equipment Corporation. *PDP-11 Software Handbook* (No. EB-21759-20). Maynard, Mass.: DEC, 1982.

Donovan, John J. *Systems Programming.* New York: McGraw-Hill, 1972, 21.

Flynn, M. J. ''Microprogramming.'' In *The Encyclopedia of Computer Science and Engineering,* A. Ralston, ed. New York: Van Nostrand Reinhold, 1983, 977–85.

Huskey, H. D. ''ENIAC.'' In *The Encyclopedia of Computer Science and Engineering,* A. Ralston, ed. New York: Van Nostrand Reinhold, 1983, 607–8.

Iliffe, J. K. *Basic Machine Principles.* New York: American Elsevier, 1972.

Pfleeger, C. P. *Machine Organization: An Introduction to the Structure and Programming of Computer Systems.* New York: Wiley, 1982.

Tanenbaum, A. S. *Structured Computer Organization.* Englewood Cliffs, N.J.: Prentice-Hall, 1976.

von Neumann, J. "Preliminary Discussion of the Logical Design of an Electronic Computing Instrument." In vol. 1 of *The Collected Works of John von Neumann,* edited by A. H. Taub, 34–79. New York: Macmillan, 1963.

2.
WAYS TO REPRESENT
NUMERIC INFORMATION

I believe that an hour of calculation is much better for me than half-an-hour of worry.

—Lewis Carroll, *Lewis Carroll's Bedside Book*

I have also found an astonishing thing: we can represent all sorts of truths and consequences with numbers.

—G. W. Leibniz, *Project d'un art d'inventeur*

2.0
AIMS

- Show the relationship between binary, hex, and decimal representations of numbers.
- Explore methods of conversion going from binary to hex, hex to binary, and decimal to other bases.
- Introduce the use of stacks and queues.
- Introduce methods of doing extended precision multiplication.
- Introduce the tens, ones and twos complement arithmetic systems.
- Introduce the use of pseudocode to represent methods of solution.

2.1
INTRODUCTION

The seventeenth century philosopher and mathematician G. W. Leibniz was among the first to suggest that we use the binary number system to represent our knowledge. He offered a novel interpretation of the base two symbols 0 and 1. He suggested that 1 represented the unity of the universe, the cosmos itself, and 0 its counterworld, its opposite.

Leibniz was the Pythagoras of the world of computing. His essays on methods of representing the terms of arguments both symbolically *and* numerically, augured the work of George Boole, Charles Babbage, and Alan Turing. His essays presage our use of codes such as ASCII and EBCDIC (Extended Binary Coded Decimal Interchange Code used by IBM) to represent concepts (and grammar) both symbolically and numerically.

The ASCII code (see Table 1.4) is used on PDP-11 and VAX-11 computers for input/output operations. An A typed on a terminal gives rise to the following sequence:

ASCII character	ASCII code	Binary representation
A	41 (hex)	0100 0001

We think in ASCII; the computer "thinks" in binary. The fundamental radix used by the machine is two. (Radix, also known as base, is the number on which a numeration system is constructed.) A set of instructions (on the machine-level) which prompt a VAX-11 computer to compute $1 + 1$ is given in the sample machine program shown in Table 2.1.

Before we can deal further with the significance of the above machine program as well as the hex and binary and symbolic instructions we can use to write programs, we first need to know something about the arithmetic for each radix commonly used, and the methods commonly used to convert numbers from one system to another.

2.2
A CROSS-REFERENCE SYMBOL TABLE FOR THREE NUMBER SYSTEMS

On VAX-11s, it is conventional to represent all binary data with hexadecimal numbers. On most large and small IBM machines these are written in hex (base sixteen) notation.

Hex is the ideal number base to use on a VAX-11 system since all VAX-11s are built around 16 registers and 32-bit addresses with four bit fields, which show up nicely in hex. On a VAX-11, a longword contains 32 bits. Each long- or doubleword can be conveniently subdivided in several ways (see Figure 2.1). A cross-reference symbol table for bases two, sixteen, and ten is given in Table 2.2.

TABLE 2.1
Sample Machine Code

Byte Addresses	Hex Instruction	Binary	Assembler Form	Interpretation
204	C1	1100 0001	ADDL3	; add
205	02	0000 0010	#1	; 1 to
206	56	0101 0110	R6	; R6, putting sum
207	57	0101 0111	R7	; in R7, a long
				; word destination
				; for the sum

The bits at the extreme left and extreme right of a longword are the most significant (MSB) and least significant (LSB) bits, respectively, of a longword. The MSB is the leftmost bit (bit 31) and is used as a sign-bit on signed integers; on unsigned numbers it can be treated as a coefficient of a power of the radix. What follows are examples of signed and unsigned integers on a VAX-11:

signed values

positive number = 4

0000 0000 0000 0000 0000 0000 0000 0100

MSB = bit 31   LSB = bit 0

negative number = −4

1111 1111 1111 1111 1111 1111 1111 1100

unsigned value

unsigned integer = 2,147,483,649

MSB   LSB

1000 0000 0000 0000 0000 0000 0000 0001

$1 \times 2^{31} = 2,147,483,648$ $1 \times 2^0 = 1$

This leads to an important restriction. The largest positive integer that can be used with VAX-11 arithmetic instructions is equal to $2^{31} - 1$ or 2,147,483,647. In this case, all of the bits *except* bit 31 will be one. A binary and hex expansion of this number appears in Figure 2.2.

Incidentally, when the MSB = 1, and the rest of the bits are 0 (turned off), we have

$$1 \times 2^{31} = 2,147,483,648$$
$$= 1\ 000\ 0000\ 0000\ 0000\ 0000\ 0000\ 0000\ 0000$$

TABLE 2.2
Cross-Reference Base Two, Sixteen,
and Ten Symbol Table

Binary	Hex	Decimal
0000	0	0
0001	1	1
0010	2	2
0011	3	3
0100	4	4
0101	5	5
0110	6	6
0111	7	7
1000	8	8
1001	9	9
1010	A	10
1011	B	11
1100	C	12
1101	D	13
1110	E	14
1111	F	15

FIGURE 2.1
Subdivisions of a Doubleword

```
long word:      00000000000000000000000000000000


bytes:          00000000    00000000    00000000    00000000
                byte 3      byte 2      byte 1      byte 0


hex groups:     0000   0000   0000   0000   0000   0000   0000   0000
                  ↑                     ↑     ↑     ↑    ↑  ↑   ↑ ↑  ↑ ↑
bits:           31                    16    15  12  11  8  7  4  3  0
```

FIGURE 2.2
31-Bit Positive Integer in Two Bases

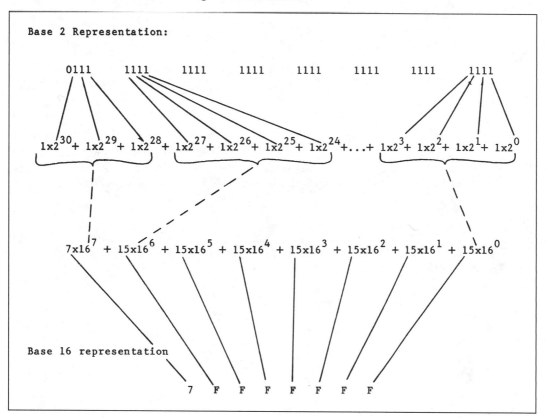

which behaves like $-2,147,483,648$. We can see this, if we take its opposite less 1 or

$$2^{31} - 1 = 2,147,483,647$$
$$= 0111\ 1111\ 1111\ 1111\ 1111\ 1111\ 1111\ 1111$$

and compute the following sum

$$4,294,967,295 = 2,147,483,648 + 2,147,483,647$$
$$= 1111\ 1111\ 1111\ 1111\ 1111\ 1111\ 1111\ 1111\ \text{(base 2)}$$

To show that

$$1\ 000\ 0000\ 0000\ 0000\ 0000\ 0000\ 0000\ 0000$$

behaves like $-2,147,483,648$, we must show that the above sum, indeed, behaves like -1 with the following playful arithmetic carried out with a VAX-11:

decimal addition	*binary addition*
-1	1111 1111 1111 1111 1111 1111 1111 1111
$+1$	$+$ 0000 0000 0000 0000 0000 0000 0000 0001
0	0000 0000 0000 0000 0000 0000 0000 0000

carry = 1, which is lost!

This oddity stems from the finite arithmetic forced on the machine by its doubleword size. After this addition, all the bits of the sum are zero. As we mentioned earlier, the carry bit is saved in another part of the machine— in bit 0 of the processor status word (PSW), which we examine later.

2.3

THE RELATIONSHIP BETWEEN HEX AND BINARY NUMBERS: FOUR-IN-ONE

The digits of a hex number such as

$$B520_{16} = 46368_{10}$$

can be represented as four binary digits

$$
\begin{array}{cccc}
B & 5 & 2 & 0 \\
\end{array}
$$
$$= $$
$$1011\ 0101\ 0010\ 0000$$

As simple as it may seem, the secret to machine and assembly language programming on a VAX-11 computer is related to our ability to determine which of four possible binary bits a hex digit represents, that is, which ones are turned on ($=1$), and which ones are turned off ($=0$). Octal numbers are used as a form of shorthand for their binary counterparts.

2.4

CONVERSION OF BINARY NUMBERS TO HEX: BUILDING BYTES

The trick to converting to hex a 32-bit number like

$$00000000000000011101101000110001$$

is to break up the binary number into groups of four digits and to use the sets of four bits to determine corresponding hex digits:

binary: 0000 0000 0000 0001 1101 1010 0011 0001

hex: 0 0 0 1 D A 3 1

We can drop the leading zeroes. Then we have

1 1101 1010 0011 0001   (base two)

= 1 D A 3 1   (hex)

In other words,

1 1101 1010 0011 0001   (base two)

$= 1 \times 2^{16}$

$$+ 1 \times 2^{15} + 1 \times 2^{14} + 0 \times 2^{13} + 1 \times 2^{12}$$
$$+ 1 \times 2^{11} + 0 \times 2^{10} + 1 \times 2^{9} + 0 \times 2^{8}$$
$$+ 0 \times 2^{7} + 0 \times 2^{6} + 1 \times 2^{5} + 1 \times 2^{4}$$
$$+ 0 \times 2^{3} + 0 \times 2^{2} + 0 \times 2^{1} + 1 \times 2^{0}$$

$= 121393$ (base ten)

Implicit in the above equation is the notion that a binary number

$$d_{31} \ldots d_{15}d_{14}d_{13}d_{12}d_{11}d_{10}d_9d_8d_7d_6d_5d_4d_3d_2d_1d_0$$

can always be rewritten as a sum of powers of 2 to obtain either its hex equivalent or its decimal equivalent:

$$d_{31}d_{30} \ldots d_1d_0 = d_{31} \times 2^{31} + d_{30} \times 2^{30} + \ldots + d_1 \times 2^1 + d_0 \times 2^0$$
$$= (\text{hex no.}) \times 16^7 + \ldots + (\text{hex no.}) \times 16^0$$

$$\uparrow \qquad\qquad\qquad\qquad\qquad \uparrow$$
$$d_{31}d_{30}d_{29}d_{28} \qquad\qquad\qquad d_3d_2d_1d_0$$

In the above example,

$$\text{IDA31 (hex)} = 1 \times 16^4 + D \times 16^3 + A \times 16^2 + 3 \times 16^1 + 1 \times 16^0$$

with the corresponding binary digits

$$d_{19}d_{18}d_{17}d_{16} = 0001 \text{ (base two)} = 1 \text{ (hex)}$$
$$d_{15}d_{14}d_{13}d_{12} = 1101 \text{ (base two)} = D \text{ (hex)}$$

FIGURE 2.3
Conversion of Hex to Binary

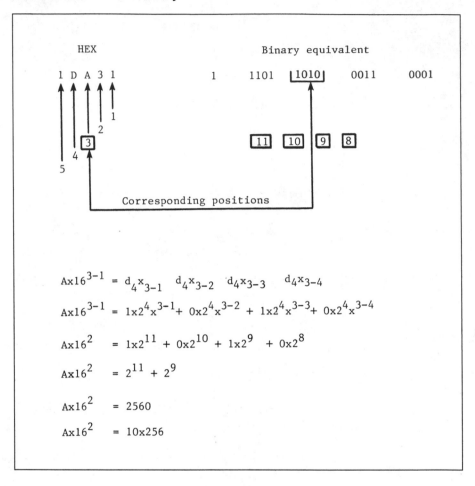

$$Ax16^{3-1} = d_4x_{3-1} \quad d_4x_{3-2} \quad d_4x_{3-3} \quad d_4x_{3-4}$$

$$Ax16^{3-1} = 1x2^4x^{3-1} + 0x2^4x^{3-2} + 1x2^4x^{3-3} + 0x2^4x^{3-4}$$

$$Ax16^2 = 1x2^{11} + 0x2^{10} + 1x2^9 + 0x2^8$$

$$Ax16^2 = 2^{11} + 2^9$$

$$Ax16^2 = 2560$$

$$Ax16^2 = 10x256$$

$$d_{11}d_{10}d_9d_8 = \quad 1010 \text{ (base two)} = A \text{ (hex)}$$
$$d_7d_6d_5d_4 = \quad 0011 \text{ (base two)} = 3 \text{ (hex)}$$
$$d_3d_2d_1d_0 = \quad 0001 \text{ (base two)} = 1 \text{ (hex)}$$

In effect, each hex digit, depending on its position, represents the sum of four separate powers of 2. Suppose the hex digit is in position K, then using H as the hex digit and d as the binary digit, it is easy to verify that

$$H_k = d_{4 \times k-1}d_{4 \times k-2}d_{4 \times k-3}d_{4 \times k-4}$$

This conversion is illustrated in Figure 2.3.

2.5

CONVERSION FROM BINARY TO DECIMAL

To convert a binary number to a decimal number, it is necessary to identify the position of each digit in a binary number. If a binary digit is in the kth position, then multiply this digit by 2^{k-1}. To find the decimal number corresponding to the binary number, add the powers of 2 related to the positions of the binary digits (see Figure 2.4).

FIGURE 2.4
Binary to Decimal Conversion

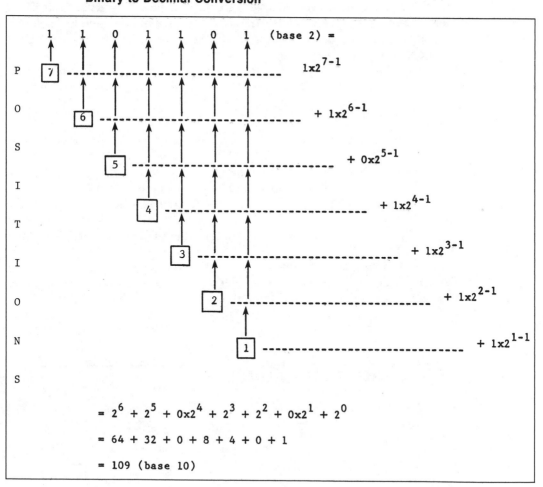

$$= 2^6 + 2^5 + 0x2^4 + 2^3 + 2^2 + 0x2^1 + 2^0$$

$$= 64 + 32 + 0 + 8 + 4 + 0 + 1$$

$$= 109 \text{ (base 10)}$$

2.5.1 Conversion of a Decimal Number to Another Base

Initially this problem can be tackled by converting base ten (decimal) numbers (both integers and mixed numbers like 1.61803) to bases less than ten. It will soon become obvious that we need a special method to handle the remainders in the following method, whenever the new base is greater than ten. The method we will use to do this employs a stack (lists governed by the LIFO rule or Last-In-First-Out rule), which was mentioned in the preceding chapter, and a queue (lists governed by the FIFO rule or First-In-First-Out rule).

Suppose, for example, we want to convert the decimal number

$$293 \underset{\underset{Y}{\uparrow}}{.} 1618$$

to its hex equivalent. We deal with the integer part Y = 293, first. To do this, we set up a stack using the LIFO rule to save the remainders each time we divide until we arrive at a quotient that is zero. We show the steps of this conversion in Figure 2.5.

Next, we set up a queue using the FIFO rule, which will be used to obtain the digits of the fraction in the new base. We illustrate this with

$$Z = .1618$$

and carry out the conversion of this fraction to its hex equivalent (Figure 2.6).

The trick now is to put together the steps shown in Figures 2.5 and 2.6. This is done graphically in Figure 2.7. We would have a better approximation of our original number, *if* we added more places to the right of the radix 16 point.

The steps in the figures are summarized in the change-base procedure given in Figure 2.8.

In this chapter, we implement the change-base procedure using a convenient high-level language. In chapter 12, we return to this idea, using an assembler program to do the same thing.

2.6

SUMS WITH HEX AND BINARY NUMBERS

In the system based on radix sixteen, the symbol 16 does not exist! The sum, for example,

$$F + 1 = 10_{16}$$

FIGURE 2.5
Integer Decimal to Hex Conversion

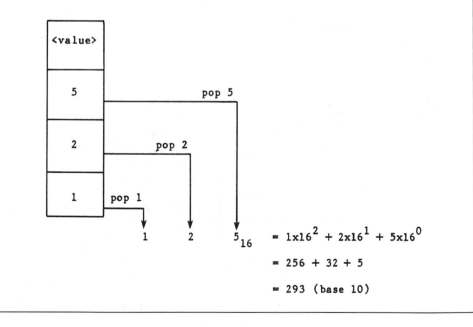

Step 0:   Push sentinel \<value\>: | \<value\> |

Step 1: 293/16   Q/18   R/5   Push 5: | 5 |

Step 2: 18/16   1   2   Push 2: | 2 |

Step 3: 1/16   0   1   Push 1: | 1 |

Stop when Q = 0

Result: (pop remainders to get number in new base):

$$1 \quad 2 \quad 5_{16} = 1 \times 16^2 + 2 \times 16^1 + 5 \times 16^0$$

$$= 256 + 32 + 5$$

$$= 293 \text{ (base 10)}$$

FIGURE 2.6
Fractional Decimal to Hex Conversion

Step 4:   enqueue ´.´

Step 5:   0.1618 x 16 = 2.58880
               enqueue 2

Step 6:   0.58880 x 16 = 9.42080
               enqueue 9

Step 7:   0.42080 x 16 = 6.73280
               enqueue 6

Step 8:   0.73280 x 16 = 11.72480
               enqueue B

        If we are content with 4 places
        to the right of the radix 16 point,
        then

Step 9:   enqueue sentinel <value>

Step 10:   dequeue ´.´ and digits:

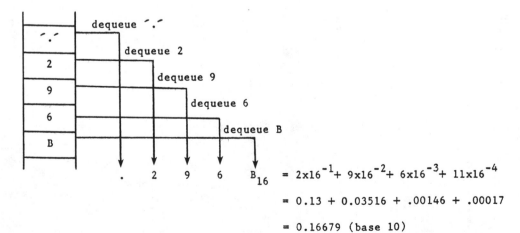

B_{16} = $2 \times 16^{-1} + 9 \times 16^{-2} + 6 \times 16^{-3} + 11 \times 16^{-4}$

= 0.13 + 0.03516 + .00146 + .00017

= 0.16679 (base 10)

FIGURE 2.7
Complete Decimal to Hex Conversion

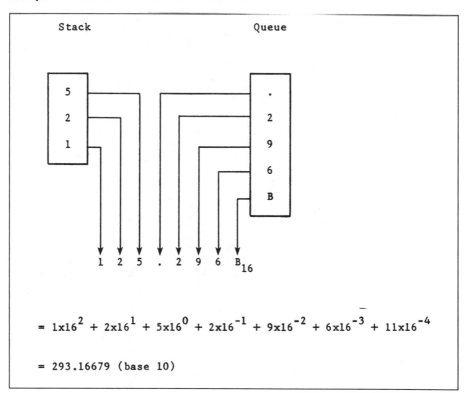

$$= 1 \times 16^2 + 2 \times 16^1 + 5 \times 16^0 + 2 \times 16^{-1} + 9 \times 16^{-2} + 6 \times 16^{-3} + 11 \times 16^{-4}$$

$$= 293.16679 \text{ (base 10)}$$

which looks like 10 decimal. Likewise, with radix two numbers, the symbol 2 does not exist, and

$$1 + 1 = 10_2$$

In computing sums and products in these bases, it helps to become familiar with the addition tables given in Table 2.3. Then summations like the ones below will be fairly straightforward:

Binary:		Hexadecimal:	
1 1 1	carries	1	carries
1 1 0 1$_2$		A 2 5 B 3 C	
1 0 1 1$_2$		A A A 1 B A	
1 1 0 0 0$_2$		1 4 C F C F 6	
$1 + 1 + 1 = 10_2 + 1 = 11_2$		$1 + 3 + B = 1 + E_{16} = F_{16}$	

FIGURE 2.8
Change-base Procedure

```
PROCEDURE        CHANGEBASE:

BEGIN

1.  Determine (READ) the decimal number (call it NO) and the new
    base (also called the radix) and call it BASE.

2.  Set up the necessary variables:
    2.1  WHOLE is assigned the TRUNC (NO), the integer-part
    2.2  FRAC is assigned the NO-WHOLE
    2.3  I,K are assigned initial values of 1
    2.4  SENTINEL is assigned the value 999
    2.5  FLAG is given a value TRUE (or 1)

3.  Begin loop to convert WHOLE to new radix:
    3.1  If WHOLE <> 0 then
         3.1.1  PUSH (SENTINEL)
         3.1.2  REPEAT the following steps UNTIL QUOTIENT = 0
                3.1.2.1  QUOTIENT assigned WHOLE DIV BASE
                3.1.2.2  REMAINDER assigned WHOLE MOD BASE
                3.1.2.3  PUSH (REMAINDER)
                3.1.2.4  WHOLE assigned the QUOTIENT

4.  Begin loop to convert FRAC to new radix:
    4.1  If FRAC <> 0 then FOR J incremented by 1 from 1 to 5 DO
         4.1.1  PRODUCT assigned FRAC * BASE
         4.1.2  PUT TRUNC (PRODUCT) into queue
         4.1.3  FRAC assigned PRODUCT - TRUNC (PRODUCT)
    4.2  Put SENTINEL in queue

5.  POP DIGIT from stack
    5.1  WHILE DIGIT <> SENTINEL perform the following steps:
         5.1.1  Write (print) DIGIT
         5.1.2  POP next DIGIT

6.  Begin steps to print out fraction:
    6.1  Print ´.´
    6.2  Pull first entry from queue
    6.3  WHILE DIGIT (from queue) <> SENTINEL perform the
         following steps:
         6.3.1  Write DIGIT
         6.3.2  PULL next item from queue

7.  END of Procedure.
```

TABLE 2.3
Binary/Hexadecimal Addition Tables

Binary:		
+	0	1
0	0	1
1	1	10

Hexadecimal:

+	0	1	2	3	4	5	6	7	8	9	A	B	C	D	E	F
0	0	1	2	3	4	5	6	7	8	9	A	B	C	D	E	F
1	1	2	3	4	5	6	7	8	9	A	B	C	D	E	F	10
2	2	3	4	5	6	7	8	9	A	B	C	D	E	F	10	11
3	3	4	5	6	7	8	9	A	B	C	D	E	F	10	11	12
4	4	5	6	7	8	9	A	B	C	D	E	F	10	11	12	13
5	5	6	7	8	9	A	B	C	D	E	F	10	11	12	13	14
6	6	7	8	9	A	B	C	D	E	F	10	11	12	13	14	15
7	7	8	9	A	B	C	D	E	F	10	11	12	13	14	15	16
8	8	9	A	B	C	D	E	F	10	11	12	13	14	15	16	17
9	9	A	B	C	D	E	F	10	11	12	13	14	15	16	17	18
A	A	B	C	D	E	F	10	11	12	13	14	15	16	17	18	19
B	B	C	D	E	F	10	11	12	13	14	15	16	17	18	19	1A
C	C	D	E	F	10	11	12	13	14	15	16	17	18	19	1A	1B
D	D	E	F	10	11	12	13	14	15	16	17	18	19	1A	1B	1C
E	E	F	10	11	12	13	14	15	16	17	18	19	1A	1B	1C	1D
F	F	10	11	12	13	14	15	16	17	18	19	1A	1B	1C	1D	1E

2.7

COMPUTING PRODUCTS

This is an important topic, especially if we want to coax the machine into computing products outside the range of its maximum integer and beyond the capabilities of its instruction set. The procedure that follows can be used to do extended arithmetic. It provides a way to compute products of large integers by repeatedly adding pairs of digits.

D. E. Knuth (1981, pp. 254–57) suggests a method for multiplying non-negative integers. A simplified version of this procedure is presented in Figure 2.9. A program to implement this algorithm in a convenient higher-level language is left as an exercise. (Chapter 11 shows how this procedure can be readily implemented in an assembly program.) Theoretically, there is no limit to the size of the product that can be produced with this method. In practical terms, we would be limited by the sizes of the arrays U, V, and W. The steps needed to compute the product

$$98765 \times 9876$$

are shown in Table 2.4. The final answer will appear in the last row of this table (shown inside the long rectangle).

TABLE 2.4
Knuth's Method of Computing 98765 × 9876

I	J	U(I)	V(J)	T	K	W1	W2	W3	W4	W5	W6	W7	W8	W9	W10	W11	W12
5	4	5	6	30	3	0	0	0	0	0	0	0	0	[0]	0	0	0
4	4	6	6	39	3	0	0	0	0	0	0	0	[9]	0	0	0	0
3	4	7	6	45	4	0	0	0	0	0	0	[5]	9	0	0	0	0
2	4	8	6	52	5	0	0	0	0	0	[2]	5	9	0	0	0	0
1	4	9	6	59	5	0	0	0	0	[9]	2	5	9	0	0	0	0
0	4	–	6	59	5	0	0	0	[5]	9	2	5	9	0	0	0	0
5	3	5	7	44	4	0	0	0	5	9	2	5	[4]	0	0	0	0
4	3	6	7	51	5	0	0	0	5	9	2	[1]	4	0	0	0	0
3	3	7	7	56	5	0	0	0	5	9	[6]	1	4	0	0	0	0
2	3	8	7	70	7	0	0	0	5	[0]	6	1	4	0	0	0	0
1	3	9	7	75	7	0	0	0	[5]	0	6	1	4	0	0	0	0
0	3	–	7	75	7	0	0	[7]	5	0	6	1	4	0	0	0	0
5	2	5	8	41	4	0	0	7	5	0	6	[1]	4	0	0	0	0
4	2	6	8	58	5	0	0	7	5	0	[8]	1	4	0	0	0	0
3	2	7	8	61	6	0	0	7	5	[1]	8	1	4	0	0	0	0
2	2	8	8	75	7	0	0	7	[5]	1	8	1	4	0	0	0	0
1	2	9	8	86	8	0	0	[6]	5	1	8	1	4	0	0	0	0
0	2	–	8	86	8	0	[8]	6	5	1	8	1	4	0	0	0	0
5	1	5	9	53	5	0	8	6	5	1	[3]	1	4	0	0	0	0
4	1	6	9	60	6	0	8	6	5	[0]	3	1	4	0	0	0	0
3	1	7	9	74	7	0	8	6	[4]	0	3	1	4	0	0	0	0
2	1	8	9	85	8	0	8	[5]	4	0	3	1	4	0	0	0	0
1	1	9	9	97	9	0	[7]	5	4	0	3	1	4	0	0	0	0
0	1	–	9	97	9	[9]	[7]	[5]	[4]	[0]	[3]	[1]	[4]	[0]	0	0	0

FIGURE 2.9
Knuth's Extended Precision Product Procedure

```
PROCEDURE KNUTH:

BEGIN

1.  Insert FACTOR NO. 1 (with M digits) into ARRAY U with
    dimension M

2.  Insert FACTOR NO. 2 (with N digits) in ARRAY V with dimension
    N

3.  Initialize the product array W so that W(M+1) through W(M+N)
    are zero

4.  Set up a counter J (for FACTOR NO. 1) equal to N

5.  Repeat the following steps UNTIL J <= 0:
    5.1  IF V(J) <> 0 Then execute the following steps:
         5.1.1 Initialize counter I (for FACTOR NO. 2) equal to M
         5.1.2 Initialize carry K equal to zero
         5.1.3 REPEAT the following steps UNTIL I <= 0:
               5.1.3.1 T:=V(I)*V(J)+W(I+J)+K
               5.1.3.2 W{I+J}:=T MOD BASE
               5.1.3.3 K: = T DIV BASE
               5.1.3.4 K: = I - 1
         5.1.4 W(J): = K
         ELSE
               W(J): = 0
    5.2  J: = J - 1

6.  Write out W(1) through W(M+N) as the answer

7.  End Procedure Knuth
```

2.8

METHODS OF DOING ARITHMETIC WITH SIGNED NUMBERS ON CALCULATORS AND COMPUTERS

Ordinary signed integers are added, if they have the same sign. If the signs differ, the integers must be subtracted. Two mechanisms would be needed to handle this arithmetic in a computer (adders and subtracters in the arithmetic unit of the processor). To get around this, *n's complement arithmetic* is used. For calculators, *n* will be 10; for computers, *n* will be either 1 or 2. We explain this method first in terms of the more familiar calculator.

2.8.1 Tens Complement Arithmetic

Assume we have a calculator capable of handling ten-digit numbers. The tens complement of a negative number x will be a number y so that

x + y = 00000 00000

For example, the tens complement of -11111 is 9999988889, since

9999988889 + 11111 = 00000 00000
(carry is lost)

Suppose we want to compute

56712 − 11111

we can replace 11111 with its tens complement and add to get the same result obtained by subtracting. That is,

56712 − 11111 = 45601
= 56712 + 9999988889
= 45601

If we start with a positive number X, its tens complement will behave like $-X$ in a sum. For example,

Tens complement of 5 = 99999 99995
= −5

since

5 − 5 = 5 + 99999 99995
= 00000 00000
(carry is lost)

Knuth (1981, p. 186) points out that "most mechanical calculators" use the tens complement to represent negative numbers. As a result, only addition is necessary to carry out subtractions on pairs of integers with opposite signs. Since the binary number system is used by computers, however, either ones complement or, more commonly, twos complement arithmetic applies here. By way of comparison, we offer side-by-side (tens and twos complement) arithmetic in Figure 2.10.

FIGURE 2.10
Tens Complement Method

```
         Base 10        Ten´s Complement
         (ten´s)            Method
    ─────────────────────────────────────────────

            4            00000 00004
           -6            99999 99994
           ───           ─────────────
           -2            99999 99998 = Ten´s complement
                                         of -2
```

2.8.2 Ones Complement Arithmetic

CDC computers (the Cyber series) as well as the PDP-15 support use ones complement arithmetic. For convenience, assume we have a 10-bit machine. Call it the PLUS-4/10. We obtain the *ones complement* of a binary number by replacing its 1s with 0s and its 0s with 1s. For example,

Ones complement of 101 = 11111 11010 (on PLUS-4/10)

since

```
    00000 00101        5
  + 11111 11010       -5
    ───────────       ──
    11111 11111       -0
```

The number 11111 11111 is called negative zero. Added to any other integer on this machine it behaves like zero. We can verify this ones complement of zero by applying the rule to zero. That is,

Ones complement of 00000 00000 = 11111 11111

$$= -0$$

To solve the problem of negative zero and the more general problem of adding a ones complement number to a positive number, if there is a carry out of the most significant bit position, do the following: *Add the carry back to the unit's place*. This is called an *end-around carry*. For example,

```
     5     00000 00101
    -0     11111 11111
    ──     ───────────
     5     00000 00100
                   + 1   (end-around carry)
           ───────────
           00000 00101
```

Other examples of ones complement numbers appear in Table 2.5.

The ones complement is not the choice of most computer manufacturers. Peterson (1978, p. 27) points to the reason: "the hardware to test for zero must check for both representations of zero, making it more complicated." Each time -0 occurs, it must be converted to $+0$.

2.8.3 Twos Complement Arithmetic

The IBM 370, PDP-11, and VAX-11 computers use twos complement arithmetic. The twos complement of a number is defined as follows:

twos complement of x = ones complement of x + 1

For example, on the PLUS-4/100, an improved version of the PLUS-4/10 (with twos complement arithmetic), we have

5	00000 00101	
-5	+ 11111 11010	(ones complement form of -5)
0	+ _____1	
	00000 00000	(-0 eliminated!)
	(carry lost)	

TABLE 2.5
Ones Complement Cross-Reference Table

POSITIVE NUMBERS			NEGATIVE NUMBERS (Ones Complement Form)		
Decimal	Hex	Binary	Decimal	Hex	Binary
0	0	0000 0000 0000	-0	FFF	1111 1111 1111
1	1	0000 0000 0001	-1	FFE	1111 1111 1110
2	2	0000 0000 0010	-2	FFD	1111 1111 1101
3	3	0000 0000 0011	-3	FFC	1111 1111 1100
4	4	0000 0000 0100	-4	FFB	1111 1111 1011
5	5	0000 0000 0101	-5	FFA	1111 1111 1010
6	6	0000 0000 0110	-6	FF9	1111 1111 1001
7	7	0000 0000 0111	-7	FF8	1111 1111 1000
8	8	0000 0000 1000	-8	FF7	1111 1111 0111
9	9	0000 0000 1001	-9	FF6	1111 1111 0110
10	A	0000 0000 1010	-10	FF5	1111 1111 0101
11	B	0000 0000 1011	-11	FF4	1111 1111 0100
12	C	0000 0000 1100	-12	FF3	1111 1111 0011
13	D	0000 0000 1101	-13	FF2	1111 1111 0010
14	E	0000 0000 1110	-14	FF1	1111 1111 0001
15	F	0000 0000 1111	-15	FF0	1111 1111 0000
16	10	0000 0001 0000	-16	FEF	1111 1110 1111
256	100	0001 0000 0000	-256	EFF	1110 1111 1111

Again, for example,

```
   4            00000 00100
  -6          + 11111 11001     (ones complement form of -6)
 ────         ─────────────
  -2          +           1
              ─────────────
              11111 11110
```

We can verify that

```
11111 11110 = twos complement form of -2
```

by adding 00000 00010 to this number:

```
    11111 11110        -2
  + 00000 00010        +2
  ─────────────       ────
    00000 00000         0
   (carry lost)
```

This can also be shown by finding the twos complement of 11111 11110:

```
Ones complement of 11111 11110 = 00000 00001
                                       + 1
                               ─────────────
                                 00000 00010
```

which is 2. In other words, the twos complement of the twos complement form of -2 is 2. The result of using twos complement arithmetic is a greatly simplified and elegant computation inside the computer. Two signed integers can be added *as if* they were unsigned. We no longer have two representations of zero, both $+0$ and -0.

As an exercise, add 1 to a ones complement binary number and give the corresponding hex equivalent of the resulting twos complement number. Look for patterns when you do this.

2.9
SUMMARY

Most computers use twos complement arithmetic to handle signed numbers. This makes it easier to handle computations involving integers with opposite signs. It also eliminates -0. Addition can be used to handle pairs of numbers that would have to be subtracted in their ordinary representations as integers because negative integers can be represented as twos complement numbers. The twos complement of an integer is the ones complement of that integer plus one. Tens complement arithmetic is used on calculators.

It is helpful to understand the methods of handling base conversion. In the case of binary numbers, the binary digits can be separated into groups of four from right to left to obtain the hex equivalent of the binary number. Put another way, a hex digit can always be represented as four binary digits. If the digit of a number in base b is in position K, then multiply this digit by b^{K-1} when converting from base b to decimal.

Using the array data structure, we give Knuth's method of computing extended precision products. Implementation of this method is left as an exercise, first in a higher-order language (HOL) in this chapter, later in assembler. Products obtained by this method are limited to single-digit integers. The individual digits of the complete product are used inside the cells of the product array W. Thus the computer does not "think" of the final result as one product. The same is true for the factors. This leaves the way open to work with products of large numbers, larger than the computer can handle by itself.

2.10

EXERCISES

1. Each of the following binary numbers represents the contents of 16-bit computer words. Convert these numbers to their hex equivalent.

   (a) 0101010101010101
   (b) 0010101010101010
   (c) 0111111111111111
   (d) 0000110111011111
   (e) 0111110111111001
   (f) 1000000111010111

2. Separate the upper and lower 8 digits of each of the binary numbers in the preceding exercise, that is, into high and low bytes of these words. Give the hex equivalent of each byte.

3. Convert the binary numbers in exercise 1 to their decimal equivalent using powers of 2.

4. Convert the hex numbers obtained in exercise 1 to their decimal equivalent using powers of 16.

5. Convert the following hex numbers to binary:

   (a) 600 (16)
   (b) 56 (16)
   (c) DO (16)
   (d) AAAA (16)

(e) A111 (16)   (h) 7FFF

(f) 1FFF FFFF   (i) 8FFFF

(g) FFFF   (j) 1FFFF

6. Using the tables for addition in Table 2.3 as a guide, write product tables for radix two and sixteen.

7. Use a calculator to convert the following numbers to radix sixteen:

   (a) 796.796   (e) 2048

   (b) 1.61803   (f) 3.1415

   (c) 0.61803   (g) $4LOG_2 10 = 13.28771_{10}$

   (d) 28657   (h) $4LOG_{10^2} = 1.20411_{10}$

8. Convert the constants in exercise 7 to radix two.

9. Write a high-level language program to implement the change-base procedure in Figure 2.8. Allow the user to enter either an integer or mixed decimal number as well as a base between 2 and 36. Convert the entered number to the new base. To do this, use uppercase letters for remainders on the stack or numbers in the queue $\rangle = 10$.

   Hint: In Pascal, for example, use the chr(X) function to do this when printing out the digits of the number in the new base. Be mindful of the locations of the digits 0 through 9 in the ASCII chart. Zero is 48 decimal in this chart, 9 is ASCII 57 (decimal). If a digit $X + 48$ is greater than 57, increase $X + 48$ by 7 to transfer to the ASCII codes for the uppercase letters.

10. Each of the numbers in the following computations is in hex for a 32-bit machine like the VAX-11. Carry out the following arithmetic *in hex* (use the twos complement representations of negative integers) and give results in hex:

    (a) 25A − C1   (g) 1 + FFFFFFFF

    (b) C1 − 25A   (h) 1 − FFFFFFFF

    (c) AAA / 25   (i) 8000 0000 + 7FFF FFFF

    (d) C2A / C1A   (j) 8000 0000 − 7FFF FFFF

    (e) A − FFFFFFFF   (k) 8000 + 7FFF

    (f) A + FFFFFFFF   (l) A − B − C − D − E − F

11. Using Table 2.5 as a guide, construct a twos complement table for the entries in Table 2.5.

12. Each of the following numbers is in base ten. Use tens complement arithmetic to carry out the following computations normally done on the PLUS-4/10 digit calculator:

(a) 5-2   (c) 1111155555-11111

(b) 32767-7129   (d) 10-5555512121

13. Using Table 2.4 (Knuth's method of computing products) as a guide, write out the steps of Knuth's extended precision method of computing 39659×32767.

2.11

LAB PROJECTS

1. It is possible to use repeated subtraction to compute quotients and remainders from ratios like 37/13. That is, repeatedly subtract the smaller from the larger number:

$$
\begin{array}{cc}
37 & 24 \\
-13 & -13 \\
\hline
24 & 11
\end{array}
$$

until the difference is smaller than the smaller of the original two numbers (that is, smaller than the divisor). Then

Remainder R = 11

Quotient Q = 2 = no. of subtractions

(a) Write a procedure in pseudocode that describes how to divide a number X by a number Y using repeated subtraction.

(b) Write a procedure in pseudocode that describes how to set up an extended precision routine to divide X by Y using repeated subtraction on a pair of digits, one from X and one from Y.

(c) Write a program in a higher-level language like C or Pascal to implement the procedure in (a). Test your program with 6765/4181.

Note: Write your program so that it will work for numbers in bases two through nine.

(d) Write a program in a higher-level language to implement the procedure in (b). Test your program with 6722026041/1286729879.

Note: Print out 10 places to the right of the decimal; your program should handle numbers in bases two through nine.

2. Using an HOL, write a program to do extended precision addition. Test your program with the following pairs of numbers:

(a) 65535, 65535   (b) 2147483647, 2147483647

3. A quick, efficient way to compute products (Huber's Method) is shown below. First load an array with the digits of the first factor, with each digit as a separate array element. Do the same for the second factor. Then, save the carry and the units place for each of the pairs of digits on separate stacks as shown below with

1057 × 142

Computation of Products of Pairs of digits		*Unit Stack*	*Carry Stack*
Step 1: 105 7 142			
7 × 2 = 14		4	1
Step 2: 10 5 7 1 4 2			
7 × 4			
+			
5 × 2 = 38 + carry		9	3
Step 3: 1 0 5 7 1 4 2			
7 × 1			
+			
5 × 4			
+			
0 × 2 = 27 + carry		0	3
Step 4: 1 0 5 7 1 4 2			
5 × 1			
+			
0 × 4			
+			
1 × 2 = 7 + carry		0	1
Step 5: 1 0 57 1 4 2			
0 × 1			
1 × 4 = 4 + carry		5	0

Step 6: 1 057   1 42

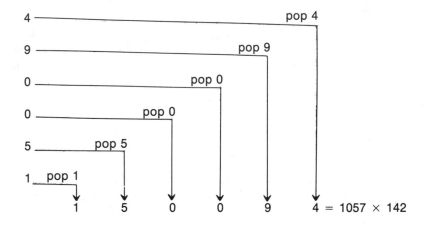

1 × 1   = 1 + carry   1   0

0

Now pop the digits in the unit stack:

4 ——————————————————————————— pop 4

9 ———————————————————————— pop 9

0 ——————————————— pop 0

0 ——————————— pop 0

5 ————— pop 5

1 ⎽ pop 1

1   5   0   0   9   4 = 1057 × 142

The pseudocode rendition of Huber's method is given next:

```
Procedure Huber;
begin
read(x,y); (factors with x1 and y1 as their digit lengths.)
if x1 > y1 then y:=x and x:=y;
load digits in reverse order into arrays a and b respectively.
array1 c:=y; (c is to be used as a counter since each digit of x is
            multiplied with each digit of y only y1 times.)
for z:=1 to (x1+y1−1) do (total amount of steps.)
        begin
        buff:=0;
        for zz:=1 to z do
                begin
                if c[zz] <>0 then
                        if zz<=y then
                                begin
                                c[zz]:=c[zz]−1:
                                buff:=buff+a[zz]*b[((z+1)−zz)];
                        end;
                end;
                if z>1 then
                        buff:=buff+d[(z−1)]; (add to buff digit from
                                        previous carry stack.)
```

```
                         d[z]:=buff div 10; (carry stack created.)
                         e[z]:=buff mod 10; (unit stack created.)
              end;
              e[x+y]:=d[x+y−1]; (pops last digit of carry stack on to
                                       unit stack.)
              print out array e in reverse order.
        END.
```

This will become the basis for an extended precision product routine that is fairly independent of the word size of the computer system.

(a) Write a procedure to implement the above method, which was suggested by Thomas Huber, Physics Department, University of Wyoming.

(b) Write a program in a higher-level language that implements your procedure.

(c) Test your program to compute

  (i) 65535×7
  (ii) 1307674368000×16

Note: this product equals 16!

  (iii) 2147483647×32

(d) Write a separate program to trace what happens during computing of one of these products (a partial trace will do). That is, show (display) the entries made to the units and carry stacks during processing.

4. Using an HOL (Knuth's method), write a program to implement Knuth's method given in Figure 2.9 to carry out extended precision multiplication. Run your program in terms of the products in parts C1, C2, and C3 of lab 2. Enhance your program in the first part to print out a trace of Knuth's method.

2.12

REVIEW QUIZ

Indicate whether the following statements are true or false:

1. The tens complement of 1 on a 10-digit display calculator is 9.

2. $\hat{}C\langle 0 \rangle = $ FFFF FFFF, if 0 is the content of a doubleword.

3. ^C⟨1⟩ = FFFF FFFF, if 1 is the content of a doubleword.

4. ^B⟨10⟩ = 1001, if 10 (decimal) is the content of a doubleword.

5. ^B⟨1⟩ = 0000 0000 0000 0000 0000 0000 0000 0001 on a VAX-11.

6. ^B⟨2⟩ = 1000 0000 0000 0000 0000 0000 0000 0010 on a VAX-11.

7. ^X⟨15⟩ = F, if 15 (decimal) is the content of a doubleword.

8. ADDL3 is VAX-11 mnemonic for C1 (hex).

9. A stack is used to hold the digits of the integer part of a base conversion from decimal to another base.

10. A queue is used to hold the digits of the integer part of the new number in a base conversion from decimal to another base.

11. Push and pop are queue operations.

12. Each time we push a number onto a stack, the other numbers in the stack move to make room for the new number (this is like putting a new cup in a paper cup dispenser—make room for the new cup).

13. The largest positive integer on a VAX-11 is 7FFF FFFF.

14. The largest unsigned number on a VAX-11 is 7FFF FFFF.

15. In a VAX-11 register, bit 31 is the MSB.

16. In a VAX-11 register, bit 31 is the LSB.

17. In a VAX-11 register, bit 0 is the MSB.

18. In a VAX-11 register, bit 0 is the LSB.

2.13

REFERENCES

Knuth, D. E. *The Art of Computer Programming, Vol. 2, Seminumerical Algorithms*. Menlo Park, CA: Addison-Wesley, 1981. See especially chap. 4. This is a classic in computing; it is detailed and provides 142 pages of solutions and alternative paths to the problems presented in the text.

Peterson, J. L. *Computer Organization and Assembly Language Programming*. New York: Academic Press, 1978. See especially section 1.2 on the computation unit (what we call the ALU).

3.

BUILDING AN ASSEMBLY LANGUAGE PROGRAM

The assembly process can be regarded as one of establishing bindings between symbolic objects (i.e., the symbolic instructions) and their values (the binary version).

—D. W. Barron, *Assemblers and Loaders*

3.0

AIMS

- Introduce the structure of assembly language source texts for main programs.
- Distinguish types of source texts.
- Show how a location counter is used by an assembler.
- Introduce some of the more commonly used VAX-11 operators and addressing modes.
- Distinguish three types of assembler operators.
- Suggest how new instructions can be created.

3.1

INTRODUCTION

The structure of a typical VAX-11 assembly language source text is shown in Figure 3.1. This chapter is about the building blocks needed to flesh out a framework like that shown in the figure. This framework is for a *main program*. Other assembly language source texts are possible: external procedures, external subroutines, external libraries of procedures, external libraries of what are known as open routines (macro definitions). A *main program* stands alone; it initiates calls to outside routines but is never called by an outside routine. The other types of assembly language source texts are dependent; they must be called by main programs or other routines or procedures. A sample VAX-11 assembly language source text for a main program is shown in Figure 3.2.

FIGURE 3.1
Structure of a VAX-11 Assembly Language Program

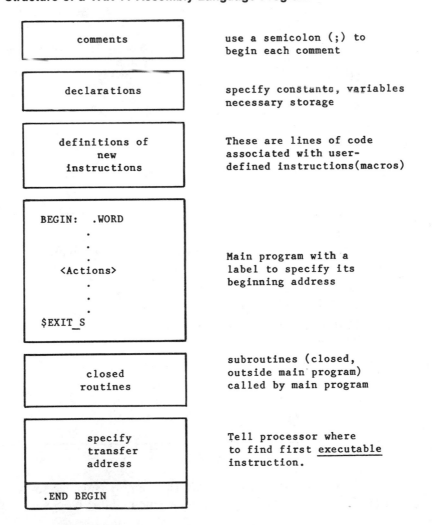

FIGURE 3.2
Sample Assembly Language Program

```
;
;Ref.:  Figure 3.2 (Sample Assembly Language Program)
;
;VAR

        MAX:       .LONG 3
        INDEX:     .LONG 0

;DEFINITION FOR USER-CREATED INSTRUCTION:

        .MACRO DRAWTRIANGLE
        WRITELN <                              *>
        WRITELN <                            ***>
        WRITELN <                          *****>
        .ENDM DRAWTRIANGLE

BEGIN:  .WORD

STATEMENT:
        DRAWTRIANGLE
        AOBLSS MAX,INDEX,STATEMENT
LOOP:   JMP LOOP

        $EXIT_S

        .END BEGIN



RUN FG32
                            *
                           ***
                          *****
                            *
                           ***
                          *****
                            *
                           ***
                          *****
```

The assembly language on VAX-11 computers is called VAX-11 Macro. This assembler supports the use of user-defined instructions called *macros*. Whenever the assembler encounters one of these instructions, the lines of code associated with the macro get inserted into a source text. The lines of code associated with a macro are given in a *macro definition*. These must appear either before the text for a main program or independently in external macro libraries. VAX-11 macro supplies its own system macro library, which we draw from each time we write a VAX-11 macro program.

3.2

COMMENTS

In an assembly language source text, comments are essential. A *comment* is used to explain the text. Each comment begins with a semicolon (;). In constructing a machine program equivalent to an assembler source text, comments (*any* characters to the right of a semicolon) are ignored by the assembler. Notice in Figure 3.2 that simple ⟨ret⟩s can be used as well. These empty lines help separate sections of the text.

3.3

THE DECLARATION PART: DEFINING LABELS AND SYMBOLS

The declaration part of an assembly language source text contains definitions of variables and constants. A *variable* is referenced in terms of a label. A *label* is a symbolic address for a memory location. Its value is its numeric address, *not* the content of the memory location named by the label. Since the content of a labelled location can vary, these symbolic addresses define (identify) variables. Notice, again, it is not the value of the label that varies but the content of the location that the label identifies. Labels are crucial to the development of an assembly language text. The mechanism used by an assembler to determine the numeric address for a label is important.

An assembler uses a *location counter* to keep track of the address of the first byte of each line of a source text containing either data definitions or instructions. It uses the location counter to tabulate the number of bytes up to the current byte at the *beginning* of the current line being translated to the binary level. Not every source text line has a label. Most do not. Labels always appear at the beginning of a source text line. The assembler begins by setting the location counter to zero—the default beginning value—which can be changed, if desired. Each time the assembler advances to the next line of text, it advances the location counter by the number of bytes used by the *preceding* line. When the assembler encounters a label, it uses the current location counter value to assign a numeric address to the label. The location counter is comparable to a pointer (think of a pencil with a built-in counter) that moves down the text as the assembler advances from line to line in its translating. This procedure is depicted in Figure 3.3.

In Figure 3.3, the label MAX is assigned the numeric address 0000 0000. The pointer advances to the line following the one containing MAX. Since MAX is defined in terms of a longword in

MAX :   .LONG 3

FIGURE 3.3
The Location Counter

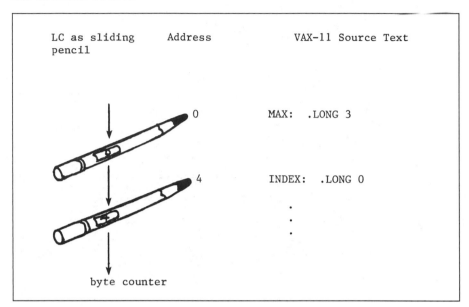

In the figure:

LC as sliding   Address   VAX-11 Source Text
pencil

0   MAX: .LONG 3

4   INDEX: .LONG 0
                             .
                             .
                             .

byte counter

4 bytes have been used by this source text line. Hence, the location counter (our fanciful pencil with a built-in counter) is advanced by 4. This becomes the numeric address for the label INDEX. When these labels are referenced in the main program, they take on a numeric value. These are examples of *relocatable addresses*. The VAX-11 reserves the first 512 bytes for its own use or the bytes in the range as shown below:

decimal	hex	
0	0	
:	:	reserved bytes
$\overline{511}$	$\overline{1FF}$	
512	200	

The preliminary addresses supplied by the assembler will be relocated later:

Assembler Address	Relocated Address	Label Address
0	200	MAX
4	204	INDEX

In VAX-11 assembly language programs, a period (.) is used to represent the current value of the location counter. This allows us to move the location counter back and forth at will within a program. For example,

```
X :  .LONG
        . = . + 1020
Y :
```

will reserve 1K (1024) bytes of memory for the variable *X*. Why? The .LONG is a storage directive. A directive instructs the assembler to do something. This directive instructs the assembler to reserve 4 bytes (one longword) *beginning* with the byte labelled *X*. Then we advance the location counter by 1020. When the assembler advances to the line labelled *Y*, it will advance the location by 4 + 1020 = 1024. This sets aside 1024 bytes addressed by *X*. We can represent the location counter symbolically with

```
LC = .
```

Any symbol could have been used. The symbol LC makes a good mnemonic. We can use this symbol, if we advance the LC later in the text. For example,

```
LC = LC + 1024
```

Labels can be 1 to 31 characters long and can have the following forms:

Form	*Example*
⟨letter(s)⟩ ⟨integer⟩	Apple2
⟨letter(s)⟩ ⟨_⟩ ⟨letter(s)⟩	Golden_section
⟨Integer⟩ ⟨$⟩	169$
⟨letter(s)⟩	Compute

VAX-11s accept source texts written in lower case, which is wonderful. The mixture of upper and lower case in a source text makes a text more readable. A colon (:) is used to separate a label from what follows. For example,

Form	*Example*
⟨label⟩ : ⟨storage directive⟩	X: .LONG2
⟨label⟩ : ⟨blank line⟩	LOOP:
⟨label⟩ : ⟨instruction⟩	COMPUTE: ADDL2 R6, R7

Commonly used storage directives are given in Figure 3.4.

A storage directive can be used to initialize the content of a memory

FIGURE 3.4
Storage Directives

Single Memory Units		Multiple Memory Units	
Directive	Bits	Directive	Bits
.BYTE	8	.BLKB <n>	n x 8
.WORD	16	.BLKW <n>	n x 16
.LONG	32	.BLKL <n>	n x 32
.QUAD	64	.BLKQ <n>	n x 64
.FLOAT	32	.BLKF <n>	n x 32

location. For example,

```
X:   .LONG 6
Y:   .LONG ^X⟨12345678⟩
```

puts 6 in the byte with address X, a 78 (hex) in the byte with address Y. If we assume $X = 200$ (an address in hex), then the above declarations set up two longwords as follows:

Label	LC	Byte Address	Byte Content	Comment
X	200	200	06	; 06 represents 0000 0110
		201	00	
		202	00	
		203	00	
Y	204	204	78	; 78 represents 0111 1000
		205	56	
		206	34	
		207	12	

The declaration part can also include the use of *pseudolabels,* which are symbols with constant values. For example, we can define

```
CR = 13
```

and give to the symbol CR the value 13. This is handy. We can move the

CR-value into a convenient location like R6 by using a #-sign prefix; for example,

        MOVL #CR, R6

A word of caution is in order here. It happens that 13 is the decimal ASCII code for a carriage return. It is not possible to use

        MOVL CR, R6

which would result in an access *violation message* from the processor. VAX-11 Macro limits symbols to values in the forbidden range 0:1FF. Errors also arise if we attempt to define a symbol with a value greater than 1FF (hex). Despite these restrictions, symbols with values (they are used as constants) are extremely useful. Features of labels are summarized in Figure 3.5.

Finally, notice how the label STATEMENT in Figure 3.2 is used in the AOBLSS loop. This time, the label identifies the boundary address of a loop. Notice that the values of all three labels MAX, INDEX, and STATE-

FIGURE 3.5
Features of Labels

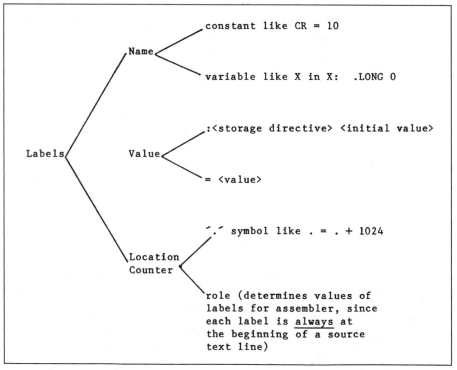

MENT control the branching and execution in

STATEMENT:

DRAWTRIANGLE

AOBLSS MAX, INDEX, STATEMENT

symbolic address used in loop

incremented by 1 until the *content* of the memory location with the symbolic address INDEX equals the *content* of MAX

label to identify memory location having upper limit of loop

repeat ⟨statement⟩ until MAX = INDEX

3.4

ASSEMBLER INSTRUCTIONS

The structure of a typical VAX-11 assembly language instruction is shown in Figure 3.6.

An *operator* specifies an action to be performed by the processor. Three types of operators are used in assembly language programs:

1. *Mnemonic* like ADDL3 for an instruction that is part of the native instruction set of the machine.

2. *Directive* like .LONG used to control assembly of a source text.

3. *User-defined operators* (macro names that are part of macro instructions) like DRAWTRIANGLE in Figure 3.2. A macro operator is associated with lines of code in a macro definition, which is inserted into the source

FIGURE 3.6
Structure of Assembler Instructions

Label	Operator	Operand	. . .	Operand	Comment
Field	Field	Field		Field	Field
⟨Symbolic address⟩	⟨Operator mnemonic⟩	⟨Specifier⟩	. . .	⟨Specifier⟩	⟨;expression⟩

text by the assembler when it encounters a macro. Actually, WRITELN is also a user-defined operator, which we explain in the next chapter.

Most VAX-11 assembly language operators have more than one form, depending on the data types of the operator(s) and the number of operators called for by the operator. Out of 105 more commonly used, elementary nonbranch operators, we can identify 28 actions. These are shown in Table 3.1.

In general, operands have two forms:

Action Specifier	Data Type	No. of Operands
ADD	L	2

TABLE 3.1
VAX-11 Operators

Forms	Operator	x	y	No. of Operands	Action Specified
8	ADDxy	B,W,L,F	2,3	2 or 3	add
1	ADWC			2	add with carry
2	ASHx	L,Q		3	shift bits
5	CLRx	B,W,L,Q,F		1	clear bits
5	CMPx	B,W,L,F		2	compare
2	CMPCy		3,5	3 or 5	compare character
13	CVTxy	B,W,L,F	B,W,L,F	2	convert (a special move)
3	DECx	B,W,L		1	decrement by 1
8	DIVxy	B,W,L,F		2 or 3	divide
1	EDIV			4	extended divide
1	EMUL			4	extended multiply
3	INCx	B,W,L		1	increment by 1
3	MCOMx	B,W,L		1	MOVe ones complement
4	MNEGx	B,N,L,F		1	MOVe twos complement
	MOVX	B,W,L,Q,F			
5	MOVAx	B,W,L,Q,F		2	MOVe address
1	MOVPSL			1	MOVe PSL
2	MOVZxy	B,W	W,L		MOVe with zero
8	MULxy	B,W,L,F	2,3	2 or 3	multiply
1	NOP			0	continue
1	POPL			1	pop value
1	POPR			1 to 15	pop registers
1	ROTL			1	rotate bits
8	SUBxy	B,W,L,F	2,3	2 or 3	subtract
4	TSTx	B,W,L,F		1	test condition codes
6	XORxy	B,W,L	2,3	2 or 3	exclusive OR

or

Action Specifier	Data Type	Data Type
MOVeZ	B	L

For example,

MOVZBL   X,   R6

source   destination

If we start with

X content = FF   .

R6 content = AAAA2121

Then executing a MOVZBL X, R6 will produce the following result:

R6 content = 0000 00FF

In this case, the action is a MOVe, which puts the *X*-content into the low byte of R6 and clears (zero extends) the bits of the upper 3 bytes of R6. This operator specifies the data type of each operand. In this instruction, *X* is an example of a *source operand*. It specifies the address of the operand to be used in calculating the result. R6 is a *destination operand*; it holds the result of the action specified by the MOVeZero extended operator. ADDxy and MOVZxy are examples of VAX-11 processor instruction mnemonics.

Directives tell the assembler to do something when it assembles a source text. They are widely used in source texts. Besides storage directives such as

.LONG or .BLKL

there is another that must be used in *every* assembly language source text:

.END ⟨label⟩

This directive specifies the transfer address, that is, the location of the byte where execution of the binary version of source text will begin *after* it is loaded into memory for execution. The .END directive is associated with

BEGIN : .WORD

which identifies the beginning of the first executable instruction of the source text.

Appendix C contains a library of macros that are easy to use. For example

WRITELN ⟨string⟩

will tell the assembler to insert into the source text the lines of code associated with the WRITELN operator, whenever it encounters this macro in the source text after the BEGIN : .WORD directive. This particular macro has lines of code that make it possible to

1. print a specified string
2. print a ⟨ret⟩

In addition, the VAX-11 has a library of system macros. One of these is used in every assembler source text for a main program:

$EXIT_S

This macro introduces lines of code into the source text to terminate execution of the program. It is possible, but not advisable, to omit this macro in a main program. *Main program* means a source text that does not depend on other source texts to specify actions to the processor.

3.5
INSTRUCTION OPERANDS

Each instruction operand specifier indicates the location of the operand to be used by an instruction. When registers are used, a variety of addressing modes are available to specify the location of the operand. Implicitly, we have used what is known as *register mode* with instructions like

MOVL #2,   R6

Register mode addressing specifies that the destination operand is in R6 itself, i.e., the number 2 is put into R6

Another addressing mode called *immediate mode addressing*. The #-sign tells the assembler what follows the #-sign is the immediate operand for the instruction

The immediate mode can be used in terms of

#⟨number⟩

The operand itself, *not* its address, is specified, using the # sign and an integer like 200 in

ADDL2 #200, R6

If we drop the # sign and use

ADDL2 ˆX⟨200⟩, R6

this adds the content of the hex location 200 to R6. Without the # sign, we have an example of the relative addressing mode. The operand

ˆX⟨200⟩

specifies the location of the source operand relative to the displacement of the PC. If we write

ADDL2 200, R6

the assembler takes the decimal value of the constant 200 as an address. It happens that the first 512 bytes

000

⋮   200 (base ten) is in this interval

1FF (hex)

200 (hex)

are reserved by DEC. These locations cannot be addressed by assembler instructions. Thus the absence of the ˆX-prefix in

ADDL2 200, R6

will be treated as an access violation by the processor when it attempts to execute this instruction. The immediate mode can also be used in terms of

⟨expression⟩

For example, suppose we have

LF = 10

which gives the symbol LF a value of 10. If we use

MOVL #LF, R6

this will put 10 into R6. It is *not* the content of location 10, but rather the value of LF we are addressing immediately after the # sign. We will see later that if, for example, we have

AX: .LONG 0

then

MOVL #AX, R6

will move the address represented by AX into R6.

It is helpful to *see* what happens to memory in the computer as a result of using some of these addressing modes. To do this, use the following steps:

1. Use an editor like TECO or EDIT to prepare a source text (call it T.MAR).

2. Assemble the source text by using

MACRO T⟨ret⟩

3. Link the resulting object module by using

LINK T ⟨ret⟩

4. Run the executable module produced by the linker (it will be called T.EXE) by using

RUN T

5. While the program is running, type

⟨CTRL⟩ ⟨Y⟩

This prevents the processor from clearing memory, once it finishes executing your program. As a rule, the processor will always clear memory before you have a chance to type ⟨CTRL⟩ ⟨Y⟩. To get around this problem, put an infinite loop in your program like

    LOOP : JMP LOOP

which will tell the processor to jump to location LOOP. Once it does this, it will execute the instruction again, make the jump to LOOP, and so on ad infinitum. Now you can examine memory to see what happened when your program was executed by the processor.

6. To do this, type EXAMINE/BYTE 200 : ⟨hex address of high byte⟩ or, for example,

    EXA/BYTE 200 : 300

to get a memory dump of the byte locations from 200 (hex) to 300 (hex). To examine memory in terms of longwords, use

    EXA 200 : 300

(the default dump is in terms of longwords). We show this in terms of a sample source text that uses some of the move instructions and the addressing modes we have mentioned thus far. The source text appears in Figure 3.7.

Figure 3.8 shows the use of the above steps as well as a memory dump. Several features of this memory dump are of interest here:

1. With a #A, 200 (base ten) is inserted into location 274 (hex).
2. With

    MOVB B, ^X⟨278⟩

we use relative addressing for both operands. This puts CC (hex) into location 278 (hex). The AA (hex) at location 275 (hex) is not affected by this operation. You might wonder what would happen to the bytes in memory, starting at 278 (hex), if we had used

    MOVL B, ^X⟨278⟩

or

    MOVW B, ^X⟨278⟩

3. With

    MOVB B, R6

FIGURE 3.7

```
;
;Ref.:  Figure 3.7 (Immediate,Relative and Register Addressing Modes)
;
        A       = 200                   ;NOTE:200(BASE 10)=C8(HEX)

;VAR
        B:      .BYTE ^X<CC>            ;PUT CC(HEX) IN LOC. B

        .       = . + 3                 ;ADVANCE LC 3 BYTES FOR MORE
                                        ;READABLE MEMORY DUMP

        D:      .LONG ^X<AAAAAAAA>      ;PUT AAAAAAAA(HEX) IN LOC. D

BEGIN:  .WORD                           ;SET UP FIRST ADDRESS OF MAIN

        MOVB    #A,^X<274>              ;Modes:
                                        ;
                                        ;   MOVB #A,^X<274>
                                        ;         ^       ^
                                        ;         |    Relative Addressing
                                        ;      Immediate Addressing


        MOVL    D,^X<278>               ;PUT COPY OF D @ LOC. 278
        MOVL    D,^X<27C>               ;PUT COPY OF D @ LOC. 27C
        MOVL    D,^X<280>               ;PUT COPY OF D @ LOC. 280
        MOVL    D,R6                    ;PUT COPY OF D IN R6
        MOVL    D,R7                    ;PUT COPY OF D IN R7

        MOVB    B,^X<278>               ;PUT BYTE INTO LOC. 278(HEX)
        MOVB    B,R6                    ;USE RIGHTMOST BYTE OF R6
        MOVL    R6,^X<27C>              ;COPY R6 TO LOC. 27C(HEX)
        MOVZBL  B,R7                    ;MOVe Zero extend B TO R7
                                        ;RESULT:
                                        ;
                                        ;R7: |0 0|0 0|0 0|C|C|
                                        ;     ^   ^   ^  ^
                                        ;     |   |   |  |__ byte 0 = CC
                                        ;     |   |   |
                                        ;     |   |   |____ byte 1 = 0
                                        ;     |   |
                                        ;     |   |_____ byte 2 = 0
                                        ;     |
                                        ;     |_____ byte 3 = 0
                                        ;
        MOVL    R7,^X<280>              ;
        MOVL    D,R6                    ;RESTORE D TO R6
        MOVL    B,R6                    ;PUT B IN R6
        MOVL    R6,^X<284>              ;PUT COPY OF R6 IN LOC. 284
                                        ;COMPARE RESULT WITH
                                        ;
                                        ;   MOVB B,R6
LOOP:   JMP     LOOP                    ;SET UP INFINITE LOOP

        $EXIT_S
        .END BEGIN
```

FIGURE 3.8
Memory Dump

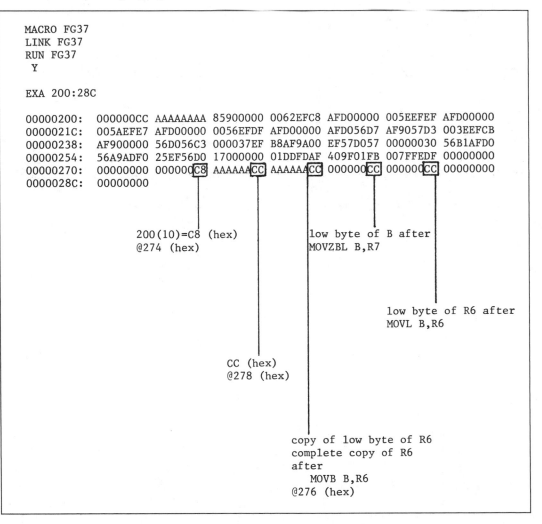

we use relative addressing in terms of the source B and register addressing in terms of the destination operand R6. Notice, again, that bytes 1, 2, and 3 are unaffected by inserting CC (hex) into byte 0 of R6. Notice what happened to bytes 1, 2, and 3 as a result of executing

MOVL B, R6

VAX-11 macro clears the bytes above byte 0, which obtains a copy of location B.

You might wonder what would happen if we used

```
CVTBL B, R6
MOVL R6, ^X⟨300⟩
```

That is, what would the CVTBL operator do to the bytes above the low byte of R6? This operator would still put ^X⟨CC⟩ in the rightmost byte of R6. This question can be solved as an exercise.

3.6

HOW TO DETERMINE THE BYTE RANGE FOR A MEMORY DUMP

The VAX-11 *assembler* treats numeric entries like 600 in

```
MOVL 600, R6
```

as decimal numbers. The VAX-11 processor also treats numeric entries like 600 in

```
MOVL 600, R6
```

as decimal numbers. However, the VAX-11 *processor* treats numeric entries in the EXAMINE instruction as hex numbers. For example,

```
EXA 600
```

tells the processor to dump (exhibit) the content of location 600 (hex). The first available location that can be examined is 600 (hex). In picking memory locations in which to put copies of data, there is a danger that you might write over the top of memory locations containing the instructions of your program. To avoid this, pick fairly high addresses like 300 (hex), if you are working with a short program like the one in Figure 3.6. It is possible to obtain a copy of the machine program and the temporary addresses used by the assembler in translating your source text down to the object module level. To do this, type

```
MACRO/LIST  ⟨source file name⟩
```

Then type, for example,

```
TY FG36.LIS ⟨ret⟩
```

or just

TY FG36 ⟨ret⟩

This will give you a copy of the list file. The beginning address will be 0000 0000. This will be relocated to 200 (hex) by the VAX-11 linker. In fact, add 200 to each of the addresses to determine the ones used by your program; for example, consider the following list module:

Machine Instr.	Assembler Instr.	Temporary Addr.	Relocated Addr.
0000	BEGIN: .WORD	0000	200
56 D4	CLR R6	2	202
57 56 02 C1	ADDL3 #2, R6, R7	4	204

3.7

OTHER ADDRESSING MODES

Table 3.2 provides a summary of VAX-11 addressing modes. In the beginning programs, the ones commonly used are

1. *Immediate Mode*   :MOVL #2, R6
2. *Relative Mode*   :MOVL X, R6
3. *Register Mode*   :MOVL R6, R7
4. *Register Deferred (Rn) Addressing Mode,* which specifies that a register contains an address that identifies the location of an operand. For example,

MOVAL X, R6

label to identify a memory address

long

address (this tells the processor to use the X-address, instead of the content of location X)

puts X-address into R6

Then

ADDL2 #233, (R6)

register deferred addressing specifies destination operand is in location X, *not* R6.

5. *Autoincrement Addressing Mode* (Rn)+ specifies two things. First, the register-content is used to determine the address of the operand. Second, after the operand has been used by the instruction, the content of the register is incremented

> by 1, if byte operands are being used
>
> by 2, if word operands are being used
>
> by 4, if longword operands are being used

For example,

CLRL (R6)+

specifies

increment

content of R6 before operation:

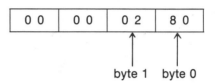

content of loc. 280 before operation:

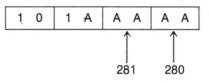

produces the following results:

first:

content of loc. 280:283 after operation:

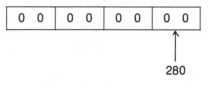

second:

content of R6 after operation:

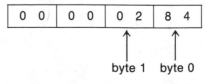

6. *Autodecrement Addressing Mode* − (Rn) specifies two things. First, the

TABLE 3.2
Addressing Mode

Hex	Mode	Symbol	Location of Operand
0–3	Immediate (PC)	#⟨number⟩ or ⟨expression⟩	following # sign
5	Register	Rn	Rn
6	Register deferred	(Rn)	@(Rn)
8	Autoincrement	(Rn)+	@(Rn)
7	Autodecrement	−(Rn)	@[(Rn)−1]
9	Autoincrement Deferred	@(Rn)+	@((Rn))
4	Index	i(Rn)	@[(Rn)+i]
B,D,F	Relative (PC)	⟨symbolic address⟩	@symbolic address
9	Absolute (PC)	@#⟨symbolic address⟩	@symbolic address
A	Byte displacement	B^D(Rn)	@[(Rn)+D]
C	Word displacement	W^D(Rn)	@[(Rn)+2xD]
E	Long displacement	L^D(Rn)	@[(Rn)+4xD]
B	Index Deferred	@i(Rn)	@[((Rn)+i)]
B	Byte Displacement Deferred	@B^D(Rn)	@[((Rn)+D)]
D	Word Displacement Deferred	@W^D(Rn)	@[((Rn)+2xD)]
F	Long Displacement Deferred	@L^D(Rn)	@[((Rn)+4xD)]

Note:

PC = program counter.
((Rn)): Rn holds address of location with address of operand without B^D, the default displacement in @i(Rn) is byte displacement.
D = constant like 5.

content of register Rn is decremented in terms of the operand specified by the instruction operator. Second, the new Rn specifies the location in memory of the operand. For example,

MOVB #5, −(R6)   content of R6 before operation:

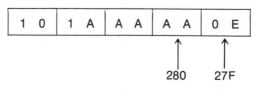

content of loc. 27F:283 before operation:

produces the following results:

first:

content of R6 after operation:

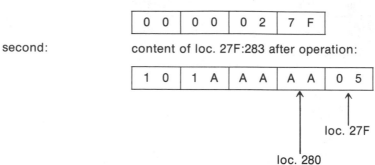

second:

content of loc. 27F:283 after operation:

7. *Index Addressing Mode* X(Rn) specifies that the address of operand is given by

(Rn) + X

For example, if there is 250 (hex) in R6, then

MOVL 10(R6), R7

puts the content of location 260 (hex) into R7.

3.8

EXAMPLE WITH AUTOINCREMENT/AUTODECREMENT MODES

An autoincrement/autodecrement instruction operator will determine the amount of autodecrement or autoincrement necessary for a register. For example, when autoincrementing R6 using a MOVe instruction, we get

1. MOVB #ˆX⟨A⟩, (R6)+ ;increments R6 by 1 *after* the MOVe
2. MOVW #ˆX⟨A⟩, (R6)+ ;increments R6 by 2 *after* the MOVe
3. MOVL #ˆX⟨A⟩, (R6)+ ;increments R6 by 4 *after* the MOVe
4. MOVQ #ˆX⟨A⟩, (R6)+ ;increments R6 by 8 *after* the MOVe

Using autodecrementing with R6, we get

5. MOVB #ˆX⟨A⟩, −(R6) ;decrements R6 by 1 *before* the MOVe
6. MOVW #ˆX⟨A⟩, −(R6) ;decrements R6 by 2 *before* the MOVe
7. MOVL #ˆX⟨A⟩, −(R6) ;decrements R6 by 4 *before* the MOVe

8. MOVQ #ˆX⟨A⟩, −(R6) ;decrements R6 by 8 *before* the MOVe

We combine autodecrementing, autoincrementing, immediate, relative and register addressing in the following example. Notice how

    ˆX⟨288⟩

is used in

    MOVL R6, ˆX⟨288⟩

        source   destination

This is *relative* addressing and it specifies a hex address for the destination operand. If we omit the ˆX, VAX-11 takes 288 as a decimal. It is possible to use decimal numbers to indicate addresses. For example,

    MOVL ˆX⟨290⟩, 768

          a decimal number:

          768 (base 10) = 300 (hex)

This will put a copy of the content of location 290 (hex) in location 300 (hex). A program to implement these ideas is shown in Figure 3.9.

FIGURE 3.9
Autoincrement, Autodecrement Addressing Modes

```
                 ;
                 ;Ref.:  Figure 3.9
                 ;
                 BEGIN:   .WORD
                          MOVL    #^X<280>,R6
                          MOVL    #5,-(R6)
                          MOVL    R6,^X<288>

                          MOVL    #^X<29A>,R6
                          MOVB    #^X<AA>,-(R6)
                          MOVL    R6,^X<29E>

                          MOVL    #^X<28C>,R7
                          MOVL    #33,(R7)+
                          MOVL    R7,^X<290>

                          MOVL    ^X<290>,768

                 LOOP:    JMP     LOOP

                          $EXIT_S

                          .END BEGIN
```

FIGURE 3.10
Memory Dump

```
EXA/LONG 200:304

00000200:   8FD00000  00000280  7605D056  75EF56D0  D0000000  00029A8F  85905600
0000021C:   56D076AA  000079EF  8C8FD000  57000002  D08721D0  005AEF57  EFD00000
00000238:   00000054  0000BFEF  FDAF1700  01FB01DD  FEDF409F  0000007F  00000000
00000254:   00000000  00000000  00000000  00000000  00000000  00000000  00000000
00000270:   00000000  00000000  00000000  00000005  00000000  00000000  0000027C
0000028C:   00000021  00000290  00000000  0000AA00  02990000  00000000  00000000
000002A8:   00000000  00000000  00000000  00000000  00000000  00000000  00000000
000002C4:   00000000  00000000  00000000  00000000  00000000  00000000  00000000
000002E0:   00000000  00000000  00000000  00000000  00000000  00000000  00000000
000002FC:   00000000  00000290  00000000
```

```
      33(10)
      @28C                                    @27C
               @290
                                         @29E

                                                        @288
      @300 (hex)=768(10)                       (288)=280-4
                                                  =27C (HEX)
               @299
           (299)=29A-1
             =299 (hex)
```

A memory dump of the longwords used by this program is given next. Notice the addresses of each destination operand relative to the addressing modes used (see Figure 3.10) These addressing modes are widely *and* easily used in assembly language programming on a VAX-11. The autoincrement, autodecrement, and index modes are useful in working with linear lists. The autodecrement and autoincrement modes make it easy to set up register stacks besides the system stack addressed by the SP. It is often handy to work with more than one stack. These modes can also be used to set up queues. (We show how to do this in chapter 6.)

For example, in the program in Figure 3.6, it would have been easier (but less obvious) to set up memory locations to save the results of operations using the autoincrement mode. Try this:

```
            CLRL R7                 ;set up AOBLSS index
            MOVL #^X⟨300⟩, R6        ;put 300 (hex) into R6
STATEMENT:
            MOVL D, (R6)+           ;(R6) ← 300 (hex)
                                    ;where (D) = AAAA AAAA
                                    ;(R6) ← (R6) + 4
```

```
        AOBLSS #3, R7, STATEMENT              ;continue executing statement
                                              ;until R7=3
```

This will load memory as follows:

location	content	R6
300	AAAAAAAA	300
304	AAAAAAAA	304
308	AAAAAAAA	308
30C	AAAAAAAA	30C
		310 (final value!)

Then, restoring the initial address to R6 will make it possible to use autoincrementing again. This time, we can use it to test the influence of some of the VAX-11 operators on memory content. After putting 300 (hex) in R6 with

```
        MOVL ˆX〈300〉, R6
```

try

```
        MOVL #A, (R6)+      ;affects loc. 300 (hex)
        MOVL B, (R6)+       ;affects loc. 304 (hex)
        MOVZBL B, (R6)+     ;affects loc. 308 (hex)
        MOVL C, (R6)+       ;affects loc. 30C (hex)
```

3.9

HOW TO INVENT NEW INSTRUCTIONS

This section presents a brief introduction to a topic we will continue to explore in later chapters. To invent new instructions, start by using an editor to install PAS.MAR given in Appendix C into a disk file. Then use

```
        LIBRARY/CREATE/MACRO PAS PAS
```

to establish a macro library, which we will use. Also install IO.MAR given in Appendix C into a disk file. Then use

```
        MACRO IO
        LIBRARY/CREATE/OBJ IO IO
```

to establish a library of I/O procedures, which we explain in the next several chapters. In this chapter, we merely want to explain how to set up new instructions like

DRAWTRIANGLE

given in Figure 3.2.

Three macros in PAS.MAR can be used to get started:

MACRO	FUNCTION
WRITELN ⟨string⟩	prints ⟨string⟩ with a ⟨ret⟩
WRITE ⟨string⟩	prints ⟨string⟩ without a ⟨ret⟩
TAB ⟨value⟩	prints a tab without a ⟨ret⟩

These macros can be used by themselves within a main program or as part of the definition of a newly created instruction. To create a new instruction (a macro) use

```
.MACRO   ⟨operator name⟩
   ⋮
⟨lines of code⟩              ;macro definition
   ⋮
.ENDM ⟨operator name⟩
```

The lines of code in the macro definition can include the macros in PAS.MAR as well as *any* of the other VAX-11 instructions mentioned so far. For example,

```
.MACRO DRAWRECTANGLE
WRITELN ⟨******⟩
WRITELN ⟨******⟩
.ENDM DRAWRECTANGLE
```

This would be put in the definition block above the

```
BEGIN :  .WORD
```

of the main program. To assemble and link a program with one of these new instructions, use the following steps:

```
MACRO FG32 + PAS/LIB
LINK FG32 + IO/LIB
RUN FG32
```

To see what the assembler does to a source text each time it finds a user-defined instruction like DRAWTRIANGLE inside the source text for the main program, type

```
MACRO/LIST/SHOW = ME FG32 + PAS/LIB
TY FG32
```

3.10

IN SEARCH OF THE ART OF ASSEMBLY LANGUAGE PROGRAMMING

Much of what we do in developing an assembly language source text for a main program hinges on an understanding of addressing. That is, it is important to know which bytes in memory are affected by an operation. It is equally important to become familiar with labels; that means knowing how to associate one or more bytes with a symbolic address specified by a label. There is a technique (an art) to be learned here in setting up labels to reserve areas of memory for future use, and in setting up instructions to manage memory contents.

In learning this technique, you should search for style in setting up source texts to make them more readable. It makes no sense to spend time writing a program unless you have some hope of reusing it. Unfortunately, it does not take long to forget what a program was about. The following tried-and-true methods can help you build a useful programming style:

1. Use *assertions* in comments—tell what the outcome of one or more operations will be.

2. Specify the *method* used.

3. Specify *test data* to be used in running an assembly language program. For example, try

   A = 768

   in Figure 3.7; in fact, try other values for A $\rangle$= 200 (hex). *Explain* the pitfalls in using certain data; *predict* results.

4. *Characterize* (in comments) *assembly language instructions* in terms of

more familiar higher-level language constructs. For example,

```
MOVL #2, X
```

is comparable to the Pascal assignment

```
X := 2
```

5. Specify *invariants* (things that will always happen) when a program is run. For example, unless MAX is initialized with a different value, the program in Figure 3.2 will always draw three triangles.

Assembly language programs are helpful in tapping the resources of a machine, in gaining insight into the organization of a computer. Assembly language programs also inspire fear—fear that they will not work. The pursuit of style will give you something to fall back on when a program does fail. Debugging becomes easier—you will find errors more readily if you check your *assertions* and look for invariants that failed to appear during a run. Finally, it is helpful to become comfortable with *looking* into memory, with checking memory dumps to see the effect assembly language instructions have had on memory contents.

3.11
SUMMARY

There are two frameworks to consider in starting a source text for a main program. First, there is the framework "expected" by the assembler for the entire text and its parts. Even though it is possible to put data declarations after the $EXIT_S, it is preferable to *start* a source text with these declarations. In other words, imitate the organization of programs written with structured languages like Pascal. This step alone will increase the readability of a source text. Introduce and explain data (variables, constants and, later, strings) *before* using them. The portion of the source text specifying operations to be carried out by the processor is bracketed by

```
BEGIN:  .WORD
          ⋮
        ⟨actions⟩
          ⋮
        $EXIT_S
        .END BEGIN
```

The label BEGIN specifies where the processor will find the first *executable* instruction. The data declarations and macro definitions are *not* executable. The $EXIT_S tells the processor when to stop executing. Before the processor can begin the instruction-execution cycle, the machine equivalent of your program must be loaded into memory. It will be brought in from secondary storage, from a disk, by the processor. The last line of code loaded into memory before the machine program is executed is the .END BEGIN. This gives the processor the address of the beginning of the executable part of the machine program. The label BEGIN is therefore called the *transfer address*.

A second framework to consider in developing an assembly language source text is the structure of the assembler instructions. The assembler reads each line from left to right. If it finds a label at the beginning of an instruction, the location counter comes into play, supplying the assembler with the numeric equivalent of the symbolic address provided by the label. Choosing operators to use in an instruction means choosing actions for the processor to perform. VAX-11 operators specify processor actions, *data types of the operands*, and, in some cases, the *number of operands*.

Finally, choosing operands means choosing addressing modes. Addressing modes specify methods to be used by the processor in *selecting* operands. A rich selection of VAX-11 Macro addressing modes is available.

3.12
EXERCISES

1. Obtain a listing (list module) for the program in Figure 3.2 by using MACRO/LIST FG32. Identify the following items in the listing:

   (a) location counter value

   (b) *relocated* address that will be assigned by the linker to each location counter value

   (c) operation code *and* its byte address

   (d) operands and their byte addresses

   Note: Follow the instructions in section 3.7 in setting up this program.

2. Obtain an *expanded* listing of the program in Figure 3.2 by using MACRO/LIST/SHOW = ME #FG32 + PAS/LIB. Identify

   (a) text inserted after each DRAWTRIANGLE (see the macro definitions and I/O procedures in PAS.MAR and IO.MAR in Appendix C to do this)

(b) text inserted for $EXIT_S system macro

3. Assume *each* label given below has 200 (hex) as its numeric address. Give the address *and* content for each byte reserved by the indicated storage directive (use hex to specify *all* addresses and byte contents):

(a) X: .BYTE 2

(b) X: .BYTE 33

(c) X_2: .LONG 65535

(d) X_3: .LONG

(e) X_4: .LONG ^X⟨ABC⟩

(f) X_5: .LONG ^B⟨1111⟩

(g) MM: .LONG ^C⟨1⟩

(h) AHA: .LONG ^C⟨0⟩

(i) AHH: .LONG ^X⟨1A2B⟩

(j) YES: .QUAD

(k) T: .QUAD ^B⟨10001000⟩

(l) TT: .QUAD 768

(m) TNT: .QUAD ^X⟨AAAA1⟩

(n) L: .QUAD ^0⟨777⟩

(o) LL: .WORD ^X⟨11⟩

(p) L_2: .WORD ^X⟨556⟩

4. In Figure 3.7, replace

        MOVB #A, ^X⟨274⟩

by

        MOVB A, ^X⟨274⟩

and run the program. Explain what happens.

5. In the original program in Figure 3.7, replace

        A = 200

by

        A = 768

and run the program without further change. Explain what happens.

6. Enhance the original program in Figure 3.7 by replacing

    MOVL D, ^X⟨278⟩
    MOVL D, ^X⟨27C⟩
    MOVL D, ^X⟨280⟩

with just two instructions, using register and autoincrement addressing modes. Replace the remaining instructions using relative addressing such as

    MOVB B, ^X⟨278⟩

with autoincrement addressing.

Hint: After loading locations 278:280 (hex), it will be necessary to *restore* the beginning address 278 (hex) in the register you use to handle the autoincrementing for the remaining instructions. Next, do the following:
(a) Run the modified program.
(b) Get a memory dump.
(c) Identify the location of *each* destination operand.

7. Remove the infinite loop from the program in Figure 3.7. Then try examining memory after running the modified program. Explain what you find.

Hint: Type RUN, then hold your hand poised over the ⟨CTRL⟩ and ⟨Y⟩ keys, pressing them just after hitting ⟨ret⟩. Now try examining memory.

8. When

    EXA 200 : ⟨high address⟩

is used after typing ⟨CTRL⟩ ⟨Y⟩ to suspend a program in memory, the memory dump is in longwords. Do the following
(a) Obtain a dump for the program in Figure 3.7, using

    EXA 200 : 28C

(b) Identify the locations and byte addresses for byte 3 (the high byte) of each longword, beginning at location 270 (hex).
(c) Obtain a dump for the program in Figure 3.7, using

    EXA/BYTE 200 : 28C

(d) Using the dump from part (c), identify the location *and* address of byte 0 (the low byte) and byte 3 of each longword, beginning with location 270 (hex).

(e) Comment on the differences between the dumps in parts (a) and (c).

(f) Using the list module for the program in Figure 3.7, identify the byte locations of the operator and operand codes for

```
MOVB #A, ^X⟨274⟩
MOVL D, ^X⟨278⟩
MOVZBL B, R7
```

The VAX-11 operator codes are given in Appendix A.

9. Using the program in Figure 3.9 as a guide, write a program to test the results of using *each* data type (B, W, L, Q) with the MOVe instruction. Use a memory dump like the one in Figure 3.10 to explain these results.

10. Use

```
X: .BLKL 20
```

and autoincrement addressing to fill the longwords, starting with location *X* and with even integers. Fill these longwords with even numbers, beginning with 2. That is, fill the first longword with 2, the second with 4, the third with 8, the fourth with 10, the fifth with 12, etc. In doing this, follow the program in Figure 3.2 to set up an AOBLSS loop.

11. The instruction

```
WRITELN ⟨string⟩
```

will print ⟨string⟩ with a ⟨ret⟩. A *string* is any sequence of ASCII characters. (Section 3.7 explains how to set up PAS.MAR and IO.MAR to use this macro.) Write a program to print your name and address.

12. A plain

```
WRITELN
```

will insert a ⟨ret⟩ into an outputted text. Write an enhanced version of the program for exercise 10 to print

Location counter:

⟨skip 1 line⟩

⟨indent 10 spaces⟩ ⟨begin definition⟩

⟨continue definition⟩

13. Write a program to test the results of using the CVTxy operator to move

a copy of the *x*-operand to the *y*-destination using register destination operands. Exhibit these results by moving the result of each CVT*xy* operation to memory locations, starting at location 300 (hcx). Explain what has happened, using a memory dump. Use data types *B*, *W*, *L*, *Q* with *x* and *y*.

14. Explain the difference between

    ADDL2 R6, R7

    ADDL3 R6, R7, R8

15. Write a program to compute the average age of members of your family, ignoring fractions. Use

    DIVL2 ⟨constant⟩, R6

to do this, after using

    ADDL3 (R7)+, (R8)

to compute the sum of the ages. Initialize R8 with the SUM-address. Initialize with an address AGES from, for example,

    AGES: .LONG 2, 10, 40, 36

Put the average in location 300 (hex). Get a memory dump to see the result.

Note: This can be done without a loop. However, if you follow the setup for an AOBLSS loop in Figure 3.2, this is easier. Try

    STATEMENT:

            ⟨compute sum⟩
        AOBLSS MAX, INDEX, STATEMENT
                  ↑   ↑
                  | Try zero as initial value
                No. of family members

16. Write a program to move a copy of the PSL into memory starting at location 300 (hex), then 304 (hex), then 308 (hex), and so on, *after* each of the following operations:

        1 − 1
        1 − 2
        ^X⟨FFFFFFFF⟩ + 1

Do the following:
(a) Run your program.
(b) Get a memory dump.
(c) Identify the N, Z, V, C bits of the PSL for each operation.
Correlate what you find with the operations performed in your program.

Hint: Use MOVPSL ⟨destination⟩.

3.13

LAB PROJECTS

1. Create an instruction operator called CUBE for a program to print 3 cubes. Do this by using CUBE only once in the main program.

2. Create an instruction called HORIZONTAL which will prompt the processor to print a row of 20 dots:

   . . . .

   when it is used inside a main program. Create a second instruction called SPIKE, which will prompt the processor to print a spike of 5 dots:

   .
   .
   .
   .
   .

   Write a program using HORIZONTAL and SPIKE to print a succession 5 U-shapes.

3.14

REVIEW QUIZ

Indicate whether the following statements are true or false:

1. The last line of every VAX-11 assembly program is $EXIT_S.
2. The last line of every VAX-11 assembly program is .END ⟨address⟩.
3. A .END ⟨address⟩ specifies a transfer address to the processor.
4. A .END ⟨address⟩ specifies a transfer address to the assembler.

5. A .END ⟨address⟩ terminates execution of an assembly language program at the indicated address.

6. Characters to the left of a semicolon (;) are taken as comments.

7. .BLKB 2 reserves 16 bits of main memory.

8. .BLKB 2 reserves one word of main memory.

9. .BLKW 2 reserves a doubleword of main memory.

10. .BLKL 10 reserves 10 doublewords of main memory.

11. .LONG 10 reserves 10 longwords of main memory.

12. . = . + 1024 advances the location counter 1024 bytes.

13. . = LC gives to LC the current value of the PC.

14. MOVB #2,R6 puts 2 into the low byte of R6.

15. MOVB #2,R6 puts 2 into the high byte of R6.

16. MOVZBL #2,R6 clears byte 0,byte 1,byte 2 and puts 2 into byte 0.

17. MOVZBL #2,R6 clears byte 3,byte 2,byte 1 and puts 2 into byte 2.

18. LOOP: JMP LOOP is an infinite loop.

3.15

REFERENCES

Barron, D. W. *Assemblers and Loaders*. New York: Elsevier North Holland, 1978.

Digital Equipment Corporation. *VAX Architecture Handbook*. Maynard, Mass., 1981. See especially chapters 2 and 5.

4.

BEGINNING I/O

Programming is designing, creating new programs.
—N. Wirth, *Programming in Modula-2*

4.0

AIMS

- Introduce a set of macros to handle input and output of integers and strings.
- Show how to use .ASCII, .ASCIC, and .ASCIZ.
- Introduce the CVT (convert), MOVAx (move address), and MOVC (move characters) instructions.
- Begin using constants to build string-arrays and to establish string lengths.
- Use the location counter to establish the length of a string.
- Begin using the indexed addressing mode.

4.1

INTRODUCTION

Memory dumps are helpful. They show precisely what the processor does when it executes a program. It would be awkward, however, if we always had to write our programs with an *infinite loop* to prevent the processor from clearing memory. The alternative to memory dumps is a set of macros to help us trace what happens inside the machine, to display the results of a processor's operation, and to build interactive programs. This chapter presents a set of macros (user-defined instructions) to handle terminal I/O.

Methods of handling integers and strings using macros taken from PAS.MAR are outlined in Appendix C. These macros have been developed using the VAX-11 QIO (Queue Input Output) system macros. (Chapter 9 examines procedures used to increase flexibility in handling both strings and numbers.)

This chapter focuses on some I/O macros that can aid in the design of new assembly language programs. These macros will help supplement memory dumps in tracing what a processor does. We will use these macros as tools in building new programs that prompt for test data entered from a keyboard and print out the results of processor operations. This exercise will also help you become more familiar with register addressing modes.

4.2

TWO STRINGHANDLING MACROS: WRITE AND WRITELN

The WRITE and WRITELN macros were introduced briefly in the previous chapter. The general format for a WRITE is

WRITE ⟨string⟩

any sequence of ASCII characters inside the pointed brackets

prints the ⟨string⟩ without a ⟨ret⟩

There is a broad range of possibilities here. If, for example, we type a tab inside the pointed brackets as follows:

WRITE ⟨TAB⟩

press the TAB key

nothing but a space will appear inside the brackets. Even so, when the processor executes the lines of code associated with this macro, an ASCII 9 for a horizontal tab will be printed.

This macro as well as WRITELN can be used in either main programs or definitions such as DRAWTRIANGLE (see chapter 3) for new macros.

If we use

    WRITELN

by itself, this will print a ⟨ret⟩, both an ASCII 10 for a linefeed and ASCII 13 for a carriage return. The next section shows how these macros can be used in combination with a macro to handle numeric input.

4.3

READVAR: A NUMERIC INPUT MACRO

The READVAR macro in PAS.MAR has the following form:

    READVAR ⟨VARIABLE⟩ . . . ⟨VARIABLE⟩ RADIX = ⟨VALUE⟩

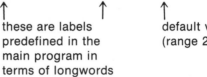

these are labels
predefined in the
main program in
terms of longwords

default value = 10
(range 2:10)

For example, we can use the following scheme to use this macro to read integers from a terminal:

    X: .LONG

          .

          .

          .

    BEGIN: .WORD
            WRITE ⟨enter an integer:⟩   ;print prompt
            READVAR X   ;get integer from keyboard

The WRITE macro is handy here. It prints the prompt without a ⟨ret⟩ so that the integer can be entered on the same line with the prompt. If the word radix does not appear in the READVAL instruction, it uses Radix = 10 as the default value (the radix range is 2 to 10). If you want to enter a binary number, then use

    READVAR X   RADIX = 2

This macro allows up to three integers to be entered together on the same line. To enter two integers X and Y, use

```
X:   .LONG
Y:   .LONG

       .

       .

       .

BEGIN:   .WORD
WRITE ⟨enter two integers in base two:⟩
READVAR X Y RADIX = 2
```

To enter three integers, using registers R6, R7, R8, for example, then use

```
BEGIN:   .WORD
WRITE ⟨enter three integers in base 10:⟩
READVAR  R6  R7  R8
```

You might be wondering how to enter these numbers at a keyboard. Type the numeric entries (in the specified base) separated by commas or spaces. Here is a sample typing session:

```
Enter three integers in base ten:
```

On the same line, you type, for example,

```
144, 233, 377 ⟨ret⟩
```

Now R6, R7, and R8 will have the values you typed! We illustrate the use of this idea in terms of loading consecutive memory locations with values entered from the keyboard. This is done using an AOBLSS loop, as illustrated in Figure 4.1.

The source text shown in Figure 4.1 illustrates the use of lower instead of upper case to prepare the text. A memory dump showing what happens to the longwords beginning with X is shown in Figure 4.2.

This program uses R6 to manage the data entry. First, we put the X-address into R6. Within the AOBLSS loop, we use register deferred addressing (R6) to load the first longword. The remaining two integers entered at a keyboard are handled using indexed addressing: 4(R6) *selects* the second longword; 8(R6) *selects* the third longword. Then #12 is added to R6 to advance the address in R6 to point to the *beginning* of the next set of three longwords. A portion of the memory dump in Figure 4.2 is interpreted graphically in Figure 4.3.

FIGURE 4.1
A Numeric Input Macro

```
;
;Ref.:  Figure 4.1 (A Numeric Input Macro)
;
;Method:  Use register deferred and indexed addressing modes with operands
;         in the READVAR macro.  Integers are loaded into consecutive long
;         words, starting at loc. X, three at a time using an AOBLSS loop.
;         The MOVA (MOVe Address) instruction is used to initialize R6, then
;         (R6) puts the first integer in the first long word location, 4(R6)
;         puts the next no. into the 2nd longword, 8(R6) puts the 3rd no.
;         into the 3rd long word location.
;
;var
        max:      .LONG 5                ;upper limit in AOBLSS loop
        index:    .LONG 0
        x:        .BLKL 20               ;Reserve 20 long words

Begin:  .word

        moval    x,R6                    ;put x-address in R6
statement:
        write <Enter 3 integers:  >
        readvar (R6) 4(R6) 8(R6)
        writeln                          ;print a <ret>
        add12    #12,R6                  ;advance address in R6
                                         ;to beginning of next 3
                                         ;long words.

        aoblss    max,index,statement

loop:   jmp loop                         ;set up infinite loop to
                                         ;make it easy to examine memory

        $exit_s

        .end begin



RUN FG41

Enter 3 integers:  1 1 2


Enter 3 integers:  3 5 8


Enter 3 integers:  13 21 34


Enter 3 integers:  55 89 144


Enter 3 integers:  233 377 610


^Y
```

103

FIGURE 4.2
Memory Dump

```
EXA 200:2E0

00000200:   00000005 00000005 00000001 00000001 00000002 00000003 00000005
0000021C:   00000008 0000000D 00000015 00000022 00000037 00000059 00000090
00000238:   000000E9 00000179 00000262 00000000 00000000 00000000 00000000
00000254:   00000000 AFDE0000 EF9F56AB 00000009 7BEF01FB 11000002 6E451314
00000270:   20726574 6E692033 65676574 203A7372 0A900120 0000BDEF EF00FB00
0000028C:   00000133 08A68BD0 04A68BD0 9F668BD0 00000AEF EF01FB00 0000023E
000002A8:   02000331 9F010D0A 00000AEF EF01FB00 0000022A 02000331 C0010D0A
000002C4:   CFF2560C 37CFFF36 AF1790FF FB01DDFD DF409F01 00007FFE 00000000
000002E0:   00000000
```

FIGURE 4.3
Graphical Interpretation of Memory Dump

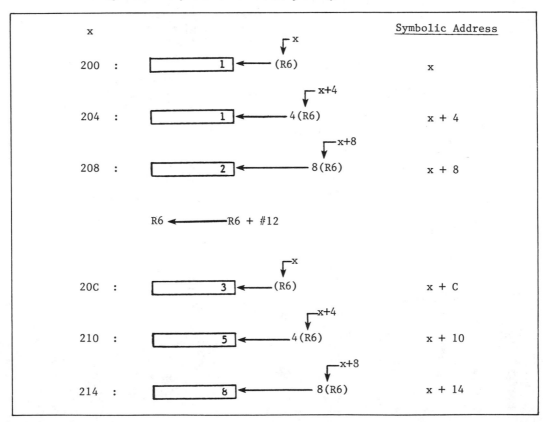

We still need a method of printing the contents of memory locations and/or registers. The next section shows how to do this.

4.4

WRITEVAL: A NUMERIC OUTPUT MACRO

The WRITEVAL macro prints copies of longword locations and registers. Its general format is

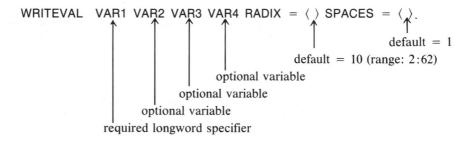

WRITEVAL   VAR1 VAR2 VAR3 VAR4 RADIX = ⟨ ⟩ SPACES = ⟨ ⟩.

default = 1

default = 10 (range: 2:62)

optional variable

optional variable

optional variable

required longword specifier

The following are some of the possible ways this macro can be used:

```
1.  X:   .LONG  ^X⟨1AA⟩
         .
         .
         .

    BEGIN:   .WORD
             WRITEVAL X
```

will print 1AA(hex) in base ten. (The default radix = 10.)

```
2.  X:   .LONG  ^⟨1AA⟩
    Y:   .LONG  ^X⟨33⟩
         .
         .
         .

    BEGIN:   .WORD
             WRITEVAL X Y Radix = 2   Spaces = 5
```

will print 1AA(hex) and 33(hex) in binary with 5 spaces between the two numbers printed.

3. X: .LONG ^X⟨1AA⟩

.

.

.

BEGIN: .WORD

.

.

.

WRITEVAL X R6 R7

will print the contents of *X* and registers R6 and R7.

This macro allows us to print memory contents or register contents in hex:

WRITEVAL X RADIX = 16

This macro is capable of converting integers in memory or registers to bases in the range of two to sixty-two.

4.5

EXAMPLE: COMBINED USE OF THE NUMERIC I/O MACROS

We can enhance the program in Figure 4.1 by replacing the infinite loop

loop: jump loop

with a sequence of WRITEVAL statements to echo-print the numbers that have been entered into memory. To do this, we restore (put back) the beginning *X*-address in R6. Then we step through the list of integers in the *X*-row of longwords. In restoring the *X*-address, we use a

movab x, R6

b = byte
a = address of the x-byte

instead of

moval x, F6

$\uparrow\uparrow$

l = longword

a = address of the x-byte = address for next 4

bytes, *beginning* with the x-byte

to call attention to an important addressing feature on the VAX-11. That is, for each set of 4 contiguous bytes in VAX-11 memory representing a longword, the address of the low byte of the longword is the same as the address for the longword.

The program that carries out these ideas is shown in Figure 4.4. This program or one like it can be used to enter numbers in base ten and print the same numbers in a different base. Since interaction is now possible, the following scheme could be used to allow the user to select a different output radix each time this program is run (see Figure 4.5).

We use the CVT (ConVerT) instruction for the first time in this enhancement of the program in Figure 4.1. Why? We use a byte for the radix and new_radix. The READVAR macro works with longword entries. The

FIGURE 4.4
Numeric Input and Output

```
;
;Ref.:   Figure 4.4 (Numeric Input and Output)
;
;Method: This is an enhancement of the program in Figure 4.1, where the
;        WRITEVAL macro from PAS.MAR in Appendix C is used to print a copy
;        of the integers that have been entered from a keyboard and stored
;        in the x-row of contiguous long words.
;
;var
        max:      .LONG 4                    ;upper limit in AOBLSS loop
        index:    .LONG 0
        x:        .BLKL 20                   ;Reserve 20 long words

Begin:  .word

        moval     x,R6                       ;put x-address in R6
statement:
        write <Enter 3 integers:  >
        readvar (R6) 4(R6) 8(R6)
        writeln                              ;print a <ret>
        addl2     #12,R6                     ;advance address in R6
                                             ; to beginning of next 3
                                             ;long words.

        aoblss    max,index,statement
```

Continued on following page.

Figure 4.4 continued.

```
writeln                                    ;print <ret>
writeln <--------------------------------------->
writeln
writeln <      Copy of x-list:>
writeln
movab     x,R6                             ;init. R6 with x-address
                                           ;notice:
                                           ;  |_|_|_|_|_|_|_|_|...
                                           ;    ^     ^ ^     ^
                                           ;    |     | |     |
                                           ;    ------- -------
                                           ;    |         @x + 4
                                           ;  x-byte addr. = x-long addr.
                                           ;
writeval (R6) 4(R6) 8(R6) 12(R6)
writeval 16(R6) 20(R6) 24(R6) 28(R6)
writeval 32(R6) 36(R6) 40(R6) 44(R6)
writeln

writeln <--------------------------------------->

$exit_s

.end begin

RUN FG44

Enter 3 integers:  1 1 2


Enter 3 integers:  3 5 8


Enter 3 integers:  13 21 55


Enter 3 integers:  89 144 233



-------------------------------------------

        Copy of x-list:

1 1 2 3 5 8 13 21 55 89 144 233
---------------------------------------
```

FIGURE 4.5
Selecting Numeric Output Radices

```
NEW_RADIX:      .BYTE  10                ;default Radix = 10
                     .
                     .
                     .

Begin:          .WORD
                     .
                     .
                     .

                Write <Enter desired output radix: >

                Readvar   R7
                                                    put in
                Cvtlb     R7, New_Base              extra spaces
                     .
                     .
                     .

New_Statement:
                Writeval R6,4(R6) 8(R6) Radix = New_Base
                     .
                     .
                     .

                AOBLSS Max, Index, New_Statement
                     .
                     .
                     .

                .END Begin
```

CVT instruction prompts the processor to convert the data type of the source operand to the data type of the destination operand *and* put a copy of the newly formed data types into the destination. In effect, what happens in the above program is shown below:

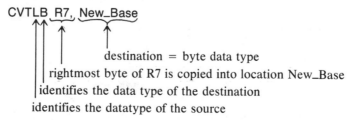

CVTLB R7, New_Base

destination = byte data type
rightmost byte of R7 is copied into location New_Base
identifies the data type of the destination
identifies the datatype of the source

This moves the selected radix into New_Base, making this variable ready for the WRITEVAL macro.

We leave the implementation of this idea as an exercise.

4.6

WRITESTRING: A STRINGHANDLING MACRO

The VAX-11 assembly language has four storage directives for setting up strings (sequences of ASCII characters). These are shown in Table 4.1.

This chapter shows how to use .ASCII and .ASCIC in building strings. Chapter 9 will show how to use the .ASCID directive in RTL (Run Time Library) procedures available on VAX-11 computers.

To work with strings, either those printed or those entered at a keyboard, it is necessary to specify the length of each string used. The *length of a string* equals the number of bytes needed to store a string in memory.

TABLE 4.1
Stringhandling Storage Directives

Directive	Format	Structure
.ASCII	.ASCII /string/	Sets up contiguous bytes, one for each character of the string inside the delimiters
.ASCIZ	.ASCIZ /string/	
.ASCIC	.ASCIC /string/	
.ASCID	.ASCID /string/	

The ASCII character set is built around 7 bits, so each of these codes can be stored in a byte ($=8$ bits). If we use

> X: .ASCIC/Eureka!/

with no spaces between the slanted line (//) delimiters, this storage tells the assembler to build a set of contiguous (side-by-side) bytes:

```
X: 7     45    75    72    65    6B    61    21
   ^     ^     ^     ^     ^     ^     ^     ^
                                            21 (hex) = !
                                      61 (hex) = a
                                6B (hex) = k
                          65 (hex) = e
                    72 (hex) = r
              75 (hex) = u
        45 (hex) = E
   7 = length of string
```

The .ASCIC storage directive or its equivalent is used by the WRITE-STRING macro given in PAS.MAR in Appendix C. This idea is illustrated in Figure 4.6.

The $X + $ 1st address in the above program identifies the beginning of a predefined string, which is a line from J. R. R. Tolkien's *Adventures of*

FIGURE 4.6
A String-Output Macro

```
;
;Ref.:  Figure 4.6 (A string-output macro)
;
;var
        x: .ascic /Tom went walking on up the Withywindle./

Begin:  .word

        writestring x

        $exit_s

        .end Begin


RUN FG47

Tom went walking on up the Withywindle.
```

FIGURE 4.7
Determining Lengths of Strings

```
;
;Ref.:   Figure 4.7 (Determining Lengths of strings)
;
         x: .ascic /Programming is designing, creating new programs (Wirth)./

Begin:   .word

         cvtbl    x,r6                     ;copy x-byte to rightmost byte of r6
         writeln
         writeln < The string that follows:>
         writeln
         write < >                         ;print tab = < >
         writestring x
         writeln
         writeln
         write < has >
         writeval r6
         write <characters.>

         $exit_s

         .end Begin



RUN FG48


 The string that follows:

         Programming is designing, creating new programs (Wirth).

 has 56 characters.
```

Tom Bombadil. Using this technique, we can construct a source text with predefined headings, messages, and so on.

Using the CVT*xy* (*x* = B, *y* = L) operator, we can tap the first byte of a .ASCII set-up to determine, work with, and print the number of characters in a string. For example, we would use

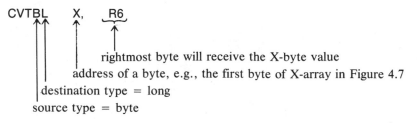

in terms of the row of bytes, starting with X in Figure 4.7. Then the WRITEVAL macro can be used to print this value. Figure 4.7 is an enhanced version of the preceding program.

4.7

BUILDING STRINGS WITH A .ASCII

The key to printing strings is the byte just before the first string-character. This is always used to hold the length of the string. If we do not use a .ASCIC storage directive, and instead use a directive like .ASCII, then we need to devise a method of computing the length of the .ASCII string. We can do this by performing arithmetic with the location counter. For example,

```
X :   .BYTE
        .ASCII /YES!/
Length  = .  − X − 1
```

will leave a 4 in length. When length is computed, the location counter has been moved by the assembler 5 bytes past the X-address. If we assume, for example, that the X-address = 200, then the progression of the location values will be as shown in Figure 4.8.

FIGURE 4.8
Using the Location Counter to Compute String Lengths

Location Counter	Line Address	Lines of Code
200	200	X: .BYTE
201	201	.ASCII /Yes!/
205	205	Length = . − X − 1

$$Length = . - X - 1$$
$$\uparrow$$
$$200$$

205

Length = 205−201 = 4

To use the WRITESTRING macro with a .ASCII directive, it is necessary to MOVe Byte the length-value into the *X*-byte in the above example. We will illustrate this in terms of multiple .ASCII directives on successive lines following the initial *empty* byte. In doing this we will exhibit an additional feature of the .ASCII or .ASCIZ or .ASCIC directive. We illustrate it here with the .ASCII:

.ASCII ⟨ASCII code⟩/string/⟨ASCII code⟩/string/ . . .

ASCII code like 32 for a space

FIGURE 4.9
The ASCII Storage Division

```
;
;
;Ref.:   Figure 4.9 (The .ASCII storage directive)
;
        x: .byte
           .ascii /Goldberry pulled Tom´s beard./<10><10><13>
        x_length = . - x - 1

        y: .byte
           .ascii /  Selections:/<10><13>
           .ascii /--1. A word with a CR + LF suffix/<10><13>
           .ascii /--2. Sounds:/<7><7>/more sounds:/<7><7><7><10><13>
        y_length = . - y - 1

Begin:  .word

        movb     #x_length,x           ;init. x-byte with length
        movb     #y_length,y           ;init. y-byte with length
                                       ;notice! the #-sign prefixes.

        writestring x

        writestring y

        $exit_s

        .end Begin



RUN FG410

Goldberry pulled Tom´s beard.
  Selections:
--1. A word with a CR + LF suffix
--2. Sounds:more sounds:
```

In other words, ASCII codes inside pointed brackets can be used to *format* a .ASCII string. For example,

```
.ASCII /Yes!/ ⟨10⟩⟨13⟩
               ↑   ↑
              LF  CR
```

will append the codes for a ⟨ret⟩ to the string inside the delimiters (/ /). These ideas are illustrated in the program in Figure 4.9.

The maximum number of bytes allowable with the WRITESTRING macro is 80. Finally, notice that the # sign is essential in moving the x_length or y_length values into the beginning bytes of the two strings. If we had used

```
movb x_length, x
```

then the processor would have considered this an access violation, since the x_length value is in the hex range 0, . . . , 1FF, which is inaccessible, for programming. In addition, we use the x_length value, not the content of the location in memory identified by x_length.

Strings can also be built without one of the string storage directives. This is done by loading the bytes *after* the initial one with ASCII codes. Furthermore, VAX-11 Macro permits multiple bytes to be defined in terms of a single ASCII code. This is done as follows:

```
X:   .BYTE
     .BYTE    7[40]
```

no. of times the ASCII code is to be put into succeeding bytes

ASCII code for a bell-sound

In effect, we have

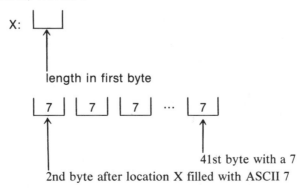

length in first byte

41st byte with a 7

2nd byte after location X filled with ASCII 7

An effective, easy-to-follow method for building byte strings is to define

FIGURE 4.10
Building Strings with BYTE

```
        ;
        ;Ref.:  Figure 4.10 (Building strings with a .BYTE)
        ;
        ;constants:

                arrowhead = 62
                vt = 11
                lf = 10
                cr = 13
                star = 42
                bell = 7
                dash = 45

        ;var

                text:      .byte
                           .byte dash[20],lf,cr
                           .byte vt
                           .byte star[10],arrowhead,bell[5]
                           .byte lf,cr,vt
                           .byte dash[20]

                length    = . - text - 1

        Begin:  .word

                movb       #length,text
                writestring text

                $exit_s

                .end Begin



        RUN FG411

        --------------------


        *********>


        --------------------
```

symbols having ASCII codes as values. Then these symbols are used instead of their numeric equivalents, as illustrated in Figure 4.10.

4.8

READSTRING: STRING INPUT

The macro library in Appendix C also includes a READSTRING macro to read strings typed at a keyboard. To use this macro, we need to set up a set of contiguous bytes that can be used to hold an input-string. This can be done with the .BLKB directive. For example, try the following scheme:

```
        X:   .BLKB 80
   BEGIN:    .WORD
             WRITELN ⟨enter your name:⟩
             READSTRING X
                  .

                  .

                  .

             $EXIT_S

             .END  BEGIN
```

The READSTRING macro will do two things once you type a ⟨ret⟩ after entering a string (your name, in the above example):

1. Put the length of the string into the first byte of the block of bytes you have reserved.
2. Put the ASCII codes for the string you enter into the reserved bytes, beginning with the byte with $X + $ 1st address.

We illustrate these ideas in the following example, which determines your position in time relative to the birth of the von Neumann machine (see Figure 4.11). This program can be improved by providing a choice of two output messages:

1. ⟨Name⟩, you were born ⟨positive no.⟩ *before* . . .
2. ⟨Name⟩, you were born ⟨positive no.⟩ *after* . . .

We will do this in the next chapter, when we show how to use the PSW

FIGURE 4.11
The von Neumann Machine Time Interval

```
;
;Ref.:   Figure 4.11 (The Von Neumann Machine time interval)
;
;var

        heading: .ascic /        A program with prompts:/
        name:    .blkb  80
        year:    .long

Begin:  .word
        writestring heading
        writeln
        writeln <-------------------------------------------->
        writeln
        write <your name:  >
        readstring name
        writeln
        writeln <Your birth year:  >
        readvar year

        sub13    #1946,year,r7
        writeln
        writeln <-------------------------------------------->
        writeln
        writestring name
        write <,you were born >
        writeval r7
        write < years before (after) the birth of the Von Neumann machine.>

        $exit_s

        .end begin




RUN FG412

        A program with prompts:
-------------------------------------------

your name:  SUE

Your birth year:
1967


-------------------------------------------

SUE,you were born 21  years before (after) the birth of the Von Neumann machine.
```

(processor status word) condition codes to select some alternative actions to be performed by the processor.

4.9

MOVC3: AN INSTRUCTION TO COPY STRINGS

VAX-11 Macro includes a MOVC instruction to put a copy of a string in one byte-row into another byte-row. A *byte-row* is a set of contiguous mem-

FIGURE 4.12
Graphical Interpretation of MOVC3

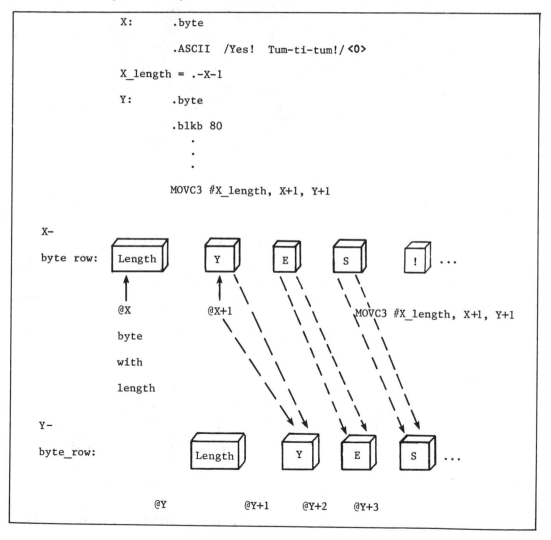

FIGURE 4.13
Copying String Arrays

```
;
;Ref.:  Figure 4.13 (Copying String Arrays)
;
        x:       .byte
                 .ascii /  Yes! Tum-ti-tum!/<0>
        x_length = . - x - 1

        y:       .byte
                 .blkb 80

Begin:  .word

        movb      #x_length,x            ;init. x-byte with length
        movc      #x_length,x+1,y+1      ;copy x-array to y-array
        movb      #x_length,y            ;init. y-byte with length

        writeln                          ;put in some empty lines:
        writeln
        write <   Original string-array:>
        writeln
        write < >                    ;< > = tab
        writestring x
        writeln
        writeln
        write <   Copy of string-array:>
        writeln
        write < >                    ;< > = tab
        writestring y

        $exit_s

        .end Begin




RUN FG413

   Original string-array:
        Yes! Tum-ti-tum!

   Copy of string-array:
        Yes! Tum-ti-tum!
```

ory locations. We have been working with string byte-rows or string arrays. The MOVC or MOVe characters instruction has the following term:

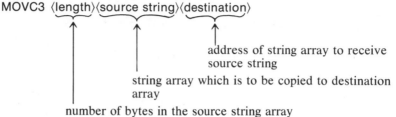

MOVC3 ⟨length⟩⟨source string⟩⟨destination⟩

address of string array to receive source string

string array which is to be copied to destination array

number of bytes in the source string array

This instruction can be seen in Figure 4.12.

After moving the contents of one string array to another byte-row, it is necessary to move the original string length into the byte just before the second byte-row with the string copy. Then it is just a matter of working with the bytes of either the original string and/or its copy. In the example in Figure 4.13 we merely print a copy of the two byte-rows after executing the MOVC3 instruction.

4.10

HOW TO IMPLEMENT THE I/O MACROS

To use the source texts given in this chapter or to create new ones using the WRITESTRING, READSTRING, READVAR, and WRITEVAL macros, it is necessary to install both the IO.MAR and PAS.MAR libraries given in Appendix C. Once these are available on a VAX-11, then use the following steps to prepare a source text for execution:

1. To assemble a source text T.MAR, use

        MACRO T + PAS/LIB
        result: T.OBJ

2. To link T.OBJ, use

        LINK T + IO/LIB
        result: T.EXE

3. To run T.EXE, use

    RUN T

4. To obtain a listing of T.MAR with an object module, use

    MACRO/LIST T + PAS/LIB
    result: T.LIS and T.OBJ

TABLE 4.2
Operator Cross-Reference Table

Operator	Usage	Example	Reference
CVTxy	ConVerT (*move* source x-data type to destination y-data type)	Fig. 4.7	DEC [1981,184–86]
.ASCII	Directive to set up byte-row for ASCII codes	Fig. 4.9	DEC [LRM,1982,5–7]
.ASCIZ	Directive to set up byte-row for ASCII codes and with ⟨o⟩ = null suffix	See comments about Fig. 4.9	DEC [LRM,1982,5–7]
.ASCIC	Directive to set up a byte-row with first byte containing the string length, the remaining ones for ASCII codes	Fig. 4.6,4.7	DEC [LRM,1982,5–7]
Writestring	Print string array specified	Fig. 4.6,4.7, 4.9,4.10	Appendix C
Readstring	Get string array from keyboard	Fig. 4.11	Appendix C
Writeval	Print integer values in various bases	Fig. 4.4	Appendix C
Readvar	Get numeric values from keyboard	Fig. 4.4,4.1, 4.7	Appendix C
MOVC3	Copy source string array to a destination byte-row	Fig. 4.12	DEC [1981,288–89]
MOVax	Move address of type x	Fig. 4.4,4.1	DEC [1981,224–25]

DEC = Digital Equipment Corporation.

5. To obtain a listing of T.MAR *without* an object module, use

    MACRO/LIST/NOOBJECT T + PAS/LIB
    result: T.LIS

6. To obtain a listing with macro definitions inserted into the source text without an object module for T.MAR, use

    MACRO/LIST/SHOW = ME/NOOBJECT T + PAS/LIB
    result: T.LIS

4.11
SUMMARY

The I/O macros given in this chapter will make it possible to write interactive assembly language programs on a VAX-11. Later chapters will show you how to enhance these macros and VAX-11 QIO procedures to tailor them to individual needs. I/O problems are among the most challenging in assembly language programming. With these macros, it will be easier to obtain printed copies of memory contents as a result of executing processor instructions.

To make it easier to use the operators given in this chapter, we cross-reference them with parts of this book and with Digital Equipment Corporation (1981, 1982). The cross-reference table appears in Table 4.2.

4.12
EXERCISES

1. Write a program to enter a pair of decimal integers that are printed out in binary. Run your program for
   (a) 2, 10
   (b) 233, 32767

2. Write a program that does the following:
   (a) Prompts for an integer to be entered.
   (b) Prompts for an output base (2:60).
   (c) Prints the entered number in the original base and in the newly selected base.

Run your program for

(d) Your age in hex;

(e) 65536 in hex;

(f) 65535 in hex;

(g) $2^{31} - 1$ in hex.

3. Write a program to fill 20 consecutive longwords starting at location X with the sequence

$$2, 4, 6, 8, \ldots, 2 \times 20$$

and then print out a copy of the contents of the X-list.

4. Obtain a memory dump for the program written in exercise no. 3 and identify the elements *and* addresses of the elements in X-list.

5. Modify the program written for exercise 3 so that 20 consecutive bytes are filled with the even numbers 2:40. Run your program and identify both the X-list elements *and* their addresses. Remember that the READVAL and WRITEVAL macros work only with longwords. Thus, some conversion will be necessary to move longword entries into byte locations or to move the x-byte-row into registers for printing.

6. Use the READSTRING and WRITESTRING macros in a program in which you prompt the user for a name that the computer will echo-print once the user has entered the name.

7. Use the .ASCIC directive and the WRITESTRING macro to print the following string:

The VAX-11 has 16 general registers.

8. Write a program to prompt for a string to be entered at a keyboard. Then echo-print the string along with an indication of the number of characters in the entered string. The program in Figure 4.7 will be helpful, here.

9. Write a program that does the following:
   (a) establishes values of constants *a, b, c* using the location counter as follows:

$$a = .$$
$$b = . + 1024$$
$$c = . + 4096$$

(b) prints the values of these constants.

10. Indicate how the location counter could be used to do the same thing as the following:

    x : .BLKB 1024

without using the .BLKB directive. That is, use the location counter to reserve 1KB (1024 bytes) for x without the .BLKB directive.

11. Write a program that uses the .BYTE and .ASCII directives to print the following sawtooth:

    Tom   Goldberry   the
       .   .   .
      .   .   .   .   .
     .   .   .   .   .
       followed   down   Withywindle.

In doing this, remember there is an 80-byte limit on the strings printed by WRITESTRING macro.

12. Write a program to do the following:
    (a) Prompt for a string to be entered at a keyboard.
    (b) Load the entered string into location X.
    (c) Use the MOVC3 instruction to put a copy of the X-string into a Y-byte-row and a Z-byte-row. Print a copy of the X-, Y-, and Z-strings.
    (d) Use the MOVC3 instruction to put the entered string into a T-byte-row, then the first half of the entered string into the bytes immediately following the T-byte-row.
    For example, try this with the quote from N. Wirth in Figure 4.7:

    P r o ... h . P r o ... r
                   ↑   ↑
             56th character   28th char.

Print the concatenated strings.

4.13

LAB PROJECTS

1. Write a program to do the following:
   (a) Prompt for a word (limit = 10 characters).
   (b) Print the entered string on successive lines (limit = 20 lines) so that on each new line (on line k, for example) the original string is printed along with a suffix made up of the first $k - 1$ letters of the preceding line. For example, assume

   YES!

   is entered, then print

   ```
   line
    1  YES!
    2  YES! Y
    3  YES! YE
    4  YES! YES
    5  YES! YES!
    6  YES! YES! Y
    .  .. .
    .  .. .
    .  .. .
   ```

   Note: You might try using two AOBLSS loops to do this, one loop inside the other. An alternative would be to use the MOVC3 instruction to build 20-byte-rows in memory first, then print them out.

2. Write a program to do the following:
   (a) Prompt for five strings, each with a different length.
   (b) Print a copy of each string indicating how many characters are in the string.
   (c) On a separate line, print out the total number of characters that were entered.

4.14

REVIEW QUIZ

Indicate whether the following statements are true or false:

1. AOBLSS requires 3 arguments.
2. The WRITELN macro can be used without an argument.
3. The following macros print something on 3 separate lines:

> write⟨a⟩
> write⟨h⟩
> write⟨a⟩

4. The following label is legal:

> yesyesyesyesyesyesyesyesyesyesyesyesyesyesyesyesyesyesyesyes:

5. A CVTLB converts a longword to a byte.
6. $EXITS does the same thing as a $EXIT_S.
7. if x is at 208(hex), then x + 4 is at 212(hex).
8. MOV #X,R6 does the same thing as MOVAL X,R6.
9. MOVAB X,R6 does the same thing as MOVAL X,R6.
10. With

> x : .byte
> length = . − x

length will equal 1.
11. With

> x : .byte
>   .ascii/Goldberry. . ./
> length = . − x

length will equal 13.

12. With

    cvtbl x,r6

    the rightmost byte of R6 will get the x-byte value.
13. .ASCIC/yes!/ and .ASCII/yes!/ use the same number of bytes.
14. .ASCIC/A way a lone a loved a long the/ uses 32 bytes.
15. In

    .ascic/riverrun,/

    the first byte has the ASCII code for a lower case r.

4.15

REFERENCES

Digital Equipment Corporation. *VAX Architecture Handbook*. Order No. EB-19580-20/31). Maynard, Mass., 1981.

Digital Equipment Corporation. *VAX-11 MACRO Language Reference Manual*. Order No. AA-DO32C-TE. Maynard, Mass., 1982.

Wirth, N. *Programming in Modula-2*. New York: Springer-Verlag, 1982.

5.
CONTROL STRUCTURES

It is a prime characteristic of computers that individual actions can be selected, repeated or performed conditionally depending on some previously computed results.

—N. Wirth, *Programming in Modula-2*

5.0
AIMS

- Introduce the concept of a control structure.
- Explain the computation of displacements used in forward and backward branching.
- Introduce conditional and unconditional branches in the VAX-11 instruction repertoire.
- Show how to build both selective and repetitive control structures.
- Implement IF/THEN, IF/THEN/ELSE, WHILE/DO, and REPEAT/UNTIL in assembly programs.
- Distinguish the role of the assembler in computing displacements from the role of the processor in checking PSW condition codes.

5.1

INTRODUCTION

This chapter introduces the components of the VAX-11 instruction set that make it possible to set up control structures within an assembly language program. Normally a processor executes instructions *sequentially* (one after the other). A *control structure* prompts the processor to depart from its normal sequential execution.

For example, a VAX-11 AOBLSS instruction used in the previous chapters sets up a *repetitive control structure*. It directs the VAX-11 processor to transfer control to an instruction identified by the label:

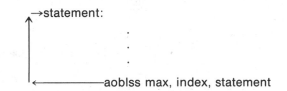

We will consider two types of control structures here:

1. selection control
2. repetition control

which can be set up by means of VAX-11 branch instructions. Finally, in this chapter we will begin making extensive use of lower case to build more readable source texts.

5.2

VAX-11 CONDITIONAL BRANCH INSTRUCTIONS

A VAX-11 conditional branch instruction prompts the processor to transfer control to a labelled instruction, provided the condition codes of the PSW satisfy the branch operator specification. These conditional branches are given in Table 5.1. Each branch instruction uses two bytes, one for the branch op code, another for the displacement to be added to the PC. The format for a branch instruction is as follows:

OP Code	Displacement
byte 0	byte 1

TABLE 5.1
Conditional Branches

Branch Operator	For Results Treated as Signed Values		
	Branch Results If x Is	With CMP (Comparison), Branch Results in Terms of x, y, If	Conditions Needed for Branch
BEQL	x = 0	x − y = 0	z = 1
BNEQ	x <> 0	x <> y	z = 0
BGTR	x > 0	x − y > 0	n = 0 and z = 0
BLEQ	x <= 0	x − y <= 0	n = 1 or z = 0
BGEQ	x >= 0	x − y >= 0	n = 0
BLSS	x < 0	x − y < 0	n = 1
	For Results Treated as Unsigned Values		
BEQLU	x = 0	x − y = 0	z = 1
BNEQU	x <> 0	x <> y	z = 0
BGTRU	x > 0	x − y > 0	c = 0 and z = 0
BLEQU	x <= 0	x − y <= 0	c = 1 or z = 0
BGEQU	x >= 0	x − y >= 0	c = 0
BLSSU	x < 0	x − y < 0	c = 1
	For Results which Trigger Overflow/carry		
BVS	(Overflow occurs when x > declared data type)		v = 1
BVC	(No overflow in obtaining result x)		v = 0
BCS	(Carry occurs when 1 is added to MSB = 1)		c = 1
BCC	(Carry does not occur)		c = 0

It is the assembler's task to compute the necessary displacement, so that

$$(PC) \leftarrow (PC) + \text{displacement}$$

will *effect* the transfer of control to the labelled instruction called for by the assembly language instruction. For example, a BEQL (Branch, if the result of a previous operation is zero and the Z-bit of the PSW is 1 or is *set*) has the following form in an assembly language program:

BEQL ⟨label⟩

The assembler must determine (a) the numeric address for the ⟨label⟩ and (b) calculate the displacement that will have to be added to the PC to complete the branch, if the PSW bit satisfies the required condition.

These conditional branches can effect a transfer of control either forward or backward in the program. For example, the following lines of code:

.

.

.

→ diminish:

          decl R6   ;R6 ← R6 − 1

          bneq diminish   ;transfer control to location

                               ;diminish, until R6 = 0

     ⟨next instruction⟩

are equivalent to

.

.

.

repeat

     x := x − 1

   until x = 0;

in Pascal. When the processor is executing the BNEQ, the current PC is loaded with the address of the ⟨next instruction⟩. The assembler takes this into account in computing how much displacement should be added to the PC to transfer control *backwards* to location *diminish*. Suppose the assembler finds that the *numeric* address for the label diminish is 204. Then the assembler uses the following scheme to compute the necessary displacement:

diminish = 204		operator	operand	instruction
−4	204	D7		decl
−3	205		56	R6
−2	206	12		bneq
−1	208			PC-content

With the displacement = −4, the assembler must use the twos complement form of −4:

   twos complement form of −4:

                   0000 0100

$$\text{ones complement of } 4 = \text{FB}$$

$$1111\ 1011$$

$$\frac{+1 \qquad +1}{\text{twos complement form of } -4} = \overline{\text{FC}} = 1111\ 1100$$

In machine code for the above segment, the assembler will use

$$\begin{array}{cc} 12 & FC \\ \uparrow & \uparrow \\ \vert & \vert \\ \text{bneq} & \text{twos complement form of } -4 \end{array}$$

When the processor executes this instruction, assume the above numeric addresses hold true and that

$$\text{current} - \text{(PC)} = 208$$

If the processor finds the Z-bit of the PSW is *not* set, it will compute the address of the next instruction it is to execute. It does address computations with 32 bits, so that it will do a sign extension on the displacement with the remaining 24 bits of the longword used for the computation; this sign extension is shown in Figure 5.1. Then the transfer address is computed as follows:

$$\begin{array}{rl} \text{displacement} = & \text{FFFF FFFC} \\ + \text{ current} - \text{(PC)} = + & \underline{\qquad 208} \\ & \text{0000 0204} = \text{new} - \text{(PC)} \end{array}$$

$$\text{carry ignored}$$

FIGURE 5.1
Sign Extension

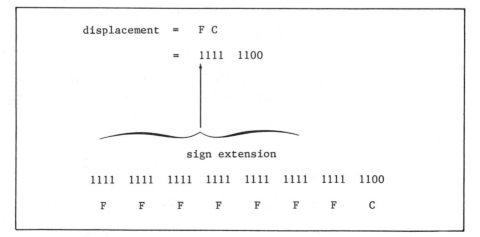

That is, the PC is assigned the value 204, which transfers control back to the decrement-long (DECL) instruction. This will happen repeatedly (4 times) *until* the Z-bit of the PSW is set by the DECL R6 instruction.

The conditional branch instructions can also be used to set up forward branches (*down* past the next instruction, instead of up in a backwards branch). Suppose we have the following situation:

```
          Subl2 #3, r6      ;r6←r6−3
          beql side_step    ;conditional
          divl2 r6, r7       ;r7←r7/r6
side_step:

          ⟨next instruction⟩
```

This is equivalent to the following lines of Pascal code:

```
x := x−3   (* let x = r6 *)
if x ⟨⟩ 0    (* let y = r7 *)
   then y := y/x
   ⟨next statement⟩
```

This time, the conditional branch is BEQL (branch, if equal). That is, processor control will transfer to location SIDE_STEP, if the processor finds that the Z-bit has been set (= 1) as a result of the instruction

```
     Subl2 #3, r6
```

This is known as a *forward reference*. When the assembler first encounters

```
     beql side_step
```

it does *not* have a numeric value to substitute for SIDE_STEP. It must first determine the numeric address for SIDE_STEP, then go back and compute the displacement for the BEQL instruction.

Assume that the BEQL instruction is at location 210. Then the following scheme will be used by the assembler to compute the necessary displacement:

	operator	operand	instruction
207	C2		Subl2
208		03	#3
209		56	r6
210	13		beql

		operator	operand	instruction
	211	3		⟨displacement⟩
0	212	C6		divl2
1	213		56	r6
2	214		57	r7
3	215			

↑
side_step numeric address

The key thing to notice here is the current PC value when the processor begins execution of the Branch, if Equal (BEQL) instruction is at location 210. That is, when the processor is dealing with the branch at location 210, the PC has been advanced to location 212. Then the correct displacement is 3, since

$$(PC) \leftarrow (PC) + 3 = 212 + 3 = 215$$

will transfer control to location 215, if r6 = 0.

Each of the VAX-11 conditional branch operators has an op code and a displacement, which is added to the current PC, *if* the branch condition is satisfied. These branch instructions have a serious limitation. Since the branch displacement is limited to one byte, the maximum branch forwards or backwards is 127 bytes. The branch instructions are appropriate only for short branches. Longer branches must be handled with an unconditional branch or jump. Before considering unconditional control transfers, however, we must first look at the assembler CMPx (CoMPare ⟨datatype⟩) instruction.

5.3

THE COMPARE INSTRUCTION: CMPx

An assembler branch instruction can be used to set up familiar control structures found in higher-level languages. This is done using the VAX-11 CMP (CoMPare) instruction.

The CMPx ($x = B, W, L, F$) has the form

CMP ⟨datatype⟩ source, destination

The following things occur, when this instruction is executed:

1. The difference source − destination is computed *without* affecting either the source or the destination operand.

2. The processor status word bits *N*, *Z* and *C* (<u>not</u> *V*) are conditionally set, depending on the computed difference.

For example, suppose we have to choose between two values to determine a course of action. Suppose we prompt the user for a value, which is compared with a fixed value. The following program illustrates two *selective* control structures. A *selective control structure* will have an if/then form, and the flow-of-control will be like that shown in Figure 5.2.

The diamond in Figure 5.2 indicates that a CMP instruction has been used to test some condition, or to adjust the condition codes in terms of a prior result. Then a conditional branch instruction can be used to transfer control to statement *A*, if the condition tested is true, else control should pass to statement *B*. Figure 5.3 shows a program that has a forward branch and a backward branch.

At this point, you may wish to test your skill in deciphering the significance of the displacement computed by the assembler and shown in the list file for the above program. Use the analysis shown earlier to verify that the control-transfers called for by the source test *do* occur relative to the numeric values of the labeled locations referenced by the branch instructions:

Again for backwards branch

Next_Q for forwards branch

You might wonder how this idea might be extended to obtain an if/then/else

FIGURE 5.2
Selective Control Structure

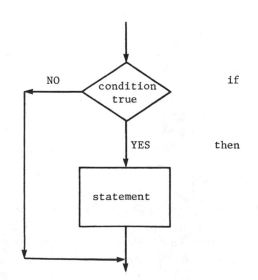

FIGURE 5.3
A Program with Forward and Backward Branching

```
;
;Ref.:  Figure 5.3 (A Program with Forward and Backward Branching)
;

Begin:   .word

again:
         write <Enter a base 10 integer: >
         readvar r6
         writeln
         write <Do you want the hex representation of this no(1=Y,0=N):  >
         readvar r7
         writeln
         writeln                        ;<ret>
         cmpl    #0,r7                   ;No?
         beql    next_question           ;if ans=no, then branch
         writeval r6 radix=16            ;write entry in hex
         write < (hex)>

next_question:
         writeln
         writeln <------------------------------------------------>
         writeln
         write <Do you wish to enter another number? (1=Y,0=N) : >
         readvar r7
         cmpl    #0,r7                   ;No?
         beql    stop                    ;if ans=no, then stop
         jmp     again                   ;go to beginning
stop:
         $exit_s

         .end Begin




RUN FG53

Enter a base 10 integer: 1984

Do you want the hex representation of this no(1=Y,0=N):  1


7C0  (hex)
------------------------------------------------
Do you wish to enter another number? (1=Y,0=N) : 0
```

FIGURE 5.4
If/then/else Control Structure

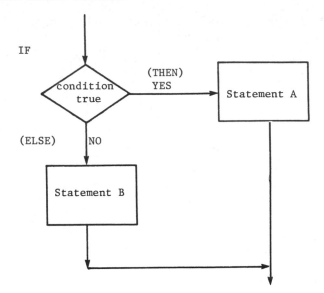

selective control structure. The flow-of-control for an if/then/else is shown in Figure 5.4.

Building an if/then/else control structure with an assembler can be made easier with the aid of unconditional branch instructions. The VAX-11 unconditional branch operators are shown in Table 5.2. Each of these branches is equivalent to

        goto ⟨label⟩

in Pascal. They differ from each other in terms of the number of bytes in the displacement allowed. The JMP (jump) is commonly used because it

TABLE 5.2
Unconditional Control Transfer Operators

Unconditional Branches	
	Bytes in Branch
BRB (Branch with byte displacement)	127
BRW (Branch with word displacement)	32767
Unconditional Jump	
JMP (Jump)	Length of Program

FIGURE 5.5
If/then/else Implementation

```
;
;Ref.:  Figure 5.5 (if/then/else implementation)
;
;var
        choice:  .long

Begin:  .word

        writeln <  Menu:>
        writeln <--1. December 1983 average temp. in Minnesota>
        writeln
        writeln <--2. January 1984 average temp. in Minnesota>
        writeln
        write <Enter choice:   >
        readvar choice
        cmpl    #1, choice              ;was it 1?
        beql    leapfrog                ;if so, then leapfrog
        jmp     else
leapfrog:
        jmp     then
else:
        write <January 1984 average temp. was +25 F.>
        jmp     doorway
then:
        write <December 1983 average temp. was -25 F.>
doorway:

        $exit_s

        .end Begin


RUN FG55

  Menu:
--1. December 1983 average temp. in Minnesota

--2. January 1984 average temp. in Minnesota

Enter choice:  1

December 1983 average temp. was -25 F.
```

permits jumps of any number of bytes within a program. To implement the
if/then/else selective control structure, we can use the following method:

```
        cmpl x, y                   ;
        B<condition> leapfrog       ;if <cond.> then leapfrog
        jmp 2$                      ;else execute 2$
```

```
leapfrog:
          jmp 1$
2$:                                    ; else-part
          ⟨action⟩
          jmp next
1$:                                    ; then-part
          ⟨action⟩
next:
          ⟨continue program⟩
```

We illustrate this in terms of a menu in the program in Figure 5.5.

You might wonder how to set up the equivalent of the following scheme:

```
if ⟨cond. A⟩ then ⟨action⟩
    else
      if ⟨cond. B⟩ then ⟨action⟩
          else
            ⟨action⟩
```

This is left as an exercise. The VAX-11 instruction set also includes a CASE operator, which provides the logical equivalent of an if/then/else statement with an indefinite number of IF/THEN/ELSE statements following the first else. This is given later.

5.4

REPETITIVE CONTROL STRUCTURES

For the most part, we have been considering how to set up if/then statements. A wide variety of loops can be set up in VAX-11 assembler. These can be divided into two groups according to the mechanism used to control branching:

1. Indexed repetitive control structures

2. Conditional repetitive control structures

5.4.1 Indexed Loops

The VAX-11 instruction has four operators for setting up indexed loops (see Table 5.3). These are not the exact counterparts of the Pascal FOR/DO, since each of these instructions effects only a *backwards* branch up to 127 bytes. This means a statement referenced by a label in one of these instructions is executed once *before* the condition is checked. In terms of flow-of-control, these instructions behave like Pascal repeat/until loops. They differ from the usual repeat/until loop, since the condition in a repeat loop is *not* indexed. Since these instructions are limited to byte displacement, they are restricted to small loops.

Probably because of its frustration with the SOB and AOB loops, DEC included the ACBx (Add, Compare, Branch) instruction in its VAX-11 instruction repertoire. The SOB (Subtract and Branch) and AOB (Add and Branch) instructions are limited to a longword index. The ACBx instruction can use byte, word, longword, or floating operands (the max, increment, and index). Since its operands can be floating points, fractional increments are now possible. Instead of a maximum of 127 bytes in SOB or AOB loops, an ACBx loop can have displacements up to 32767 bytes. Finally, the ACBx instruction can be used in place of the SOBGEQ and AOBLEQ instructions.

Thus, the VAX-11 assembler equivalent of a

```
for index := min to max do ⟨statement⟩
```

is

```
        movl min, index
do:
        ⟨actions⟩
for:    acbl max, step, index, do
```

Figure 5.6 illustrates the mechanics of setting this loop up in terms of the sum

$$1 + 2 + 3 + 4 + 5 + \ldots + 1000$$

5.4.2 Nested Indexed Loops

VAX-11 ACBx loops can be nested. For example, we can set up nested loops equivalent to

```
for i := min1 to max1 do
    for j := min2 to max2 do
        ⟨statement⟩
```

This can be illustrated in printing what Arthur Keller (1982, p. 39) calls

TABLE 5.3
Indexed Loop Instructions

Downward Indexing	
Instruction	Pascal Equivalent
SOBGEQ index, displacement	for index := max down to 0 do ⟨statement⟩
SOBGTR index, displacement	for index := max down to 1 do ⟨statement⟩
Upward Indexing (Byte Displacement)	
AOBLSS max, index, displacement	for index := min to max-1 do ⟨statement⟩
AOBLEQ max, index, displacement	for index := min to max do ⟨statement⟩
Downward or Upward Indexing (Word Displacement)	
ACBx max, increment, index, displacement x = B,W,L,F	
(a) if increment is negative, this gives:	for index := max down to min do ⟨statement⟩
(b) if increment is positive, this gives:	for index := min to max do ⟨statement⟩

Floyd's triangle, which was suggested by R. W. Floyd:

```
rows                columns
            1   2   3   4   5   6   7  . . .
 1          1
 2          2   3
 3          4   5   6
 4          7   8   9  10
 5         11  12  13  14  15
 6         16  17  18  19  20  21
 7         22  23  24  25  26  27  28
 .
 .
 .
```

If we take i to be the row number, and j the column number, then we can set up a pair of nested loops in Pascal to build Floyd's triangle:

```
for i := 1 to rowmax do
    begin
        for j := 1 to i do
            begin
                Floydentry := Floydentry + 1;
                write (Floydentry)
            end;
        writeln;
    end;
```

A VAX-11 assembly language program that can be used to build Floyd's triangle is given in Figure 5.7.

FIGURE 5.6
For/do Implementation

```
        ;
        ;Ref.:   Figure 5.6 (for/do implementation)
        ;
        ;var
                sum:        .long 0
                max:        .long
                step:       .long 1
                index:      .long 1

        Begin:  .word
                write <Enter max in 1 + ... + max:  >
                readvar max
                writeln
        do:
                writeval index
                write < + >
                add12       index,sum
        for:
                acbl        max,step,index,do

                write <= >
                writeval sum

                $exit_s

                .end Begin


        RUN FG56

        Enter max in 1 + ... + max:   10

        1  + 2  + 3  + 4  + 5  + 6  + 7  + 8  + 9  + 10  + = 55
```

5.4.3 Conditional Loops: WHILE and REPEAT

The difference between a WHILE/DO and a REPEAT/UNTIL loop is shown in Figure 5.8.

The VAX-11 assembly language equivalent of a WHILE loop can be

FIGURE 5.7
Floyd's Triangle

```
;
;Ref.:   Figure 5.7 (Floyd's triangle with nested for/do loops)
;
;var
        Floyd_entry:        .long
        row_max: .long
        i:                  .long
        j:                  .long
        step:               .long

Begin:  .word

again:
        movl    #0,Floyd_entry
        movl    #1,i
        movl    #1,j
        movl    #1,step
        write <Enter no. of rows you wish in Floyd's triangle: >
        readvar row_max

do_1:
        do_2:
                incl       Floyd_entry
                writeval Floyd_entry
        for_2:
                acbl       i,step,j,do_2
        writeln
        movl    #1,j
for_1:
        acbl    row_max,step,i,do_1

        writeln
        writeln <------------------------------------->
        write <Do wish another run? 1=Y, 0=N:  >
        readvar r6
        cmpl    #0,r6
        beql    doorway
        jmp     again
doorway:

        $exit_s

        .end Begin
```

Figure 5.7 continued.

```
RUN FG57

Enter no. of rows you wish in Floyd's triangle: 20

1
2  3
4  5  6
7  8  9  10
11 12 13 14 15
16 17 18 19 20 21
22 23 24 25 26 27 28
29 30 31 32 33 34 35 36
37 38 39 40 41 42 43 44 45
46 47 48 49 50 51 52 53 54 55
56 57 58 59 60 61 62 63 64 65 66
67 68 69 70 71 72 73 74 75 76 77 78
79 80 81 82 83 84 85 86 87 88 89 90 91
92 93 94 95 96 97 98 99 100 101 102 103 104 105
106 107 108 109 110 111 112 113 114 115 116 117 118 119 120
121 122 123 124 125 126 127 128 129 130 131 132 133 134 135 136
137 138 139 140 141 142 143 144 145 146 147 148 149 150 151 152 153
154 155 156 157 158 159 160 161 162 163 164 165 166 167 168 169 170 171
172 173 174 175 176 177 178 179 180 181 182 183 184 185 186 187 188 189 190
191 192 193 194 195 196 197 198 199 200 201 202 203 204 205 206 207 208 209
210


-------------------------------------
Do wish another run? 1=Y, 0=N:  1

Enter no. of rows you wish in Floyd's triangle: 13

1
2  3
4  5  6
7  8  9  10
11 12 13 14 15
16 17 18 19 20 21
22 23 24 25 26 27 28
29 30 31 32 33 34 35 36
37 38 39 40 41 42 43 44 45
46 47 48 49 50 51 52 53 54 55
56 57 58 59 60 61 62 63 64 65 66
67 68 69 70 71 72 73 74 75 76 77 78
79 80 81 82 83 84 85 86 87 88 89 90 91


-------------------------------------
Do wish another run? 1=Y, 0=N:  0
```

FIGURE 5.8
WHILE/DO and REPEAT/UNTIL Control Structures

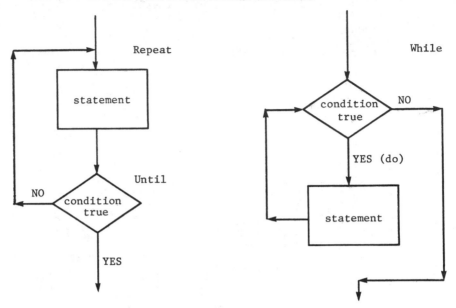

built using the CMPx and conditional instructions as follows:

```
while:
            cmpl x, y              ;x,y are longwords
            b⟨condition⟩ do        ;condition = NEQ, for example
            brw next_statement
do:
            ⟨actions⟩
            brw while
next_statement:
```

In Figure 5.9 we illustrate the use of a WHILE/DO loop in a VAX-11 assembly language program in terms of printing the terms of the following sequence:

2, 4, 6, 8, 10, 12, . . .

A generalized REPEAT/UNTIL statement can also be characterized using

FIGURE 5.9
WHILE/DO Implementation

```
;
;Ref.:  Figure 5.9 (While/do implementation)
;
;var
        term:     .long
        n:        .long
        max:      .long
        i:        .long

Begin:  .word

Again:
        movl      #2,term
        movl      #0,i
        write <Enter n in 2,4,6, ... ,2n :  >
        readvar   n
        mull3     #2,n,max
        writeln
        writeln

while:
        cmpl      term,max
        blss      do
        brw       next_statement
do:
        incl      i
        mull3     #2,i,term
        writeval  term
        brw       while

next_statement:

        writeln
        writeln <------------------------------------------------->
        writeln
        write <Do you wish another run? 1=Y,0=N:  >
        readvar   r6
        cmpl      #0,r6
        beql      doorway
        jmp       again
doorway:

        $exit_s

        .end Begin

RUN FG59

Enter n in 2,4,6, ... ,2n :  25


2 4 6 8 10 12 14 16 18 20 22 24 26 28 30 32 34 36 38 40 42 44 46 48 50
-----------------------------------------------

Do you wish another run? 1=Y,0=N:  0
```

the VAX-11 assembler CMPx and branch instructions:

```
            .
            .
            .

repeat:
                ⟨actions⟩
                cmpl x, y
until:
                b⟨condition⟩ next_statement
                brw repeat
next_statement:

            .
            .
            .
```

A REPEAT/UNTIL can be used whenever it does not matter if the action is performed *before* the condition is checked. It would be unwise to use a REPEAT/UNTIL loop in situations where division is used, for example. A WHILE/DO loop could be set up in such cases to avoid possible zero divisors.

We illustrate the use of nested REPEAT/UNTIL loops in terms of a small graphics problem—that is, in drawing a pointilistic interpretation of Floyd's triangle:

```
.
.  .
.  .  .
.  .  .  .
.  .  .  .  .
.  .  .  .  .  .
```

We also want to let the user select the number of rows of dots printed. We show the Pascal equivalent of this idea next:

```
Repeat
  Repeat
  count := count + 1;
  write ('.')
  until count = index;
```

FIGURE 5.10
Pointilistic Floyd Triangle

```
        ;
        ;Ref.:   Figure 5.10 (Pointilistic Floyd triangle)
        ;
        ;var
                row_count:              .long
                row_max: .long
                index:                  .long

Begin:  .word

again:
                clrl    index
                movl    #1,row_count
                write <Enter no. of rows you wish in dot triangle :  >
                readvar row_max

repeat_1:
        repeat_2:

                        incl    index
                        write < . >
                        cmpl    index,row_count
                until_2:

                        blss    repeat_2
                writeln
                incl    row_count
                clrl    index
until_1:

                cmpl    row_count,row_max
                bleq    repeat_1

                writeln
                writeln <-------------------------------->
                write <Do you wish another run? 1=Y,0=N:  >
                readvar r6
                cmpl    #0,r6
                beql    doorway
                jmp     again
doorway:

                $exit_s

                .end Begin
```

Continued on following page.

Figure 5.10 continued.

```
        RUN FG510

        Enter no. of rows you wish in dot triangle :   10

          .
          .   .
          .   .   .
          .   .   .   .
          .   .   .   .   .
          .   .   .   .   .   .
          .   .   .   .   .   .   .
          .   .   .   .   .   .   .   .
          .   .   .   .   .   .   .   .   .
          .   .   .   .   .   .   .   .   .   .

        ---------------------------------
        Do you wish another run? 1=Y,0=N:   0
```

```
            writeln;
            count := 0;
            index := index + 1
        Until index = max;
```

A VAX-11 assembly language program to implement this idea is given in Figure 5.10.

5.4.4 Difficulties with Conditional Loops

The VAX-11 assembler renditions of WHILE/DO and REPEAT/UNTIL loops depend on unconditional branches, which are limited to word displacements. As a result, the number of actions that can be performed within one of these loops is quite limited. It is possible to remedy this situation by using short jumps for loop exits and long jumps (JMP) to transfer control to the beginning of a loop. For example, we can use

```
              .
              .
              .

    while:
              cmpl x, y
              b⟨condition⟩ do
              jmp next_statement
```

```
    do:

            <actions>
    next_statement:
                    .
                    .
                    .
```

These enhancements are left as exercises.

5.5

SUMMARY

Control structures are useful because they provide the flexibility needed in executing a program. It is important to be able to select the next instruction to be executed. The branch instructions in the VAX-11 instruction repertoire are complete.

Loops are easy to set up. Each of the typical conditional control structures found in higher-level languages can be built using the CMPx instruction, along with the conditional *and* unconditional branch instructions. To maximize the number of actions inside these loops, it is necessary to use the JMP instruction. Later, we show how to use macros to generalize the conditional loops set up in this chapter (see chapters 16 and 17).

Indexed loops are also easy to set up. The SOBGEQ (subtract, and branch, if greater than or equal) and AOBLEQ (add, and branch, if less than or equal) can be used for short loops (ones with no more than a byte displacement). The ACBL can be used in place of these instructions for longer loops (ones with no more than a word displacement). The ACBx instruction is an extremely powerful one, since it allows *both* integer and floating point (fractional) operands.

Selective control structures (IF/THEN or IF/THEN/ELSE) are set up using a conditional branch to assess the result of a previous operation. To do this, the processor checks the condition code-values of the PSW.

In each case, the execution of the conditional branch instructions depends on two factors:

1. PSW condition code-values
2. branch displacement

It is the assembler that computes the correct displacement needed for a particular branch. The conditional branches make it possible to set up both forward *and* backward branches.

The more complex SOBx, AOBx, and ACBx instructions also use a displacement computed by the assembler and the PSW condition codes. These instructions have a third feature *not* present in the simpler conditional branch instructions like BEQL:

3. computation relative to an index

In each case, these branch instructions depend on the use of a labelled location, which the branch instruction will reference.

5.6

EXERCISES

1. Use

```
diminish:                    ; diminish is @300 (hex)
        addl3 r6, r7, r8
        decl r6
        bneq diminish
```

to do the following:

(a) With *diminish* representing 300 (hex) calculate the twos complement displacement computed by the assembler for the BNEQ instruction.

(b) Follow the set-up shown in section 5.1 for the fragment beginning with the same label. Give the machine equivalent of the above fragment.

(c) Give the value of the current (PC) when the processor executes the branch instruction.

2. Use

```
        addl2 #233, r6
        beql side_step      ; beql @ loc. 350
        divl2 r6, r7
        movl r7, r8
side_step:
        ⟨next instruction⟩
```

to do the following:

(a) With the BEQL branch at location 350 (hex), calculate the twos complement displacement computed by the assembler for the BEQL instruction.

(b) Follow the instructions in 1(b) to set up the SIDE_STEP fragment in section 5.1.

(c) Follow the instructions in 1(c).

3. Prepare a flow-of-control diagram like the one in Figure 5.4 for the following sequence:

```
if ⟨condition1⟩ then ⟨statement1⟩
    else
if ⟨condition2⟩ then ⟨statement2⟩
    else
if ⟨condition3⟩ then ⟨statement3⟩
```

4. Give the VAX-11 assembler equivalent of the IF/THEN/ELSE sequence in exercise 3.

5. Write an assembly language program to do the following:

(a) Prompt the user to choose one of the items in the following menu:

```
1.  December, 1983 low temp in the USA
2.  December, 1983 high temp in the USA
3.  December, 1982 low temp in the USA
4.  December, 1982 high temp in the USA
```

(b) Depending on the menu item chosen, print a message.

(c) Check if the user wishes to make another menu item. If so, transfer control back to the beginning of the program.

6. Write an assembly language program to do the following:

(a) Prompt for three integers.

(b) Print the largest of the three numbers entered.

(c) Allow the user to rerun the program.

7. Enhance the program in exercise 6 to select the largest number among 2 to 15 numbers that the user enters. In other words,

(a) Determine how many numbers the user wishes to enter (assign k this value).

(b) Set up a loop based on the value of k to read the entered numbers, checking each pair of entries until the largest is found.

(c) Store the entered numbers in an x-list.

(d) Print out the x-list with an indication of the biggest entry.

8. Write an assembly language program that

(a) Uses a newly created macro called star to print

inside a WHILE loop.

(b) Prompts the user for the number of stars to be printed.

(c) Allows the user to rerun the program.

Hint: Use the DRAWTRIANGLE macro as a guide to create the STAR macro.

9. Construct an example in which the displacement called for by an AOB-LEQ loop is too large (more than 127 bytes).

10. Correct the example in exercise 9 by substituting an ACBL instruction.

11. Write an assembly language program to print the following sequence:

1, 3, 5, 7, 9, 11, . . . , 99

12. Write an assembly language program to print the following alphabet triangle:

```
a
b  c
d  e  f
g  h  i  j
k  l  m  n  o
```

Allow the user to choose the number of rows to be printed.

Hint: The WRITESTRING macro can be used to do this, if you initialize a register with 97 (decimal code for a lower case *a*) and increment the register by 1 inside nested loops.

13. Enhance the program in exercise 13 to allow the user to choose

    (a) upper case alphabet triangle

    (b) lower case alphabet triangle

    (c) number of rows in each triangle printed

    (d) choose to rerun the program

Note: (a) and (b) can be handled with a menu; (d) with an IF/THEN at the end of the program.

14. Enhance the definition of a WHILE/DO in VAX-11 assembler in section 5.4.3 using the JMP.

15. Enhance the definition of a REPEAT/UNTIL in VAX-11 assembler in section 5.4.3 using the JMP.

5.7

LAB PROJECTS

1. Write an assembly program to do the following:

    (a) Print a Lucas triangle (see note below) as follows:

```
2
1   3
4   7   11
18  29  47  76
.
.
.
```

Note: Lucas numbers start with $L(0) = 2$, $L(1) = 1$, $L(2) = L(1) + L(0) = 3$. In general, $L(n) = L(n - 1) + L(n - 2)$, giving the sequence

    2, 1, 3, 4, 7, 11, 18, 29, 47, . . .

(b) Allow the user to choose the number of rows in the Lucas triangle.

(c) Allow the user to rerun the program with another choice of rows.

2. Enhance the program in exercise 13 so that

(a) The user can choose the starting ASCII code with a minimum of 33 for an (!).

Note: You must detect when the increment by 1 of the *preceding* code in the triangle jumps past 126 (the last ASCII code). If this happens, make the next code 33 and start over again. The range of printable ASCII codes is

$$33, \quad 34, \quad \ldots, \quad 125, \quad 126$$
$$\uparrow \quad \uparrow \qquad \uparrow \quad \uparrow$$
$$! \qquad " \qquad \quad \} \qquad \sim$$

(b) Allow the user to choose the number of rows to be printed.

(c) Allow the user to rerun the program.

5.8

REVIEW QUIZ

Indicate whether the following statements are true or false:

1. The ones complement of 4 = FB, if this is the ones complement of a byte whose content is 4.
2. If the address of the instruction currently being executed is 204 and the current instruction uses 10 bytes, then the current (PC) is 2E0.
3. Branch displacement is limited to one byte.
4. The maximum branch forward is 32767 bytes.
5. The maximum branch forward is 127 bytes.
6. A CMP tells the processor to subtract the destination from the source.
7. The PSW bits N, Z, and C are conditionally set by a CMP instruction.
8. The PSW V bit is not conditionally set by execution of a CMP instruction.
9. The x in CMPx stands for hex.
10. Selection control will have a WHILE/DO form.

11. Indexed repetition will have a FOR/DO form.

12. IF/THEN/ELSE offers an example of a repetition control statement.

13. Three actions are possible with an IF/THEN/ELSE statement.

14. The loop condition is checked first with a REPEAT/UNTIL loop.

15. An ACBx instruction allows maximum forward displacements of 512 bytes.

5.9

REFERENCES

A. Keller, *A First Course in Computer Programming Using Pascal,* McGraw-Hill, Inc., N.Y., 1982.

Wirth, N. *Programming in Modula-2*. New York: Springer-Verlag, 1983.

6.
STACKS AND QUEUES

Many a scene that looks desert and rock-bound from the distance, will unfold itself into rare valleys.

—Thomas Carlyle, *Sartor Resartus* (1830)

6.0
AIMS

- Introduce the basic operations for stacks and queues.
- Distinguish between efficient and inefficient, downward and upward, system and register stacks.
- Illustrate the uses of the VAX-11 stack and queue instructions.
- Introduce singly linked and doubly linked lists in terms of the INSQUE and REMQUE instructions.
- Show how stacks and queues can be used to handle base conversions.

6.1
INTRODUCTION

Stacks and queues are among the most useful data structures in computing. Each can be characterized as a list of elements. They are distinguished by the manner in which insertions and deletions are made.

VAX-11s depend on the use of hardware stacks and queues. These lists are implemented on a computer by means of contiguous memory locations. VAX-11 system stacks are in the control (P1) region of main memory, which is set aside for its operating system called Virtual Memory System (VMS) and is used to handle addressing problems. An *operating system* is a program that is used to manage the resources of a computer system. VMS uses queues to manage user requests for system devices such as disk drives, terminals, card readers, and so on. This is called Queue Input Output or QIO. It sets up queues for tasks awaiting system services because more than one user may need the *same* system services at the *same* time.

VAX-11s depend on the use of the system stack to handle addressing problems related to procedure calls and return from procedures to a calling program or routine. It is necessary to save the current (PC) when a procedure call is made. A procedure call entails giving the PC a new address, the *beginning* address of the procedure being called. When a return from the end of a procedure is in initiated, the old PC is popped off the system stack. This becomes the new PC value. We explain this in more detail in the next chapter.

Stacks and queues are also useful in assembly language programming. This chapter presents some of the techniques used in stack- and queue-handling. The VAX-11 instruction is richly endowed with instructions to handle typical and some atypical stack and queue operations. We also begin using these instructions here. We start with stacks.

6.2

STACKS

Stacks can be found everywhere in the physical world—for example, in layered structures like the cambium rings of a tree, in the tiers of arctic ice, in geologic formations, and so on. These components of the physical world appear to be a collection of "stacks" where the latest layer (ring, tier) we encounter is the newest layer and subsequent ones are progressively older—the basic last in, first out rule.

Some stacks are more efficient than others. A cafeteria tray stacker is an example of an inefficient stack. Why? Each time a tray is added to the stacker, the other trays are pushed down in the stack. That is, the trays already in the stack do not stay in the same position when either a tray is pushed on or popped off the stack. This is not the way the system stack on a VAX-11 works. The VAX-11 system stack is managed more like a stack of plates on a shelf or a pile of letters; in other words, insertions and deletions do not disturb the other elements of the stack. The contrast between these two types of stacks is illustrated in Figure 6.1.

FIGURE 6.1
Efficient and Inefficient Stacks

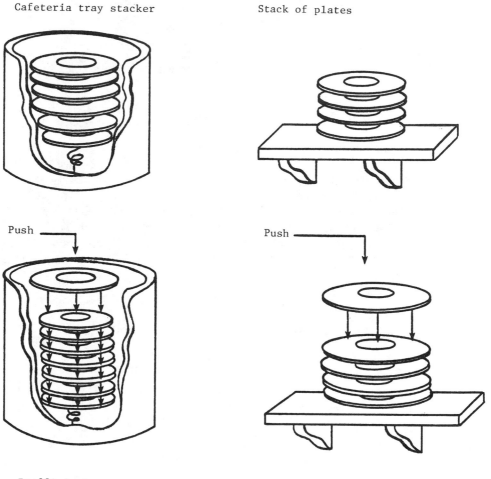

Cafeteria tray stacker

Stack of plates

Push

Push

Inefficient
Stack

Efficient
Stack

Initially, the system stack pointer SP (= R14) on a VAX-11 holds the address of the *stack head*, the location in memory just above the first stack location. To push an element onto the stack, autodecrement addressing is used. For example, to push a 3 onto the system stack, we can use

movl #3, − (SP)

Each push inserts an element immediately *below* the preceding stack entry in memory. The VAX-11 system stack is an example of a *downward stack*, since successive pushes move *down* in memory, approaching the user program P0 region of memory. Instead of using the above autodecrement for a push, we can use

    pushl #3

to do the same thing. Similarly, if we want to pop a stack element, we can use

    popl r6

which accomplishes the same thing as

    movl (SP)+, r6

which pops a system stack entry into R6. The VAX-11 instruction set includes a rich selection of stack operators, as shown in Table 6.1.

These operators simplify the use of the system stack. They take the place of the necessary autodecrement needed for a push, and autoincrement

TABLE 6.1
VAX-11 Stack Instructions with Memory Contents

pushl ⟨value⟩ equivalent to movl ⟨value⟩, −(SP)
popl ⟨value⟩ equivalent to movl (SP)+, ⟨destination⟩

With Registers

pushr ⟨register⟩ equivalent to movl ⟨register⟩, −(SP)
pushr #^M⟨r6,r7,...⟩ equivalent to movl r6, −(SP)
                                        movl r7, −(SP)
                                        .
                                        .
                                        .

popr ⟨destination register⟩ equivalent to movl (SP)+, ⟨register⟩
popr #^M⟨r6,r7,...⟩ equivalent to movl (SP)+, r6
                                        movl (SP)+, r7
                                        .
                                        .
                                        .

With Addresses

pushax ⟨address⟩ equivalent to movax ⟨label⟩, r6
                                        pushl r6

x = B, W, L, Q, F

needed for a pop. Figure 6.2 illustrates the mechanism implicit in these stack operations in terms of pushing the elements of the sequence

5, 8, 13, 21, . . .

and popping several of these elements off the stack.

FIGURE 6.2
Sample Push/Pop Cycles

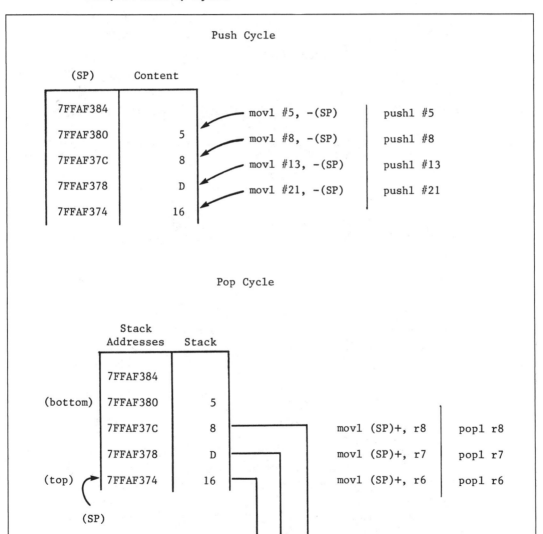

If the contents of one or more registers are pushed, VAX-11 provides a unary operator M (for Mask). This is used to tell the assembler that the registers inside the angle brackets will be masked (saved). For example, if we want to push R6, R7, R8, R9, we would use

```
pushr #ˆM⟨r6, r7, r8, r9⟩
```

To restore (pop) the old register contents use

```
popr #ˆM⟨r6, r7, r8, r9⟩
```

These two operations are useful if we want to preserve the current register contents *and* free the same registers for new uses.

6.2.1 How to Examine System Stack Addresses and Contents

The VAX-11 assembler accepts SP as an identifier for R14, but *not* R14 itself. The following operation will print a copy of the *current* SP (an address in the P1 control region of memory):

```
writeval SP
```

To print the content of the stack top *without* moving the SP "up" in the stack, use

```
writeval (SP)
```

Figure 6.3 illustrates this idea by printing the initial SP, *before* any stack operations are used, as well as successive SP-contents during a sequence of pushes.

6.2.2 Downward Register Stack

A register stack moves downward if a push puts the pushed element below the preceding one. The "top" moves downward. The address of the stack bottom is always greater than or equal to the top address. To set up a register stack, initialize a register with the address (MOVAx) of the stack head, which is the location immediately above the stack bottom. Then use autodecrementing to handle pushes, autoincrementing to handle pops.

We illustrate this by filling the first 20 positions of a stack with Lucas numbers. The procedure we will use in the push cycle is shown in Figure

FIGURE 6.3
SP Values

```
;
;Ref.:   Figure 6.3 (System stack pointer values)
;
;var
        max:      .long 10
        step:     .long 1
        index:    .long 1
        number:   .long 1

Begin:  .word

        Write <System stack head address = >
        writeval sp radix = 2
        writeln
        writeln
        writeln <----------------------------------------------------->
        writeln
        writeln <            Push cycle:>
        writeln
        writeln <            (sp) top address top entry>
        writeln <----------------------------------------------------->
        writeln

push_cycle:

        pushl     number
        writeval sp radix = 2
        write < >                                ;< > = tab
        writeval (sp)
        incl      number
        writeln
        acbl      max,step,index,push_cycle

        movl      #1,index
        writeln
        writeln <            Pop cycle:>
        writeln
        writeln <            Location of top    Popped value>
        writeln <----------------------------------------------------->
        writeln
pop_cycle:

        writeval sp radix = 2
        write < >                                ;< > = tab
        popl      number
        writeval number
        writeln
        acbl      max,step,index,pop_cycle

        $exit_s

        .end Begin
```

Continued on following page.

Figure 6.3 continued.

```
RUN FG63

System stack head address = 11111111111101011110011100000100

--------------------------------------------------------

        Push cycle:

        (sp) top address      top entry
--------------------------------------------------------

11111111111101011110011100000000   1
11111111111101011110011101111100   2
11111111111101011110011101111000   3
11111111111101011110011101110100   4
11111111111101011110011101110000   5
11111111111101011110011101101100   6
11111111111101011110011101101000   7
11111111111101011110011101100100   8
11111111111101011110011101100000   9
11111111111101011110011101011100   10

        Pop cycle:

        Location of top          Popped value
--------------------------------------------------------

11111111111101011110011101011100   10
11111111111101011110011101100000   9
11111111111101011110011101100100   8
11111111111101011110011101101000   7
11111111111101011110011101101100   6
11111111111101011110011101110000   5
11111111111101011110011101110100   4
11111111111101011110011101111000   3
11111111111101011110011101111100   2
11111111111101011110011100000000   1
```

6.4 (assume the label *stack* symbolizes 304 [hex]). A program employing the complete technique is shown in Figure 6.5.

6.2.3 Why Use Register Stacks?

Once elements have been popped from the system stack, the original stack entries are lost. The VAX-11 will have used the same locations for some other task. To verify this, save the stack-top address after pushing elements onto the system stack. Pop the entries. Restore the top address and pop the stack contents. This is left as an exercise.

In contrast, popping register stack entries does not destroy the stack

FIGURE 6.4
Downward Register Stack Illustration

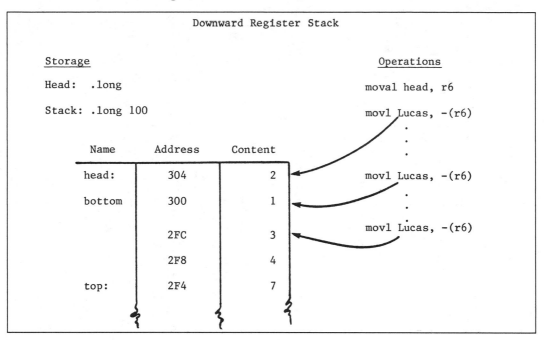

contents. They can be reused, if necessary. We illustrate this in Figure 6.6 by making two copies of an R6-stack after loading the stack. In addition, register stacks are not limited to longwords. Since a MOVe is used, each of the data types available for a push or pop can be used.

6.2.4 Upward Register Stacks

The graphic interpretation of an upward register stack is given in Figure 6.7. In other words, each push places the pushed element *above* the last stack entry. The "top" moves up in the stack, although you would intuitively expect it to be at the bottom.

A push is handled by

mov⟨type⟩ ⟨item⟩, (register)+

A pop is handled by

mov⟨type⟩ − (register), ⟨destination⟩

This provides a handy alternative to the downward stack. Why? If we were to set up two register stacks—one upward, one downward—there would be no danger of one stack "bumping" into the other. In addition, the address

FIGURE 6.5
A Program with a Downward Register Stack

```
;
;Ref.:   Figure 6.5 (A downward register stack)
;
;var
        max:       .long 10
        step:      .long 1
        index:     .long 1
        Lucas:     .long 3
        x:         .long 1
        y:         .long 3
        stack:     .blkl 30
        stack_head:
                   .long

Begin:  .word

        moval stack_head, r6                    ;init. r6 with stack head ptr

        write <Register stack head address: >
        writeval r6 radix=16
        writeln
        writeln
        writeln <------------------------------------------------------->
        writeln
        writeln <            Push cycle:>
        writeln
        writeln <              (r6) top address     top entry>
        writeln <------------------------------------------------------->
        writeln

push_cycle:

        movl     Lucas,-(r6)                    ;push Lucas no. down
        write <               >                 ;<  > = 2 tabs
        writeval r6 radix = 16
        write <               >                 ;<  > = 2 tabs
        writeval (r6)
        writeln
        add13    x,y,Lucas                      ;Lucas:=x + y
        movl     y,x                            ;x := y
        movl     Lucas,y                        ;y := Lucas
        acbl     max,step,index,push_cycle

        movl     #1,index

        writeln
        writeln <            Pop cycle:>
        writeln
        writeln <            Location of top      Popped value>
        writeln <------------------------------------------------------->
        writeln

pop_cycle:
```

Figure 6.5 continued.

```
        write <                    >              ;<  > = 2 tabs
        writeval r6 radix = 16
        write <                    >              ;<  > = 2 tabs
        movl     (r6)+,r7                         ;pop Lucas no.
        writeval r7
        writeln
        acbl     max,step,index,pop_cycle

        $exit_s

        .end Begin


RUN FG65

Register stack head address: 290

------------------------------------------------------------

        Push cycle:

        (r6) top address        top entry
------------------------------------------------------------

                28C                 3
                288                 4
                284                 7
                280                 11
                27C                 18
                278                 29
                274                 47
                270                 76
                26C                 123
                268                 199

        Pop cycle:

        Location of top         Popped value
------------------------------------------------------------

                268                 199
                26C                 123
                270                 76
                274                 47
                278                 29
                27C                 18
                280                 11
                284                 7
                288                 4
                28C                 3
```

FIGURE 6.6
Reusing Register Stack Entries

```
;
;Ref.    Figure 6.6 (Reusing register stack entries)
;
;var
        max:        .long 20
        step:       .long 1
        index:      .long 1
        number:     .long 1
        stack:      .blkl 25
        stack_head:
                    .long
        stack_top:
                    .long


Begin:  .word

        moval    stack_head,r6

push_cycle:

        movl     number,-(r6)                        ;push number
        incl     number
        acbl     max,step,index,push_cycle

        movl     r6,stack_top                        ;save top-address
        movl     #1,index                            ;restore original index
        writeln
        writeln <              First use of stack:>
        writeln
        writeln <--------------------------------------------------------->
        writeln

pop_cycle:

        movl     (r6)+,r7                            ;pop number
        writeval r7
        acbl     max,step,index,pop_cycle

        movl     #1,index                            ;restore original index
        movl     stack_top,r6                        ;restore stack_top to r6
        writeln
        writeln
        writeln <           Reuse of original stack entries:>
        writeln
        writeln <--------------------------------------------------------->
        writeln

new_pop_cycle:

        movl     (r6)+,r7                            ;pop number
        writeval r7
        acbl     max,step,index,new_pop_cycle

        $exit_s
        .end Begin
```

Figure 6.6 continued.

```
RUN FG66

        First use of stack:

-----------------------------------------------------------

20 19 18 17 16 15 14 13 12 11 10 9 8 7 6 5 4 3 2 1

        Reuse of original stack entries:

-----------------------------------------------------------

20 19 18 17 16 15 14 13 12 11 10 9 8 7 6 5 4 3 2 1
```

head could be used for both stacks. We can use the following storage setup here:

```
    stack_up  :  .blkl 1024

        head  :  .long

stack_down  :  .blkl 1024
```

FIGURE 6.7
Upward Register Stack Illustration

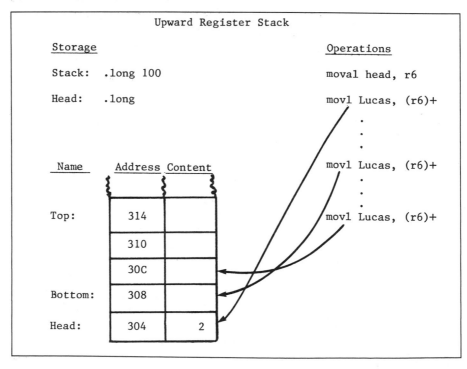

The alternative is to set up max-position addresses, each with the address of the location past the last allowable stack-top address. In this case, a push would be executed only if the stack pointer to be used did not exceed a set limit on its address range.

    max_length + 1

For example, we can use the following scheme:

    head_1   :   .long
    stack_1 :   .blkl 1024
    max1   :   .long
    head_2   :   .long
    stack_2 :   .blkl 100
    max2   :   .long
             .
             .
             .
    head_k   :   .long
    stack_k :   .blkl 5
    maxk   :   .long

Then it is just a matter of checking the individual stack pointer against a max address. To do this, use the VAX-11 TST⟨type⟩ (Test) instruction to advance the stack pointer *before* attempting a push. That is, use the following scheme:

```
                              ;assume r6 has stack pointer
    test: tst1 (r6)+          ;advance pointer
          cmpl r6, maxk
          bgtr push
          write ⟨stack full!⟩
          jump doorway
    push: movl ⟨element⟩, (r6)
          jump test
    doorway:
             .
             .
             .
```

The TSTx (TeST) instruction in the above example merely advances the stack pointer. (In general, this instruction can be used to set the PSW condition codes [*N* and *Z* bits] in terms of an operand, *without* affecting the operand.)

You might be wondering whether it is possible to set up 10 register stacks with 6 general registers (R6:R11). To do this, use the PUSHR and POPR instructions to save and restore register contents as needed. Try setting up 6 register stacks using R6:R11. Then

> pushr #ˆM⟨r6, r7, r8, r9⟩

and free R6:R9 to set up 4 new stacks, *without* losing track of the address tops of each of the first stacks.

6.2.5 Application: Changing Integer Bases

We will use the change-base procedure given in chapter 2 to determine a new base for a given integer. We can do this with a downward register stack by using the VAX-11 extended division instruction:

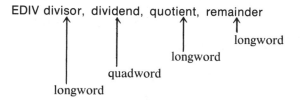

A convenient way to set up the quadword for the dividend is to use a pair of registers. If we use R6, for example, then R7 will be the second longword in the quadword (=8 bytes). Even if we only want to work with longword dividends, we must use a quadword dividend for this instruction. If, for example, R6 is used, it is necessary to clear R7 before using R6 as the dividend in the EDIV instruction. Otherwise, any stray content in R7 will produce erroneous results. A base conversion procedure which uses the EDIV instruction and a register stack is given in Figure 6.8.

This method hinges on a thorough understanding of the ASCII table and what happens when we divide a number by a base—that is, the remainder will always be less than or equal to the base. If the base is sixteen, then remainders greater than 9 must be treated in a special way. Suppose, for example, the remainder is 11:

> no = 59
>
> base = 16
>
> $\dfrac{59}{16} = 3 +$ a remainder of 11

FIGURE 6.8
NEW_BASE Assembler Procedure

```
            Procedure Integer Base Conversion

            var

                number, base, quotient, remainder:  integer;
                r7, r6, count:  integer;

            Begin

            1.  Initialize number, base;
                        r6 := number

            2.  Set up quadword for ediv:
                      r7 := 0;

                2.1  ediv base, r6, quotient, remainder;

                2.2  Adjust remainder for ASCII bias:
                        remainder := remainder + 48;
                        if remainder > 57 (= ASCII code for 9)
                           then
                              remainder := remainder + 7

                    2.3  push remainder;

                    2.4  count := count + 1;

                    2.5  if quotient <> 0
                             then
                                 begin
                                 r6 := quotient;
                                 repeat step 2
                                 end
                             else
                                 repeat
                                 pop digit;
                                 count := count-1
                                 until count = 0
            End.
```

Adding the ASCII bias 48 to 11 gives

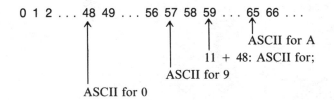

FIGURE 6.9
Integer Base Conversion Program

```
;
;Ref.:   Figure 6.9 (Integer Base Conversions)
;
;var
        quotient:               .long
        remainder:              .long
        no:                     .long
        max:                    .long
        step:                   .long 1
        index:                  .long 1
        reg_stack:              .blkl 20
        stack_head:             .long
        answer:                 .long

Begin:  .word

again:
        write <Enter base 10 integer:  >
        readvar no
        movl      no,r6
        movab     stack_head,r9
        writeln
        writeln <--------------------------------------------------->
        writeln
        writeval no
        write <(base 10)  =   >

push_cycle:

        clrl      r7                        ;set up quad for ediv
        ediv      #16,r6,quotient,remainder
        movl      remainder,-(r9)           ;push remainder into reg. stack
        incl      max                       ;set up for/do loop range
        movl      quotient, r6              ;get quotient
                                            ;is it zero?
        bneq      push_cycle                ;if not, push new digit
                                            ;else
pop_cycle:                                  ;begin pop cycle

        movl      (r9)+,r7
        writeval r7 radix=16,spaces=0
        acbl      max,step,index,pop_cycle

        writeln
        writeln <--------------------------------------------------->
        writeln
        write <  Do want another run?--1=Y,0=N :  >
        readvar answer
        cmpl      #0,answer
        beql      doorway
        jmp       again
doorway:
        $exit_s
        .end Begin
```

Continued on following page.

Figure 6.9 continued.

```
RUN FG69

Enter base 10 integer:   512


------------------------------------------------------

512 (base 10)  =   200
------------------------------------------------------

          Do want another run?--1=Y,0=N :   0
```

There are 7 characters between ASCII 57 (for 9) and ASCII 65 (for *A*). To replace 11 + 48 by the correct hex letter, it is necessary to add 7 to obtain

$$11 + 48 + 7 = 66 = B$$

ASCII symbol

ASCII code

This explains the need for step 2.2 in the NEW_BASE procedure in Figure 6.8. A program that is designed to carry out this idea appears in Figure 6.9. In this program, step 2.2 is hidden in the WRITEVAL macro. It relies on a numeric output procedure, which we explain in chapter 9. In the meantime, we use the WRITEVAL macro to handle the problem of adjusting the ASCII bias of the remainders when they are greater than 9.

6.3
QUEUES

The last entry in a queue occurs at the queue *tail*. The leading or first entry is at the queue *front*. *Dequeue* operations (deletions from a queue) are made from the queue front. *Enqueue* operations (insertions into a queue) are made at the tail end. Common examples of queues are grocery store lines, carwash lines, cafeteria lines, and so on. To set up a queue in memory, it is helpful to set up a *list head* (a location with the address of the queue front). We illustrate this idea graphically in terms of enqueuing

20, 30, . . . , 100

We will put the list head at location 300. Once the queue is built, we will dequeue the same elements, as shown in Figure 6.10.

FIGURE 6.10
Queue Operations Illustrated

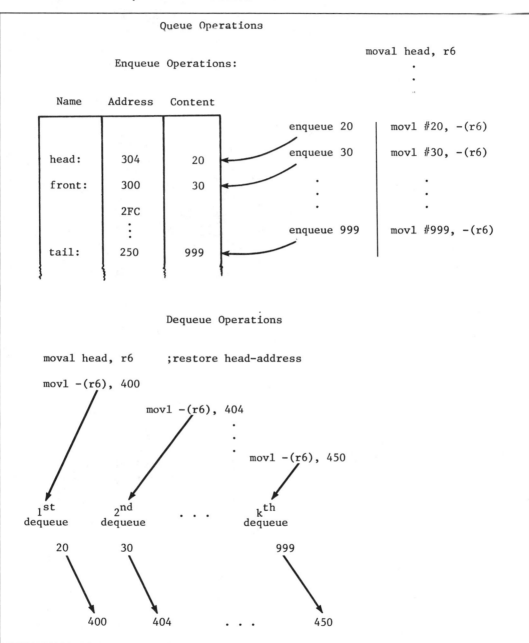

FIGURE 6.11
Dequeueing Even Lucas Numbers

```
;
;Ref.:   Figure 6.11 (Dequeueing even Lucas numbers)
;
;var
        max:                    .long 20
        step:                   .long 1
        index:                  .long 1
        total_found:            .long
        Lucas:                  .long 3
        x:                      .long 1
        y:                      .long 3
        queue:                  .blkl 25
        queue_head:             .long
        reg_stack:              .blkl 25
        stack_head:             .long

Begin:  .word

        movab       queue_head,r6

        writeln <                Lucas numbers in queue:>
        writeln
        writeln <                Queue address             Entry>
        writeln <-------------------------------------------------------->
        writeln

enqueue:

        movl        Lucas,-(r6)                         ;enqueue Lucas no.
        write < >
        writeval r6 radix = 16
        write <              >
        writeval (r6)
        writeln
        addl3       x,y,Lucas                           ;compute new Lucas no.
        movl        y,x                                 ; x := y
        movl        Lucas,y                             ; y := Lucas
        acbl        max,step,index,enqueue

        movab       queue_head,r6                       ;restore queue_head to r6
        movab       stack_head,r11                      ;set up r11 with stack ptr
        movl        #1,index                            ;restore original index

dequeue:

        movl        -(r6),r7                            ;dequeue Lucas no.
        clrl        r8                                  ;set up quad for ediv
        ediv        #2,r7,r9,r10
        tstl        r10                                 ;r10 = remainder will be
                                                        ;zero, if Lucas no. is even
        beql        save
        jmp         next_Lucas_no
save:
        incl        total_found                         ;adjust range of for/do loop
        movl        r7,-(r11)                           ;push even Lucas no.
                                                        ;been found?
```

Figure 6.11 continued.

```
next_Lucas_no:

        acbl       max,step,index,dequeue

report:

        writeln
        writeln <-------------------------------------------------->
        writeln
        movl       #1,index
        writeln
        write < >                                          ;< > = tab
        writeval total_found
        write <  even Lucas numbers found in queue: >
        writeln
        writeln

pop:

        movl       (r11)+,r7                              ;pop even Lucas no.
        writeval r7
        acbl total_found,step,index,pop

        $exit_s

        .end Begin

        RUN FG611


                Lucas numbers in queue:


                Queue address          Entry
        ---------------------------------------------------------

                27C                   3
                278                   4
                274                   7
                270                   11
                26C                   18
                268                   29
                264                   47
                260                   76
                25C                   123
                258                   199
                254                   322
                250                   521
                24C                   843
                248                   1364
                244                   2207
                240                   3571
                23C                   5778
                238                   9349
                234                   15127
                230                   24476

        ----------------------------------------------------

                7   even Lucas numbers found in queue:

        24476 5778 1364 322 76 18 4
```

The enqueue and dequeue operations can both be handled with the autodecrement addressing mode. To enqueue, put the head address into a register (try R6), and use the following instruction:

```
movl ⟨entry⟩, − (r6)
```

To dequeue, restore the queue head address to the register being used. To find an element in a queue, it is usually necessary to go to the queue front and dequeue until the desired element is found. We illustrate this idea in a simple way, first. We enqueue 20 Lucas numbers and then we dequeue from the queue entries, pushing the even-valued Lucas numbers into a register stack (see Figure 6.11).

Remember, it is important to restore the original index-value of 1 before beginning another ACBL-loop.

6.3.1 Application: Getting Fractional Results

We illustrate the use of a queue in terms of determining fractional results. (This idea was discussed in chapter 2.) Suppose, for example, we want to change 0.61806 (base ten) to hex. Figure 6.12 outlines a method that can be used to do this. To get the hex fraction from the queue, restore the address of the list head and dequeue the digits. Figure 6.13 shows a program that will do this.

In the above example, we dequeue the "normal" way by restoring the list head address. We dequeue from the front of the queue. It would be just as easy to set up a queue that would allow us to dequeue from the tail. To do this, just use the autoincrement mode to work *backwards* through the queue to the queue front. Included in the VAX-11 instruction set are instructions that make it easier to scan a queue backwards and forwards, or anywhere between the front and tail of a queue. To understand how these queue instructions work, we must look at linked lists.

6.3.2 Linked Lists

A *list* is any finite sequence of elements. The elements of a list—like the names in a telephone directory—are identified according to their *position* in the list:

$$name_1, name_2, name_3, \ldots, name_k$$

It is possible to build a list so that each element of the list, called a *node*, contains information as well as the location of the next element of the list. These locations are called *links* of the nodes. The result is what is known as a *linked list*. For example, suppose we want to identify the names of

FIGURE 6.12
Sample Decimal to Hex Fraction Conversion

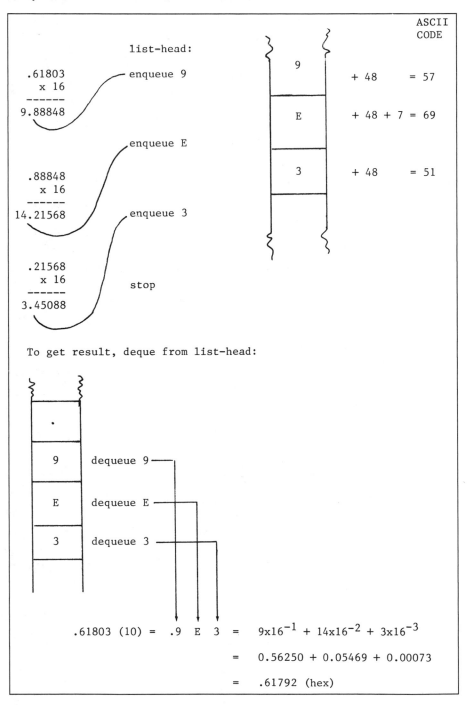

FIGURE 6.13
Fraction Conversion Program

```
;
;Ref.:   Figure 6.13 (Fraction base conversion)
;
;var
        answer:                 .long
        max:                    .long 6
        step:                   .long 1
        index:                  .long 1
        quotient:               .long
        remainder:              .long
        divisor: .long
        new_base:               .long 16
        queue:                  .blkl 20
        queue_head:             .long


Begin:  .word

again:

        write <Enter integers x,y to compute ratio of x to y in hex: >
        readvar r8 divisor
        writeln
        write <                 >               ;< > = 2 tabs
        writeval r8
        write < : >
        writeval divisor
        write < = >
        clrl    r9                              ;set up quad for ediv
        ediv    divisor,r8,quotient,remainder
        writeval quotient radix = 16, spaces = 0
        write < . >
        movab   queue_head,r10                  ;init. r10 queue ptr

enqueue:

        mull3   new_base,remainder,r6           ;shift digits left
        clrl    r7
        ediv    divisor,r6,quotient,remainder
        movl    quotient,-(r10)                 ;enqueue digit of fraction
        acbl    max,step,index,enqueue

        movl    #1,index                        ;restore original index
        movab   queue_head,r10                  ;restore queue ptr

dequeue:

        movl    -(r10),r6                       ;dequeue digit
        writeval r6 radix = 16, spaces = 0
        acbl    max,step,index,dequeue

        writeln
        writeln <------------------------------------------------------->
        writeln
        writeln
```

Figure 6.13 continued.

```
write <Do you wish to enter another pair of numbers? 1=Y,0=N: >
readvar answer
cmpl     #0,answer
beql     doorway
jmp      again

doorway:

     $exit_s

     .end Begin


RUN FG613

Enter integers x,y to compute ratio of x to y in hex: 233.144

          233  : 144  = 1 . 9E38E3
-----------------------------------------------------------


Do you wish to enter another pair of numbers? 1=Y,0=N: 1
Enter integers x,y to compute ratio of x to y in hex: 144.233

          144  : 233  = 0 . 9E38E3
-----------------------------------------------------------


Do you wish to enter another pair of numbers? 1=Y,0=N: 1
Enter integers x,y to compute ratio of x to y in hex: 2,3


          2  : 3  = 0 . AE38E3
-----------------------------------------------------------


Do you wish to enter another pair of numbers? 1=Y,0=N: 0
```

computer scientists and their location in a directory. We could devise the scheme shown in Figure 6.14.

The last node of this example contains a null pointer *nil*; it points to nothing. Before you begin using a linked list, it is helpful to set up a *list head node* that contains a pointer (link) to the beginning node of the list. This is an example of a *singly linked list*. The links of the nodes in the directory linked list in Figure 6.14 are *forward links* or FLINKS. Each one points forward to the next list node. If to each of the above list-nodes we add a link pointing backwards to the *previous* node, then we will have a *doubly linked list*. The new links are *backward links* or BLINKS (see Figure 6.15). Now the list head contains a pointer to the *front* or beginning of the list, as well as a pointer to the last node or *tail* of the list.

FIGURE 6.14
Sample Singly Linked List

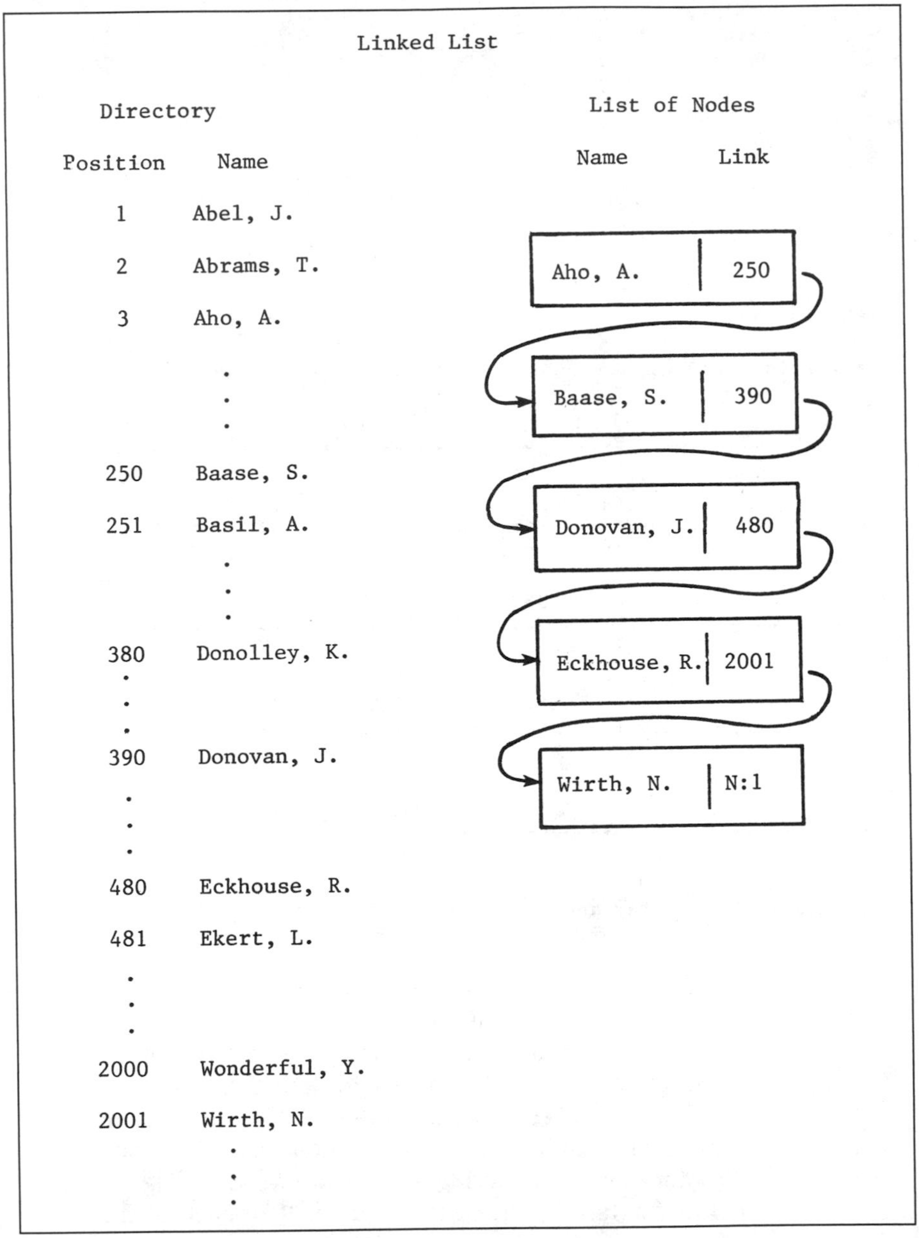

FIGURE 6.15
Sample Doubly Linked List

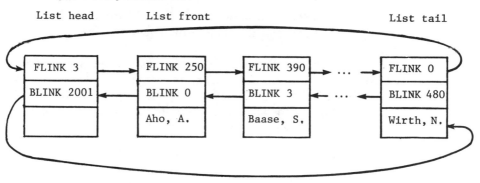

TABLE 6.2
Two VAX-11 Queue Instructions

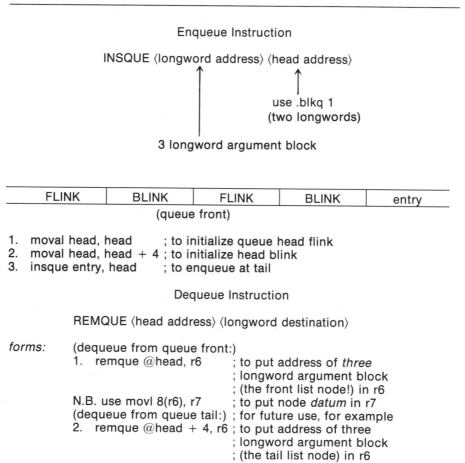

Enqueue Instruction

INSQUE ⟨longword address⟩ ⟨head address⟩

use .blkq 1
(two longwords)

3 longword argument block

FLINK	BLINK	FLINK	BLINK	entry

(queue front)

1. moval head, head   ; to initialize queue head flink
2. moval head, head + 4 ; to initialize head blink
3. insque entry, head   ; to enqueue at tail

Dequeue Instruction

REMQUE ⟨head address⟩ ⟨longword destination⟩

forms: (dequeue from queue front:)
        1. remque @head, r6   ; to put address of *three*
                                   ; longword argument block
                                   ; (the front list node!) in r6
        N.B. use movl 8(r6), r7   ; to put node *datum* in r7
        (dequeue from queue tail:) ; for future use, for example
        2. remque @head + 4, r6 ; to put address of three
                                   ; longword argument block
                                   ; (the tail list node) in r6

The queue set up with the VAX-11 queue instructions is a doubly linked list. Two of these instructions and their features are summarized in Table 6.2.

Each time the INSQUE (enqueue) instruction is executed by the processor, the FLINK of the list head node points to the queue front (the first list node with data). The processor updates the BLINK of the head node so that it contains the address of the tail node. The following steps are used to set up a queue with two nodes on the VAX-11:

1. Initialize the head node with the addresses as follows:

```
moval head, head
moval head, head + 4
```

FIGURE 6.16
Sample VAX-11 Doubly Linked Queue

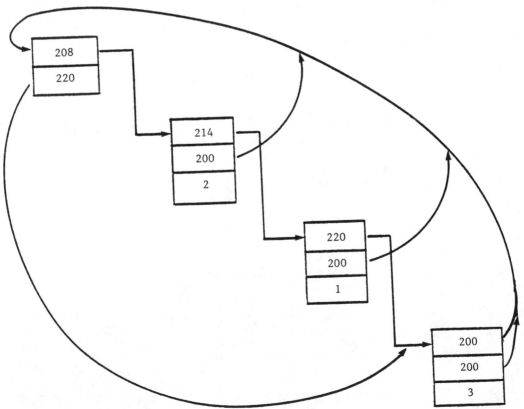

2. Initialize the *queue front* as follows:

```
insque entry, head
```

3. Initialize the *queue tail* as follows:

```
insque entry, @head + 4
```

4. Additional enqueuing is done at the tail end using the instruction format in step 3.

This idea can be illustrated by enqueuing the following numbers:

```
2, 1, 3
```

Each time the processor executes

```
insque ⟨node address⟩, @head + 4
```

it updates the predecessor node so that its FLINK has the address of the next node (the tail, until another insertion is made). Each BLINK points back to the list head. Both the BLINK and FLINK of the tail node point to the list head node, as shown in Figure 6.16. A program illustrating this idea is presented in Figure 16.17.

We have printed out both the links and the datum in each node. It is helpful to trace the links shown by obtaining a memory dump for the above program. This is left as an exercise. It is easy to dequeue moving backwards from the queue tail by using the following instruction:

```
dequeue:
        remque @h + 4, r6
```

The above program illustrates the need to address the *beginning* of each Lucas node, when we use the INSQUE instruction. Each set of longwords at location Lucas represents a queue node. The leading pair of longwords are used by the processor to set up the FLINK and BLINK addresses.

The following is an enhanced version of the above program. This time we isolate a Lucas node (three longwords), which we use to store members of the Lucas sequence:

```
2, 1, 3, 4, 7, 11, 18, . . . , L(n)
```

Before enqueing, we must assign a Lucas number to the third longword of each queue node. Once the INSQUE instruction is used for the first time

FIGURE 6.17
A Program with INSQUE/REMQUE Instructions

```
;
;Ref.:   Figure 6.17 (How to use the insque and remque instructions)
;
        h:         .blkq 1
        lucas:     .long      0,0,2,0,0,1,0,0,3,0,0,4,0,0,7,0,0,11,0,0,18
        max:       .long      5
        index:     .long      1
Begin:  .word

        moval      h,h
        moval      h,h+4

        insque     lucas,h
        insque     lucas+12,@h+4
        insque     lucas+24,@h+4
        insque     lucas+36,@h+4
        insque     lucas+48,@h+4

        writeln
        writeln <           Queue head node:>
        writeln
        writeln <                   flink        blink>
        writeln
        write<              >
        writeval h h+4 radix = 16 spaces = 14
        writeln
        writeln <-------------------------------------------------->
        writeln
        writeln <           Queue nodes:>
        writeln
        writeln <                   flink        blink        entry>
        writeln
        writeln <-------------------------------------------------->
        writeln

dequeue:
        remque     @h,r6
        write <              >
        writeval h h+4 8(r6) radix=16 spaces = 14
        writeln
        acbl       max,#1,index,dequeue

        $exit_s

        .end Begin

        RUN FG617

                Queue head node:

                        flink        blink

                        208          238
```

Figure 6.17 continued.

```
    --------------------------------------------------

        Queue nodes:

                  flink          blink          entry

    --------------------------------------------------

                  214            238              2
                  220            238              1
                  22C            238              3
                  238            238              4
                  200            200              7
```

FIGURE 6.18
Enhanced Enqueue/Dequeue Program

```
;
;Ref.:  Figure 6.18 (Enhanced insque/remque program)
;
;var
        h:        .blkq 1                       ;queue head node
        queue:    .blkl 200                     ;queue nodes
        lucas:    .long 0,0,3                   ;Lucas node
        x:        .long 1
        y:        .long 3
        max:      .long 20
        step:     .long 1
        index:    .long 1

Begin:  .word

        moval     h,h                           ;init. head node flink
        moval     h,h+4                         ;init. head node blink
        movl      lucas+8,queue+8              ;init. front node datum
        insque    queue,h                       ;enqueue
        moval     queue,r6                      ;init. r6 with queue
                                                ;front address

enqueue:

        addl2     #12,r6                        ;advance queue ptr to next node
        addl3     x,y,lucas+8                   ;compute new Lucas number
        movl      lucas+8,8(r6)                 ;init. queue node with no.
        insque    (r6),@h+4                     ;enqueue
        movl      y,x                           ; x := y
        movl      lucas+8,y                     ; y := Lucas no
        acbl      max,step,index,enqueue        ;repeat enqueue procedure
                                                ;until index = max

        movl      #1,index
        writeln <------------------------------------------------>
        writeln
        writeln <dequeueing at front:>
        writeln
```

Continued on following page.

```
                    Figure 6.18 continued.

 dequeue:

   remque    @h,r6                        ;dequeue from queue front
   writeval  8(r6)                        ;print copy dequeued no.
   acbl      max,step,index,dequeue       ;repeat dequeue procedure
                                          ;until index = max


   $exit_s

   .end Begin

   RUN FG618

 --------------------------------------------------------

 dequeueing at front:

 3 4 7 11 18 29 47 76 123 199 322 521 843 1364 2207 3571 5778 9349 15127 24476
```

and a number inserted in the second node, we will have a list of the form:

```
     200   200   3   0   0   4
      ↑            ↑   ↑   ↑
      |            |   |   └ insert 4
      |            |   └ BLINK which is empty
      |            └ FLINK which is empty
      └ FLINK of queue front
```

That is, the second node will not be linked to the queue front until the processor executes the instruction

insque (r6), @ h+4

The enhanced program appears in Figure 6.18.

6.4

SUMMARY

In writing assembly language programs, try to get used to checking memory dumps after a processor has performed stack or queue operations. This habit should be cultivated. A check of a memory dump for these operations should be coupled with a check of the list module. The list module machine (binary) addresses will save time in determining where to look in memory beyond location 200 (hex).

You should also learn to handle fractions and use queues, rather than rely entirely on the floating point instructions in the VAX-11 repertoire. We cover the floating point instructions later. They are fairly easy to use and they offer some powerful tools, but they also hide some of the more important methods used in number handling on the assembly language level.

We have introduced methods for setting up both stacks and queues with and without the VAX-11 stack and queue operators. You should be able to set up a register stack as an alternative to the system stack. A register stack is especially helpful if you have to reuse stack entries. Popping the elements of a register stack leaves the original entries intact. After popping elements from the system stack, there is no guarantee that the original entries will be available for reuse. This is true on both PDP-11s and VAX-11s.

The simplicity of queues set up with the autodecrement addressing mode is attractive. Autodecrementing is used for both the enqueue and dequeue operations. This provides a *downward queue*. These queues are downward since each enqueue operation moves the queue tail down in memory. The new tail will sit immediately below the old tail. The enqueue and dequeue operations are simplified by maintaining a list head.

It is possible to set up an upward queue by using autoincrement addressing for both enqueue and dequeue operations. In this case, the list head will sit below the queue front.

Before the VAX-11 INSQUE and REMQUE instructions can be used, a double linked list must be set up. The list head will be a quadword, instead of a longword, as in the case of user-defined queues. The REMQUE instruction makes it possible to dequeue from either the front or tail of the queue. If the address of a queue node's predecessor is known, it is possible to dequeue a node without a sequential search from the ends of the queue.

6.5

EXERCISES

1. Give a *physical* model for each of the following:

   (a) inefficient downward stack
   (b) efficient downward stack
   (c) inefficient upward stack
   (d) efficient upward stack
   (e) queue

2. The programming language ALGOL60 was designed using a hardware stack. Check how this was done.

3. The cambium rings of a tree are not a good example of a stack. Why?

4. Assuming there is water under the tiers of arctic ice, then the arctic ice is also not a good example of a stack. Why?

5. Is a stack of plates on a shelf an upward or a downward stack? Why?

6. Is a paper cup dispenser an upward or a downward stack? Is it efficient or inefficient? Why?

7. Write an assembly language program to do the following:

   (a) Use the PUSHL instruction to insert the numbers in the following sequence into the system stack:

   1, 1, 2, 3, 5, 8, 13, 21, 34, 55

   (b) Save the current SP; then use the POPL instruction to pop and print contents of the stack.

   (c) Restore the old SP (stack-top pointer) and use autoincrementing to pop and print the contents of the stack.

8. Write an assembly language program that uses a downward register stack to carry out (a), (b), (c) in exercise 7. Comment on what you find in part (c).

9. Write an assembly language program that uses an upward register stack to carry out (a), (b), (c) in exercise 7.

10. Why use register stacks?

11. Use a stack to print the ASCII characters with ASCII codes 33 through 126. Print the list backwards, then forwards.

12. Write a program to do the following:

   (a) Enqueue the following Lucas numbers:

   2, 1, 3, 4, 7, 11, 18, 29, 47, 123, 199, 322

   (b) Dequeue the Lucas numbers in the queue, and enqueue the odd-valued Lucas numbers in a second queue.

   (c) Dequeue and print the contents of each of the queues, starting from the queue front.

13. Enhance the program in Figure 6.13 as follows:

   (a) Set up a doubly linked list for the remainders.

(b) Use the INSQUE and REMQUE instruction to handle the enqueue and dequeue operations.

Run your program for

(c) 233, 144, base 10;

(d) 144, 233, base 8.

6.6

LAB PROJECTS

1. Combine the programs in Figure 6.9 and exercise 13 into one program. Run your program for

   (a) 2207, 1364, base = 16
   (b) 5778, 843, base = 16
   (c) 24476, 521, base = 2
   (d) 2207, 1364, base = 2
   (e) 5778, 843, base = 2

2. Set up a doubly linked list in which each node has a FLINK, BLINK, plus 10 bytes to hold the ASCII codes for the letters of people's last names. Then do the following in an assembly language program:

   (a) Use the INSQUE instruction to enqueue the names.
   (b) Use the REMQUE instruction to dequeue and print the names from the tail.
   (c) Allow the user to enter the names to be enqueued.

   Run your program for

   (d) The names of the computer scientists in Figure 6.14.
   (e) Ten names of persons you know.

6.7

REVIEW QUIZ

Indicate whether the following statements are true or false:

1. A cafeteria tray stacker is an example of a downward stack.

2. POPL R6 does the same thing as MOVL R6, $-$(SP).

3. PUSHL R6 does the same thing as MOV (SP)$+$, R6.

4. The PUSHL and POPL instructions use register 14.

5. A downward register (non-SP) stack is stored in the P0 region of memory.

6. The stack head is always the bottom of a downward register stack.

7. The bottom of a downward register stack has the highest stack address.

8. The bottom of an upward register stack has the lowest stack address.

9. The address of the top changes with each push or pop.

10. A stack with one entry has no top.

11. A queue front moves after each enqueue or dequeue operation.

12. Stack insertions are made at the stack top.

13. Queue insertions are made at the queue front.

14. Queue deletions are made at the queue tail.

15. Each node of a singly linked list has two links, a BLINK and FLINK.

7.
CLOSED ROUTINES

When the operation to be done is more complex, write a separate subroutine or function. The ease of later comprehending, debugging, and changing the program will more than compensate for any overhead caused by adding the extra modules.

—B. W. Kernighan and P. J. Plauger,
The Elements of Programming Style

7.0
AIMS

- Distinguish between open and closed routines, subroutines, and procedures; internal and external subroutines.
- Introduce coroutines, the resume mechanism used on VAX-11s.
- Distinguish flow-of-control between ordinary subroutines and coroutines that call each other.
- Show how to use global variables.
- Show how to build and use argument lists for subroutines.

7.1
INTRODUCTION

Up to now we have used macros rather freely in each of the assembly language programs given so far. A macro definition is also called an *open rou-*

tine. Since a macro call like WRITELN appears on any line of an assembly language main program or, as we shall see, subroutine or procedure, the corresponding open routine will be inserted by the assembler directly into the source text wherever a macro call appears. Once inserted, it will be indistinguishable from the other lines of code that the processor will execute.

An open routine is inserted *in-line*. In a main program, for example, the lines of code and the rest of the instructions of the program will be executed sequentially. No transfer-of-control occurs from the main program to the open routine. A *closed routine,* by contrast, requires a transfer-of-control from the main program or calling routine to the closed routine. Closed routines are not part of main programs. They are not in-line. Their position is fixed—they either appear in the source text between the $EXIT_S and .END, or they reside in an external file. The processor's normal sequential execution of a main program, for example, will be diverted to another location in memory by a call to a closed routine.

A closed routine will contain the typical lines of assembler code needed to carry out a separate task. The physical separation of a closed routine from a main program or another calling routine is coupled with the logical separation of programming tasks needed to be carried out.

On a VAX-11 there are two classes of closed routines: subroutines and procedures. A *subroutine* is a closed routine without parameters being passed by the caller. If parameters are needed by the subroutine, they are either global (common to the subroutine and caller), or they are available on the system stack (a register stack or queue) or in registers. A procedure is a closed routine with a CALL_FRAME set up on the system stack that makes it possible for the caller to pass parameters to the procedure. We explain how to use procedures in the next chapter.

Subroutines can be called with

    jsb ⟨subroutine name⟩

This instruction does the following:

1. Saves (pushes!) the current (PC) on the system stack; the current (PC) has the address of the next instruction following the jsb.
2. Assigns to the (PC) the address of the subroutine corresponding to the subroutine name.

The return from a subroutine is accomplished by using

    rsb

which does the following:

1. Pops the old (PC) off the system stack.
2. Assigns the old (PC) to the PC, and thus transfers control back to the caller.

These ideas are illustrated in Figure 7.1 in a main program which calls a subroutine A. At the time of the JSB A, the (PC) is pointing to the NOP on the next line. This (PC) is saved on the system stack. When the processor reaches the RSB, it pops the old (PC) and control passes back to the caller. We illustrate this idea in a program with one subroutine, which can be used to build a sequence of Lucas numbers that can be "fed" to the main program (see Figure 7.2).

FIGURE 7.1
Processor Control Transfers with Subroutines

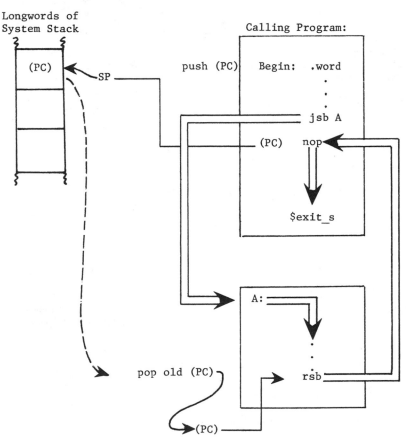

FIGURE 7.2
An Internal Subroutine

```
;
;Ref.:   Figure 7.2 (An internal subroutine)
;
;var
        Lucas:     .blkl 30
        x:         .long 3
        y:         .long -1
        sum:       .long
        max:       .long
        step:      .long 1
        index:     .long 1

Begin:  .word

        jsb      builder                    ;call routine to build list
        moval    Lucas,r6                   ;use r6 as Lucas list selector
        movl     #1,index                   ;restore original index
        writeln

compute:

        writeval (r6)
        write < + >
        addl2    (r6)+,sum                  ;compute sum
        acbl     max,step,index,compute

        write < = >
        writeval sum

        $exit_s

builder:

        write <Enter max in L(0),L(1), ... ,L(max) : >
        readvar max
        moval    Lucas,r6                        ;use r6 to select list entries

sequence:

        addl3    x,y,(r6)
        movl     y,x
        movl     (r6)+,y
        acbl     max,step,index,sequence    ;repeat computations to
                                            ;build sequence until max=index
        rsb

        .end Begin


RUN FG72

Enter max in L(0),L(1), ... ,L(max) : 10

2  + 1  + 3  + 4  + 7  + 11  + 18  + 29  + 47  + 76  +  = 198
```

7.2

INTERNAL AND EXTERNAL SUBROUTINES

The Builder subroutine in Figure 7.2 is an example of an *internal routine*. It is part of the same file that contains the source text for the main program. The above program could have been split into two subroutines, one to build the Lucas sequence, the other to handle summing the terms of the sequence. In that case the main program would have been reduced to reporting the results.

When more than one subroutine is needed by a program and, especially, when it is desirable to share one routine among many programs and/or users, then it makes sense to construct a routine in a separate file. An *external subroutine* is a closed routine in a separate file, apart from calling a main program or routine. The .GLOBAL directive is normally used in a main program to declare names of external routines and associated data. This directive has the form:

    .GLOBAL ⟨name₁⟩, . . . , ⟨nameₖ⟩

The label in an external routine has a double colon (::) suffix. For example, if A is an external routine, it has the following form:

```
;declarations of local variables and constants
;
            .
            .
            .

A::
            .
            .
            .

    ⟨lines of code⟩
            .
            .
            .

        rsb
        .end
```

To prepare an external routine, use the following steps:

1. Use an editor to put together a source text for the external routine. If A

is the external routine, then

A.MAR

is its designation.

2. Assemble the external routine A, for example, with

FIGURE 7.3
Linking an External Subroutine

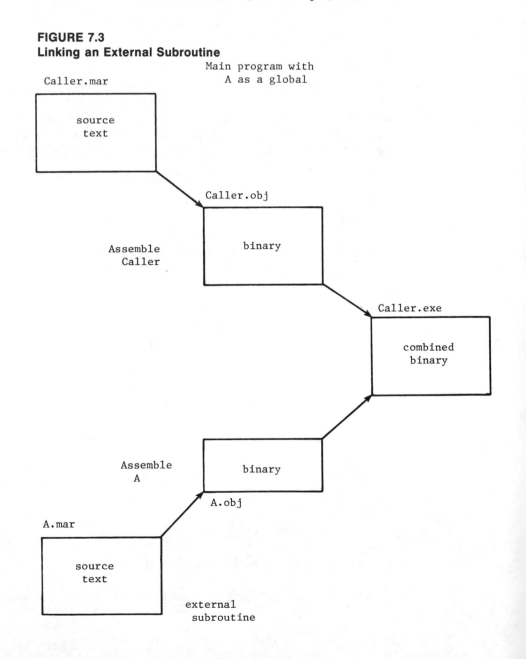

MACRO A

Result: A.OBJ

3. If CALLER is a main program that calls A, then link the two object modules for CALLER and A as follows:

LINK CALLER, A

Result: CALLER.EXE

FIGURE 7.4
A Program with Two External Subroutines

```
;
;Ref.:   Figure 7.4 (A program with two external subroutines)
;
;var

        .global             builder,compute_sum

        Lucas::             .blkl 20
        x::                 .long 3
        y::                 .long -1
        max::               .long
        step::              .long 1
        index::             .long 1
        sum::               .long
        answer:             .long

Begin:  .word

again:

        jsb       builder                       ;call external routine
                                                ;to build list of Lucas nos.
        moval     Lucas,r6                      ;init. r6 as list selector
        movl      #1,index

        jsb       compute_sum                   ;call external routine to
                                                ;compute sum
        write <Another run?--1=Y,0=N : >
        readvar answer
        cmpl      #0,answer
        beql      doorway
        movl      #3,x                          ;restore original x-value
        movl      #-1,y                         ;restore original y-value
        movl      #1,index                      ;restore original index
        clrl      sum                           ;get ready for new sum
        jmp       again

doorway:

        $exit_s

        .end Begin
```

Continued on following page.

Figure 7.4 continued.

```
;
;Ref.:  Figure 7.4 (continued)
;
;Content:            Two external subroutines

        .global              builder, compute_sum

builder::

        write <Enter max in L(0),L(1), ... ,L(max) : >
        readvar max
        moval   Lucas,r6                         ;init. r6 as list selector

sequence:

        addl3   x,y,(r6)                         ;compute sum
        movl    y,x
        movl    (r6)+,y
        acbl    max,step,index,sequence

        rsb

compute_sum::

next:
        writeval (r6)
        write < + >
        addl2   (r6)+,sum
        acbl max,step,index,next

        write < = >
        writeval sum
        writeln
        writeln

        rsb

        .end


RUN FG74

Enter max in L(0),L(1), ... ,L(max) : 5
2  + 1  + 3  + 4  + 7  + = 17

Another run?--1=Y,0=N : 1
Enter max in L(0),L(1), ... ,L(max) : 10
2  + 1  + 3  + 4  + 7  + 11  + 18  + 29  + 47  + 76  + = 198

Another run?--1=Y,0=N : 0
```

FIGURE 7.5
Graphical Interpretation of Linking External Routines

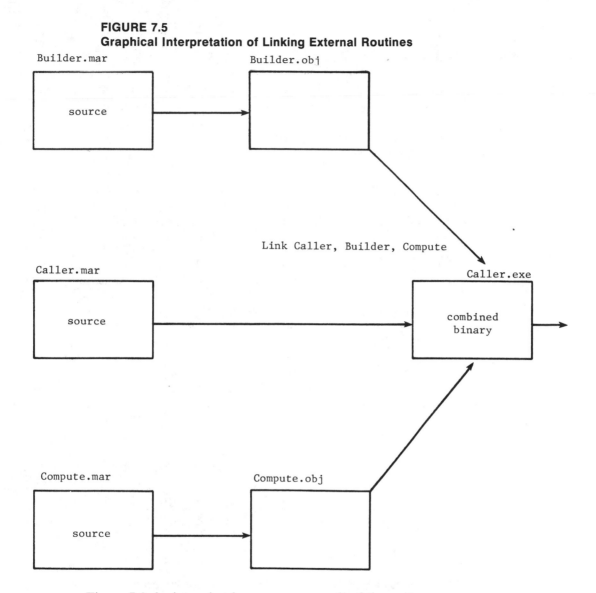

Figure 7.3 depicts what happens as a result of these steps.

Any internal subroutine can easily be converted into an external routine. This makes it possible to link the object module for an external routine into object modules for various calling programs so that the external routines can be shared by other programs and system users. We illustrate this in a revision of the program in Figure 7.4. In this program, all but the answer variable are global variables shared by the two external routines Builder and Compute Sum. What happens at link time is shown in Figure 7.5.

7.3

ARGUMENT LISTS

It is possible to use the system stack or a register stack to build an argument list that can be used by a subroutine. The steps are as follows:

1. Use PUSH arguments. There are two types:

   1.1 Push *values*. For example,

   ```
   pushl x
   ```

   will put the content of location *x* onto the system stack.

   1.2 Push *references*. For example,

   ```
   pushal x
   ```

   will put the *x*-address onto the system stack.

2. Call a routine.

3. Use the SP in the following ways:

   3.1 Use values on the system stack. For example, use the *first* argument with

   ```
   movl 4(sp), r6
   ```

   The index 4 is used, since the subroutine call in step 2 puts the old (PC) on the stack after pushing the last argument.

   3.2 Use references to data. For example, if *apple* is an address two long-words above the return address on the stack, then use

   ```
   movl @8(sp), r6
   ```

The program in Figure 7.6 illustrates the use of an argument list.

When the references (addresses) from Lucas, *x*, *y* are pushed onto the system stack, they will sit *above* the return address pushed onto the stack by

```
jsb enqueue
```

The arrangement of these items on the system stack relative to their original arrangement is shown in Figure 7.7. In other words, the first argument

FIGURE 7.6
A Subroutine with an Argument List

```
;
;Ref:    Figure 7.6 (A subroutine with a system stack argument list)
;
;Method: Set up a queue filled with Lucas numbers, using arguments pushed
;        onto the system stack, which are referenced from the external
;        enqueue routine with the sp.  The pushed arguments are addresses
;        (references) of memory locations containing Lucas numbers.  After
;        enqueueing 20 Lucas numbers, the user chooses between dequeueing
;        from the queue-tail or queue-front.

        .global            dequeue_tail,dequeue_head,enqueue

h::        .blkq      1
queue::    .blkl      100
Lucas:     .long      2
x:         .long      3
y:         .long      -1
max::      .long      20
step::     .long      1
index::    .long      1
choice:    .long

Begin:  .word

again:

        moval      h,h                          ;init. flink
        moval      h,h+4                        ;init. blink
        moval      Lucas,queue+8                ;init. front datum
        moval      queue,r6
        pushal     Lucas                        ;begin arg. list
        pushal     y
        pushal     x
        jsb        enqueue                      ;call enqueue

        write <Enter choice: 1=dequeue from front,2=dequeue from tail: >
        readvar choice
        writeln                                 ;<ret>
        writeln                                 ;   <ret> for more
                                                ;readable run

        cmpl       #2,choice
        beql       tail
        jsb        dequeue_head
        jmp        doorway

tail:
        jsb        dequeue_tail

doorway:

        $exit_s

        .end Begin
```

Continued on following page.

Figure 7.6 continued.

```
;
;Ref.:   Figure 7.6 (continued)
;
        .global                  dequeue_tail,dequeue_head,enqueue

dequeue_head::

        movl      #1,index                        ;init. index
mmm:
        remque @h,r6                               ;dequeue from head
        writeval 8(r6)
        acbl      max,step,index,mmm

        rsb

dequeue_tail::

        movl      #1,index                        ;init. index
mmmm:

        remque @h+4,r6                             ;dequeue from tail
        writeval 8(r6)
        acbl      max,step,index,mmmm

        rsb

enqueue::

        movl      #1,index                        ;make sure index=1
entry:

        addl2     #12,r6                           ;move list selector
        addl3     @4(sp),@8(sp),@12(sp)            ;Lucas := x + y
        movl      @12(sp),8(r6)                    ;init. queue node datum
        insque    (r6),@h+4                        ;enqueue at tail
        movl      @8(sp),@4(sp)                    ; x := y
        movl      @12(sp),@8(sp)                   ; y := Lucas
        acbl      max,step,index,entry

        rsb

        .end

RUN FG76
Enter choice: 1=dequeue from front,2=dequeue from tail: 1

2 1 3 4 7 11 18 29 47 76 123 199 322 521 843 1364 2207 3571 5778 9349


RUN FG76
Enter choice: 1=dequeue from front,2=dequeue from tail: 2

9349 5778 3571 2207 1364 843 521 322 199 123 76 47 29 18 11 7 4 3 1 2
```

FIGURE 7.7
Graphical Interpretation of an Argument List

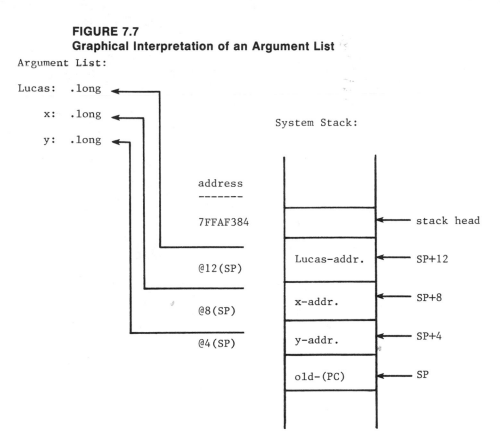

pushed is furthest away from the SP when the subroutine call is made. The instruction

    pushl step

puts a value in the argument list above the SP during execution of the enqueue routine. If this value had been pushed before the list of addresses of the argument list, then we could have used

    acbl max, 16(sp), index, enqueue

since the step-value will be 16 bytes above the SP during execution of the enqueue routine. This change is left as an exercise.

To see what an argument list of references and values looks like when we process a subroutine, we set up a dummy list of values in the next program. In doing this, we push values using both immediate and relative addressing (see Figure 7.8). The 3ED (hex) at location 7FFAF364 is the return

FIGURE 7.8
A Program to Exhibit an Argument List

```
;
;Ref.:  Figure 7.8 (A program to exhibit an argument list)
;
        a:          .long ^x<aaa>
        b:          .long ^x<23>
        c:          .long ^x<abc>
        max:        .long 8
        step:       .long 1
        index:      .long 1

Begin:  .word

        writeln
        writeln <              Initial sp address:>
        writeln
        write < >
        writeval sp radix=16
        writeln
        writeln <--------------------------------------------->
        writeln
        writeln <            sp               argument>
        writeln
        writeln <--------------------------------------------->
        writeln

        pushl    c
        pushl    b
        pushl    a
        pushal   c
        pushal   b
        pushal   a
        pushl    #^x<aaaaaa>

        jsb      storage

        $exit_s

storage:

        movl     sp,r6                         ;init. r6 with current sp

argument_list:

        write < >                             ;< > = tab
        writeval r6 (r6) radix=16 spaces=14
        writeln
        add12    #4,r6                         ;advance sp
        acbl     max,step,index,argument_list

        rsb

        .end Begin
```

208

Figure 7.8 continued.

```
RUN FG78

    Initial sp address:

    7FFAF384
-----------------------------------------------------

    sp                    argument

-----------------------------------------------------

    7FFAF364              3F9
    7FFAF368              AAAAAA
    7FFAF36C              200
    7FFAF370              204
    7FFAF374              208
    7FFAF378              AAA
    7FFAF37C              23
    7FFAF380              ABC
```

address (the old (PC)). This can be verified by getting a copy of the list file for the above program.

7.4

COROUTINES

Subroutines can call each other. However, as a rule, when one subroutine calls another, the PC is assigned the beginning address of the called routine. This situation is illustrated in terms of routines *a* and *b* in Figure 7.9. Each time routine *a* calls routine *b*, flow-of-control transfers back to the beginning of routine *b*. There are times when it is more efficient to use a set of two or more routines so that on a return the processing transfers to the instruction immediately following the call to a routine. This is what happens in a main program. Also, it is sometimes advantageous to have one routine call a second routine so that processing transfers *within* rather than *to the beginning* of the called routine. Two routines that are set up to call each other in this way are known as coroutines. If *a* and *b* are coroutines, then when *a* calls *b*, it is said to

resume b

When *b* returns control to *a*, it is said to

resume a

FIGURE 7.9
Flow-of-Control Between Two Subroutines

```
;main program:
```

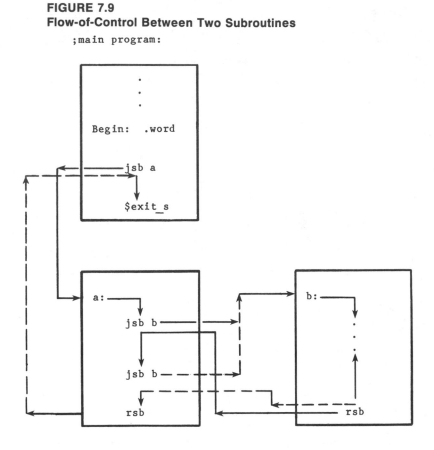

This is easy to set up on either a VAX-11 or a PDP-11 using an initial

```
jsb b (first call)
```

followed by autoincrement deferred addressing:

```
jsb @(sp)+ (to resume a)
```

and

```
jsb @(sp)+ (to resume b)
```

The second and third of the above calls take advantage of the return address put on the system stack by the SP. The processor will carry out the following

FIGURE 7.10
Tracing Flow-of-Control with Two Coroutines

```
;
;Ref.:  Figure 7.10 (Tracing flow-of-control with two coroutines)
;

Begin:  .word

        jsb      Crusoe

        writeln
        writeln <...Return to mainland.>

        $exit_s

Crusoe:

        jsb      Friday

        writeln
        writeln <           Friday's footprint!>

        jsb     @(sp)+                                  ;resume Friday

        writeln
        writeln <            Another Friday print!>

        rsb

Friday:

        writeln
        writeln <               Crusoe visited here.>

        jsb     @(sp)+                                  ;resume Crusoe

        writeln
        writeln <                  Crusoe again!>

        jsb     @(sp)+                                  ;resume Crusoe

        rsb

        .end Begin


RUN FG710

                         Crusoe visited here.

        Friday's footprint!

                               Crusoe again!

             Another Friday print!
...Return to mainland.
```

steps when it executes a resume instruction:

1.	movl @(sp)+, temp	;save return address in temporary
		;location
2.	movl r15, −(sp)	;push current (PC)
3.	movl temp. r15	;transfer control by initializing
		;the PC with old (PC)

In the next program we trace the flow-of-control back and forth between two coroutines. Each time the processor visits one coroutine or returns from a coroutine, we print a message. In some respects, this trace is analogous to Defoe's rendition of Robinson Crusoe's experience. Crusoe does not see Friday at first, but he does see Friday's footprint in the wet sand. Hence the use of the Crusoe/Friday messages in Figure 7.10.

7.5
USES FOR COROUTINES

O.-J. Dahl (1972, pp. 184–90) distinguishes two types of coroutines. Pairs of coroutines can be set up for games so that each routine carries out the moves of opposing players. For example, we can have coroutine *a* bid and play against coroutine *b* in a game of stud poker. This is possible if the main program takes the dealer's role, dealing cards (entries in separate lists) to each player. Routine *a* is given access only to one list, or one hand. Its behavior dictates, in part, what moves routine *b* makes.

Producer and consumer routines can also be set up. Routine *a* (the producer) can be used, for example, to obtain information from files or from the user. Each time routine *a* obtains new data, it transfers control to routine *b*, which uses (consumes) it to produce a result. An example of this type of coroutine is given by S. E. Sevcik (1975, pp. 27–30) in terms of building a bibliography. The producer coroutine will determine the next part of a bibliographic entry to be printed. The consumer coroutine will take the findings of *a* and format the bibliographic output. One coroutine *gets* needed information, the other *uses* the information.

We can illustrate the producer/consumer coroutine pair in building a message. The producer routine will determine the correct part of the message to build. The consumer routine will use the choice supplied by its coroutine to assign an input string. In the example in Figure 7.11 the consumer routine also produces; it gets the entry that will be used.

FIGURE 7.11
A Program with Producer/Consumer Coroutines

```
;
;Ref.:  Figure 7.11 (A program with producer/consumer coroutines)
;
;Method:  The producer coroutine determines your choice in building
;         the parts of a message (the heading and body); the consumer
;         coroutine is fed the choice, which it uses to determine which
;         byte row to fill with a readstring macro.  It then returns
;         control to the producer routine, which finds out if there is
;         another insertion.

;var
        heading:
                .blkb 80
        message:
                .blkb 80
        null:   .long
        choice: .long

Begin:  .word

        jsb producer

        writestring heading
        writeln
        writestring message

        $exit_s

producer:

again:
        write < Enter choice:    1=heading,2=message,3=null: >
        readvar choice

one:
        cmpl    choice,#1               ;a heading?
        bneq    two                     ;if not, check other choices
                                        ;else
        jsb     consumer                ;resume consumer

        jmp     check                   ;transfer control to check

two:
        cmpl    choice,#2               ;a message?
        bneq    last                    ;if not, then branch to 3rd choice
                                        ;else
        jsb     consumer                ;resume consumer

        jmp     check                   ;transfer control to check

last:
        jsb     @(sp)+                  ;resume consumer

check:
```

Continued on following page.

Figure 7.11 continued.

```
        write  <Do you want to make another choice?--1=Y,0=N:  >
        readvar  choice
        cmpl     #0,choice
        beql     doorway
        jmp      again

doorway:

        rsb

consumer:

        cmpl     #1,choice
        bneq     next
        write    <Enter heading: >
        readstring            heading
        writeln
        jsb      @(sp)+
next:

        cmpl     #2,choice
        bneq     another_doorway
        write    <Enter message: >
        readstring            message
        writeln
        jsb      @(sp)+

another_doorway:

        rsb

        .end Begin


RUN FG711

        Enter choice:        1=heading,2=message,3=null: 1

Enter heading: January 13,1984 message:

Do you want to make another choice?--1=Y,0=N:  1

        Enter choice:        1=heading,2=message,3=null: 2

Enter message: If this is winter, can spring be far behind?

Do you want to make another choice?--1=Y,0=N:  0

January 13,1984 message:
If this is winter, can spring be far behind?
```

Both coroutines in Figure 7.11 allow the user to go back to make a new entry. Why use coroutines? To answer this question we must look back at the last program. The producer coroutine transfers control to the consumer coroutine as soon as it determines a choice. Based on this choice, the consumer routine fills a byte row. Once the byte row is filled, the consumer routine transfers control back to the instruction in the producer routine immediately *following* the consumer routine call:

```
producer:                          consumer:

         .                              .

         .                              .

         .                              .

jsb consumer                       ⟨fill byte row⟩
jmp check                              .

         .                              .

         .                              .

         .                         jsb @ (sp)+
```

Without the coroutine mechanism, the transfer-of-control from the consumer routine to the producer routine would make processing resume at the *beginning* of the producer routine.

In other words, in situations where coroutines can work as partners, the *resume* mechanism is more efficient than the control transfer mechanism in ordinary routines. This is especially true in more complex programs, such as a program used to handle assembly of a source text. A common method used to assemble a source text is known as the *two-pass* method. One pass is used to scan a source text and build a symbol table with the corresponding numeric addresses for labels that have been used. A second pass is used to replace symbolic with numeric addresses, using the symbol table built during the first pass. Dahl (1972, p. 185) suggests using coroutines to replace two complete scans of a source text with the two-pass method. Two coroutines would pass control back and forth, helping each other determine numeric addresses and to translate the source text down to the binary level. The result would be a more efficient one-pass method of handling the translation.

7.6
SUMMARY

Subroutines are designed to be called. Their execution depends on their being called by a main program and/or another routine. External subroutines are more useful than internal subroutines. External subroutines can be shared. They can be called by more than one program *and* by more than one user. An *internal subroutine* is a subroutine that is part of the source text in the same file as a main program. An *external* subroutine is a subroutine in a file that does not include a main program.

Subroutines are closed routines. Before they can be used by a main program or by another subroutine, the PC is used to transfer control away from the calling structure to the subroutine. Both the subroutine call using the JSB and a return from subroutine using an RSB rely on the use of a stack. The stack used is the system stack. The return address—the old (PC)—is pushed onto the system stack *before* the processor transfers control to a subroutine. The return from a subroutine to the caller requires a pop of the old (PC). The old (PC) on the stack was the current (PC) when the processor *began* execution of a JSB.

Subroutines can call each other. As a rule, when one subroutine calls another, control transfers back to the *beginning* of the called routine. This is not the case with coroutines.

Coroutines use a resume mechanism to call each other. After the initial

    jsb ⟨coroutine name⟩

a resume is made possible with a

    jsb @ (sp)+

In a sense, one is put into a wait-state (its operation is suspended) when a RESUME call is made. A RESUME call allows the called coroutine to resume its operation. In cases where coroutines can be set up to perform complementary tasks, coroutines are more efficient than ordinary subroutines. Why?

The system stack or a register stack can be used to set up argument lists for subroutines. These argument lists can be set up with references to memory locations and with values pushed immediately onto the stack. In terms of the system stack, subroutines use the stack pointer SP to manage an argument list. Care must be used in setting up an argument list. To put argument *a* in

    a: .long
    b: .long
    c: .long

onto the stack immediately *above* the (SP), it is necessary to push these arguments in the following way:

```
pushl c
pushl b
pushl a
```

Then, for example,

```
movl 4 (sp), r6
```

puts a copy of *a* into R6. We can also push the above in the following way:

```
pushl a
pushl b
pushl c
```

Then, to manipulate the argument *a*, we would need to use, for example,

```
movl 12 (sp), r6
```

to put a copy of *a* into R6. In setting up argument lists for subroutines, the frame pointer (R13) and argument pointer (R12) are not used. These registers are used to set up argument lists for procedures. We discuss this operation in the next chapter.

7.7

EXERCISES

1. Suppose a main program calls subroutine *a*, which *midway* through its execution calls subroutine *b*, which *midway* through its execution calls subroutine *c*. Then execution continues in subroutine *c* until the processor reaches the RSB. Use Figure 7.1 as a guide and give a flow-of-control diagram for main, *a*, *b*, *c*. Include a picture of the system stack and how it is used to manage returns. Assume *a*, *b*, *c* are internal subroutines.

2. Suppose the subroutines *a*, *b*, *c* in exercise 1 are made into external subroutines. Give the command string and each step needed to assemble main, *a*, *b*, *c* as well as link main to *a*, *b*, and *c*. Assume *a*, *b*, *c* are each in a separate file.

3. Using the assumptions in exercise 2, and Figure 7.5 as a guide, give

a graphical interpretation of linking A.OBJ, B.OBJ, C.OBJ to MAIN.OBJ.

4. Add an external subroutine to the program in Figure 7.4. Call the subroutine Lucas_Differences. This subroutine should do the following:

(a) Compute differences $L(n) - L(n - 1)$ for successive pairs of Lucas numbers, starting with the first pair: $L(2) - L(1)$. That is, do the following:

> *Lucas numbers:*
>
> 1, 3, 4, 7, 11, 18, 29, . . .
> 3-1
>   4-3
>   7-4
>   11-7
>   18-11
>   29-18

(b) Print a difference table of the form:

> *Difference Table*
>
> 2
> 2 1
> 2 1 3
> 2 1 3 4
> 2 1 3 4 7

(c) Drop the subroutine to print the sum.

(d) Put Lucas_Differences and Builder Routines in separate files.

5. Enhance the program in exercise 4 so that

(a) The Lucas_Differences, Builder, and Compute Sum subroutines are put into one file forming a mini subroutine library. Use the following framework:

> .global Lucas_Differences, Builder, Compute Sum

```
        Lucas_Differences::

                            .
                            .
                            .

                        rsb
        Builder::

                        .
                        .
                        .

        Compute Sum::

                        .
                        .
                        .

                        rsb
                        .end
```

(b) Print a menu and allow the user to choose

  1. Lucas Difference Table

  2. Sum of Lucas Numbers

  after using the Builder routine in response to the user's choice of the number of Lucas numbers to put into the Lucas sequence.

6. Write an assembly language program to set up the following argument list on the system stack:

```
        argument 1: value of a
        argument 2: value of b
        argument 3: value of c
        argument 4: address of d
        argument 5: address of 3
        argument 6: #ˆX⟨233⟩
```

  in terms of

```
        a: .byte 5
        b: .byte 6
        c: .byte 7
        d: .long ˆX⟨aaa⟩
        e: .long ˆX⟨bbb⟩
```

Then do the following:

(a) Write an external subroutine that does the following *in terms of* the items in the argument list:

    1.   compute a + b + c   ;print sum;

    2.   compute d + e   ;print sum;

    3.   compute d + e − argument 6   ;print result;

(b) Print a copy of the argument list and return address as well as the stack address for each argument.

7. Using Figure 7.7 as a guide, give a graphical interpretation of the argument list in exercise 6.

7.8

LAB PROJECTS

1. Write a program with two coroutines *a* and *b*. Coroutine *a* prints the odd-numbered rows and coroutine *b* prints the even-numbered rows in a triangle like the following one:

       .   printed by a

      . .   printed by b

     . . .   printed by a

    . . . .   printed by b

Your program should do the following:

(a) Allow the user to choose the symbol to be used in printing the triangle.

(b) Allow the user to choose the number of rows in the printed triangle.

Run your program with

(c) Symbol = '.' with 20 rows

(d) Symbol = 'A' with 60 rows

2. Write a program with two or more coroutines to do the following (Sevcik's Problem):

(a) Get the entries for a bibliographic reference.

(b) Format the printing of the reference as follows:

Author's last name, first name

Title

Includes (index)

1. topic

2. subtopic

I. title

II. title:

LC no. date

ISBN no.

Run your program for

Kernighan, Brian W.

The Elements of Programming Style.

Bibliography: p.

Includes Index.

1. Electronic digital computers–programming.

I. Plauger, P.J., date joint author

II. Title

QA76.6.K47 1978

ISBN 0-07-034207-5

3. Write a program with 2 coroutines (Player *A* and Player *B*) that does the following:

(a) Prompts for a poker hand for player *A* (the user deals the cards and types in the cards in player *A*'s hand).

(b) Prompts for a poker hand for player *B* (the user deals).

(c) Player *A* and player *B* both check their hands; request more cards, if needed, and place bet.

(d) Give player *A* and player *B* a starting amount to use in betting. The game is over when the kitty held by one of the players is depleted.

7.9

REVIEW QUIZ

Indicate whether the following statements are true or false:

1. A closed routine is out-of-line relative to a main program that calls it.

2. The VAX-11 uses a queue to manage transfers to and from closed routines.

3. A double colon (::) is used for globals.

4. Closed routines can be external.

5. A program with an external closed routine is assembled together with its external closed routine.

6. At link time, a linkage editor saves a copy of the final, executable module on the disk. When we link an object module on the VAX-11, a linkage editor is not used.

7. The system stack can be used to set up an argument list for a closed routine.

8. 4(SP) points to stack content.

9. @4(SP) points to stack content.

10. Addl2 4(SP),@4(SP) adds the content of the doubleword on the system stack to the content of a doubleword somewhere else on the system stack.

11. 8(SP) is another way of referring to the stack content at location 8 + SP.

12. @8(SP) is another way of referring to location 8 + (SP).

13. Coroutines are comparable to colleagues.

14. Producer/consumer coroutines always have a symbiotic relationship.

7.10

REFERENCES

Dahl, O.-J., E. W. Dijkstra, and C. A. R. Hoare. *Structured Programming.* New York: Academic Press, 1972.

Kernighan, B. W. and P. J. Plauger. *The Elements of Programming Style.* New York: McGraw-Hill, 1978.

Sevcik, S. E. *An Analysis of Uses of Coroutines.* Ann Arbor, Mich.: University Microfilms, 1976.

8.
PROCEDURES

Actually, the procedure is one of the few fundamental tools in the art of programming whose mastery has a decisive influence on the style and quality of a programmer's work. The procedure serves as a device to abbreviate the text and, more significantly, as a means to partition and to structure a program into logically coherent, closed components.

— N. Wirth, *Systematic Programming: An Introduction*

8.0
AIMS

- Introduce the structure of procedures and argument lists used by procedures.
- Distinguish between internal and external procedures, call by value, call by reference, CALLS and CALLG instructions.
- Show how to use the AP (argument pointer) and FP (frame pointer) relative to call frames used by procedures.
- Show how to access and use arguments, either for a CALLG or for a CALLS instruction.
- Introduce procedure libraries.

8.1
INTRODUCTION

A *procedure* is a closed routine. It is separate from (outside, not a part of) the lines of code of the caller. The *caller* can be a main program, a subroutine, or another procedure. The system stack is used by the processor to save the return address—that is, the current (PC), henceforth called the old (PC)—before it transfers control to a procedure.

The structure of a procedure is shown in Figure 8.1.

The beginning address of a procedure (its entry point) is established using the .ENTRY directive. The .ENTRY name is the procedure name; it is referred to in calling a procedure. The .ENTRY mask is a powerful

FIGURE 8.1
Structure of a Procedure

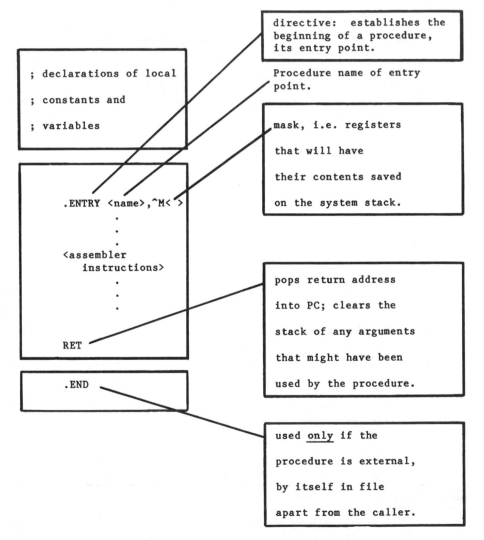

tool. A *procedure call mask* is a specification of *general* registers the contents of which are to be pushed onto the system stack by the processor before the processor begins execution of the procedure. Registers R0:R11 (any of these) can be masked as part of a procedure call. At the time a procedure is called, registers R0:R11 (any of these) indicated inside the pointed brackets will have their contents saved on the system stack. For example, if we want to save the contents of R6, R7, R8, R9, we would use the following .ENTRY setup for a procedure called *T*:

```
.ENTRY T, ^M⟨r6, r7, r8, r9⟩
```

Saved registers are part of a structure on the system stack called a *call frame*. Associated with every procedure is a call frame, which is a sequence of contiguous longwords on the system stack. The call frame consists of a minimum of 5 longwords and a maximum of 144 system stack longwords. The structure of a typical call frame is shown in Figure 8.2.

The minimum call frame has the following longwords on the system stack, starting with the longword at the *lowest* address in the call frame:

1. Beginning longword used by the processor whenever an exception condition occurs while processing a procedure. Initially, this longword is zero. Notice that the *current* (FP) points to this longword.

2. A longword used to hold the PSW at the time of the procedure call. Part of this longword (the high bits) is used to indicate the registers in the mask, the type of call (the S-bit), and any longword alignment (the SPA, which is four bits). This is at 4(FP).

3. The old (AP) and old (FP). Notice that the current AP (argument pointer) has the address of the beginning of the argument list for a procedure, if one has been set up.

4. This longword has the old (PC), the return address, which the processor will pop into the PC when it is ready to return from a procedure.

An argument list for a procedure contains two types of arguments: values and addresses. If we want to pass a value *x* to a procedure, we use

```
pushl x      ;value taken from location x
```

or

```
pushl #⟨immediate value⟩
```

This is known as a *call by value*. If we want to pass an address (reference

FIGURE 8.2
Structure of a Call Frame

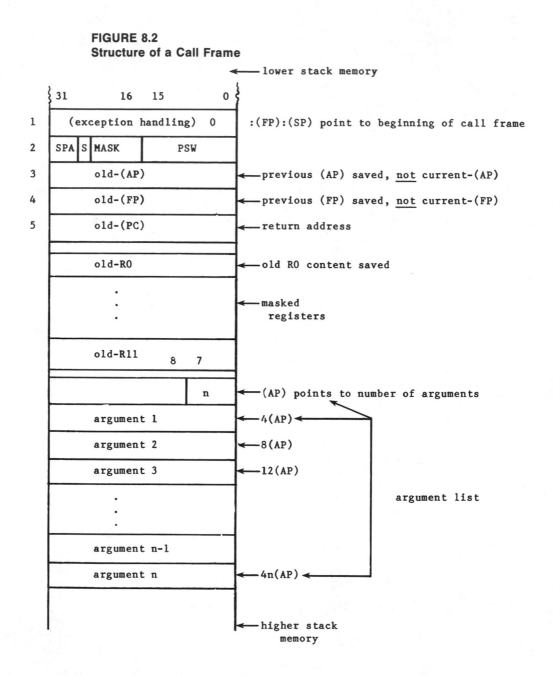

to a value in memory) to a procedure, we use

    pushal ⟨label⟩

This is known as a *call by reference*. These arguments are used within a procedure in terms of the argument pointer. For example, suppose we push the following arguments:

    pushal x   ;furthest from (AP)
    pushal y
    pushal z
    pushl a
    pushl b
    pushl c   ;closest to (AP)

Figure 8.3 shows how these arguments will be arranged relative to the stack head and the (AP):

There are two types of procedure calls: CALLS and CALLG. A CALLS has the following form:

    calls #⟨number⟩, ⟨name⟩
          ↑   ↑
          │   This identifies the entry point, its beginning address.
          This specifies the number of arguments that have been passed to
          the procedure, prior to the procedure call.

Notice that the number of arguments is in the longword pointed to by the argument pointer. Bits 0:7 of this longword are set aside for this number. This allows for n in the range

    $0 \leq n \leq 127$

A procedure T can be called with zero arguments with

    calls #0, T

If, for example, 6 arguments are pushed onto the stack prior to the procedure call, then we would use

    calls #6, T

Suppose the following variables have been defined at the beginning of a program:

```
x:    .long ^X⟨283⟩
y:    .long 1
a:    .long ^X⟨aaaabb⟩
b:    .long ^X⟨CDC⟩

        ⋮

Begin:   .word

        ⋮
```

Then, to pass values x and y, references a and b, and an immediate value 2001 (hex), we can use

```
pushl #^X⟨2001⟩
pushal b
pushal a
pushl  y
pushl  x
```

If these arguments are passed to a procedure T, then

```
calls #5, T
```

would be used. Notice that #5 will be closest to the argument pointer. That is,

ap   will be the stack address for the location in the argument list with
      5 = number of arguments

4ap   will be the stack address for the location of the x-content 283 (hex)

8ap   the stack location of 1 (from y)

and so on. To get at the arguments themselves from within a procedure, we can use the scheme shown in Figure 8.4.

The use of a CALLG to call a procedure requires the use of an argument list, which remains in the P0 region of main memory. The arguments are not pushed onto the system stack. The structure of a CALLG instruction is

FIGURE 8.3
Sample System Stack Argument List

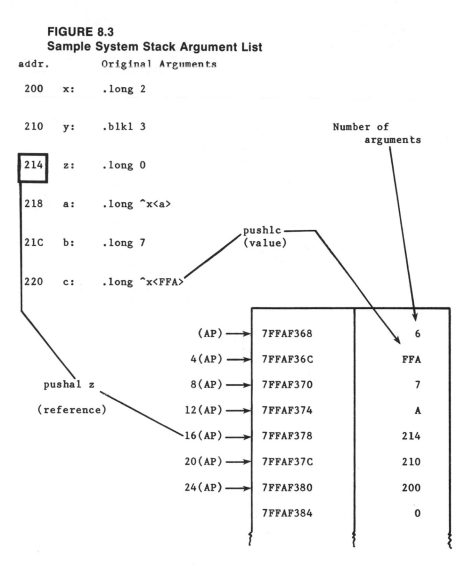

addr.   Original Arguments

200   x: .long 2

210   y: .blkl 3   Number of
                                                          arguments

214   z: .long 0

218   a: .long ^x<a>

                                      pushlc
                                      (value)

21C   b: .long 7

220   c: .long ^x<FFA>

                              (AP) ──▶ 7FFAF368   6

                            4(AP) ──▶ 7FFAF36C   FFA

          pushal z   8(AP) ──▶ 7FFAF370   7

          (reference)   12(AP) ──▶ 7FFAF374   A

                           16(AP) ──▶ 7FFAF378   214

                           20(AP) ──▶ 7FFAF37C   210

                           24(AP) ──▶ 7FFAF380   200

                                       7FFAF384   0

shown next:

    callg ⟨label⟩, ⟨name⟩

            This identifies the entry point of the procedure.
    This identifies a memory location containing the *number* of
    arguments in an argument list.

To set up the argument list for a CALLG, a .ADDRESS directive is used

FIGURE 8.4
Calls by Reference and by Value

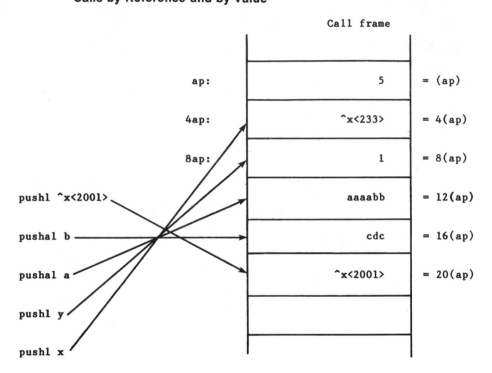

to identify the addresses of the arguments, which is a sequence of longwords. For example, suppose we want to have *a, b, c, d* in argument list:

```
a:   .long 1     ;@4(ap) = 1
b:   .long 1     ;@8(ap) = 1
c:   .long 2     ;@12(ap) = 2
d:   .long 3     ;@16(ap) = 3
list:
```

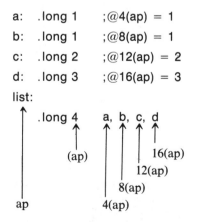

If we want to call a procedure *T* with a CALLG, with the above list we would use

    callg list, T

The argument pointer will be given the address list. Its content or (AP) will be 4. The address 4AP will itself identify an address! That is, 4(AP) will contain the address of the first argument; 4(AP) will contain the argument *a*-address. Then 8(AP) will contain the *b*-address, and so on. To get at the first argument, itself, we need to use displacement deferred addressing:

    @4(ap) = first argument
           = 1

For example, if we want to move the *a*-content to R6 inside the procedure *T*, we would use

    movl @4(ap), r6

To move the *a*-address into R7, we would use

    movl 4(ap), r7

We illustrate the use of these two types of procedure calls in a bit. So far, we have distinguished two types of argument lists, one on the system stack for a CALLS, and one in memory for a CALLG. In general, a CALLS is easier to use for short argument lists, a CALLG for longer ones. Each time the processor returns from a CALLS procedure, it clears the call frame (eliminates the argument list on the stack). When the processor returns from a CALLG procedure, it leaves the argument list used *intact*. Therefore, if an argument list is going to be used by more than one procedure, it is better to use a CALLG. We will illustrate the use of both types of argument lists.

In both cases—with either a CALLS or a CALLG—the processor will eliminate the call frame when it returns from a procedure. There are two types of procedures: *internal* and *external* procedures. An *internal procedure* will be part of the same file as the main program that initiates procedure CALLS. An *external procedure* is contained in a separate file, apart from the caller. It is attached to the object module for a main program at link time. External procedures can be shared by more than one program or user. Internal procedures are limited to calls from the callers inside the file that contains them. When a procedure is being developed, it is better to start it as an internal procedure because debugging is easier and variables can be managed more readily. Later, a useful internal procedure can easily be made into an external procedure, which can be shared. The ultimate goal is to build procedure libraries like IO.MAR in Appendix C.

8.2

THE STACK FORM OF AN ARGUMENT LIST: USING A CALLS

This section explains how to set up an internal procedure that will show us its stack call frame, its saved register contents, and its argument list. In doing this, we pass arguments to the procedure both by calls by value and calls by reference. There are two forms of calls by value: relative addressing with

> pushl ⟨label⟩

and immediate addressing with

> push #⟨value⟩

Figure 8.5 shows both types of calls by value.

In the example in Figure 8.5, when the processor executes the procedure call frame, it first prints the current call frame. Then it prints a whimsical message before it returns to the main program. It is left as an exercise to print the *same* system stack locations after the processor has returned from the call frame procedure. To do this, save a copy of the procedure FP (frame pointer) in a general register. Do this inside the call frame procedure *before* returning to the main program. Then use the old FP to go back and examine the system stack that has replaced the procedure call frame. The parts of the call frame printed above are examined in Figure 8.6.

In addition to the stack contents shown in Figure 8.6, we also printed part of another call frame higher up in the system stack. This is unrelated to the program in Figure 8.5.

8.3

NONSYSTEM STACK FORM OF AN ARGUMENT LIST: USING A CALLG

In the following example, we call a procedure T with a CALLG. We use the procedure T to show us its argument list relative to the three types of information given by the AP:

1. The AP, itself, which identifies the beginning of the argument list;
2. n(AP), where n = 4, 8, 12, 16, . . . , 4k, which gives the address of an argument, following the first one, which is the number of entries in the

FIGURE 8.5
A Procedure to Exhibit Its own Call Frame

```
;
;Ref.:   Figure 8.5 (A procedure to exhibit its own call frame)

;
;Method:  Use an acbl loop in terms of successive values of ap,(ap), the
;         argument pointer address and the content of the stack location it
;         points to(the parts of the argument list) as well as the sp and (sp),
;         the stack pointer address and the content of the stack location it
;         points to (the parts of the procedure call frame).


         a:         .long ^x<aaaaaa>
         b:         .long ^x<233>
         c:         .long ^x<bbbbbb>
         d:         .long ^x<2010>
         e:         .long ^x<2020>
         f:         .long ^x<2001>
         max:       .long 16
         step:      .long 1
         index:     .long 1

Begin:   .word

         pushl      f
         pushl      e
         pushl      d
         pushl      c
         pushal     b
         pushal     a
         pushl      #^x<eeeeee>

         movl       #^x<cb>,r7
         movl       #^x<fcc>,r8
         movl       #^x<abc>,r9

         calls      #7,call_frame

         $exit_s

         .entry call_frame,^m<r7,r8,r9>

         writeln
         writeln <                  System stack entries:>
         writeln
         writeln <         sp   (sp)-content   ap              (ap)-content>
         writeln
         writeln <------------------------------------------------------------>
         writeln

         movl       sp,r6
         movl       ap,r7

loop:

         write < >
```

Continued on following page.

Figure 8.5 continued.

```
        writeval r6 (r6) radix=16 spaces=7
        write <  >
        writeval r7 (r7) radix=16 spaces=7
        writeln
        addl2    #4,r6
        addl2    #4,r7
        acbl     max,step,index,loop

        writeln
        writeln

        write <Tum-ti-tum-ti!  Tum-ti-tum-ti-tum-toes!>

        ret

        .end Begin
```

RUN FG85

System stack entries:

sp	(sp)-content	ap	(ap)-content
7FFAF344	0	7FFAF364	7
7FFAF348	23800000	7FFAF368	EEEEEE
7FFAF34C	7FFAF3CC	7FFAF36C	200
7FFAF350	7FFAF384	7FFAF370	204
7FFAF354	25A	7FFAF374	BBBBBB
7FFAF358	CB	7FFAF378	2010
7FFAF35C	FCC	7FFAF37C	2020
7FFAF360	ABC	7FFAF380	2001
7FFAF364	7	7FFAF384	0
7FFAF368	EEEEEE	7FFAF388	0
7FFAF36C	200	7FFAF38C	7FFAF3CC
7FFAF370	204	7FFAF390	7FFAF3B8
7FFAF374	BBBBBB	7FFAF394	-7FFE98FA
7FFAF378	2010	7FFAF398	BFF
7FFAF37C	2020	7FFAF39C	5
7FFAF380	2001	7FFAF3A0	224

Tum-ti-tum-ti! Tum-ti-tum-ti-tum-toes!

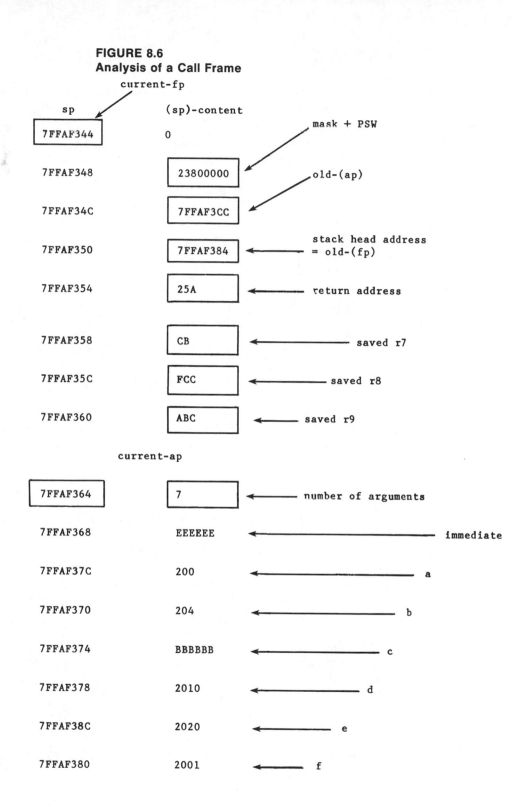

FIGURE 8.6
Analysis of a Call Frame

current-fp

sp	(sp)-content	
7FFAF344	0	mask + PSW
7FFAF348	23800000	old-(ap)
7FFAF34C	7FFAF3CC	
7FFAF350	7FFAF384	stack head address = old-(fp)
7FFAF354	25A	return address
7FFAF358	CB	saved r7
7FFAF35C	FCC	saved r8
7FFAF360	ABC	saved r9

current-ap

7FFAF364	7	number of arguments
7FFAF368	EEEEEE	immediate
7FFAF37C	200	a
7FFAF370	204	b
7FFAF374	BBBBBB	c
7FFAF378	2010	d
7FFAF38C	2020	e
7FFAF380	2001	f

list. Notice that 4(AP) actually points to a memory address which is *below* the AP. This is the opposite of the relationship between the first argument in a stack frame and its AP;

3. @n(AP), where n = 4, 8, 12, 16, . . . , 4k, which gives the argument, itself.

In setting up the example in Figure 8.7, we include a memory location labeled *place*, which contains the address of a row of longwords, otherwise known as an array. This is necessary, since the processor uses the argument number to identify each argument address. The use of an array itself, rather than a location loaded with the array address, would create an addressing conflict.

    At the beginning of the procedure *T*, we first print a copy of the AP and (AP). We avoid printing @(AP). Why? Recall how memory is organized on a VAX-11. The first 512 bytes or locations 0 through 1FF are unavailable. Since (AP) = 5, if we used, for example,

    movl @(ap), r6

we would be attempting to print the content of location 5. After printing the AP and its content (the number 5), we increment the AP by 4 to make it point to the first argument. Finally, notice that the first argument is an address, namely, the address of the NOS array. It is the basic framework of the above argument in *T* that we use in the next example.

8.4

EXAMPLE: REPEATED USE OF THE SAME ARGUMENT LIST

In the next program, the arguments are manipulated by means of several procedures, all internal. This program first builds a list of triangular numbers: 1, 3, 6, 10, 15, ... A *triangular number* can be represented as a triangle of dots. This is an example of what the ancient Greeks called a geometric number, which they defined as a number associated with a fundamental geometric shape. Examples of the geometric interpretation of triangular numbers are shown in Figure 8.8.

    Each succeeding dot triangle contains each of the preceding or lower dot triangles for lower triangular numbers. A formula for computing triangular numbers is given by

    Triangular Number = i(i + 1)/2, i = 1, 2, 3, . . .

Just let *i* be a natural number. In the program that follows, we use a CALLG to call a geometric NOS procedure, which puts together a list of triangular

FIGURE 8.7
Arguments for a CALLG

```
;
;Ref.:   Figure 8.7 (Arguments for a callg)

        index:    .long 1
        nos:      .blkl     30                    ;referenced by place-arg

argument_list:

        place:    .long nos                       ;put nos-addr in place
        i:        .long 1                         ;this will start the
                                                  ;triangular no. sequence
                                                  ;in Figure 8.9

        a:.long 4
        b:.long 5
        c:.long ^x<aaa>

        arg:                                      ;ap points here
                  .long 5
                  .address place,i,a,b,c

Begin:  .word

        callg     arg,t                           ;call t procedure

        $exit_s

        .entry t,0

        writeln
        writeln <               Argument list:>
        writeln
        writeln <               ap    (ap)-content @(ap)-content>
        writeln
        writeln <------------------------------------------------------------->
        writeln

        movl ap,r6
        write < >                                 ;< > = tab
        writeval r6 (r6) radix=16 spaces=9
        addl2     #4,r6
        writeln

loop:

        movl      @(r6),r7
        write < >                                 ;< > = tab
        writeval r6 (r6) r7 radix=16 spaces=9
        writeln
        addl2     #4,r6
        acbl      #5,#1,index,loop

        ret

        .end Begin
```

Continued on following page.

Figure 8.7 continued.

```
RUN FG87

    Argument list:

    ap      (ap)-content    @(ap)-content

------------------------------------------------------------

    290     5
    294     27C             204
    298     280             1
    29C     284             4
    2A0     288             5
    2A4     28C             AAA
```

FIGURE 8.8
Geometric Numbers

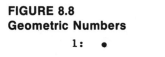

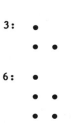

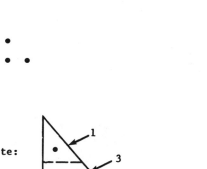

FIGURE 8.9
A Triangular Numbers Program

```
;
;Ref.:   Figure 8.9 (Geometric numbers with three callgs with one list)
;
;Method:
;        Use the formula
;                                  i(i+1)/2, i = 1,2,3,...,n (n=natural no.)
;
;        to produce a list of triangular numbers and to use certain list
;        entries to print corresponding triangles.  Each triangular number
;        becomes the limit on the outside of three nested acbl loops.

        index:    .long 1
        nos:      .blkl 30                    ;referenced by place-arg.

argument_list:

        place:    .long nos                   ;place references nos. list
        i:        .long 1                     ;used in generating nos
        a:.long 4                             ;not used
        b:.long 5                             ;not used
        c:.long ^x<aaa>                       ;not used

        arg:                                  ;ap points here!
                  .long 5
                  .address place,i,a,b,c

Begin:  .word

        callg     arg,geometric_nos           ;build list

        callg     arg,echo                    ;echo what's been done

        callg     arg,pictures                ;draw pictures

        $exit_s

        j:        .long                       ;local variable

        .entry geometric_nos,0

        movl      @4(ap),r6                   ;get address of list
        movl      @8(ap),r7                   ;get value of i (note:
                                              ;in enhanced versions of
                                              ;this pgm, this will be
                                              ;selected by the user
        movl      #2,j                        ;init. j
        movl      #1,index                    ;set up loop index

triangular_nos:

        clrl      r9                          ;set up quad for ediv
        movl      j,r8                        ;set up factor
        mull2     r7,r8                       ;i(i + 1)
        ediv      #2,r8,r10,r11               ;get quotient
```

Continued on following page.

Figure 8.9 continued.

```
        movl    r10,(r6)+                       ;save no. in list
        incl    r7                              ;new i
        incl    j                               ;new i + 1
        acbl    #20,#1,index,triangular_nos     ;repeat production
                                                ;until index = 20

        ret

        .entry echo,0

        movl    @4(ap),r6                       ;get list address
        movl    #1,index                        ;init. index
        writeln
        writeln <              Triangular numbers:>
        writeln
        writeln <----------------------------------------------------->
        writeln

copy:

        writeval (r6)
        add12   #4,r6
        acbl    #20,#1,index,copy

        ret

local_variables:

        x:      .long 1                          ;dot-determiner
        triangle:
                .long 1                          ;row-determiner
        limit:  .long 5                          ;no-of-triangles-1
        index1: .long 1                          ;innermost loop
        index2: .long 1                          ;second loop
        index3: .long 1                          ;outer loop
        step:   .long 1

        .entry pictures,0

        movl    @4(ap),r6                        ;get list address

        next_triangle:

                no:

                        row:

                        write < . >
                        acbl x,step,index1,row
```

Figure 8.9 continued.

```
        movl        #1,indexl
        incl        x
        writeln
        acbl        triangle,step,index2,no
        movl    #1,index2
        writeln
        writeln
        movl    #1,x
        movl    (r6)+,triangle
        acbl    limit,step,index3,next_triangle

        ret

        .end Begin
```

RUN FG89

        Triangular numbers:

----

1 3 6 10 15 21 28 36 45 55 66 78 91 105 120 136 153 171 190 210

        .

        .
      . .
      . . .

        .
      . .
      . . .
      . . . .
      . . . . .
      . . . . . .

        .
      . .
      . . .
      . . . .
      . . . . .
      . . . . . .
      . . . .
      . . . .
      . . . .
      . . . .

numbers. We use a procedure echo to print a copy of the newly constructed list. Then we use a procedure PICTURES to print some of the corresponding dot triangles for the triangular numbers that have been computed. In doing this, we keep a longer argument list than is needed. Notice that each procedure feeds on different parts of the list. The implication here is that different procedures can use different parts of the same list. The same CALLG format can be used over and over, the same list passed to different procedures. This simplifies the use of the CALLG. The program for this is shown in Figure 8.9.

8.5
LOCAL VS. GLOBAL VARIABLES

Implicit in the structure of a procedure (see Figure 8.1) is the presence of local variables. A *local variable* is restricted in scope, its use limited to a procedure. A *global variable* is unlimited in scope; it can be shared throughout a main program as well as in any internal or external procedure. A global variable is declared with a double colon (::). Technically, all of the variables in the program in Figure 8.9 are local. Even so, we have separated from the main program those variables that are *only* used by a procedure. Notice, for example, the extensive list of variables for the pictures procedure:

```
x:          .long 1
triangle:
            .long 1
limit:      .long 5
index1:     .long 1

    ⋮
```

These are local to the pictures procedure since they are not used by the other procedures or main program. Similarly, the variable *j* is used only by the geometric NOS procedure. If these procedures are made external, their local variables will also be made external.

The use of global variables presents an alternative to the argument list. They are easy to set up and easy to use. However, they should be used sparingly, since they tend to hide (and be hidden by) what is happening, especially in the case of a main program that has global variables used by an external procedure. Notice that some of the variables in the I/O procedures in Appendix C are global. This makes the values of these variables available to calling programs. We show how this works in the next chapter.

8.6

PROCEDURES CAN CALL EACH OTHER

One procedure can call another one, forming a chain of calls. We illustrate this in the next example, where we use a procedure to build the list and then fill it with triangular numbers. This will be an enhanced version of the geometric NOS procedure given earlier. We will use this procedure to call another procedure called sampler. The arrangement of the procedures relative to the main program is illustrated in Figure 8.10.

FIGURE 8.10
Flow-of-Control Between Two Procedures

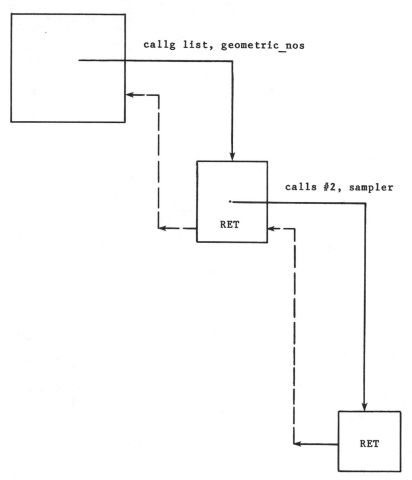

FIGURE 8.11
A Program with Two External Procedures

```
;
;Ref.:   Figure 8.11 (A chain of Procedure Calls)
;
;Method:
;       Use the formula
;                               i(i+1)/2, i = 1,2,3,...,n (n=natural no.)
;
;       to load a list with triangular numbers using the geometric_nos
;       procedure; use the sampler procedure called from the geometric_nos
;       procedure to print a copy of the newly created list.  Both procedures
;       are external, each in a separate file.

        index:  .long 1
        nos:    .blkl 30                        ;referenced by place-arg.

argument_list:

        place:  .long nos                       ;place references nos. list
        i:      .long 1                         ;used in generating nos
        a:.long 4                               ;not used
        b:.long 5                               ;not used
        c:.long ^x<aaa>                         ;not used

        arg:                                    ;ap points here!
                .long 5
                .address place,i,a,b,c

Begin:  .word

        callg   arg,geometric_nos               ;build list

        $exit_s

        .end Begin


;Ref.:   Figure 8.11 (continued)
;Note:   This is an external procedure called from a main program with a callg.


        j:      .long
        index1: .long 1

        .entry  geometric_nos,0

        movl    @4(ap),r6                       ;get list address
        movl    @8(ap),r7                       ;get initial i-value
        movl    #2,j                            ;get i + 1

triangular_nos:

        clrl    r9                              ;set up quad for ediv
        movl    j,r8                            ;set up i + 1
        mull2   r7,r8                           ;i(i + 1)
```

Figure 8.11 continued.

```
        ediv    #2,r8,r10,r11                    ;r10 = i(i + 1)/2
        movl    r10,(r6)+                        ;put no. in list
        incl    r7                               ;new i
        incl    j                                ;new i + 1
        acbl    #20,#1,index1,triangular_nos

        movl    @4(ap),r6                        ;restore list address
        pushl   r6                               ;push it!
        calls   #1,sampler                       ;call sampler

        ret

        .end


;Ref.:  Figure 8.11 (continued)
;
;Note:  This is an external procedure called from the geometric_nos
;       procedure, which is also external.  It is called with a calls
;       instruction.


        index2: .long 1

        .entry sampler,0

        movl    4(ap),r6                             ;get list address
        writeln
        writeln <             Triangular numbers:>
        writeln
        writeln <----------------------------------------------------->
        writeln

copy:

        writeval (r6)
        addl2   #4,r6
        acbl    #20,#1,index2,copy

        ret

        .end


RUN FG811

        Triangular numbers:

----------------------------------------------------

1 3 6 10 15 21 28 36 45 55 66 78 91 105 120 136 153 171 190 210
```

We make both procedures external and use a mixture of calling methods. Notice that we carry along the local variable *j* in the file containing the geometric NOS procedure. This will govern the ACB1 loops inside the procedures. And the geometric numbers procedure passes to the sampler procedure in the beginning address of the list. The new program together with its external procedures is shown in Figure 8.11.

In setting up the geometric NOS and sampler procedures as external procedures, we have made the index used by each procedure a local variable. Thus the geometric NOS procedure uses INDEX1 to control its ACB1 loop; the sampler procedure uses INDEX2. In doing this, we have eliminated the variable index that was in the earlier version of the main program. An alternative to this approach would be to make index a global variable:

```
index:: .long 1
```

in the main program. This would eliminate the local variables INDEX1 and INDEX2 in the two external procedures. You may wish to try this alternative as an exercise. A word of caution is needed here, however: a comment should be put into each external procedure to indicate the presence of a global variable and how it is to be set up in the main program. Notice, also, since geometric NOS would use index, first, it would have to be given a new value of 1 before the index could use it. The call frames related to the above procedures have some special features, which are discussed in the next section.

8.7

CALL FRAMES FOR TWO PROCEDURES

When one procedure calls another, the processor sets up a second call frame on the system stack. The second call frame will be below the first one used by the first procedure. The old (FP) of the second call frame will be the stack address of the beginning of the first call frame. The old (AP) in the second call frame will be the AP used by the first call frame. We show this by modifying the geometric NOS procedure in Figure 8.11 so that it prints its call frame. Then we modify the sampler procedure to print a copy of its call frame from its beginning to the top stack address of the geometric NOS call frame. The technique we use to do this is shown in Figure 8.5. Figure 8.12 shows the output from the modified program.

Notice that the frame pointer is used differently in a CALLG call frame. That is, if a CALLG is used, then the FP points to a system stack address containing the number of arguments in the CALLG argument list. In ad-

FIGURE 8.12
Call Frames for Two Procedures

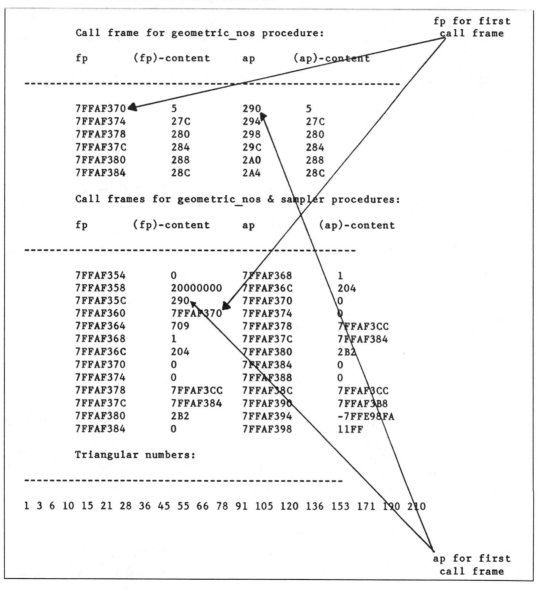

Call frame for geometric_nos procedure:

fp for first
call frame

fp	(fp)-content	ap	(ap)-content
7FFAF370	5	290	5
7FFAF374	27C	294	27C
7FFAF378	280	298	280
7FFAF37C	284	29C	284
7FFAF380	288	2A0	288
7FFAF384	28C	2A4	28C

Call frames for geometric_nos & sampler procedures:

fp	(fp)-content	ap	(ap)-content
7FFAF354	0	7FFAF368	1
7FFAF358	20000000	7FFAF36C	204
7FFAF35C	290	7FFAF370	0
7FFAF360	7FFAF370	7FFAF374	0
7FFAF364	709	7FFAF378	7FFAF3CC
7FFAF368	1	7FFAF37C	7FFAF384
7FFAF36C	204	7FFAF380	2B2
7FFAF370	0	7FFAF384	0
7FFAF374	0	7FFAF388	0
7FFAF378	7FFAF3CC	7FFAF38C	7FFAF3CC
7FFAF37C	7FFAF384	7FFAF390	7FFAF3B8
7FFAF380	2B2	7FFAF394	-7FFE98FA
7FFAF384	0	7FFAF398	11FF

Triangular numbers:

1 3 6 10 15 21 28 36 45 55 66 78 91 105 120 136 153 171 190 210

ap for first
call frame

dition, the addresses of the CALLG argument list are stored on the system stack above the frame pointer address.

In the above example, 7FFAF370 is the FP address for the geometric NOS procedure call frame. The AP address for this procedure is 290 (hex).

These addresses become the old (FP) and old (AP) in the call frame for the sampler procedure.

8.8

LIBRARIES OF PROCEDURES

The VAX-11 has a librarian program that makes it possible to set up a collection of external procedures inside one file. The following steps are used to build such a library:

1. Use an editor to prepare the source text for the library. (Call it *T*.) The extension on the source text file will be .MAR.

2. Assemble the library file with

   MACRO T ⟨ret⟩

3. Produce a final version, using the system librarian, with

   LIBRARY/CREATE/OBJ T T ⟨ret⟩

Step 3 will produce an OLB (Object Library) module:

   T.OLB

The structure of the source text for a procedure library is shown in Figure 8.13.

The VAX-11 also has a substantial library of procedures available to assembly language programs. It has an RTL (Real-Time Library), which gives a wide variety of procedures to handle system communications, input/output, and memory management problems. An RTL procedure has the form

   LIB$ ⟨name⟩ ⟨argument list⟩

For example,

   LIB$ PUT_OUTPUT ⟨source⟩

prints an ASCII source string at a terminal when it is called. To use this RTL procedure, it is necessary to use the .ASCID directive to establish a string to be printed. The setup required by this procedure is as follows:

FIGURE 8.13
Structure of a Library of Procedures

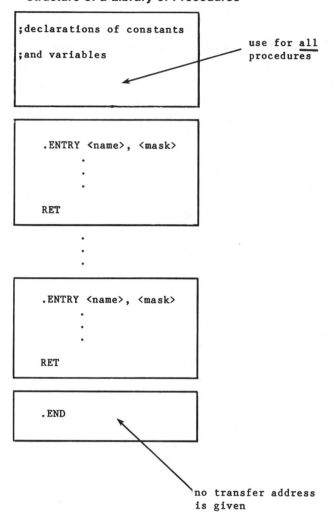

1. Establish string:

   X: .ASCID/⟨string⟩/

2. Push the address of X onto the system stack:

   pushal X

FIGURE 8.14
An RTL Procedure: LIB$PUT_OUTPUT

```
;
;Ref.:   Figure 8.14 (An RTL procedure: lib$put_output)
;
        x:          .ascid /Did George Orwell have a big brother?/

Begin:  .word

        pushal x
        calls   #1,g^lib$put_output

        $exit_s

        .end Begin


RUN FG814

Did George Orwell have a big brother?
```

3. Use a CALLS instruction to transfer control to this procedure:

> calls #1, G^LIB$PUT_OUTPUT

The unary operator $G^$ is used to tell the processor that the address specified is the address of the RTL procedure. The G stands for general mode. Without the $G^$ unary operator, the linker returns an error message. This RTL procedure is illustrated in Figure 8.14.

Learning to use the RTL procedures requires a course in itself. Each RTL procedure has its own quirks. A complete description of this library has been compiled by the Digital Equipment Corporation (1982*a,b*).

Our chief concern in this text is with setting up an I/O library of procedures, which is needed to do serious assembly language programming on a VAX-11. We show how to do this in the next chapter.

8.9
SUMMARY

Procedures can be either internal or external. In developing a procedure for a program, it is better to start with an internal procedure. This simplifies the addressing problems and organization of the new procedure. It also simplifies the assembling and linking that must be done. The ultimate goal is to make generally useful procedures external so that they can be shared by more than one program and more than one user. Linking can be made easier by clustering external procedures together in procedure libraries.

In developing the external procedures for Figure 8.11, for example, the procedures and main program were put into separate files:

geometric_nos   in file   fg811a.mar

sampler   in file   fg811b.mar

main   in file   fg811.mar

Then, to assemble these files, we used

macro fg811 + pas/lib

macro fg811a + pas/lib

macro fg811b + pas/lib

Finally, to link these files together, we used

link fg811, fg811a, fg811b + io/lib

If we had put the two procedures FG811a and FG811b into the I/O library, we could have used

link fg811 + io/lib

Even with this last simplification, it is better not to put external procedures into a library until they are working. In other words, take the bugs out of an external procedure before putting it into a library. This is especially true of IO.MAR, which is used by every program requiring input/output services. This library, or any library, for that matter, should be handled with great care.

The argument lists for procedures are diverse. The flexibility of an argument list used with a CALLG is shown in Figure 8.9, which illustrates three procedures that use parts of the *same* argument list. The system stack argument list for a CALLS instruction must be recreated every time a CALLS is used. That is, the necessary arguments must be pushed onto the system stack before a CALLS is used. There are pros and cons here. The argument list for a CALLS is easier to set up if there are few arguments. The AP for a CALLS is only once removed from the argument. That is, 4AP is the stack address of the first argument and @4(AP) is the argument itself, either a value or a reference. The AP for a CALLG is twice removed from the argument. That is, 4AP is the memory address of the first argument address. The argument itself is located by using displacement deferred addressing with @4(AP).

The argument list used with a CALLG is very attractive, since it can be reused by more than one procedure. It is not destroyed when the processor returns from a procedure that has been called with a CALLG.

The distinction between *call by value* and *call by reference* for a CALLS instruction is important. A call by reference passes an address to the procedure. If this is the first argument on the system stack, then 4(AP) identifies the operand address, and @4(AP) identifies the operand itself. A call by value passes a value to the procedure. Either relative or immediate addressing can be used to do this. If the first argument on the system stack is a value, then 4(AP) identifies the operand (the value).

It is helpful to become comfortable with the AP (R12) and FP (R13) and SP (R14) in checking the structure of argument lists *and* call frames used by procedures. We have shown how this is done. Some questions about call frames have been left unanswered. We need to look more closely at the call frame which a CALLG requires. Fortunately, this is easy to do. We do this in the exercises, and in the labs.

8.10

EXERCISES

1. Write an assembly language program to do the following:

   (a) Obtain from the user the starting number in the sequence

   $$1, 2, 4, 8, 16, 32, \ldots, 2^n$$

   Store this value in R6.

   (b) Obtain from the user the maximum value of n to use in computing powers of 2. Store this value in R7.

   (c) Call an internal procedure called sum with the entry mask ^M⟨R6,R7⟩;

   (d) Use a CALLS to call sum, passing to sum the contents of R6, R7.

   (e) Inside the sum procedure, do the following:

      1. Print the call frame for sum.

      2. Compute the sum.

      $$1 + 2 + 4 + \ldots + 2^n \qquad \text{(store in R8)}$$

3. Return to main.

(f) in the main program, use R6, R7, R8 to print

$$\langle\text{beginning term}\rangle + \ldots + 2^{\langle\text{value}\rangle} = \langle\text{value}\rangle$$

Run your program for

(g) beginning term $= 4 = 2^2$, $n = 20$ in 2^n

2. Identify the parts of the call frame for the sum procedure in Exercise 1.
3. Enhance the program in Exercise 1 in the following ways:

   (a) Establish a second internal procedure called report, which is called by main, once the processor returns from the sum procedure. Have the report procedure print the results.
   (b) Have the report procedure print its call frame.
   (c) Call report using a CALLS, using a

      ```
      calls #0, report
      ```

      since it can use the values in R6, R7 and R8 to print its report.
   (d) Explain the report procedure call frame.

4. Enhance the program in exercise 3 so that the sum and report procedures are made external. Run your program for

   (a) beginning term $= 16$, $n = 22$, in 2^n
   (b) analyze the resulting call frames

5. The following variables are to be used in an argument list:

   ```
   a:   .long ^X⟨ffa⟩
   b:   .long ^X⟨999⟩
   c:   .long a
   d:   .long b
   e:   .long ^X⟨377⟩
   ```

   (a) Pass a, b, e to a procedure T as values.
   (b) Pass c, d to procedure T as references.
   (c) Pass

$$\#^{\wedge}X\langle aabbcc\rangle$$

to procedure T as an immediate value.

(d) Use procedure T to do the following:

1. Print its complete call frame (include the arguments).

2. Compute the sum:

$$a + b + e + \langle\text{the immediate value} = aabbcc\rangle$$

3. Print the result.

4. Print the contents c and d, using the argument list on the stack.

6. Use the variables in exercise 5 and set up an argument list for a CALLG. Then do the following:

(a) use a CALLG to call a procedure SUM to compute the sum

$$a + b + e + \langle\text{value} = aabbcc\rangle$$

Take the *aabbcc* (hex) value from the argument list, this time. (Use a variable x for this.) Store the sum in R6.

(b) Use the same argument list in a CALLG to a procedure *exhibit* to do the following:

1. Print a copy of the argument list table in terms of the following heading:

    ap   (ap)-content   @(ap) content

2. Print the sum in R6.

3. Print the content of c and d.

(c) Allow the user to rerun this program. To do this, use the same argument list in a CALLG to a *procedure* enquiry. Use the enquiry procedure to allow the user to fill the variables a, b, e, and x with new values.

Rerun your program with

(d) a = 9000 (hex), b = 25555 (hex), e = ab(hex), x = 2.

7. Enhance the three procedures in exercise 6 so that each one prints out its call frame. Explain these.

8. Modify the program in exercise 6, so that the sum procedure calls the

exhibit procedure. Use the technique presented in Figure 8.12 to print out the call frames for the two procedures. Explain the result.

9. Modify the program in Figure 8.11 to duplicate the call frames in Figure 8.12.

10. When a CALLS instruction is used, what is the maximum number of arguments that can be passed to a procedure? Why?

11. When a CALLG instruction is used, what is the maximum number of arguments that can be used relative to the CALLG instruction? Why?

12. If procedure A has an argument list X on the system stack set up relative to a CALLS, is X available to a procedure B after the processor returns control from A to main? Why?

13. Make a list of differences between a CALLS and CALLG instruction.

14. How is the AP used with a CALLG?

15. How is the AP used with a CALLS?

16. How is the FP used with a CALLG?

17. How is the FP used with a CALLS?

18. Explain the difference between a *call by value* and a *call by reference*.

19. Explain the difference between an external and an internal procedure.

20. What is a global variable?

21. What is a local variable relative to a procedure?

22. What is the purpose of the .ENTRY directive?

23. Which general registers can be masked?

24. Use the RTL procedure LIB$PUT_OUTPUT to print a 10-line autobiography.

8.11

LAB PROJECTS

1. Put the three procedures used in Figure 8.9 into a procedure library called graphics. Add to this library a fourth procedure called *enquiry*. Use enquiry to do the following:

   (a) See if the user wishes another run.

   (b) Obtain a starting value for i in

   $$i\,(i\,+\,1)/2$$

(c) Obtain from the user the number of triangular numbers to be computed.

Note: Increase the number of longwords in the NOS array to allow for more than 30 numbers.

(d) Obtain from the user the number of triangle pictures to be printed.

Run your program for

(e) $i = 5$, number $= 25$, pictures $= 6$

2. Enhance the pictures procedure in Figure 8.9 so that it prints *consecutive* triangles instead of skipping triangles the way it does now. Put the enhanced procedure into the graphics library. To print pictures of 10 triangular numbers, run the program in lab 1 for $i = 1$, number $= 10$, pictures $= 10$.

3. Add a new procedure called CHOICE to the graphics library built in labs 1 and 2. Then modify the program in lab 1 to do the following:

(a) Print a menu:

1. Print triangular numbers (the values).
2. Print pictures of consecutive triangular numbers (use the enhanced pictures procedure from lab 2 to do this).
3. Print the picture of a particular triangular number (use the CHOICE procedure to print this single picture).

(b) In terms of the menu item chosen, transfer control to the correct procedure.

Run your program to

(c) Print a picture of 91.

8.12
REVIEW QUIZ

Indicate whether the following statements are true or false:

1. A procedure mask specifies general registers to be saved on the system stack.
2. The minimum VAX-11 procedure call frame has 6 longwords.
3. The FP is used to point to the beginning of a call frame.

4. PUSHL #⟨immediate value⟩ is a call by value.

5. PUSHAL ⟨label⟩ is a call by reference.

6. procedures can be either internal or external.

7. With either a CALLS or CALLG, the processor will eliminate the call frame when it returns from a procedure.

8. A CALLS uses a nonsystem stack form of an argument list.

9. A CALLG uses a nonsystem stack form of an argument list.

10. A local procedure variable is limited in scope to that procedure.

11. Procedures can call each other.

12. The same argument list can be used by more than one CALLG.

13. Either relative or immediate addressing can be used in calls by value.

14. Assume a, b, c, d are procedures where a calls b and b calls d and d calls c. When the processor returns from c, it returns to b, first.

8.13

REFERENCES

Digital Equipment Corporation. *VAX/VMS Run-Time Library Reference Manual.* Order No. AA-D036C-TE. Maynard, Mass., 1982*a*.

Digital Equipment Corporation. *VAX/VMS System Services Reference Manual.* Order No. AA-D018C-TE. Maynard, Mass., 1982*b*.

Wirth, N. *Systematic Programming: An Introduction.* Englewood Cliffs, N.J.: Prentice-Hall, 1973.

9.
I/O PROCEDURES

Programs do not spring ready-made like Athena from Zeus's forehead. . . .

—R. S. Forsyth, *Pascal at Work and Play*

9.0
AIMS

- Introduce the use of queue input/output (QIO) on a VAX-11.
- Develop procedures to handle both string and numeric I/O via a terminal.
- Show how to use a constant to determine the maximum length of an input string.
- Distinguish between the simplified $OUTPUT macro and more complex $QIO macro.
- Show varying uses for argument lists with the CALLS instruction.
- Show how to build a whole number from separate ASCII codes for each digit of an integer.

9.1

INTRODUCTION

Up to now we have used I/O macros found in the macro library in Appendix C. In this chapter we go behind the scenes to look at the input/output procedures used by these macros. This will make it possible to tailor the I/O procedures to individual needs.

In setting up I/O procedures, we rely on the VAX-11 system macros to get started. The VAX-11 system macro library is substantial. It is also fairly easy to use, once the arguments used by the system macros are understood. Our initial concern is to learn how to use existing system macros to set up I/O procedures. In later chapters we explain how to build new I/O macros and how to enhance the procedures given in this chapter.

The VAX-11 associates a request for input or output with a channel between the processor and the I/O device requested. A *channel* is a communication path associated with a physical device such as a terminal or a disk drive. Before an I/O request can be made in a program, the physical device to be used must be assigned to a channel. There is a system macro to do this: $ASSIGN, which is introduced in this chapter. All VAX-11/VMS I/O requests are made using a Queue I/O request system device. There is a system macro to issue a Queue I/O request: $QIO, which is also introduced in this chapter.

Typically, more than one user will request I/O services relative to the same I/O device. These requests are fed to a queue, which the VAX-11 dequeues each time a physical device requested becomes available.

The Queue I/O macro will build what is known as an I/O Request Packet or IRP. Each acceptable IRP will be inserted into a device queue by the queue I/O service.

9.2

READING STRINGS

A procedure to read strings 80 bytes long from a keyboard is given in Figure 9.1.

This procedure uses a simplified form of the $QIO macro. It specifies the following:

1. TTNAME (I/O Device Name). This is used by QIO to identify the device that has been requested. Normally, this will be a logical name assigned

FIGURE 9.1
String Input Procedure

```
;
;Ref.:  Figure 9.1 (String input procedure)

instr:  .blkb 80
ttname: .ascid/sys$input:/
        .even
ttchan: .blkw 1
ttiosb: .blkw 1
ttiolen:
        .word
        .long
ferror: blbs r0,10$
        $exit_s r0
10$:    rsb


        .entry input,0
        $assign_s devnam = ttname chan = ttchan
        bsbb error

        $input chan = ttchan length = #80 buffer = instr iosb = ttiosb

        cvtlb     ttiolen,@4(AP)              ;init. input string with
length
        movl      4(ap),r6                    ;r6 gets input string address
        incl      r6                          ;advance addr. past length
byte
        movc3     ttiolen,instr,(r6)          ;copy instr to input string

        $dassgn_s chan = ttchan

        ret

        .end
```

by the system manager. In this procedure, we have used

SYS$INPUT

QIO will then identify the physical device requested.

2. TTCHAN (Device Channel). This is used by QIO to assign a device channel relative to the requested I/O device. Notice that each of the I/O macros ($ASSIGN, $INPUT, $DASSGN) must specify this channel to QIO.

3. TTIOSB (I/O Status Block). This is the location used by QIO to give the completion status of the I/O request.

4. TTIOLEN (Length of Input String). QIO will count the number of char-

acters in the entered string and put this count in the first word labelled TTIOLEN.

5. ERROR. QIO uses this location to handle I/O errors.

6. $ASSIGN. This macro assigns a channel to a device.

7. $INPUT. This macro identifies the maximum string length and the memory location where the input string is to be put. It also tells QIO what locations to use to assign a channel and to keep track of QIO completion status. Longer strings can be entered by changing the length parameter. If this is done, a corresponding change must be made in the *X*-string.

8. $DASSGN. This deassigns the opened I/O channel.

After the $INPUT macro moves the entered characters into INSTR, this information must be transferred to the byte row specified by the caller. The caller will push the address of the string to be used by this procedure. Since the TTIOLEN has the string length, TTIOLEN is moved to the first byte of the string specified by the caller. This is done with

```
cvtlb ttiolen, @4(ap)
```

The newly entered string is copied to the byte row specified by the caller,

FIGURE 9.2
A Program with String Input

```
;
;Ref.:  Figure 9.2 (A program with string input)
x:
        .byte                           ;use to store length
        .blkb 80                        ;use for characters

Begin:  .word

        write <Enter a string: >

        pushal x                        ;string address = arg.
        calls #1,input                  ;get string from terminal

        writestring x                   ;print copy of new string
        $exit_s

        .end Begin



RUN FG92

Enter a string: George Orwell´s real name was Eric Arthur Blair.
George Orwell´s real name was Eric Arthur Blair.
```

using

```
movc3 ttiolen, instr, (r6)
```

Notice the importance of adjusting the address supplied by the caller, so that the *second* byte of the caller's string is used to put the first byte of INSTR.

We illustrate the use of this string input procedure in the following program. In this program, we pass the address of the *x*-byte row (a call by reference) to the output procedure (see Figure 9.2).

For now, we rely on the WRITESTRING macro to print a copy of the entered string. In the next section, we show a procedure to print strings.

All QIO on a VAX-11 depends on the use of a channel to pass character codes back and forth between main memory and a physical device. In the above program, a channel is opened (made available) by the $ASSIGN macro so that the character codes that were typed will have a reserved path to follow. A simplified graphical interpretation of the use of a channel set up by QIO relative to the above program is shown in Figure 9.3.

FIGURE 9.3
Simplified Graphical Interpretation of a Channel

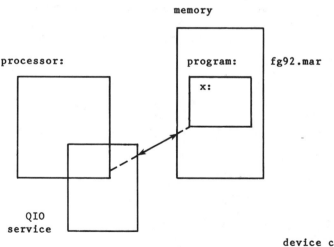

```
                         memory

processor:              program:     fg92.mar

                          x:


QIO
service

                                device channel:  ASCII
                                codes passed along this
                                channel by QIO.



                    device
```

QIO will transfer the ASCII codes it gets from a terminal along a channel to designated memory locations. It passes these codes to the INSTR byte-row in the above example.

9.3

WRITING STRINGS

A procedure called output that can be used to write strings from main memory to a terminal is shown in Figure 9.4.

The output procedure uses the $ASSIGN and $DASSGN macros to assign and deassign a channel for the output. The $OUTPUT macro is essentially the same as the $INPUT macro, except that now the ASCII code traffic is directed *to* the terminal being used. It also uses an INSTR byte-row, which holds a copy of the ASCII codes set up in the main program. We use OUTLEN to hold the number of bytes in the original string. We use the GET-loop to build a copy of the original string.

Again, we have made the output procedure external, even though it was developed as an internal procedure. Figure 9.5 shows a program that uses both the input and the output procedures. It uses the output procedure to handle the prompt, instead of the WRITELN macro. It then uses the input procedure to get a string from the terminal, and uses the output procedure to echo-print the entered string.

Up to now, we have limited the length of the I/O string to 80 characters. We can change this by introducing a constant, which allows the user to preselect the maximum size of the I/O string. We do this as follows:

1. Define

    number of bytes = ⟨constant⟩

2. Inside the input procedure, we define a variable INLEN:

    inlen: .blkl 1

3. The argument list for the input procedure is expanded as follows:

    pushl number of bytes
    pushal x
    calls #2, input

4. Inside the input procedure, the length argument is passed to INLEN as follows:

          movl 8(sp), inlen

The rest of the input procedure is the same as before. A program to implement this idea is shown in Figure 9.6.

    We built into this program an illustration of a drawback to the $OUTPUT macro. That is, the $OUTPUT macro volunteers a ⟨cr⟩ and ⟨lf⟩ at the end of each string it prints. This works against us if we want to use a string

FIGURE 9.4
String Output Procedure

```
;
;Ref.:   Figure 9.4 (String output procedure)

         instr:   .blkb 80
         ttname:  .ascid/sys$input:/
                  .even
         ttchan:  .blkw 1
         ttiosb:  .blkw 1
         ttiolen:
                  .word
                  .long
error:   blbs r0,10$
         $exit_s r0
10$:     rsb

         outlen:  .blkl 1

         .entry output,^m<r6,r7,r8>

         $assign_s devnam = ttname chan = ttchan

         bsbw      error

         movzbl    @4(ap),outlen       ;get string length
         movl      outlen,r6           ;set up sob loop counter
         movl      4(ap),r7            ;get string address
         incl      r7                  ;get addr. of 1st char.
         movab     instr,r8            ;set up autoincrement
get:
         movb      (r7)+,(r8)+         ;insert char.
         sobgeq    r6,get

         $output chan = ttchan length = outlen buffer = instr iosb = ttiosb

         $dassgn_s chan = ttchan

         ret

         .end
```

FIGURE 9.5
A Program with String I/O

```
;
;Ref.:   Figure 9.5 (A program with string I/O)

prompt: .ascic / Enter a string--limit = 80 characters: /<10><13><13>

x:
        .byte                               ;for string length
        .blkb 80                            ;for characters

Begin:  .word

        pushal    prompt
        calls #1,output                     ;prompt for string

        pushal    x
        calls #1,input                      ;get string

        pushal    x
        calls     #1,output                 ;print copy of string

        $exit_s

        .end Begin


RUN FG95

  Enter a string--limit = 80 characters:

        Tom went walking on up the Withywindle.
        Tom went walking on up the Withywindle.
```

to prompt for numbers on the *same* line with the prompt. In other words, the $OUTPUT macro does not give an assembly language programmer complete control of the format of the output.

We remedy the drawback to the $OUTPUT macro by substituting a form of the $QIO macro: $QIOW. First, we show the modified output procedure in Figure 9.7.

In the $QIOW macro, an EFN (event flag) is used. An *event flag* is used by the $QIOW macro to post (declare) status bits. It uses the

    efn = #1

when the output process is complete, that is, when the last ASCII code in the output string has been passed along the designated channel to a terminal. In effect, this prevents the system macro from volunteering a ⟨ret⟩, when it reaches the last ASCII code of the output string.

FIGURE 9.6
Modifying the I/O String Length

```
;
;Ref.:  Figure 9.6 (Modifying the length of an I/O string)

;constant:

        number_of_bytes = 256                 ;use to adjust str.-length
prompt_1:
        .ascic / Enter a string--limit = 256 characters: /<10><13><13>

prompt_2:
        .ascic<10><13><13>/Enter your name: /

x:
        .byte                                 ;use this byte for length
        .blkb number_of_bytes                 ;use for character codes
                                              ;notice! constant value
                                              ;sets the number of bytes

Begin:  .word

        pushal    prompt_1
        calls     #1,output                   ;prompt for string

        pushl     #number_of_bytes            ;push length into arg. list
        pushal    x                           ;push str. addr. into list
        calls     #2,input                    ;get string

        pushal    x                           ;push str. addr. into list
        calls     #1,output                   ;print string

        pushal    prompt_2                     ;push output str. addr.
        calls     #1,output                   ;prompt for 2nd string

        pushl     #number_of_bytes            ;push length arg.
        pushal    x                           ;push input str. addr.
        calls     #2,input                    ;get string

        pushal    x                           ;push output str. addr.
        calls     #1,output                   ;print new string

        $exit_s

        .end Begin

RUN FG96

  Enter a string--limit = 256 characters:

Goldberry pulled Tom´s beard down by the Withywindle.
Goldberry pulled Tom´s beard down by the Withywindle.

Enter your name:

J.R.R. Tolkien
J.R.R. Tolkien
```

FIGURE 9.7
Enhanced String Output Procedure

```
;
;Ref.:   Figure 9.7 (Enhanced string output procedure)

         instr:   .blkb 512
         ttname:  .ascid /sys$input:/
                  .even
         ttchan:  .blkw 1
         ttiosb:  .blkw 1
         ttiolen:
                  .word
                  .long
         error:
                  blbs       r0,10$
                  $exit_s r0
10$:     rsb

         outlen:  .blkl 1

         .entry output,^m<r6,r7,r8>

         $assign_s devnam = ttname chan = ttchan

         bsbw       error

         movzbl     @4(ap),outlen             ;get string length
         movl       outlen,r6                 ;set up sob loop counter
         movl       4(ap),r7                  ;get string address
         incl       r7                        ;get address of 1st byte
         movab      instr,r8                  ;init. r8 with output addr.
get:
         movb       (r7)+,(r8)+               ;build output string
         sobgeq     r6,get

         $qiow_s  efn = #1 chan = ttchan func = #io$_writevblk -
                  p1 = instr p2 = outlen

         $dassgn_s chan = ttchan

         ret

         .end
```

The other new feature of the $QIOW macro is

    func = #io$_writevblk

This gives QIO a *function code,* which is device dependent. This code indicates that information will be written to the specified device, a byte at a

FIGURE 9.8
A Program with Enhanced String Output

```
;
;Ref.:   Figure 9.8 (A program with enhanced string-output)

         number_of_bytes = 256

prompt:
         .ascic <10><13><13><13><11>/ Enter your name: /

x:
         .byte
         .blkb number_of_bytes

Begin:   .word

         pushal    prompt
         calls #1,output

         pushl     #number_of_bytes
         pushal    x
         calls     #2,input

         pushal    x
         calls     #1,output

         $exit_s

         .end Begin


RUN FG98

 Enter your name: J.R.R. Tolkien
J.R.R. Tolkien
```

time. In general, a *function code* specifies the QIO operation to be performed relative to the specified device. This procedure is illustrated in Figure 9.8.

This time, notice that the prompt

enter your name:

is not accompanied by a ⟨ret⟩. That is, the entered string is given on the *same* line as the prompt. This tiny advance over the $OUTPUT macro is tremendously important in dealing with numeric input. We illustrate this in the next section.

9.4

NUMERIC INPUT

Figure 9.9 shows a simplified procedure called numeric input.
This procedure takes the entered number as a string of ASCII codes.

FIGURE 9.9
Numeric-Input Procedure

```
        ;
        ;Ref.:   Figure 9.9 (Numeric input procedure)

                instr:    .blkb 80
                ttname:   .ascid/sys$input:/
                          .even
                ttchan:   .blkw 1
                ttiosb:   .blkw 1
                ttiolen:

                          .word
                          .long
                outlen: .blkl 1
                error:  blbs  r0,10$
                        $exit_s r0
        10$:    rsb

                .entry   numeric_input,^m<r6,r7,r8,r9>

                $assign_s devnam = ttname chan = ttchan

                bsbw     error

                $input   chan = ttchan length = #80 buffer = instr iosb = ttiosb

                movzwl   ttiolen,r9               ;get no. of digits entered
                movab    instr,r8                 ;get address of first digit
                clrl     r6                       ;use r6 to hold sum
        remove:

                subb2    #48,(r8)                 ;remove ASCII bias
                movzbl   (r8)+,r7                 ;save digit in r7
                mull2    #10,r6                   ;sum times 10
                addl2    r7,r6                    ;add unit digit
                sobgtr   r9,remove                ;until last digit

                movl     r6,@4(ap)

                $dassgn_s chan = ttchan

                ret

                .end
```

If we type 233, it puts the following information into the INSTR byte row:

2   3   3
↑   ↑   ↑
| | ASCII 51 (base ten)
| ASCII 51 (base ten)
ASCII 50 (base ten)

In other words, the INSTR byte row is loaded as follows:

instr: 50, 51, 51

The trick is now to take these ASCII codes for the separate digits of the entered number and convert them to one number, namely 233. We do this inside the remove loop in the above procedure. The steps used in this loop are summarized in Figure 9.10.

We illustrate the use of all three procedures introduced so far in the next program (see Figure 9.11). We use the entered value to govern the number of times a string is printed.

FIGURE 9.10
String-to-Number Conversion

instr: 50 , 51 , 51	r6 is clear
50−48 = 2	r7 2
	r6 r6*10 = 0
	r6 r6+2 = 2
51−48 = 3	r7 3
	r6 r6*10 = 20
	r6 r6+3 = 23
51−48 = 3	r7 3
	r6 r6*10 = 230
	r6 r6+3 = 233

FIGURE 9.11
A Program with Numeric Input

```
    ,
    ;Ref.:   Figure 9.11 (A program with numeric input)

            index:    .long

            prompt:   .ascic /Enter number of times to print Yes!: /

            x:        .long

            y:        .ascic / Yes! /

    Begin:  .word

            pushal prompt
            calls     #1,output

            pushal  x
            calls     #1,numeric_input

    echo:

            pushal y
            calls     #1,output
            acbl      x,#1,index,echo

            $exit_s

            .end Begin


    RUN FG911

    Enter number of times to print Yes!: 10
      Yes!  Yes!  Yes!  Yes!  Yes!  Yes!  Yes!  Yes!  Yes!  Yes!  Yes!
```

9.5

NUMERIC OUTPUT

Figure 9.12 shows a simplified procedure called *numeric output* that uses the base conversion technique shown in chapter 2. That is, we start with an integer in hex, which we convert to base ten by repeatedly dividing, each time replacing the old dividend by the new quotient until the quotient is zero. Each time we divide, we add the ASCII bias to the remainder and push the remainder into a stack. We use the INSTR byte row to do this, starting with the 80th byte. Once we have built up a complete row of remainders, we are not done. To avoid leading zeros, we copy the remainders into the beginning

FIGURE 9.12
Numeric-Output Procedure

```
;
;Ref.:   Figure 9.12 (Numeric output procedure)

        instr:   .blkb 80                        ;use to construct output
        ttname:  .ascid /sys$input:/
                 .even
        ttchan:  .blkw 1
        ttiosb:  .blkw 1
        ttiolen:
                 .word
                 .long
        outlen:  .blkl 1
        error:   blbs        r0,10$
                 $exit_s r0
10$:    rsb

        .entry numeric_output,^m<r6,r7,r9,r10,r11>

        $assign_s devnam = ttname chan = ttchan

        bsbw error

        movl    4(ap),r6                  ;get number to be printed
        movab   instr,r9                  ;init. r9 with no.-builder array
        addl2   #80,r9                    ;adjust for length
        clrl    outlen                    ;outlen will equal no. of digits

digit:
        clrl    r7                        ;set up quad for ediv
        ediv    #10,r6,r10,r11
        addl2   #48,r11                   ;adjust remainder w. ASCII bias
        cvtlb   r11,-(r9)                 ;push digit

        incl    outlen                    ;count digit
        movl    r10,r6                    ;get new dividend
        bneq    digit                     ;if quotient <> 0 , get next
digit
                                          ;else
        movl    outlen,r7                 ;get no. of digits
        movab   instr,r6                  ;get instr address

new_copy:

        movb    (r9)+,(r6)+               ;pop digit into instr
        sobgtr  r7,new_copy

        $qiow_s  efn=#1 chan=ttchan func=#io$_writevblk p1=instr p2=outlen

        bsbw    error

        $dassgn_s chan = ttchan

        ret

        .end
```

FIGURE 9.13
A Program with Numeric I/O

```
;
;Ref.:   Figure 9.13 (A program with numeric I/O)

         prompt:  .ascic /    Enter your age in years: /
         result:  .ascic <10><13><13>/Approximate no. of days you have lived:
         x:       .long

Begin:   .word

         pushal   prompt
         calls    #1,output                  ;prompt for age

         pushal   x
         calls    #1,numeric_input           ;get age

         mull2    #365,x                     ;compute days lived

         pushal   result
         calls    #1,output                  ;print explanation

         pushl    x
         calls    #1,numeric_output          ;print days

         $exit_s

         .end Begin


RUN FG913

         Enter your age in years: 21
Approximate no. of days you have lived:  7665
```

of INSTR, then print the remainders as the digits of the base ten number. Figure 9.13 illustrates how this new procedure is used in the program.

9.6
I/O PROCEDURE LIBRARIES

To simplify the use of the above procedures, we have put them into an I/O library. We call it BEGIN I/O. This library is given in Appendix C. Notice that each of the above procedures makes use of the same variables. This simplifies the use of these procedures.

A more advanced version of this library is also given in Appendix C. The more advanced version is used in later chapters to handle numbers in different bases. This is the familiar IO.MAR used by the I/O macros we have given so far.

Why bother treating I/O procedures at all, once a complete set of I/O macros is available? Up to now we have freely used the following macros:

write	(to print a string w/o a ⟨ret⟩)
writeln	(to print a string with a ⟨ret⟩)
writestring	(to print a string)
readstring	(to read a string)
writeval	(to print an integer)
readvar	(to read an integer)

These macros are built in accordance with the procedures in the I/O library. By treating the I/O procedures themselves, it becomes possible to modify the I/O macros later. It gives us fairly complete control of input and output. The challenge is to become comfortable with making changes in the I/O procedures. The challenge is to gain control of the strings sent to and from an I/O device.

9.7
SUMMARY

The emphasis in this chapter has been on methods of tailoring I/O to the needs of a programmer. Each of the procedures in this chapter can be enhanced and further changed to cultivate new I/O. Also, each procedure in this chapter was first developed as an *internal* procedure to speed up development. It was made external after it was found to be working correctly.

Perhaps it is still not apparent that both strings and numbers start off as ASCII codes inside the machine. When numbers are entered at a keyboard, they are taken as strings of ASCII codes. Once entered, a number must be built in terms of the codes that have been entered.

I/O between a terminal and a program thus becomes a matter of managing the bytes of strings. In showing how this is done, we started with I/O procedures in their simplest forms. It soon becomes obvious that these procedures can be enhanced. One of the more satisfying enhancements has to do with modifying the length of the input string.

We used a constant number of bytes to do this. We used this constant to specify the extent of the byte row in Figure 9.6:

```
x:
    .byte
    .blkb number of bytes
```

In addition, this constant becomes an argument in the list set up for the input procedure. This is done by using the following instruction (see Figure 9.6):

```
pushl #number of bytes
```

Finally, these I/O procedures should be clustered together into a procedure library simplifying the linking needed. This elementary I/O procedure library is given in Appendix C.

9.8
EXERCISES

1. What is the path that QIO uses called?
2. What does the $ASSIGN macro do?
3. What is the difference between the $OUTPUT macro and the $QIOW macro?
4. What variable is used only by the enhanced input procedure called by the program in Figure 9.6? That is, this variable is not used by the other procedures introduced in this chapter.
5. Give the meanings of the following acronyms:

   (a) QIO   (b) DEC

   (c) IRP   (d) VAX

   (e) IOSB   (f) ASCII

   (g) EFN

6. If *message* is a label for a string to be printed by the output procedure, then

   (a) How is the first byte of the message byte-row used?

   (b) How are the bytes after the first one used in the message byte-row?

7. Write an assembly language program that uses *only* procedures to do the

following:

(a) Obtain the user's name.

(b) Obtain the user's age in years.

(c) Compute the number of months, days, hours, minutes, seconds that the user has lived up to the beginning of the current year.

(d) Print out the message:

⟨name⟩, you have lived:

Months   Days   Hours   Minutes   Seconds

(e) Print the values below the solid line in the above message.

8. Give the enhanced input procedure used by the program in Figure 9.6. That is, enhance the procedure in Figure 9.1 so that it uses a variable INLEN, which gets its value from the argument list for the procedure.

9. Write a program that does the following:

(a) Uses the enhanced input procedure in exercise 8.

(b) Prompts for a two-sentence (160 bytes) description of the VAX-11.

(c) Prints a copy of the entered sentences.

9.9

LAB PROJECTS

1. Enhance the numeric output procedure so that it has a variable called BASE. Then set up the procedure to get the value for the BASE variable from the argument list for the procedure. Then write an assembly language program that prints out the first 20 natural numbers

1, 2, 3, . . . , 19, 20

in

(a) binary

(b) octal

(c) radix = nine

2. Enhance the numeric output procedure from Lab 1 so that it can print a number in hex. To do this, use the following steps:

(a) In Figure 9.12, get remainder from EDIV base, R6, R7, R10, R11. See if the remainder (new digit or R11) is greater than 9.

(b) If it is, then add 7 to the remainder.

(c) Then add 48 to take care of the ASCII bias.

(d) Save the digit the same way.

(e) Repeat step (a) until the quotient (R10) is zero.

Then write an assembly language program to print

(f) the first 20 naturals in base 10 and

(g) the first 20 naturals in hex.

9.10
REVIEW QUIZ

Indicate whether the following statements are true or false:

1. A channel is a communication path.
2. VAX-11 system macros have a $ prefix.
3. The $ASSIGN macro is used to assign values to procedure variables.
4. The I in QIO stands for Interface.
5. EFN stands for event flag.
6. A 6-digit number typed at a keyboard is taken by the VAX-11 as six separate integers.
7. The $OUTPUT macro volunteers a ⟨ret⟩ at the end of each string it prints.
8. $QIOW can be used to inhibit a ⟨ret⟩ after a string is printed.
9. All QIO on a VAX-11 does not depend on the use of a channel.
10. $QIOW does not depend on the use of a channel.

9.11
REFERENCE

Forsyth, R. S., *Pascal at Work and Play*. London: Chapman and Hall, 1982. p. 19.

10.
ASSEMBLY: AN INTRODUCTION

The assembly process can be regarded as one of establishing bindings between symbolic objects (i.e., symbolic instructions) and their values (the binary version).

—D. W. Barron, *Assemblers and Loaders*

10.0
AIMS

- Define the notion of *assembly*.
- Show the framework for a two-pass assembler.
- Give step-by-step procedures used by a two-pass assembler.
- Compare the use of macros in PDP-11 Macro-11 and VAX-11 Macro.

10.1
INTRODUCTION

We have yet to discuss the question of what actually happens at assembly time. The text has presented assembly programs and their companion ML (Machine Language) translations repeatedly but has not explored the intermediate steps by which an assembler translates a symbolic program to the machine level. This chapter tackles these intermediate assembly procedures (the assembly time process). That is, we want to see how the symbolic expressions of an assembly language program are translated to the ML level. We must therefore look at the steps needed to convert a source file written in assembly language to the machine readable, binary code.

10.2
WHAT IS AN ASSEMBLER?

An assembler is a program that assists a programmer in developing symbolic representations of machine-level programs. An assembler will take symbolic representations like

    addl2 r6, r7

and translate them into machine code to obtain

    57 56 C0

Typically, it takes several steps to complete such a translation before an executable module is built. This translation is also known as *program assembly*.

10.3
WHAT HAPPENS AT ASSEMBLY TIME?

What we call *assembly time* might also be called *binding time*, taking the cue from D. W. Barron's description of the *assembly process* quoted at the beginning of this chapter. At assembly time an assembler binds symbolic expressions to their corresponding numeric codes (for operators) and addresses (for labels).

There are two types of classical assemblers. They are distinguished by the number of times the assembler scans a source text in an effort to pair up labels with numeric addresses and to replace mnemonics like ADDl2 or MOVl with op codes. Two-pass assemblers are the most commonly used type, but a one-pass assembler is also possible. Both types rely on the use of a location counter to determine numeric addresses of labels. We consider the two-pass assembly method first.

10.3.1 A Two-Pass Assembler

First, we should examine the framework of the two passes:

Pass 1. Scan the source text; collect labels that have numeric addresses supplied by the location counter, which advances from line to line. Eventually, each label should appear by itself on a separate line. The location counter-value for a particular line containing a label (its definition) supplies a numeric address representing a memory location. Usually this is a virtual, relocatable address adjusted (relocated) later by a loader program.

Pass 2. Scan the source text a second time, line by line. During the second scan (pass), the assembler supplies op codes for mnemonics, using a predefined op code table. Each time a label is encountered, the symbol table constructed during the first pass supplies the companion numeric address. The end result of assembly is a preliminary ML module called an *object module*.

This method of assembly has been in use the longest, no doubt because it is very convenient. Why? The construction of a symbol table containing (label, numeric address) pairs is forced upon an assembler by the presence of *forward references*. That is, instruction operands often use symbols that are defined at the beginning of a line later in a program. A two-pass assembler continues scanning, only making a symbol table entry whenever a label has a corresponding numeric address.

Calingaert (1979, p. 14) explains why the two-pass method works: "Each symbol used in an operand field must also appear as a label." By *label* we mean a symbol followed by a ':' used at the beginning of a source text line to name that line. Once we have carried out a complete scan of the source text, we should have all the necessary labels with corresponding addresses that have been referenced as operands within instructions.

10.3.2 Procedure for Pass One

What follows is a more detailed rendition of the steps used in Pass 1. We use LC for Location Counter, Line for Line Counter. The procedure follows:

Procedure Symbol Table Builder (Pass 1):

VAR LC, Line: INTEGER;

Begin

    1. (LC) ← 0, (Line) ← 1

2. Get line from source code:

    2.1 If instruction is not a HALT
    THEN

        2.1.1 IF line contains a label and is in the symbol table, flag line with an error for *multiply defined symbol*
        ELSE
        Establish pair (label, (LC)) in symbol table

        2.1.2 (LC) ← (LC) + Instruction length

        2.1.3 (Line) ← (Line) + 1

    2.2 REPEAT SCAN LOOP (at step 2) UNTIL HALT is found

End Proc. (Pass 1).

10.3.3 Procedure for Pass Two

The next step is to do a complete translation of the source text. The step-by-step procedure follows:

Procedure Object Module Builder (Pass 2):

VAR LC, Line: INTEGER;

Begin

    1. (LC) ← 0, (Line) ← 1

    2. Get line from source code.

        2.1 If instruction is not a HALT,
        THEN construct corresponding ML line by checking

            2.1.1 If op code mnemonic is not defined in the assembler op code table,
            THEN flag line with error
            ELSE
            Obtain binary op code

            2.1.2 Replace any symbolic operands by finding corresponding numeric addresses in the symbol table from Pass 1.

            2.1.3 Construct complete ML line with

Line No.	Line Address	Length of Instr	Binary Op Code	Operand Address	Operand Address
	(from LC)		(from op code table)	(from sym table)	(from sym table)

2.1.4 (LC) ← (LC) + Instruction length

2.1.5 (Line) ← (Line) + 1

2.2 REPEAT Scan-Loop (at step 2) UNTIL HALT is found.

End Proc. (Pass 2).

10.3.4 Example: Assembly on a PLUS-4/16

To simplify interpretation of the two-pass assembler procedures, we illustrate them in terms of the hypothetical PLUS-4/16 computer. This machine is being featured this week at Bertha's Kitty Boutique in the dales near Lake Woebegon, Minnesota. This is the home of powdermilk biscuits, which has been sung about on The Prairie Home Companion by Garrison Keiler. Bertha's PLUS-4/16 is a 16-bit machine. Its 16-bit words can be used for addresses, instructions, and data. Bertha's PLUS-4/16 has a limited instruction set (see Table 10.1).

We illustrate assembly of the following PLUS-4/16 assembly language program using the two-pass procedure:

```
MAIN: ADD A, B
      HALT
A:    5
B:    177777
```

The two-pass rendition of this program is shown in Figure 10.1.
On a PDP-11,

```
ADD A, B
```

would entail the use of relative addressing with relative addresses computed in terms of the corresponding numeric addresses for *A* and *B* in the symbol table. The relative addresses would be stored in locations 000002 and 000004. Bertha's PLUS-4/16 does not have relative addressing. The ML code

```
06 000010 000012
```

just means add the contents of location 10 (octal) to location 12 (octal). This works like the immediate addressing mode on a VAX-11. Lake Woebegoners are expected to release their PLUS-4/16e (*e* = extended), which will have a relative addressing PC-mode as well as CMP and CMPB instructions.

TABLE 10.1
PLUS-4/16 Opcode Table

Mnemonic	Opcode	Explanation
MOV	01	Load word-S to word-D
MOVB	21	Load byte-S to byte-D
ADD	06	Add word-S to word-D
ADDB	26	Add byte-S to byte-D
ZAP	02	Change all 0-bits of word-D to 1
ZAPB	22	Change all 0-bits of byte-D to 1
HALT	000000	Halt execution, not system!

Legend:
S: Contents of Source
D: Contents of Destination
word: 16 bits
byte: 8 bits

10.3.5 What Happens after Assembly?

Before a complete, executable machine program can be built, two more programs come into play. The object module addresses assigned to labels during the second pass are not necessarily the final, physical addresses. In addition, one object module may reference others. For example, we might use a subroutine call to a routine external to a given source file. Unresolved references to external object modules are handled by a linker program. The required modules are linked in, or brought together with the original object module to build an expanded ML file. The linker program does not deal with the problem of relocatable addresses, changing virtual addresses to physical memory addresses at which the final ML coded can be inserted.

The output from the linker program is a load module that usually still has relocatable addresses. A second program called a loader takes care of producing the final ML code, which can be loaded and executed. The steps leading from the source module to the final executable module are shown in Figure 10.2.

It turns out that the two logically separate linking and loading routines can be combined into one program called a linker/loader.

10.3.6 One-Pass Assemblers

D. W. Barron (1978, p. 49) suggests that the one-pass idea did not flourish at the time it was introduced in the mid-1950s because ''the classical two pass assembler commanded the sort of respect customarily accorded to the

FIGURE 10.1
Graphical Interpretation of a Limited Two-Pass Assembler

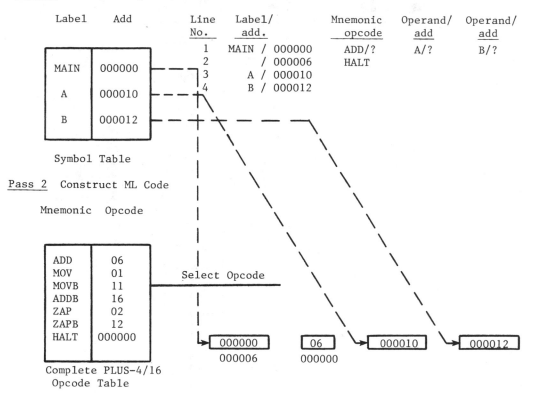

Pass 1 Construct Symbol/Add Table

Label	Add	Line No.	Label/ add.	Mnemonic opcode	Operand/ add	Operand/ add
		1	MAIN / 000000	ADD/?	A/?	B/?
MAIN	000000	2	/ 000006	HALT		
A	000010	3	A / 000010			
B	000012	4	B / 000012			

Symbol Table

Pass 2 Construct ML Code

Mnemonic   Opcode

ADD	06
MOV	01
MOVB	11
ADDB	16
ZAP	02
ZAPB	12
HALT	000000

Complete PLUS-4/16
Opcode Table

Select Opcode

| 000000 | | 06 | | 000010 | | 000012 |
| 000006 | | 000000 | | | | |

Legend:

------->   Select label address from symbol table
———————>   Select ML opcode corresponding to mnemonic

Old Testament.'' The original idea for a one-pass assembler came from D. J. Wheeler.

Barron (1978, pp. 48–49) reduces the problem of assembly to binding. Binding occurs later in a two-pass system. There are delays in binding symbols (labels) to numeric addresses whenever labels referenced in a symbolic instruction are defined in later lines of an assembly language program. This happens with labels A and B (but not with MAIN) in the PLUS-4/16 assembly in Figure 10.1. To get around this in a one-pass system, a linked list is set

FIGURE 10.2
Steps from Source to Final Machine Language Code

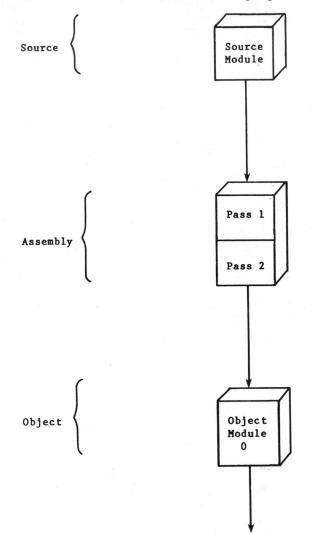

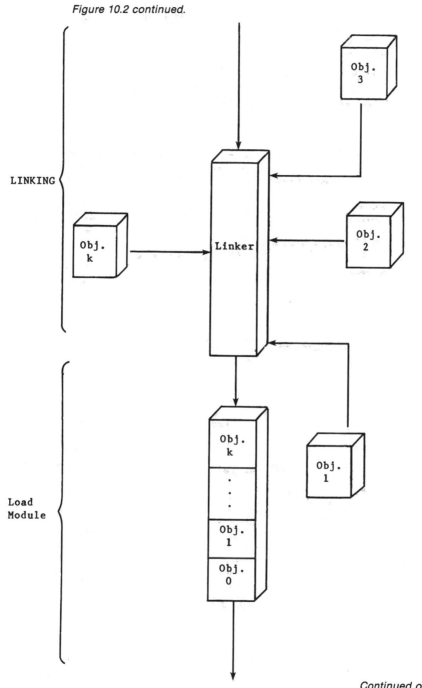

Figure 10.2 continued.

LINKING

Load
Module

Continued on following page.

Figure 10.2 continued.

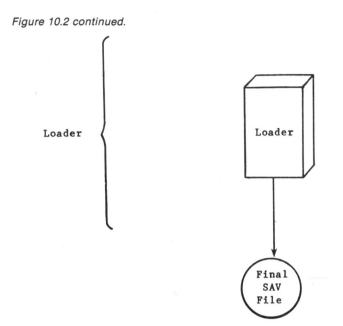

up (Barron calls it a fix-up table). Pointers tell where to replace an undefined label later with the true value of the label, if it is found.

10.3.7 Assembly on a VAX-11

Digital Equipment Corporation (DEC) provides few details about how its VAX-11 macro language assembles a source text. DEC (1982, p. 203) does say, however, that "the VAX-11 macro language is similar to the PDP-11 macro language, but its instruction mnemonics correspond to the VAX native instructions."

The PDP-11 assembly language is called MACRO-11. It is a two-pass assembler. It includes the features of a classical two-pass assembler plus a provision for macro processing. MACRO-11 incorporates a provision for macro processing as part of its first pass. The key task of its macro processing is text insertion. During the first pass, if MACRO-11 encounters a macro call like

    writeln ⟨aha!⟩

it looks for the corresponding macro text in any user-defined macro libraries or in its own system macro library. The source text is expanded by the corresponding macro definition. Logically, a macro processor is the front end to a macro assembler (see Figure 10.3).

FIGURE 10.3
Macro Assembly

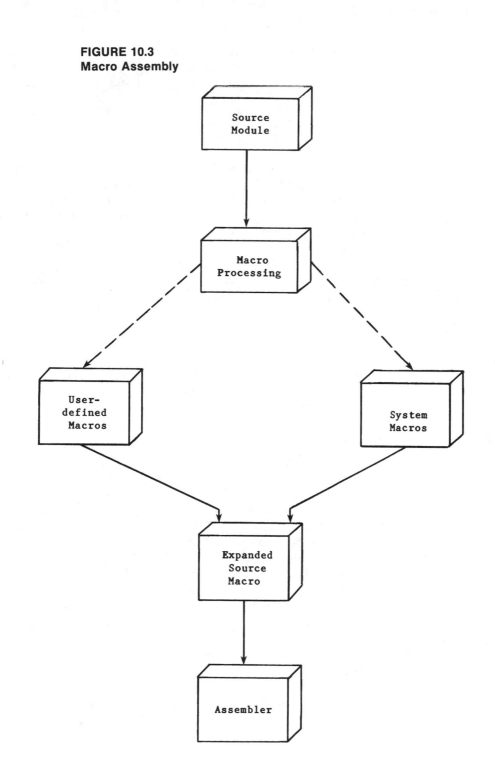

VAX-11 differs sharply from MACRO-11 in terms of macros. MACRO-11 requires an .MCALL directive (to list macros to be used) at the head of a source text that uses macros. At least one macro is always used, a .EXIT in the .MCALL list:

```
.MCALL   .EXIT
```

This appears *before* the first executable instruction in the source text. It is not necessary to use the .MCALL directive in a VAX-11 macro program. MACRO-11 requires that macro definitions like the one for DRAWTRI-ANGLE in chapter 1 be given at the beginning of the source text, before the first executable instruction. In VAX-11 macro, a macro definition of the form

```
.MACRO T
⟨definition⟩
.endm T
```

can appear *after* the first executable instruction, provided it appears *before* the first time it is called within the source text. In general, VAX-11 macro is more flexible than MACRO-11 in its guidelines for the usage of macros.

10.4

SUMMARY

This chapter discusses the procedures used in a classical two-pass assembler. A first pass wrestles with unresolved forward references. This delays binding labels in forward references to their numeric addresses. Collecting (label, address) pairs inside a symbol table resolves this problem. It also delays assembly of source code until a complete symbol table has been produced. Complete assembly of the source code occurs during a second complete scan of the source text. A predefined op code table and a newly constructed symbol table make this possible. This method of assembly is both orderly and easy to implement.

The key notion tied to assembly is binding, a concept introduced by Barron. That is, source symbols are *bound* to numeric content at assembly time.

VAX-11 macro is similar to MACRO-11, which is a two-pass assembler. Both allow for macro processing, but in different ways.

10.5

EXERCISES

1. In terms of PLUS-4/16 (without relative addressing), and using Table 7.1 and the method shown in Figure 7.1, give a graphical interpretation of the assembly of

    (a) MAIN: ZAP A

                ZAPB B

                HALT

        A: 000000

        B: 177777

Note: Assume (LC) is initialized at 000000.

    (b) MAIN: ADD A, B

                MOVB B, C

                ADDB C, D

                HALT

        A: 5

        B: 177770

        C: 25

        D: 25

Note: Assume (LC) is initialized at 001000.

    (c) MAIN: MOV A, B

                ADDB A, B

                HALT

        A: 12777

        B: 10001

        MOV: 13

    (d) MAIN: ZAP A

                ZAPB B

                ADDB A, B

                HALT

        A: 10357

```
B:      45
C:      111111
```

2. In terms of the newer PLUS-4/16e (with relative addressing), use the technique shown in Figure 10.1 to assemble the program in part (a) of the preceding exercise.

3. Using the technique shown in Figure 10.1, show the MACRO-11 two-pass assembly of the following:

Note: The line with the .MCALL does not become part of the object module.

```
        .MCALL   .EXIT
MAIN:   NEG  A
        NEG  B
        COMB  C
        MOVB  B, X
        MOVB  C, Y
        ADD  X, Y
A:      1
B:      377
C:      177000
X:      0
Y:      0
        .END  MAIN
```

4. Elementary flowcharting is built around the five symbols shown below:

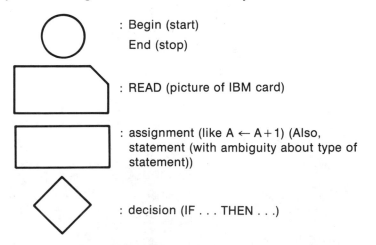

: Begin (start)
End (stop)

: READ (picture of IBM card)

: assignment (like A ← A+1) (Also, statement (with ambiguity about type of statement))

: decision (IF . . . THEN . . .)

 : print (torn piece of paper)

For example, an IF . . . THEN . . . ELSE . . . statement can be represented with

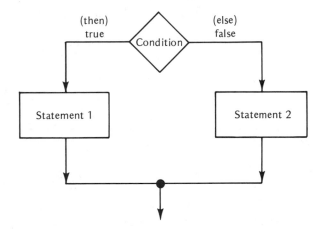

The arrows are used to represent flow-of-control during processing. In the above rendition of IF/THEN/ELSE, statement A and/or B could also be an IF/THEN/ELSE statement, depending on the program. Give flowchart interpretations of

(a) The first-pass procedure in section 10.3.2.

(b) The second-pass procedure in section 10.3.3.

10.6

LAB PROJECTS

1. Write a program in a higher-level language to carry out the procedure in the first pass of a two-pass assembler. Your program should

   (a) Allow for assembly language programs up to 10 lines long.

   (b) Allow for 0, 1, and 2 operand instructions.

   (c) Allow only single-letter labels for operands.

   (d) Distinguish between 'A' (forward reference) and 'A:' (definition of label), for example.

(e) Use a string variable like A$(I) = 'A:' to determine memory location M(I). The subscript I can be used as the LC.

Produce a symbol table using the PLUS-4/16 program in exercise 10.7.1(a), 10.7.1(c), and 10.7.1(d).
To simplify this program, load each part of a line into a separate string array variable. A two-dimensional array would be helpful.

2. Write a program in a higher-level language that uses the program in lab 1 as a routine to produce a list module. Print out this module.

10.7
REVIEW QUIZ

Indicate whether the following statements are true or false:

1. In VAX-11 Macro, macro definitions can appear immediately before the first corresponding macro calls.
2. MACRO-11 is a one-pass assembler.
3. Logically, a macro processor is the front end of a macro assembler.
4. An assembler uses the PC to assign numeric values to symbolic addresses.
5. An assembler defines operand symbols in terms of labels.
6. Source text symbols are recognizable in terms of a point (.) suffix.
7. Source text labels are recognizable in terms of a semicolon (;) suffix.
8. One-pass assemblers are commonly used.
9. The addresses supplied by VAX-11 macro are relocatable.
10. Symbol tables are necessary to take care of forward references.

10.8
REFERENCES

Barron, D. W. *Assemblers and Loaders*. New York: North-Holland, 1978. Take this book to bed. It can be read in one evening.

Calingaert, P. *Assemblers, Compilers, and Program Translation*. Rockville, Md.: Computer Science Press, 1979.

Digital Equipment Corporation. *VAX Software Handbook*. Maynard, Mass., 1982.

Digital Equipment Corporation. *PDP-11 MACRO-11 Language Reference Manual*. Order No. (AA-V027A-TC). Maynard, Mass., March 1983. This is the version 5 manual.

11.
ARRAYS

*Democritus, although he did not name "things" as such, but
supposed "atoms" only, seems to have spoken of them as such
because although they may be separated out, they are not damaged
nor destroyed, nor cut up into parts, but retain in themselves forever
a perfect solidity. Since therefore from these, being in
correspondence, all things seem to come together and be born. . . .*
—Vitruvius on Architecture, Book II, circa 27 B.C.

11.0
AIMS

- Introduce the concept of arrays and array selectors.
- Distinguish between arrays of characters and arrays of numbers (integers) in terms of string- and numberhandling.
- Focus on stringhandling.
- Introduce methods of sorting and searching in terms of strings.
- Introduce string concatenations.
- Introduce an AL program to handle extended precision products.

11.1
INTRODUCTION

Hearkening back to the bricks of Vitruvius's buildings to open a chapter on
arrays is stretching things a bit. He, in turn, hearkens back to Democritus

to talk about the building blocks of the universe. Even so, analogies abound between the structures underpinning Democritus's universe, Vitruvius's buildings and our uses of arrays in programming.

In some ways, array elements are to programmers what the "perfect solidity" of atoms was to Democritus. Just as the tissue of the world can have its atoms separated out, so too arrays can have their array elements separated out—*selected* with adequate *selectors* (Niklaus Wirth's term) or *pointers*. It is easy to think of array elements as building blocks, perhaps like the sturdy bricks of a building engineered by Vitruvius.

Again, the atoms of the universe and the bricks of Vitruvius's buildings *aggregate* —that is, come together—to form useful structures. Aho et al. (1983, p. 13) speak of one-dimensional arrays (rows of elements) as "the simplest aggregating mechanism in Pascal and most other programming languages." In the computer, the cells of an array are memory locations that are contiguous. Arrays in assembler programming are put together by setting aside contiguous bytes or words or multiples of words (doublewords, quadwords, octawords). We select individual cells by starting with a pointer that is assigned the addresses of an end cell. Then, according to certain criteria, we slide the pointer sequentially from cell to cell to select the one(s) we want. We can also access array elements *directly* rather than sequentially by adjusting the value of the pointer beforehand.

We begin the aggregation with a declaration of a little "universe" with, for example,

        L: .BLKW 1024

which puts the symbolic address L at the beginning of 1024 or 1K contiguous word locations in memory.

11.2

SOME PROGRAMMING TOOLS

We set up one-dimensional arrays in many ways. Here are some common ways of doing this.

- .WORD 0, 0, 0, 0, 0, 0, 0, 0, 0, 0 reserves 10 contiguous words.
- .BLKW 10 does the same thing as tool 1.
- .BYTE 0, 0 reserves 2 contiguous bytes.
- .BLKB 2 does the same thing as method 3.

Another useful method is INDEX MODE. In the little AL segment shown in Figure 11.1, the address of the first array element is the address of L (called the base address) plus the content of R6 (called the index) or

$$\#L + (R6) = base + index$$

or, in the initial tap of the L array, it is

$$\#L + 0 = L_0$$

since R6 has been cleared before we enter the TAP-loop.

Looking at Figure 11.1, you might wonder what would be printed, how many and which bytes would have their contents exhibited. This will depend on the value of the variable LIMIT. The completion of the fragment in Figure 11.1 is left as an exercise. You might also wonder how we go about selecting portions of the array shown. Even more important, you might wonder what mechanism we could use to determine when we have reached the end of the array, when the pointer has slipped past the last byte. This is easy. Append a byte following the last array byte and give the appended byte a label (call it EDGE). That is, use

```
        ⋮
L:      .BYTE 65, 66, 67, 68, 69, 70

        ⋮
        .ASCII /BELLS, BELLS, BELLS, THE TINTINNABULATIONS OF THE/
        .BYTE 7, 7, 7, 7, 7, 7, 7, 7, 7, 7   ; = BELL[10]
EDGE:   .BYTE
        .EVEN
        .END MAIN
```

Then, each time we advance the selector (array pointer), compare it with #EDGE to determine when we have reached the edge. Rather than use a loop like the one shown in Figure 11.1, it would be better to allow processing in the loop to continue as long as the array pointer has not reached the EDGE (what is commonly known as a sentinel or flag). This enhancement of Figure 11.1 is also treated later in an exercise.

Another tool useful in array-handling is to develop a device (mechanism) that allows us to select a particular array element. Assume, for ex-

FIGURE 11.1
Tapping an Array of Bytes

```
;
;Ref.:      Figure 11.1 (Tapping an Array of Bytes)
;
;TASK:      SET UP A LABEL L AS AN ARRAY-SELECTOR AND A LABEL X FOR AN ARRAY
;           WHICH CAN SERVE AS ´EXPRESS´ IN SENDING BYTES OF L CONTAINING ASCII
;           CODES, SELECTIVELY, TO A PRINT PROCEDURE.
;
BELL       = 7
;
L:          .BYTE 65,66,67,68,69,70
            .BYTE 48,49,50,51,52,53
            .BYTE 97,98,99,100,101,102
            .BYTE BELL[10]
            .ASCII/EDGAR ALLEN POE´S BELL´S:/
            .ASCII/BELLS,BELLS,BELLS,THE TINTINNABULATIONS OF THE/
            .BYTE BELL[20]
;
X:          .BYTE 1,0                    ;EXPRESS ARRAY
LIMIT:      .BYTE
;
            .ENTRY BEGIN,0
                    .
                    .
                    .
;           <PROCESS: SET LIMIT USED BELOW>
                    .
                    .
                    .

;           <TAP PART OF L-ARRAY>
            CLRL      R6                 ;SET UP ARRAY-POINTER
ARRAY_TAP:
            MOVB      L(R6),X+1          ;COPY L-BYTE INTO X-ARRAY
            PUSHAB    X                  ;EXPRESS:
                                         ;SET UP STACK FRAME,
                                         ;BEGIN ´EXPRESSING´ COPY
                                         ;OF L-BYTE TO PRINTER
            CALLS     #1,WRITESTR        ;PRINT CHARACTER
            CMPL      LIMIT,R6           ;CHECK FOR LIMIT
            BNEQ      ARRAY_TAP          ;IF LIMIT NOT REACHED
                                         ;THEN CONTINUE TAPPING ARRAY
                                         ;ELSE <BEGIN NEW ACTION>
                    .
                    .
                    .
            $EXIT_S
            .END BEGIN                   ;IDENTIFY TRANSFER ADDRESS
```

ample, that we have an array of bytes with

```
L:   .BYTE 45, 45, 46, 45 [3]
     .BYTE 46, 45, 46, 46, 45, 46, 46
     .BYTE 45, 46 [5], 45, 46
     .BYTE 46, 45, 46, 45, 46, 45, 45
```

where 45 is the ASCII code for a hyphen (or short dash) and 46 the code for a dot (the combination of dashes and dots in this array gives the Morse Code for a familiar word). Suppose, in addition, we want to get at the fifth byte of the array or the

```
#L + 4th
```

byte (#L points to the *first* byte). Then VAX-11 macro lends itself to this problem in each of the following cases:

Case 1: Try using the index mode in terms of a register Rn:

base address		(index) register		Effective Address
L	+	(Rn)	=	Address of operand

That is, use R6, for example, in

```
CLRL  R6
ADDL2 #4, R6
MOVB  L(R6), ⟨destination⟩
```

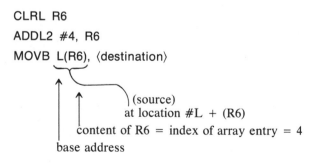

(source)
at location #L + (R6)
content of R6 = index of array entry = 4
base address

Case 2: The above steps can be condensed into

```
CLRL  R6
MOVB  L+4 (R6), ⟨destination⟩
```

0 = index of array entry ⎱ source at
displacement = L + 4   ⎰ location #L + 4 + 0

Levy and Eckhouse (1980, p. 80) emphasize that the index mode is "one of the most powerful addressing features of the VAX-11." What is hidden in the above examples is a mechanism supplied by this addressing mode. That is, the base address points to an array of elements, each of the same type. In the above example, each element of the *L*-array is a byte. Suppose, however, that we have an array

```
A:   .BLKL 20
```

of 20 longwords, and that we use R6 as the index register. If we initialize R6 with a 4, then VAX-11 macro computes the *effective* address of the array element being selected with

```
L (R6)
```

by

$$L + (R6) * \text{(no. of bytes of each element)}$$
$$= L + (R6) * 4$$
$$= L + 4 * 4$$
$$= L + 16$$

That is, we have the situation shown in Figure 11.2.

Case 3: An alternative to the above two methods is suggested next in terms of two registers, R6 and R7, which are used as pointers of separate arrays:

```
MOVAB L+4, R6
MOVAB ⟨destination⟩, R7
MOVB (R6), (R7)
```

Case 4: Yet another way to tap one of the bytes of an array is to use relative PC addressing. We can suggest a couple of ways to do this:

```
MOVB B^L+4, B^ ⟨destination address⟩
```

or

Case 5:

```
MOVB L+4, ⟨destination address⟩
```

For example, if we assume $X + 1$ points to the destination, then we would

FIGURE 11.2
The Index Mode with Arrays

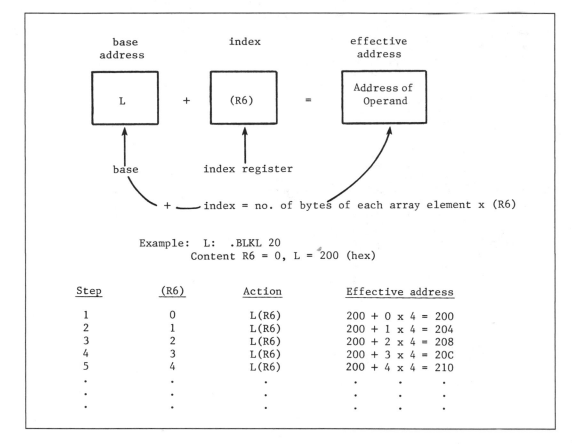

write

      MOVB B^L+4, B^X+1

or

      MOVB L+4, X+1

Case 6 (Displacement Mode): Unlike the index mode, the displacement mode relies on the use of a register to hold the base address (the beginning address of a array). Since management of the displacement is left to the programmer, great care must be used in addressing array elements that are multiples of bytes. The *effective address* (the one used to select an array element) is computed as the sum of a displacement supplied by the programmer and the base address. For example, if *L* is an array of bytes like the one in Figure 11.1 and the label *X* is used to reference the displace-

FIGURE 11.3
Ways to Tap an Array of Bytes

```
;
;REF.:       FIGURE 11.3 (WAYS TO TAP A ARRAY OF BYTES)
;
L:           .BYTE 45,45,46,45[3]
             .BYTE 46,45,46,46,45,46,46
             .BYTE 45,46[5],45,46
             .BYTE 46,45,46,45,46,45,45
X:           .BYTE 1,0
;
             .ENTRY BEGIN,0
;
CASE_1:      CLRL R6
             ADDL2 #4,R6              ;SHIFT PTR TO 5TH BYTE OF
             MOVB L(R6),X+1          ;ARRAY L & COPY BYTE TO 2ND BYTE OF X
             PUSHAB X               ;SET UP X FOR PRINTING WITH
             CALLS #1,WRITESTR      ;WRITESTR PROCEDURE
;
CASE_2:      CLRL R6                 ;SET UP ARRAY PTR &
             MOVB L+4(R6),X+1       ;COPY 5TH BYTE OF L TO 2ND BYTE OF X
             PUSHAB X
             CALLS #1,WRITESTR
;
CASE_3:      MOVAB L+4,R6           ;SET UP L+4 PTR IN R6
             MOVAB X+1,R7           ;SET UP X+1 PTR IN R7 &
             MOVB (R6),(R7)         ;COPY 5TH BYTE OF L TO 2ND BYTE OF X
             PUSHAB X               ;GET READY TO
             CALLS #1,WRITESTR      ;SHOW RESULT OF COPYING L+4TH BYTE
;
CASE_4:      MOVB B^L+4,B^X+1       ;USE RELATIVE ADDRESSING FOR
             PUSHAB X               ;COPYING & THEN
             CALLS #1,WRITESTR      ;PRINT IT!
;
CASE_5:      MOVB L+4,X+1           ;USE RELATIVE ADDRESSING &
             PUSHAB X               ;SET UP FOR
             CALLS #1,WRITESTR      ;PRINTING
;
             $EXIT_S
             .END BEGIN
```

ment (try $X = 4$), then

```
        MOVAB L, R6
        MOVB #4, X
        MOVB X(R6), ⟨destination⟩
```

where

$$\text{effective address} = X + (R6)$$
$$= X + \#L$$
$$= 4 + \#L$$

The first five cases just given are illustrated in Figure 11.3. We take care of implementation of the displacement mode mechanism in case 6 later in an exercise.

11.3

ANOTHER TOOL

Suppose, for example, that we want to clear the fourth byte of the array L in Figure 11.1. Try

```
CLRB L+3    ;This is relative addressing, again!
```

Why do we increment L by 3 to clear the *fourth* byte of the L-array?

11.4

TWO WAYS TO HANDLE ARRAY INDICES

```
            Instead of:                    Use:

            CLRL R6                        MOVL #L, R6
     LOOP:  ADDL2 L(R6),SUM         LOOP:  ADDL2 (R6)+,SUM
            ADDL2 #1, R6                   CMPL R6, LIMIT
            CMPL R6,LIMIT                  BNEQ LOOP
            BNEQ LOOP              ;
     L:     .BLKL 90               L:     .BLKL 90
     LIMIT: .LONG ⟨VALUE⟩          LIMIT: .LONG ⟨VALUE⟩
```

That is, by using the *autoincrement mode* after initializing R6 with the base address L, we can move across the array without having to add 1 to R6 each time to point to the next array element. In the autoincrement mode the assembler takes into account the nature of the array elements. It will increment by 4 in this example, since the array elements are longwords. Although the index mode is a bit awkward to use at times, autoincrementing is a handy device in dealing with arrays.

11.5

HOW TO UTILIZE ARRAYS

Initially, we need to deal with the problem of loading an array we wish to use. This can be handled directly by the programmer with, for example, the following declaration:

```
L:    .WORD −34, −33, −12, −2, −2, 0, 0, 1, 2
      .WORD 45, 36, 456, 7216, 7777, 7676
```

or we can write a routine to load an array from a terminal in much the same way we would do this, for example, in Pascal or BASIC:

```
;
LIST:      .BLKL 1000
COUNT:     .LONG ⟨VALUE⟩
PROMPT:    .ASCIC /YOUR ENTRY?/
;

            ⋮
           .ENTRY BEGIN, 0
           MOVAB LIST, R6        ;Init. R6 with base address
BUMP:      PUSHAB PROMPT         ;set up stack frame to
           CALLS #1, WRITESTR    ;print prompt
           PUSHAL (R6)+          ;set up stack frame to get array
           CALLS #1, READVAL     ;element from terminal
           AOBLSS #⟨value⟩,COUNT,BUMP

            ⋮
           ⟨PROCESS⟩

            ⋮
           $EXIT_S
           .END BEGIN
```

The trick is to determine ahead of time how many array elements will be put into an array. It is always a good idea to allow some slack in the array size, assuming the number of array entries will vary. That is, allow for slightly larger array than what you might otherwise use.

11.5.1 Echo-printing

Next, we have to contend with the problem of echo-printing an array we have loaded. We can do this by following the above loop with a routine like the one that follows:

```
                    :
        PUSHAB ECHO              ;say what
        CALLS #1, WRITESTR       ;it is!
        MOVAB LIST,R6            ;initialize R6 with the array base
                                 ;address
LOOP:   PUSHL (R6)+              ;set up stack frame to
        CALLS #1, WRITEVAL       ;print entry
        AOBLSS #⟨value⟩,COUNT,LOOP
```

This echo-print will output the list from the first "atom" to the last one (the natural order).

11.5.2 Puzzle

How would we write the above echo-print routine so that the elements of the array LIST would be echo-printed in reverse order?

Hint: When we complete the array-load loop (we call it the BUMP-loop), what word address is pointed to by the array pointer R6? (This is a measure of your assembly-computing maturity!)

11.5.3 How to Load an Array of Characters

It is possible to set up an array of ASCII characters with the following declaration:

```
CH:   .ASCII/    /  ;Array of contiguous characters
```

as opposed to the typical array of numbers:

```
NO:   .BYTE 0, 0, 0, . . . , 0   ;Array of contiguous characters
```

Two features of this new data structure should be noted. First, before trying to use this structure, take a close look at the storage allocation set up by the .ASCII directive. Since only character codes are "expected" between the / . . ./, contiguous bytes, *not* contiguous words or longwords or some other byte multiple, are set aside by the .ASCII directive for its string of characters (or character array). Second, the number of spaces (blanks) between the slanted lines (/) following the .ASCII represent the number of contiguous bytes associated (set aside) with the label CH.

FIGURE 11.4
Procedure to Build a Character Array

```
Procedure Char. Array Builder:

VAR   Ch:  ARRAY OF BYTES;

      I, Edge:  INTEGER;

BEGIN

1.  Initialize Ch-array, Edge- at byte following Ch-array, I = 0

2.  Begin building character array:

    2.1  Get character

    2.2  Ch[I] <----- character

    2.3  Advance Ch-selector:  I <--- I + 1

    2.4  REPEAT Ch-loop at 2.1 UNTIL

         Edge is reached.

END Procedure
```

To load the CH-character array, use the procedure given in Figure 11.4.

11.5.4 MacEwen's Method

Suppose we want to fill a string array with the ASCII codes for the digits stripped off an integer. This is sometimes useful. For example, suppose we want to test the randomness of the individual digits of a sequence of numbers. Again, suppose we want to isolate certain digits of a number (the leading digits of an identity number, for example).

To do this we use a method suggested by G. H. MacEwen (1980, pp. 71–72), which has a measure of elegance. Suppose, for example, we try stripping the digits from right to left from the Fibonacci number 1597. The steps used to do this are shown in Figure 11.5.

It is fairly easy to interpret the logic of this method in terms of an assembly program, as illustrated in Figure 11.6.

This VAX-11 macro representation of MacEwen's method (a digit-strip, string-filled algorithm) is a bit crude. Several improvements can make this program more useful (and elegant):

FIGURE 11.5
MacEwen's Method: Stripping Digits

Step 1. Compute X = 1597/10;
Step 2. Isolate the remainder;
Step 3. Adjust for the ASCII bias of the remainder by adding 48 (decimal) to the remainder;
Step 4. Tack the resulting ASCII code onto the righthand side of the string array;
Step 5. Repeat steps 1-4 until array index is zero.

If you follow this procedure, you will discover

Pass:		1		2		3		4
No.	Step	Result	Step	Result	Step	Result	Step	Result
1	1597/10		159/10		15/10		1/10	
2	7		9		5		1	
3	55		57		53		49	
4	TACK: /	55/	TACK: /	5755	TACK: /	535755/	TACK:	/49535755/
5	Repeat		Repeat		Repeat		Stop!	

1. Try moving the CH-address into R8 and use the autodecrement mode to manage the selection of bytes within the CH-string. In effect, eliminate

   SUBL2 #1, R8

2. Use a READ routine to submit an integer to be "sliced up" by this program. Try using the READVAL procedure given earlier. This change would entail our prompting for one or more integers, which we would take from a keyboard, and move to an array. Try

   X: BLKQ   (array of quadwords)

3. Allow the user to select the digits to be stripped off. The second of the above suggestions entails the use of an array of quadwords. Why?

In the program in Figure 11.6, we have made special use of registers R6 and R7, which are adjacent longwords inside the central processor of the VAX-11. Taken together, these two registers make up a quadword. Even though the integer 1597 fits comfortably inside R6, the EDIV (Extended

FIGURE 11.6
Implementation of MacEwen's Method

```
;Ref.: Figure 11.6 (Implementation of MacEwen's Method)
;
;TASK:    STRIP THE DIGITS FROM AN INTEGER AND STORE THEM (THEIR
;         ASCII CODES) SEPARATELY INSIDE A STRING ARRAY FOR FUTURE
;         MANIPULATION.
;
SPACE     =32
;
CH:       .BYTE 0
          .ASCII/
LEN_CH    =. - CH - 1
Q:        .LONG                   ;Q=QUOTIENT
R:        .LONG                   ;R=REMAINDER
;
          .ENTRY   BEGIN,0   ;
                                  ;USE WRITE & WRITELN MACROS TO
                                  ;SET UP HEADING
                                  ;
          WRITE<--------------------------------------->
          WRITELN
          WRITE<SEPARATED DIGITS OF 1597:>
          WRITELN
          WRITELN
          TAB<4>
                                  ;
          MOVZWL   #1597,R6       ;USE R6 TO HOLD NO. WHICH WE
                                  ;'TAKE APART'(WHOSE DIGITS WE
                                  ;WILL STRIP OFF & STORE IN
                                  ;THE CH-STRING
          CLRL     R7             ;CLEAR R7 AND USE THIS REGISTER
                                  ;AS THE SECOND LONG WORD IN THE
                                  ;QUAD WORD USED BY THE EDIV
                                  ;(EXTENDED DIVIDE) INSTRUCTION
          MOVL     #12,R8         ;SET UP R8 AS A COUNTER
                                  ;TO KEEP TRACK OF HOW MANY BYTES
                                  ;OF THE CH-ARRAY HAVE BEEN USED
TACK:     EDIV     #10,R6,Q,R     ;WHAT THIS INSTRUCTION DOES:
                                  ;
                                  ;(1)DIVIDES NO. IN R6 BY 10
                                  ;(2)PUTS QUOTIENT IN Q
                                  ;(3)PUTS REMAINDER IN R
                                  ;EXAMPLE:
                                  ;  NO.    Q      R
                                  ;------------------
                                  ;  233    23     3
                                  ;
          ADDL2    #48,R          ;ADJUST ASCII BIAS OF REMAINDER
          CVTLB    R,CH(R8)       ;CONVERT R(A LONG WORD) TO
                                  ;BYTE-LENGTH OPERAND & PUT IN CH-ARRAY
          MOVL     Q,R6           ;OLD NO. IN R6 <-- QUOTIENT
          CLRL     R7             ;SAFETY MEASURE: CLEAR HIGH LONGWORD
                                  ;OF THE R6,R7 COMBINATION
          SUBL2    #1,R8          ;DECREMENT COUNTER
```

Figure 11.6 continued.

```
        MOVB      #SPACE,CH(R8)   ;PUT 2 SPACES BETWEEN THE ASCII
                                  ;CODES IN THE CH-ARRAY:
        SUBL2     #1,R8           ;
        MOVB      #SPACE,CH(R8)   ;
        SUBL2     #1,R8           ;DECREMENT COUNTER,AGAIN!
        BNEQ      TACK            ;REPEAT TACK-LOOP
                                  ;UNTIL R8-COUNTER = 0
        MOVB      #LEN_CH,CH      ;PUT LENGTH OF CH-ARRAY (LESS 1)
                                  ;INTO THE FIRST BYTE OF THIS ARRAY
                                  ;(IN OTHER WORDS, SIMULATE A
                                  ;.ASCIC SET-UP, WHICH WE CAN USE
                                  ;IN THE WRITESTR-PROCEDURE)
        PUSHAB CH                 ;SET UP STACK FRAME TO
        CALLS #1,WRITESTR         ;PRINT THE CONTENTS OF THE CH-ARRAY
                                  ;(IN EFFECT, EXHIBIT THE SEPARATED
                                  ;DIGITS OF OUR NUMBER)
;
        $EXIT_S
        .END BEGIN


RUN FG11.6

-----------------------------------------
SEPARATED DIGITS OF 1597:

                        1   5   9   7
```

DIVide) instruction calls for a quadword for its dividend. Although we only reference R6 (a longword) in the dividend spot in

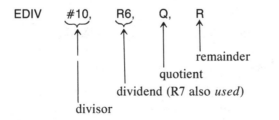

the machine will use the bits of R7 to compute the quotient and remainder of this operation.

The R6 + R7 quadword in the EDIV instruction in the above program can be eliminated if some *X*-array of quadwords becomes a direct supplier of dividends in the EDIV instruction. This would tend to simplify the program in Figure 11.6. The hidden feature in the R6 + R7 quadword mechanism is its efficiency. Using an array *X* of quadwords to supply dividends in the EDIV instruction is less efficient than using registers.

If we choose to scrap the R6 + R7 quadword mechanism suggested in the above program, then we need to set up

```
X:  .BLKL    (array of longwords)
```

to hold dividends we take in from a keyboard. The efficiency of these methods can be determined later, once we have a random number generator as a supplier of dividends. We can then use the internal clock of the machine and a fairly unbiased supplier of dividends to play with the efficiency of the above two methods.

11.5.5 Sorting an Array of Characters

Sorting problems offer yet another hunting ground for arrays. In this section we tackle the problem of sorting an array of characters. Initially, we will illustrate how a bubblesort procedure can be implemented to handle this problem. Later in the exercises, we will look at alternative sorting procedures both in terms of characters and in terms of numbers. A bubblesort procedure to handle a character array (call it L) is shown in Figure 11.7.

Suppose, for example, we have the following character array:

```
L:  .ASCIC/Leibniz lived in Hannover./
```

The program that follows implements the above bubblesort procedure in terms of this L-array (see Figure 11.8).

This program is specialized in terms of just one string. We can enhance this program so that a user can load the L-array from a keyboard, for example. We leave this as an exercise.

The swap section of the above program makes use of the index mode. The entire sort pivots around three comparisons, especially the third one:

```
CMPL  R8, #NEXT−1
```

where R8 is used to check on the position of the left-hand pointer. Initially, R6 (the index) plus the base address (array-L) points to the *leftmost* character of the L-array. Each time we drop through the swap loop, this index is advanced and added to $L + 1$ inside R8, and is compared with the last character of the array. The sort is complete when

```
L+1 + R6
```

matches

```
#NEXT−1
```

which is the address of the last character of L. In a somewhat longer program we show a refinement of this method. We introduce a flag to tell us when a pass through the swap loop has not resulted in a swap (this will tell us sooner that the sort is complete). We also make use of *K* as a symbol with a value, which we repeatedly increase each time we drop through the swap loop. In addition, we compare our position relative to the rightmost instead of the leftmost characters. Each time we pass through the swap loop, the highest order character will "float" to the right end of the list. This alternative bubblesort is shown in Figure 11.9.

11.5.6 Working with Pairs of Arrays

Next, we show the use of the register deferred and autoincrement modes to handle more than one array. The trick is to move the *beginning addresses* of the arrays into separate registers. Once the registers have been initialized with the array addresses, we can use the autoincrement (or autodecrement) mode to slide back and forth across the contiguous memory locations of one

FIGURE 11.7
Procedure to Bubblesort

```
Procedure Bubble Sort:

VAR  L:  ARRAY [0..K] OF CHAR;  Buff: CHAR;
      I, J, Max: INTEGER;

BEGIN
1.  Load L-array; Initialize I := 0, J := I+1; Max :=K;
2.  BEGIN Sort:
    2.1  Compare L[I] and L[J]:
         IF L[I] <= L[J]
         THEN branch to step 2.2
         ELSE (swap elemens)
         2.1.1  Buff <--- L[I]
         2.1.2  L[I] <--- L[J]
         2.1.3  L[J] <--- Buff
    2.2  Check for end of string:
         2.2.1  Increment J by 1:
                IF J < Max
                THEN REPEAT Loop at step 2.1
                ELSE
         2.2.2  Increment I by 1
                IF I< Max - 1
                THEN
                2.2.2.1  J := I + 1
                2.2.2.2 REPEAT Loop at step 2.1
                ELSE exit
    END Procedure
```

FIGURE 11.8
Bubblesort of a Character Array

```
;
;REF.: Figure 11.8 (BUBBLE SORT OF A CHARACTER ARRAY)
;
BUFF:   .BYTE
L:      .ASCIC/LEIBNIZ LIVED IN HANNOVER/
NEXT:   .BYTE
;
ARRAY_L=L+1
;
BEGIN:  .WORD                           ;START:
        CLRL    R6                      ;Set up R6 for the index mode
LOOP:
        MOVL    R6,R7                   ;Set up R7 as 2nd array pointer
        INCL    R7                      ;Slide pointer over one
SWAP:   CMPB    ARRAY_L(R6),ARRAY_L(R7) ;See if swap is necessary
        BLEQ    CORK                    ;If not, side right ptr over one
                                        ;Else
        MOVB    ARRAY_L(R6),BUFF        ;  Begin swap: put ele. in buffer
        MOVB    ARRAY_L(R7),ARRAY_L(R6) ;  put copy of 2nd ele. in
                                        ;  lead spot
        MOVB    BUFF,ARRAY_L(R7)        ;  replace 2nd ele. by buffer ele.
                                        ;  which was in the lead spot
CORK:   INCL    R7                      ;Float to right, one
        MOVAL   L+1,R8                  ;Get beginning address &
        ADDL2   R7,R8                   ;add current rt. ptr value to it &
        CMPL    R8,#NEXT                ;see if we have reached the end
                                        ;of the array being sorted
        BLSS    SWAP                    ;If not, continue swap-loop
                                        ;Else
;
;
        SPURT   <L>                     ;exhibit current state of array
        WRITELN                         ;& print a <ret>
        INCL    R6                      ;slide left pointer over one
        MOVAL   L+1,R8                  ;get beginning array address
        ADDL2   R6,R8                   ;add to it the left ptr value
        CMPL    R8,#NEXT-1              ;& see if we have reached
                                        ;the 2nd to the last ele.
                                        ;of the array being sorted
        BLSS    LOOP                    ;If not, return to swap loop
                                        ;  Else exit
        $EXIT_S
        .END BEGIN
```

Figure 11.8 continued.

```
                    RUN FG118
            LIENIZBLIVED IN HANNOVER
             LINIZELIVEDBIN HANNOVER
             LNIZILIVEEDINBHANNOVER
             ANLZILIVIEEINDHBNNOVER
             ABNZLLIVIIEINEHDNNOVER
             ABDZNLLVIIIINEHENNOVER
             ABDEZNLVLIIINIHENNOVER
             ABDEEZNVLLIINIIHNNOVER
             ABDEEEZVNLLINIIINNOVHR
             ABDEEEHZVNLLNIIINNOVIR
             ABDEEEHIZVNLNLIINNOVIR
             ABDEEEHIIZVNNLLINNOVIR
             ABDEEEHIIIZVNNLLNNOVIR
             ABDEEEHIIIIZVNNLNNOVLR
             ABDEEEHIIIILZVNNNNOVLR
             ABDEEEHIIIILLZVNNNOVNR
             ABDEEEHIIIILLNZVNNOVNR
             ABDEEEHIIIILLNNZVNOVNR
             ABDEEEHIIIILLNNNZVOVNR
             ABDEEEHIIIILLNNNNZVVOR
             ABDEEEHIIIILLNNNNOZVVR
             ABDEEEHIIIILLNNNNORZVV
             ABDEEEHIIIILLNNNNORVZV
             ABDEEEHIIIILLNNNNORVVZ
```

or more arrays. This can be fun (and useful), once you know how registers can be used to scan, compare, swap, shift, insert, delete, move and, in general, *manage* array elements.

We illustrate this in terms of computing the sum of corresponding elements of two arrays, where corresponding array elements are added together. The simplicity of the program that follows might obscure its subtlety. First, look at the program given in Figure 11.10.

R6 gets the address of SUM (the *beginning* address of the SUM-array), while R5 gets the *L*-array address. A sum is computed with

ADDL2 (R5)+,   (R6)

Register deferred mode used, since we want to use the *same* sum-array address to set up a stack frame to print the sum.

Really, two steps: (1) (R5) points to the desired operand; (2) the autoincrement mode array pointer shifts over to the adjacent array element *after* the operand has been fetched and added.

There is a better way to do this. We could introduce a third array (call it

FIGURE 11.9
Refinement of Bubblesort of a Character Array

```
;
;REF.: FIG. 11.9 (REFINEMENT OF BUBBLE SORT OF A CHARACTER ARRAY)
;
BUFF:   .BYTE
L:      .ASCIC/LEIBNIZ LIVED IN HANNOVER/
NEXT:   .BYTE
;
ARRAY_L=L+1
K=0
FLAG:   .BYTE 0
;
BEGIN:  .WORD                               ;Start:
LOOP:   CLRL    R6                          ;set up R6 as left-pointer
        CLRB    FLAG                        ;set up FLAG to tell us
                                            ;a complete pass through
                                            ;the swap loop has not
                                            ;resulted in a swap

        MOVL    R6,R7                       ;set up R7 as right-pointer
        INCL    R7                          ;slide ptr over one
                                            ;Begin swap loop:
SWAP:   CMPB    ARRAY_L(R6),ARRAY_L(R7)     ;check if swap is needed
        BLEQ    CORK                        ;If not, prepare to ´float´
                                            ;left-ptr over one
                                            ;   Else
        MOVB    ARRAY_L(R6),BUFF            ;   store left ele. in buffer
        MOVB    ARRAY_L(R7),ARRAY_L(R6)     ;   & copy rt ele. in left
                                            ;   ele. spot &
        MOVB    BUFF,ARRAY_L(R7)            ;   replace rt ele. with
                                            ;   left ele. stored in buffer

        MOVB    #1,FLAG                     ;Set flag
CORK:   INCL    R7                          ;Slide rt ptr over one
        MOVAL   L+1,R8                      ;get beginning array address
        ADDL2   R7,R8                       ;& add to it rt index
        CMPL    R8,#NEXT-K                  ;& see if we have ´crept´
                                            ;to right-end limit
                                            ;note:
                                            ;
                                            ;L:|_||_||_|...|_||_||_||_|
                                            ;                   ^
                                            ;
                                            ;                   |
                                            ;
                                            ;           #NEXT-3,for example
                                            ;           (the variable K
                                            ;           shifts this end-limit
                                            ;           over one to the left
                                            ;           each time we reenter
                                            ;           the swap-loop)
        BEQL    BUMP                        ;If the right ptr stored in R7
                                            ;has not reached the limit-position,
                                            ;then we continue inside the swap
                                            ;loop with
        INCL    R6                          ;slide left ptr over one
        BRW     SWAP                        ;continue swap loop
                                            ;   Else
BUMP:   SPURT   <L>                         ;exhibit current state of array
```

316

Figure 11.9 continued.

```
            WRITELN                        ;print a <ret>
            CMPB    #1,FLAG                ;see if a swap was made
            BNEQ    LAST                   ;if not, exit
                                           ; Else
K=K+1                                      ;   reset left-hand limit
            CMPL    #L+1,#NEXT-K           ;   & see if we have reached
                                           ;   the beginning of the array
            BNEQ    LOOP                   ;If not, continue with new
LAST:       NOP
            $EXIT_S
            .END BEGIN


RUN FG119

EIBLIN LIVED IN HANNOVERZ
EBIIL LINED IN HANNOVERVZ
BEII LILED IN HANNNOERVVZ
BEI IILED IL HANNNNEORVVZ
BE IIIED IL HALNNNENORVVZ
B EIIED II HALLNNENNORVVZ
 BEIED II HAILLNENNNORVVZ
 BEED II HAIILLENNNNORVVZ
 BED EI HAIIILELNNNNORVVZ
 BD EE HAIIIIELLNNNNORVVZ
 B DE EAHIIIEILLNNNNORVVZ
  BD EAEHIIEIILLNNNNORVVZ
  B DAEEHIEIIILLNNNNORVVZ
  BADEEHEIIIILLNNNNORVVZ
  ABDEEEHIIIIILLNNNNORVVZ
  ABDEEEHIIIIILLNNNNORVVZ
```

LL) to *refine* the above program. In doing so, we can preserve the contents
of the original arrays and then still compute their sum. Try using the following
method:

```
MOVAL L, R5        (array of addends)
MOVAL LL, R6       (array of addends)
MOVAL SUM, R7      (array of zeros, initially)
```

and compute the sum with

```
LOOP:  ADDL3 (R5)+, (R6)+, (R7)+
       PUSHL (R7)+
       CALLS #1, WRITEVAL
       SOBGTR COUNT, LOOP
```

FIGURE 11.10
Program to Compute the Sum of Two Arrays

```
;
;REF.: FIG. 11.10 (SUM TWO ARRAYS OF INTEGERS)
;
TITLE:      .ASCIC<10><10><13><9>/LUCAS NOS.:/<10><10><13>
SPACE:      .ASCIC<32><32>
L:          .LONG 1,1,2,3,5,8,13,21,34,55,89,144
SUM:        .LONG 2,3,5,8,13,21,34,55,89,144,233,377
COUNT:      .LONG 12
;
BEGIN:      .WORD                     ;Start:
            SPURT <TITLE>             ;print title
            MOVAL SUM,R6              ;use R6 as sum-array pointer
            MOVAL L,R5                ;use R5 as L-array pointer
;
LOOP:       ADDL2 (R5)+,(R6)          ;add L-array ele. to sum-ele. &
                                      ;autoincrement pointer

            PUSHL (R6)                ;set up stack frame
            CALLS #1,WRITEVAL         ;to print out sum
            TSTL (R6)+                ;slide sum-array ptr over also
                                      ;using autoincrement
            SPURT <SPACE>             ;print 2 spaces
            SOBGTR COUNT,LOOP         ;repeat sum-loop until count = 0
;
            $EXIT_S
            .END BEGIN



RUN FG1110

            LUCAS NOS.:

3   4   7   11   18   29   47   76   123   199   322   521
```

Implementation of this refinement is left as an exercise. A further refinement of the program in Figure 11.10 would make it possible for a user to load the *L*- and *LL*-array from a keyboard. The program could also be enhanced to allow you to choose one or both of the following array operations:

L + LL

and/or

L − LL

to subtract corresponding array elements.

11.6

SUBSTRINGS

You might wonder what VAX-11 macro does at assembly time to establish the validity of an expression in a source text (its syntax). For example, if it encounters

```
AOBLSS #5, R6, LOOP
```

it first finds the AOBLSS, then it checks for the #5 following the space delimiter (ASCII 32), then the R6 following the comma delimiter, and so on.

In a similar fashion we can check for the presence of substrings in a string array. For example, we could check for the presence of the substring *LL* in the string

```
POE:   .ASCIC/
BELLS,BELLS,BELLS,THE TINTINNABULATIONS OF THE BELLS/
```

At the same time we do this, we can keep a tally of the number of occurrences of *LL* inside the string POE. We might first try writing out the steps of the method used to do this:

Step 0: Determine the target (substring) like *L* in *LL*.

Step 1: Compare a character of POE with the target *L*. If the character = target, then do

Step 1.1: Compare the adjacent character with the target. If the adjacent character = target,

(a) PRINT "EUREKA!" and

(b) increment frequency counter for matching pairs of L's

ELSE

Step 1.2: If the adjacent character is not the 2nd-to-the-last character, then repeat step 1

ELSE

STOP!

This idea is illustrated in Figure 11.11.

FIGURE 11.11
Graphical Interpretation of Substring Searcn

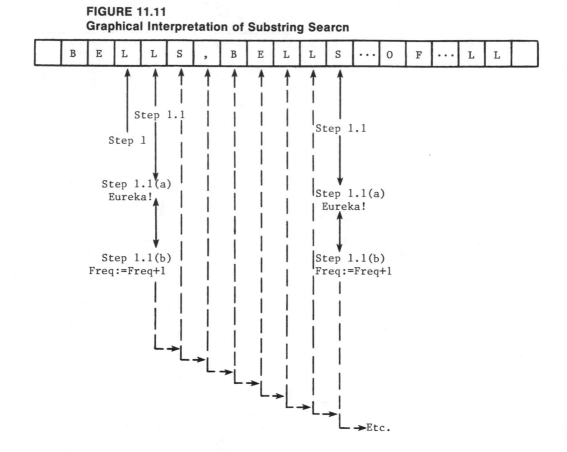

11.6.1 Programming Hint

Suppose we have a string with 20 characters. Then we would set up two string arrays:

```
      L:   .ASCII /       /   ;first 19 characters
   NEXT:   .ASCII /     /     ;last character
```

Then #NEXT (the address represented by the label NEXT) can be used as a flag to signal the end of the string of 20 characters. In the following program, we use this trick. We search for substrings with matching pairs of characters shown in the Figure 11.11.

11.6.2 Example: Substring Search

The program that follows uses a linear search for a target substring within a given string. It also searches for matching adjacent characters that correspond to the target character supplied by the user. To carry out this search, we introduce a tracking procedure in terms of a variable TARGET and a flag NEXT, which is the address of the memory location immediately after the last location in an array *L*. We show the steps for this procedure in Figure 11.12.

Next we show a program that uses this tracking procedure (see Figure 11.13). This program illustrates how to build the equivalent of what might be called an .ASCIC-array. That is, we construct character arrays like the

FIGURE 11.12
Program to Perform a Substring Search

```
;Ref.: Figure 11.12 (Tracking Procedure)
;
Procedure Track:

Var
        L: Array[1..k] of CHAR;
        NEXT,FREQ,I: INTEGER;
        TARGET: CHAR;

Begin

1. Load L-array;
2. Initialize
        NEXT:=K+1; I:=0;FREQ:=0;TARGET:=<character>;
3. I:=I+1;
4. If I = NEXT
    Then exit!
        Else
        4.1 Track:
                If L[I] <> TARGET
                Then Repeat step 3
                  Else
                    4.2 Track:
                        4.2.1 I:=I+1;
                        4.2.2 If L[I] <> TARGET
                                Then Repeat step 3
                                  Else
                                    4.3 Continue tracking
                                        4.3.1 I:=I-1;
                                        4.3.2 Write ´Eureka!´;
                                        4.3.3 FREQ := FREQ + 1;
                                        4.3.4 Repeat step 3
End procedure track.
```

FIGURE 11.13
Tracking Procedure

```
;
;REF.:   FIGURE 11.13 (SEARCH FOR MATCHING PAIRS OF CHARACTERS)
;
;NOTE: LINK FG1113,OBJ WITH THE WRITESTR,READSTR,WRITEVAL PROCEDURES GIVEN EARLIER
;
DASH      =45
TAB       =9
;
TOP:      .BYTE 0,10,13
          .ASCII/SUBSTRING SEARCH FOR MATCHING PAIRS OF CHAR´S/
          .BYTE 10,13,DASH[20]
LEN_TOP  =. - TOP - 1
P1:       .ASCIC<10><13>/TARGET CHAR:/<32>
P2:       .ASCIC/STRING (WITHOUT LAST CHARACTER):/<10><13>
P3:       .ASCIC/LAST CHAR. OF STRING:/<32>
DEF_N:    .BYTE 0,DASH[20],10,10,13
          .ASCII/NO. MATCHING PAIRS IN STRING = /
          .BYTE 32
LEN_DEF_N=. - DEF_N - 1
CR:       .ASCIC<10><13>
GOLD:     .ASCIC<9><9><9>/EUREKA!/<10><13>
TARGET:   .BYTE
L:        .BLKB 80
NEXT:     .BYTE
FREQ:     .BYTE
COPY:     .LONG
;
          .ENTRY    BEGIN,0
          MOVB      #LEN_TOP,TOP     ;INIT. 1ST BYTE OF TOP WITH LENGTH
                                     ;TO SIMULATE A .ASCIC
          PUSHAB    TOP              ;SET UP STACK FRAME TO
          CALLS     #1,WRITESTR      ;PRINT HEADING
          PUSHAB    P1               ;SET UP STACK FRAME TO
          CALLS     #1,WRITESTR      ;PROMPT FOR TARGET CHARACTER
          CALLS     #0,READSTR       ;TAKE TARGET FROM TERMINAL
          MOVAB     X,R7             ;SET UP R7 AS X-STRING PTR
          MOVAB     TARGET,R8        ;SET UP R8 AS TARGET-STR PTR
          JSB       BUILD            ;CALL ROUTINE TO BUILD COPY OF
                                     ;X-STR (IT HOLDS TARGET) IN
                                     ;TARGET STRING
          PUSHAB    CR               ;SET UP STACK FRAME TO
          CALLS     #1,WRITESTR      ;PRINT CR
          PUSHAB    P2               ;SET UP STACK FRAME TO
          CALLS     #1,WRITESTR      ;PROMPT FOR STRING TO SCAN FOR TARGET
          CALLS     #0,READSTR       ;CALL ROUTINE TO GET STRING
          MOVAB     X,R7             ;SET UP R7 AS X-STRING PTR
          MOVAB     L,R8             ;SET UP R8 AS L-STRING PTR
          JSB       BUILD            ;COPY STRING (IN X-STRING BUFFER) TO L-STR
          PUSHAB    CR               ;PRINT A
          CALLS     #1,WRITESTR      ;CR
          PUSHAB    P3               ;SET UP
          CALLS     #1,WRITESTR      ;PROMPT FOR TRAILING CHAR
          CALLS     #0,READSTR       ;TO MOVE FROM TTY TO X-STR BUFFER
          MOVAB     X,R7             ;SET UP X-PTR
```

Figure 11.13 continued.

```
          MOVAB     NEXT,R8          ;SET UP NEXT-PTR &
          JSB       BUILD            ;COPY X-BUFFER INTO NEXT-STRING
;
          MOVAB     L-1,R6           ;LET R6 POINT L-1ST BYTE
TRACK:    INCL      R6               ;SLIDE L-PTR OVER ONE &
          CMPL      R6,#NEXT         ;CHECK FOR END-OF-STRING
                                     ;CAUTION: WE ARE COMPARING ADDRESSES
                                     ;     OF BYTES, NOT BYTES THEMSELVES
          BEQL      STAT             ;IF SO, BEGIN PRINTING RESULTS
                                     ;ELSE
          CMPB      (R6),TARGET      ;CHECK FOR PRESENCE OF TARGET
          BNEQ      TRACK            ;IF (R6)<>TARGET,THEN CONTINUE TRACKING
                                     ;ELSE
          INCL      R6               ;SHIFT L-PTR OVER ONE &
          CMPB      (R6),TARGET      ;CHECK REPETITION OF TARGET (A MATCH!)
          BNEQ      TRACK            ;IF (R6)<>TARGET,CONTINUE TRACKING
                                     ;ELSE
          DECL      R6               ;SHIFT PTR TO ALLOW FOR
                                     ;ADJACENT MATCHING TARGET PAIRS
          PUSHAB    GOLD             ;GET READY TO PRINT
          CALLS     #1,WRITESTR      ;EUREKA!
          INCB      FREQ             ;AUGMENT FREQUENCY
          JMP       TRACK            ;CONTINUE TRACKING
;
STAT:     MOVB      #LEN_DEF_N,DEF_N
                                     ;INIT. 1ST BYTE OF DEF_N WITH
                                     ;LENGTH OF DEF_N STRING
          PUSHAB    DEF_N            ;GET READY TO PRINT
          CALLS     #1,WRITESTR      ;DESCRIPTION OF FREQUENCY
          MOVZBL    FREQ,COPY        ;COPY FREQ TO LONG-WORD LOC.
          PUSHL     COPY             ;GET READY TO PRINT
          CALLS     #1,PRINT         ;FREQ.
;
          $EXIT_S
;
BUILD:    CMPB      #13,(R7)         ;CHECK FOR CR
          BEQL      AHA              ;IF SO,QUIT BUILDING X-STRING
          MOVB      (R7)+,(R8)+      ;ELSE
          BRW       BUILD            ;CONTINUE BUILD X-STRING
AHA:      NOP                        ;PREPARE TO RETURN
          RSB
;
          .END BEGIN
RUN FG1113
```

Continued on following page.

Figure 11.13 continued.

```
          SUBSTRING SEARCH FOR MATCHING PAIRS OF CHAR´S
          --------------------
          TARGET CHAR: L

          STRING (WITHOUT LAST CHARACTER):
          BELLS,BELLS,BELLS,THE TINNABULATIONS OF THE BELLS

          LAST CHAR. OF STRING: .
                                    EUREKA!
                                    EUREKA!
                                    EUREKA!
                                    EUREKA!

          --------------------
          NO. MATCHING PAIRS IN STRING =  4
```

TOP-array where the first byte eventually gets the length of the array (its dimension) from the second byte to the last byte. This gives us a little more flexibility in preparing strings to be printed at a terminal by the WRITESTR procedure shown earlier.

This program will count, for example,

$$\underbrace{3 \quad 3}_{} \quad 3$$

matching pair of 3s

matching pair of 3s

as two matching pairs of 3s.

11.6.3 Concatenating Strings

If we have two strings, it will be helpful to have some method to "attach" one string to another one; three cases are shown in Figure 11.14.

The first and third cases are fairly easy to handle. Here are the steps for case (1):

Step 0: Determine address of the last char. of L1; say #L1+N (move #L1 over byte-by-byte until a NULL (or some flag) is encountered).

Step 1: @ L1+N+1 = #L2 (place to start concatenating).

Step 2: Append a character of the L2-array to the L1-array (move a leading byte-content of L2 into a trailing byte of the L1-array).

Step 3: Slide L1 pointer over one (increment the L1 pointer). Do the same for the L2 pointer. If the L2-pointer has not reached a null (or some post L2-array flag) then repeat step 2; else stop.

FIGURE 11.14
Ways to Concatenate Strings

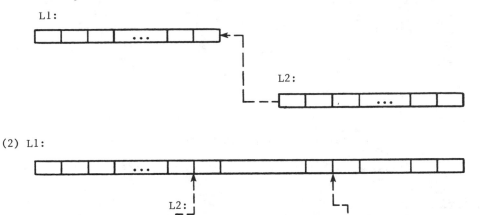

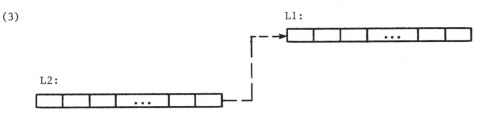

Here is a different strategy for case two. This time we need a TARGET character to look for in the first string (L1), then

Step 0: Determine address of TARGET in L1 and #TARGET + 1.

Step 1: Move the substring from #L1 . . . #TARGET to a buffer.

Step 2: Repeat steps of method for case 1 and append L2 to this substring.

Step 3: Repeat steps of method for case 1 and append to

#L1 . . . #TARGET#L2 . . . #L2+K

the tail end of L1 from #TARGET+1 to the end of L1.

The assembly program given next shows how to handle the first case shown in this section. This program takes advantage of the BUILD routine given

FIGURE 11.15
Program to Concatenate Strings

```
;
;Ref.: Figure 11.15 (How to Concatenate Strings)
;
;NOTE: LINK FG1115.OBJ WITH THE READSTR,WRITESTR PROCEDURES GIVEN EARLIER
;
DASH=45
SPACE=32
CR=13
LF=10
TAB=9
;
P1:        .ASCIC <10><13>/STRING?/<10><13>
P2:        .ASCIC<10><13>/STRING TO BE CONCATENATED:/<10><13>
TOP:       .BYTE 0,10,13
           .ASCII/TASK: CONCATENATING TWO STRINGS/<10><13>
           .BYTE DASH[20]
LEN_TOP=.-TOP+1
RESULT:    .BYTE 0
           .ASCII<10><13>/CONCATENATED STRINGS:/<10><10><13>
           .BYTE DASH[20]
           .BYTE 10,13
LEN_RESULT=.-RESULT+1
;
SIZE:      .BYTE
BUFF:      .BYTE
L1:        .BLKB    80
L2:        .BLKB    40
;
           .ENTRY  BEGIN,0
           MOVB    #LEN_TOP,TOP ;SIMULATE .ASCIC & INIT. TOP WITH
                                    ;LENGTH OF TOP BYTE-ARRAY
           PUSHAB  TOP
           CALLS   #1,WRITESTR
           PUSHAB  P1                  ;PROMPT FOR 1ST STRING
           CALLS   #1,WRITESTR
           CALLS   #0,READSTR          ;GET STRING FROM TERMINAL
           MOVAB   X,R7                ;SET UP R7 AS X-PTR
           MOVAB   L1+1,R8             ;SET UP R8 AS L1-PTR (SKIP PAST 1ST BYTE!)
           JSB     BUILD               ;CALL STRING-BUILDER ROUTINE
           MOVB    SIZE,L1             ;INIT. 1ST BYTE OF L1 WITH LENGTH
           MOVB    SIZE,BUFF           ;SAVE THE SIZE OF L1-STRING
           CLRB    SIZE                ;INIT. SIZE WITH 0
;
           PUSHAB  P2                  ;PROMPT FOR 2ND STRING
           CALLS   #1,WRITESTR         ;
           CALLS   #0,READSTR          ;GET 2ND STRING FROM TERMINAL
           MOVAB   X,R7                ;SET UP R7 AS X-PTR
           MOVAB   L2,R8               ;SET UP R8 AS L2-PTR
           JSB     BUILD               ;COPY X-STRING INTO L2-STRING
           TSTB    (R8)                ;SLIDE PTR OVER TO NEXT L2-BYTE
           MOVB    #0,(R8)             ;SET UP NULL-FLAG IN L2
           ADDB2   SIZE,L1             ;ADJUST FOR L2-LENGTH AFTER
                                       ;CONCATENATING IT TO L1-STRING
           INCB    L1                  ;ALLOW FOR SPACE TO BE INSERTED, NEXT
```

Figure 11.15 continued.

```
        MOVAB   L1+1,R6              ;SET UP R6 AS L1-PTR (SKIP PAST 1ST BYTE)
        ADDB2   BUFF,R6             ;SLIDE PTR TO END OF L1-STRING
        MOVB    #32,(R6)            ;INSERT SPACE
        MOVAB   L2,R7               ;SET UP R7 AS L2-PTR
;
CONCATENATE:
        CMPB    #0,(R7)             ;ARE WE POINTING TO A NULL?
        BEQL    REPORT              ;IF SO, THEN PRINT REPORT
                                    ;ELSE
        MOVB    (R7)+,(R6)+         ;COPY L2-BYTE TO L1
                                    ;--CONCATENATE!
        BRB     CONCATENATE         ;REPEAT LOOP
                                    ;UNTIL A NULL IS FOUND
;
REPORT:
        MOVB    #LEN_RESULT,RESULT
        PUSHAB  RESULT              ;SET UP STACK FRAME TO
        CALLS   #1,WRITESTR         ;PRINT HEADING FOR RESULT
        PUSHAB  L1                  ;SET UP STACK FRAME TO
        CALLS   #1,WRITESTR         ;PRINT CONCATENATED STRINGS
;
        $EXIT_S
;
BUILD:
        CMPB    #13,(R7)            ;A CR?
        BEQL    AHA                 ;IF SO, QUIT
                                    ;ELSE
        MOVB    (R7)+,(R8)+         ;COPY X-BYTE TO STRING POINTED TO BY R8
        INCB    SIZE
        BRW     BUILD               ;REPEAT BUILD-LOOP
                                    ;UNTIL A CR IS FOUND
AHA:    NOP
        RSB                         ;RETURN
;
        .END    BEGIN


RUN FG1115

TASK: CONCATENATING TWO STRINGS
--------------------
STRING?
TUMTY

STRING TO BE CONCATENATED:
TUMTYTUMTOES

CONCATENATED STRINGS:
--------------------

TUMTYTUMTYTUMTOES
```

in the program in Figure 11.11 (the substring search). This is shown in Figure 11.15.

11.6.4 Programming Hint

The program given in Figure 11.15 utilizes a variable BUFF, which carries a copy of the value of the SIZE variable found in the BUILD routine. Each time BUILD is called, it tallies how many characters are in the string it is building in an array. This is handy. It gives us a way of computing the address of the last character of a string array. For example, the address of the last character of L1 (after leaving the BUILD routine the *first* time) is given by

    #L1 + SIZE

This tells us where to start appending the second string.

11.7

EXTENDED PRECISION PRODUCTS WITH ARRAYS

Using either an AL or an HOL, we can set up arrays to compute products in such a way that the computer does not "know" it is dealing with numbers larger than its own words. We can do this in computing factorials like 20! or sums like

$$514229 + 832040 = f_{29} + f_{30}$$

or products like

    514229 * 233

Here is how we can use a pair of arrays. We can represent a fairly generalized method for doing this, for example, in computing the product

$$a^*x = x + x + x + \ldots + x \quad \text{(a additions)}$$

We will display this method first in steps:

Step 1: Set up an array X of bytes containing the K digits of x

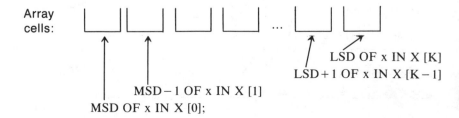

FIGURE 11.16
Program to Compute Extended Precision Products

```
;
;Ref.: Figure 11.16 (Computing Extended Precision Products)
;
;NOTE: FACTOR-A IS USED AS A COUNTER IN THE FOLLOWING PROGRAM.  IF
;      THE FACTORS ARE UNEQUAL, ENTER THE LARGER ONE, FIRST( THIS
;      WOULD BE X, THE FIRST NUMBER WE PROMPT FOR).
;
           .ENABLE GBL
;
BUFF:      .LONG
BUMP:      .LONG
MPLR:      .LONG
L:         .BLKB 30
X:         .BLKB 30
RESULT:    .BLKB 60
NO:        .BYTE 1,0
;
;
           .ENTRY  BEGIN,0          ;
           WRITE   <X = ? IN A*X   >
;
           CALLS   #0,READCH
           MOVAB   X,R7             ;USE R7 AS X-ARRAY PTR
           MOVAL   BUMP,R8
           JSB     CAPTURE_DIGITS ;GET DIGITS
;
           WRITELN
           WRITE   <A = ?  >
;
           CALLS   #0,READCH
           MOVAB   L,R7             ;USE R7 AS L-ARRAY PTR
           MOVAL   MPLR,R8
           JSB     CAPTURE_DIGITS
;
           JSB     COMPUTE          ;BEGIN COMPUTING PRODUCT A*X
;
           WRITELN
           WRITELN <------------------------------------------>
           WRITELN
           WRITE   <PRODUCT:    >
;
           MOVAB   RESULT,R6        ;USE R6 AS RESULT-ARRAY PTR
           MOVL    #60,R7           ;USE R7 TO KEEP TRACK OF NO. DIGITS
                                    ;IN THE PRODUCT
           JSB     REPORT
           $EXIT_S
;
CAPTURE_DIGITS:
           MOVAB   CH,R10           ;USE R10 TO HOLD INPUT-ARRAY ADDR.
                                    ;FROM THE READSTR PROC.
           MOVZWL  TTIOLEN,R9       ;USE R9 TO HOLD LENGTH OF INPUT-
                                    ;ARRAY DIM.
           MOVL    R9,(R8)          ;STORE DIM FOR COMPUTE ROUTINE
           ADDL2   #30,R7           ;SLIDE PTR TO RIGHT END OF FACTOR ARRAY
```

Continued on following page.

Figure 11.16 continued.

```
           SUBL2    R9,R7              ;SLIDE PTR BACK DIM-BYTES
PUSH:      MOVB     (R10)+,(R7)        ;LOAD FACTOR ARRAY FROM INPUT-ARRAY
           SUBB2    #48,(R7)+          ;DROP ASCII BIAS
                                       ;
                                       ;|_||_||_| · · · |_||_|
                                       ;                  ^
                                       ;                  |
                                       ;                  LAST DIGIT PUSHED
                                       ;                  GOES INTO ´LSB´ SPOT
                                       ;                  OF NO.-ARRAY
           SOBGTR   R9,PUSH            ;REPEAT PUSH LOOP UNTIL COUNT=0
           RSB
;
COMPUTE:
           MOVAB    L,R7               ;USE R7 AS L-ARRAY PTR
           ADDL2    #30,R7             ;SLIDE PTR TO ´LOW´ END OF L-ARRAY
CKOP:
           DECB     -(R7)              ;SEE IF
           BGEQ     NOWCMP             ;BORROW IS NECESSARY
           ADDB2    #10,(R7)           ;BORROW 10
           MOVAB    L,R10              ;USE R10 AS DUPLICATE L-ARRAY PTR
           ADDL2    #29,R10            ;SLIDE PTR TO RIGHT
           SUBL2    MPLR,R10           ;SLIDE PTR BACK TO LEFTMOST DIGIT
           CMPL     R10,R7             ;COMPARE ARRAY POINTERS
                                       ;AND STOP WHEN DIFF. < 0
           BNEQ     CKOP               ;IF DIFF. <> 0, CHECK NEXT LEFTMOST
                                       ;FOR POSSIBLE BORROW
                                       ;ELSE
           RSB                         ;RETURN
;
NOWCMP:
           MOVAB    RESULT,R9          ;USE R9 AS RESULT-ARRAY PTR
           ADDL2    #60,R9             ;SLIDE PTR TO RIGHT
           MOVAB    X,R6               ;USE R6 AS X-ARRAY PTR
           ADDL2    #30,R6             ;SLIDE PTR TO RIGHT
;
SUM:       ADDB2    -(R6),-(R9)        ;COMPUTE SUM OF CORRESPONDING DIGITS
           MOVL     R9,BUFF            ;SAVE RESULT-PTR
;
EXTEND:
           CMPB     #9,(R9)            ;CHECK FOR CARRY
           BGEQ     CHECK              ;IF NOT, BYPASS CARRY ROUTINE
                                       ;ELSE
           SUBB2    #10,(R9)           ;ADD TEN TO MAKE POSITIVE
           ADDB2    #1,-(R9)           ;BORROW ONE FRON NEST SIG. DIGIT
           CMPL     R9,#RESULT         ;DONE WITH CARRIES?
           BNEQ     EXTEND             ;IF NOT, CONTINUE GETTING CARRIES
                                       ;ELSE
;
CHECK:     MOVL     BUFF,R9            ;RESTORE RESULT-PTR
;
NEXT:      CMPL     #X,R6              ;SEE IF WE HAVE REACHED 30TH DIGIT
           BNEQ     SUM                ;IF NOT, CONTINUE SUMMING
                                       ;ELSE
```

Figure 11.16 continued.

```
            JMP     COMPUTE             ;REDUCE COUNTER TO SEE IF
                                        ;WE ARE DONE
;
REPORT:     TSTB    (R6)                ;IS DIGIT A LEADING ZERO?
            BNEQ    NOT_ZERO            ;NO, SET UP FOR PRINTING
            DECL    R7                  ;SLIDE RESULT-PTR BACK ONE BYTE
            BLSS    ERR                 ;PRINT 0, IF NECESSARY
                                        ;ELSE
            TSTB    (R6)+               ;SET UP FOR CHECKING NEXT DIGIT
                                        ;FOR LEADING ZERO
            JMP     REPORT              ;IF CONTENT = 0, LOOK FOR NEW DIGIT
                                        ;ELSE
NOT_ZERO:
            MOVL    R6,R11              ;GET THE ADDRESS OF FIRST NONZERO DIGIT
            MOVB    R7,-(R11)           ;STORE LENGTH-1 OF STRING
            ADDB2   #48,(R6)+           ;ADJUST FOR ASCII BIAS ON STRING
            TSTL    R7                  ;IS COUNT = 0?
            BEQL    SINGLE
DIGIT:      ADDB2   #48,(R6)+           ;TAKE CARE OF ASCII BIAS
            SOBGTR  R7,DIGIT            ;CONTINUE REPORTING UNTIL COUNT = 0
SINGLE:     NOP
            PUSHL   R11
            CALLS   #1,WRITESTR
            RSB
ERR:        NOP
            MOVB    #48,NO+1
            SPURT   <NO>
            RSB
;
            .END    BEGIN


RUN FG1116

X = ? IN A*X    211321532853138

A = ?   233

------------------------------------------

PRODUCT:    49237917154781154
```

(where MSD = 'most significant digit' and LSD = 'least significant digit') and record *K*.

Step 2: Set up a second array called *L*, which is loaded with the digits of the second factor *a*. Record the number of digits of *a* (call it MPLR).

Step 3: Compute sums of pairs of digits (a digit from the *X*-array added to itself), keeping track of the necessity of possible carries after each addition.

Step 4: Print the result.

Although this method taken at face value is simple, its implementation is tricky. We need to use considerable care in managing the bytes of the various arrays we set up. A program to carry out this method is presented in Figure 11.16.

We can do essentially the same thing much more directly with either Huber's or Knuth's method (shown earlier). We leave the implementation of these methods as exercises.

11.8
SUMMARY

This chapter deals with methods for setting up, accessing, loading, echo-printing, and managing one-dimensional arrays. We can set up an array L of bytes filled with 100 ASCII codes for a dash, for example,

    L: .BYTE 45 [100]

This convenient way to fill array locations with the same value. We can also set up an array with varied entries using, for example,

    L: .BYTE 45, 1, 1, 45, 2, 3, 45

These are contiguous bytes that will be filled with values we have indicated in the source text. The .BYTE directive specifies that each array element is of the same type, a byte-length memory location. We have four other alternatives for arrays of integers (.WORD, .LONG, .QUAD, and .OCTA).

The alternative to preselecting array-element values is to use one of the following .BLKx forms to set up an array L:

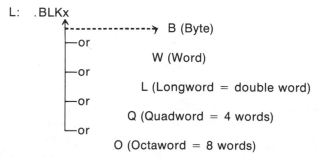

where, by default, an array would begin with null entries.

Arrays rank high in the list of data structures available to programmers. Their use in AL programs depends on two things. First, we need to set aside contiguous memory cells (locations). Second, we need to set up one or more pointers to use in *selecting* array elements. Arrays can be used for either number- or stringhandling.

Arrays also entail the use of a wide variety of addressing modes. Besides the obvious index mode, there is also the register deferred mode, autoincrementing and autodecrementing. The latter two modes make it easy to slide an array pointer back and forth across an array of bytes or words.

In setting up arrays, you must first consider the nature of the data that will be loaded into an array. In the substring search presented in Figure 11.11, for example, we could have used an array of words or doublewords instead of an array of bytes for the array *L* and gotten the same result after adjusting the instructions. This procedure would be inefficient, since the ASCII codes for characters require only 7 bits. In this case, we make better use of memory by using contiguous bytes, rather than contiguous words, for an array of ASCII codes.

The secret to the successful use of arrays is careful use of array pointers. It is necessary to gain control of pointers used to *select* array elements. This selection requires *complete* control of the addressing method, the management of the pointers used in selecting array elements. The importance of this control becomes apparent when we try to sort (rearrange) array elements or perform a substring search in terms of some target substring.

Managing array pointers demands care and will become a straightforward practice with experience.

11.9

EXERCISES

1. The 5th programming tool in section 11.2 has an *L*-array. Write an AL program to

   (a) Print out the content of each of the bytes in this array.

   (b) Print, on a separate line, the content of the 3rd byte of this array.

   (c) Print, on a separate line, the content of the 8th byte of

   ```
   T:   .ASCII/BELLS,BELLS,BELLS,THE TINTINNABULATIONS OF
        THE BELLS/
   ```

   taken by itself as a separate array apart from the *L*-array in Figure 11.1.

(d) Print, on a separate line, the content of the last 5 bytes of the *T*-array in part (c).

(e) Test each of the first five cases in the 6th tool of section 11.2 by printing, on a separate line, the content of the 4th byte of the *T*-array in part (c) in five different ways (follow Figure 11.3).

(f) Use the displacement mode (case 6) to print out the 4th, then the 6th, then the 8th byte content of the *L*-array.

2. Write an AL program to echo (print a copy of) all the bytes in the array in Figure 11.3. What does the morse code say?

3. Write an AL program with a TABLE array with

TABLE: .BYTE ⟨ASCII character code⟩,⟨45/46⟩, . . . ,⟨45/46⟩

.BYTE ⟨ASCII character code⟩,⟨45/46⟩, . . . ,⟨45/46⟩

⋮   ⋮   ⋮   ⋮

where TABLE contains a character code followed by the corresponding morse code (45 = dash, 46 = dot). Prompt the user for a word and print out the corresponding morse code by selecting the part of the TABLE array having this code.

Run your program with the word "Eureka." Be sure to insert (print) one or two spaces between the morse codes for each letter.

4. Write an AL program to

(a) Prompt the user for a string.

(b) Maintain a count of the number of characters in the string, excluding the CR and LF.

(c) Echo-print the string entered.

(d) Print the number of characters in the string.

(e) Check whether the user has another string to enter. If so, repeat steps (b), (c), (d).

Run your program for

Another example of coroutine structuring is provided in a two pass compiler for a programming language. ⟨RET⟩

First, the second pass is executed until it reaches its first request for an input message. ⟨RET⟩

The first pass program is then executed until it produces its first output message. ⟨RET⟩

which is a quotation from O. J. Dahl and C. A. R. Hoar (1972, p. 185).

5. Enhance the program in the preceding exercise so that it prints the following table:

String No.	Target Char.	First 5 Words of Each String	Number of Characters	Frequency of Target

so that

(a) The user is prompted for (i) a string, (ii) a target character whose frequency within the string you will determine (this is easy: each time a character is to be loaded into a string array, compare it with the target character beforehand).

(b) The user can rerun the program for a different set of strings, if need be.

Note: allow each string entered to have either the same or a different target character to check.

6. Write an AL program to implement MacEwen's method shown in Figure 11.6. That is,

(a) Prompt the user for base 10 integer.

(b) Strip off the digits of the number *after* it has been read from KB buffer by a READ procedure.

(c) Echo-print the original number on one line.

(d) Print the separate digits in a column, starting on the next line with the leftmost digit of the original number.

Run your program with

(e) 28657

(f) 17711

7. Rewrite the sort routine in Figure 11.9 so that

(a) You prompt the user for the string array to be sorted.

(b) You use the register deferred addressing mode instead of the index mode to handle the sort.

(c) After the sort is complete, print the ordered list in ascending order, then, on the next line, in descending order. (The secret to this step is to move the array pointer to the opposite end of the list to print the sorted elements in descending order.)

Run your program for

(d) computing is best in wintertime.

(e) the PC is a sliding arrow.

8. Write an AL program to sort up to 500 integers. Prompt for entries, echo-print the entries, print on successive lines the numbers after a swap, until sort is complete. Run your program for

(a) 44, 55, 12, 42, 94, 18, 6, 67

(b) 99, 5, 5, 62, 56, 6, 56, 56, 71, 16, 17, 4, 0, 1, 1, 5.

9. Implement the refinement suggested earlier in section 11.4.6 for the program in Figure 11.10. Also, allow the user to

(a) Load the L and LL arrays.

(b) Compute $L + LL$.

(c) Compute $L - LL$ or subtract corresponding array elements.

Careful: if a difference is negative (check for this after computing each difference!), find the twos complement of the difference (try the MCOML instruction, for example) and print out the new number with a minus sign prefix.

10. Enhance the program in Figure 11.11 so that the user can choose from the following menu:

(a) Enter string, a target and learn frequency of occurrence of the target.

(b) Enter more than one string (limit = 5), one or more targets (limit = 5), and learn the frequency of occurrence of each target in the strings entered.

(c) Enter string, a target and learn frequency of matching pairs of the target (what this program does, now!).

(d) Do none of these.

Also, allow the user to rerun this program before discontinuing execution. Also, echo-print the string(s) entered *before* printing the frequency counts. Run your program for

(i) The string used in Figure 11.11 (the quote from Poe's *Bells*) in terms of case (a). Enter the target *L* to determine its frequency.

(ii) The string used in Figure 11.11 in terms of case (b). Enter the targets *I*, *L*, *N* to determine their frequency of occurrence.

11. Write an AL program to insert a substring into a given string. This is a variation of the program in Figure 11.10. Prompt for a sentinel word (maximum number of letters = 10) or character contained in the parent string that will precede the insertion.

Caution: If the sentinel is not unique, then your program should insert the "child" substring after *each* occurrence of the sentinel in the parent string.

Run your program for

(a) *parent-string:*
Dark came under. Tom, he lit a candle, upstairs creaking went, turned the door-handle.
sentinel: under
child-string: hill

(b) *parent-string:* Dawn broke.
sentinel: broke
child-string: ,grey

(c) *parent-string:*
Old Tom Bombadil was a merry fellow; bright blue his jacket and his boots were yellow; green were his girdle and his breeches all of leather; he wore in his tall hat a swan-wing feather.
sentinel: his
child-string: own

11.10

LAB PROJECTS

1. Write an AL program that uses Huber's method to compute extended precision products. (This method is explained in lab 3 of chapter 1). Run your program for

(a) 2147483647 × 23 (this is 23 times the largest integer on the VAX-11.)

(b) 2147483647 × 233

(c) 2147483647 × 1597

2. Write an AL program that uses Knuth's method to compute extended precision products. (This method is explained in section 1.9 and goes back to lab 4 of chapter 1). Run your program for

   (a) the products in parts (a), (b), (c) of the preceding exercise
   (b) 2147483647×65535

3. Write an AL program to compute a table of factorials from $0! = 1$ to $20!$

	NOTE:		
	$1! = 1$	$= 1$
	$2! = 1 \times 2$	$= 2$
	$3! = 1 \times 2 \times 3$	$= 6$
	$4! = 3! \times 4$	$= 24$
	$5! = 4! \times 5$	$= 120$
	$6! = 5! \times 6$	$= 720$

   and so on.

   Hint: Extend either of the methods shown in labs 1 or 2 or the one shown in Figure 11.15 by using a loop, each time using the preceding product times a loop counter plus 1. That is, use

   ```
   procedure factorial:
   VAR X, COUNT, MAX:INTEGER;
   BEGIN
   1. Initialize X:=1, COUNT:=2
   2. Begin computing factorials
        2.1 X:=X * COUNT (*Use product routine, here!*)
        2.2 COUNT: = COUNT + 1
        2.3 Compare COUNT with MAX:
             IF COUNT < MAX
             THEN REPEAT steps starting with 2.1
             ELSE stop
   End procedure
   ```

4. Write an AL program to print out a table with the following:

F(I)	No.
F(1)	1

F(I)	No.
F(2)	1
F(3)	2
⋮	⋮
F(50)	12586269025

where the entries are Fibonacci numbers. That is, use a technique similar to the one used in one of the extended precision product routines to compute sums using pairs of arrays and adding the numbers digit by digit.

5. Write an enhanced version of the search program in Figure 11.13 to print out a frequency table for vowels used in a text and the distance between like vowels (include spaces in count). To test your program, use the following sentence from James Joyce's *Ulysses*:

> Ever he would wander, self-compelled, to the extreme limit of his cometary orbit, beyond the fixed stars and variable suns and telescopic planets, astronomical waifs and strays, to the extreme boundary of space, passing from land to land, among peoples, amid events. Somewhere imperceptibly he would hear and somehow reluctantly, suncompelled, obey the summons of recall.

Your program should print out a table like the following one:

Vowel	Sentence	Frequency	Distances between Occurrences
a	1	24	1,3,11,3,6,2,7 . . .
a	2		
e	1		
e	2		
⋮	⋮		

11.11

REVIEW QUIZ

Indicate whether the following statements are true or false:

1. With

.byte 10[7]

we put the ASCII code for the keyboard bell into 10 consecutive bytes.

2. With

> byte 7[20],7

we put the ASCII code for the keyboard bell into 21 consecutive bytes.

3. With

> movab x + 4,r4

we put the content of loc. x + 4 into R4.

5. X + (R6) is the effective address of an operand specified by X(R6).

6. With

> x: .ascii/   /

we set up an array of contiguous bytes.

7. With

> x: .blkq 1

we do the same thing as

> x: .quad

8. With

> ediv r6,r7,r9,r10

a quadword is used for the dividend represented by R7.

9. With the EDIV instruction, the 3rd argument is used for the quotient.

10. The following array represents an efficient use of memory for a string array:

> x: blkw 80

11. String arrays use contiguous bytes.

12. .BLKB 1 does the same thing as .ASCII/   /.

13. .BYTE 65,65,65 does the same thing as .ASCII/AAA/.

14. .BYTE 65,12,15,65,12,15,65 does the same thing as

> ascii/A/⟨12⟩⟨15⟩/A/⟨12⟩⟨15⟩/A/

15. Byte rows cannot be used for integer arrays.

11.12

REFERENCES

Aho, A. V., J. E. Hopcroft, and J. D. Ullman. *Data Structures and Algorithms*. Reading, Mass.: Addison-Wesley, 1983.

Dahl, O.-J., and C. A. R. Hoare. "Hierarchical Program Structures." In *Structured Programming,* edited by O.-J. Dahl et al., 175–220. New York: Academic Press, 1972.

Levy, H. M. and R. H. Eckhouse, Jr. *Computer Programming and Architecture: The VAX-11*. Bedford, Mass.: Digital Press, 1980.

MacEwen, G. H. *Introduction to Computer Systems Using the PDP-11 and Pascal*. New York: McGraw-Hill, 1980.

12.
ADVANCED I/O

In the world of the shaping spirit, save for its patterns, there is nothing new that was not old.

—J. L. Lowes, *The Road to Zanadu*

12.0
AIMS

- Enhance the numeric entry procedure.
- Introduce the ASH and MOVC instructions.
- Show how to load an array of numbers.
- Introduce a scanner routine.
- Enhance the numeric output procedure.
- Illustrate the combined use of the new I/O procedures.
- Give an enhanced I/O procedure library.

12.1
INTRODUCTION

Up to this point we have used fairly primitive routines to handle terminal I/O of numbers. It is often necessary and convenient to enter more than one number on a single line of input. It is also helpful to keep track of how many numbers are entered on each input line. This chapter shows how to enhance the READVAL routine so that you can do both of these things. It also includes a variable base that will enable you to change the base relative to the numbers being entered.

We have used base ten as the default base for all numeric I/O so far. This chapter explains how to enhance the WRITEVAL routine to permit printing of numbers in bases two through sixty-two.

These enhancements give us, for example, more efficient ways to load arrays of numbers and conversions of results from one base to another. We incorporate the newer I/O routines in our earlier library of procedures.

This chapter also shows how to use the ASH (arithmetic shift) instruction to compute products, how to use the MOVC (move characters) to copy one string to another, and how to obtain the radix point representation of ratios of numbers in different bases.

12.2

ENHANCEMENT OF THE NUMERIC INPUT ROUTINE

Thus far we have relied on a numeric input routine that took a single number from the keyboard buffer in terms of the ASCII codes for each digit of the number. The ASCII bias was removed successively for each digit and a single number built up in a register (we used R6). Once all the ASCII codes had been removed from the keyboard buffer, the final number in R6 was copied into the location whose address was stored in the stack frame with

```
MOVL      R6,     @4     (ap)
```

argument pointer (ap)

4 bytes over from the beginning address of the ap
displacement deferred mode where displacement = 4 and
address of the destination is given in the longword
location immediately following the ap

number built by READVAL routine

This procedure is primitive. It allows us access to one number per line entered at a keyboard. In building this number, we have limited numeric entry to base ten. This is awkward, since we often need to work with numbers in other bases.

To remedy the problem of single-entry input, we introduce a register stack inside the input routine itself. We introduce a global variable STACK, which will serve as the address of the bottom of the numeric entry stack.

We also introduce a global variable COUNT to maintain a tally of how many numbers are given on each input line. This information will be useful later in determining when we have emptied the numeric input stack.

Finally, we introduce a global variable BASE. We give BASE a default value of 10, which will be used in building numeric input stack entries, unless the user specifies otherwise. This BASE variable can be changed within a program by calling the new READVAL routine or by prompting for a new base during program execution. The READVAL routine can be used to get the new base, which, in turn, can be used by the program to change the BASE variable. This is illustrated later in the chapter.

Basically, the key to the enhancement of the READVAL routine is recognition of the presence of a comma or a space between numbers on an input line. Since the ASCII codes for a comma (ASCII 44 [base ten]) or a space (ASCII 32 [decimal]) are less than the ASCII codes for the digits 0 through 9, fishing for commas or spaces on the input line is straightforward with

CMPB ⟨input code⟩, #48

The ASCII code 48 (decimal) is the code for zero. If the above CMPB statement detects that ⟨input⟩ is less than #48, this will serve as a signal to push the number built up in R6 onto the numeric input stack. The framework for the READVAL procedure is shown in Figure 12.1.

For example, suppose we enter

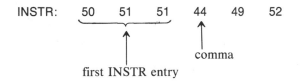

so that in the INSTR array we have

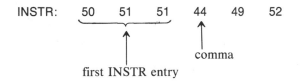

The steps outlined in the procedure in Figure 12.1 lead to the results shown in Figure 12.2 (assume BASE = ten).

Notice in Figure 12.2 the state of the R11 stack when the reading is

FIGURE 12.1
Procedure for Numeric Input

```
;
;Ref.: Figure 12.1 (Enhanced Numeric Input Procedure)
;
Procedure for Numeric Input;
Var
        TTIOLEN,COUNT,BASE: Integer;
        INSTR: Array [1..80] of Char;
        STACK: Array [1..80] of Integer;
Begin
1. Initialize COUNT:=0,I,J:=1,BASE and TTIOLEN;
2. Load INSTR with ASCII codes for input digits and delimiters;
3. Begin constructing number:
        3.1 INSTR[I] := INSTR[I] - 48;
        3.2 STACK[J] := STACK[J] * BASE;
        3.3 STACK[J] := STACK[J] + INSTR[I];
        3.4 I := I + 1;
        3.5 If INSTR[I] >= 48
            then
                3.5.1 TTIOLEN := TTIOLEN - 1;
                3.5.2 If TTIOLEN > 0
                        then repeat step 3.1
                        else
                        3.5.2.1 COUNT := COUNT + 1;
                        3.5.2.2 TTIOLEN := TTIOLEN - 1;
                        3.5.2.3 If TTIOLEN = 0
                                    then exit
                                    else
                                    3.5.2.3.1 I := I + 1;
                                    3.5.2.3.2 TTIOLEN := TTIOLEN - 1;
                                    3.5.2.3.3 If TTIOLEN > 0
                                                  then repeat step 3.1
                                                  else exit
    end.
```

complete:

```
        ─────
          ⋮
        ─────
        ─────
        ─────
         14       STACK +8 (stack top)
         233      STACK +4 (stack bottom)
                  STACK (address that precedes initial
                          stack entry)
        ──────
R11 - stack entries
```

The enhanced READVAL procedure reflects the steps shown in Figures 12.1 and 12.2. The actual READVAL routine is shown in Figure 12.3. Remember, however, that the labels STACK, COUNT, and BASE are global and *reserved*. Since they are defined inside the READVAL procedure, they do need to be defined again in a program that calls READVAL. Their contents can be *shared* by both the READVAL procedure and the calling program. Notice, also, that R11 points to the top of the numeric entry stack when the reading is complete. This can be used to advantage in a main program.

FIGURE 12.2
Calculations with the READVAL Procedure

REMOVE Loop:

$|\overline{50}|$ - 48 = 2

Save 2 in R7

R6: = R6*10 = 0*10

R6: = R6+R7 = 0+2

Check for comma in next byte

Decrement TTIOLEN (6-1)

$|\overline{51}|$ - 48 = 3

Save 3 in R7

R6: = R6*10 = 2*10 = 20

R6: = R6+R7 = 20+3 = 23

Check for comma in next byte

Decrement TTIOLEN (5-1)

$|\overline{51}|$ - 48 = 3

Save 3 in R7

R6: = R6*10 = 23*10 = 230

R6: = R6+R7 = 230+3 = 233

Check for comma in next byte

$|\overline{44}|$ is detected!

NEWNUM Loop:

Push R6 into R11-stack

Decrement TTIOLEN (4-1)

(advance to comma)

Clear R6

(get ready for

next number)

Advance INSTR pointer

to next byte

Decrement TTIOLEN (3-1)

(advance part

comma)

REMOVE Loop:

$|\overline{49}|$ - 48 = 1

Save 1 in R7

R6: = R6*10 = 0*10 = 0

R6: = R6+R7 = 0+1 = 1

Check for comma in next byte

Decrement TTIOLEN (2-1)

$|\overline{52}|$ - 48 = 4

Save 4 in R7

R6: = R6*10 = 1*10 = 10

R6: = R6+R7 = 10+4 = 14

Check for comma in next byte

Decrement TTIOLEN (1-1)

And exit (TTIOLEN = 0, now!)

NEWNUM Loop, again:

Push R6 into R11-stack

Detect zero in TTIOLEN

And exit from READVAL

routine

FIGURE 12.3
Enhanced Numeric Input Routine

```
;
;Ref.: Figure 12.3 (Enhanced Numeric Entry Routine)
;
          . = . + 100                        ;storage for downward stack
STACK:: .LONG
COUNT:: .LONG                                ;tally of no. of entries
                                             ;on STACK
BASE::  .LONG 10                             ;default base for entries
INSTR:: .BLKB 80                             ;storage for entered codes
TTNAME::.ASCID/_TTD6:/                       ;device name (this will vary)
TTCHAN::.BLKW 1                              ;I/O channel
TTIOSB::.BLKW 1                              ;I/O status block
TTIOLEN::
        .WORD
        .LONG                                ;length of entered string
                                             ;(this counts the bytes
                                             ;containing the char. codes)
OUTLEN::.BLKL 1                              ;length of string
ERROR:  BLBS R0,10$                          :I/O error routine
        $EXIT_S R0
10$:    RSB
;
        .ENTRY READVAL,^M<R6,R7,R8,R9>
;
        $ASSIGN_S
                DEVNAM=TTNAME,-              ;device name
                CHAN=TTCHAN                  ;I/O channel used
        BSBW ERROR
;
        $INPUT -                             :system input macro
                CHAN=TTCHAN,-               ;channel used
                LENGTH=#80,-                :size of input buffer
                BUFFER=INSTR                 ;use for KB buffer
                                             ;to hold codes entered

                IOSB=TTIOSB
;
        MOVAB   STACK,R11                    ;set up R11 stack pointer
        MOVZWL  TTIOLEN,R9                   ;save size of entered
                                             ;string in R9
        MOVAB   INSTR,R8                     ;set up R8 as pointer
                                             ;to char. codes
        CLRL    R6
        CLRL    COUNT
REMOV:  SUBB2   #48,(R8)                     ;drop ASCII bias from code
        MOVZBL  (R8)+,R7                     ;save adjusted value in R7
        MULL2   BASE,R6                      ;times base
        ADDL2   R7,R6                        ;add unit's place digit
        CMPB    (R8),#48                     ;see if next char. code
                                             ;represents a digit
        BLSS    NEWNUM                       ;if not, it's a delimiter
                                             ;separating 2 nos. or the
                                             ;end of the string
                                             ;else
        SOBGTR  R9,REMOV                     ;continue removing char.
```

Figure 12.3 continued.

```
                                            ;codes until TTIOLEN = 0
        NEWNUM:
                MOVL     R6,-(R11)          ;push no.
                INCL     COUNT              ;increment stack tally
                DECL     R9                 ;adjust byte count
                TSTL     R9                 ;last byte?
                BEQL     LEAVE              ;if so, exit
                                            ;else
                CLRL     R6                 ;get R6 ready for next no.
                TSTB     (R8)+              ;slide pointer over to next code
                SOBGTR   R9,REMOV           ;continue until TTIOLEN = 0
        ;
        LEAVE:  $DASSGN_S -
                         CHAN=TTCHAN        ;close I/O channel
        ;
                RET
                .END
```

12.2.1 Applications of the New READVAR Procedure

The interaction between a main program and the READVAL routine is illustrated first in terms of loading an array of numbers. What we do is pop the R11-stack entries into an array, using the value of COUNT to tell us when to stop popping. Then we echo-print the NOS-array we have loaded. The program in Figure 12.4 takes advantage of the fact that STACK points to the bottom of the R11 stack. We restore the bottom STACK pointer before we *start* loading the NOS array each time in a pop loop. This allows us to build the NOS array with the numeric entries in the order they were entered from a keyboard. In effect, we are using the stack array as a circular list. That is, we return to the *beginning* of the list each time we reach the end of this list; we travel in a circle. This is to our advantage if we want to work with an ordered list. Also, notice that we maintain a separate variable TOTAL, which we use to keep track of the total number of entries. This is to our advantage if we have more than one line of input.

Try this program without the circular list feature

```
MOVAB STACK, R11      ;restore the address
                      ;of the stack bottom
```

Try this revised version of the above program in terms of several lines of input. Suppose we entered K lines of numbers. What would we need to do to allow us to print even-numbered rows in reverse order, odd-numbered rows in the original order? The secret, here, is to save the COUNT value for each line (try pushing the COUNTs onto a separate register stack). Then, depending on the row, we must decide when to restore the R11-stack bottom in popping numbers into the NOS array. If the R11-stack bottom address is

FIGURE 12.4
Loading an Array of Numbers

```
;
;Ref.: Figure 12.4 (LOADING AN ARRAY OF NOS. WITH THE ENHANCED
;                   READVAL ROUTINE)
;
NOS:      .BLKL 50
TOTAL:    .LONG
;
BEGIN:    .WORD
          MOVAB   NOS,R6
LOAD:     WRITELN <ENTER ROW OF NOS--A 999 BY ITSELF TO QUIT>
          WRITELN
          CALLS   #0,READVAL             ;get row of nos.
          CMPL    #999,(R11)             ;see if sentinel has been
                                         ;entered
          BEQL    NEXT                   ;if so, start echo-printing
                                         ;else
          ADDL2   COUNT,TOTAL            ;update TOTAL no. of entries
                                         ;with COUNT variable maintained
                                         ;by the READVAL routine
;
          MOVAB   STACK,R11              ;restore addr. of BOTTOM
                                         ;of stack which is set up
                                         ;by the READVAL routine
BUILD:
          MOVL    -(R11),(R6)+           ;copy entries into NOS-array
          SOBGTR  COUNT,BUILD            ;& continue until COUNT = 0
;
          JMP     LOAD                   ;continue data-entry
;
NEXT:     MOVAB   NOS,R6                 ;restore beginning address
                                         ;of NOS array
;
          WRITELN
          WRITELN
          WRITELN <--------------------------------->
          WRITELN
          WRITELN
          WRITELN <    Echo-print of entries:>
          WRITELN
          WRITELN
ECHO:
          PUSHL   (R6)+                  ;set up stack frame to
          CALLS   #1,WRITEVAL            ;print entries
          SPACE   <2>
          SOBGTR  TOTAL,ECHO
;
          WRITELN
          WRITELN
          WRITELN <--------------------------------->
          $EXIT_S
          .END BEGIN
```

Figure 12.4 continued.

```
RUN FG124

ENTER ROW OF NOS--A 999 BY ITSELF TO QUIT

2,3,45,1,2,2,2,3,44,233
ENTER ROW OF NOS--A 999 BY ITSELF TO QUIT

144,13,377,610,29,47
ENTER ROW OF NOS--A 999 BY ITSELF TO QUIT

999

---------------------------------------


   Echo-print of entries:


2   3   45   1   2   2   2   3   44   233   144   13   377   610   29   47

---------------------------------------
```

FIGURE 12.5
Procedure for a Scanner

```
;
;Ref.: Figure 12.5 (Procedure for a Numeric Array Scanner)
;
Procedure for a Scanner;
Var
        I,BUFF,N,MAX,RESULT,COUNT: Integer;
        L: Array [1..n] of Integer;
Begin
1. Load L; Initialize I := 1;J := 1;RESULT := L[I];MAX;
2. Begin scan:
        2.1 (outer loop:) BUFF := 0;
        2.2 (inner loop:) BUFF := BUFF + 1;I := J;J := I + 1;
        2.3 (compare J and MAX):
            If J = MAX
               then exit to step 3
               else (compare L[I] and L[J])
                 If L[I] = L[J]
                    then repeat step 2.2
                    else (compare BUFF and COUNT)
                      If BUFF <= COUNT
                         then repeat step 2.1
                         else
                            COUNT := BUFF;
                            RESULT := L[I];
                            Repeat step 2.1
3. print RESULT and COUNT
End.
```

351

FIGURE 12.6
A Scanner Program

```
;
;REF.: FIG. 12.6 (Scanner Program)
;
NOS:      .BLKL 200
EDGE:     .LONG
TOTAL:    .LONG
ELEMENT:.LONG
NEW_COUNT:
          .LONG
OLD_COUNT:
          .LONG
;
BEGIN:    .WORD
          WRITELN
          WRITE <--------------------------------------------------->
          WRITELN
          TAB <1>
          WRITE<THIS PROGRAM ALLOWS YOU TO ENTER ROWS OF POS. INTEGERS>
          WRITELN
          WRITELN <(UP TO 20 PER LINE WITH A MAXIMUM OF 200 NOS.).  ENTER A>
          WRITELN <999 BY ITSELF ON A LINE TO TERMINATE DATA ENTRY.  THIS >
          WRITELN <PROGRAM THEN ECHO-PRINTS WHAT WAS ENTERED AND, THEN, PRINTS>
          WRITELN <THE FREQUENCY OF THE NO. THAT OCCURS MOST OFTEN.  ENTER THE>
          WRITELN <NOS. IN ASCENDING ORDER.  LATER, THIS PROGRAM CAN BE REFINED>
          WRITELN <TO ALLOW THE USER TO ENTER THE NOS. IN ANY ORDER.>
          WRITELN
          WRITELN <--------------------------------------------------->
          WRITELN
          WRITELN
;
          MOVAB   NOS,R6              ;set up R6 as a nos.-array
                                      ;pointer
;
LOAD:     WRITELN <ENTER ROW OF NOS--A 999 BY ITSELF TO QUIT>
          WRITELN
          CALLS   #0,READVAL          ;get row numbers, which
                                      ;will be pushed onto a
                                      ;register-stack using R11
          CMPL    #999,(R11)          ;check for sentinel=999
          BEQL    NEXT                ;if found, then stop data-entry
                                      ;else
          ADDL2   COUNT,TOTAL         ;update tally of entries made
                                      ;using COUNT maintained by
                                      ;the READVAL routine
;
          MOVAB   STACK,R11           ;restore the address of the
                                      ;BOTTOM of the R11 stack
                                      ;(note: the STACK variable
                                      ;is set up in the READVAL
                                      ;routine)
BUILD:
          MOVL    -(R11),(R6)+        ;save entries in the NOS
                                      ;array (they are PUSHED
                                      ;from the R11 stack into the
```

Figure 12.6A continued.

```
                                     ;NOS array)
          SOBGTR  COUNT,BUILD        ;continue until COUNT = 0
;
          JMP    LOAD                ;return to READVAL routine
;
NEXT:
          WRITELN
          WRITELN
          WRITE <    Echo print:>
          WRITELN
          MOVAB  NOS,R6              ;restore the beginning addr.
                                     ;of the NOS array
;
ECHO:
          PUSHL  (R6)+               ;set up stack frame to
          CALLS  #1,WRITEVAL         ;print entry
          SPACE  <2>                 ;2 spaces
          SOBGTR TOTAL,ECHO          ;continue until TOTAL = 0
          WRITELN
          WRITELN
          WRITE <-------------------------------------->
          WRITELN
;
          MOVAB  NOS,R6              ;restore beginning addr.
                                     ;of NOS array
;
OUTER_LOOP:
          CLRL   NEW_COUNT           ;init. temporary counter
;
INNER_LOOP:
          INCL   NEW_COUNT           ;begin count
          CMPL   R6,#EDGE            ;see if we have reached
                                     ;the edge of the NOS array
          BEQL   STATISTICS          ;if so, print results
                                     ;else
BUMP:
          CMPL   (R6)+,(R6)          ;compare adjacent entries
          BEQL   INNER_LOOP          ;if equal, update counter
                                     ;else
          CMPL   NEW_COUNT,OLD_COUNT ;compare counters
          BLEQ   OUTER_LOOP          ;if NEW_COUNT <= OLD_COUNT
                                     ;then continue with outer
                                     ;loop with init. NEW_COUNT
                                     ;else
          MOVL   NEW_COUNT,OLD_COUNT ;update OLD_COUNT &
          MOVL   -(R6),ELEMENT       ;save ele. with current freq.
          BRW    OUTER_LOOP          ;& continue with outer loop
;
STATISTICS:
          WRITELN
          TAB <1>
          PUSHL  ELEMENT             ;set up stack frame to
          CALLS  #1,WRITEVAL         ;print ele.
          WRITE < OCCURS MOST OFTEN, WITH A FREQUENCY OF  >
```

Continued on following page.

Figure 12.6C continued.

```
        PUSHL   OLD_COUNT                ;set up stack frame to
        CALLS   #1,WRITEVAL              ;print frequency of ele.
        WRITELN
        WRITELN
;
        $EXIT_S
        .END BEGIN


RUN FG126


--------------------------------------------------
        THIS PROGRAM ALLOWS YOU TO ENTER ROWS OF POS. INTEGERS
(UP TO 20 PER LINE WITH A MAXIMUM OF 200 NOS.).  ENTER A
999 BY ITSELF ON A LINE TO TERMINATE DATA ENTRY.  THIS
PROGRAM THEN ECHO-PRINTS WHAT WAS ENTERED AND, THEN, PRINTS
THE FREQUENCY OF THE NO. THAT OCCURS MOST OFTEN.  ENTER THE
NOS. IN ASCENDING ORDER.  LATER, THIS PROGRAM CAN BE REFINED
TO ALLOW THE USER TO ENTER THE NOS. IN ANY ORDER.


--------------------------------------------------


ENTER ROW OF NOS--A 999 BY ITSELF TO QUIT

3,3,3,3,3,3,5,6,77,77,77,88,88,88
ENTER ROW OF NOS--A 999 BY ITSELF TO QUIT

144,144,144,144,144,144,144,32767
ENTER ROW OF NOS--A 999 BY ITSELF TO QUIT

999


   Echo print:
3  3  3  3  3  3  5  6  77  77  77  88  88  88  144  144  144  144  144  144
144  32767


-----------------------------------------

        144  OCCURS MOST OFTEN, WITH A FREQUENCY OF  7
```

not restored in R11 before popping, then the R11-stack entries would be loaded into the NOS array in reverse order relative to the way they were entered from a keyboard. This will be demonstrated later in an exercise.

12.2.2 Another Application: A Scanner Routine

We can extend the idea in Figure 12.4 by building a program to scan an ordered list of numeric entries to determine the frequency of the entry that occurs most often. What follows is an assembly language problem inspired by a problem in Gill (1983, p. 66). The scanner procedure is shown in Figure 12.5.

The trick here is to maintain two counters, one for the frequency of occurrence of one element being compared with its neighbors, the other for the frequency of the element occurring most often. The algorithm in this scanner routine depends on an ordered list being fed to it. The two counters maintain tallies on the current pair of elements and its predecessors, only. We use the new READVAL procedure to build a copy of the ordered list in the NOS array. Once the array is built, the beginning address of the NOS array is retrieved and a scan of the list begins (see Figure 12.6).

A later exercise will show you how to enhance this program to obtain frequency counts for the other numbers in the list. We also allow the user to load the NOS array with an unordered list, which we sort and then scan for frequencies. Each enhancement should add flexibility to a program. Enhancements tend to make a program more readable and, often, more understandable.

12.3
ENHANCEMENT OF THE NUMERIC OUTPUT PROCEDURE

Up to now we have used a default base of ten in converting the digits of numbers to their corresponding ASCII codes. We have used the following steps:

1. Divide a number by 10.
2. Save the quotient Q, then obtain the remainder R.
3. Restore the ASCII bias by adding 48 to R.
4. Save the new R.
5. Repeat step 1 until Q = 0.
6. Copy the digits into INSTR for printing by the QIO macro.

We introduce a global variable BASE and add some extensions to step 3 in the above procedure for the WRITEVAL routine. That is, we include

> 3) restore the ASCII bias by adding 48 to R
>> 3.1) see if the new R ⟩ ASCII 57 (for a 9)
>>> if so, add 7 to the new R to obtain an upper case letter code from the ASCII table

FIGURE 12.7
Enhanced Numeric Output Procedure

```
;
;Ref.:  Figure 12.7 (Enhanced Numeric Output Routine)
;
BASE::  .BYTE   10
INSTR:: .BLKB   80                      ;storage for entered codes
TTNAME::.ASCID/_TTD6:/                   ;device name
TTCHAN::.BLKW   1                       ;I/O channel to be used
TTIOSB::.BLKW   1                       ;I/O status block
TTIOLEN::
        .WORD
        .LONG
OUTLEN::
        .BLKL   1                       ;length of string
ERROR:  BLBS    R0,10$
        $EXIT_S R0
10$:    RSB
;
        .ENTRY WRITEVAL,^M<R6,R7,R8,R9>
;
        $ASSIGN_S -                     ;system macro to
                DEVNAM=TTNAME,-         ;assign an I/O device &
                CHAN=TTCHAN             ;I/O channel to be used
        BSBW    ERROR
;
        MOVAB   INSTR,R9                ;set up R9 as string ptr
        MOVL    4(AP),R6                ;store no. to be printed
                                        ;in R6
        ADDL2   #80,R9                  ;start with 1´s place of no.
        CLRL    OUTLEN                  ;set up for printing string
FETCH:  MOVL    R6,R7                   ;copy value into R7
        DIVL2   BASE,R6                 ;divide by base desired to get quotient
        MOVL    R6,R8                   ;copy quotient
        MULL2   BASE,R6                 ;multiply by base
        SUBL2   R6,R7                   ;and subtract to get remainder
        ADDL2   #48,R7                  ;add ascii bias
        CMPL    #57,R7                  ;see if we need more ascii bias
        BGEQ    NEXT                    ;if not, go to store digit
        ADDL2   #7,R7                   ;provides for bases 11-36
        CMPL    #90,R7                  ;more ascii bias?
        BGEQ    NEXT                    ;
        ADDL2   #6,R7                   ;provides for bases 37-62
NEXT:   MOVB    R7,-(R9)                ;place ascii digit in string
        INCL    OUTLEN                  ;increment length of string
        MOVL    R8,R6                   ;get old quotient back
        BNEQ    UNLOAD                  ;if it is not zero, more computation
        MOVL    OUTLEN,R8               ;else, prepare to print
        MOVAB   INSTR,R7                ;prepare to move digits from end of
LOOP:   MOVB    (R9)+,(R7)+             ;string to beginning
        SOBGTR  R8,LOOP

        $QIOW_S -                       ;output macro, queue I/O request, wait
                EFN=#1, -               ;event flag
                CHAN=TTCHAN, -          ;specify channel
                FUNC=#IO$_WRITEVBLK, -  ;specify I/O function
```

356

Figure 12.7A continued.

```
              P1=INSTR, -              ;specify string to be printed
              P2=OUTLEN, -             ;specify length of string
      BSBW    ERROR

      $DASSGN_S -                      ;macro to deassign
              CHAN=TTCHAN              ;channel

      RET
      .END
```

    3.2) see if the new *R* (after adding 7) is greater than ASCII 90 (for a Z). If so, add 6 to the new *R* to obtain a lower case letter code from the ASCII table

The rest of the WRITEVAL routine is the same as that given earlier. The enhanced routine appears in Figure 12.7.

The combination of the new READVAL *and* WRITEVAL routines produce some nice results. The potential of this combination is hinted at in the program presented in Figure 12.8. We take in a single number, then take in a selection of bases to which we convert the initial number. The result is a somewhat impressive medley of representations of the original number.

This time we do not tamper with the order of the entries of the bases on the R11-stack. Hence the reversed order of the results. A later exercise shows how to improve the display of these results. In the results shown, base forty has the following symbols:

$$0, \ldots, 9, \underset{10}{A}, \underset{11}{B}, \ldots, \underset{33}{X}, \underset{34}{Y}, \underset{35}{Z}, \underset{36}{a}, \underset{37}{b}, \underset{38}{c}, \underset{39}{d}, \underset{40}{e}$$

That is,

34 (base ten) = Y (base forty)

12.3.1 The ASH (Arithmetic SHift) Instruction

If it is necessary to multiply or divide a quantity by a power of 2, then the ASH instruction is handy. As a rule, the ASH instruction will take a third less time to execute than the corresponding MUL instructions. We show below the options possible with an ASH in terms of multiplying a number by a power of 2:

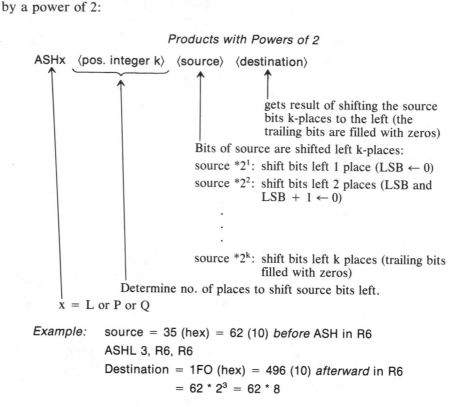

Products with Powers of 2

ASHx ⟨pos. integer k⟩ ⟨source⟩ ⟨destination⟩

gets result of shifting the source bits k-places to the left (the trailing bits are filled with zeros)

Bits of source are shifted left k-places:

source $*2^1$: shift bits left 1 place (LSB ← 0)

source $*2^2$: shift bits left 2 places (LSB and LSB + 1 ← 0)

.
.
.

source $*2^k$: shift bits left k places (trailing bits filled with zeros)

Determine no. of places to shift source bits left.

x = L or P or Q

Example: source = 35 (hex) = 62 (10) *before* ASH in R6

ASHL 3, R6, R6

Destination = 1FO (hex) = 496 (10) *afterward* in R6

$= 62 * 2^3 = 62 * 8$

A graphical interpretation of the ASH instruction is presented in Figure 12.9.

The same instruction can be used to divide a number by a power of 2. This time we use a negative integer:

ASHx ⟨neg. k⟩ ⟨source⟩ ⟨destination⟩

shift source bits to the *right* k place with the high bits filled with zeros

This instruction can be illustrated in terms of producing a radix point representation of two octal integers. The trick in the program that follows is to

1. Obtain a quotient and remainder by dividing two integers.

2. Repeatedly multiply the remainder by 8 to isolate *successively* (by division by 8) the digits that follow the radix 8 point. In effect

(Remainder * 8)/8 to get digit $/8^{-1}$

(Remainder * 8 * 8)/8 to get digit $/8^{-2}$

(Remainder * 8 * 8 * 8)/8 to get digit $/8^{-3}$

FIGURE 12.8
Medley of Representations of an Integer

```
;
;Ref.:  Figure 12.8 (Medley of representations of an integer)
;
NUMBER: .LONG
Begin:  .word
        WRITELN
        WRITE <Enter the number you want printed:  >
        WRITELN
        CALLS   #0,READVAL
        MOVL    (R11)+,NUMBER
        WRITELN
        WRITELN <Enter bases for medley of representations of entered no.: >
        WRITELN
        CALLS   #0,READVAL
        MOVL    COUNT,R10
        WRITELN <--------------------------------------------->
        WRITELN
        WRITELN
LOOP:   MOVL    (R11)+,BASE
        PUSHL   NUMBER
        CALLS   #1,WRITEVAL
        SPACE   <3>
        SOBGTR  R10,LOOP
        $EXIT_S
        .END Begin


RUN FG128

Enter the number you want printed:
34

Enter bases for medley of representations of entered no.:

2,16,34,40
---------------------------------------------


Y    10   22   100010
```

and so on.

Figure 12.10 illustrates this in a specialized program using a single pair of integers.

It happens that successive ratios of Fibonacci numbers tend to approach the golden ratios or

1.61803

FIGURE 12.9
Graphical Interpretation of ASH Instruction

Step 0:

Content of location 250 <u>before</u> ASH: A000007A

Bits:

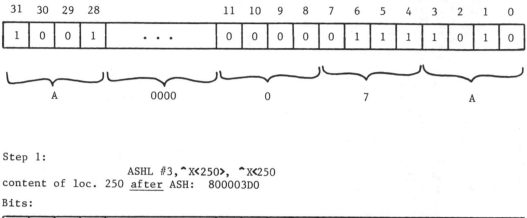

Step 1:

ASHL #3, ˆX‹250›, ˆX‹250

content of loc. 250 <u>after</u> ASH: 800003D0

Bits:

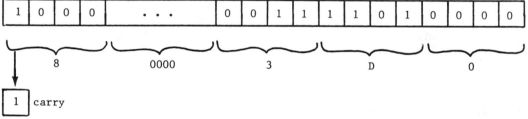

The result in the above program can be interpreted as follows:

1.4743357156 (octal)

$$= 1 + 4 \times 8^{-1} + 7 \times 8^{-2} + 4 \times 8^{-3} + 3 \times 8^{-4} + 3 \times 8^{-5}$$
$$+ 7 \times 8^{-6} + 1 \times 8^{-7} + 5 \times 8^{-8} + 6 \times 8^{-9}$$
$$= 1 + 0.5 + 0.11 + 0.000781 + 0.0007 + 0.00009 + \ldots$$
$$= 1.16157 \text{ (decimal)}$$

For efficiency, the ASH instruction can be used to enhance earlier programs to replace the

MULL2 #10, ⟨operand⟩

in terms of the ASH instruction. That is, we can interpret the above product

FIGURE 12.10
A Program to Compute Ratios

```
;
;Ref.: Figure 12.10 (A Program to Compute Ratios)
;
Q:        .LONG                           ;quotient
R:        .LONG                           ;remainder
X:        .LONG 2178309                   ;Fibonacci no. f(32)
Y:        .LONG 3524578                   ;Fibonacci no. f(33)
                                          ;(Note: the ratio f(33)/f(32)
                                          ;approx. the golden ratio
                                          ;or (1 + sqrt(5))/2
;
BEGIN:    .WORD
          WRITELN
          WRITELN
          WRITE < golden ratio is approximately    >
          CLRL    R7                      ;set up R7 to form the
                                          ;double-double or quad word
                                          ;with R6 and R7
          MOVL    Y,R6                    ;put dividend in R6
COMPUTE:
          EDIV    X,R6,Q,R                ;get quot. & remainder
;
          PUSHL   Q                       ;set up stack frame to
          CALLS   #1,WRITEVAL             ;print quotient
;
          WRITE < . >                     ;print radix point
;
          .REPEAT 10                      ;begin REPEAT loop
          ASHL    #3,R,R                  ;shift R-bits to left 3 bits
                                          ;which is the same as finding
                                          ;product R * 8
          MOVL    R,R6                    ;init. dividend
          CLRL    R7                      ;clear high double word
                                          ;of R6-R7 quad word
          EDIV    X,R6,Q,R                ;get new remainder
          PUSHL   Q                       ;set up stack frame to
          CALLS   #1,WRITEVAL             ;print digit of ratio
          SPACE   <1>                     ;space
          .ENDR
          WRITE <( BASE 8 )>
          WRITELN
          WRITELN
          WRITE <---------------------------------------->
          WRITELN
          WRITELN
          $EXIT_S
          .END BEGIN


RUN FG1210

 golden ratio is approximately    1 . 4 7 4 3 3 5 7 1 5 6 ( BASE 8 )

----------------------------------------
```

FIGURE 12.11
A Program to Compute Radix Point Representations

```
;
;REF.: FIGURE 12.11 (RADIX POINT REPRESENTATIONS OF RATIOS)
;
Q:      .LONG                         ;Q=quotient
R:      .LONG                         ;R=remainder
;
BEGIN:  .WORD
        WRITELN
        WRITE <--------------------------->
        WRITELN
        WRITELN
        WRITELN <THIS PROGRAM ALLOWS YOU A RADIX POINT REPRESENTATION>
        WRITELN <OF A PAIR OF INTEGERS.  YOU CAN SELECT THE BASE FOR>
        WRITELN <THE RATIO.>
        WRITELN
        WRITELN
        WRITE <--------------------------->
        WRITELN
        WRITELN
        WRITE <INPUT BASE FOR NOS. IN RATIO:  >
;
        CALLS  #0,READVAL             ;get base from keyboard
        MOVL   (R11)+,BASE            ;init. BASE variable
;
        WRITELN
        WRITE <PAIR OF INTEGERS IN NEW BASE:  >
;
        CALLS  #0,READVAL                 ;get pair of integers
                                          ;in new base
        WRITELN
        WRITELN
        MOVL   (R11)+,R8              ;init. R8 with divisor
        MOVL   (R11)+,R6              ;init. R6 with dividend
        CLRL   R7                     ;clear R7 as 2nd double
                                      ;word in R6-R7 combination
                                      ;(a quadword)
        EDIV   R8,R6,Q,R              ;get quot. & remainder
        PUSHL  Q                      ;set up stack frame to
        CALLS  #1,WRITEVAL            ;print quotient
        WRITE <.>                     ;print point
        .REPEAT 8                     ;begin REPEAT block:
        MULL2  BASE,R                 ;compute base * remainder
                                      ;to isolate leading digit
        MOVL   R,R6                   ;use remainder as new
                                      ;dividend
        CLRL   R7                     ;set up R6-R7 combination
        EDIV   R8,R6,Q,R              ;get digit = Q
        PUSHL  Q                      ;set up stack frame to
        CALLS  #1,WRITEVAL            ;print digit to right
                                      ;of the point
        .ENDR
;
        WRITE < base >
        PUSHL  BASE
```

Figure 12.11 continued.

```
                        CALLS  #1,WRITEVAL
                        $EXIT_S
                        .END BEGIN


        RUN FG1211


        -------------------------------


        THIS PROGRAM ALLOWS YOU A RADIX POINT REPRESENTATION
        OF A PAIR OF INTEGERS.  YOU CAN SELECT THE BASE FOR
        THE RATIO.


        -------------------------------


        INPUT BASE FOR NOS. IN RATIO:  16

        PAIR OF INTEGERS IN NEW BASE:  5,3


        1.AAAAAAAA  base  16

        RUN FG1211


        -------------------------------


        THIS PROGRAM ALLOWS YOU A RADIX POINT REPRESENTATION
        OF A PAIR OF INTEGERS.  YOU CAN SELECT THE BASE FOR
        THE RATIO.


        -------------------------------


        INPUT BASE FOR NOS. IN RATIO:  10

        PAIR OF INTEGERS IN NEW BASE:  28657,17711


        1.61803399  base  10
```

as a sum of products with powers of 2:

$$10 * \langle \text{quantity} \rangle = (8+2) * \langle \text{quantity} \rangle$$
$$= 8 * \langle \text{quantity} \rangle + 2 * \langle \text{quantity} \rangle$$

Assume the quantity we wish to multiply by 10 is in location X. Then using R6 to hold the partial sums, we get

```
ASHL #3, X, R6    (X * 8)
ASHL #1, X, X     (X * 2)
ADDL2 X, R6       (8x + 2x = 10x)
```

The above program can be improved by allowing the user to enter the numbers in the ratio from the keyboard. We do this later in an exercise.

12.3.2 Computing Ratios in Different Bases

Next we combine the use of the READVAL and WRITEVAL routines to compute ratios of numbers in different bases. This is an enhancement of the program in the preceding section. The trick is to prompt for the base of the ratio, first. This will allow us to change the BASE variable in the READVAL routine to accommodate the base of the numbers in the ratio entered by the user. This also allows us to generalize the mechanism for computing radix point representations of the remainders (see Figure 12.11).

The program can be made more efficient by replacing

    MULL2 BASE, R

with a combination of ASH and ADD instructions determined by the BASE-value. This enhancement is left as a challenge to the reader.

12.4

LOADING STRINGS: THE MOVC INSTRUCTION

VAX-11 macro includes an instruction that allows us to copy a string from one location to another. Although the mechanism to do this is simple, the result is fairly extraordinary. The format for the MOVC instruction is shown below:

MOVC ⟨source length⟩⟨source str.⟩⟨destin. str.⟩

k bytes of source = length

source: _____

_____

_____

destin.: _____

_____

What we need to do is utilize the TTIOLEN-value taken from the READSTR procedure routine after a string has been brought into the keyboard buffer by the READSTR procedure. We use INSTR for this buffer. We can use

FIGURE 12.12
A Program to Copy Strings with MOVC

```
;
;Ref.:  Figure 12.12 (COPYING ONE STRING TO ANOTHER)
;
X:        .BYTE
          .BLKB 80
BEGIN:    .WORD
          WRITELN<ENTER STRING:>
          PUSHAB X+1
          CALLS   #0,READSTR          ;load string into INSTR array
                                      ;copy INSTR-array into X-array
                                      ;using the TTIOLEN variable set
                                      ;up by the READSTR routine
                                      ;(note: we start loading at 2nd
                                      ;byte of the X-array to begin
                                      ;setting up simulated .ASCIC
                                      ;string-array
          MOVB    TTIOLEN,X           ;load first byte of X-array
                                      ;with the length of input-string
          SPURT   <X>                 ;display X-array!
          $EXIT_S
          .END BEGIN


RUN FG1212

ENTER STRING:
TUMTYTUMTYTUMTOES!
TUMTYTUMTYTUMTOES!
```

this value to advantage in the MOVC instruction. Then we can copy the
INSTR bytes into another byte array. This idea is illustrated in Figure 12.12.
In effect, this instruction greatly simplifies the BUILD routine given earlier
in the string handling program in Figures 11.13 and 11.15.

12.5

ENHANCED I/O PROCEDURE LIBRARY

We can now incorporate the changes discussed so far in the I/O library (see
Figure 12.13).

The global labels STACK::, BASE::, TTIOLEN::, INSTR::,
COUNT:: are reserved from now on. The trick is to learn to use the information they provide to main programs. Since we call procedures regularly,
we reserve the system stack for stack frames used by procedures. If we
need a stack, we set up our own register stack. We reserve R11 for I/O work
relative to READVAL.

FIGURE 12.13
Enhanced I/O Library

```
;
;Ref.: Figure 12.13 (Enhanced I/O Procedure Library)
;
;METHOD:
;
;          MACRO IO <RET>
;          LIB/CREAT/OBJ IO IO<RET>
;          LINK IOTEST+IO/LIB
;          RUN IOTEST
;
;          .ENABLE GBL
;
;DATA USED BY ALL PROCEDURES:
;
.              =. + 100                      ;storage for downwards stack
STACK::  .LONG                               ;label stack
COUNT::  .LONG                               ;counter for read routine
BASE::   .BYTE   10                          ;default base value for subroutines
INSTR::  .BLKB   80                          ;storage for strings going in and out

                   t
TTNAME:: .ASCID/_TTD6:/                      ;device name
TTCHAN:: .BLKW   1                           ;channel
TTIOSB:: .BLKW   1                           ;I/O Statue Block
TTIOLEN::
         .WORD
         .LONG
OUTLEN:: .BLKL   1                           ;length of string

ERROR:   BLBS    R0,10$                      ;error routine for I/O
         $EXIT_S R0
10$:     RSB

         .ENTRY  READVAL,^M<R6,R7,R8,R9>     ;reads in 1 or more values

         $ASSIGN_S -                         ;macro to specify
                 DEVNAM=TTNAME, -            ;device
                 CHAN=TTCHAN                 ;and channel

         BSBW    ERROR

         $INPUT -                            ;macro to read in string
                 CHAN=TTCHAN, -
                 LENGTH=#80, -
                 BUFFER=INSTR, -
                 IOSB=TTIOSB

         MOVAB   STACK,R11                   ;use R11 as pointer to stack
         MOVZWL  TTIOLEN,R9                  ;length of string read goes in R9
         MOVAB   INSTR,R8                    ;use R8 as pointer to chars of string
         CLRL    R6                          ;clear for number
         CLRL    COUNT                       ;reset count for new subroutine call
REMOV:   SUBB2   #48,(R8)                    ;remove ascii bias from 1st char
         MOVZBL  (R8)+,R7                    ;put value obtained in R7
```

Figure 12.13 continued.

```
            MULL2    BASE,R6                ;multiply number by base desired
            ADDL2    R7,R6                  ;and add value to it
            CMPB     (R8),#48               ;is next char a digit?
            BLSS     NEWNUM                 ;if not, it's a separator, so a new #
            SOBGTR   R9,REMOV               ;else, get value of next char
NEWNUM:     MOVL     R6,-(R11)              ;store the 1st number
            INCL     COUNT                  ;we have one (more) number on the
stack
            DECL     R9                     ;we have one less char in the string
            TSTL     R9                     ;are there more characters?
            BEQL     LEAVE                  ;if not, leave subroutine
            CLRL     R6                     ;else, clear R6 for a new number
            TSTB     (R8)+                  ;move to next char in string
            SOBGTR   R9,REMOV               ;go to evaluate nest char

LEAVE:      $DASSGN_S -                     ;end of subroutine, deassign
                     CHAN=TTCHAN            ;the channel


            RET

            .ENTRY   WRITEVAL,^M<R6,R7,R8,R9>;subroutine to write numbers

            $ASSIGN_S -                     ;macro to specify
                     DEVNAM=TTNAME, -       ;device
                     CHAN=TTCHAN            ;and channel

            BSBW     ERROR
            MOVAB    INSTR,R9               ;use R9 as pointer to string
            MOVL     4(AP),R6               ;get value of number to be printed
            ADDL2    #80,R9                 ;go to end of string, because we
                                           ;will start with 1's place on #
            CLRL     OUTLEN                 ;clear for length of string created
UNLOAD:     MOVL     R6,R7                  ;copy value in R7
            DIVL2    BASE,R6                ;divide by base desired to get
quotient
            MOVL     R6,R8                  ;copy quotient
            MULL2    BASE,R6                ;multiply by base
            SUBL2    R6,R7                  ;and subtract to get remainder
            ADDL2    #48,R7                 ;add ascii bias
            CMPL     #57,R7                 ;see if we need more ascii bias
            BGEQ     NEXT                   ;
            ADDL2    #7,R7                  ;provides for bases 11-36
            CMPL     #90,R7                 ;more ascii bias?
            BGEQ     NEXT
            ADDL2    #6,R7                  ;provides for bases 37-62
NEXT:       MOVB     R7,-(R9)
            INCL     OUTLEN
            MOVL     R8,R6
            BNEQ     UNLOAD
            MOVL     OUTLEN,R8
            MOVAB    INSTR,R7
LOOP:       MOVB     (R9)+,(R7)+
            SOBGTR   R8,LOOP
            $QIOW_S -
```

Continued on following page.

Figure 12.13 continued.

```
                        EFN=#1, -
                        CHAN=TTCHAN, -
                        FUNC=#IO$_WRITEVBLK, -
                        P1=INSTR, -
                        P2=OUTLEN

            BSBW        ERROR

            $DASSGN_S -
                        CHAN=TTCHAN

            RET

            .ENTRY   WRITESTR,^M<R6,R7,R8>

            $ASSIGN_S -
                        DEVNAM=TTNAME, -
                        CHAN=TTCHAN

            BSBW        ERROR

            MOVZBL      @4(AP),OUTLEN
            MOVL        OUTLEN,R6
            MOVL        4(AP),R7
            INCL        R7
            MOVAB       INSTR,R8
GET:        MOVB        (R7)+,(R8)+
            SOBGEQ      R6,GET

            $QIOW_S -
                        EFN=#1, -
                        CHAN=TTCHAN, -
                        FUNC=#IO$_WRITEVBLK, -
                        P1=INSTR, -
                        P2=OUTLEN

            BSBW        ERROR

            $DASSGN_S -
                        CHAN=TTCHAN

            RET

            .ENTRY   READSTR,0
;
            $ASSIGN_S -
                        DEVNAM=TTNAME, -
                        CHAN=TTCHAN

            BSBW        ERROR

            $INPUT -
                        CHAN=TTCHAN, -
                        LENGTH=#80, -
```

Figure 12.13 continued.

```
        BUFFER=INSTR, -
        IOSB=TTIOSB

$DASSGN_S -
        CHAN=TTCHAN

RET

.END
```

12.6
SUMMARY

To be useful, I/O procedures must be flexible. In a sense, I/O procedures must be built so that they can "reflect" on the data they are processing. This can be done with the READVAL routine by including a count of the number of numeric entries it finds in the keyboard buffer. We also set up two stack pointers, one for the top of the stack (the *current* address in R11) and one for the bottom of the stack. These are convenience features. They allow us to manage the numeric input more easily.

Another "hidden" feature of the new I/O routines is the global character of the procedure variables. We have already seen how useful TTI-OLEN can be to a main program in copying string from one location to another (Figure 12.12). The trick is to learn to use this information to advantage in main programs or in other procedures that call the I/O procedures.

12.7
EXERCISES

1. Assume location 250 has FOOAA80E in it. Assume each of the following instructions begins with this content. Give (i) the content of location 250 after executing the instruction, and (ii) a graphical interpretation of the action taken by the instruction (show what happens to the carry bit of the PSW; see Figure 12.9).

   (a) ASH *3, ^X⟨250⟩, ^X⟨250⟩

   (b) ASH #32, ^X⟨250⟩, ^X⟨250⟩

   (c) ASH #33, ^X⟨250⟩, ^X⟨250⟩

   (d) ASH #−3, ^X⟨250⟩, ^X⟨250⟩

(e) ASH # − 6, ˆX⟨250⟩, ˆX⟨250⟩

(f) ASH # − 30, @#ˆX⟨250⟩, @#ˆX⟨250⟩

2. Assume the user enters one of the following sets of numbers on a single line (use Figure 12.2 as a guide to show step by step how the READVAL routine handles the ASCII codes in the keyboard buffer):

   (a) 377,29

   (b) 29,377

   (c) 6001,1

3. If a negative integer like − 233 is entered, will this be "recognized" by the READVAL routine as a negative number? If not, why not?

4. Write a program to prompt the user to enter more than one line of numbers. Then print odd-numbered lines in the order entered, the even-numbered rows in reverse order. Run your program with the following sample data:

   Line 1: 1, 1, 2, 3, 5, 8, 13, 21, 34
   Line 2: 1597, 987, 610, 377, 233, 144, 89, 55
   Line 3: 2584, 4181, 6765, 10946, 17711, 28657

5. Write a program that will allow the user to enter a number and a base to use in printing the number in the desired base alongside the original number. In the output, include the old base and new base in parentheses next to the identity of the bases of the printed numbers. Run your program with

   (a) 32767, new base = sixteen

   (b) 2^{30}, new base = two (enter expanded form of 2^{30})

   (c) 2^{30}, new base = sixteen

   (d) 65536, new base = two

6. Enhance the program in exercise 5 to allow the user to enter more than one number at a time; get the output base; echo-print the entries; and print the entries in the new base.

7. Improve the scanner program in Figure 12.6 so that routines are added to

   (a) Determine the numeric entry with the lowest frequency.

   (b) Compute the average frequency of the numbers in the list (express this average with 3 places to the right of the decimal point).

(c) Print out the following table:

Scanner Statistics:

Element _____ with highest frequency = _____

Element _____ with lowest frequency = _____

Average frequency of appearance = _____

Element	Frequency	Element	Frequency
E[1]	C[1]	E[middle + 1]	C[middle + 1]

Note: Divide the list in two, so that half appears in the first column, the other half in the third column of the table. To compute the average, maintain counters for each distinct list element. You can do this with an array C[1], C[2], . . . , C[n]. Store the element corresponding to the first count C[1] in array element E[1], the element corresponding to C[2] in E[2], and so on. The C-elements will supply both the basis for computing the average A in

$$A = (C[1] + \ldots + C[n])/n$$

The C-elements will also supply the frequencies for your table. The E-elements allow you to build the rest of your table.

(d) Allow the user to rerun this program.

Run your program with

(e) The list in Figure 12.4 entered by the user.

(f) The following list:

> 0, 0, 0, 1, 5, 5, 5, 8, 13, 13, 13, 13, 21, 34, 34, 35, 35, 40, 40, 40, 40, 40, 41, 42, 43, 1000, 1001, 1001, 1001, 1002, 1050, 2200, 5000, 5000, 5000, 5002, 10000, 10001, 10001, 10001, 10001, 10005, 12000, 12000, 12000, 32000, 32001, 32001, 32001, 32767

8. Enhance the program in exercise 7 to allow the user to enter an unordered list, which produces the scanner statistics given in exercise 7. Run your program with the following list of numbers:

(a) 9, 33, 1, 1, 1, 0, 44, 55, 69, 44, 44, 233, 13, 13, 13, 21, 13, 21, 377, 610, 0, 1, 1, 2, 2, 0, 1, 1, 9, 33, 44, 610, 610, 610

(b) 55555, 5, 6, 5, 5, 55555, 1, 1, 1, 214214214, 21, 21, 3, 3, 3, 3, 1, 1, 55, 214214214, 5, 13, 21, 29, 29, 47, 29

9. Using the ASH instruction, given the assembly language equivalent of

the following instructions without the MUL instruction:

(a) MULL2 #12, R6

(b) MULL2 #544, R6

(c) MULL2 #8192, R6

(d) MULL2 #8448, R6

10. Enhance the program in Figure 12.10 to allow the user to select the numbers to be printed in the octal ratio. Run your program with the following numbers, which can be obtained from Appendix D:

(a) F(36)/F(37)

(b) F(37)/F(36)

(c) L(36)/L(37)

(d) L(37)/L(36)

11. Write a program to allow the user to enter two or more strings that are concatenated in an echo-print. Use the MOVC instruction to handle string constructions.

12.8

LAB PROJECTS

1. Write a well-structured program to

   (a) Prompt the user for a list of characters (allow a maximum of 10 strings, each with a maximum length of 70 columns) either ordered or unordered.

   (b) Carry out the steps in exercises 7 and 8 in scanning the list of characters. That is,

      1. Determine the frequency of each character.

      2. Determine the characters with the highest and lowest frequencies.

      3. Print a table showing the characters and their respective frequencies.

      4. Determine the average frequency.

      5. Allow the user to rerun the program.

2. Write an AL program that

   (a) Prompts the user for an input radix.

(b) Prompts the user for an output radix.

(c) Prompts the user for a pair of numbers in the input radix (be sure to include an indication of the input radix in your prompt).

(d) Prints the ratio of the input numbers in the output radix, along with an echo-print of the input numbers.

Run your program for

(e) Input radix = 16
Input 1AA1 and BE3
Output radix = 10

(f) Input radix = 16
Input 1AA1 and BE3
Output radix = 16

(g) Input radix = 16
Input 1AA1 and BE3
Output radix = 8

12.9

REVIEW QUIZ

Indicate whether the following statements are true or false:

1. ASHL #3,R6,R6 shifts the bits in R6 to the right 3 bits.

2. ASHL #32,R6,R6 leaves each bit in R6 zero.

3. The C bit of the PSW is conditionally set by the ASH instruction.

4. ASHL − 32,R6,R6 leaves each bit in R6 zero.

5. ASHL − 3,R6,R6 does the same thing as MULL2 #8,R6.

6. CALLS #0,READVAL is a call-by-value without a value for READVAL.

7. CALLS #1,WRITEVAL is a call-by-value with 1 value for WRITEVAL.

8. The following is a legal label for a procedure:

   A_way_a_lone_a_last_a_loved_a_long_the_riverrun:

9. With

   .entry writeval

there is no mask.

10. The double colons in Figure 12.7 designate the corresponding variables as global.

11. RSB means read-only substitution.

12. The W in BSBW designates the maximum displacement used in the branch.

13. INCB 2000 does the same thing as INCL 2000.

14. On a VAX-11, clrl r7 does the same thing as CLRL R7.

15. By default, numbers in VAX-11 programs are decimal.

12.10

REFERENCE

Gill, A. *Machine and Assembly Language Programming of the PDP-11.* 2d ed. Englewood Cliffs, N.J.: Prentice-Hall. 1983.

13.
THE LINKER

"Find the jewels or the map!" cried Black and Littlejack.
—The King's Men in James Thurber,
The 13 Clocks and the Wonderful O

13.0
AIMS

- Introduce the mechanics of the linker.
- Illustrate the use of load maps.
- Examine memory dumps of executable images.
- Show how to concatenate psects with common attributes.
- Show the use of the NOEXE psect attribute.

13.1
INTRODUCTION

This chapter explores some of the procedures in the VAX-11 and PDP-11 linker programs that enable us to decipher the final, executable image produced by the linker. It also introduces some ways to concatenate program sections in separate object modules (results of assembly of separate source texts).

This leads us to some of the hidden benefits of having a linker. What may not be obvious is that the linker program makes it possible to separate programmable tasks into separate modules that can be linked together in a variety of ways. The separation of program modules facilitates program development. It allows us to share modules among *different* main programs and among different users.

Another hidden feature of this linker is that it provides program sections (psects) with changeable attributes. Key among these is a provision for global psects, which allows us to link such psects with common attributes into larger psects. This feature is especially helpful in concatenating sets of data from psects in separate object modules.

The main objective of this chapter is to help you gain an understanding of the structure of the final, executable image produced by the linker. This will make it easier to pinpoint trouble spots in a program with errors. An understanding of the significance of the linker load map will enable you to understand the executable images themselves, which we reproduce with main memory dumps. This chapter shows how to obtain these maps and memory dumps of executable images. First, we consider how the linker works (what it does to obtain an executable image).

13.2
THE LINKER

Linking on a VAX-11 requires two passes (scans) of the object modules specified in the linker command string:

LINK ⟨/⟨options⟩⟩⟨obj. module⟩, . . . , ⟨obj. module⟩

results of assembly of
separate source texts

possible lead map plus optional enhancements

A graphical interpretation of the linker procedure is given in Figure 13.1.

The linker program used by PDP-11s and VAX-11s carries out two complete scans (passes) of the various object modules referenced in the command string. Apart from the separate passes the linker carries out three tasks.

Pass 1

Task 1: Resolve global symbolic references (references to subroutines, external procedures, to labels used in external procedures, such as the

FIGURE 13.1
The Two Passes of the Linker

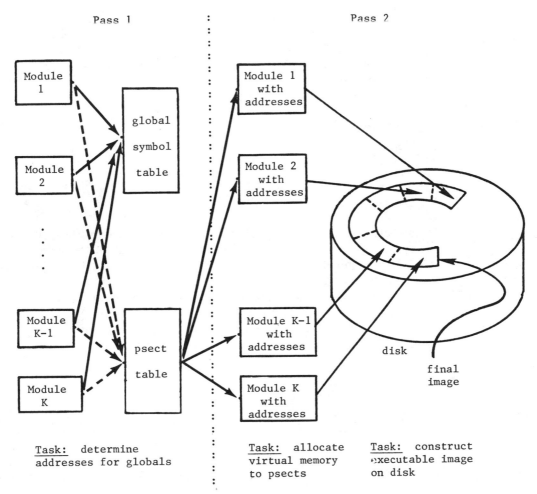

Pass 1   Pass 2

Module 1 → global symbol table

Module 2

Module K-1

Module K → psect table

Module 1 with addresses

Module 2 with addresses

Module K-1 with addresses

Module K with addresses

disk

final image

Task: determine addresses for globals

Task: allocate virtual memory to psects

Task: construct executable image on disk

label COUNT in READVAL, which shows up as

COUNT ********X

in the list module using COUNT and READVAL).

Pass 2

Task 2: Allocate virtual memory to the separate images (the length of each psect of each image cluster).

Task 3: Construct a complete, executable image (this image will have the .EXE extension and will be stored on an auxiliary storage medium, usually a disk).

The first task is carried out during Pass 1 of the linker, the second and third tasks during Pass 2. The result of these passes is the construction of an executable image, which the Digital Equipment Corporation (1982, p. 1–5) defines as an "image that is executed by the DCL command RUN." (DCL stands for Digital Command Language.)

13.2.1 Pass 1 of the Linker

During this pass, two tables are built by the linker program:

- global symbol table (symbols like TTIOLEN, STACK, COUNT, etc.)
- psect table

The global symbol table allows the linker to resolve all global symbol references in any of the separate object modules (task 1 of the linker). The psect table comes into play later, during Pass 2, when the linker uses this table to link together psects with common attributes. The linker will place psects in the final image in alphabetical order. The one exception to this rule are psects with the NOEXE attribute (they are not executable images). These are moved to the beginning of the final image built during Pass 2. The resolution of symbolic references is the principal task of this first pass.

13.2.2 Pass 2 of the Linker

The outcome of this pass is a final, executable image (the one with the .EXE extension), which is usually saved on a disk. This part of the linker program relies on a psect table built during Pass 1 to assign virtual memory to each psect of each object module listed in the command string. The image sections itemized in the psect table contribute to the final image with the final run-time virtual addresses.

Final memory addresses of the executable image are dealt with later by an image activator program brought into play when we type

RUN ⟨image name⟩

Then the memory management unit takes over in assigning the pages to be used in physical memory to execute the Pass 2 image stored on the disk. The RUN statement initiates the actual transfer of the executable image (with virtual addressing) to actual addresses in main memory. The memory management parcels out the .EXE-image in terms of available pages (each 512 bytes long) in main memory.

13.2.3 Optional Load Map

We can include in the linker command string a request for a load map. This supplies a valuable profile of the *executable* image, its virtual addresses, program sections, their names, order, length, and characteristics. This can be illustrated in terms of the program given in the list module in Figure 13.2.

This program is set up to work with a larger array than is shown. The section labeled LOOP controls the printing of the NOS array. It uses the COUNT variable to limit the printing of the array elements to 10 numbers per line. The tally routine runs a check on how many numbers are in the array. This routine will be useful later when we concatenate the DATA psect in this program with other psects with identical attributes, that is, psects contained in other object modules outside the one in Figure 13.2.

To obtain a load map for the object module for the above program, use

LINK/MAP FG132 + IO/LIB

This produces a default load map, which gives the following sections:

Load Map	*Section*
1. Object module synopsis	Lists the object modules found in the final, executable image.
2. Program section synopsis	Gives the psects and the virtual memory boundaries found in the final load module.
3. Symbols by name	Global symbol names and their virtual addresses.
4. Image synopsis	Extensive profile of the final image (its transfer address, number of psects, global symbols, map length, etc.).
5. Link-run statistics	CPU time used in constructing each part of the final image.

Actually, three principal types of load maps can be obtained: (1) *brief* (with parts 1, 4, and 5 shown above); (2) *default* (with the above parts); and (3) *full* (with three additional sections besides the ones in the default map). A full load map will contain

6. Module synopsis	Number of .ADDRESS directives used in each module.
7. Symbols by value	Hexadecimal symbol values.
8. Image synopsis	More statistics about the final image.

FIGURE 13.2
List Module of Program with a Data Psect

```
;
;Ref: Figure 13.2 (List module for a program with a data psect)
;
;tasks: (1) determine the number of entries in the NOS array (maintain
;           a tally for the number of entries in COUNT and in COPY_
;           OF_COUNT); (2) print a copy of the entries in the NOS
;           array, using the EDIV instruction to control the no. of
;           elements printed on each line.
;
```

```
                                    0000    1         .TITLE Figure 13.1 w/o c
omments
                                    0000    2         COPY_OF_COUNT:

                    00000000        0000    3         .LONG

                            0000    0004    4         .ENTRY MAIN,0
                                    0006    5 ;
        56    00000000´EF    9E     0006    6         MOVAB NOS,R6

              00000151´EF    16     000D    7         JSB TALLY
                                    0013    8 ;
                                    0013    9         WRITELN
                                    0027    10        WRITELN
        56    00000000´EF    9E     003B    11        MOVAB NOS,R6
                            86  DD  0042    12 LOOP:   PUSHL (R6)+
              00000000´EF    01  FB  0044    13        CALLS #1,WRITEVAL
                                    004B    14        SPACE <2>
        57    00000000´EF    D0     006B    15        MOVL COUNT,R7
                            58  D4  0072    16        CLRL R8
        5A  59  57    0A    7B     0074    17        EDIV #10,R7,R9,R10
                            5A  D5  0079    18        TSTL R10
                            28  12  007B    19        BNEQ NEXT_NO
                                    007D    20        WRITELN
                                    0091    21        WRITELN
                                    00A5    22 NEXT_NO:
        96 00000000´EF      F5     00A5    23        SOBGTR COUNT,LOOP
                                    00AC    24        WRITELN
                                    00C0    25        WRITELN <---------------
----------------------->
                                    00F9    26        WRITELN
                                    010D    27        WRITELN
                                    0121    28        WRITE <COUNT = >
                    FEC2 CF    DD  013A    29        PUSHL COPY_OF_COUNT
              00000000´EF    01  FB  013E    30        CALLS #1,WRITEVAL
                    FD AF    17     0145    31 T:      JMP T
                                    0148    32        .SHOW ME
                                    0148    33        $EXIT_S
                                    0148               .GLOBL  SYS$EXIT

                            01  DD  0148              PUSHL      #1
              00000000´GF    01  FB  014A              CALLS    #1,G^SYS
$EXIT
```

Figure 13.2 continued.

```
                        0151
                        0151   34        .NOSHOW ME
                86  D5  0151   35 TALLY: TSTL (R6)+
                08  13  0153   36        BEQL LAST
        00000000´EF  D6  0155   37        INCL COUNT
                F4  11  015B   38        BRB TALLY
FE9A CF 00000000´EF  D0  015D   39 LAST:  MOVL COUNT,COPY_OF_COUNT

                05  0166   40        RSB
            00000000      41        .PSECT DATA,GBL,NOEXE
                0000      42        .SUBTITLE SAMPLE DATA
00000002 00000001 00000001  0000  43 NOS:   .LONG 1,1,2
                000C      44        .END MAIN
```

The default load map is the most useful one. Figure 13.3 shows the default map for the program just given.

As a rule, the most useful part of a map is the program section (psect) synopsis. This is helpful in pinpointing run-time errors and in getting an overview of the final, executable image with the EXE extension. The beginning and ending address of each psect can be used in examining a memory dump of the final image. Figure 13.4 presents a graphical interpretation of the psect synopsis of the above map.

Notice that the beginning address is 200 (hex). The psect synopsis tells us the following:

Section Name	Content	Beginning or Base Address	Ending Address
.BLANK.	Except for the DATA psect, this is the complete main program plus complete I/O library	200	679
FIGURE	Beginning module (the main program *without* the DATA psect)	200	366
.MAIN.	I/O library module	367	679
DATA	The data psect (12 bytes!)	67A	685

The .BLANK psect synopsis gives an overview of the entire load module, apart from the data psect. To understand what is happening in the entire final image, we must look at two things. First, it is helpful to determine the beginning and the final address (the last address of the data psect or 685 [hex]). These addresses can be used to obtain a memory dump.

FIGURE 13.3
Load Map

```
RUN FG13

1   1   2
-------------------------------------


COUNT = 3


;
;Ref.:  Figure 13.3 (Complete default load map, cf. Fig. 13.2)
;
FG13                                                    21-NOV-1983 14:2
7          VAX-11 Linker V03-03            Page    1
                                        +------------------------+
                                        ! Object Module Synopsis !
                                        +------------------------+

Module Name     Ident          Bytes      File
  Creation Date        Creator
-----------     -----          -----      -----
  -------------        -------
FIGURE          0                  371 SJU:[SJU1]FG13.OBJ;2              2
1-NOV-1983 14:27  VAX-11 Macro V03-00
.MAIN.          0                  787 SJU:[SJU1]IO.OLB;22               1
6-NOV-1983 01:17  VAX-11 Macro V03-00


                                      +--------------------------+
                                      ! Program Section Synopsis !
                                      +--------------------------+

Psect Name      Module Name      Base     End          Length        Align
                Attributes
----------      -----------      ----     ---          ------        -----
                -----------
. BLANK .                        00000200 00000679 0000047A (    1146.) BYTE 0
 NOPIC,USR,CON,REL,LCL,NOSHR,    EXE,  RD,  WRT,NOVEC
                FIGURE           00000200 00000366 00000167 (     359.) BYTE 0

                .MAIN.           00000367 00000679 00000313 (     787.) BYTE 0

DATA                             0000067A 00000685 0000000C (      12.) BYTE 0
 NOPIC,USR,CON,REL,GBL,NOSHR,    EXE,  RD,  WRT,NOVEC
                FIGURE           0000067A 00000685 0000000C (      12.) BYTE 0
                                      +-----------------+
                                      ! Symbols By Name !
                                      +-----------------+

Symbol          Value           Symbol       Value            Symbol
      Value            Symbol       Value
------          -----           ------       -----            ------
      -----           ------       -----
```

Figure 13.3 continued.

```
BASE            000003D3-R
COUNT           000003CF-R
INSTR           000003D7-R
MAIN            00000204-R
OUTLEN          0000043F-R
READNO          0000061E-R
READSTR         000005D6-R
READVAL         00000450-R
STACK           000003CB-R
TTCHAN          00000435-R
TTIOLEN         00000439-R
TTIOSB          00000437-R
TTNAME          00000427-R
WRITESTR        00000573-R
WRITEVAL        000004D2-R
```

```
              Key for special characters above:
                   +------------------+
                   ! *  - Undefined   !
                   ! U  - Universal   !
                   ! R  - Relocatable !
                   ! X  - External    !
                   +------------------+
SJU:[SJU1]FG13.EXE;3                              21-NOV-1983 14:2
7        VAX-11 Linker V03-03          Page    2

                                    +----------------+
                                    ! Image Synopsis !
                                    +----------------+


Virtual memory allocated:                  00000200 000009FF 00000800 (20
48. bytes, 4. pages)
Stack size:                                    20. pages
Image header virtual block limits:             1.           1. (1. block)
Image binary virtual block limits:             2.           4. (3. blocks)
Image name and identification:             FG13 0
Number of files:                               4.
Number of modules:                             3.
Number of program sections:                    5.
Number of global symbols:                      20.
Number of image sections:                      3.
User transfer address:                     00000204
Debugger transfer address:                 7FFEDF68
Image type:                                EXECUTABLE.
Map format:                                DEFAULT in file SJU:[SJU1]FG13
.MAP;2
Estimated map length:                          13. blocks
                                    +--------------------+
                                    ! Link Run Statistics !
                                    +--------------------+
```

Continued on following page.

Figure 13.3 continued.

```
Performance Indicators                              Page Faults   CPU Time
Elapsed Time
----------------------                              -----------   --------
------------
     Command processing:                                  33      00:00:00.07
00:00:00.14
     Pass 1:                                             137      00:00:00.40
00:00:00.97
     Allocation/Relocation:                               22      00:00:00.05
00:00:00.24
     Pass 2:                                               34      00:00:00.18
00:00:00.72
     Map data after object module synopsis:               14      00:00:00.08
00:00:00.08
     Symbol table output:                                  2      00:00:00.02
00:00:00.17
Total run values:                                        242      00:00:00.80
00:00:02.32

Using a working set limited to 450 pages and 33 pages of data storage (excluding
  image)

Total number object records read (both passes):   126
     of which 46 were in libraries and 4 were DEBUG data records containing 213
bytes
178 bytes of DEBUG data were written,starting at VBN 6 with 1 blocks allocated

Number of modules extracted explicitly         = 0
     with 2 extracted to resolve undefined symbols

5 library searches were for symbols not in the library searched

A total of 0 global symbol table records was written

/MAP FG13+IO/LIB
```

In this case, we would use

EXAMINE/BYTE 200: 685

Second, we must look beyond the outside edges of the map and determine the byte boundaries of the individual modules. The addresses of the boundaries are needed to determine the sources of errors. As it stands, the load map addresses for the main program in the list module in Figure 13.2 do not correspond to the addresses for this module in the above load map. The linker has relocated the object module addresses. Each one is 200 (hex) greater than the original ones.

Later we show how to force the main program to have list module

FIGURE 13.4
Graphical Interpretation of a Load Map

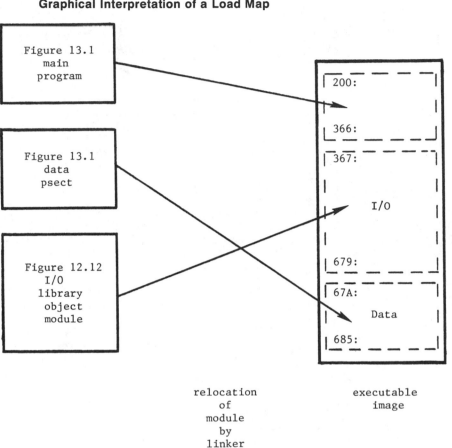

addresses that are the same as the corresponding load map. For now, it is necessary to subtract 200 (hex) from load map addresses to see corresponding addresses in the list module.

Obtaining a memory dump of the final, executable image depends on the use of a trick shown earlier. That is, we put an infinite loop

```
T: JMP T
```

at the end of the source text. This prevents the VAX-11 operating system from clearing memory before we press a ⟨CTRL⟩ ⟨Y⟩. This will leave the executable image in main memory. Otherwise it would be lost. Main memory would be cleared by VMS (Virtual Memory operating System on the VAX). Next, Figure 13.5 shows a sample run of the above program, followed by the memory dump for the final image described by the above map.

FIGURE 13.5
Memory Dump of an Executable Image

```
;
;Ref.:     Figure 13.5(EXA/BYTE 200:685)
;
00000200:  03 00 00 00 00 00 9E EF 6E 04 00 00 56 16 EF 3E 01 00 00 9F EF 0A
00000216:  00 00 00 FB 01 EF 53 03 00 00 31 03 00 02 0A 0D 01 9F EF 0A 00 00
0000022C:  00 FB 01 EF 3F 03 00 00 31 03 00 02 0A 0D 01 9E EF 39 04 00 00 56
00000242:  DD 86 FB 01 EF 87 02 00 00 9F EF 17 00 00 00 FB 01 EF 1B 03 00 00
00000258:  9F EF 0A 00 00 00 FB 01 EF 0E 03 00 00 31 02 00 01 20 01 D0 EF 5E
0000026E:  01 00 00 57 D4 58 7B 0A 57 59 5A D5 5A 12 28 9F EF 0A 00 00 00 FB
00000284:  01 EF E9 02 00 00 31 03 00 02 0A 0D 01 9F EF 0A 00 00 00 FB 01 EF
0000029A:  D5 02 00 00 31 03 00 02 0A 0D 01 F5 EF 24 01 00 00 96 9F EF 0A 00
000002B0:  00 00 FB 01 EF BA 02 00 00 31 03 00 02 0A 0D 01 9F EF 0A 00 00 00
000002C6:  FB 01 EF A6 02 00 00 31 28 00 27 2D 2D 2D 2D 2D 2D 2D 2D 2D 2D 2D
000002DC:  2D 2D 2D 2D 2D 2D 2D 2D 2D 2D 2D 2D 2D 2D 2D 2D 2D 2D 2D 2D 2D 2D
000002F2:  2D 2D 2D 2D 0A 0D 01 9F EF 0A 00 00 00 FB 01 EF 6D 02 00 00 31 03
00000308:  00 02 0A 0D 01 9F EF 0A 00 00 00 FB 01 EF 59 02 00 00 31 03 00 02
0000031E:  0A 0D 01 9F EF 09 00 00 00 FB 01 EF 45 02 00 00 11 09 08 43 4F 55
00000334:  4E 54 20 3D 20 01 DD CF C2 FE FB 01 EF 8D 01 00 00 17 AF FD DD 01
0000034A:  FB 01 9F 40 DF FE 7F D5 86 13 08 D6 EF 74 00 00 00 11 F4 D0 EF 6C
00000360:  00 00 00 CF 9A FE 05 00 00 00 00 00 00 00 00 00 00 00 00 00 00 00
00000376:  00 00 00 00 00 00 00 00 00 00 00 00 00 00 00 00 00 00 00 00 00 00
0000038C:  00 00 00 00 00 00 00 00 00 00 00 00 00 00 00 00 00 00 00 00 00 00
000003A2:  00 00 00 00 00 00 00 00 00 00 00 00 00 00 00 00 00 00 00 00 00 00
000003B8:  00 00 00 00 00 00 00 00 00 00 00 00 00 00 00 00 00 00 00 00 00 00
000003CE:  00 00 00 00 00 0A 00 00 00 33 4F 55 4E 54 20 3D 20 01 2D 2D 2D 2D
000003E4:  2D 2D 2D 2D 2D 2D 2D 2D 2D 2D 2D 2D 2D 2D 2D 2D 2D 2D 2D 2D 2D 2D
000003FA:  2D 2D 0A 0D 01 00 00 00 00 00 00 00 00 00 00 00 00 00 00 00 00 00
00000410:  00 00 00 00 00 00 00 00 00 00 00 00 00 00 00 00 00 00 00 00 00 00
00000426:  33 06 00 0E 01 2F 04 00 00 5F 54 54 44 36 3A 20 00 00 00 00 00 00
0000043C:  00 00 00 01 00 00 00 E8 50 09 DD 50 FB 01 9F 40 DF FE 7F 05 C0 03
00000452:  7C 7E 3F AF DE 7F AF CD FB 04 9F 50 DE FE 7F 30 DF FF 7C 7E 7C 7E
00000468:  DD 8F 50 00 00 00 DF CF 65 FF 7C 7E 7F AF C0 3C 31 7E 3C AF B8 7E
0000047E:  DD 00 FB 0C 9F 00 DE FE 7F 9E CF 40 FF 5B 3C AF AA 59 9E CF 43 FF
00000494:  58 D4 56 D4 CF 34 FF 82 30 68 9A 88 57 C4 CF 2E FF 56 C0 57 56 91
000004AA:  68 30 19 03 F5 59 EA D0 56 7B D6 CF 17 FF D7 59 D5 59 13 07 D4 56
000004C0:  95 88 F5 59 D6 3C CF 6C FF 7E FB 01 9F E0 DE FE 7F 04 C0 03 7C 7E
000004D6:  3F CF 5B FF 7F CF 49 FF FB 04 9F 50 DE FE 7F 30 5B FF 9E CF EB FE
000004EC:  59 D0 AC 04 56 C0 8F 50 00 00 00 59 D4 CF 43 FF D0 56 57 C6 CF D0
00000502:  FE 56 D0 56 58 C4 CF C8 FE 56 C2 56 57 C0 30 57 D1 39 57 18 0F C0
00000518:  07 57 D1 8F 5A 00 00 00 57 18 03 C0 06 57 90 57 79 D6 CF 12 FF D0
0000052E:  58 56 12 CA D0 CF 09 FF 58 9E CF 9C FE 57 90 89 87 F5 58 FA 7C 7E
00000544:  7C 7E DD CF F5 FE DF CF 89 FE 7C 7E DD 00 3C 30 7E 3C CF DC FE 7E
0000055A:  DD 01 FB 0C 9F 00 DE FE 7F 30 DD FE 3C CF CB FE 7E FB 01 9F E0 DE
00000570:  FE 7F 04 C0 01 7C 7E 3F CF BA FE 7F CF A8 FE FB 04 9F 50 DE FE 7F
00000586:  30 BA FE 9A BC 04 CF B0 FE D0 CF AC FE 56 D0 AC 04 57 D6 57 9E CF
0000059C:  39 FE 58 90 87 88 F4 56 FA 7C 7E 7C 7E DD CF 92 FE DF CF 26 FE 7C
000005B2:  7E DD 00 3C 30 7E 3C CF 79 FE 7E DD 01 FB 0C 9F 00 DE FE 7F 30 7A
000005C8:  FE 3C CF 68 FE 7E FB 01 9F E0 DE FE 7F 04 00 00 7C 7E 3F CF 57 FE
000005DE:  7F CF 45 FE FB 04 9F 50 DE FE 7F 30 57 FE 7C 7E 7C 7E DD 8F 50 00
000005F4:  00 00 DF CF DD FD 7C 7E 7F CF 37 FE 3C 31 7E 3C CF 2E FE 7E DD 00
0000060A:  FB 0C 9F 00 DE FE 7F 3C CF 20 FE 7E FB 01 9F E0 DE FE 7F 04 C0 03
00000620:  7C 7E 3F CF 0F FE 7F CF FD FD FB 04 9F 50 DE FE 7F 30 0F FE 7C 7E
00000636:  7C 7E DD 8F 50 00 00 00 DF CF 95 FD 7C 7E 7F CF EF FD 3C 31 7E 3C
0000064C:  CF E6 FD 7E DD 00 FB 0C 9F 00 DE FE 7F 3C CF DC FD 59 9E CF 75 FD
```

Figure 13.5 continued.

```
00000662:   58 82 30 88 D6 CF 65 FD F5 59 F6 3C CF C4 FD 7E FB 01 9F E0 DE FE
00000678:   7F 04 01 00 00 00 01 00 00 00 02 00 00 00
```

13.2.4 Changing Default Beginning Addresses

The default beginning addresses seen up to this point are

Module	Default Beginning Address
List module	00000000 = 0 (hex)
Load module	00000200 = 200 (hex)

It is possible to align the addresses of the list module with those of the load map. First, obtain a load map. Second, modify the source text by inserting

    . = . + ^X⟨200⟩   ;advance the location counter

at the beginning of the source text. Then obtain a list module for the modified source text. The addresses of the map and the list module will match. (They will begin with 200 [hex].)

There is a sandtrap here. If you obtain a load map for the modified source module, its beginning address will be 400 (hex)! To get the list module addresses to correspond to those in the load map, get the load map *first*. Then go back and make the above change in the source and obtain a list module for the modified text.

For a complex program, the above trick will be helpful, if errors occur when the linker is used. Often errors will occur not when a program is assembled or linked, but when it is run. The addresses in the error messages will reference final addresses, ones given in the load map. In such cases, the above strategy is helpful.

13.3

PSECTS

The final, executable image built by the linker is organized in terms of psects. As a rule psects are useful in beginning programming (1) to identify (name!) program sections in extensive programs and (2) to allow psects in separate object modules to be concatenated (put together) by the linker. The attributes of a psect are shown in Table 13.1.

A plain

    .PSECT ⟨name⟩

TABLE 13.1
Psect Attributes

Psect	Attributes	Explanation
default attribute	/ alternative / attribute	(* = used in this chapter)
* REL	/ ABS	REL = relocatable psect ABS = psects for comments
* CON	/ OVR	CON = psects which can be concatenated, OVR = overlay psects
* LCL	/*GBL	LCL = local psect, GBL = global psects that are put together in final load image
* EXE	/*NOEXE	EXE = executable psect NOEXE = data psect (nonexecutable)
* WRT	/ NOWRT	WRT = modifiable psect
RD	/ NORD	Not used
PIC	/*NOPIC	PIC = position independent code
SHR	/*NOSHR	SHR = sharable image
USR	/ LIB	Not used
VEC	/*NOVEC	VEC = psect has message vectors

will carry along all of the default psects shown in the table. For now, we will examine two of these attributes. The LCL (local) attribute limits a psect to a segment (or cluster) boundary. To make concatenation of psects in separate object modules possible, this needs to be changed to GBL (global). For example, we can use

.PSECT DATA, GBL

↑   ↑

replacement for LCL attribute

psect name

13.3.1 How to Concatenate Psects

To illustrate the technique for concatenating psects, we build a tiny source text with a dummy (empty) main program and an "attached" data psect with the GBL attribute. The list module for this is shown in Figure 13.6.

The data psect of this text has attributes *identical* to the ones in Figure 13.2. This means we can use the linker to concatenate these separate psects. Next, we show the psect synopsis for the load map linking the object modules for these separate source texts. This is given together with a sample run in Figure 13.7.

Now notice the data psect of the load map is expanded. The hex addresses 688 and 702 represent the boundaries of the second data psect. The sample run in the above figure shows that, in fact, there is a new tally for the NOS array. It was 3, earlier. Now it is 33! The print loop of the original program in Figure 13.2 now uses this tally (the value of the COUNT-variable) to print several lines of numbers. A graphical interpretation of the psect

FIGURE 13.6
Another Program with a Data Psect

```
                                    0000  1 ;
                                    0000  2 ;Ref.: Figure 13.6 (Another pro
                                                   gram with a data psect)
                                    0000  3 ;
                                    0000  4 ;       .ENTRY X,0
                                    0000  5 ;       NOP
                                    0000  6 ;       RET
                                    0000  7 ;
                                    0000  8 ;       .PSECT DATA,GBL
                                    0000  9 ;NOS:   .LONG 3,5,8,13,21,34,55,
                                                   89,144,233,377,610,987,1597
                                    0000 10 ;       .LONG 2,1,3,4,7,11,18,29
                                                   ,47,76,123,199,322,521,843,1364
                                    0000 11 ;
                                    0000 12 ;       .END
                                    0000 13 ;
                          0000 0000 14         .ENTRY X,0
                            01 0002 15         NOP
                            04 0003 16         RET
                                                             .PSECT DATA,GBL
0000000D 00000008 00000005 00000003 0004 17 NOS:   .LONG 3,5,8,13,21,34,55,
                                                   89,144,233,377,610,987,1597
00000059 00000037 00000022 00000015 0014
00000262 00000179 000000E9 00000090 0024
                  0000063D 000003DB 0034
00000004 00000003 00000001 00000002 003C 18        .LONG 2,1,3,4,7,11,18,29
                                                   ,47,76,123,199,322,521,843,1364
0000001D 00000012 0000000B 00000007 004C
000000C7 0000007B 0000004C 0000002F 005C
00000554 0000034B 00000209 00000142 006C
                                    007C 19        .END

PSECT name                 Allocation          PSECT No.  Attributes
----------                 ----------          ---------  ----------
. ABS   .                  00000000 (    0.)   00 (  0.)  NOPIC  USR  CON
   ABS   LCL NOSHR NOEXE NORD  NOWRT NOVEC BYTE
. BLANK .                  0000007C (  124.)   01 (  1.)  NOPIC  USR  CON
   REL   LCL NOSHR  EXE   RD   WRT NOVEC BYTE
                                   +------------------------+
                                   ! Performance indicators !
                                   +------------------------+
There were no errors, warnings or information messages.

/LIST FG131C+PAS/LIB
```

FIGURE 13.7
Load Map with Concatenated Psects

```
1   1   2   3

5   8   13   21   34   55   89   144   233   377

610   987   1597   2   1   3   4   7   11   18

29   47   76   123   199   322   521   843   1364
--------------------------------------

COUNT = 33

;
;Ref.:   Figure 13.7 (Partial default load map with concatenated psects)
;
;Note:   This map displays the link of the object modules for the programs
;        shown in figures 13.2(= FG13, below) and 13.6(= FG131C, below).
;
FG13                                                    21-NOV-1983 15:0
6          VAX-11 Linker V03-03             Page    1

                                   +------------------------+
                                   ! Object Module Synopsis !
                                   +------------------------+

Module Name     Ident          Bytes     File
   Creation Date        Creator
-----------     -----          -----     -----
 -------------        -------
FIGURE          0                 371 SJU:[SJU1]FG13.OBJ;2                2
1-NOV-1983 14:27  VAX-11 Macro V03-00
.MAIN.          0                 124 SJU:[SJU1]FG131C.OBJ;3              2
1-NOV-1983 14:50  VAX-11 Macro V03-00
.MAIN.          0                 787 SJU:[SJU1]IO.OLB;22                 1
6-NOV-1983 01:17  VAX-11 Macro V03-00

                                   +-------------------------+
                                   ! Program Section Synopsis !
                                   +-------------------------+

Psect Name      Module Name     Base     End         Length        Align
                Attributes
----------      -----------     ----     ---         ------        -----
                 ----------
. BLANK .                       00000200 000006F5 000004F6 (     1270.) BYTE 0
  NOPIC,USR,CON,REL,LCL,NOSHR,  EXE,  RD,   WRT,NOVEC
                FIGURE          00000200 00000366 00000167 (      359.) BYTE 0

                .MAIN.          00000367 000003E2 0000007C (      124.) BYTE 0

                .MAIN.          000003E3 000006F5 00000313 (      787.) BYTE 0
```

390

Figure 13.7 continued.

```
DATA                            000006F6 00000701 0000000C (        12.) BYTE 0
    NOPIC,USR,CON,REL,GBL,NOSHR,  EXE,  RD,   WRT,NOVEC
                    FIGURE      000006F6 00000701 0000000C (        12.) BYTE 0

User transfer address:                              00000204
Estimated map length:                               14. blocks

/MAP FG13,FG131C+IO/LIB
```

synopsis in the above map showing concatenated psects is given next in Figure 13.8.

Concatenating psects in separate object modules allows us to share data among many files or by other users having access to each other's accounts. This must be set up with care. Notice that the second data psect (the one in Figure 13.6) is part of a procedure, not a main program. Psects from different main programs cannot be shared. Why? Only one transfer address can be used by the linker. Except for the initial main program, concatenated psects must come from external procedures or subroutines.

The memory dump for the above concatenation is given in Figure 13.9. Notice that the second psect (its numbers inside longwords) trails the first psect at the end of the final image. This is awkward. We can change this and get the linker to move all nonexecutable data sections to the beginning of the load module. We do this with the NOEXE attribute.

13.3.2 The NOEXE Attribute

The above data psects have used the default attribute EXE, which implies that these sections contain executable instructions. This should be changed. We do this with

    .PSECT DATA, GBL, NOEXE

Now, if we concatenate the above psects, they will appear at the beginning of the load module. This is true for all psects with the NOEXE attribute, which separated from the executable psects by the linker. This is advantageous because it makes the load map easier to decipher, especially if, unlike the above examples, there are a large number of psects.

Next, we show the result of changing the data psects of the above two programs. We change the EXE to the NOEXE attribute in *each* data psect. The psect synopsis for the new map is given in Figure 13.10.

Obtaining a memory dump for the new executable image is left as an exercise. In the figure, notice the separation of the NOEXE and EXE psects is more than a mere rearrangement of the psects. The beginning address of the data psect is 200, whereas the beginning of the EXE psect is 400.

FIGURE 13.8
Graphical Interpretation of Concatenation Map

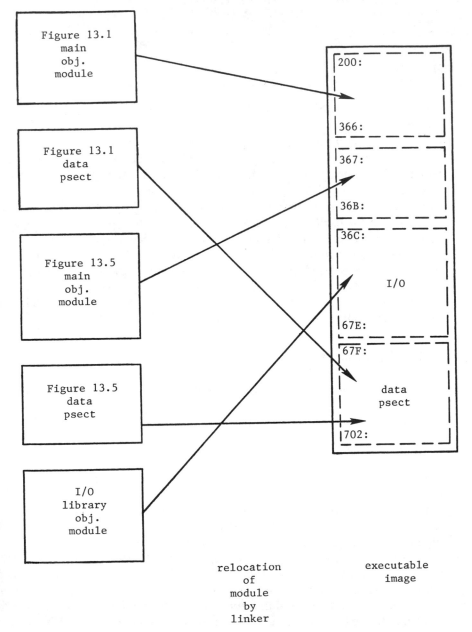

relocation
of
module
by
linker

executable
image

FIGURE 13.9
Executable Image with Concatenated Psects

```
;
;REF.:    Figure 13.9(EXA/BYTE 200:702)
;
00000200:  21 00 00 00 00 00 9E EF 72 04 00 00 56 16 EF 3E 01 00 00 9F EF 0A
00000216:  00 00 00 FB 01 EF 57 03 00 00 31 03 00 02 0A 0D 01 9F EF 0A 00 00
0000022C:  00 FB 01 EF 43 03 00 00 31 03 00 02 0A 0D 01 9E EF 3D 04 00 00 56
00000242:  DD 86 FB 01 EF 8B 02 00 00 9F EF 17 00 00 00 FB 01 EF 1F 03 00 00
00000258:  9F EF 0A 00 00 00 FB 01 EF 12 03 00 00 31 02 00 01 20 01 D0 EF 62
0000026E:  01 00 00 57 D4 58 7B 0A 57 59 5A D5 5A 12 28 9F EF 0A 00 00 00 FB
00000284:  01 EF ED 02 00 00 31 03 00 02 0A 0D 01 9F EF 0A 00 00 00 FB 01 EF
0000029A:  D9 02 00 00 31 03 00 02 0A 0D 01 F5 EF 28 01 00 00 96 9F EF 0A 00
000002B0:  00 00 FB 01 EF BE 02 00 00 31 03 00 02 0A 0D 01 9F EF 0A 00 00 00
000002C6:  FB 01 EF AA 02 00 00 31 28 00 27 2D 2D 2D 2D 2D 2D 2D 2D 2D 2D 2D
000002DC:  2D 2D 2D 2D 2D 2D 2D 2D 2D 2D 2D 2D 2D 2D 2D 2D 2D 2D 2D 2D 2D 2D
000002F2:  2D 2D 2D 2D 0A 0D 01 9F EF 0A 00 00 00 FB 01 EF 71 02 00 00 31 03
00000308:  00 02 0A 0D 01 9F EF 0A 00 00 00 FB 01 EF 5D 02 00 00 31 03 00 02
0000031E:  0A 0D 01 9F EF 09 00 00 00 FB 01 EF 49 02 00 00 11 09 08 43 4F 55
00000334:  4E 54 20 3D 20 01 DD CF C2 FE FB 01 EF 91 01 00 00 17 AF FD DD 01
0000034A:  FB 01 9F 40 DF FE 7F D5 86 13 08 D6 EF 78 00 00 00 11 F4 D0 EF 70
00000360:  00 00 00 CF 9A FE 05 00 00 01 04 00 00 00 00 00 00 00 00 00 00 00
00000376:  00 00 00 00 00 00 00 00 00 00 00 00 00 00 00 00 00 00 00 00 00 00
0000038C:  00 00 00 00 00 00 00 00 00 00 00 00 00 00 00 00 00 00 00 00 00 00
000003A2:  00 00 00 00 00 00 00 00 00 00 00 00 00 00 00 00 00 00 00 00 00 00
000003B8:  00 00 00 00 00 00 00 00 00 00 00 00 00 00 00 00 00 00 00 00 00 00
000003CE:  00 00 00 00 00 00 00 00 0A 00 00 00 33 33 55 4E 54 20 3D 20 01
000003E4:  2D 2D 2D 2D 2D 2D 2D 2D 2D 2D 2D 2D 2D 2D 2D 2D 2D 2D 2D 2D 2D 2D
000003FA:  2D 2D 2D 2D 2D 2D 0A 0D 01 00 00 00 00 00 00 00 00 00 00 00 00 00
00000410:  00 00 00 00 00 00 00 00 00 00 00 00 00 00 00 00 00 00 00 00 00 00
00000426:  00 31 33 33 33 06 00 0E 01 33 04 00 00 5F 54 54 44 36 3A 20 00 00
0000043C:  00 00 00 00 00 00 00 02 00 00 00 E8 50 09 DD 50 FB 01 9F 40 DF FE
00000452:  7F 05 C0 03 7C 7E 3F AF DE 7F AF CD FB 04 9F 50 DE FE 7F 30 DF FF
00000468:  7C 7E 7C 7E DD 8F 50 00 00 00 DF CF 65 FF 7C 7E 7F AF C0 3C 31 7E
0000047E:  3C AF B8 7E DD 00 FB 0C 9F 00 DE FE 7F 9E CF 40 FF 5B 3C AF AA 59
00000494:  9E CF 43 FF 58 D4 56 D4 CF 34 FF 82 30 68 9A 88 57 C4 CF 2E FF 56
000004AA:  C0 57 56 91 68 30 19 03 F5 59 EA D0 56 7B D6 CF 17 FF D7 59 D5 59
000004C0:  13 07 D4 56 95 88 F5 59 D6 3C CF 6C FF 7E FB 01 9F E0 DE FE 7F 04
000004D6:  C0 03 7C 7E 3F CF 5B FF 7F CF 49 FF FB 04 9F 50 DE FE 7F 30 5B FF
000004EC:  9E CF EB FE 59 D0 AC 04 56 C0 8F 50 00 00 00 59 D4 CF 43 FF D0 56
00000502:  57 C6 CF D0 FE 56 D0 56 58 C4 CF C8 FE 56 C2 56 57 C0 30 57 D1 39
00000518:  57 18 0F C0 07 57 D1 8F 5A 00 00 00 57 18 03 C0 06 57 90 57 79 D6
0000052E:  CF 12 FF D0 58 56 12 CA D0 CF 09 FF 58 9E CF 9C FE 57 90 89 87 F5
00000544:  58 FA 7C 7E 7C 7E DD CF F5 FE DF CF 89 FE 7C 7E DD 00 3C 30 7E 3C
0000055A:  CF DC FE 7E DD 01 FB 0C 9F 00 DE FE 7F 30 DD FE 3C CF CB FE 7E FB
00000570:  01 9F E0 DE FE 7F 04 C0 01 7C 7E 3F CF BA FE 7F CF A8 FE FB 04 9F
00000586:  50 DE FE 7F 30 BA FE 9A BC 04 CF B0 FE D0 CF AC FE 56 D0 AC 04 57
0000059C:  D6 57 9E CF 39 FE 58 90 87 88 F4 56 FA 7C 7E 7C 7E DD CF 92 FE DF
000005B2:  CF 26 FE 7C 7E DD 00 3C 30 7E 3C CF 79 FE 7E DD 01 FB 0C 9F 00 DE
000005C8:  FE 7F 30 7A FE 3C CF 68 FE 7E FB 01 9F E0 DE FE 7F 04 00 00 7C 7E
000005DE:  3F CF 57 FE 7F CF 45 FE FB 04 9F 50 DE FE 7F 30 57 FE 7C 7E 7C 7E
000005F4:  DD 8F 50 00 00 00 DF CF DD FD 7C 7E 7F CF 37 FE 3C 31 7E 3C CF 2E
0000060A:  FE 7E DD 00 FB 0C 9F 00 DE FE 7F 3C CF 20 FE 7E FB 01 9F E0 DE FE
00000620:  7F 04 C0 03 7C 7E 3F CF 0F FE 7F CF FD FD FB 04 9F 50 DE FE 7F 30
00000636:  0F FE 7C 7E 7C 7E DD 8F 50 00 00 00 DF CF 95 FD 7C 7E 7F CF EF FD
0000064C:  3C 31 7E 3C CF E6 FD 7E DD 00 FB 0C 9F 00 DE FE 7F 3C CF DC FD 59
```

Continued on following page.

Figure 13.9 continued.

```
00000662:  9E CF 75 FD 58 82 30 88 D6 CF 65 FD F5 59 F6 3C CF C4 FD 7E FB 01
00000678:  9F E0 DE FE 7F 04 01 00 00 00 01 00 00 00 02 00 00 00 03 00 00 00
0000068E:  05 00 00 00 08 00 00 00 0D 00 00 00 15 00 00 00 22 00 00 00 37 00
000006A4:  00 00 59 00 00 00 90 00 00 00 E9 00 00 00 79 01 00 00 62 02 00 00
000006BA:  DB 03 00 00 3D 06 00 00 02 00 00 00 01 00 00 00 03 00 00 00 04 00
000006D0:  00 00 07 00 00 00 0B 00 00 00 12 00 00 00 1D 00 00 00 2F 00 00 00
000006E6:  4C 00 00 00 7B 00 00 00 C7 00 00 00 42 01 00 00 09 02 00 00 4B 03
000006FC:  00 00 54 05 00 00 00
```

FIGURE 13.10
Load Map of Psects with NOEXE Attribute

```
;
;Ref.:  Figure 13.10 (Load map for concatenated psects with NOEXE attribute)
;
FG13                                                          21-NOV-1983 16:2
4        VAX-11 Linker V03-03            Page    1


                                     +------------------------+
                                     ! Object Module Synopsis !
                                     +------------------------+


Module Name      Ident              Bytes      File
   Creation Date      Creator
-----------      -----              -----      -----
   -------------      -------
FIGURE           0                    371 SJU:[SJU1]FG13.OBJ;4                 2
1-NOV-1983 16:24  VAX-11 Macro V03-00
.MAIN.           0                    124 SJU:[SJU1]FG131C.OBJ;4               2
1-NOV-1983 16:16  VAX-11 Macro V03-00
.MAIN.           0                    787 SJU:[SJU1]IO.OLB;22                  1
6-NOV-1983 01:17  VAX-11 Macro V03-00


                                     +-------------------------+
                                     ! Program Section Synopsis !
                                     +-------------------------+


Psect Name       Module Name       Base     End           Length          Align
                 Attributes
----------       -----------       ----     ---           ------          -----
                 ----------
DATA                               00000200 00000283 00000084 (     132.) BYTE 0
   NOPIC,USR,CON,REL,GBL,NOSHR,NOEXE,  RD,  WRT,NOVEC
                 FIGURE            00000200 0000020B 0000000C (      12.) BYTE 0

                 .MAIN.            0000020C 00000283 00000078 (     120.) BYTE 0

. BLANK .                          00000400 0000087D 0000047E (    1150.) BYTE 0
   NOPIC,USR,CON,REL,LCL,NOSHR,  EXE,  RD,  WRT,NOVEC
                 FIGURE            00000400 00000566 00000167 (     359.) BYTE 0

                 .MAIN.            00000567 0000056A 00000004 (       4.) BYTE 0

                 .MAIN.            0000056B 0000087D 00000313 (     787.) BYTE 0

/MAP FG13,FG131C+IO/LIB
```

13.4
SUMMARY

The significance of the linker tends to remain hidden if its use is limited to single, isolated object modules. Its usefulness becomes more apparent when we try joining modules of separate object module clusters like our I/O library or psects in separate figures. The linker allows us to construct executable images by concatenating separate modules. In effect, its utility becomes apparent when we start linking together several modules inside entirely separate object modules.

In this chapter we built up several load maps with corresponding executable images given in memory dumps. List modules, load maps, psect synopsis, memory dumps of images become useful tools. They contribute to an understanding of the final versions of our programs. Load maps, in particular, are useful in pinpointing the sources of our run-time errors. The trick is to get used to setting them up and to cross-reference load map addresses with corresponding list module relocatable addresses.

13.5
EXERCISES

1. Add

   . = . + ^X⟨200⟩

   to the top of the source text for Figure 13.2. Obtain a new list module for this program, and compare the beginning and ending addresses of this list module with the load map in Figure 13.3. Comment on what you see.

2. Obtain a default load map for the modified source text in Exercise 1. Contrast this with the map in Figure 13.3. Comment on what you see.

3. Obtain a memory dump for the image obtained in Exercise 2. With a highlighter, identify the psects of the executable image in the memory dump.

4. Add

   . = . + ^X⟨367⟩

   to the top of the I/O procedure library given in Figure 12.12 and linked in exercise 2. Obtain a list module for this library. Compare the beginning addresses of each procedure of the new list module with those given in the symbols-by-name section of the load map in Figure 13.3. Comment on what you see.

5. Using the list module in Exercise 4, highlight the beginning of each pro-

cedure in the memory dump given in Figure 13.5. To obtain a copy of this dump, link the program in Figure 13.2 and

(a) Run FIG132

(b) ⟨CTRL⟩ ⟨Y⟩

(c) EXA/BYTE 200:685

6. Link the object module for the following source text:

```
        .ENTRY X, 0
        NOP
        RET
        .PSECT DATA, GBL
NOS:    .LONG 3, 3, 3, 1, 5, 1, 8, 1, 13, 1, 21
        .LONG 1, 34, 1, 55, 1, 89, 1, 1, 5
        .LONG 1, 1, 2, 5, 1, 1, 2, 3, 5, 333
        .END
```

with the object modules for the source texts in Figures 13.2 and Figure 13.6. Obtain

(a) a brief load map

(b) a default load map

(c) a full load map

7. Obtain the memory dump for the image constructed in exercise 6. Highlight the psects *and* module boundaries of the image in the dump.

8. Obtain a modified load map for the modules in Exercise 6 by using the NOEXE attribute with the data psects.

13.6

LAB PROJECTS

1. Form five separate data psects in five separate object modules. Write a program to scan a NOS array built up by concatenating separating psects. The scan should determine the frequency of the number occurring most often in the NOS array.

   (a) Do this for NOS array with the data psects concatenated from Figures 13.2, 13.6, and exercise 6 in this chapter.

(b) Do this for NOS array with the five data psects formed in the first part of this lab and the one in Exercise 6.

(c) Give the load maps for parts 1(a) and 1(b).

(d) Obtain a memory dump for the executable image for this program and highlight (and label) each section of the map, including the various psects concatenated together in the NOS array.

13.7
REVIEW QUIZ

Indicate whether the following questions are true or false:

1. By default, the VAX-11 linker constructs a load map each time we link.
2. Linking on a VAX-11 requires two passes.
3. The VAX-11 linker takes care of globals during its first pass.
4. The VAX-11 linker is really a linkage editor, since it puts a copy of the load image into secondary storage when it finishes linking.
5. RUN is a DCL command.
6. The VAX-11 linker supplies the .EXE extension on the load image during the second pass.
7. The second pass of the VAX-11 linker has two key tasks.
8. psect stands for procedure section.
9. A load map provides a profile of a load image.
10. The default load map does not include a symbols-by-value section.
11. The default load map does include a symbols-by-name section.
12. The link run statistics are concerned with CPU time.
13. It is possible to concatenate psects.
14. GBL is a default attribute of every psect.
15. psects contain a default NOEXE attribute.

13.8
REFERENCE

Digital Equipment Corporation. *VAX-11 Linker Reference Manual.* Order No. AA-D019C-TE. Maynard, Mass., May 1982.

14.

RESULTS

And all games and puzzles (excepting of course whist*) allow, and even encourage,* talking—*which in itself is one of the best and healthiest mental recreations.*

—Lewis Carroll, *Symbolic Logic* (1896)

14.0

AIMS

- Introduce a random number generator.
- Introduce the use of the CVT, ACB, and CASE instructions.
- Show how to build tables of random numbers.
- Illustrate the use of random numbers in terms of cryptography, graphics, and drawing from a hat.

14.1

INTRODUCTION

This chapter brings together many of the methods and assembly language tools we have seen so far. We add some new instructions (variations of CVT, ACB, CASE) and two new system macros ($GETTIM and $NUMTIM) to our repertoire. We add tools to the toolbox! We construct a random number generator and develop its use in a variety of applications of the assembly language. For example, we use random numbers in selecting ciphers in the encryption (encoding) of a message. The program we develop is easily extended to enable us to construct system passwords. We also learn how to use random numbers to control the size and frequency of graphic images. And, we use random numbers to determine the selection of a case (action to carry out) using the VAX-11 macro CASE statement. (This simulates drawing from a hat.) Finally, we show how to use the $NUMTIM system macro to time actions within a program.

14.2
RANDOM NUMBERS

When are numbers in a distribution random? The notion of randomness is elusive. As D. E. Knuth (1981) has pointed out, "People who think about this topic almost invariably get into philosophical discussions about what the word *random* means." If a distribution contains numbers that are randomly distributed, such a distribution has built into it a measure of disorder, a measure of entropy. The numbers will appear helter-skelter with no number appearing more often than another one. We will not, for example, find more 5s than 6s if the range of random numbers is between 0 and 10, and these numbers are part of a sequence of 5,000 numbers in this range. Each number in a random distribution has just as much chance as any other of occurring in any given spot in the distribution.

Richard Von Mises (1919) has been credited with introducing the notion of randomness during his search for a definition of *probability*. He associated randomness with what he called the Principle of Excluded Gambling Systems. Von Mises (1957) also defined probability in terms of random sequences.

For example, a periodic binary sequence contains 0s and 1s of the form

1 1 0 0 0 0 0 1 1 0 0 0 0 0 1 1 0 0 0 0 0 1 1 0 0 0 0 0 . . .

which is said to be both 2-distributed (in terms of 1s) and 5-distributed (in terms of zeros).

Von Mises would say that a binary sequence is random if *every infinite subsequence obtainable by some rule is 1-distributed*. His notion of randomness parallels the one given by D. E. Knuth (1981, p. 145), who has pointed out that "*a truly random sequence will exhibit local nonrandomness.*"

This chapter brings random number generators to your attention because they are the basis of some challenging as well as interesting AL routines. Random, or, better yet, pseudorandom numbers are useful in (a) testing programs to handle sorts and searches, (b) simulations—game programs like repeated rolls of a pair of dice, (c) development of cryptography programs (ways to construct "secret" passwords, to encode messages, and so on), and (d) statistics programs.

Random numbers can be explained intuitively in terms of the likelihood of their occurrence. If these numbers (say, in the range of 0 to 99) were coming up on slips of paper drawn from a large hat, the selection would be random whenever each number in the given range was equally likely to occur. If we continued to pick and tabulate, the number N of each of the 0s, 1s, . . . , 98s, 99s, should be fairly equal. For example, suppose we pick 100,000 of these slips of paper from a hat containing 10 million slips of paper. If the selections are made randomly, tallies of the number of 0s selected, of 1s, . . . , of 99s should be close to 1,000 (1,000 0s, 1,000 1s, and so on). Whenever this happens, the distribution of the selections is said to be *uniform*. We want to obtain a fairly uniform distribution from any random number generator we construct.

14.2.1 Linear Congruential Method

We have followed Knuth's lead in the selection of a random number generator. We use

RND:= (aX + b) mod m

as a random number generator. This is known as a *linear congruence,* where RND is the remainder after division of $(aX + b)$ by m, and a, X, b and m are positive integers. For judiciously chosen values for these integers in the linear congruence, the resulting distribution of remainders tends to be uniform. Knuth (1981, p. 170) mentions that this method "gives the *nicest* and *simplest* random number generator for the machine language of most computers." The trick is to choose appropriate values for a, X, b, and m.

The integer m is known as the *modulus*. Knuth recommends choosing m to be a power of 2, preferably the word-size of the machine. X is known as the *seed*. Each time we compute a new remainder, X will be set equal to the preceding RND. The question is, *What do we choose for the initial value of X?* There is a simple solution. That is, start with X set equal to the current time of day, which can be lifted from the computer clock. (This is also Knuth's idea!) The number b should have no factor in common with m. Finally, the multiplier a should be in the range

.01 〈= a 〈= .99m

and the digits in its binary representation should be as haphazard as possible.

14.2.2 VAX-11 System Time

The Virtual Memory System (VMS) maintains the current date and time. It is given in a 64-bit format in 100 nanosecond units offset from the system base date and time. Its base date and time are taken from the Smithsonian Institution base date (or November 17, 1858) at 00:00 o'clock. The current system time can be obtained by using the system service macro $GETTIM. To do this, we need to set up a quadword location to hold the current time. We could use the scheme

```
TIME:   .quad

         .
         .

       $GETTIM_S TIMADR = TIME
```

when the $GETTIM macro is executed, the current date and time are loaded into the TIME-quadword we have set up beforehand. This can become the source of the seed for a random number generator.

14.2.3 Alternative to the $GETTIM Macro: $NUMTIM

The $NUMTIM macro gives a more detailed look at the current time. Its information becomes a convenient source of a random number generator seed. When the $NUMTIM macro appears in a program, it returns the current date and time in seven parts. It determines the current year, month, day (this starts from year 0, instead of the geophysical year, 1858). It also determines the current hour, minute of the hour, second of the hour, and hundredths of second for the current second. Beforehand, we need to set up a seven-word buffer where this information can be stored. The structure of this buffer is shown in Figure 14.1.

The format for this macro is

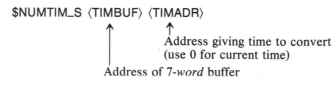

Besides supplying seeds for a random number generator, this macro can also be used to check the efficiency (run-time but *not* CPU time) of a procedure within a program. Figure 14.2 illustrates how to use this macro in terms of how long it takes a VAX-11 computer to go through an SOB Loop 10,000 times (a little more than ½ second in the following example).

FIGURE 14.1
The $NUMTIM Buffer Structure

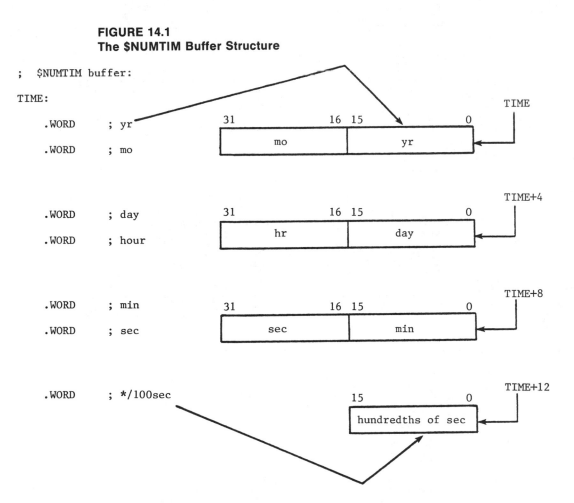

```
;   $NUMTIM buffer:

TIME:

    .WORD       ; yr
    .WORD       ; mo


    .WORD       ; day
    .WORD       ; hour


    .WORD       ; min
    .WORD       ; sec


    .WORD       ; */100sec
```

In effect, we use the following framework to time a process within a program:

Procedure for a Timer;

VAR

    x,y: INTEGER;

BEGIN

1. Get the time in seconds (assign this to x) and hundredths of seconds (assign this to y)

2. Execute a process (example: loading an array with 10,000 random numbers, or sorting an array of random numbers)

3. Get the new time, using $NUMTIM

    3.1 x: = new seconds − x (old seconds)

FIGURE 14.2
A Timer Program

```
;
;REF.: FIGURE 14.2 (A TIMER PROGRAM)
;
A:                                              ;FIRST PART OF $NUMTIM BUFFER
        .WORD                                   ;YEAR
B:      .WORD                                   ;MONTH
C:      .WORD                                   ;DAY
D:      .WORD                                   ;HOUR
E:      .WORD                                   ;MINUTE
SECONDS:                                        ;
        .WORD 0                                 ;SECOND
HUNDREDTHS:                                     ;
        .WORD 0                                 ;100TH OF SECOND
;
X:      .WORD                                   ;FOR INITIAL TOTAL 100THS
Y:      .WORD                                   ;FOR 2ND TOTAL 100THS
;
        .ENTRY BEGIN,0
        $NUMTIM_S -
                TIMBUF = A,-                    ;ASSIGN 5 WORD TIME BUFFER
                TIMADR = 0                      ;GIVE ADDRESS OF TIME TO
                                                ;TO BE CONVERTED--0 SENDS
                                                ;THIS MACRO TO CURRENT TIME
;
        JSB COPY                                ;SHOW OLD TIME
;
        MULW2 #100,SECONDS                      ;COMPUTE:
        ADDW2 SECONDS,HUNDREDTHS                ;
                                                ; 100*SECONDS + HUNDREDTHS
                                                ;
        MOVW HUNDREDTHS,X                       ;SAVE OLD TIME
;
        MOVL #100000,R9                         ;SET UP T-LOOP COUNTER
T:      SOBGTR R9,T                             ;CONTINUE LOOP UNTIL T = 0
;
        $NUMTIM_S -                             ;GET NEW TIME:
                TIMBUF = A,-
                TIMADR = 0
;
        JSB COPY                                ;SHOW NEW TIME
;
        MULW3 #100,SECONDS,Y                    ;COMPUTE NEW TOTAL
        ADDW2 HUNDREDTHS,Y                      ;100THS
        CVTWL X,R6                              ;SWITCH TO LONG FOR OLD
        CVTWL Y,R7                              ;& NEW TOTAL 100THS
        SUBL3 R6,R7,R8                          ;ADJUST FOR OLD TOTAL
        CLRL R9                                 ;SET UP R8-R9 QUADWORD
        EDIV #100,R8,R10,R11                    ;GET
                                                ;  R10=SEC PART OF 100THS
                                                ;  R11=100THS LEFT OVER
;
        PUSHL  R10
        CALLS  #1,WRITEVAL                      ;PRINT ELAPSED SECONDS
        SPACE  <2>                              ;PRINT 2 SPACES, THEN
```

Figure 14.2 continued.

```
        WRITE <SECONDS>
        SPACE <5>
        PUSHL  R11                        ;SET UP STACK FRAME TO
        CALLS  #1,WRITEVAL                ;PRINT ELAPSED 100THS
        SPACE <2>                         ;OF A SECOND
        WRITE < HUNDREDTHS OF A SECOND>
;
        $EXIT_S
;
COPY:
        CVTWL  A,R6                       ;CONVERT YR-WORD TO LONG
        PUSHL  R6                         ;&
        CALLS  #1,WRITEVAL                ;PRINT YR
        SPACE <2>
        MOVZWL B,R6                       ;CONVERT MO-WORD TO LONG
        PUSHL  R6                         ;&
        CALLS  #1,WRITEVAL                ;PRINT MO
        SPACE <2>
        MOVZWL C,R6                       ;CONVERT DAY-WORD TO LONG
        PUSHL  R6                         ;&
        CALLS  #1,WRITEVAL                ;PRINT DAY
        SPACE <2>
        MOVZWL D,R6                       ;CONVERT HR-WORD TO LONG
        PUSHL  R6                         ;&
        CALLS  #1,WRITEVAL                ;PRINT HR
        SPACE <2>
        MOVZWL E,R6                       ;CONVERT MIN-WORD TO LONG
        PUSHL  R6                         ;&
        CALLS  #1,WRITEVAL                ;PRINT MIN
        SPACE <2>
        MOVZWL SECONDS,R6                 ;CONVERT SEC-WORD TO LONG
        PUSHL  R6                         ;&
        CALLS  #1,WRITEVAL                ;PRINT SEC
        SPACE <2>
        MOVZWL HUNDREDTHS,R6              ;CONVERT 100THS-WORD TO LONG
        PUSHL  R6                         ;&
        CALLS  #1,WRITEVAL                ;PRINT 100THS
        WRITELN
        WRITELN <-------------------------------------------->
        WRITELN
        RSB                               ;RETURN FROM ROUTINE
;
        .END BEGIN


RUN FG142

1983  12  1  17  15  23  65
-------------------------------------------

1983  12  1  17  15  24  37
-------------------------------------------

0  SECONDS    72   HUNDREDTHS OF A SECOND
```

3.2 begin computing 100ths:

    3.2.1 y: = 100 − y

    3.2.2 y: = new hundredths of sec + y

    3.2.3 x: = y DIV 100 + x

    3.2.4 Y: = y MOD 100

END Timer.

The process time from the above procedure would then be

x seconds and y hundredths of a second.

This procedure would need to be enhanced to time processes taking more than 59 seconds.

14.2.4 A Random Number Generator

The following routine will sit by itself, external to any of the programs and/or routines that call it. Later we show how it can be made into a procedure and added to our procedure library. Any program, routine, or procedure that calls this generator routine must supply an initial value of m, which will lead to random numbers in the range

0, . . . , m−1

They are the remainders after dividing $aX + b$ by m or, initially,

[a*(seed) + b] mod m

To compute $aX + b$, we use the EMUL (Extended MULtiply) instruction in the VAX-11 repertoire:

EMUL factor, factor, addend, product
        ↑   ↑   ↑   ↑
        a   X   b   aX + b
   (long) (long) (long) (quadword)

This instruction computes $a*X$, adds b to the product, and puts the result in a quadword location (we call it PRODUCT). Each of the terms (a, X, b) is stored in *long* words.

In the routine that follows, we go to great lengths to avoid results that are negative, where the MSB is set. If the sign bit (or bit 31 of the low *long* word of PRODUCT), we take its twos complement instead before continuing

We do this with

```
MNEGL  SEED, SEED
```

twos complement of the source

aX + b gives new seed

The routine for this operation is shown in Figure 14.3.

14.2.5 How to Produce Random Numbers

In the program that follows we repeatedly obtain integers in the range 0 through 9. In doing so, we use the EDIV instruction to control the printout of the random numbers, 20 per line in this example. Later, we will extend this idea in order to represent an array of random numbers printed in tabular form. The main point to notice is that we supply a value of m used in

(aX + b) mod m

each time we call the generator routine (see Figure 14.4).

We have yet to measure the efficiency of this random number generator. We do this next by measuring how evenly the generated numbers are distributed.

14.2.6 Random Number Frequency Polygons

We can set up a frequency polygon by loading an array with frequencies. If we are producing random numbers in the range 0, . . . , 9, then we can use the random numbers *themselves* as array indices. Each time a 3 is produced by our generator routine, for example, increment the corresponding array frequency or

array [3]

In the program that follows, we print star-spikes to give a graphical interpretation of the frequency of each random number. Figure 14.5 illustrates this program together with a sample frequency polygon.

This program can be enhanced. Each star could be used to represent ten occurrences of a random number, instead of a star for each occurrence of a random number. An alternative to a star polygon would be a table of frequencies relative to a larger set of random numbers (that is, where $m >$ 10). These enhancements are handled later in the exercises.

FIGURE 14.3
A Random Number Generator Routine

```
        ;
        ;Ref.: Figure 14.3 (A RANDOM NUMBER GENERATOR ROUTINE)
        ;
        ;METHOD: LINEAR CONGRUENTIAL
        ;
            .GLOBAL RANDOM,RND,M
RESULT: .LONG                           ;FOR TRIAL REMAINDER
M::     .LONG                           ;MODULUS
RND::   .LONG                           ;REMAINER IN
                                        ;
                                        ; (A*SEED + B) MOD M
                                        ;   ^         ^
A:      .LONG 48593                     ;48593        |
B:      .LONG 1726939                   ;           1726939
TIME:
        .BLKW 5                         ;BEGIN 7-WORD TIME
SEED:   .WORD                           ;BUFFER FOR THE
        .WORD                           ;$NUMTIM SYSTEM MACRO
PRODUCT::
        .LONG                           ;QUAD (=2 LONG WORDS)
        .LONG 0                         ;FOR EMUL INSTRUCTION
Q:      .LONG                           ;QUOTIENT
        ;
RANDOM::                                ;BEGIN EXTERNAL ROUTINE
        TSTL SEED                       ;CHECK IF SEED IS NEEDED
        BGTR NEWRND                     ;IF NOT, GET NEW RND
                                        ;ELSE
        $NUMTIM_S TIMBUF=TIME TIMADR=0  ;GET TIME
        ADDL2 TIME,SEED                 ;INIT. SEED
        ADDL2 TIME+8,SEED               ;MAKE SEED LARGER
NEWRND:

        EMUL A,SEED,B,PRODUCT           ;COMPUTE A*SEED + B
        MOVL PRODUCT,SEED               ;USE AS NEW SEED
        BGEQ NONEG                      ;WAS IT < 0 ?
        MNEGL SEED,SEED                 ;IF SO, GET 2´S COMPLEMENT
                                        ;ELSE
        ;
NONEG:
        MOVL SEED,PRODUCT               ;INIT. A*SEED + B > 0
        CLRL PRODUCT + 4                ;CLEAR HIGH LONGWD OF QUAD
        EDIV M,PRODUCT,Q,RESULT         ;COMPUTE TRIAL RND
        TSTL RESULT                     ;WAS IT < 0 ?
        BLSS ERROR                      ;IF SO, REJECT RND
                                        ;ELSE
        MOVL RESULT,RND                 ;INIT. NEW RND
        RSB
        ;
ERROR:  $EXIT_S
        .END
```

FIGURE 14.4
Sample Random Numbers

```
;
;Ref.: Figure 14.4 (SAMPLE RANDOM NUMBERS)
;
;METHOD: REPEATED USE OF THE ROUTINE IN FIGURE 14.3, USING THE
EDIV
;          INSTRUCTION TO CONTROL THE NO. OF RND´S PRINTED ON EACH
LINE.
;
        .GLOBAL RANDOM,RND,M,PRODUCT
;
        .ENTRY BEGIN,0
        MOVL    #200,R6                 ;INIT. COUNT OF RND´S
        CLRL    R7                      ;USE R7 FOR COLUMN COUNTER
LOOP:
        MOVL    #10,M                   ;INIT. MODULUS, GIVING RND´S
                                        ;IN THE RANGE 0, ... ,9
        JSB     RANDOM                  ;GET RND
        PUSHL   RND                     ;SET UP STACK FRAME
        CALLS   #1,WRITEVAL             ;& PRINT RND NO.
        SPACE   <2>
        INCL    R7                      ;INCREMENT COLUMN COUNTER
        CLRL    R8                      ;CLEAR R8 IN R7-R8 QUADWORD
        EDIV    #20,R7,R9,R10           ;COMPUTE REMAINDER
        TSTL    R10                     ;SEE IF COL-COUNT IS
                                        ;MULTIPLE OF 20
        BNEQ    NEXT_NO                 ;IF NOT, CONTINUE PRINTING
                                        ;ELSE
;
        WRITELN                         ;<RET>
        WRITELN                         ;      <RET>
        CLRL R7
;
NEXT_NO:
        SOBGEQ R6,LOOP                  ;CONTINUE UNTIL R6 < 0
;
        $EXIT_S
        .END BEGIN
```

8	3	0	5	6	7	0	7	2	1	2	1	4	1	2	1	0	5	4	3
6	7	4	1	2	5	0	9	4	1	2	1	0	7	0	1	6	1	6	1
2	7	2	5	6	7	2	5	2	7	2	9	2	1	2	5	4	1	8	5
8	9	0	1	2	7	2	7	6	7	6	3	4	9	2	9	8	1	6	9
6	9	2	3	6	5	2	3	8	9	2	7	2	5	6	3	8	3	6	7
2	3	4	1	6	1	6	9	0	1	0	9	4	9	4	5	8	3	0	5
8	7	2	3	4	7	4	9	0	7	8	3	0	1	0	5	6	1	6	9
4	5	2	5	2	7	6	5	2	9	4	5	2	9	0	1	8	7	0	3
0	9	2	1	6	1	4	7	8	5	8	3	2	9	6	5	6	5	4	3
8	3	0	1	6	9	4	3	0	3	6	7	6	7	2	3	6	9	0	7
0																			

FIGURE 14.5
Frequency Polygon Program

```
;
;Ref.: Figure 14.5 (Frequency polygon program)
;
;Task: Obtain random numbers in the range 0, ... ,m-1, and tabulate the
;      frequency that each random number occurs in n trials.  Then (1)
;      display a table with each random number obtained, its frequency,
;      and (2) a corresponding frequency polygon.
;
        .GLOBAL WRITEVAL,RANDOM
MAX:    .LONG                           ;UPPER LIMIT IN RND RANGE
ARRAY:  .LONG 0[776]                    ;RND TABLE
;
        .ENTRY BEGIN,0
        WRITELN
        WRITELN
        WRITE <ENTER MAX. IN THE RANGE 0,...,MAX:  >
        WRITELN
        CALLS #1,READVAL
        MOVL (R11)+,R7                  ;COPY OF MAX
        MOVL R7,MAX                     ;INIT. MAX
        WRITELN
        WRITE <ENTER NO. OF TRIALS TO USE IN GETTING RND´S: >
        WRITELN
        CALLS #1,READVAL
        MOVL (R11)+,R6                  ;INIT. R6 WITH NO. OF TRIALS
;
LOOP:
        NOP
        MOVL    R7,M                    ;INIT. M IN 0, ... ,M-1
        BSBW    RANDOM                  ;GET RND
        MOVL    RND,R3                  ;INIT. TABLE INDEX
        INCL    ARRAY[R3]               ;INCREMENT RND-FREQ-COUNT
        SOBGEQ  R6,LOOP                 ;CONTINUE UNTIL COUNT=0
;
        WRITELN
        WRITELN
        WRITE <RND    FREQ.             FREQ. POLYGON>
        WRITELN
        WRITELN<------------------------------------------------------------>
        WRITELN
        WRITELN
;
        CLRL    R6                      ;INIT. ARRAY INDEX
OUTLP:
        PUSHL   R6                      ;SET UP STACK FRAME TO
        CALLS   #1,WRITEVAL             ;PRINT INDEX
        SPACE   <5>
        PUSHL   ARRAY[R6]               ;SET UP STACK FRAME TO
        CALLS   #1,WRITEVAL             ;PRINT FREQUENCY
        SPACE   <1>
        TAB     <2>
        WRITE   <|>                     ;BEGIN FREQ POLYGON SPIKE
        MOVL    ARRAY[R6],COUNT         ;SET UP STAR-COUNT
STAR:   WRITE <*>                       ;PRINT STAR IN SPIKE
```

Figure 14.5 continued.

```
        SOBGTR    COUNT,STAR              ;CONTINUE BUILDING SPIKE
                                          ;UNTIL STAR-COUNT = 0
;
        WRITELN
        WRITELN
;
        INCL    R6                        ;INCREMENT INDEX
        CMPL    MAX,R6                    ;IS INDEX < MAX
        BEQL    LAST                      ;IF NOT, EXIT
                                          ;ELSE
        JMP     OUTLP                     ;CONTINUE PRINTING POLYGON
LAST:   NOP
        $EXIT_S
;
        .END BEGIN

RUN FG145

Enter max. in the range 0,...,max:
20

Enter no. of trials to use in getting rnd´s:
600

rnd   freq.              freq. polygon
-----------------------------------------------------------

0     29      |****************************
1     35      |**********************************
2     30      |*****************************
3     28      |***************************
4     29      |****************************
5     32      |*******************************
6     36      |***********************************
7     29      |****************************
8     39      |**************************************
9     33      |********************************
10    25      |************************
11    25      |************************
```

Continued on following page.

Figure 14.5 continued.

12	28	|*****************************
13	37	|*************************************
14	22	|**********************
15	34	|**********************************
16	39	|***************************************
17	28	|****************************
18	23	|***********************
19	20	|********************

14.3

RANDOM NUMBER TABLES

Building a random number table is made easier by storing the random numbers in an array. We do this next. We build a NOS array with random entries contributed by the routine in Figure 14.3. Then, using the EDIV instruction to control the row length of the table, we echo-print the new array, as shown in Figure 14.6.

An obvious enhancement to this would be to print the digits 0, . . . , 9 in clusters, depending on the number of digits desired in the numbers in column of the random number table. That is, the clusters can be taken as new random numbers. An alternative to this would be to increase the size of m in the random number range

$$0, \ldots, m-1$$

We allow for this (the NOS array consists of longwords). These enhancements are tested later in an exercise.

14.4

CRYPTOGRAPHY: ENCODING A MESSAGE

We can use random numbers to encode a message. This is done by setting up an array of symbols (such as the letters of the alphabet and punctuation marks). This will be our symbol table. Then we set up a second array of

FIGURE 14.6
Random Number Table Program

```
;
;Ref.:   Figure 14.6 (Building a random number table)
;
;Task:   use the random number generator in Figure 14.3 to build and an
;        array of random numbers, then use the EDIV instruction to print
;        the array in tabular form.
;
MAX:     .LONG 100                           ;upper limit in rnd range
ARRAY:   .LONG 0[1000]                       ;rnd array
TALLY:   .LONG 300                           ;no. of trials in searching
                                             ;for rnd´s
;
         .ENTRY BEGIN,0
;
         MOVL    TALLY,R7                    ;limit on array entries
         MOVAB   ARRAY,R6                    ;set up array pointer
BUILD:
         MOVL    MAX,M                       ;init. max in
                                             ;
                                             ;  0, . . . ,max-1
                                             ;
                                             ;random no. range

         JSB     RANDOM
         MOVL    RND, (R6)+                  ;put rnd into array slot
         SOBGTR R7,BUILD
;
         MOVAB   ARRAY,R6                    ;restore beginning array addr.
;
COPY_OF_RND_NOS:
         MOVL    TALLY,R8                    ;now used tally to
                                             ;control line-length
         CLRL    R9                          ;use R9 in R8,R9 quadword
         EDIV    #20,R8,R10,R11
         TSTL    R11                         ;check for zero remainder
         BNEQ    NEXT_NO                     ;if not, continue printing
                                             ;else
         WRITELN                             ; <ret>
         WRITELN                             ;   twice!
;
NEXT_NO:
         PUSHL   (R6)+
         CALLS   #1,WRITEVAL                 ;print entry
         SPACE   <2>
         SOBGTR TALLY,COPY_OF_RND_NOS
;
         $EXIT_S
;
         .END BEGIN
```

Continued on following page.

Figure 14.6 continued.

```
RUN FG146

43  78  67  94  99  90  77  68  61  28  85  96  33  40  93  20  39  62  51  70

9   76  71  22  91  46  19  94  13  32  93  12  69  96  63  94  5   68  11  18

91  74  93  36  25  32  87  34  53  40  79  14  9   68  59  66  99  66  13  16

69  88  1   60  29  48  33  44  67  90  23  86  33  20  59  86  77  68  55  94

15  22  5   28  47  70  61  8   59  18  59  42  47  82  53  20  51  6   97  72

79  34  73  96  65  44  41  24  23  50  65  88  45  48  79  58  17  12  9   36

19  78  31  50  37  72  81  44  57  44  51  30  9   88  15  74  75  30  21  76

7   18  55  66  5   48  61  36  11  10  91  14  25  96  33  88  23  10  13  44

7   86  63  50  93  16  47  90  13  68  77  4   37  60  3   90  99  94  91  78

87  30  7   50  45  72  7   10  9   52  39  38  9   92  33  36  87  46  3   50

59  22  71  46  95  30  77  48  39  98  35  46  31  66  61  76  11  2   31  38

95  34  33  32  23  62  85  72  97  88  39  38  33  88  55  6   55  50  3   38

77  64  33  0   83  82  3   94  55  58  67  82  41  4   7   86  89  8   7   50

15  42  91  74  11  6   45  40  71
```

random entries (a cipher table). The position of a symbol in the symbol table (array) can be used to determine which random number will be its replacement. We do this with three arrays of bytes: a message, symbol, and random number array. (The symbol table will contain ASCII codes for the necessary symbols.) The procedure we use to encrypt a message is shown graphically in Figure 14.7.

We have implemented the procedure shown in Figure 14.7 without being concerned about the uniqueness of a cipher. The same number can be used as the cipher for more than one message symbol. This is easily changed later. For the moment we reproduce a predetermined message, its encryption, and a dictionary that makes decryption possible. The dictionary contains both the complete symbol table and complete cipher table. Later, we deal with the problem of allowing the user to enter a new message each time the encryption program is run. A further enhancement would be a routine to decrypt a message, which means a cipher table would need to be predefined (it could be in an external psect linked together with the decryption routine or entered from a keyboard). A beginning encryption program is shown in Figure 14.8.

FIGURE 14.7
Graphical Interpretation of Encryption

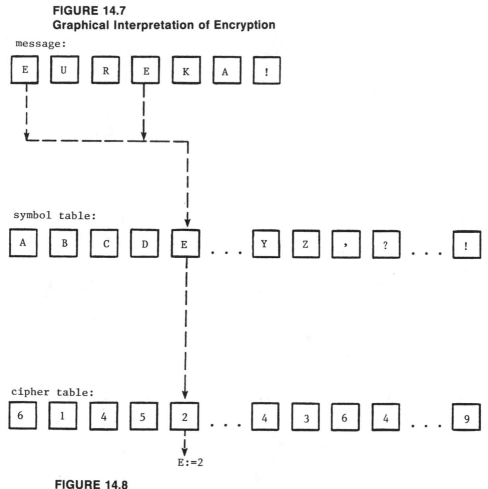

FIGURE 14.8
Cryptography Program with Dictionary

```
;
;Ref.:   Figure 14.8 (Cryptography program with decryption dictionary)
;
;Task:   Set up three tables: (1)message table (array of bytes with message),
;        (2)symbol table with symbols found in messages (array of bytes with
;        ASCII codes for symbols, and (3) cipher table containing random
;        numbers.  A message symbol maps to symbol table ASCII code:
;
;                        message symbol :---> symbol table code
;
;        and the symbol table code maps to a random number cipher in terms
;        of the position of the symbol table code in the symbol table:
```

Continued on following page.

Figure 14.8 continued.

```
;
;                                symbol table code :---> cipher
;
;          |_||_||_|  ...  |_||_|  ...  |_||_||_||_||_||_|
;          ^                ^
;          |                |
;       symbol[0]
;                    symbol[i]
;                                        ^
;                                        |
;          |_||_||_|  ...  |_||_| ...  |_||_||_||_||_||_|
;                                 ^
;       ciphers:                  |
;                         cipher[i] = rnd no.
;
        .GLOBAL RANDOM,M
TALLY:  .LONG 29
MAX:    .LONG 29
MESSAGE:                                ;message table
        .ASCIC/EUREKA!/
        .BYTE 0
SYMBOL_TABLE:
        .BYTE 65,66,67,68,69,70,71,72,73,74,75,76,77,78,79,80,81,82,83
        .BYTE 84,85,86,87,88,89,90,44,46,63,33
;
;       Symbol table with codes for capitals and , . ? !
;
ENCRYPTION_TABLE:
        .BYTE 0[30]
CODE:
        .BYTE 1,0                       ;use to print out single-
                                        ;digit codes
;
        .ENTRY BEGIN,0
        JSB BUILD_E_TABLE               ;fill encryption table with
                                        ;randomly selected entries
;
        WRITELN
        WRITELN
        WRITE <  Original message:   >
        SPURT <MESSAGE>
        WRITELN

        WRITELN
        WRITELN<------------------------------------------------->
        WRITELN
        WRITE <  Ecryption:  >
        SPACE <6>
;
        CLRL    R6                      ;set array indices:
        INCL    R6                      ;slide pointer past first
                                        ;byte of the .ASCIC array
        CLRL    R7
```

Figure 14.8 continued.

```
;
SEARCH:
        CMPB    MESSAGE[R6],SYMBOL_TABLE[R7]
        BEQL    ENCRYPT                 ;if message symbol matches
                                        ;symbol-table entry,
                                        ;    then encrypt symbol
                                        ;       else
        INCL    R7                      ;       advance s-table index
        BRW     SEARCH                  ;       & continue searching
ENCRYPT:
        CVTBL   ENCRYPTION_TABLE[R7],R8
        PUSHL   R8                      ;init. code to be
        CALLS   #1,WRITEVAL             ;printed
        SPACE   <2>
        INCL    R6                      ;advance message index
        CMPB    #0,MESSAGE[R6]          ;check for null
        BEQL    DICTIONARY              ;if so, print dictionary
                                        ;else
        CLRL    R7                      ;   init. encrypt-table index
        JMP     SEARCH                  ;   & continue encryption
;
DICTIONARY:
        WRITELN
        WRITELN<------------------------------------------------------->
        WRITELN
        WRITELN<  Symbol              Encryption code>
        WRITELN
        WRITELN<------------------------------------------------------->
        CLRL    R6
        CLRL    R7
        MOVL    TALLY,R8
ECHO:
        SPACE   <6>
        MOVB    SYMBOL_TABLE[R6],CODE + 1  ;get symbol
        SPURT   <CODE>
        SPACE   <15>
        CVTBL   ENCRYPTION_TABLE[R7],R9
        PUSHL   R9
        CALLS   #1,WRITEVAL
        WRITELN
        INCL    R6
        INCL    R7
        DECL    R8
        BLSS    AGAIN
        JMP     ECHO
;
AGAIN:
        NOP
        $EXIT_S
;
BUILD_E_TABLE:
        CLRL    R6
```

Continued on following page.

Figure 14.8 continued.

```
        MOVL    TALLY,R7
;
TABLE:
        MOVL    MAX,M
        JSB     RANDOM
        CVTLB   RND,ENCRYPTION_TABLE[R6]
        INCL    R6
        SOBGEQ  R7,TABLE
        RSB
;
        .END BEGIN

RUN FG148

  Original message:   EUREKA!

--------------------------------------------

  Ecryption:         1   5   5   1   26   14   5
--------------------------------------------------

  Symbol             Encryption code

--------------------------------------------------

        A               14
        B               15
        C               0
        D               3
        E               1
        F               27
        G               14
        H               22
        I               7
        J               26
        K               26
        L               26
        M               5
        N               13
        O               0
        P               2
        Q               23
        R               5
        S               8
        T               16
        U               5
        V               27
        W               4
        X               20
        Y               7
        Z               11
        ,               9
        .               5
        ?               24
        !               5
```

In this program we use

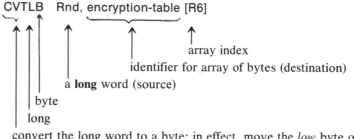

convert the long word to a byte; in effect, move the *low* byte of Rnd (the source) to a byte location (the destination)

This makes it easier to determine the correct cipher to use relative to an ASCII code in the symbol table. We need to use the CVT instruction in this way, since the random number RND is in a *long* word. As it stands, the WRITEVAL relies on the use of a *long* word that has been pushed onto a stack frame before the

    CALLS #1, WRITEVAL

To print the numeric ciphers, we use

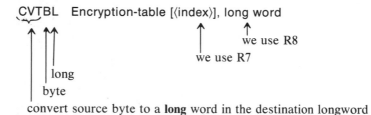

convert source byte to a **long** word in the destination longword

The above program produces what is known as a plaintext (the original message) and a ciphertext (random numbers in place of plaintext symbols). This program could be used to produce what B. Bosworth (1982, p. 91) calls a polyalphabetic cipher system. That is, we could use the random entries to construct a rearranged alphabet, which, in turn, could be used to replace the letters in the original message. We might also randomly select symbols from a symbol table to construct keywords of varying length. Then symbols in the original message would be replaced by corresponding keywords. We try some of these things later, in a lab project.

14.5

GRAPHICS: RANDOMLY SELECTED IMAGES

We can use random numbers to determine the dimensions of a printed image and the frequency with which it is printed. We do this by using the ACB instruction, which functions like a FOR/DO in Pascal, or a DO loop in Fortran. The ACB and Pascal FOR/DO instructions are compared below:

Pascal	Assembly Language
FOR I: = LIMIT DOWNTO K	ACTION:
DO	⋮
BEGIN	⟨process⟩
⋮	⋮
⟨action(s)⟩	ACBL K, # − 1, LIMIT, ACTION
⋮	Limit: = Limit − 1
END;	step (downward)
	lower limit

The action inside the ACBL loop continues *until* the limit is less than *K*, or *while* the limit is greater than or equal to *K*. We use this instruction to advantage in the next example. We use it, first, to print a spike of random length. Then we use it to regulate the printing of rows of spikes. We embellish the resulting graph by ringing a bell once an arrowhead has been "attached" to each spike (see Figure 14.9).

FIGURE 14.9
Random Images Program

```
;
;Ref.:   Figure 14.9 (Graphics: Random images)
;
;Task:   Using random numbers, both the length and frequency of spikes
;        printed are determined randomly.  Capping each arrow is a bell
;        sound.
;
ARROW    = 62
RING     = 7


;
MAX:     .LONG 40
NO_OF_ROWS:
         .LONG
SPIKE:
         .BYTE 0,0[70]                  ;spike table
BELL:
         .BYTE 1,RING[3]                ;simulated .ASCIC
ARROWHEAD:
         .BYTE 1,ARROW[2]               ;simulated .ASCIC
;
         .ENTRY BEGIN,0
```

Figure 14.9 continued.

```
;
NO:
        MOVL    MAX,M                   ;INIT. M FOR RND ROUTINE
        JSB     RANDOM                  ;CALL RND ROUTINE
                                        ;ELSE
;
        MOVL    RND,NO_OF_ROWS          ;USE RND TO DETERMINE
;
GRAPH:
        MOVL    MAX,M                   ;init. m in 0, ... ,m-1 range
        JSB     RANDOM                  ;get rnd
        MOVL    RND,R6                  ;set up limit on for-loop
        MOVAB   SPIKE+1,R7              ;set up spike table pointer
        CVTLB   RND,SPIKE              ;set up count of stars in spike
                                        ;using the rnd to set the count
                                        ;of the no. of stars in table
;
STARS:
        MOVB    #42,(R7)+              ;put star code in spike table
        ACBL    #1,#-1,R6,STARS        ;equivalent to
                                        ;
                                        ; for i:=rnd downto 1 do
                                        ;    <put star code in spike>
                                        ;
;
        SPURT   <SPIKE>                 ;print spike
        SPURT   <ARROWHEAD>             ;print arrowhead
        SPURT   <BELL>                  ;ring bell
        WRITELN
;
        ACBL    #1,#-1,NO_OF_ROWS,GRAPH ;Pascal equivalent:
                                        ; for i:=rnd downto 1 do
                                        ;    <graph loop, above>
;
        $EXIT_S
        .END BEGIN


RUN FG149

***************>
*********************>
*****************>
************>
*******>
****************************************>
*>
********************>
*************************>
********************>
******************************>
************************************>
*****************************************>
**********>
```

Continued on following page.

Figure 14.9 continued.

```
*****>
********************************>
***>
*****************************>
*******>
**************************>
*********************>
************************>
***************************>
**>
****************************************>
>
*********************>
************************>
**************************>
******>
***********************>
**********************>
*********>
************>
***************>
******>
******************>
****>
```

This program can be enhanced by allowing the user to select the image to be printed, and what is done with it when it is printed. We explore this later. It should be noted that this program actually has nested loops:

graph:

   0. get Rnd

star loop:

   1. print spike (inner loop)

   2. print arrowhead (outer loop)

   3. turn on keyboard bell (outer loop)

get new spike until limit < k = 1

The size of each loop has been determined randomly.

14.6

RANDOM SELECTION OF CASES: DRAWING FROM A HAT

This final example depends on the use of the CASE statement in VAX-11 macro instruction repertoire. This statement functions somewhat like an ON/GOTO:

ON x ⟨statement no.⟩, . . . , ⟨statement no.⟩

in BASIC, but is actually closer to the case statement in Pascal, where x determines which action among a set of possible actions is executed. Levy and Eckhouse (1980, p. 105) compare the VAX-11 CASE to a computed GOTO in FORTRAN. We show the VAX-11 instruction in parallel with the Pascal case statement:

Pascal	*VAX-11*
Case x of	Case x, base, limit
0: action 0	Items:
1: action 1	Case 0
	Case 1
⋮	
limit − 1: action limit − 1	⋮
otherwise	Case limit + base − 1
: alternate action	otherwise
	Case limit + base (max)

When the VAX-11 CASE instruction is executed, the base value is subtracted from the selector x. If the computed value of x is in the range

base, base + 1, . . . , base + limit

an item (action) inside the case-table will be executed. The setup for this instruction is complex. The illustration of this statement by Digital Equipment Corporation (1981, p. 274) is riddled with misprints, errors, and omissions, with the result that it is difficult to implement. Key among the omissions is a provision for *leaving* the case statement after a case has been selected and execution is made to continue with the instruction following the case statement. We show this in outline form first (assume Limit = 7, which implies 8 cases, if the base = one):

```
CASE X, 1, LIMIT
ITEMS:
            .WORD 10$ – ITEMS      ;displacement 0
            .WORD 20$ – ITEMS      ;displacement 0

                ⋮

            .WORD 70$ – ITEMS      ;displacement 6
```

FIGURE 14.10

Random Case Selections: Drawing from a Hat

```
;
;Ref.:   Figure 14.10 (DRAWING FROM A HAT)
;
;TASK:   USE RANDOM NUMBERS TO DETERMINE THE SELECTION OF AN ACTION, WHICH
;        IS TIED TO THE VAX-11 CASE STATEMENT.
;
MAX:     .LONG 7                          ;UPPER LIMIT IN RND RANGE
BUFFER:
         .LONG
SELECTION:
         .LONG                            ;CASE SELECTOR
;
         .ENTRY BEGIN,0
;
NO:
         MOVL    MAX,BUFFER               ;SAVE A COPY OF MAX
         MOVL    MAX,M                    ;INIT M IN 0, ... ,M-1 RANGE
         JSB     RANDOM                   ;GET RND IN ABOVE RANGE
         TSTL    RND                      ;CHECK FOR ZERO-RND
         BEQL    NO                       ;IF RND = 0, THEN GET NEW RND
                                          ;  ELSE
         MOVL    RND,SELECTION            ;INIT. CASE SELECTOR
;
         DECL    BUFFER                   ;DO THIS, SINCE THE RND
                                          ; NOS. ARE IN 0..MAX-1 RANGE
         CASEL   SELECTION,#1,BUFFER      ;EQUIVALENT TO
                                          ;
                                          ; CASE SELECTION OF
                                          ;  <LIST OF CASES>
                                          ;
                                          ;IN EFFECT:
                                          ;
                                          ;  if selection = 0 then
                                          ;    <execute case 0>
                                          ;    else
                                          ;    if selection = 1 then
                                          ;      <execute case 1>
                                          ;      else
                                          ;        <consider next case>
ITEMS:
         .WORD   10$-ITEMS                ;DISPLACEMENT 0
         .WORD   20$-ITEMS                ;DISPLACEMENT 1
         .WORD   30$-ITEMS                ;DISPLACEMENT 2
         .WORD   40$-ITEMS                ;DISPLACEMENT 3
         .WORD   50$-ITEMS                ;DISPLACEMENT 4
         .WORD   60$-ITEMS                ;DISPLACEMENT 5
         .WORD   70$-ITEMS                ;DISPLACEMENT 6
         JMP ENQUIRE                      ;otherwise enquire about
10$:     WRITELN
         WRITELN < 0! Bother! says Winnie-the-Pooh when he gets stuck.>
         WRITELN
         JMP ENQUIRE
20$:     WRITELN
         WRITELN < Winnie-the-Pooh loves honey!>
```

Figure 14.10 continued.

```
                WRITELN
                JMP ENQUIRE
30$:            WRITELN
                WRITELN < A way a last a loved along the riverrun...>
                WRITELN
                JMP ENQUIRE
40$:            WRITELN
                WRITELN <                    Eureka!>
                WRITELN
                JMP ENQUIRE
50$:            WRITELN
                WRITELN <                     *>
                WRITELN <                    * * >
                WRITELN <                   * * *>
                WRITELN <                  * * * *>
                WRITELN <                     *>
                WRITELN
                JMP ENQUIRE
60$:            WRITELN
                WRITELN < EDIV divisor,dividend,quotient,remainder>
                WRITELN <                    ^>
                WRITELN <               |>
                WRITELN <          quad word>
                WRITELN
                JMP ENQUIRE
70$:
                BRW ENQUIRE
;
ENQUIRE:
                WRITE <Again?--Type 1 for yes, 0 for no:    >
                CALLS  #0,READVAL
                CMPL   #1,(R11)               ;CHECK RESPONSE
                BNEQ   LAST_BYTE
                JMP    NO
;
LAST_BYTE:
                NOP
                $EXIT_S
                .END BEGIN


RUN FG1410


                    *
                   * *
                  * * *
                 * * * *
                    *


Again?--Type 1 for yes, 0 for no:    1

 Winnie-the-Pooh loves honey!

Again?--Type 1 for yes, 0 for no:    1
```

Continued on following page.

Figure 14.10 continued.

```
     Winnie-the-Pooh loves honey!

     Again?--Type 1 for yes, 0 for no:   1


                           *
                         *  *
                       *  *  *
                     *  *  *  *
                           *


     Again?--Type 1 for yes, 0 for no:   1

       O! Bother! says Winnie-the-Pooh when he gets stuck.

     Again?--Type 1 for yes, 0 for no:   1

       O! Bother! says Winnie-the-Pooh when he gets stuck.

     Again?--Type 1 for yes, 0 for no:   1

       EDIV divisor,dividend,quotient,remainder
                           ^
                 |
                 quad word

     Again?--Type 1 for yes, 0 for no:   0
```

```
     OTHERWISE:
             JMP ⟨next instruction⟩
     10$:    ⟨action(s)⟩              ;case 0
             JMP ⟨exit to next instruction⟩
     20$:    ⟨action(s)⟩              ;case 1
             JMP ⟨exit to next instruction⟩

               ⋮

     70$:    ⟨action(s)⟩              ;case 6
             JMP ⟨exit to next instruction⟩
```

Figure 14.10 illustrates the use of this instruction in conjunction with the production of random value of x in selecting the case to be executed. In effect, this program simulates random selection of items (from a hat!).

14.7

SUMMARY

The random number generator discussed in this chapter uses the system time for its initial value. This time is its seed. It comes to us as a gift from the $NUMTIM system macro, or the more amorphous result of the $GET-TIM macro. Without this, we would have to choose the generator seed each time we wanted to produce a random number sequence. The EMUL (Extended MULtiply) and EDIV (Extended DIVide) are just the right tools for implementing the linear congruential algorithm suggested by Knuth. The resulting random number routine is a truly useful tool. As Aho (1983, p. 27) would say, it is "a program with a variety of uses."

We not only investigate the randomness of the random number distributions produced, but we also exhibit the application of random numbers in cryptography, graphics, filling arrays with numbers without a seeming bias or excessive weight in terms of one number rather than another, and in random selections (from "a hat"). Along the way, we have illustrated the use of added instructions shown in the cross-reference table given in Table 14.1.

TABLE 14.1
Cross-reference Table of VAX-11 Instructions

Instruction	Structure	Comparable Instruction	Example	Reference
CVTxy	CVTxy S, D x = B, y = L x = L, y = B	MOVZBL S, D Cf. CVTBL S, D	Figures: 14.8 14.9	DEC [1981, 184–86]; Levy, Eckhouse [1980, p. 156]

ACBx	ACBx lim,step,No,label
	lim = lower limit
	step = amt added to
	　　NO
	NO = loop control
	If Step < 0, then
	
	execution continues
	while step + NO > lim.
	If step > 0, then
	execution continues
	while step + NO < lim.
		step = −1:
		For No: = ⟨value⟩
		　DOWNTO lim
		　DO
		　⟨action⟩
		For step = + 1:
		For NO: = ⟨value⟩
		　to lim
		　DO
		　⟨action⟩
			Figure
			14.9
			
			(x = L
			
			for
			long)
				DEC [1981, 268–69];
				Levy, Eckhouse
				[1980, p. 108]

CASE	CASE x,base,limit	Case statement in Pascal; ON × GOTO __,__ in BASIC	Figure 14.10	Levy, Eckhouse [1980, 106–7]

DEC = Digital Equipment Corporation.

Patience and care are needed in fashioning an adequate random number generator. The VAX-11, for example, is finicky. It does unwanted things to negative integers when we attempt to divide them. It does a sign extension on the high longword if the MSB is set in the lower longword of the quadword in

EDIV   divisor, dividend, quotient, remainder

(long)   (quad)   (long)   (long)

That is, it does not treat the lower longword of the dividend as an unsigned integer. If we let this go unchecked, the random generator given in Figure 14.1 would produce many spikes of unequal length (often, many zeros).

14.8

EXERCISES

1. Give an example of a finite sequence that is

   (a) 8-distributed

   (b) 2-distributed as well as 3-distributed

2. Illustrate the use of the $NUMTIM macro to time how long it takes a machine to load an array with

   (a) 10,000 random numbers in the range 0, . . . , 9 (m = 10)

   (b) 10,000 random numbers in the range 000, . . . , 999 (m = 1000);

   Hint: Try using a variation of the program in Figure 14.6 to do this.

3. Adjust the program in Figure 14.5 so that each star printed represents 10 occurrences of a random number in range 0, . . . , 9.

4. Enhance the program in Exercise 3 so that the user can select the number of occurrences of a random number a star will represent in the spikes printed for the frequency polygon. Run your program for

   (a) Print a star for each 2 occurrences with m = 100; trials = 400.

   (b) Print a star for each 10 occurrences with m = 1000; trials = 1000.

5. Enhance the program in Figure 14.6 so that it allows the user to *select*

   (a) the number of digits of each number

(b) the number of columns of random numbers printed

(c) the number of rows printed

Run your program

(d) a random number table with 40 rows, 10 columns of 5-digit random numbers, with each column separated by two blank columns

6. Write an improved frequency polygon program where

   (a) There is more than one set of random numbers (e.g., 5 sets with each set representing the use of a new initial system time (or seed) and 1,000 trials).

   (b) For *each* of the sets of random numbers, the number of times a particular number occurs is tabulated.

   (c) The average number of occurrences of a random number is computed. For example, if 0(1) represents the number of occurrences of a 9 in set 1; 0(2), the number of occurrences in set 2, and so on. Then use

   $$\text{average} = \frac{0(1) + 0(2) + \cdots + 0(k)}{k}$$

   for *k* sets of random numbers

   Run your program for

   (d) 5 sets of random numbers in the range

   $$0, \ldots, 9 \quad (m = 10)$$

   with each set containing 200 elements (they were obtained after 200 trials or visits to a random number generator);

   (e) 10 sets of random numbers in the range

   $$00, \ldots, 99 \quad (m = 100)$$

   with each set containing 500 elements.

7. Write a graphics program to print a flat stellar pyramid (filled-in triangle) of the form

```
      *
    *  *
   *  *  *
  *  *  *  *
```

so that the number of rows in the flat pyramid varies randomly (will be different each time the program is run).

8. Enhance the program so that it prints a menu, allowing the user to choose

(a) flat pyramid

(b) stellar diamond

```
      *
    *  *
  *  *  *
    *  *
      *
```

where the sizes of the figures printed vary randomly. The lines of code in Pascal that can be used to do this are given below:

```
BEGIN
        TOPLINES: = NOOFLINES DIV 2 + 1;
        FOR I: = 1 TO TOPLINES DO
            BEGIN
            WRITE(' ' :NOOFLINES − I + 1);
            FOR J: = 1 TO I*2 − 1 DO
                WRITE ('*');
            WRITELN
            END;
        FOR I: = TOPLINES − 1 DOWNTO 1 DO
            BEGIN
            WRITE (' ': NOOFLINES − I + 1);
            FOR J: = 1 TO I*2 − 1 DO
                WRITE ('*');
            WRITELN
            END
    END.
```

(This technique was suggested by Dr. H. M. Sallam in the computer science department at Saint John's University.)

9. Write a variation of the random number generator in Figure 14.3 that

(a) Uses the $GETTIM system macro instead of the $NUMTIM macro.

(b) Uses the $GETTIM macro to supply a time to $NUMTIM macro.

(c) Uses

(i) a = 1726939 (a prime)
    b = 48593 (a prime)
    m = 10   ; trials = 200

(ii) a = 1726939
     b = 1
     m = 2^{30} ; trials = 200

(iii) a = 48593
      b = 1
      m = 2^{30} ; trials = 200

10. Rewrite the random number generator in Figure 14.3 as an external procedure, leaving RND and M global. Add this routine to the I/O library.

11. Enhance the cipher program in Figure 14.8 so that it does the following:

(a) Uses a unique random number cipher for each symbol (no two symbols should have the same cipher).

(b) Allows the user to enter a message to be enciphered.

Run your program for

(c) Message: A program is a piece of text. (See N. Wirth, 1983, p. 6.)

(d) Message: A compiler is a program translating programs from their source form to specific computer codes. (See Wirth, 1983, p. 6.)

14.9

LAB PROJECTS

1. Shift-Register Generator of Random Numbers: G. Marsaglia (1983, p. 1260) gives the shift register RND generator method. We represent the framework of Marsaglia's method in the following procedure:

Procedure Shift Register Generator:

var x, y, Rn RND: Integer;

BEGIN

    1. Initialize X (with $NUMTIM, for example); Rn:=X;

    2. Begin generating random numbers:

        2.1 ASHL ⟨shift Rn to right 3 places⟩

2.2 Rn: = Rn + X

2.3 Y: = Rn

2.4 ASHL ⟨shift Rn to left 4 places⟩

2.5 Rn: = Rn + Y

2.6 RND: = Rn

2.7 X: = Rn

2.8 REPEAT Loop at Step 2

End Proc.

Do the following:

(a) Use the $NUMTIM macro to supply the initial value for X in the above procedure. Write an assembler routine to implement the above procedure.

(b) Write an assembly language program to print 1000 values of RND.

(c) Write a new version of the routine in part (a) so that the routine produces remainders in the interval

$$0 \le RND \le 0.999969482$$

(d) Run the frequency polygon program in Figure 14.5 in terms of the new generator.

2. Midsquare Generator, suggested by John von Neumann in 1946: The procedure for this random number generator is given next.

Procedure Mid-Square:

VAR X, MID, RND: Integer;

BEGIN

   1. Initialize X: = 45086273, for example;

   2. Begin computing random numbers;

     2.1 X: = X²

     2.2 RND: = middle 8 digits (call new no. MID)

     2.3 X: = MID

     2.4 REPEAT Loop at step 2

End Proc.

Do the following:

(a) Use the $NUMTIM macro to initialize X (the seed) and write a routine to implement this generator.

(b) Write an assembly program to print 1,000 values of RND.

3. Write an assembly program with the following menu:

(a) 3-digit random numbers table;

(b) 4-digit random numbers table;

(c) 5-digit random numbers table;

(d) 6-digit random numbers table;

which allows the user to choose one of these base 10 random number tables and, then, prints out the corresponding table.

Hint: Build each number in terms of random selection of the digits of each number rather than attempt to compute a single number.

4. Enhance the program in the preceding lab so that the user can choose the base for the numbers in the table. Run your program using the shift register generator with

(a) numbers in hex with 5-digit random entries in the table

(b) numbers in octal with 5-digit random entries in the table

5. Write an assembly program to generate automobile license numbers consisting of 3 letters and 3 digits. Your program should prompt the user to enter a certain number of 3-letter combinations that should be excluded and the number of licenses desired. Run your program with the following conditions:

(a) Generate 100 licenses.

(b) Exclude the following 3 letter combinations:

MOO, DAD, BAD, SAD, RUN, MUD, DUD, and WON

Print out the results subdivided into columns with a centered heading.

6. Write an assembly program that allows the user to build a short vocabulary of words (10 to 150 words) stored in an array. Then your program

should randomly select words from the vocabulary list and print 10 verses (each one containing a maximum of 5 words). The trick is to develop a vocabulary that can produce fairly interesting verses. Include in your vocabulary table the following words from REV-UP (Recursion Enumeration of Verse Universing Program) given by N. Pourboireki (1972, pp. 94–104):

BIT	TOWARD	DESIGN	BRIGHT
WORD	LINE	COUPLED	I
BY	LEFT	TIGHT	SILENT
FIT	RIGHT	TIGER	MACHINE
TENDING	VERSE	BURNING	ALERT
TO	YOUR	ORDER	ANSWER
QUERY	DANGEROUS	BORDER	MACHINING
VERSE-ED	REDUCTION	NO	INTERVENING
POETIC	CONSTRUCTION	MECHANICS	METERED
ALONG	LINES	ALGORITHMICALLY	WRONG
PANICS	PRODUCES	THE	FALLING
LINES	RECUR	ENDLESSLY	SOMETHING
IN	LOVE	WITH	BLUE
OUT	OF	THE	WORLD
MOON	MOTH	SOMBER	

Run your program (try using the concatenating ideas in chapter 11 to build poems) with

(a) 5 groups (stanzas) of 4-line verses

(b) 2 groups (stanzas) of 6-line verses

7. Write an assembly program to simulate the rolls of a pair of dice. Print a graphical representation of the results. Run your program more than once. Compute the sum each time and print

(a) "You win!" if the sum is 7 or 11.

(b) "You lose!" if the sum is a 2, 3, or 12.

(c) Roll again until the sum is (a) or (b).

14.10

REVIEW QUIZ

Indicate whether the following statements are true or false:

1. Von Mises introduced the notion of randomness.
2. A truly random sequence will exhibit local nonrandomness.
3. A random number distribution should be nonuniform.
4. Random number generators produce nonuniform distributions.
5. A linear congruence uses a modulus.
6. A random number generator requires a seed.
7. If we use the same seed each time, a random number generator will always produce the same sequence of numbers on the same computer.
8. VMS stands for virtual memory system.
9. The $GETTIM macro uses the Smithsonian Institution base date.
10. The $NUMTIM macro starts from year 0.
11. The $NUMTIM macro requires a seven-word buffer.
12. The spikes of a frequency polygon for the random number distribution should not be the same length if the numbers in the distribution are truly random.

14.11

REFERENCES

Aho, A. V., J. E. Hopcroft, and J. D. Ullman. *Data Structures and Algorithms*. Reading, Mass.: Addison-Wesley, 1983. See especially chap. 1.

Bosworth, B. *Codes, Ciphers, and Computers*. New York: Hayden Book Co., 1982. See especially chap. 5.

Digital Equipment Corporation. *VAX Architecture Handbook*. Maynard, Mass., 1981, chap. 13.

Knuth, D. E., *The Art of Computer Programming*. Vol. 2. *Seminumerical Algorithms*. Reading, Mass.: Addison-Wesley, 1981, pp. 1–176. See especially pp. 170–76, 101–5.

Levy, H. M., and R. H. Eckhouse. *Computer Programming and Architecture: The VAX-11*. Bedford, Mass.: Digital Press, 1980, chap. 4.

Marsaglia, G. "Random Number Generation." In *Encyclopedia of Computer Science and Engineering,* edited by A. Ralston, pp. 1260–64. New York: Van Nostrand Reinhold, 1983.

Pourboireki, N. "Artificial Intelligence and Intelligent Artifice." Chap. 10 in R. M. Baer. *The Digital Villian: Notes on the Numerology, Parapsychology, and Metaphysics of the Computer.* Reading, Mass.: Addison-Wesley, 1972.

Von Mises, R. "Grundlagen der wahrscheinlichkeitsrechnung." *Mathematische Zeitschrift.* Vol. 5. Berlin: J. Springer, 1919, pp. 52–99.

Von Mises, R. *Probability, Statistics and Truth.* New York: Macmillan, 1957.

Wirth, N. *Programming in Modula-2.* New York: Springer-Verlag, 1983.

15.
MACRO ASSEMBLY

The combination of macros with assembler language provides an extremely powerful and versatile tool. It is, in fact, possible to define a rich enough set of macro instructions so that programs for a given application area can be written using only these macro instructions. In effect, this amounts to creating a new special purpose language for the application.

—W. Kent, "Assembler Language Macroprogramming:
A Tutorial Oriented Toward the IBM 360"

15.0
AIMS

- Introduce the terms macro, macro instruction, macro definition, and macro processor (MP).
- Introduce the classical two-pass MP.
- Introduce the one-pass MP used in the first pass of a macro assembler.

15.1
INTRODUCTION

The term *macro* is derived from the Greek word *makros,* which means long or large. The *Oxford English Dictionary* notes that the prefix *macro* has two connotations in English. In words like *macrography* (abnormally large writing like James Thurber's) or *macrocosm* (large world), the implication is an "individual of unusual size." This is not the sense in which this word is used in computing.

In words like *macrosporange* (a capsule containing macrospores) or *macronucleus* (containing a micronucleus), the prefix means "containing a number of smaller individuals." This meaning of the term is somewhat closer to that used in computing. An example here would be *macro instruction,* which refers to a group of instructions, or to an *open subroutine.* However, the "individuals" represented by a macro instruction are not necessarily smaller. They themselves (the instructions of the open routine) can be macro instructions. Thus, the meaning of *macro* applicable to computing departs from standard usage.

In computing the term *macro* may be used by itself (see, for example, M. Campbell-Kelly, 1973, p. 27, p. 29) or as a prefix in the term *macro instruction* (see P. J. Brown, 1983; Calingaert, 1979). Calingaert (1979, p. 74) puts it this way: a macro instruction represents "a group of assembler language instructions." This group of instructions is also known as an *open subroutine.*

When an open subroutine call (or *macro call*) is used in building a source text, it is later "expanded" into a group of instructions that make up the corresponding open routine. The open routine instructions are injected into the text immediately after the macro call. They are placed *inline.* The source text is made longer. Unlike the execution of a closed routine, the execution of an open routine does not require transfer-of-control away from the main program. Open routines offer a means of saving time during execution. (This is the principal advantage of macros.)

Each occurrence of a macro call means a subsequent expansion of the main program. The open routines use up program memory. (This is a disadvantage of macros.) The trade-offs of more space vs. less execution time need to be balanced off against two other features of macros.

First, macro calls include parameters that are substituted into the open routine. This feature distinguishes open from closed routine calls. Parameter substitutions can be set up by the macro call, whereas closed routine calls are limited to transfers-of-control. The variables to be chewed on by a closed routine need to be set up *before* the closed routine call.

Second, macros can be used to build special-purpose languages. Brown (1983, p. 905) suggests that "macros can be thought of as forming a new language in their own right." M. D. McIlroy (1960) originally suggested using macros to build special-purpose assembler instructions tailored to various applications. W. Kent (1969, p. 183) went a step further: it is "possible to define a rich enough set of macro instructions so that programs can be written using only these macro instructions." This view was echoed by Erik Roberts at Harvard. As H. R. Lewis (1981) has noted, Roberts "coined the phrase 'MACRO-11 as a high-level language.'" MACRO-11 on PDP-11s and VAX-11 macro make it possible to use macros in a complete way.

W. Kent (1969, p. 183) lists the following advantages of macros:

1. Reduced coding effort [Calingaert, 1979, p. 73, would probably disagree, since he says an open routine "offers a faster alternative at the cost of space *and* effort"; my emphasis];

2. Flexibility and adaptability of programs [this is McIlroy's point];

3. Fewer coding bugs and easier debugging [this is not explained];

4. Standardized coding conventions and interfaces [this is part of the second advantage in terms of macro instructions using HOL terms];

5. Less detailed thinking required;

6. Less programming training needed [the opposite is more likely to be true, since we often "create" instructions belonging neither to any HOL or to the parent assembler];

7. Better program documentation and more uniform code [really, the code of the source text will probably be less uniform when contrasted with usual assembler source code; the term *documentation* is not explained].

15.2

MACRO PROCESSORS

A macro processor (MP) is a program. What such a program does can be described in a straightforward fashion. On the flat side, an MP makes it possible to insert one or more lines of code in place of a shorthand (oblique) reference to the lines of code. According to C. B. Hsieh (1980, p. 3), it is a program that is used "to define and process macro definitions." J. Cole (1982) speaks of an MP as a program that performs text replacement (it replaces the macro call by the corresponding open routine). Calingaert (1979, p. 74), meanwhile, notes that a macro instruction will specify how an open routine is to be generated, while an MP is "a translator which accomplishes this task."

What an MP program makes possible (that is, the creation of a macro language) is another question. The MP handles *only* text insertion. This says nothing about what an MP does for an assembly programmer. S. S. Black (1974, p. 1) defines an MP both in terms of what it *allows,* as well as what it *does*: MP "allows the user to add new instructions of his own design to existing software by substituting sequences of codes for prespecified abbreviations for that code." Brown (1983, p. 905) goes a bit further, arguing that macros and their attendant MPs can be used "as an end in themselves."

15.2.1 The Macro Definition

Each macro instruction used in a program corresponds to a macro definition that has several parts. A macro definition has the following structure:

1. *Delimiters* (call them MCDEF for the beginning of the definition, MCEND for the end of the macro definition); these are the boundaries of the definition; that is, they signal to the MP the start and finish of the definition.

2. *Prototype statement*, which contains two parts: macro name; and macro parameters (arguments). These are formal.

3. *Skeleton,* which *is* the open subroutine to be inserted into the main program.

The macro definition in Figure 15.1 embodies these parts. It is accompanied by the parallel of the definition written in VAX-11 Macro.

In part (b), a .MACRO directive is used in place of MCDEF in VAX-11 Macro, the .ENDM directive in place of MCEND. This contrasts with the IBM OS/360 form of a macro definition, which uses MACRO and ENDM as delimiters instead. Also notice that the VAX-11 macro definition, unlike part (a) of the above figure or OS/360 assembler, combines the beginning delimiter (.MACRO) with the prototype statement, itself.

The terms *prototype* and *skeleton* were proposed by Calingaert. What Calingaert (1979, p. 75) calls the prototype statement is referred to as a template by W. M. Waite (1967, p. 433). Waite's use of this term is unusual, however, since the term *template* is used by Kent (1969), Calingaert, and others to refer to the skeleton, or what Waite calls the macro *code body*. When the prototype statement appears with actual rather than formal parameters in a main program source text, it is known as a *macro call*. Waite identifies macro calling with "pattern matching against a set of templates

FIGURE 15.1
Structure of a Macro Definition

```
Delimiter    MCDEF
Prototype    Computesum A,B,C,D          .MACRO Computesum a, b, c, d
             ADD A, B                    add13 a, b, c
Skeleton     ADD B, C                    add12 c, d
             ADD C, D
             MOV D, R0                   movl d, r0
Delimiter    MCEND                       .ENDM Computesum


         (a) Macro definition           (b) VAX-11 MACRO definition
```

FIGURE 15.2
Macro Definition Table Entry

```
        Source Text:              MCDEF Table Entry

    MCDEF
    Compute A, B, C           Compute A, B, C
    ADD  A, B                 ADD  #1, #2
    ADD  B, C                 ADD  #2, #3
    MOV  C, R0                MOV  #3, R0
    MCEND                     MCEND
```

defined by the user.'' This is an apt description of macro calling, if we include both the prototype statement and the skeleton of the macro definition in the matching. We will see that the prototype parameters within the skeleton are usually interpreted in terms of matching skeleton statement parameters relative to their *position* in the prototype statement.

Macro processing can be summed up in terms of the following steps if we consider an MP apart from the needs of an assembler (its passes):

1. Scan the source text until a MCDEF delimiter or a macro is found. If an MCDEF delimiter is found, set up a special form of the macro definition in a MCDEF table, ELSE build an intermediate text containing only the macro call.

2. Construct an intermediate text minus any macro definitions.

3. Add to the MCDEF table any system macros that are needed.

4. Follow up the first complete source text scan by a second one, where the actual parameters of macro calls dictate text insertions of specialized versions of the skeleton found in the MCDEF table.

When an MP sets up a MCDEF table, the parameters of each line of the skeleton are identified in terms of the *position* of the parameters in the prototype statement. Figure 15.2 illustrates this in terms of the macro definition in Figure 15.1.

If we had used the macro call,

COMPUTE X, Y, Z

then the formal parameters A, B, C would be replaced by the actual parameters X, Y, Z in the lines of the open routine during the expansion (text insertion) following the macro call. The positional representation of the parameters in the MCDEF table entry would dictate which actual parameters would be used in a given line of the open routine. Figure 15.3 illustrates the macro expansion mode of an MP.

FIGURE 15.3
Output from a Macro Processor

Input to MP:

```
MAIN:   MOV #MAIN, SP
          .
          .
          .

        COMPUTE X,Y,Z
          .
          .
          .
        .EXIT
```

Output to Assembler:

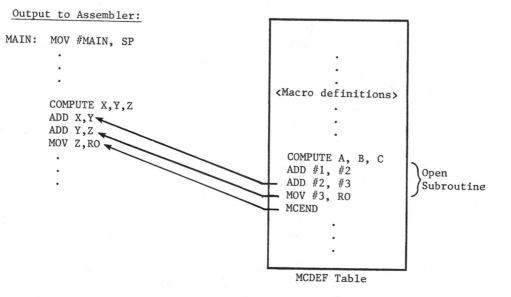

```
MAIN:   MOV #MAIN, SP
          .
          .
          .

        COMPUTE X,Y,Z
        ADD X,Y
        ADD Y,Z
        MOV Z,RO
          .
          .
          .
```

```
          .
          .
          .
<Macro definitions>
          .
          .
          .

        COMPUTE A, B, C
        ADD #1, #2
        ADD #2, #3        } Open
        MOV #3, RO        } Subroutine
        MCEND
          .
          .
          .
```

MCDEF Table

      IBM OS/360 (F-level) assembler relies on four separate passes, two for the MP and two for the assembly of a source text. Black (1974, p. 86) describes the OS/360 MP program in terms of two passes, one to scan the source text, the other to expand the source text "before assembly begins." Calingaert gets closer to the OS/360 macro assembler process. He distinguishes Pass 1, which is done by the assembler to construct a preliminary symbol table. Pass 2 does the macro processing and text expansion relative to the Pass 1 symbol table. Pass 3 builds a new (revised) symbol table based on the expanded source text from Pass 2 of the MP. Finally, Pass 4 is Pass 2 of the assembler.

The classical two-pass macro processor allows a source text with macro calls to come *before* the corresponding macro definitions. It allows for forward references. The procedure to do this is discussed next.

15.2.2 The Classical Two-Pass Macro Processor

The input to an MP is a source text containing macros and macro definitions. The output from a two-pass MP is an intermediate text, which contains the macro calls with corresponding *specialized* text insertions (specialized in terms of the actual parameters used in the macro call). This becomes the input to an assembler. The two-pass procedure is shown in Figure 15.4.

15.2.3 Example

Bertha's kitty boutique has been busy. It has a new PLUS-4/16e model t (or PLUS-4/16et) computer with an expanded op code table, a small system

FIGURE 15.4
Procedure for a Two-Pass Macro Processor

```
Procedure Two Pass MP:
VAR  Mcdef: ARRAY [1..N1] OF WORD;
     Text: ARRAY [1.. N2] OF WORD;
BEGIN
1.  Copy source text to TEXT, line by line;
    IF source line begins with Mcdef delimiter
    THEN
        1.1  (Insert macro definition into Mcdef table, replacing formal
             parameters of open routine lines by positional parameters
             relative to the position of the parameters in the prototype
             statement)
    ELSE
        IF source line calls for a system macro,
        THEN
            1.2  Insert system macro definition into TEXT
        ELSE
            1.3  continue step 1
2.  Scan Intermediate Text line by line;
    IF a Text line contains a macro call
    THEN
        2.1  Find prototype statement in Mcdf tables
            2.1.1 Based on macro call actual parameter list, copy instructions
                  of the skeleton into the new TEXT, replacing each
                  occurrence of the #i (position parameter) of each open
                  routine line by the ith value in the actual parameter list.
```

FIGURE 15.5
PLUS-4/16et Tables

Mnemonic	Op Code	Length	No. of Operands	Action
ADD s,d	06	3	2	d ⟵ d + s
ADDB s,d	26	3	2	d ⟵ d + s (in bytes)
MOV s,d	01	3	2	d ⟵ s
MOVB s,d	21	3	2	d s (in bytes)
ZAP d	02	2	1	BIS d
ZAPB d	22	2	1	BIS d (byte)
DEC d	03	2	1	d ⟵ d - 1
BR <label>	05			Branch (goto)
BNE <label>	15			Branch if Z-bit <> 0
INC d	13	2	1	d ⟵ d + 1

System Macros

```
.EXIT                      ;suspend execution
.NO                        ;print numerical value of R0 in decimal
```

System Directives

```
.MCALL <list>              ;list system macros needed
                           ;in MCDEF Table
:                          ;mark label
.END                       ;supply transfer address to PLUS-4/16et CPU
```

macro library and a macro assembler called MACROet. The expanded op code table and system macro library for the PLUS-4/16et is shown in Figure 15.5.

The PLUS-4/16et also has two PC modes (immediate and relative) and each of the register modes found on a PDP-11.

If Pass 1 of an assembler has as input the intermediate text from a two-pass MP, then it has an expanded version of the original source text to scan in building its symbol table. Assume that the program given in Figure 15.6 is designed to run on the PLUS-4/16et.

You can imagine what the PLUS-4/16et MP program does to the source text (see Figure 15.7).

FIGURE 15.6
Program for the PLUS-4/16et

```
        .MCALL  .NO  .EXIT
        MCDEF
        BEGIN X
        MOV #X, SP
        MCEND
MAIN:   BEGIN MAIN               ;macro call
        SETUP X,Y,Z              ;macro call (forward reference)
        .NO                      ;system macro call
        MCDEF                    ;macro definition
        SETUP A,B,C
        ADD A,B
        ADD B,C
        MOV C, R0
        MCEND
        .EXIT                    ;system macro call
X:      1
Y:      1
Z:      0
        .END MAIN
```

FIGURE 15.7
MP Pass 2 Output

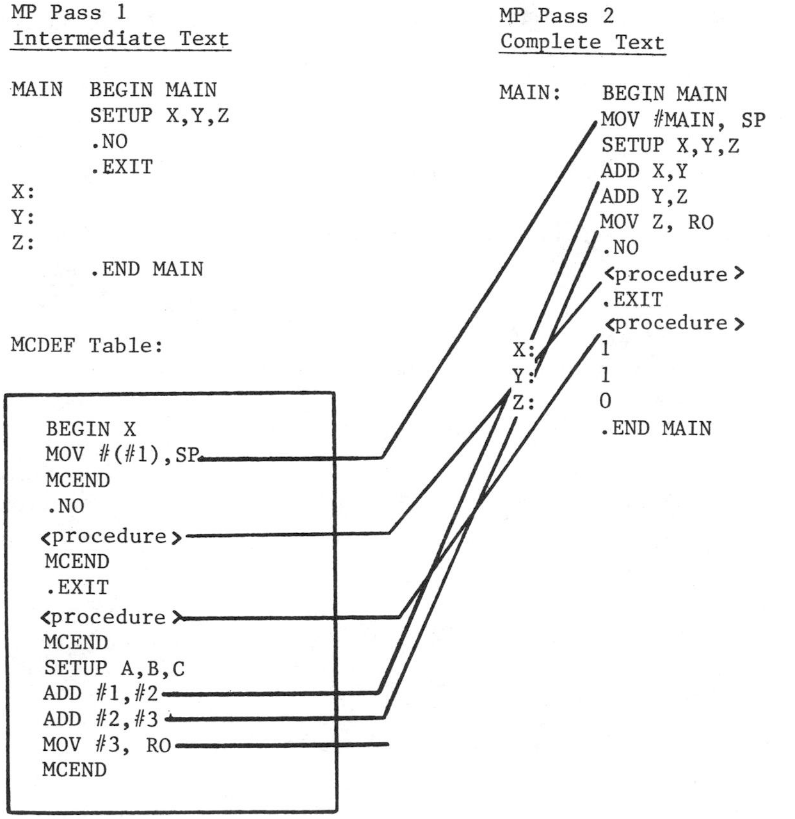

MP Pass 1
Intermediate Text

```
MAIN  BEGIN MAIN
      SETUP X,Y,Z
      .NO
      .EXIT
X:
Y:
Z:
      .END MAIN
```

MCDEF Table:

```
BEGIN X
MOV #(#1),SP
MCEND
.NO
<procedure>
MCEND
.EXIT
<procedure>
MCEND
SETUP A,B,C
ADD #1,#2
ADD #2,#3
MOV #3, RO
MCEND
```

MP Pass 2
Complete Text

```
MAIN:  BEGIN MAIN
       MOV #MAIN, SP
       SETUP X,Y,Z
       ADD X,Y
       ADD Y,Z
       MOV Z, RO
       .NO
       <procedure>
       .EXIT
       <procedure>
X:     1
Y:     1
Z:     0
       .END MAIN
```

15.3

MACRO ASSEMBLY

When an MP is combined with an assembler, the result is termed a macro assembler. In the more usual combination of assemblers with MPs, the MP is reduced to one pass embodied in Pass 1 of the assembler. This prohibits the use of macro calls that come before the corresponding macro definitions in the source text, as is the case with the CDC COMPASS, PDP-11 MACRO-11, or VAX-11 macro assemblers. Also, instead of developing an intermediate text, the source text is transformed line by line, after a macro definition table has been set up. This explains the

    .MCALL ⟨list⟩

at the head of PDP-11 MACRO-11 programs. VAX-11 dispenses with the .MCALL ⟨list⟩. During the first pass, MACRO-11 actually builds the necessary definition tables from macro libraries and any predefined macros in the source text. VAX-11 macro works essentially the same way. Digital Equipment Corporation (1982, p. 43) requires that a macro be defined *before* it is called; it is preferable to place all VAX-11 macro definitions before the

    .ENTRY BEGIN,0

15.3.1 Pass 1 of a Macro Assembler

When the MP functions are made part of Pass 1 of an assembler, the following steps are used:

1. Scan a source text line.
2. Let the op code determine which process to use:

   (a) Add to MCDEF table, if a macro definition is encountered; or, if a macro call is found, expand the source text with the corresponding open routine (skeleton) with appropriate *actual* parameters.

   (b) Augment symbol table, if possible, and begin scan of next source text line with step 1.

The CDC COMPASS assembler relies on the use of three tables by the MP:

      MCDEF Table (macro definitions)
      MCARGS Table (macro arguments)
      MARDIS Table (argument descriptors)

FIGURE 15.8
Procedure for Macro Assembler Pass 1

```
Procedure Macro Assembler Pass 1:

VAR  Word : ARRAY [1..N] OF CHAR;
     Mcname : ARRAY [1..N1] OF Word;
     Mcdef : ARRAY [1..N2] OF Word;
     Mcargs : ARRAY [1..N3] OF Word;
BEGIN
1.  Read line from source file;
2.  Scan line:
    IF line contains HALT instruction, begin pass 2
    ELSE
        CASE Opcode of
            2.1  Macroinstruction:  Scan Mcname:
                2.1.1  IF name present, insert new occurrence in Mcname with
                       pointer to new macrodefinition
                    2.1.1.1  insert new definition ahead of old one in
                             Mcdef
                    2.1.1.2  insert macro arguments in Mcargs
                2.1.2  ELSE insert name in Mcname
                    2.1.2.1  insert Mcdef
                    2.1.2.2  insert Mcargs
            2.2  Valid opcode: Perform regular assembler pass 1
            2.3  Macro call: Get line from Mcdef
                 IF not Mcend THEN replace #arguments by arguments(labels)
                 in Mcargs
                 ELSE continue Step 1
END Procedure
```

FIGURE 15.9
MACROet/2.0 Program

```
                        MCDEF
                        BEGIN X
                        MOV #X, SP
                        MCEND
                        MCDEF
                        LUCAS A,B,C
                        ADD B,C
                        MOV B,A
                        MOV C,B
                        MOV C,R0
                        MCEND
                        .MCALL  .EXIT  .NO
            MAIN:       BEGIN MAIN
            LOOP:       LUCAS X,Y,Z
                        .NO
                        BR LOOP
                        .EXIT
            X:          2
            Y:          1
            Z:          3
                        .END MAIN
```

FIGURE 15.10
Macro Assembler Expanded Source Text

Tables Produced by Pass 1 of the MA

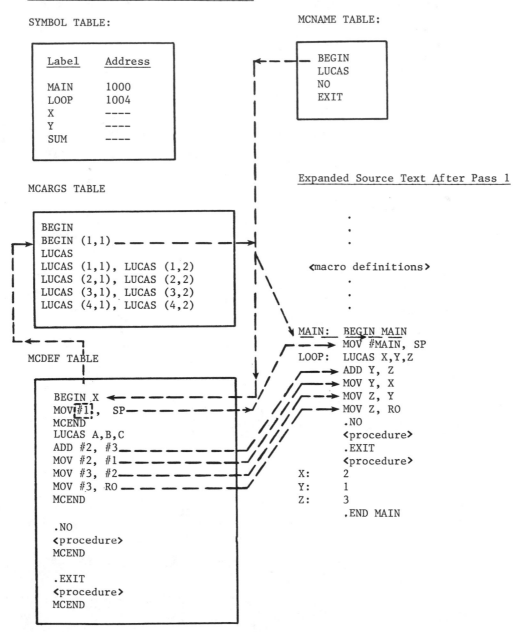

SYMBOL TABLE:

Label	Address
MAIN	1000
LOOP	1004
X	----
Y	----
SUM	----

MCNAME TABLE:

BEGIN
LUCAS
NO
EXIT

MCARGS TABLE

BEGIN
BEGIN (1,1)
LUCAS
LUCAS (1,1), LUCAS (1,2)
LUCAS (2,1), LUCAS (2,2)
LUCAS (3,1), LUCAS (3,2)
LUCAS (4,1), LUCAS (4,2)

MCDEF TABLE

BEGIN X
MOV #1, SP
MCEND
LUCAS A,B,C
ADD #2, #3
MOV #2, #1
MOV #3, #2
MOV #3, RO
MCEND

.NO
<procedure>
MCEND

.EXIT
<procedure>
MCEND

Expanded Source Text After Pass 1

<macro definitions>

MAIN: BEGIN MAIN
        MOV #MAIN, SP
LOOP: LUCAS X,Y,Z
        ADD Y, Z
        MOV Y, X
        MOV Z, Y
        MOV Z, RO
        .NO
        <procedure>
        .EXIT
        <procedure>
X: 2
Y: 1
Z: 3
        .END MAIN

The following Pass 1 procedure for a MA is in terms of the use of the first two of the above tables as well as a MCNAME table. An entry in the MCDEF table would include both the prototype statement and the open routine with positional representations of the arguments. The procedure is given in Figure 15.8.

In effect, the output of Pass 1 looks like the output shown in Figure 15.3, except that more has happened. That is, if Pass 1 of an assembler uses the procedure shown in Figure 15.7, then (1) Pass 2 of the assembler has an expanded version of the source text to scan and (2) Pass 1 has produced a symbol table (which will be used by Pass 2 to replace symbolic addresses by numeric addresses).

15.3.2 Example

MACROet 2.0 on the PLUS-4/16et uses the procedure shown in Figure 15.8 to produce an expanded source text. Forward references by macros are no longer possible. In fact, the programs are organized very much like those on the PDP-11. The following program, which recurses endlessly, produces the Lucas numbers

2, 1, 3, 4, 7, 11, 18, 29, 47, . . .

as shown in Figure 15.9.

The expansion of this source text is shown in Figure 15.10.

15.4
SUMMARY

For every macro or macro instruction there is a corresponding macro definition having three principal parts:

1. *delimiters* like MACRO/ENDM

2. *prototype statement* like

    COMPUTE A, B, C

3. *Skeleton* or template that is the open routine to be inserted in-line as a result of a corresponding macro call.

A macro processor is a program that can expand macro calls by inserting in-line corresponding open subroutines. The insertion of the open routine is specialized each time it occurs in a source text in terms of the actual parameters of the macro call. This is one of the most powerful features of macros; it is known as *parameter substitution*.

Macro processors allow and encourage the design of new statements and a new language. This is painstaking work, which tends to be its own reward, an "end in itself."

A complete two-pass macro processor makes it possible to have macro calls precede macro definitions in a source text. This does seem to run counter to a top-down approach to program development. Forward references would be eliminated if macro definitions were all placed ahead of the main program. In such cases a one-pass macro processor comes into play.

The combination of MP + AL produces what is known as a macro assembler. The one-pass procedure is embedded within the first pass of the assembler. Both CDC COMPASS, PDP-11 MACRO-11 and VAX-11 Macro are examples of this. Source text expansion as a result of a macro call depends on the use of a macro definition table.

15.5

EXERCISES

1. Give an example of an English word having macro as a prefix whose meaning is close to that in the term macro instruction (that is, implying a number of individuals but not necessarily *smaller* individuals).

2. How does an open routine *differ* from and how is an open routine the *same* as a closed routine? Give your answer in table form:

Open Routine Features	Closed Routine Features

3. How does a macro call differ from a closed routine call? Explain your answer in table form:

Macro Call Features	Closed Routine Call Features

15.6

LAB PROJECTS

1. Using an HOL, write a program to implement the two-pass procedure in Figure 15.4. Your program should

   (a) Print out the MCDEF table set up by the Pass 1 of the MP program.

(b) Print out the intermediate text produced by Pass 1.

(c) Print out the expanded text produced by Pass 2.

Run your program in terms of

(d) The PLUS-4/16et program in Figure 15.6.

(e) The following program

```
              .MCALL   .EXIT   .NO
              MCDEF
              BUMP X, Y
              INC X
              INC Y
              MCEND
    MAIN:     BEGIN MAIN
    LOOP:     BUMP X, Y
              THREAD X, Y, Z
              .NO
              BR LOOP
              MCDEF
              THREAD X, Y, Z
              MOV X, Y
              MOV Y, Z
              MOV Z, RO
              MCEND
              MCDEF
              BEGIN X
              MOV #X, SP
              MCEND
              .EXIT
    X:   2
    Y:   1
    Z:   3
              .END MAIN
```

2. Using an HOL, write a program to implement the one-pass MP embedded in Pass 1 of a macro assembler as given in Figure 15.8. Your program should

(a) Produce the complete MCDEF table produced during Pass 1.

(b) Print out the symbol table resulting from Pass 1.

(c) Print out the expanded source text.

Run your program in terms of

(d) The program in Figure 15.9.

(e) The following MACROet/2.0 program

```
            MCDEF
            STOP
            .EXIT
            MCEND
            MCDEF
            SUPERLUCAS A, B, C
            ADD B, C
            MOV B, A
            MOV C, B
            INC A
            INC B
            INC C
            MCEND
            .MCALL   .EXIT   .NO
    MAIN:   BEGIN MAIN
    LOOP:   SUPERLUCAS X, Y, Z
            MOV C, RO
            .NO
            BR LOOP
            STOP
      X:    3
      Y:    1
      Z:    2
            .END MAIN
```

15.7

REVIEW QUIZ

Indicate whether the following statements are true or false:

1. "Macro" is a shortened form of "macro instruction."

2. A macro call is an open subroutine call.

3. A macro call is the same as a closed subroutine call.

4. An assembler handles a macro call the same way it handles a closed subroutine call.

5. Macro calls can include parameters.

6. Each occurrence of a macro call in a program means a subsequent expansion of the program.

7. A macro represents a group of assembly language instructions.

8. A macro processor is a program.

9. The chief task carried out by a macro processor is text insertion.

10. A prototype statement has two parts.

11. .MACRO and .ENDM are VAX-11 macro definition delimiters.

12. A macro assembler is a program that combines an assembler with a macro processor.

13. A key feature of macros is parameter substitution.

14. Every macro definition has three parts.

15.8
REFERENCES

Black, S. S. *A Comparative Analysis of Two Macro Assemblers.* Ann Arbor, Mich.: University Microfilms, 1974.

Brown, P. J. "Macroinstruction." *Encyclopedia of Computer Science and Engineering,* edited by A. Ralston. New York: Van Nostrand Reinhold, 1983.

Calingaert, P. *Assemblers, Compilers and Program Translation.* Potomac, Md.: Computer Science Press, 1979.

Campbell-Kelly, M. *An Introduction to Macros.* New York: MacDonald, 1973.

Cole, A. J. *Macroprocessors.* 2d ed. New York: Cambridge University Press, 1982.

Digital Equipment Corporation. *VAX-11 Macro User's Guide.* Maynard, Mass., 1982.

Hsieh, C. B. *An On-Line Macro Processor for the Motorola 6800 Microprocessor.* Ann Arbor, Mich.: University Microfilms, 1980.

Kent, W. "Assembler-Language Macroprogramming: A Tutorial Oriented Toward the IBM 360." *Computing Surveys* 1, no. 4 (December 1969):183–96.

Lewis, H. R. *An Introduction to Computer Programming and Data Structures Using MACRO-11*. Reston, Va.: Reston Publishing, 1981.

McIlroy, M. D. "Macro Instruction Extension of Compiler Languages." *Communications of the ACM* (April, 1960):214.

Waite, W. M. "A Language Independent Macro Processor." *Communications of the ACM* 10, no. 7 (July 1967):433–40.

16.

MACROS

*Water divides into a dark evaporation, becoming earth, and into what
is pure, sparkling fire and burning in the solar sphere; what is fiery
becomes meteors, planets and stars, theorizes the pre-Socratic
philosopher Heraclitus concerning the origin of the universe.*

—Hegel, *Lectures on the History of Philosophy* (1805)

16.0

AIMS

- Introduce the use of VAX-11 Macro to set up macros.
- Introduce the framework for open routines (the skeleton of a macro definition).
- Illustrate the use of positional and keyword parameters.
- Illustrate concatenation and conditional assembly.
- Suggest ways to set up macro definitions using familiar control structures.

16.1

INTRODUCTION

Macros and subroutines are the meteors, planets, and stars of assembly
language programs. The logic of most main programs depends on a variety
of tasks. There are usually subtasks that naturally separate themselves from

455

the principal thrust (logic, task) of a main program. Macros and subroutines offer elegant mechanisms for carrying out these subtasks. They also help to focus the logic of a main program and make it more intelligible.

Subtasks such as swapping (the bubblesort), pushing and popping (stack operations), and so on, are commonly used by many different main programs and subprograms. And, appropriately, both macros and subroutines can be developed as collections (libraries) that are separate from any one main program. We have already seen this in subroutines used to pass data to and from a keyboard ring buffer. In the case of external (or internal) subroutines, flow-of-control switches back and forth between a main program and its subroutines during program execution. This switching back and forth can significantly slow down the execution cycle in large-scale assembly programs.

Macros offer an alternative way to handle the subtasks carried out by programs. It is possible to build a program embodying sundry macro calls (requests) for subtasks to be carried out by macros. Then, at assembly time, each of these macro calls will be replaced by appropriate lines of code (will be expanded) from the skeleton of a macro that will carry out the particular subtask being requested. That is, instead of transferring control between the main program and a subroutine or procedure, and back (after the subtask has been carried out), these macro calls summon lines of code that are inserted *in-line* during macro assembly of the source text. Later the fleshed-out macro skeleton is executed in-line. No transfer-of-control takes place. This gives macros or open routines an edge over closed routines in terms of execution time or efficiency.

For example, we can use macros to streamline (and simplify!) the beginning and ending of a source text for a main program. We can use the following macros:

```
        Beginning:              Ending
     .MACRO BEGIN X        .MACRO TUMTY
 X:  .WORD                 $EXIT.S
     .ENDM                 .ENDM
```

The structure of these macros can be seen in Figure 16.1.

A main program using these two macros would have the following form:

```
BEGIN ⟨MAIN⟩
   ⋮
⟨process⟩
   ⋮
TUMTY
.END MAIN
```

FIGURE 16.1
Structure of Two Macro Definitions

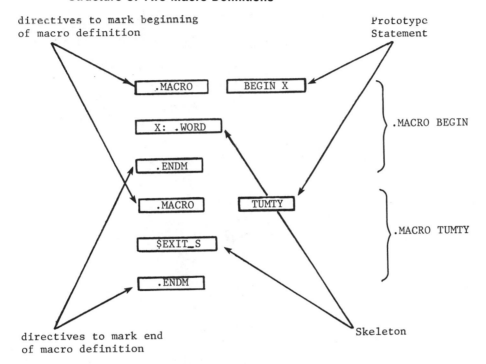

directives to mark beginning
of macro definition

Prototype
Statement

.MACRO BEGIN

.MACRO TUMTY

directives to mark end
of macro definition

Skeleton

The macro definitions for BEGIN and TUMTY will replace the above calls during macro assembly of this text.

For now, we will place all macro definitions at the head of a source text. Later, these will be put into a macro library like the one we have been using to handle strings (WRITE and WRITELN). When a source text is expanded in terms of the macro calls, the calls are replaced by the texts referenced by the calls. We illustrate this in terms of

```
BEGIN ⟨MAIN⟩
WRITE ⟨pinggg! is an onomatopoetic word for rain.⟩
TUMTY
.END MAIN
```

The actual complete source text together with a run for the above "macro-fied" program is given in Figure 16.2.

To see the results of macro assembly (the expanded source text), use

```
.SHOW ME
```

FIGURE 16.2
Program with Two Macro Definitions

```
        ;
        ;REF.:   Figure 16.2 (List file with two macros)
        ;
                .SHOW ME                        ;PUT MACRO EXPANSIONS IN
                                                ;LIST MODULE

                .MACRO BEGIN X                  ;PROTOTYPE STATEMENT
        X:      .WORD                           ;SKELETON: INIT. MAIN PROGRAM
                .ENDM

                .MACRO TUMTY                    ;PROTO-ST.:O TUMTYTUMTYTUMTOES!
                $EXIT_S                         ;SKELETON: TERMINATE EXECUTION
                .ENDM

                BEGIN <HERE>

                WRITE <PINGGG! IS AN ONOMATOPOEIC WORD FOR RAIN.>

                TUMTY
                .END HERE


        RUN FG162

        Pinggg! is an onomatopoeic word for rain.
```

to insert the macro expansions into the list module for a source text. This is illustrated in Figure 16.3.

What happens to the source text after it is macro assembled is shown in Figure 16.4.

Macros give us a shorthand notation for frequently used constructions. They allow us to develop a new notation for particular problems. G. Berglass (1970, p. 12) comments that a new notation will "tend to clarify the problem for the writer as well as for other readers. In principle, an entire higher level language could be written in a macro language, as is, in fact, suggested by Halpern [1968]." The combination of a macro processing facility like the one provided by VAX-11 macro and a collection of system and user-defined macros forms what Berglass (1970, p. 15) calls a macro system. In this chapter, we build the basis for a macro language. This language will contain macros that imitate constructions that will handle control structures (FOR/ DO, WHILE/DO, REPEAT/UNTIL) and conditionals (IF/THEN, IF/ THEN/ELSE, CASE) found in Pascal or Modula-2. It will also contain I/O macros to make it easier to handle terminal I/O, which is fairly complex on a VAX-11. This will lead us, in the next chapter, to the construction of a complete, non-system macro library.

FIGURE 16.3
Results of Macro Assembly

```
                                    0000      1  ;
                                    0000      2  ;REF.:      Figure 16.3 (List file
                                                            with two macros)
                                    0000      3  ;
                                    0000      4           .show me
                                    0000      5
                                    0000      6           .macro begin x
                                    0000      7  x:        .word
                                    0000      8           .endm
                                    0000      9
                                    0000     10           .macro tumty
                                    0000     11  $exit_s
                                    0000     12           .endm
                                    0000     13
                                    0000     14           begin <here>
                            0000    0000         here:    .word
                                    0002
                                    0002     15
                                    0002     16           write <Pinggg! is an ono
                                                           matopoetic word for rain.>
              00000011´EF    9F     0002              PUSHAB 30000$
              00000000´EF    01  FB 0008              CALLS #1,WRITESTR
                             2B    11 000F              BRB 30001$
20 73 69 20 21 67 67 67 6E 69 50 00´ 0011     30000$:  .ASCIC/Pinggg! is an ono
                                                        matopoetic word for rain./
6F 70 6F 74 61 6D 6F 6E 6F 20 6E 61  001D
6F 66 20 64 72 6F 77 20 63 69 74 65  0029
            2E 6E 69 61 72 20 72     0035
                               2A    0011
                             01      003C     30001$:  NOP
                                    003D
                                    003D     17
                                    003D     18           tumty
                                    003D              $exit_s
                                    003D                      .GLOBL   SYS$EXIT
                     01    DD     003D                    PUSHL   #1
              00000000´GF  01  FB 003F                    CALLS   #1,G^SYS
$EXIT
                                    0046
                                    0046
                                    0046     19           .end here
Symbol table                                                  8-DEC-
1983 00:10:26   SJU:[SJU1]FG163.MAR;2          (1)

HERE             00000000 R     01
SYS$EXIT         ******** GX    01
WRITESTR         ********  X    01

There were no errors, warnings or information messages.

/LIST FG163+PAS/LIB
```

FIGURE 16.4
Graphical Interpretation of Macro Assembly

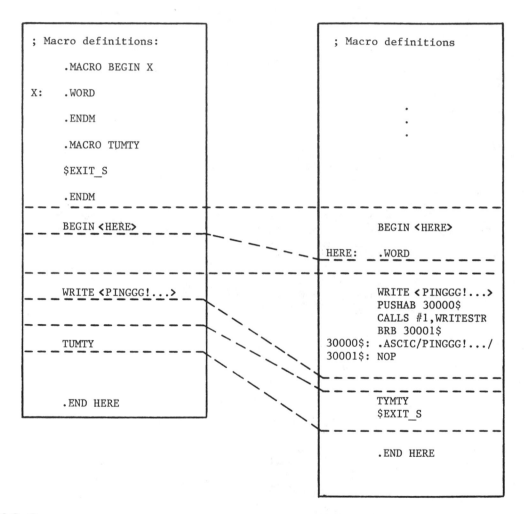

Before Macro Assembly: After Macro Assembly:

```
; Macro definitions:                    ; Macro definitions

        .MACRO BEGIN X
                                                    .
X:      .WORD                                       .
                                                    .
        .ENDM

        .MACRO TUMTY

        $EXIT_S

        .ENDM
- - - - - - - - - - - - - - - - - - - - - - - - - - - - -
        BEGIN <HERE>                          BEGIN <HERE>

                                        HERE:   .WORD
- - - - - - - - - - - - - - - - - - - - - - - - - - - - -
        WRITE <PINGGG!...>                    WRITE < PINGGG!...>
                                              PUSHAB 30000$
                                              CALLS #1,WRITESTR
                                              BRB 30001$
        TUMTY                         30000$: .ASCIC/PINGGG!.../
                                      30001$: NOP
- - - - - - - - - - - - - - - - - - - - - - - - - - - - -
                                              TYMTY
        .END HERE                             $EXIT_S

                                              .END HERE
```

16.2

OPEN VS. CLOSED ROUTINES

A macro definition is also called an open routine. Unlike closed routines (procedures and subroutines)—which always reside outside the source text for a main program that calls closed routines—open routines are always in-line. Open routines are always part of the source text for a main program.

FIGURE 16.5
Flow-of-Control with Open and Closed Routines

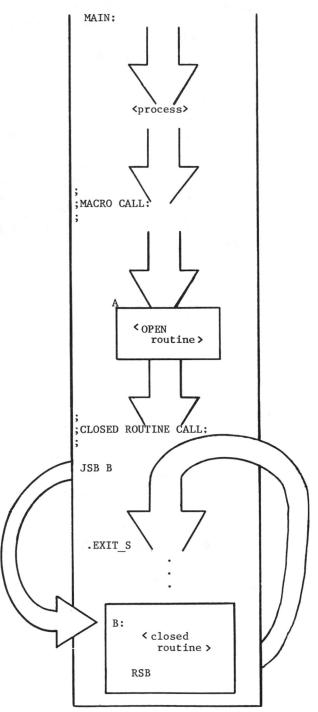

Closed routines can appear more than once inside a main program. Open routines do not have a *fixed* position. Closed routines, on the other hand, always have a fixed position.

After macro assembly, the flow-of-control within a main program that has macro expansions (open routines) contrasts sharply with that governed by closed routines. This is shown in Figure 16.5 in terms of an assembly language program with a macro *A* and closed routine *B*.

An open routine consumes space while a closed routine consumes execution time. These trade-offs (less memory vs. swifter execution) have to be measured against the constraints of a particular computer and the immensity of the particular program. As a rule, macros are used in combination with subroutines. Macros are handy for carrying out shorter subtasks and to save on assembly (conditional assembly is possible with macros), while subroutines are handy for carrying out more complex subtasks (they themselves will typically have macro calls as well). Macros can also be used to improve the readability of a program or a subroutine.

16.3

THE STRUCTURE OF MACROS

What we call the prototype statement or macro instruction has a fairly rich structure:

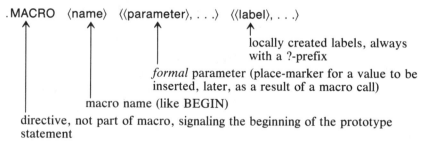

.MACRO ⟨name⟩ ⟨⟨parameter⟩, . . .⟩ ⟨⟨label⟩, . . .⟩

locally created labels, always with a ?-prefix

formal parameter (place-marker for a value to be inserted, later, as a result of a macro call)

macro name (like BEGIN)

directive, not part of macro, signaling the beginning of the prototype statement

16.3.1 Positional and Keyword Parameters

There are two types of parameters. In

```
.MACRO EXADD A B C D WITH TYPE = L
ADD'TYPE'3 A,B,C
ADD'TYPE'2 C,D
PUSH'TYPE D
.ENDM EXADD
```

the parameters are separated by spaces (commas or tabs can also be used). The parameters A,B,C, D are *positional parameters*. Their order in the macro must be adhered to strictly in an EXADD macro call like

        EXADD #2, Y, X, SUM

which will lead to the following expansion

        ADDL3 #2, Y, X
        ADDL2 X, SUM
        PUSHL SUM

The word 'WITH' in the above macro is known as a *noise word*. It serves to improve the readability of the macro. Nothing else. The parameter TYPE is a *keyword parameter*, which will be explained shortly.

Text expansion of EXADD in terms of the positional parameters depends entirely on the placement of these parameters in the call. If we had used

        EXADD #2, Y, SUM, X

then its expansion would have been

        ADDL3 #2, Y, SUM
        ADDL2 SUM, X
        PUSHL X

Changing the order of the positional parameters in a macro call changes the expansion of the macro. In the second call above, *X* gets pushed instead of SUM, which may or may not be desirable.

Keyword parameters like TYPE in the EXADD macro are position independent. TYPE has a default value of *L*. If TYPE is not referenced in the call, the default value is used. If the two types of parameters are used together in a macro, it is advisable to put keyword parameters after positional parameters. The mechanism used to "attach" TYPE to ADD and PUSH in

        ADD 'TYPE' 3

and

        PUSH' TYPE

is called *concatenation*. This is explained later. The macro processor will take the single quote (') as a signal to attach the TYPE value to a text-term. PUSH'TYPE becomes PUSHL, for example.

Unlike positional parameters, keyword parameters can appear in a macro call *without* regard to the original order of the keyword parameters. For example,

```
.MACRO EXMOV X = R6 Y = R7 Z = R8 TYPE = L
MOV'TYPE X, Y
MOV'TYPE X, Z
.ENDM EXMOV
```

We can use

```
EXMOV TYPE = W, Z = R11, Y = R10
```

to produce the same expansion as

```
EXMOV Y = R10, Z = R11, TYPE = W
```

namely,

```
MOVW R6, R10
MOVW R6, R11
```

Notice that this time, $X = R6$ is used by default in the EXMOV macro expansion, since the keyword parameter is not used in the above macro calls.

We illustrate the above idea in terms of three EXMOV macro calls in the following program. Notice in what follows that a

```
EXMOV
```

by itself will prompt the macro assembly of the source text with the default values for X, Y, Z and TYPE (see Figure 16.6).

16.3.2 Noise Words

Berglass (1970, p. 43) uses the term *noise words* to indicate terms used in macros to make macro calls more readable. If they are not used in the skeleton of the definition, they are ignored by the macro processor. For

FIGURE 16.6
A Macro with Keyword Parameters

```
;
;REF.:  FIGURE 16.6 (A EXTENDED MOVE MACRO WITH KEYWORD PARAMETERS)
;
        .MACRO EXMOV X=R6 Y=R7 Z=R8 WITH TYPE=L
        MOV´TYPE X,Y                    ;concatenate type to MOV
        MOV´TYPE X,Z                    ;concatenate type to MOV
        .ENDM EXMOV
;
        BEGIN   <WITH:       .WORD>     ;estab. trans. address
        MOVL    #377,R6                 ;init. r6
        SPACE   <10>                    ;macro call to get
                                        ;10 spaces

        EXMOV                           ;notice!
                                        ;this call uses the
                                        ;default parameters

        PUSHL   R7                      ;set up stack frame to
        CALLS   #1,WRITEVAL             ;print partial result
                                        ;of EXMOV call
        SPACE   <5>                     ;insert 10 spaces

        EXMOV   Z=R11 Y=R10             ;this call assigns new
                                        ;arguments to keywords,
                                        ;leaving 2 with default
                                        ;values

        PUSHL   R11                     ;set up stack frame to
        CALLS   #1,WRITEVAL             ;print partial result
                                        ;of EXMOV call
        SPACE   <5>                     ;insert 5 spaces

        EXMOV   Y=R10 Z=R11             ;this call assigns the
                                        ;same pair of arguments
                                        ;as in the preceding call,
                                        ;but in reverse order

        PUSHL   R11                     ;set up stack frame to
        CALLS   #1,WRITEVAL             ;print partial result

        TUMTY                           ;insert $exit_s
        .END    WITH


RUN FG166

        377     377     377
```

465

example,

.MACRO COMPUTE R EQUAL X MOD Y

↑noise↑

EDIV Y, X, R10, R
.ENDM COMPUTE

For a macro call we can use, for example,

COMPUTE R := A MOD B

which leads to the expansion

EDIV B, A, R10, A

Neither EQUAL nor MOD (the so-called noise words) appears in the macro expansion. Nonetheless, these words do contribute to the *readability* of the macro, as illustrated in Figure 16.7.

16.3.3 Local Labels

Labels are an acute problem for macros. If a macro definition like

```
        .MACRO STORE X
L:      .LONG
        MOVL X, L
        .ENDM STORE
```

is set up, it can be used (called) only *once* in any program. Why? The label is fixed. Two STORE macro calls within the same source text would produce an addressing error. Both MACRO-11 on PDP-11s and VAX-11 make provision for *locally created labels,* using the question mark (?) prefix to identify labels in the macro. For example, we can revise the above macro with

.MACRO STORE X ?L

Now, each time STORE is called in the *same* source text, a new and different

FIGURE 16.7
A Mod Macro with Noise Words

```
;
;REF.:  FIGURE 16.7 (A MOD MACRO)
;
        .MACRO COMPUTE R EQUAL X MOD Y          ;proto st. uses
                                                ;EQUAL & MOD as noise
                                                ;words
        EDIV Y,X,R10,R                          ;get R=remainder
        WRITELN                                 ;<ret>
        WRITE <                 X MOD Y = >      ;notice!
                                                ;the values of X,Y
                                                ;passed in COMPUTE call
                                                ;are printed
        PUSHL R                                 ;set up stack frame
        CALLS #1,WRITEVAL                       ;to print remainder
        .ENDM COMPUTE

        BEGIN   <WITH:          .WORD>          ;estab. transfer addr.

        COMPUTE R9 := #13 MOD #7                ;call
        COMPUTE R9 := #32767 MOD #7             ;call
        COMPUTE R9 := #2141111 MOD #17711       ;call

        TUMTY                                   ;insert $exit_s
        .END WITH


RUN FG167

                #13 MOD #7 = 6
                #32767 MOD #7 = 0
                #2141111 MOD #17711 = 15791
```

value for *L* will be created. The range of local labels is

$$30000\$, \ldots, 65535\$$$

For example, if we use

```
.ENTRY BEGIN, 0
STORE COUNT
STORE LIMIT

      ⋮

.EXIT_S
.END BEGIN
```

then when this text is expanded by the VAX-11 macro processing facility, we get

```
            .ENTRY BEGIN, 0
30000$:     .LONG
            MOVL COUNT, 30000$
30004$:     .LONG
            MOVL LIMIT, 30004$
                    ⋮
            $EXIT_S
            .END BEGIN
```

16.3.4 Macro Calls

There is considerable flexibility here. The following situations are possible:

1. A macro definition using only assembler instructions (EXADD, EXMOV and STORE given are examples). Thus a macro call, in this case, leads to an expanded source text in terms of these instructions and the actual arguments used to replace the formal parameters in the macro;

2. A macro definition can include macro calls. For example,

```
    .MACRO TUMTY
    $EXIT_S
    .ENDM
```

where $EXIT_S is a system macro call. These lead to some powerful extensions of the native assembler. Again the COMPUTE macro in Figure 16.7 illustrates this (WRITE and WRITELN are macro calls!).

3. Macro calls from within procedures and subroutines.

We can illustrate case 2 in a somewhat more tantalizing way in terms of two macros, one for a FOR/DO and one for a new BEGIN. We explain the FOR/DO macro first (see Figure 16.8).

In this macro, INDEX, IS, TO, and DO are noise words. The default step is +1. The new BEGIN macro is given in Figure 16.9.

This BEGIN macro is limited to six actions. This number is easily

FIGURE 16.8
A FOR/DO Macro Definition

```
        ;
        ;Ref.:  Figure 16.8 (A for/do macro definition)
        ;
                .MACRO FOR INDEX IS MIN TO MAX DO ACT,-
                        STEP=1 TYPE=L ?LOOP ?BYE ?CHECK
                MOV´TYPE MIN,INDEX
        CHECK:  CMP´TYPE INDEX,MAX
                BEQL     LOOP
                .IF IDN TO DOWNTO
                CMP´TYPE INDEX,MAX
                BGTR     LOOP
                .IF_FALSE
                CMP´TYPE INDEX,MAX
                BLSS     LOOP
                .ENDC
                JMP      BYE
        LOOP:   ACT
                .IF IDN TO DOWNTO
                .REPEAT ´C<STEP>+1
                SUB´TYPE´2                #1,INDEX
                .ENDR
                .IF_FALSE
                .REPEAT STEP
                ADD´TYPE´2                #1,INDEX
                .ENDR
                .ENDC
                JMP      CHECK
        BYE:
                .ENDM    FOR
```

FIGURE 16.9
A Generalized BEGIN Macro

```
        ;
        ;Ref.:  Figure 16.9 (A Generalized BEGIN macro definition)
        ;
                .MACRO BEGIN ACT1 ACT2 ACT3 ACT4 ACT5 ACT6
                ACT1
                ACT2
                ACT3
                ACT4
                ACT5
                ACT6
                .ENDM BEGIN
```

increased. We could use the following macro call to illustrate case 2:

```
FOR I := #1 TO #5 DO -
        ⟨BEGIN -
            ⟨INCL X⟩-
            ⟨PUSHL X⟩-
            ⟨CALLS #1, WRITEVAL⟩-
            ⟨SPACE⟨5⟩⟩⟩
```

FIGURE 16.10
A Program with Nested Macro Calls

```
;
;Ref.:  Figure 16.10 (Macro definition with nested macro calls)
;
;Method: In this program, we use the hyphen (-) to advantage in
;         formatting the FOR macro call; also, notice the use of
;         the pointed brackets (< >) to enclose arguments representing
;         actions to be performed.  For example,
;
;             <INCL X>  TAKES THE PLACE OF THE ACT1 FORMAL PARAMETER
;             <PUSHL X> TAKES THE PLACE OF THE ACT2 FORMAL PARAMETER
;             ETC.
;
;         IN THE BEGIN MACRO DEFINITION.
;
;         TO ASSEMBLE THIS PROGRAM, USE
;
;             MACRO FG1610 + PAS/LIB
;
;         (NOTE: THE FOR MACRO DEFINITION IS EXTERNAL; IT IS IN PAS.MAR
;          GIVEN IN THE APPENDICES.)
;
X:      .LONG 233
;
        BEGIN <MAIN:          .WORD>
        WRITELN
        TAB <2>
        FOR I := #1 TO #5 DO -
                <BEGIN-
                        <INCL X>-
                        <PUSHL X>-
                        <CALLS #1,WRITEVAL>-
                        <SPACE <5>>>
        TUMTY
;
        .END MAIN

RUN FG1610

            234     235     236     237     238
```

FIGURE 16.11
Macro Expansion of a FOR/DO Loop

```
                              0000  1  ;Ref.:     Figure 16.11 ( nested macro calls
                                                                listing)
                              0000  2
             000000E9         0000  3  x:         .long 233
                              0004  4
                              0004  5             begin <main:       .word>
                      0000    0004                main:      .word
                              0006  6             writeln
          00000016^EF    9F  0006                 PUSHAB 30000$
          00000000^EF 01 FB  000C                 CALLS #1,WRITESTR
                    0003  31  0013                 BRW 30001$
              0D 0A 00^       0016     30000$:    .ASCIC//<10><13>
                       02     0016
                       01     0019     30001$:    NOP
                              001A
                              001A  7             tab <2>
                              001A                FOR I := #1 TO 2 DO
                                                  <WRITE<          >>
         0000005C^EF    01 D0 001A                MOVL       #1,30003$
00000002^EF  0000005C^EF D1   0021     30005$:    CMPL       30003$,2
                    13  13    002C                BEQL       30002$
                              002E                .IF IDN TO DOWNTO
                              002E                CMPL       30003$,2
                              002E                BGTR       30002$
                              002E                .IF_FALSE
00000002^EF  0000005C^EF D1   002E                CMPL       30003$,2
                    06  19    0039                BLSS       30002$
                       003B                       .ENDC
         00000060^EF    17    003B                JMP        30004$
                              0041     30002$:    WRITE<     >
         00000050^EF    9F    0041                PUSHAB     30006$
         00000000^EF 01 FB    0047                CALLS #1,WRITESTR
                    02  11    004E                BRB        30007$
                 09 00^       0050     30006$:    .ASCIC/    /
                       01     0050
                       01     0052     30007$:    NOP
                              0053
                              0053                .IF IDN TO DOWNTO
                              0053                .REPEAT ^C<1>+1
                              0053                DECL       30003$
                              0053                .ENDR
                              0053                .IF_FALSE
                              0053                .REPEAT 1
                              0053                INCL       30003$
                              0053                .ENDR
         0000005C^EF    D6    0053                INCL       30003$
                              0059
                              0059                .ENDC
                 C5 AF  17    0059                JMP        30005$
             00000000         005C     30003$:    .LONG 0
                              0060     30004$:
                              0060
                              0060
                              0060  8             for i := #1 to #5 do -
```

Continued on following page.

Figure 16.11 continued.

```
                              0060      9                        <begin-
                              0060     10                              <incl x>-
                              0060     11                              <pushl x>-
                              0060     12                              <calls #
                                                                      1,writeval-
                              0060     13                              <space <5>>>
  000000DE´EF    01    D0     0060                      MOVL      #1,30009$
05   000000DE´EF    D1        0067        30011$:       CMPL      30009$,#5
              0F    13        006E                      BEQL      30008$
                              0070                      .IF IDN to DOWNTO
                              0070                      CMPL      30009$,#5
                              0070                      BGTR      30008$
                              0070                      .IF_FALSE
05   000000DE´EF    D1        0070                      CMPL      30009$,#5
              06    19        0077                      BLSS      30008$
                              0079                      .ENDC
  000000E2´EF    17           0079                      JMP       30010$
                              007F        30008$: begin
                                                       <incl x>
                                                       <pushl x>
                                                       <calls #1,writeval>
                                                       <space <5>>
      FF7D CF    D6           007F                      incl x
      FF79 CF    DD           0083                      pushl x
00000000´EF    01    FB       0087                      calls #1,writeval
                              008E                      space <5>
                              008E                      .REPEAT 5
                              008E                      PUSHAB 30012$
                              008E                      CALLS #1,WRITESTR
                              008E                      .ENDR
  000000D2´EF    9F           008E                      PUSHAB 30012$
00000000´EF    01    FB       0094                      CALLS #1,WRITESTR
                              009B
  000000D2´EF    9F           009B                      PUSHAB 30012$
00000000´EF    01    FB       00A1                      CALLS #1,WRITESTR
                              00A8
  000000D2´EF    9F           00A8                      PUSHAB 30012$
00000000´EF    01    FB       00AE                      CALLS #1,WRITESTR
                              00B5
  000000D2´EF    9F           00B5                      PUSHAB 30012$
00000000´EF    01    FB       00BB                      CALLS #1,WRITESTR
                              00C2
  000000D2´EF    9F           00C2                      PUSHAB 30012$
00000000´EF    01    FB       00C8                      CALLS #1,WRITESTR
                              00CF
          0002    31          00CF                      BRW 30013$
              20 00´          00D2        30012$: .ASCIC<32>
                    01        00D2
                    01        00D4        30013$: NOP
                              00D5                      .IF IDN to DOWNTO
                              00D5                      .REPEAT ^C<1>+1
                              00D5                      DECL      30009$
                              00D5                      .ENDR
                              00D5                      .IF_FALSE
```

Figure 16.11 continued.

```
                          00D5                .REPEAT 1
                          00D5                INCL       30009$
                          00D5                .ENDR
     000000DE^EF    D6    00D5                INCL       30009$
                          00DB
                          00DB                .ENDC
              89 AF  17   00DB                JMP        30011$
                 00000000 00DE      30009$:   .LONG 0
                          00E2      30010$:
                          00E2
                          00E2   14           tumty
                          00E2                $EXIT_S
                          00E2                .GLOBL     SYS$EXIT
                    01 DD 00E2                PUSHL      #1
     00000000^GF   01 FB  00E4                CALLS      #1,G^SYS
                                              $EXIT
                          00EB
                          00EB
                          00EB   15
                          00EB   16           .end main
```

What comes after the DO in FOR/DO definition is a single ACT. In the call, this ACT is replaced by the string inside the pointed brackets (⟨. . .⟩). In this case ACT includes 2 macro calls (BEGIN and SPACE) as well as some familiar assembly language instructions. In effect, we have nested macro calls, one call "inside" the other. VAX-11 macro allows the use of the hyphen (-) to continue a call on the next line. This makes the resulting call more readable and more elegant. We put the FOR/DO and BEGIN macros inside our own macro library, which we call PAS. This shortens (and cleans up) the resulting source text. We discuss how this is done in the next chapter. The program shown in Figure 16.10 is assembled in the usual way with

MACRO ⟨source name⟩ + PAS/LIB

To cap this introduction to macro definitions containing macro calls, we look at the list module for the above program. We use a

```
.SHOW ME
FOR I := #1 TO #5 DO -
         ⋮
.NOSHOW ME
```

in terms of just the FOR/DO macro to shorten the listing. This is given in Figure 16.11.

16.4

ITERATIVE ASSEMBLY

VAX-11 and PDP-11 macro assembly provides three repeat block directives that can be used to build macro definitions:

directive	function
.REPEAT ⟨no.⟩ ⟨text⟩ .ENDR	Insert No.-copies of ⟨text⟩ into the source text and/or macro having a .REPEAT.
.IRP X, ⟨sequence ⟨text⟩ .ENDR	Expand the ⟨text⟩ in terms of the X-value assigned to X for each element of the ⟨sequence⟩.
.IRPC X, ⟨string⟩ ⟨text⟩ .ENDR	Expand the ⟨text⟩ in terms of the X-value assigned to X for each *character* of the ⟨string⟩.

We illustrate the use of a .REPEAT block *inside* a macro definition, which provides a surprisingly simple way to produce powers tables. In the example in Figure 16.12 each macro call produces a different powers table. For example,

Directive	Expansion
.REPEAT 3	PUSHL R6
PUSHL R6	PUSHL R6
.ENDR	PUSHL R6

The text 'PUSHL R6' is inserted into the source text without change three times. We can use the IRP directive to change the repeat-block text *each* time it is inserted into the source text:

Directive	Expansion
.IRP RX, ⟨R6,R7,R8⟩	ADDL2 R6, SUM
ADDL2 RX, SUM	ADDL2 R7, SUM
.ENDR	ADDL2 R8, SUM

FIGURE 16.12
A Powers Table Macro

```
;Ref.:   Figure 16.12 (Powers table macro with iterative assembly)
;
;method:
;        The prototype statement of the mcdef uses OF and TABLE
;        as noise words for clarity.  The formal parameter no
;        begins the computation of the table in terms of successive
;        products of the form
;                                    no * no * ... * no = no^k
;                                                         ^
;                                                         |
;                                            kth copy of no
;
         .MACRO POWERS OF NO TABLE
         WRITELN <          POWERS OF NO TABLE>
         WRITELN <--------------------------------------->
         WRITELN
         MOVL #1,R6
         MOVL #1,R7
         .REPEAT 19                      ;BEGIN REPEAT BLOCK
         MULL2 NO,R6                     ;COMPUTE NO^K
         SPACE <5>                       ;INSERT 5 SPACES
         WRITE < NO ^ >                  ;PRINT DESCRIPTION
                                         ;NOTICE!
                                         ;NO=ACTUAL ARGUMENT

         PUSHL R7
         CALLS #1,WRITEVAL
         WRITE <             >           ;PRINT 2 TABS
                                         ;(INVISIBLE RESULT OF
                                         ;PRESS TAB KEY TWICE)

         PUSHL R6
         CALLS #1,WRITEVAL
         WRITELN
         INCL R7                         ;R7 = EXPONENT
         .ENDR
         .ENDM POWERS
;
         BEGIN <BEGINNING:    .WORD>
         POWERS OF <#2> TABLE            ;2^K TABLE
         WRITELN
         POWERS OF <#3> TABLE            ;3^K TABLE
         TUMTY
;
         .END BEGINNING
```

Continued on following page.

Figure 16.12 continued.

```
RUN FG1612

              powers of #2 table
---------------------------------------------

       #2 ^ 1              2
       #2 ^ 2              4
       #2 ^ 3              8
       #2 ^ 4              16
       #2 ^ 5              32
       #2 ^ 6              64
       #2 ^ 7              128
       #2 ^ 8              256
       #2 ^ 9              512
       #2 ^ 10             1024
       #2 ^ 11             2048
       #2 ^ 12             4096
       #2 ^ 13             8192
       #2 ^ 14             16384
       #2 ^ 15             32768
       #2 ^ 16             65536
       #2 ^ 17             131072
       #2 ^ 18             262144
       #2 ^ 19             524288

              powers of #3 table
---------------------------------------------

       #3 ^ 1              3
       #3 ^ 2              9
       #3 ^ 3              27
       #3 ^ 4              81
       #3 ^ 5              243
       #3 ^ 6              729
       #3 ^ 7              2187
       #3 ^ 8              6561
       #3 ^ 9              19683
       #3 ^ 10             59049
       #3 ^ 11             177147
       #3 ^ 12             531441
       #3 ^ 13             1594323
       #3 ^ 14             4782969
       #3 ^ 15             14348907
       #3 ^ 16             43046721
       #3 ^ 17             129140163
       #3 ^ 18             387420489
       #3 ^ 19             1162261467
```

What may not be apparent here is the more general form this directive would have in a macro definition. We can have

```
.MACRO BUILD REGISTERS TOTAL
.IRP RX, ⟨registers⟩
ADDL2 RX, SUM
.ENDR
.ENDM STORE
```

Then, in a source text, we can vary the call. For example,

Source Text	Expansion
BUILD ⟨R6,R7⟩ TOTAL	ADDL2 R6, SUM
	ADDL2 R7, SUM
⋮	
BUILD ⟨R9, R10, R11⟩ TOTAL	⋮
	ADDL2 R9, SUM
	ADDL2 R10, SUM
	ADDL2 R11, SUM

The implementation of this idea is illustrated in Figure 16.13.

The third of these repeat block directives strips characters one by one from a string, a different character for each new text insertion. For example, suppose we want to fill a NOS array of longwords with single-digit values. We could use

```
.MACRO CONSTRUCT INTEGER ARRAY WITH DIM Y
MOVAB NOS, R6
.IRPC X, ⟨INTEGER⟩
MOVL #X, (R6)+
.ENDR
.ENDM CONSTRUCT
```

To call this macro, we can use, for example

Source Text	Expansion
CONSTRUCT ⟨1,3,4,7⟩ ARRAY	MOVAB NOS, R6
	MOVL #1, (R6)+
	MOVL #3, (R6)+
	MOVL #4, (R6)+
	MOVL #7, (R6)+

FIGURE 16.13
Iterative Assembly with .IRP

```
;
;REF.:   FIGURE 16.13 (Iterative assembly with .IRP)
;
         .MACRO BUILD REGISTERS TOTAL ?SUM ?LAST        ;notice!
                                                        ;proto-st uses
                                                        ;local labels

         WRITELN
         WRITELN
         SPACE      <15>                         ;insert 15 spaces
         .IRP RX,<REGISTERS>                      ;iterate,picking off
                                                  ;1-by-1 the reg. no.
         ADDL2    RX,SUM                          ;build sum
         WRITE    <RX + >                         ;print RX-name
         .ENDR
;
         WRITE    < = >                           ;=
         PUSHL    SUM                             ;set up stack frame
         CALLS    #1,WRITEVAL                     ;to print sum
         BRB      LAST                            ;branch around labels
SUM:     .LONG
LAST:    NOP
         .ENDM
;
         BEGIN    <WITH:        .WORD>            ;estab. transfer addr.
         MOVL     #5,R6                           ;init. r6
         MOVL     #317811,R7                      ;init. r7
         MOVL     #514229,R8                      ;init. r8
         MOVL     #222222,R9                      ;init. r9
         MOVL     #1111111,R10                    ;init. r10
         MOVL     #3333,R11                       ;init. r11
;
         BUILD    <R6,R7,R8> TOTAL                ;compute sum
         BUILD    <R6,R6,R6> TOTAL                ;compute new sum
         BUILD    <R6,R8,R9,R10,R11> TOTAL        ;compute new sum
;
         TUMTY                                    ;insert $exit_s
         .END     WITH


RUN FG1613

                 R6 + R7 + R8 +  = 832045

                 R6 + R6 + R6 +  = 15

                 R6 + R8 + R9 + R10 + R11 +  = 1850900
```

FIGURE 16.14
Iterative Assembly with .IRPC

```
;
;Ref.:  Figure 16.14 (Iterative assembly with .IRPC)
;
;method:
;        Use the .IRPC iterative assembly directive to fill an array
;        of integers.  ARRAY,WITH and DIM are noise words.  The trick
;        is to pass a string containing the desired entries.  These
;        are successively stripped off the string, each being assigned
;        to X.  The beauty of this macro is its use of the numeric
;        equivalent of a numeric symbol.
;
        .MACRO CONSTRUCT INTEGER ARRAY WITH DIM Y ?ECHO ?COUNT ?NOS ?LAST
        MOVAB NOS,R6
        .IRPC   X,<INTEGER>
        MOVL    #X,(R6)+
        .ENDR
        MOVAB   NOS,R7
        MOVL    Y,R8
        JMP     LAST
NOS:    .BLKL   100
LAST:   NOP
        .ENDM
;
        BEGIN   <WITH:      .WORD>
;
        CONSTRUCT <116739> ARRAY WITH DIM #6
;
        JSB     ECHO
;
        CONSTRUCT <34343455> ARRAY WITH DIM #8
;
        JSB     ECHO
;
        TUMTY
;
ECHO:   WRITELN                         ;this routine exhibits
                                        ;the new array
        WRITE   <           ENTRIES: >
COPY:
        PUSHL   (R7)+
        CALLS   #1,WRITEVAL
        SPACE   <2>
        SOBGTR  R8,COPY
        RSB
;
        .END WITH   `


RUN FG1614


        ENTRIES: 1  1  6  7  3  9
        ENTRIES: 3  4  3  4  3  4  5  5
```

Figure 16.14 illustrates the use of the CONSTRUCT macro in a program to print copies of the newly constructed arrays.

16.5

CONCATENATION

Concatenating or "attaching" one symbol to another is accomplished in a simple way in either PDP-11 or VAX-11 macro assembly. Either a single (') or a double quotation mark ('') is used. If we pass an argument in a macro call, it can be attached as a symbol to a macro definition symbol with a single quotation mark. For example, suppose we use

```
.MACRO SAVE X IN Y WITH TYPE=L
MOV'TYPE X,Y
.ENDM SAVE
```

If we use the macro call

```
SAVE A IN COUNT
SAVE RO IN FREQ WITH TYPE=B
```

this would be expanded as

```
MOVL A, COUNT
MOVB RO, FREQ
```

The pointed brackets are used to preserve clarity and delimit the argument passed. They are optional in this case. Two arguments can be concatenated with a double quotation mark (''). For example, we can use the following macro:

```
.MACRO EXECUTE INSTR TYPE WITH NO X Y VARIABLES
INSTR''TYPE'NO X,Y
.ENDM EXECUTE
```

Then the following macro calls

```
EXECUTE ADDL2 WITH 2 R6, R7 VARIABLES
EXECUTE DIVW2 WITH 2 X, SUM VARIABLES
```

will be expanded as follows:

    ADDL2 R6, R7
    DIVW2 X, SUM

The

    INSTR''TYPE'2

in effect, concatenates two arguments (INSTR and TYPE) together, while 2 is concatenated to TYPE.

16.6

CONDITIONAL ASSEMBLY

This feature of macro assemblers is an economy feature. It allows us to insert *selectively* the parts of a macro definition. This is done by setting up a conditional of the form

    .IF ⟨condition⟩

        ⋮

    ⟨actions⟩

        ⋮

    .ENDC

The instructions (specifications for actions) will be inserted into the macro-assembled (expanded) source text, provided the ⟨condition⟩ is satisfied. The complete set of conditional tests usable on a VAX-11 is shown in Table 16.1.

These are all useful. The BLANK test is especially useful in setting up macros. For example, we could use

    .MACRO MULTIPLY X1 X2 X3 AND ADD X4 TYPE=L ?RESULT ?LAST
    MUL'TYPE'3 X1,X2,RESULT
    .IF NOT_BLANK X3
    MUL'TYPE'3 X3,RESULT,RESULT
    .ENDC
    .IF NOT_BLANK X4
    ADD 'TYPE'3 RESULT,X4,RESULT
    .ENDC
    .ENDM COMPUTE

TABLE 16.1
Condition Tests to Use in Conditional Assembly

| Test | | Opposite Test | | | |
Complete Form	Short Form	Complete Form	Short Form	Significance	Example
EQUAL	EQ	NOT_EQUAL	NE	Expression = 0	.IF EQ X (if x = 0)
GREATER	GT	LESS_EQUAL	LE	Expression > 0	.IF GT X (if x>0)
LESS_THAN	LT	GREATER_EQUAL	GE	Expression < 0	.IF LT X (if x<0)
DEFINED	DF	NOT_DEFINE	NDF	Legitimate symbol or not	.IF DF X (if x is defined)
BLANK	B	NOT_BLANK	NB	Argument is blank or not	.IF B X (if x is blank)
IDENTICAL	IDN	DIFFERENT	DIF	Two arguments are the same or not	.IF IDN X Y (if x and y are identical)

If we call this with

    MULTIPLY A,B

the above macro would contribute

    MULL3 A, B, RESULT

to the macro-assembled source text, whereas

    MULTIPLY A,B,C AND ADD C

would be expanded as

    MULL3 A, B. RESULT
    MULL3 C, RESULT, RESULT
    ADDL3 RESULT, C, RESULT

Another implementation of conditionals is given next in terms of printing numerical results (a souped up version of the old SPURT macro). This new numeric output macro called WRITEVAL is given in Figure 16.15.

Figure 16.16 illustrates the use of this macro (an expanded version to

FIGURE 16.15
Numeric Output Macro

```
;
;Ref.:   Figure 16.15 (Numeric output macro)
;
         .MACRO  WRITEVAL VAR1 VAR2 VAR3 VAR4 RADIX=10 SPACES=1
         MOVB    #RADIX,BASE

         .IF     NOT_BLANK VAR1
         PUSHL   VAR1
         CALLS   #1,WRITEVAL
         SPACE   SPACES
         .ENDC

         .IF     NOT_BLANK VAR2
         PUSHL   VAR2
         CALLS   #1,WRITEVAL
         SPACE   SPACES
         .ENDC

         .IF     NOT_BLANK VAR3
         PUSHL   VAR3
         CALLS   #1,WRITEVAL
         SPACE   SPACES
         .ENDC

         IF      NOT_BLANK VAR4
         PUSHL   VAR4
         CALLS   #1,WRITEVAL
         SPACE   SPACES
         .ENDC

         .ENDM   WRITEVAL
```

handle output, also using conditional assembly) in terms of computing

ab

abc + c

$a^3 + a$

(610)*b*c + c

16.7

SUBCONDITIONALS

Both MACRO-11 and VAX-11 macro have four subconditionals, as outlined in Table 16.2.

FIGURE 16.16
Conditional Assembly

```
;
;Ref.:  Figure 16.16 (Conditional Assembly)
;
;Method:
;       This MULTIPLY macro definition makes generous use of
;       conditional assembly, testing as it goes along which
;       arguments are blank.  This influences both the computations
;       and the printing of the results.  If X3 is blank, this
;       tells us not to compute X1*X2*X3.  We illustrate how this
;       varies in the macro calls given.
;
;Note:
;       Use
;
;                        MACRO FG1616 + PAS/LIB
;
;       to assemble this program.  PAS.MAR is given in the appendices.
;
        .MACRO MULTIPLY X1 X2 X3 AND ADD X4 TYPE=L ?RESULT ?LAST
        MUL´TYPE´3              X1,X2,RESULT
        .IF       NB X3
        MUL´TYPE´3              X3,RESULT,RESULT
        .ENDC
        .IF       NB X4
        ADD´TYPE´3              RESULT,X4,RESULT
        .ENDC
        WRITELN
        WRITELN
        SPACE     <10>
        WRITEVAL X1                     ;Notice!
                                        ;This is a macro call
                                        ;to an external macro
                                        ;in PAS.MAR; it is also
                                        ;inside the MULTIPLY
                                        ;macro
        WRITE    < * >
        WRITEVAL X2                     ;Notice!
                                        ;This is a macro
                                        ;call to routine
                                        ;PAS.MAR
        .IF       NB X3                 ;inhibit printing
                                        ;if! X3 is blank.
        WRITE    < * >
        WRITEVAL X3                     ;macro call, again.
        .ENDC
        .IF       NB X4                 ;inhibit printing
                                        ;if! X4 is blank
        WRITE    < + >
        WRITEVAL X4                     ;macro call, again.
        .ENDC
        WRITE < = >
        WRITEVAL RESULT                 ;macro call, again.
        JMP LAST                        ;jump past labels
RESULT: .LONG
LAST:   NOP
```

Figure 16.16 continued.

```
            .ENDM MULTIPLY
;
A:      .LONG 144
B:      .LONG 233
C:      .LONG 377
;
        BEGIN    <WITH:       .WORD>
        MULTIPLY A,B
        MULTIPLY A,B,C AND ADD C
        MULTIPLY A,A,A AND ADD A
        MULTIPLY #610,B,C AND ADD C
        TUMTY
        .END WITH


RUN FG1616

        144  *  233  = 33552

        144  *  233  *  377  +  377  = 12649481

        144  *  144  *  144  +  144  = 2986128

        610  *  233  *  377  +  377  = 53583387
```

TABLE 16.2
Subconditionals

Condition	Read	Example	Explanation
.IFF (.IF_FALSE)	"If False"	.IF GT X ADDL2 X, R6 .IFF MNEGL X, R7 .ENDC	X is added to R6, if X > 0, else twos complement of x is moved to R7
.IIF	"Immediate If"	.IIF LE X MNEGL X, R7	If X <= 0, then put twos comple- ment of X in R7
.IFT (.IF_TRUE)	"If True"	⟨test condition, earlier⟩ .IFT ⟨action⟩ .ENDC	Action is executed, if conditional tested, earlier, is true
.IFTF	"If True or False"	⟨ test condition, earlier⟩ .IFTF ⟨action⟩ .ENDC	*UN*conditional execution

Among the subconditionals shown in Table 16.2, one of the simplest and most commonly used is the Immediate If (.IIF). No .ENDC is necessary to close the conditional block. It is useful for single actions that should be executed if a condition is true. For example,

```
.IIF GT X DIVL X, R6        ;compute R6/x
.IIF EQ X JMP LAST          ;exit
.IFF LT X MNEGL X, X        ;take care of negatives
```

The final .ENDC pertained to just the third conditional.

16.8

NUMERIC VALUES OF SYMBOLIC ARGUMENTS

The numeric values of arguments are passed in a macro using a backslash (\) prefix. Suppose, for example, we have

```
.MACRO PROC NO ENTRYMASK =^?^M⟨⟩?
.ENTRY BEGIN 'NO, ENTRYMASK
.ENDM
```

We use \X (assume X = 6) in

```
PROC \X
```

to obtain

```
.ENTRY BEGIN6, ^M⟨⟩
```

Normally, the pointed brackets (⟨ ⟩) are delimiters for arguments passed to a macro definition. By using

```
^ ? ^ M⟨⟩ ?
```

we can pass the pointed brackets as part of the formal parameter, using a question mark (?) as a parameter delimiter. To change this mask, we can use

```
PROC 7 ^?^M⟨R6,R7,R8⟩?
```

Notice the single circumflex (^) on the left; this is necessary. This time we pass a 7 rather than a *value* of *X*.

16.9

TRANSFORMATION OF THE UGLY DUCKLING

Until now, we have said little about macro libraries. We have been content to write

```
.MACRO ⟨name                    ;MCDEF

    ⋮

.ENDM
.MACRO BEGIN ACT 1 ACT2 . . .   ;MCDEF
ACT1
ACT2

    ⋮

.ENDM
.MACRO TOMTY                    ;MCDEF
$EXIT_S
.ENDM
BEGIN ⟨MAIN: .WORD⟩             ;macro call

    ⋮

TUMTY                           .macro call
END MAIN
```

A program framework like this is cumbersome. The trick, now, is to tuck the macro definitions we want to use or let others use into a macro library. This will allow us to streamline our programs, using only macro calls. We can transform the ugly duckling. In effect, we can begin to create a macro language. We can enhance the macro assembler according to our needs. This is desirable. Its implementation is also straightforward. We do this in the next chapter.

16.10

SUMMARY

This chapter provides specific details about macros, and about the corresponding open routines. Since they are in-line (part of the main source text), transfers-of-control are not necessary with open routines. Open routines tend to be efficient.

If nothing else, macros make programming in assembler easier. Macros can be tailored to the needs of a particular application.

A macro assembler as rich as VAX-11 macro or MACRO-11, or even the tinier but impressive ORCA/M macro assembler for the Apple IIe, encourages the creation of new language constructions. It encourages the shaping of new instructions. It provides for the storage of macros in libraries, which makes it possible to use only the macro calls within a source text. The resulting programs tend to be elegant and concise.

This chapter shows the framework for a macro definition and discusses the methods used in handling parameters (formal as well as actual) and labels. We repeatedly show macro calls in various contents together with the corresponding text insertions during macro assembly.

Finally, it is the little things that make macros easier to handle. Notice, for example, that the hyphen (-) enables us to use more than one line for a macro call. The single quotation mark (') is used in concatenating. We can concatenate to form labels, complete operators and operands. Mastery of these details is essential. "The devil hides in details," says Wirth (1976).

16.11

EXERCISES

1. Give the conditional assembly statements needed to test each of the following conditions:

   (a) $A = B$

   (b) $X <= 12$

   (c) $X < 12$

   (d) $X + 5 > 12$

   (e) $X >= 0$

   (f) $X < 0$

   (g) X not defined

   (h) TYPE is blank

   (i) $x - 6 <= 233$

   Hint: If, for example, we have

   $$T <= 144$$

then use

.IFF LE T − 144

2. Give the .IFF equivalent of

    (a) clear R6, if X > 5

    (b) Add R6 to R7, if X >= 10

3. Give a macro to set up an array of integers. Call it BUILD. Set it up to load the array with random numbers, using conditional assembly to determine if random numbers are to be used.

4. Write a program to implement the macro BUILD in exercise 3, filling an array with random numbers and printing a copy of the completed array.

5. Write a macro called RATIO to print out decimals having the form

    $\langle$integer$\rangle$. $\langle$fraction$\rangle$

Try using the technique shown in chapter 12 to handle fractions.

6. Write a program to implement the macro in exercise 5 to print a table of negative powers of 2.

7. Write a program that uses macros to obtain a summation. Run your program for

    (a)

$$1 + 2 + 3 + \cdots + 5000 = \sum_{i=1}^{i=5000} i$$

    (b)

$$1^2 + 2^2 + 3^2 + \cdots 100^2 = \sum_{i=1}^{i=100} i^2$$

Note: ('Σ' or sigma, the Greek symbol used as a shorthand for sum).

8. Why is it not possible to branch to a .ENDM from inside a macro?

9. Why is it necessary to branch around a storage directive inside a macro (see Figure 16.5, for example)?

10. Write a program that uses a macro that uses an .IRPC directive to print

    ITEM: $\langle$characters$\rangle$

Run your program to print

    ITEM: 2.05
    ITEM: 22.05
    ITEM: 222.05
    ITEM: 2222.05

as a result of four macro calls.

11. Write an assembly language program to print

    NOS: 1,1,2,3
    NOS: 1,2,3,5
    NOS: 2,3,5,8
    NOS: 3,5,8,13

as a result of three (*not* four!) separate macro calls in this program.

16.12

LAB PROJECT

1. Write a macro to do the equivalent of an

    IF ⟨condition⟩ THEN ⟨ACTION⟩ ELSE ⟨ACTION⟩

in Pascal. Implement this macro in terms of the following rendition of a Pascal statement found in C. Hawksley (1983, p. 55) to determine if a year after 1752 represents a leap year:

    ⟨enter year⟩
    If year mod 400 = 0
       then Leap: = 1
       else
         if (year mod 4 = 0) and (year mod 100 ⟨⟩ 0)
         then leap: = 1
         else
           leap: = 0
    ⟨print result, test the value of the variable leap⟩

Hint: This IF macro can be set up using concatenation of the conditional tests. That is, try

```
.MACRO IF arg1 condition arg2 then act1 . . .
CMPL arg1, arg2
B' condition ⟨label for arg1⟩
```

⋮

16.13

REVIEW QUIZ

Indicate whether the following statements are true or false:

1. With

```
.macro r equal x op y
```

the words "equal" and "op" can be used as noise words.
2. Noise words are ignored by a macro processor.
3. The question mark (?) is used to indicate local labels in macro prototype statements.
4. The range for local labels on a VAX-11 is 65$ to 128$, inclusive.
5. Parameters are an optional part of macros.
6. In VAX-11 macro, macros cannot call themselves.
7. .IRP is a repeat-block directive in VAX-11 Macro.
8. .IRPc is not a repeat-block directive in VAX-11 Macro.
9. .REPEAT does the same thing as .IRP.
10. VAX-11 Macro does have conditional assembly.
11. Parameters in VAX-11 macro prototype statements can be either positional or keyword parameters.
12. The colon (:) is used to set up keyword parameters in VAX-11 Macro prototype statements.
13. Macro calls can be made within macro definitions.
14. Macro calls can be made within closed routines.

16.14

REFERENCES

Berglass, G. R. A Generalization of MacroProcessing. Ann Arbor, Mich.: University Microfilms International, 1970.

Hawksley, C. *Pascal Programming*. Cambridge, England: Cambridge University Press, 1983.

Wirth, N. *Algorithms + Data Structures = Programs*. Englewood Cliffs, N.J.: Prentice-Hall, 1976.

17.

MACRO LIBRARIES

Macro library facilities can serve to augment a macro processor. A macro library serves as a general purpose macro definition tool, permitting the user to insert a block of macro statements automatically by calling the macro without defining it in the first place.

—C.-B. Hsieh, *An On-Line Macro Processor for the Motorola 6800 Microprocessor*

17.0

AIMS

- Introduce the framework for a macro library, its preliminary setup, and its relation to programs by its author and other users.
- Prepare a handbook for a fairly complete macro library that can be used as a model for other libraries.
- Show how syntax diagrams for Pascal statements can be used as templates for macros.
- Illustrate macros not given previously.
- Show how to make a macro library sharable.

17.1

INTRODUCTION

A workable, useful macro library takes considerable time to build. It is worth the effort. A macro library facility justifies the use of open routines on a broad scale. Since the macro definitions reside in a library, we can write source texts *without* macro definitions and still use macro calls liberally. The macro object library (Digital Equipment Corporation uses an .OLB for Object LiBrary on a VAX-11) is "tapped" by the macro processor each time it encounters a macro library call. The MP will construct its macro definition table using library definitions. This produces an economy in our assembly programs that is often desirable. Otherwise the inclusion of macro definitions in a source text tends to make a source text top-heavy and more error-prone. A working open routine should be prepared (and typed in) only once, when we insert it into a macro library. In practical terms, a macro library tends to cut down the preparation time for each new program we write.

Another major benefit to having a macro library is its sharability. The macro definitions in an unprotected OLB-file can be inserted into programs by other system users. Other users include calls like

    WRITE ⟨string⟩

in their source text and the macro processor can be directed to retrieve the corresponding macro definition from the unprotected macro library. We explain how to set the protection codes for a sharable macro library in this chapter.

Added to these features (that is, practicality and sharability) is the fact that a macro library can become the basis for a *macro language*. Although such a language is difficult to obtain, it is also a tantalizing feature of workable macro libraries. Assembly language programmers who have crafted their macro libraries over a number of years speak in terms of their own language. Why? In just about any programming environment, a macro library can be built to take care of most of the program constructions needed for problem solving in that environment. A library becomes the source of a demand language for the special-purpose problems. Since it can be shared, it becomes a *lingua franca* for a particular set of problems.

In building a macro language, it is wise to combine special-purpose macros with control structures and conditionals found in a commonly accepted language like Pascal or C, as we do in this chapter.

In all of this, not one bit of the efficiency of assemblers is lost. Their efficiency stays in place and preparation time is cut down by the tools in sharable macro libraries.

In this chapter, we first show how to set up, insert, augment, edit, and use personal macro libraries. We also set up a handbook for a fairly complete macro library. We have used part of this library throughout this text.

17.2

HOW TO SET UP A MACRO LIBRARY

A macro library is structurally separate from a main program or routine that has macro calls to library macros. Suppose, for example, we have programs like the ones shown in chapter 16, which use BEGIN and TUMTY macro calls. The relation between a main program and a macro library is depicted in Figure 17.1.

A macro library is a separate indexed file with an .MLB extension. It is set up with the librarian utility program by using

LIBRARY/CREATE/MACRO PAS PAS

The librarian builds into this MLB file information about the location of each module in the file. This aids the macro assembler in constructing its macro definition tables relative to the macro calls of a particular program. The structure of a VAX-11 macro library is *not* the same as that for a MACRO-11 macro library. Unlike a MACRO-11 macro library, a VAX-11 macro library does not include a

.END

as its last entry. Rather, a VAX-11 macro library contains a sequence of macro definitions:

.MACRO X1, . . .

⋮

.ENDM X1
.MACRO X2, . . .

⋮

.ENDM X2

⋮

.MACRO X99, . . .

⋮

.ENDM X99

FIGURE 17.1
Source Text Relative to a Macro Library

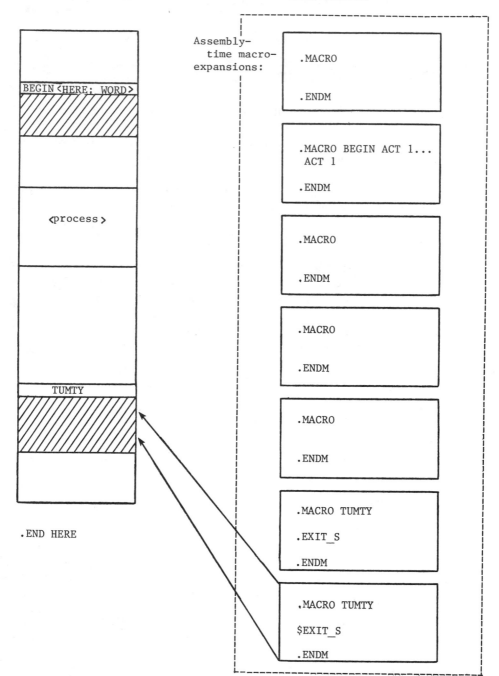

What we have done, initially, is use an editor (try TECO or EDIT, for example) to create a scratch library, which will contain trial definitions, ones which have not been entirely perfected. For example, we would put the provisional

```
.MACRO BEGIN
.WORD
.ENDM BEGIN
```

in SCRATCH.MLB. Later, we would put the more generalized version of this macro

```
.MACRO BEGIN ACT1 . . . ACTK
ACT 1

  ⋮

ACTK
.ENDM BEGIN
```

in the more permanent PAS.MLB. Each of these libraries begins with a .MAR extension, which is turned into a .MLB file with the LIBRARY/ CREAT/. . . command string. In either case, with libraries like the SCRATCH or the PAS library, we are constantly enhancing a library. And in either case, insertions into and/or enhancements of these libraries is done by editing the source text (the MAR file, *not* the MLB file!) for the library. To change PAS.MLB using EDIT, we would type

```
EDIT PAS.MAR ⟨ret⟩

  ⋮

* CH ⟨ret⟩

  ⋮

etc.
```

Then we would invoke the librarian utility *again,* in terms of the revised source text, to produce a new PAS.MLB file.

17.2.1 The Content of a Macro Library

There are choices to make here. In some ways, it is better to have a *single,* fairly large macro library with most of the open routines we would ever use. Why? First, this simplifies the command string we need to assemble a program with macro calls. For example, for a source text called *T* with macros defined in PAS.MLB, we use

```
MACRO T + PAS/LIB
```

If we have more than one MLB file, this means we have to add these references in the macro assembly command string (we have to remember which libraries we are calling, also!). For example, if we have PAS.MLB and TNT.MLB, and a source text ZZZ.MAR calling macros defined inside these two libraries, then we use

```
MACRO ZZZ + PAS/LIB + TNT/LIB
```

Second, each new macro library we set up has a minimum of 100 disk blocks (each block has 512 bytes) set aside on the disk by the librarian. This happens even if a macro library contains only *one* three-line macro definition like TUMTY. This alone discourages the use of many macro libraries.

17.2.2 The Art of Constructing Macro Libraries

It is desirable to organize the macros in a macro library into clusters, one cluster for I/O, another cluster for numberhandling and so on. There is a danger in having one library with everything in it. A library can become a hodgepodge of open routines—some to do one thing, some to do another. There is a need for what I. Kant (1787) terms an architectonic in constructing macro libraries. By *architectonic,* Kant meant an art of constructing systems, a method of isolating "various modes of knowledge as they differ in kind and origin, and to secure that they not be confounded owing to the fact that usually, in our employment of them, they are combined."

There is a way to avoid the proliferation of space-consuming macro libraries and yet avoid building a library that is a hodgepodge. First, put together a working library of open routines; then arrange the macros inside the library in terms of obvious subdivisions. As a rule, it is easier to "attach" a new open routine to the end of a macro library using the editor. Even so, it is preferable to add an open routine to the end of *a subdivision* of a library (the end of the I/O or control or conditional or statistical subdivisions) instead of the end of the library, itself.

There is an art to this. There is an art to setting up the structure of a macro library. The easiest way to begin arranging the macros inside a library is to take a top-down approach. First, identify the principal subdivisions. Next, make a sketch of a tree exhibiting the pigeonholes for the open routines (the children of the parent nodes). Figure 17.2 shows a sketch of this idea in terms of PAS.MAR.

FIGURE 17.2
Macro Language Tree

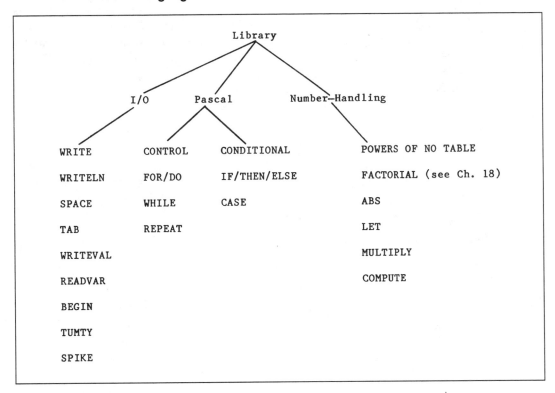

17.2.3 Example with Two Libraries

In this section we set up a second macro library called MATH and a program with macro calls relative to both the MATH and familiar PAS.MLB macro library.

Suppose we put the POWER and MULTIPLY macros from chapter 16 in a MATH.MLB library:

```
;MATH.MLB:
        .MACRO POWER OF NO TABLE WITH MIN=1 MAX=10

        ⋮

        .ENDM POWER
        .MACRO MULTIPLY . . .

        ⋮

        .ENDM MULTIPLY
```

This is shown in Figure 17.3 (notice that the original POWER macro has been enhanced).

Then, in the program shown in Figure 17.4 we call POWER from the MATH.MLB and the BEGIN and TUMTY libraries. Notice that the definition for POWER includes macro calls to open routines found in the PAS.MLB. Also notice that a third library comes into play, since TUMTY invokes a system macro, $EXIT_S. Now we can begin to see the extraordinary versatility of this macro assembler.

The command string we use to macro assemble the above program is

FIGURE 17.3
A Math Macro Library

```
;
;Ref.:  Figure 17.3 (Macro library of math routines)
;
;Method: to assemble, use
;
;                       library/create/macro math math
;
        .macro power of no table with min=1 max=10
        movl    #1,r6                   ;init. beginning factor
        .repeat min-1
        mull2   no,r6
        .endr
        movl    #min,r7                 ;init. beginning exponent
        writeln
        writeln <powers of no table>
        writeln <------------------------------------------------->
        writeln
        .repeat max-min+1
        mull2   no,r6                   ;compute product
        write   <       no^>
        writeval r7
        write   <               >
        writeval r6
        writeln
        incl    r7
        .endr
        .endm   power

        .macro multiply x1 x2 x3 and add x4 with type=1 ?result ?bye
        mul^type^3      x1,x2,result
        .if     nb x3
        mul^type^3      x3,result,result
        .endc
        .if     nb x4
        add^type^3      result,x4,result
        .endc
        .endm   multiply
```

FIGURE 17.4
A Program with Calls to Several Macro Libraries

```
        ;
        ;Ref.:  Figure 17.4 (macro calls to two separate libraries)
        ;
        ;Method: to assemble, use
        ;
        ;               macro fg174 + fg173/lib + pas/lib
        ;
                begin <here:          .word>
                power of #4 table
                writeln
                power of #5 table with-
                        min=5-
                        max=12
                tumty
                .end here


        RUN FG174

        powers of #4 table
        ---------------------------------------------

                #4^1              4
                #4^2              16
                #4^3              64
                #4^4              256
                #4^5              1024
                #4^6              4096
                #4^7              16384
                #4^8              65536
                #4^9              262144
                #4^10             1048576


        powers of #5 table
        ---------------------------------------------

                #5^5              3125
                #5^6              15625
                #5^7              78125
                #5^8              390625
                #5^9              1953125
                #5^10             9765625
                #5^11             48828125
                #5^12             244140625
```

given next:

MACRO FG174 + PAS/LIB + MATH/LIB

17.3

A COMPLETE MACRO LIBRARY

This section is concerned with the development of a fairly complete macro library. A complete listing for this library, called PAS, is given in Appendix C. It has more than 20 macros. It includes the standard control and conditional constructs found in Pascal, C, Ada, or Modula-2. It also includes I/O routines that are nonstandard at this point, since we have separate stringhandling routines (WRITE and WRITELN) to print strings and separate numeric output and input routines (WRITEVAL and READVAR) to print and read numbers. Normally, in Pascal, for example, a

Write ('your average score = ', average);

will handle both strings ('your average score = ') and numbers (*average*, for example). It is entirely possible to enhance the WRITE macro we have so that it can handle *both* strings as well as numeric output. This can be set up using conditional assembly to check the arguments used in the macro call. This is left as an exercise. The current version of WRITE does mimic one helpful feature of the Pascal WRITE statement. It prints a string *without* a ⟨ret⟩. This is particularly important in printing the parts of an output line, especially one that splices together strings and numbers. By inhibiting a ⟨ret⟩ after printing a string, we can continue displaying further strings as well as numeric output on the same line. (Figure 16.16 exhibits an extreme example of this.)

As it turns out, the formation of a macro definition often springs from the syntax of typical programming language instructions. The syntax diagrams used to represent the structure of a statement in Pascal make perfect templates, almost blueprints, for macro definitions. Importing a construct from an HOL into a macro library is advantageous. That is, we retain control of memory given to us by the assembler while utilizing the well-wrought constructs of an HOL.

17.3.1 Using a Pascal Syntax Diagram as Macro Template

A Pascal syntax diagram is a directed graph that uses

1. arrows (→) to show direction, starting with a '.' to begin the graph and leading to

2. a box with rounded corners

to enclose instruction symbols like FOR and DO; with

FIGURE 17.5
Step-by-Step Trace of a Syntax Diagram

Repeat

1.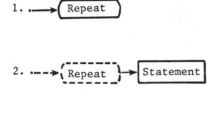

Point to initial;

Connect initial symbol to what immediately follows (prescription for an action);

2.

Statement separators

3.

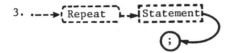

Flow of control passes to next statement;

4.

5.

Show position of 2nd Repeat statement symbol;

6.

Point to position of expression (a Boolean condition!) which controls the continuation of the Repeat loop

3. plain boxes to enclose expressions (Boolean conditions) and statements like

and

4. circles to enclose "punctuation" symbols (separators) like

;

or

:=

FIGURE 17.6
A REPEAT/UNTIL Macro Relative to a Syntax Diagram

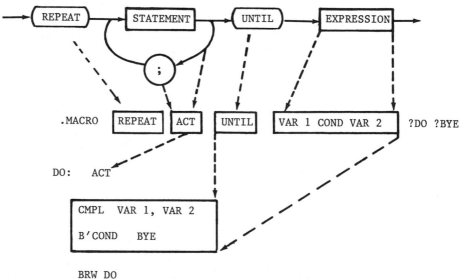

FIGURE 17.7
A Procedure for Lucas Numbers

```
;
;Ref.:   Figure 17.7 (A recursive procedure for Lucas numbers)
;
        Procedure Lucas;

        Var
                 i,j,sum,max:       integer;
        Begin

        1. Initialize i:=2 (this is L(0) in the Lucas sequence);
                      j:=1 (this is L(1));
                      max:=9999 (this is a trial upper limit);

        2. Repeat
                 sum := i + j;
                 write(sum);
                 i := j;
                 j := sum
             until sum > max

        End procedure Lucas.
```

Figure 17.5 shows the step-by-step trace of the syntax diagram for the Pascal statement REPEAT/UNTIL.

17.3.2 Example: A REPEAT/UNTIL Macro

A macro to implement the framework given by the REPEAT/UNTIL syntax diagram is given in Figure 17.6.

That is, continue performing the action(s) specified by ACT until the condition becomes true. We can illustrate this idea in terms of the procedure to print Lucas numbers given in Figure 17.7.

That is, using the above procedure we produce the sequence

$$2, \quad 1, \quad 3, \quad 4, \quad 7, \quad 11, \quad 18, \qquad \ldots \qquad 9349$$
$$L_0, \ L_1, \ L_2 \ (= \text{first number printed}), \ldots, \qquad L_{19}$$

named after the nineteenth century number theorist E. Lucas. An assembly language program to implement this idea is given in Figure 17.8.

You might wonder what the list module for this program would look like. We explore this in the exercises.

FIGURE 17.8
Implementation of the Lucas Procedure

```
        ;
        ;Ref.:  Figure 17.8 (Implementation of the Lucas Procedure)
        ;
        ;Var
                i:          .long 2
                j:          .long 1
                max:        .long 9999
                sum:        .long
                index:      .long 2

        begin   <here:    .word>
                writeln
                writeln <          Lucas numbers:>
                writeln <------------------------------------------
                writeln
                repeat-
                        <begin-
                                <addl3 i,j,sum>-
                                <write <    L( >>-
                                <writeval index>-
                                <write < )  >>-
                                <writeval sum>-
                                <writeln>-
                                <incl index>-
                                <movl j,i>-
                                <movl sum,j>>-
                until     sum gtr max
                tumty

                .end here

        RUN FG178
                Lucas numbers:
        --------------------------------------------------

                L( 2  )          3
                L( 3  )          4
                L( 4  )          7
                L( 5  )          11
                L( 6  )          18
                L( 7  )          29
                L( 8  )          47
                L( 9  )          76
                L( 10 )          123
                L( 11 )          199
                L( 12 )          322
                L( 13 )          521
                L( 14 )          843
                L( 15 )          1364
                L( 16 )          2207
                L( 17 )          3571
                L( 18 )          5778
                L( 19 )          9349
                L( 20 )          15127
```

17.4

PAS LIBRARY HANDBOOK

This handbook pulls together the assorted macros we have discussed in terms of the typical syntactic constructs appearing in statements using macros in the library given in Appendix C. Contrary to what Kent (1969, p. 184) says, it is necessary to *think* about the possible syntactic constructs that can be used in building complete statements with macro calls, especially those with chains of macro calls implicit in the macro instruction. We have seen this already with the implementation of the word ACT in the REPEAT/UNTIL macro. That is, we replace ACT with BEGIN (a call), which is spliced together with other ACTs.

17.4.1 ABS

```
        .MACRO ABS TERM WITH TYPE = L ?BYE
        TST'TYPE TERM
        BGEQ BYE
        MNEG'TYPE TERM, TERM
BYE:    NOP
        .ENDM ABS
```

This macro guarantees that TERM will be positive or zero, even if it is negative to begin with. We illustrate this in the tiny program in Figure 17.9.

17.4.2 LET

```
        .MACRO LET VAR1 EQ VAR2 WITH TYPE = L
        MOV'TYPE VAR2, VAR1
        .ENDM LET
```

This is our assignment macro. Since ':=" is taken as a string by the macro processor, we can use

```
        LET X := Y
```

as a macro call. This is fortunate, since it closely parallels the Pascal state-

FIGURE 17.9
An Absolute Value Macro

```
;
;Ref.:  Figure 17.9 (Implementing the absolute value macro)
;
;Method:
;       This program feeds an alternating sequence into the abs macro.
;
x:      .long -2584,1597,-987,610,-377,233,-144,89,-55
sentinel:
        .long 0

begin   <here:   .word>
        movab   x,r6                      ;set up array ptr
        writeln
        writeln <              Sequence with alternating signs removed>
        writeln <------------------------------------------------------->
        writeln
        repeat-
                <begin-
                        <abs (r6)>-
                        <writeval (r6)+ spaces=2>>-
        until (r6) eql sentinel
        tumty

        .end here


RUN FG179

        Sequence with alternating signs removed
--------------------------------------------------------
2584   1597   987   610   377   233   144   89   55
```

ment

    X := Y

despite the LET macro name. It is probably obvious by now that the macro name for any macro must be given in a macro call. This is unfortunate in this case, since it is sometimes unneeded baggage. It is probably also obvious that we *cannot* use

  .MACRO X EQ Y WITH TYPE=L

  MOV'TYPE Y,X

  .ENDM X

That is, a macro name cannot take on a value, or be used as part of an instruction.

17.4.3 POWER

```
.MACRO POWER OF NO TABLE with MIN = 1 MAX = 10
MOVL #1, R6                    ;init. beginning factor
.REPEAT MIN  −  1
MULL2 NO, R6
.ENDR
MOVL #MIN, R7                  ;init. beginning exponent
WRITELN
WRITELN ⟨POWERS OF NO TABLE⟩
WRITELN ⟨————————————⟩
WRITELN
.REPEAT MAX  −  MIN + 1
MULL2 NO, R6                   ;compute product
WRITE ⟨    NO^⟩
WRITEVAL R7
WRITE ⟨           ⟩
WRITEVAL R6
WRITELN
INCL R7
.ENDR
.ENDM POWER
```

See Figures 16.10 and 17.4 for illustrations of the use of this macro. This is a refinement of the earlier (see chapter 16) version of this macro. Now we allow for a starting point above a number raised to the first power. Assume MIN = 5, MAX = 10. Then

```
.REPEAT MIN − 1
MULL2 NO, R6
.ENDR
```

gives

```
MULL2 NO, R6  =  NO¹ in R6
MULL2 NO, R6  =  NO² in R6
MULL2 NO, R6  =  NO³ in R6
MULL2 NO, R6  =  NO⁴ in R6
```

Then

$$\text{.REPEAT MAX} - \text{MIN} + 1 \quad (= 10 - 5 + 1 = 6)$$
$$\text{MULL2 NO, R6}$$

$$\vdots$$

$$\text{.ENDR}$$

gives

$$\text{MULL2 NO, R6} = \text{NO}^5 \text{ in R6}$$
$$\text{MULL2 NO, R6} = \text{NO}^6 \text{ in R6}$$
$$\text{MULL2 NO, R6} = \text{NO}^7 \text{ in R6}$$
$$\text{MULL2 NO, R6} = \text{NO}^8 \text{ in R6}$$
$$\text{MULL2 NO, R6} = \text{NO}^9 \text{ in R6}$$
$$\text{MULL2 NO, R6} = \text{NO}^{10} \text{ in R6}$$

For example, if we use

$$\text{POWER OF \#6 TABLE WITH MIN} = 5 \text{ MAX} = 10$$

this macro will produce the powers of 6 in the range

$$6^5, \ldots, 6^{10}$$

17.4.4 FACTORIAL

```
.MACRO Factorial ?BYE
.IF NE N
FACTORIAL N - 1
MOVL A,R6
MULL2 #N,R6
MOVL R6,A
.ENDC
WRITELN
WRITE ⟨n! = ⟩
WRITEVAL A SPACES = 5
.ENDM FACTORIAL
```

This is explained in chapter 18. This is an example of a rather extraordinary recursive macro (it calls itself repeatedly and the calls and continued expansions are regulated by conditional assembly). The call

FACTORIAL 5

will produce the result $5! = 1*2*3*4*5 = 120$ in location A predefined in the calling program.

17.4.5 COMPUTE

```
        .MACRO COMPUTE VAR1 IS VAR2 OP VAR3 ?QUO ?BYE
        .IF IDENTICAL DIV ⟨OP⟩      ;if Op = DIV, then
        DIVL3 VAR3, VAR2, VAR1      ;compute quotient
        .IF FALSE                   ;else
        PUSHR #ˆM⟨R7,R8⟩            ;save R7,R8 contents on stack
        MOVL VAR2, R7               ;init. R7
        CLRL R8                     ;set up EDIV quad
        EDIV VAR3, R7, QUO, VAR1    ;get remainder
        POPR #ˆM⟨R7,R8⟩             ;restore R7,R8 contents
                                    ;notice! the order is the same
        .ENDC
        BRW BYE
QUO:    .LONG
BYE:    NOP
        .ENDM COMPUTE
```

This macro will take care of computing either the quotient or remainder after division. For example,

COMPUTE X := Y DIV Z

will put the quotient in X, while

COMPUTE X := Y MOD Z

will put the remainder in X after dividing Y by Z. We illustrate this in Figure 17.10. This macro can be generalized by allowing for operands of more than one type. This is left as an exercise.

FIGURE 17.10
Computing with a MOD and DIV Macro

```
    ;
    ;Ref.:  Figure 17.10 (Computing remainders and quotients)
    ;
    ;var
          x:        .long
          a:        .long
          b:        .long

begin     <here:    .word>
          write     <enter pair of integers: >
          readvar a,b
          writeln
          compute x := a DIV b
          write     <                >
          writeval a
          write     < div >
          writeval b
          write     < = >
          writeval x
          writeln
          write     <                >
          writeval a
          write     < mod >
          writeval b
          write     < = >
          compute x := a MOD b
          writeval x
          tumty

          .end here


RUN FG1710

enter pair of integers: 32767,7


                32767  div 7  = 4681
                32767  mod 7  = 0


RUN FG1710

enter pair of integers: 32768,7


                32768  div 7  = 4681
                32768  mod 7  = 1
```

17.4.6 TAB

```
.MACRO TAB X
FOR I := #1 TO X DO ⟨WRITE⟨   ⟩⟩
.ENDM
```

This is one of the more elegant examples of a macro call within a macro definition (the skeleton). This replaces the earlier version of TAB, which was cumbersome. This one has a hidden feature. When it is constructed (typed in), the keyboard tab key is pressed to put the ASCII code for a tab inside the pointed brackets in

```
WRITE ⟨     ⟩
```

We illustrate the use of the TAB macro in connection with the following macro.

17.4.7 SPIKE

```
.MACRO SPIKE X
FOR I := #1 TO X DO ⟨WRITE *⟩
.ENDM SPIKE
```

This macro will be useful in drawing pictures. The choice of the star (or asterisk) is provisional. This macro should be enhanced to allow the user to select a character (there is complete freedom, here, if a CHAR formal parameter is introduced in the prototype statement so that

```
⟨WRITE CHAR⟩
```

would be executed. The following program prints a solid rectangle (the user selects the dimensions). It utilizes a new READVAR macro, which is shown in Figure 17.11.

17.4.8 READVAR

```
.MACRO READVAR VAR1 VAR2 VAR3 RADIX = 10
MOVB #RADIX, BASE        ;init.base
CALLS #0, READVAL        ;get nos. from keyboard
.IF NOT_BLANK VAR3       ;if there is a 3rd no.,
```

514 CHAPTER 17

FIGURE 17.11
Graphics with a FOR/DO Macro

```
        ;
        ;Ref.:  Figure 17.11 (Using the spike macro)
        ;
        ;var
               width:    .long
               length:   .long

begin          <here:    .word>
               writeln
               write     <enter desired width & length of box:  >
               readvar   width,length
               writeln
               writeln
               for i := #1 to width do-
                         <begin-
                                  <tab 2>-
                                  <spike length>-
                                  <writeln>>
               tumty

               .end here


        RUN FG1711

        enter desired width & length of box:  6,30


                     ******************************
                     ******************************
                     ******************************
                     ******************************
                     ******************************
                     ******************************
```

```
MOVL (R11)+,VAR3          ;pop it!
.ENDC
.IF NOT_BLANK VAR2        ;if there is a 2nd no.,
MOVL (R11)+, VAR2         ;pop it!
.ENDC
.IF NOT_BLANK VAR1        ;if there is a 1st no.,
MOVL (R11)+, VAR1         ;pop it!
.ENDC
.ENDM READVAR
```

This macro is roughly equivalent to a Pascal read statement restricted to integers. You might wonder how it can be generalized. Figure 17.11 illustrates its use.

17.4.9 WRITEVAL

```
.MACRO WRITEVAL VAR1 VAR2 VAR3 VAR4 RADIX = 10 SPACES = 1
MOVB ERADIX,BASE
.IF NOT_BLANK VAR1
IF VAR1 LSS #0 THEN ⟨BEGIN ⟨WRITE ⟨ − ⟩⟩ ⟨ABS VAR1⟩-
        ⟨PUSHL VAR1⟩ ⟨CALLS #1,WRITEVAL⟩ ⟨MNEGL VAR1,VAR1⟩⟩-
        ELSE ⟨BEGIN ⟨PUSHL VAR1⟩ ⟨CALLS #1,WRITEVAL⟩⟩
SPACE  SPACES
.ENDC
.IF NOT_BLANK VAR2
IF VAR2 LSS #0 THEN ⟨BEGIN ⟨WRITE ⟨ − ⟩⟩ ⟨ABS VAR2⟩-
        ⟨PUSHL VAR2⟩ ⟨CALLS #1,WRITEVAL⟩ ⟨MNEGL VAR2,VAR2⟩⟩-
        ELSE ⟨BEGIN ⟨PUSHL VAR2⟩ ⟨CALLS #1,WRITEVAL⟩⟩
SPACE  SPACES
.ENDC
.IF NOT_BLANK VAR3
IF VAR3 LSS #0 THEN ⟨BEGIN ⟨WRITE ⟨ − ⟩⟩ ⟨ABS VAR3⟩ -
        ⟨PUSHL VAR3⟩ ⟨CALLS #1,WRITEVAL⟩ ⟨MNEGL VAR3,VAR3⟩⟩-
        ELSE ⟨BEGIN ⟨PUSHL VAR3⟩ ⟨CALLS #1,WRITEVAL⟩⟩
SPACE  SPACES
.ENDC
IF NOT_BLANK VAR4
IF VAR4 LSS #0 THEN ⟨BEGIN ⟨WRITE ⟨ − ⟩⟩ ⟨ABS VAR4⟩ -
        ⟨PUSHL VAR4⟩ ⟨CALLS #1,WRITEVAL⟩ ⟨MNEGL VAR4,VAR4⟩⟩-
        ELSE ⟨BEGIN ⟨PUSHL VAR4⟩ ⟨CALLS #1,WRITEVAL⟩⟩
SPACE  SPACES
.ENDC
.ENDM WRITEVAL
```

The basic feature for this numeric output macro is

```
PUSHL X
CALLS #1, WRITEVAL
```

which puts the number to be printed into a stack frame which the WRITEVAL procedure uses. The WRITEVAL procedure is the same one used in earlier chapters. In its present state this macro will handle up to four numbers. For example, if we have

```
w:   .long 3
x:   .long 281
y:   .long −2001
z:   .long −5
```

then the macro call

```
WRITEVAL x y
```

gives

```
281  − 2001
```

while the macro call

```
WRITEVAL w x y z SPACES=5
```

gives

```
3    281    −2001    −5
```

We use the BEGIN macro to set up a compound statement with respect to *each* parameter in the call. We include the ABS macro inside this statement to guarantee that only positive integers are sent to the WRITEVAL procedure if an argument is negative to begin with. Notice that a

```
MNEGL X, X   (X − VAR1 or VAR2 or VAR3 or VAR4)
```

is used to restore the sign on the argument *after* it is printed. The minus sign (−) is printed as a prefix for a negative number. This macro also permits us to vary the base on the output.

17.4.10 Other I/O Macros

In earlier sections we introduced WRITE, WRITELN and WRITEVAL. It would be helpful to put WRITE and WRITEVAL together into one macro that would print either strings or numbers or both. This is possible. The result would be equivalent to the WRITE statement in Pascal. The same can be done with WRITELN and WRITEVAL to produce the equivalent of the WRITELN statement in Pascal. These new macros are left as exercises. Finally, the SPACE macro has been used repeatedly, before. Even so, in its present form it is awkward. It would be better to redo the skeleton for the SPACE macro definition using the FOR/DO macro. Its new structure would be similar to the TAB macro. This enhancement is left as an exercise.

17.4.11 Boundary Macros

The BEGIN and TUMTY (or the more upbeat tum-ti-tum!) macros help bracket the boundaries of a program. The BEGIN macro also allows us to construct compound statements like

⟨Begin-
⟨writeln⟩-
⟨writeln ⟨tumtytumtytumtoes!⟩⟩⟩

It is desirable to introduce END as a concluding noise word in the prototype statement for the BEGIN macro. Why? Then we can either omit END in

BEGIN ⟨here : .word⟩

to set up a program transfer address or, appropriately, use

⟨Begin-
        ⟨act1⟩-
        ⟨act2⟩-
        ⟨act3⟩-

            ⋮

        ⟨actk⟩-
    end⟩

to show the complete structure of a compound statement. This enhancement is left as an exercise. It would also be helpful to introduce a register mask inside the skeleton of the BEGIN macro, so that R6, . . . , R11 would be masked immediately before the first ACT. Then, after the last ACT, the original register contents should be restored. This can be handled with an initial PUSHR and a concluding POPR. This enhancement is also left as an exercise.

17.4.12 WHILE

```
            .MACRO WHILE VAR1 COND VAR2 DO ACT ?LOOP ?BYE-
            ?AGAIN
AGAIN:  CMPL VAR1, VAR2        ;check condition
        B'COND LOOP            ;if true, do action
        BRW BYE
 LOOP:  ACT
        BRW AGAIN              go back to check condition
 BYE:   NOP

            .ENDM WHILE
```

Except for the semicolon (;), the structure of this macro matches that given by the syntax diagram for a Pascal WHILE/DO statement. This syntax diagram and a corresponding diagram for the WHILE/DO macro are shown in Figure 17.12.

Using the BEGIN macro, we can construct a compound statement in place of ACT in the WHILE/DO call. We illustrate this first in a straightforward way in terms of ACT with a repetitious printing of a familiar expression: tumtytumtytum, which is an onomatopoeic word for strumming a guitar; the *Oxford English Dictionary* renders this word as

tum-ti-tum-ti-tum

Figure 17.13 shows a program to exhibit this "music."

17.4.13 FOR

```
            .MACRO FOR INDEX IS MIN TO MAX DO ACT, STEP=#1-
            ?LOOP ?TALLY ?BYE
        MOVL MIN, TALLY
 LOOP:  ACT
        ACBL MAX, STEP, TALLY, LOOP
        BRB BYE
TALLY:  .LONG
 BYE:   NOP
            .ENDM FOR
```

FIGURE 17.12
WHILE/DO Syntax Diagram

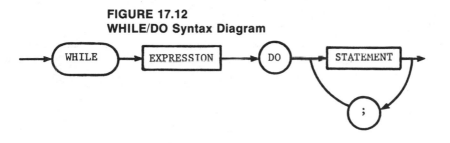

Syntax Diagram for Pascal While/Do

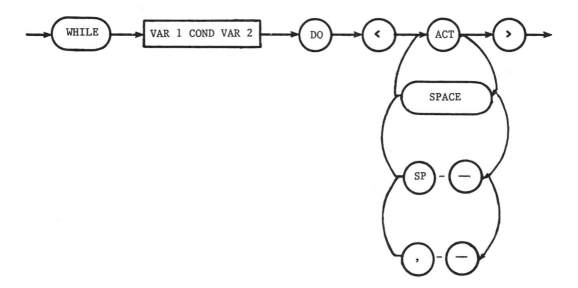

With one important exception, the structure of this macro is comparable to the structure shown in the syntax diagram for a Pascal FOR/DO loop given in Figure 17.14.

The sketch of the corresponding syntax diagram for the FOR/DO macro is left as an exercise. Again, instead of a semicolon (;), we use a hyphen (-) to separate the parts of a compound statement. Also, the statement that replaces the ACT formal parameter itself is enclosed in pointed brackets (⟨ ⟩). This macro is illustrated in Figure 17.11. In addition, we can nest FOR/DO calls, one inside the other, as illustrated in Figure 17.15.

FIGURE 17.13
Strumming a Guitar with a WHILE/DO Macro

```
        ;
        ;Ref.:   Figure 17.13 (Strumming a guitar with a while/do loop)
        ;
        ;var
                x:          .long 0
                strum:      .long 1

        begin   <here:      .word>
                writeln
                write <  How many strums of the guitar do you wish?  >
                readvar x
                writeln
                writeln
                while     strum neq x do-
                          <begin-
                                    <tab strum>-
                                    <writeln <tum-ti-tum-ti-tum!>>-
                                    <incl strum>>
                tumty

                .end here


        RUN FG1713

          How many strums of the guitar do you wish?  8



                    tum-ti-tum-ti-tum!
                        tum-ti-tum-ti-tum!
                            tum-ti-tum-ti-tum!
                                tum-ti-tum-ti-tum!
                                    tum-ti-tum-ti-tum!
                                      tum-ti-tum-ti-tum!
                                        tum-ti-tum-ti-tum!
```

FIGURE 17.14
FOR/DO Syntax Diagram

FIGURE 17.15
Nested FOR/DO Macro Calls

```
;
;Ref.:   Figure 17.15 (Nested for/do macro calls)
;
begin    <here:    .word>
         for i := #1 to #2 do -
                 <begin -
                             <write <mm..>>-
                             <writeln>-
                             <for j := #5 downto #1 do -
                                 <write <*>> step = -1>-
                             <for k := #1 to #5 do -
                                 <for l := #1 to #5 do -
                                     <for m := #1 to #5 do -
                                     <write <mm..>>>>>>>
         tumty
         .end here


RUN FG1715

mm..
*****mm..mm..mm..mm..mm..mm..mm..mm..mm..mm..mm..mm..mm..mm..mm..mm..mm..mm.
.mm..mm..mm..mm..mm..mm..mm..mm..mm..mm..mm..mm..mm..mm..mm..mm..mm..mm..mm.
.mm..mm..mm..mm..mm..mm..mm..mm..mm..mm..mm..mm..mm..mm..mm..mm..mm..mm..mm.
.mm..mm..mm..mm..mm..mm..mm..mm..mm..mm..mm..mm..mm..mm..mm..mm..mm..mm..mm.
.mm..mm..mm..mm..mm..mm..mm..mm..mm..mm..mm..mm..mm..mm..mm..mm..mm..mm..mm.
.mm..mm..mm..mm..mm..mm..mm..mm..mm..mm..mm..mm..mm..mm..mm..mm..mm..mm..mm.
.mm..mm..mm..mm..mm..mm..mm..mm..mm..mm..mm..mm..mm..mm..mm..mm..mm..mm..mm.
.mm..mm..mm..mm..mm..mm..mm..
*****mm..mm..mm..mm..mm..mm..mm..mm..mm..mm..mm..mm..mm..mm..mm..mm..mm..mm.
.mm..mm..mm..mm..mm..mm..mm..mm..mm..mm..mm..mm..mm..mm..mm..mm..mm..mm..mm.
.mm..mm..mm..mm..mm..mm..mm..mm..mm..mm..mm..mm..mm..mm..mm..mm..mm..mm..mm.
.mm..mm..mm..mm..mm..mm..mm..mm..mm..mm..mm..mm..mm..mm..mm..mm..mm..mm..mm.
.mm..mm..mm..mm..mm..mm..mm..mm..mm..mm..mm..mm..mm..mm..mm..mm..mm..mm..mm.
.mm..mm..mm..mm..mm..mm..mm..mm..mm..mm..mm..mm..mm..mm..mm..mm..mm..mm..mm.
.mm..mm..mm..mm..mm..mm..
```

17.4.14 REPEAT

```
        .MACRO REPEAT ACT UNTIL VAR1 COND VAR2 ?DO ?BYE
DO:     ACT
        CMPL VAR1, VAR2
        B'COND BYE
        BRW DO
BYE:    NOP
        .ENDM REPEAT
```

This is illustrated in Figures 17.7, 17.8, and 17.9.

17.4.15 IF

```
            .MACRO IF ARG1 COND ARG2 THEN ACT1 ELSE ACT2-
            ?FIRST ?SECOND
            CMPL ARG1, ARG2
            B'CONDITION FIRST
            ACT2
            JMP SECOND
    FIRST:  ACT1
    SECOND: NOP
            .ENDM IF
```

This macro has the same syntax as the IF/THEN/ELSE statement in Pascal. In the program that follows we use the IF/THEN/ELSE macro inside a WHILE/DO loop macro to advantage. We use a WHILE/DO loop to generate Fibonacci numbers to the left of $F_0 = 0$. The signs of these numbers alternate. For example,

$$F_2 = F_1 + F_0 = 1 + 1 = 2$$
$$F_1 = F_0 + F_{-1} = 1 + 0 = 1$$
$$F_0 = F_{-1} + F_{-2} = 1 - 1 = 0$$
$$F_{-1} = F_{-2} + F_{-3} = -1 + 2 = 1$$
$$F_{-2} = F_{-3} + F_{-4} = 2 - 3 = -1$$
$$\vdots \qquad \vdots \qquad \vdots \qquad \vdots$$

This recursion produces the sequence

$$\ldots, 233, -144, 89, -55, 34, -21, 13, -8, 5, -3, 2, -1, 1, 0, 1, 1, 2 \ldots$$

The program in Figure 17.16 illustrates this recursion.

17.4.16 CASE

```
            .MACRO CASE SELECTOR OF A ACT1 B ACT2 C ACT3 D ACT4
            E ACT5-
            OTHERWISE=NOP ?FLAG ?A2 ?A3 ?A4 ?A5-
            ?NOT_DONE ?BYE
    CLRB    FLAG
    CMPL    SELECTOR,A
    BNEQ    A2
    ACT1 ·
    MOVB    #1,FLAG
```

FIGURE 17.16
Fibonacci Numbers with Alternating Signs

```
;
;Ref.:  Figure 17.16 (Fibonacci Numbers with Alternating Signs)
;
;Method:
;       This program illustrates the use of the while/do macro together
;       with the if/then/else macro to produce Fibonacci numbers with
;       alternating signs (these are the Fibonacci numbers to the left
;       of F(0)=0 in
;
;               ...,-21,13,-8,5,-3,2,-1,1,0,1,1,2,3,5,8,13,21,...
;                        ^                      ^
;                        |            |         |
;                        |          F(0)        |
;       F(8)
;                        |
;               F(-8) = F(-6) - f(-7)
;
;
;
;       We use a while/do loop, which starts with computing the difference
;       F(-1)=F(1)-F(0).  With each difference, if the sign is negative, we
;       obtain its absolute value (inside the if/then/else statement) and
;       print the difference with a minus(-) prefix.
;
x:      .long 0
y:      .long 1
diff:   .long 0

begin   <here:   .word>
        writeln
        writeln <             Fibonacci numbers with alternating signs:>
        writeln <------------------------------------------------------------->
        writeln
        writeln
        while diff lss #4181 do -
                <begin -
                <subl3 x,y,diff>-
                <movl x,y>-
                <movl diff,x>-
                <if diff lss #0 then -
                        <begin -
                        <abs diff>-
                        <write <->>-
                        <writeval diff>>-
                        else -
                        <writeval diff>>>
        writeln
        tumty
        .end here

RUN FG1716

        Fibonacci numbers with alternating signs:
-------------------------------------------------------------

1 -1 2 -3 5 -8 13 -21 34 -55 89 -144 233 -377 610 -987 1597 -2584 4181
```

```
A2:     .IF NOT_BLANK B
        CMPL    SELECTOR,B
        BNEQ    A3
        ACT2
        MOVB    #1,FLAG
        .ENDC
A3:     .IF NOT_BLANK C
        CMPL    SELECTOR,C
        BNEQ    A4
        ACT3
        MOVB    #1,FLAG
        .ENDC
A4:     .IF NOT_BLANK D
        CMPL    SELECTOR,D
        BNEQ    A5
        ACT4
        MOVB    #1,FLAG
        .ENDC
A5:     .IF NOT_BLANK E
        CMPL    SELECTOR,E
        BNEQ    NOT_DONE
        ACT5
        MOVB    #1,FLAG
        .ENDC
NOT_DONE:
        CMPB    #1,FLAG
        BEQL    BYE
        OTHERWISE
        BRB     BYE
FLAG:   .BYTE
BYE:
        .ENDM CASE
```

This CASE macro is an alternative to the CASE instruction in the VAX-11 instruction set illustrated earlier. The CASE macro is easier to use and can accomplish the same thing as the VAX-11 case instruction. A VAX-11 macro instruction can have up to thirty-one formal arguments. This means we can easily expand this macro to handle more cases, if necessary.

This macro has the framework of the case statement in Pascal. It also includes a nonstandard OTHERWISE feature, which allows for selections outside the required range. If the range in a CASE macro call is 1, 2, 3 and a higher number is selected (one outside this range), the macro defaults to a NOP. In place of a NOP, we can assign a different action (OTHERWISE is a keyword parameter). The use of this macro is illustrated in Figure 17.17.

FIGURE 17.17
A Case Macro

```
;
;Ref.:   Figure 17.17 (How to use the case macro)
;

;var

        choice:   .long

begin   <here:    .word>
again:  write <pick a number in the range 1,2,3: >
        readvar choice
        case choice of -
                #1 <write <       aha!>>-
                #2 <write <       aha2!>>-
                OTHERWISE=<WRITE <      MMM...>>
        WRITELN
        WRITELN
        WRITE <PICK ANOTHER NO. IN THE RANGE 1,2,3,4  >
        READVAR CHOICE
        WRITELN
        WRITELN
        CASE CHOICE OF -
                #1 <WRITE <       M...>>-
                #2 <WRITE <       M2...>>-
                #3 <WRITE <       M3...>>-
                #4 <BEGIN -
                        <FOR 3 := #1 TO #5 DO <WRITELN <       EUREKA!>>>-
                        <WRITELN>>-
                otherwise = <write <   Case selection error!>>
        writeln
        write    <Again?--type 1 for yes, 0 for no:  >
        readvar  choice
        if choice eql #1 then <jmp again>

        tumty

        .end here
```

Continued on following page.

Figure 17.17 continued.

```
RUN FG1717

pick a number in the range 1,2,3: 2

                        aha2!

PICK ANOTHER NO. IN THE RANGE 1,2,3,4  4


        EUREKA!
        EUREKA!
        EUREKA!
        EUREKA!
        EUREKA!

Again?--type 1 for yes, 0 for no:  1

pick a number in the range 1,2,3: 5

            MMM...

PICK ANOTHER NO. IN THE RANGE 1,2,3,4  44


                    Case selection error!
Again?--type 1 for yes, 0 for no:  0
```

17.5

HOW TO SET UP A SHARABLE MACRO LIBRARY

If a macro library like the one given here needs to be shared by a group, it is easy to adjust the library protection codes to make it sharable. There are several ways to do this. Assume, for example, that we want each member of a group to be able to read (get a copy, call library macros) from a library in *one* group member's account. Then type

SET PROTECTION = (GROUP:R) PAS.*;*

This allows any member of a group to use the PAS.MAR (and PAS.MLB) library. If a group member has a program called *T* with macro calls to PAS.MLB, then assemble the source text for *T* by typing

MACRO T + [account name]PAS/LIB

For example, SJU is the group name for those using the VAX-11/780 at St. Cloud State University. PAS.MLB is in SJU1 and a group member with a different account (SJU3, for example) calls macros in the group library. Then, for example, use

MACRO T + [SJU1]PAS/LIB

It is also possible to change the protection on a file to allow others to add (contribute!) to a library. To allow this, type

SET PROTECTION = (GROUP:RW) PAS.*;*

To prevent members outside the group from accessing a library, type

SET PROTECTION = (SYSTEM) *.*;*

to protect all account files. By default, group members cannot read from or write to each other's files. To make a library sharable, it is necessary to change the protection as shown above.

The absentminded will run into a problem here. *Each* time a library is edited by a library owner, the library protections are reset to the default, *nonsharable* state. After editing a library, change the protection with the SET command to make a library sharable again. This will become easy after a while.

17.6

SUMMARY

Macro libraries tend to be centers of creativity. They tend to encourage a creative approach to assembly programming. With the help of a macro processor, assembly programs with macro calls can "borrow" from a macro library just those lines of code that are needed to expand a source text. So, even though a macro library may be fairly long, programs with macro calls can make selective use of macro definitions. By being separate from any one source text like those shown in chapter 16, these library macros are easily shared.

The sharability of a macro library should not be discounted or passed over lightly. There is a practical concern about available disk storage for many users wanting to use the more convenient macro calls, instead of creating or recreating the assembly language code to carry out a task. The sharability feature of macro libraries on systems like the VAX-11 series eliminates the need for duplicating effort, libraries, and consuming disk storage in 100-block chunks.

Finally, with the start of a workable macro library, it is possible to look forward to building a macro language. The macro library constructed in this chapter parallels the one developed for the PDP 11/70 by J. Peters (1984).

17.7

EXERCISES

1. Write a macro to read strings typed at a keyboard. Call it READSTR. Write a second macro to print a copy of what has been read by READSTR. Call it ECHO. Write a program to

   (a) Prompt for a string.

   (b) Use READSTR to read it.

   (c) Use ECHO to print a copy of what has been entered.

   Run your program for

   (d) Coroutines are processes . . . (Wirth, 1983).

2. Write a macro that allows either of the following calls:

   CALC X := Y − Z   (subtract Z from Y and put result in X)

   CALC X := Y + Z   (add Y to Z)

   Hint: Use conditional assembly to determine which operation is called for. Write a program using these calls.

3. Is it possible to assign values to macro names? Could we use *X* as the macro name, for example, instead of CALC in the macro in exercise 2? In other words, can we ever write

   X := Y − Z
   ↑
   macro name

4. In its current state, the WHILE/DO macro is primitive. That is, we need to enter part of a branch, a suffix like

Suffix		Branch		Symbol
LSS	in	BLSS	for	<
NEQ	in	BNEQ	for	<>
GTR	in	BGTR	for	>
EQL	in	BEQL	for	=
GEQ	in	BGEQ	for	>=
LEQ	in	BLEQ	for	<=

in a call like

```
While X LSS Y Do -
        ⟨Begin -
            ⋮
        ⟨      ⟩⟩
```

Use conditional assembly to allow the user to use a relational symbol instead of a suffix to set up a branch in the macro definition. Allow macro calls of the form

```
While X < Y Do . . .
```

5. The WRITEVAL macro is set up to print numbers in the base specified in the WRITEVAL call. Use this together with macros to write a program that produces a table of the form

decimal	binary	hex
1		
2		
3		
⋮		
50		

6. Lucas numbers are derived by starting with $L(0) = 2$, $L(1) = 1$, and

$$L(n) = L(n-1) + L(n-2)$$

For example,

2,	1,	3,	4,	7,	11,	18,	29,	. . .
↑	↑	↑	↑	↑	↑	↑	↑	
L(0)	L(1)	L(2)	L(3)	L(4)	L(5)	L(6)	L(7)	

Write a macro called LUCAS that does the following:

(a) Allows the user to select the starting Lucas number for numbers *above* L(1). This will be the MIN parameter. Let the default be MIN = 2 for L(0).

(b) Allows the user to specify the top end of the sequence. Let the default be MAX = 10.

(c) Allows the user to select the base the Lucas numbers will be printed in.

Then write a program to

(d) Print a table of base sixteen (hex) Lucas numbers in the range L(0), . . . , L(15).

(e) Print a table of base two (binary) Lucas numbers in the range L(5), . . . , L(12).

7. Write a program using macros to print the sequence

$$2,2,2,2,1,1,1,1,0,0,0,0,-1,-1,-1,-1,-2,-2,-2,-2,-3,-3,-3,-3$$
↑↑ ↑↑
a b c d

if you start with sequence seeds

    a: .long 3

    b: .long 3

    c: .long 3

    d: .long 3

8. Enhance the BEGIN macro so that it has an END as a trailing noise word, so that a macro call with this macro would have the form

    Begin -

          ⟨act1⟩ -

          ⟨act2⟩ -

              ⋮

          ⟨actk⟩ -

    End

Revise the program in Figure 17.16 so that it uses this new BEGIN macro. Run the new program.

9. Make a further enhancement of the BEGIN macro so that registers R6, . . . , R11 are pushed with PUSHR first, *before* any actions are given and then afterward popped with a POPR to restore the original register contents.

10. Write an AL program to print inverted *T*s and allow the user to select the

(a) height and

(b) the width of

```
    *  ⎫
       ⎪
    *  ⎪
       ⎬   height = 4
    *  ⎪
       ⎪
    *  ⎭

 *   *   *   *   *
   width = 5
```

17.8

LAB PROJECTS

1. Enhance the write macro in the PAS library so that it is capable of printing both strings and numbers. This can be done by *requiring* a fixed prefix (try a single quotation mark [']) and an identical trailing suffix to signal the beginning and ending of a string. Use your macro to print the table in Figure 17.8 by combining

   ⟨write ⟨   L(⟩⟩-
   ⟨writeval index⟩ -
   ⟨write ⟨)   ⟩⟩-
   ⟨writeval sum⟩

   into *one* macro call

   write ⟨   L(⟩ ⟨index⟩⟨) ⟩⟨sum⟩

2. Using macros write a program to print all possible moves of the bishop on a chessboard, once the user has supplied the row and column the bishop is currently in.

3. Figure 17.18 presents a Pascal program to

   (a) Enter an ordered list of numbers.

   (b) Echo-print the list.

   (c) Prompt the user for any insertions.

   (d) Do a binary search to find the place the new entry is to be inserted.

   (e) Prompt for other possible insertions.

FIGURE 17.18
Binary Insertion Program

```
;
;Ref.: Figure 17.18 (Binary Insertion Program)
;
PROGRAM BINARY(INPUT, OUTPUT);

  VAR
    LOW, MAX, HIGH, M: INTEGER;
    TARGET: REAL;
    ANS: CHAR;
    NOS: ARRAY [0..20] OF REAL;
    FLAG: BOOLEAN;


  PROCEDURE SWITCH;

    VAR
      K: INTEGER;


    BEGIN
      MAX := MAX + 1;
      FOR K := MAX DOWNTO M + 1 DO
        NOS[K] := NOS[K - 1];
      NOS[M] := TARGET;
      FLAG := TRUE
    END;


  BEGIN
    MAX := 1;
    WRITELN;
    WRITELN('INPUT THE NUMBERS ON SEP. LINES WITH A ^Z AS THE SENTINEL.');
    WHILE NOT EOF DO
      BEGIN
      READLN(NOS[MAX]);
      MAX := MAX + 1
      END;
    MAX := MAX - 1;
    WRITELN;
    REPEAT
      HIGH := MAX;
      LOW := 1;
      FLAG := FALSE;
      WRITELN('BEFORE INSERTION:');
      FOR M := 1 TO MAX DO
        BEGIN
        WRITE(NOS[M]: 1: 1);
        WRITE(' ': 2);
        END;
      WRITELN;
      WRITELN;
```

Figure 17.18 continued.

```
      WRITE(´NUMBER TO INSERT? ´);
      RESET(INPUT);
      READLN(TARGET);
      REPEAT
       M := TRUNC((LOW + HIGH) / 2);
       IF (HIGH - LOW) = 1 THEN
         IF TARGET <= NOS[LOW] THEN
           BEGIN
           M := LOW;
           SWITCH;
           END
         ELSE IF TARGET >= NOS[HIGH] THEN
           BEGIN
           M := HIGH + 1;
           SWITCH;
           END
         ELSE
           BEGIN
           M := HIGH;
           SWITCH;
           END;
        IF NOT FLAG THEN
           IF TARGET >= NOS[M] THEN
             LOW := M
           ELSE
             HIGH := M;
      UNTIL FLAG;
      WRITELN;
      WRITELN(´AFTER INSERTION:´);
      FOR M := 1 TO MAX DO
        BEGIN
        WRITE(NOS[M]: 2: 1);
        WRITE(´ ´: 2);
        END;
      WRITELN;
      WRITELN;
      WRITE(´ DO YOU WISH ANOTHER RUN?  ´);
      READLN(ANS);
      WRITELN;
   UNTIL ANS <> ´Y´;
END.
RUN V2

INPUT THE NUMBERS ON SEP. LINES WITH A ^Z AS THE SENTINEL.
2
2
3
11
13
13
13
44
```

Continued on following page.

Figure 17.18 continued.

```
230
233
^Z
BEFORE INSERTION:
2.0   2.0   3.0   11.0   13.0   13.0   13.0   44.0   230.0   233.0

NUMBER TO INSERT? 13

AFTER INSERTION:
2.0   2.0   3.0   11.0   13.0   13.0   13.0   13.0   44.0   230.0   233.0

  DO YOU WISH ANOTHER RUN?   Y

BEFORE INSERTION:
2.0   2.0   3.0   11.0   13.0   13.0   13.0   13.0   44.0   230.0   233.0

NUMBER TO INSERT? -33

AFTER INSERTION:
-33.0   2.0   2.0   3.0   11.0   13.0   13.0   13.0   13.0   44.0   230.0   233.0

  DO YOU WISH ANOTHER RUN?   Y

BEFORE INSERTION:
-33.0   2.0   2.0   3.0   11.0   13.0   13.0   13.0   13.0   44.0   230.0   233.0

NUMBER TO INSERT? 233.5

AFTER INSERTION:
-33.0   2.0   2.0   3.0   11.0   13.0   13.0   13.0   13.0   44.0   230.0   233.0   233.5

  DO YOU WISH ANOTHER RUN?   N
```

Using only macros, rewrite the program in Figure 17.18 in assembly language. Run the new assembly program using

(f) the list and entries shown in the sample run in Figure 17.18

(g) list: 8, 13, 21, 34, 55, 89, 144, 377
insertion: 233
next insertion: 610
next insertion: 5

4. We show a complete BASIC program to draw a selection of geometric figures in Figure 17.19. Using only macros, rewrite the BASIC program in Figure 17.19 in assembly language.

FIGURE 17.19
Graphics Program

```
100!        Ref.:  Figure 17.19 (Graphics Program)
110!
120!
130!
140         EXTEND
150         PRINT TAB (20%); ´1) AN L´
                \PRINT TAB (20%); ´2) A RECTANGLE´
                \PRINT TAB (20%); ´3) A DIAMOND´
160         PRINT \ INPUT ´WHICH MENU ITEM DO YOU WISH´;M%
170         ON M% GOSUB 190,280,380
180         STOP
190!
200!    SUBROUTINE FOR AN L
210!
220         INPUT ´HORIZONTAL LENGTH´; BASE%
                \INPUT ´VERTICAL LENGTH´; HEIGHT%
230         GOSUB 510 \ !GRAPHICS CHOICE
240         GOSUB 580 \ !DETERMINE CENTER
250         GOSUB 630 \ !DRAW VERTICLE
260         GOSUB 680 \ !DRAW HORIZONTAL
270         RETURN
280!
290!    SUBROUTINE FOR A RECTANGLE
300!
310         INPUT "HORIZONTAL LENGTH";BASE%
                \INPUT "VERTICAL LENGTH";HEIGHT%
320         GOSUB 510 \ !GRAPHICS CHOICE
330         GOSUB 580 \ !DETERMINE CENTER
340         GOSUB 680 \ !DRAW HORIZONTAL
350         GOSUB 730 \ !DRAW DOUBLE VERTICAL
360         GOSUB 680 \ !DRAW HORIZONTAL
370         RETURN
380!
390!    SUBROUTINE FOR A DIAMOND
400!
410         INPUT ´DIAMOND SIZE´;SIZE%
420         GOSUB 510
430         PRINT \ PRINT
440         PRINT TAB(SIZE%);Z$
450         PRINT TAB(SIZE% - I%);Z$;TAB(SIZE% + I%);Z$   FOR I% = 1% TO SIZE%
460         FOR I% = (SIZE% - 1%) TO 1% STEP -1
470         PRINT TAB(SIZE% - I%);Z$;TAB(SIZE% + I%);Z$
480         NEXT I%
490         PRINT TAB(SIZE%);Z$
500         RETURN
510!
520!SUBROUTINE CHOICE OF GRAPHICS
530!
540         PRINT TAB(20%); ´CHOICES:´
                \PRINT ´1) PRINT WITH A *´
                \PRINT ´2) PRINT WITH A .´
                \PRINT ´3) PRINT WITH A !
550         PRINT \ INPUT ´CHOICE´;CHOICE%
560         IF CHOICE% = 1% THEN Z$ = ´*´ ELSE
```

Continued on following page.

Figure 17.19 continued.

```
                IF CHOICE% = 2% THEN Z$ = ´.´ ELSE
                IF CHOICE% = 3% THEN Z$ = ´!´
570     RETURN
580!
590!SUBROUTINE CENTER
600!
610     CENTER% = 40% - INT(BASE% / 2%)
620     RETURN
630!
640!SUBROUTINE VERTICAL
650!
660     PRINT TAB(CENTER%);Z$  FOR K% = 1% TO HEIGHT%
670     RETURN
680!
690!SUBROUTINE HORIZONTAL
700!
710     PRINT TAB(CENTER%);Z$;  FOR K% = 1% TO BASE%
             \PRINT
720     RETURN
730!
740!SUBROUTINE DOUBLE VERTICAL
750!
760     PRINT TAB(CENTER%);Z$; SPACE$(BASE% - 2%);Z$  FOR K% = 1% TO HEIGHT%
770     RETURN
780 END
```

```
RUN FG1718
                    1) AN L
                    2) A RECTANGLE
                    3) A DIAMOND

WHICH MENU ITEM DO YOU WISH? 1
HORIZONTAL LENGTH? 4
VERTICAL LENGTH? 3
                    CHOICES:
1) PRINT WITH A *
2) PRINT WITH A .
3) PRINT WITH A !

CHOICE? 2

                         .
                         .
                         .
                         ....

Stop at line 180



RUN
```

Figure 17.19 continued.

```
                    1) AN L
                    2) A RECTANGLE
                    3) A DIAMOND

WHICH MENU ITEM DO YOU WISH? 2
HORIZONTAL LENGTH? 5
VERTICAL LENGTH? 4
                        CHOICES:
1) PRINT WITH A *
2) PRINT WITH A .
3) PRINT WITH A !

CHOICE? 1
                                         *****
                                         *   *
                                         *   *
                                         *   *
                                         *   *
                                         *****
Stop at line 180



RUN
                    1) AN L
                    2) A RECTANGLE
                    3) A DIAMOND

WHICH MENU ITEM DO YOU WISH? 3
DIAMOND SIZE? 2
                        CHOICES:
1) PRINT WITH A *
2) PRINT WITH A .
3) PRINT WITH A !

CHOICE? 3


    !
   ! !
  !   !
   ! !
    !
Stop at line 180



RUN
                    1) AN L
                    2) A RECTANGLE
                    3) A DIAMOND
```

Continued on following page.

Figure 17.19 continued.

```
WHICH MENU  ITEM DO YOU WISH? 3
DIAMOND SIZE? 16
                        CHOICES:
1) PRINT WITH A *
2) PRINT WITH A .
3) PRINT WITH A !

CHOICE? 2
```

```
Stop at line 180
```

5. Write a graphics macro to print a concentric squares macro so that the call

        SQUARES

will produce

```
*   *   *   *   *   *
*   *   *   *   *   *
*   *           *   *
*   *           *   *
*   *   *   *   *   *
*   *   *   *   *   *
```

where the dimension of the central square will be determined randomly (by default), unless the user specifies a fixed dimension with

        SQUARES INNER = ⟨integer⟩

Note: Use one of the random number generators given earlier to obtain a default dimension (use a MAX = 10). Write a program to

(a) print randomly selected image
(b) SQUARES INNER = 4

17.9

REVIEW QUIZ

Indicate whether the following statements are true or false:

1. .OLB is the extension used for macro libraries on VAX-11s.
2. The source text for a VAX-11 macro library has a .MAR extension.
3. Including macro definitions in a macro assembly language source text for a main program can make the source text top-heavy.
4. A macro library on a VAX-11 does not terminate with a .END.
5. A macro library on a VAX-11 can contain just one macro definition.
6. The word "while" is a noise word in the WHILE macro.

7. The word "for" is a noise word in the FOR macro.

8. The word "do" is not a noise word in the WHILE macro.

9. "cond" is used as a noise word in the WHILE macro.

10. The word "act" is used as a noise word in the WHILE macro.

11. With

    step = #1

    in the FOR macro, we have a keyword parameter.

12. A keyword parameter can be given a default value in a prototype statement.

13. A keyword parameter in a prototype statement can be changed each time a corresponding macro call is made within the same program.

14. It is possible for one user to use a macro library in another user's account.

17.10

REFERENCES

Hsieh, C.-B. *An On-line Macro Processor for the Motorola 6800 Microprocessor.* Ann Arbor, Mich.: University Microfilms International, 1980. See especially chap. 1.

Kant, I. *Critique of Pure Reason,* 2nd ed. New York: Dutton, 1979.

Kent, W. "Assembler Language Macroprogramming: A Tutorial Oriented Toward the IBM 360." *Computing Surveys,* 1, no. 4 (December 1969).

Peters, J. F. The Digital Way: *MACRO-11 Assembly Language Programming (PDP-11).* Reston, Va.: Reston Publishing Company, 1984. See especially chap. 17 and Appendix H.

Wirth, N. *Programming in Modula-2.* New York: Springer-Verlag, 1983.

18.
RECURSION

Recursion simplifies the structure of many programs. . . . Most often the structural simplicity is well worth the running time.

—A. V. Aho et al., *Data Structures and Algorithms*

18.0
AIMS

- Introduce the basic ideas concerning recursion, recurrence relations, iterative, nonrecursive routines, recursive open routines, and recursive closed routines.
- Illustrate the implementation of some of the more common recurrence relations.
- Show the side effects resulting from recursive calls in both open and closed routines.

18.1
INTRODUCTION

This chapter introduces ideas concerning recursive open and closed routines. A recursive routine is one that contains calls to itself. It does this with the help of a stack, which is used to keep track of the return address whenever a routine calls itself. This allows the recursive routine to find its way back to where it left off when the recursive call was made and, eventually, back to the original program or routine that called the recursive routine.

First, we explore the general notion of recursion. We do this both in terms of the recursive routines used to implement recurrence relations and in terms of recursive routines that merely call themselves.

In general a *recurrence relation* defines the current (most recent) term of a sequence in terms of preceding elements of the sequence. There are some well-known examples of this. For example, the last words of James Joyce's novel *Finnegan's Wake* are

A way a lone a last a loved a long the

which revert back to *and* are explained by earlier words, the opening words of this novel:

riverrun, past Eve and Adam's, from swerve of shore to bend of bay, brings us by a commodius vicus of recirculation back to Howth Castle and Environs.

Joyce never really wants you to finish reading his book! A more graphic example of a recursion is given by Dutch painter Vermeer in his 1665 painting called *De Schilderkunst* (Picture of the Artist) depicting himself painting a picture of himself. Figure 18.1 shows yet another example of a picture depicting a recursion, which was suggested by R. Pletcher (1983).

Again, we find the familiar recurrence relation

$$f(n) = f(n-1) + f(n-2)$$

for Fibonacci numbers, each one definable in terms of the preceding two terms of the sequence. We can set up a recursive procedure that calls itself until a specific Fibonacci number is found. First, we set up variables a and b with consecutive Fibonacci values (try $(a) = f(-1) = 1$ and $b = f(0) = 0$) as well as a variable I for the index. The recursive procedure we set up is based on the scheme shown in Figure 18.2.

Suppose we want to determine $f[35]$. Then a recursive procedure can be set up to implement the Fibonacci recurrence relation to find the desired $f[n]$. We name it after V. E. Hoggatt, Jr. (1921–80), cofounder of the Fibonacci Association in 1963. This procedure is presented in Figure 18.3.

Before we illustrate the implementation of this procedure in an assembly language closed routine, we want to suggest an alternative way to find $f[n]$ without resorting to a recursive procedure.

We do this with an iteration. If we need only one or more terms of this sequence in ascending order, we can use a FOR/DO loop like the following

FIGURE 18.1
A Modular Computer Recursion

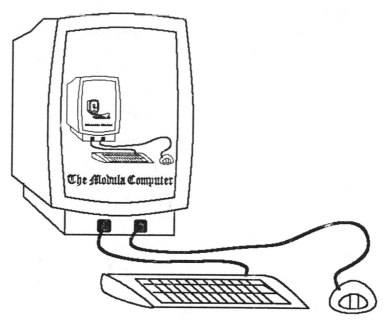

one:

```
for i:=1 to 35 do
    begin
    f(i) := a+b;
    a := b;
    b := f(i)
    end;
```

This is an *iterative* as opposed to a recursive implementation of a recurrence relation. In this case, an iteration will take less time than a recursive routine, since a stack is not used to keep track of the return addresses. There would be thirty-six return addresses on the stack once the above recursion is completed and $f[35]$ is found.

Often a recursive procedure is a way to obtain a concise implementation of a recurrence relation, especially one that is slightly more complex than the above example. Recursion is also often the easier tool to choose. The rule of thumb is to use an iteration instead of recursion if an iteration is easy to set up.

FIGURE 18.2
A Fibonacci Recurrence

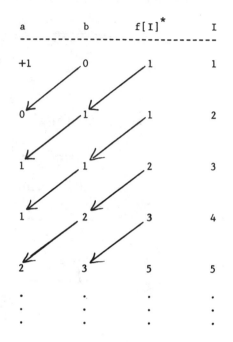

$$f[I] := a + b$$

FIGURE 18.3
A Fibonacci Recursive Procedure

```
Procedure Hoggatt;

F[I] := a+b;

a := b;

b := F[I];

I := I+1;

if I <= 50 then call Hoggatt;

End Proc.
```

There are times when recursive procedures produce beautiful as well as useful results. It is advantageous and desirable to use the recursive stack mechanism to make it easy to do such things as printing the terms of a sequence in forward as well as reverse order. That is, the extra running time demanded by a recursive routine is a small price to pay if a recursive routine produces desirable results, ones obtained dearly with a more complex coding scheme.

Each of the recursive routines we explore in this chapter can be rewritten as nonrecursive iterations. We take advantage of this in the exercises, since it is beneficial to go back and forth, to experiment with recursive vs. nonrecursive iterative routines. Most assemblers make provision for both recursive open as well as closed routines. Macro-11 on the PDP-11 series and VAX-11 Macro on VAX-11 computers are examples.

18.2

RECURSIVE PROCEDURES WITHOUT RECURRENCE RELATIONS

We can set up a recursive procedure that calls itself without having a recurrence relation governing the recursion. This is easy to set up. It is worthwhile to consider such a recursion, since it reveals the recursive procedure

FIGURE 18.4
Graphical Interpretation of a Recursion

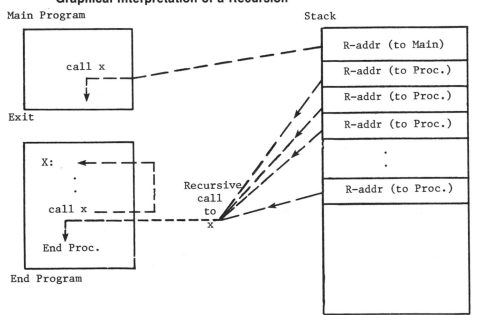

stack usage *without* extra machinery. The basic mechanism at work in a recursive procedure is a stack. Each time a procedure calls itself, a return address (call it R-addr) is pushed onto the stack. The first recursive call will put the R-addr above the return address put on the stack when the recursive routine itself was called, as illustrated in Figure 18.4.

The PC (Program Counter) in each case supplies the particular return address:

calls	*PC-addr*
To proc. X from Main	instruction following call *in* Main
To proc. X from Proc. X	instruction following Proc. call

$$\vdots \qquad\qquad\qquad\qquad\qquad\qquad \vdots$$

In a recursive assembler routine, the RET pops a return address from the stack. This is popped *into* (assigned to) the PC. The first time a return address

FIGURE 18.5
A Bare Bones Recursive Procedure

```
;
;Ref.:   Figure 18.5 (An external recursive procedure w/o a recurrence relation)
;
;Method:
;        Continue the recursion until the count (the x-value) = zero.
;
x:       .long 5

         .entry recurs,0
         decl x
         beql bye
         calls #0,recurs
         writeln <                             Eureka!>
bye:     nop
         ret
         .end



;
;Ref.:   Figure 18.5 (continued)
;
begin    <here:    .word>
         calls #0,recurs
         tumty
         .end here



RUN FG185
                              Eureka!
                              Eureka!
                              Eureka!
```

is popped, control transfers via the PC to the instruction *immediately* following the recursive call instruction. If two recursive calls are made, the above cycle is repeated when execution reaches the RET a second time. This means the process immediately following the recursive call instruction is executed as many times as there were recursive calls made. The last return address popped returns execution to the main program or routine that began the recursion.

We can demonstrate this in terms of a procedure that calls itself while a counter is not zero, as shown in Figure 18.5.

Notice that the printed message Aha! is printed four times since the RECURSE procedure called itself four times. We also print a message exhibiting when control is transferred back to the main program, once the PC is loaded with the final return address. Also, notice that the RECURSE procedure is external, in a file separate from the main program.

18.3
RECURSIVE PROCEDURES WITH RECURRENCE RELATIONS

We can set up an elegant recursive procedure to compute the greatest common divisor (g.c.d.) of a pair of integers. A recurrence relation to do this was suggested by Euclid in the fifth century B.C. The basic idea for this procedure is given in Figure 18.6.

FIGURE 18.6
Euclid's Method

```
Procedure Euclid;

var

    x, y, quotient, remainder:  Integer;


Begin

quotient := x DIV y;

remainder := x MOD y;

y := remainder;

x := y;

if remainder <> 0 then call Euclid

End Proc.
```

The g.c.d. is the last nonzero remainder obtained, namely, Y. In effect,

if R1<>0, compute quotient Q1, R1 remainder from x/y;

compute quotient A2, remainder R2 from y/R1

else   g.c.d. = y

$$\vdots$$

if R(k−1)<>0, compute quotient A(k), remainder R(k) from

R(k−2)/R(k−1)

else   g.c.d. = R(k−1)

This gives the sequence

R(k), R(k−1), R(k−2), . . . , x,y

where each new term of the sequence is defined in terms of the preceding terms (all of them!). We can illustrate this in terms of a pair of friendly numbers (the factors of one friendly number add up to the other number) 220 and 284:

$$
220 \ \frac{1}{\overline{|284}}
$$

$$
\frac{220 \quad\ \ 3}{\text{R1 } 64\,|\,220}
$$

$$
\frac{192 \quad\ \ 2}{\text{R2 } 28\,|\,64}
$$

$$
\frac{56 \quad\ \ 3}{\text{R3 } 8\,|\,28}
$$

$$
\frac{24 \quad 2}{\text{R4 } 4\,|\,8}
$$

$$
\frac{8}{\text{R5 } = 0}
$$

Since R5 = 0, then

R4 = 4 = g.c.d. of 220, 284

since

$$220 = 2^2 * 5 * 11$$
$$284 = 2^2 * 71$$

As a sidelight, notice how "friendly" these numbers are:

$$220 = 1 + 2 + 4 + 71 + 142 \text{ (factors of 284)}$$
$$284 = 1 + 2 + 4 + 5 + 10 + 11 + 20 + 22 + 44 + 55 + 110$$
$$\text{(factors of 220)}$$

Next, Figure 18.7 shows a recursive VAX-11 macro procedure to implement Euclid's method.

What we do next is write a main program that allows us to initialize x and y from a keyboard. Notice that since an NOP follows the recursive call, the repeated return to the instruction immediately following the recursive call does not manifest itself. No action is performed between the recursive call

FIGURE 18.7
Recursive Euclidean Procedure

```
;
;Ref.:  Figure 18.7 (An external recursive procedure for Euclid's method)
;
;Method:
;       Starting with an initial value for x (the divisor) and y (the dividend)
;       the quotient and remainder from y/x are computed, then
;
;                   dividend <-- old divisor
;                   old divisor <-- remainder
;
;       until the remainder = 0.  The last non-zero remainder = g.c.d.

        .global x,y,remainder

;var
        x::         .long
        y::         .long 0
                    .long 0
        quotient:
                    .long
        remainder::
                    .long

        .entry Euclid,0
        ediv x,y,quotient,remainder
        if remainder eql #0 then <jmp bye>
        clrq    y
        movl    x,y
        movl    remainder,x
        calls #0,Euclid
bye:
        nop
        ret
        .end
```

FIGURE 18.8
Implementing Euclid's method

```
;Ref.:  Figure 18.8 (Computing the GCD using an external recursive proc.)
;
;Method:
;       First, we get a pair of integers, assigning entered values to
;       global variables.  The global variable x becomes the divisor in
;       y/x and the algorithm we use to obtain the gcd(greatest common
;       divisor) of x and y goes back to Euclid.  In brief,
;
;                 Obtain remainder from y/x
;                 If the remainder <> 0
;                    then
;
;                                  y <-- x
;                                  x <-- remainder
;
;       and recursively call the Euclid procedure, until remainder = 0.
;       The last non-zero remainder equals the gcd, or the final x-value.

;var
        ans:      .long

        .global x,y,remainder

begin   <here:    .word>

Again:
        write <enter pair of integers to compute gcd:  >
        readvar x,y
        writeln
        writeln
        writeln <--------------------------------------------->
        writeln
        write <The gcd for >
        writeval x,y spaces=3
        write <  is   >
        calls #0,Euclid
        writeval x
        writeln
        writeln <--------------------------------------------->
        write <Again?--enter 1 for yes, 0 for no:  >
        readvar ans
        if ans eql #1 then <jmp again>
        tumty
        .end here
```

Figure 18.8 continued.

```
RUN FG188

enter pair of integers to compute gcd:  32767,7


-----------------------------------------------

The gcd for 32767    7       is    7
-----------------------------------------------
Again?--enter 1 for yes, 0 for no:  1
enter pair of integers to compute gcd:  32768,7


-----------------------------------------------

The gcd for 32768    7       is    1
-----------------------------------------------
Again?--enter 1 for yes, 0 for no:  1
enter pair of integers to compute gcd:  220,284



-----------------------------------------------

The gcd for 220     284       is    4
-----------------------------------------------
Again?--enter 1 for yes, 0 for no:  0
```

and the RET in Figure 18.7. The program that follows allows us to revisit the Euclidean procedure more than once with different pairs of integers, as shown in Figure 18.8.

18.4

RECURSIVE SUBROUTINES

With VAX-11 Macro it is sometimes advantageous to set up a recursive subroutine instead of a procedure. This avoids the use of the cumbersome and, sometimes, clumsy and bothersome stack frame. By using a subroutine instead, we use the system stack only for return addresses. We illustrate this in terms of the Fibonacci recurrence relation. We put it in an internal recursive routine and use registers to take care of the terms of the recurrence relation. The routine for this is shown in Figure 18.9.

This is a busy routine. It does the following:

1. Prints the terms of the Fibonacci sequence in ascending order.
2. Pushes Fibonacci triples onto the stack before each recursive call.
3. Uses the IF/THEN macro to control the recursion.
4. Pops the most recent Fibonacci triple and prints it.
5. Drops through to RET to pop the most recent return address, which

FIGURE 18.9
A Fibonacci Recursive Subroutine

```
;Ref.:  Figure 18.9 (A recursive internal subroutine)
;
;Method:
;       This program relies on the use of the recursive formula
;
;                       f(n) = f(n-1) + f(n-2)
;
;to set up a routine which recurses (calls itself) repeatedly and
;obtains successive terms of the Fibonacci sequence.
;
        .entry here,0
        let r6 := #0                    ;init. f(-1)
        let r7 := #1                    ;init. f(0)
        let r8 := #0                    ;init. r8 for sum
        jsb leaves                      ;call recursive routine
        tumty

leaves:
        add13    r6,r7,r8               ;compute f(n)
        writeval r6,r7,r8               ;print f(n-2),f(n-1),f(n)
        pushr    #^m<r6,r7,r8>          ;save registers
        let      r6 := r7               ;set up Fibonacci recursion:
                                        ;
                                        ;...,1, 0 , 1 , 1 , 2 , ...
                                        ;          /   /
                                        ;         /   /
                                        ;        r6 + r7 = 2
                                        ;
        let      r7 := r8               ;
        if r8 neq #514229 -
                then <jsb leaves>       ;recurse, if new sum < max
                                        ;else
        popr #^m<r6,r7,r8>              ;restore registers
        writeln
        write <                    >
        writeval r6,r7,r8 spaces=5      ;print restored registers
        rsb
        .end here
```

Figure 18.9 continued.

```
0  1  1  1  1  2  1  2  3  2  3  5  3  5  8  5  8  13  8  13  21  13  21  34  21  34  55  34  55  89  55  89  14
4  89  144  233  144  233  377  233  377  610  377  610  987  610  987  1597  987  1597  2584  1597
2584  4181  2584  4181  6765  4181  6765  10946  6765  10946  17711  10946  17711  28657  177
11  28657  46368  28657  46368  75025  46368  75025  121393  75025  121393  196418  121393  1
96418  317811  196418  317811  514229
```

196418	317811	514229
121393	196418	317811
75025	121393	196418
46368	75025	121393
28657	46368	75025
17711	28657	46368
10946	17711	28657
6765	10946	17711
4181	6765	10946
2584	4181	6765
1597	2584	4181
987	1597	2584
610	987	1597
377	610	987
233	377	610
144	233	377
89	144	233
55	89	144
34	55	89
21	34	55
13	21	34
8	13	21
5	8	13
3	5	8
2	3	5
1	2	3
1	1	2
0	1	1

moves the PC to

POPR #^M⟨R6,R7,R8⟩

In effect, this routine will print the same sequence in both ascending and descending order.

18.5

RECURSIVE MACROS

Most macro assemblers support macro definitions that contain recursive macro calls. That is, the macro definition for a macro *X* can include a call

X:

    .MACRO X

       ⋮

    X   ;recursive call

       ⋮

    .ENDM X

In doing so, the arguments associated with a recursive macro call are saved on a stack. Calingaert (1979) calls this a macro expansion stack. Once the last recursive call has been made, the macro in the source text is expanded in terms of the most recent arguments on the macro expansion stack. Once this first expansion is complete, the macro assembler expands the macro in the source text in terms of the next most recent set of arguments on the stack, as shown in Figure 18.10.

We illustrate this in terms of a recurrence relation to compute factorials shown in Figure 18.11.

That is, if we define

$$0: = 1$$

then

$$n! = 1*2*3*4*5* \ldots *(n-1) * n$$

For example,

n	$n!$
0	$0! = 1$
1	$1! = 1$
2	$2! = 1*2 = 2$
3	$3! = 1*2*3 = 6$
4	$4! = 1*2*3*4 = 24$
5	$5! = 1*2*3*4*5 = 120$
6	$6! = 1*2*3*4*5*6 = 720$
⋮	⋮

The above procedure can easily be implemented as either a recursive pro-

FIGURE 18.10
Graphical Interpretation of a Macro Recursion

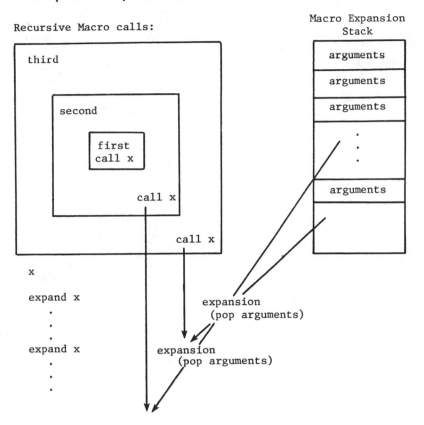

FIGURE 18.11
A Factorial Recursion

```
          Procedure Factorial:

          Begin

          If I<N then

                Begin

                    I  := I+1;

                    F  := F*I;

                    Factorial      (*recursive call*)

                End

          End Proc.
```

cedure or subroutine. It is also easy to compute *n*! without resorting to a recursion, using an iteration like the FOR/DO loop shown earlier for Fibonacci numbers. We leave these interpretations of the factorial recurrence relation for the exercises. Instead, we have chosen to show how the factorial recurrence can be used in a recursive macro (see Figure 18.12). We do this concisely with conditional assembly.

Notice that nothing is calculated or printed during macro assembly except the calculation in

> factorial n − 1

FIGURE 18.12
A Factorial Macro

```
        ,
        ;Ref.:   Figure 18.12 (Recursive macro call)
        ;
        .macro factorial n
        .if ne n
        factorial n-1
        movl     a,r6
        mull2    #n,r6
        movl     r6,a
        .endc
        writeln
        write <              n!>
        write <               >
        writeval a
        .endm factorial

a:      .long 1

        begin <with:          .word>
        factorial 12
        tumty
        .end with

    RUN FG1812

                    12-1-1-1-1-1-1-1-1-1-1-1-1!              1
                    12-1-1-1-1-1-1-1-1-1-1-1!                1
                    12-1-1-1-1-1-1-1-1-1-1!                  2
                    12-1-1-1-1-1-1-1-1-1!            6
                    12-1-1-1-1-1-1-1-1!             24
                    12-1-1-1-1-1-1-1!              120
                    12-1-1-1-1-1-1!               720
                    12-1-1-1-1-1!               5040
                    12-1-1-1-1!           40320
                    12-1-1-1!            362880
                    12-1-1!            3628800
                    12-1!        39916800
                    12!          479001600
```

FIGURE 18.13
Macro Recursion List Module

```
;
;Ref.:   Figure 18.13 (Partial copy of the list file for the factorial
;                 recursion in Figure 18.12)
;
;
                    0000      4      .macro factorial n
                    0000      5      .if ne n
                    0000      6      factorial n-1
                    0000      7      movl        a,r6
                    0000      8      mull2       #n,r6
                    0000      9      movl        r6,a
                    0000     10      .endc
                    0000     11      writeln
                    0000     12      write <          n!>
                    0000     13      write <       >
                    0000     14      writeval a
                    0000     15      .endm factorial
                    0000     16
        00000001    0000     17 a:   .long 1
                    0004     18
                    0004     19      begin <with: .word>
             0000   0004            with:       .word
                    0006     20      factorial 12
        0000000C    0006            .if ne 12
                    0006            factorial 12-1
        0000000B    0006            .if ne 12-1
                    0006            factorial 12-1-1
        0000000A    0006            .if ne 12-1-1
                    0006            factorial 12-1-1-1
        00000009    0006            .if ne 12-1-1-1
                    0006            factorial 12-1-1-1-1
        00000008    0006            .if ne 12-1-1-1-1
                    0006            factorial 12-1-1-1-1-1
        00000007    0006            .if ne 12-1-1-1-1-1
                    0006            factorial 12-1-1-1-1-1-1
        00000006    0006            .if ne 12-1-1-1-1-1-1
                    0006            factorial 12-1-1-1-1-1-1-1
        00000005    0006            .if ne 12-1-1-1-1-1-1-1
                    0006            factorial 12-1-1-1-1-1-1-1-1
        00000004    0006            .if ne 12-1-1-1-1-1-1-1-1
                    0006            factorial 12-1-1-1-1-1-1-1-1-1
        00000003    0006            .if ne 12-1-1-1-1-1-1-1-1-1
                    0006            factorial 12-1-1-1-1-1-1-1-1-1-1
        00000002    0006            .if ne 12-1-1-1-1-1-1-1-1-1-1
                    0006            factorial 12-1-1-1-1-1-1-1-1-1-1-1
        00000001    0006            .if ne 12-1-1-1-1-1-1-1-1-1-1-1
                    0006            factorial 12-1-1-1-1-1-1-1-1-1-1-1-1
        00000000    0006            .if ne 12-1-1-1-1-1-1-1-1-1-1-1-1
                    0006            factorial 12-1-1-1-1-1-1-1-1-1-1-1-1
                    0006            movl        a,r6
                    0006            mull2       #12-1-1-1-1-1-1-1-1-1-1-1-1,r6
                    0006            movl        r6,a
                    0006            .endc
                    001A
                    001A            write <        12-1-1-1-1-1-1-1-1-1-1-1-1!>
```

Continued on following page.

Figure 18.13 continued.

```
                        0049              write <        >
                        005C              writeval a
                        00CA
56    FF32 CF    D0      00CA              movl       a,r6
      56   01    C4      00CF              mull2      #12-1-1-1-1-1-1-1-1-1-1-1,r6
FF29 CF    56    D0      00D2              movl       r6,a
                        00D7              .endc

                        00EB              write <        12-1-1-1-1-1-1-1-1-1-1-1!>
                        0118              write <        >
                        012B              writeval a
                        019B
56    FE61 CF    D0      019B              movl       a,r6
      56   02    C4      01A0              mull2      #12-1-1-1-1-1-1-1-1-1-1,r6
FE58 CF    56    D0      01A3              movl       r6,a
                        01A8              .endc
                        01BC
                        0A12              $EXIT_S
                        0A1B    22        .end with
```

Each call decrements *n* by 1. That value of *n* (the macro argument) is pushed onto the macro expansion stack. The final argument in the last recursive call is

$$12-1-1-1-1-1-1-1-1-1-1-1-1$$

which is zero. This terminates the recursion. The macro assembler then expands the source text in terms of the last argument on the stack. It fleshes out the macro definition in terms of this argument, then the next one, and then the next one, until the argument stack is emptied. The list module for the above program (see Figure 18.13) shows the complete expansion of the factorial macro.

18.6
SUMMARY

Recursive procedures can be used to advantage. This has been shown in terms of concise interpretations of recurrence relations like the one for Euclid's method. They can also be used in terms of the side effects from the restoration of the return addresses put on the stack as a result of the recursive calls. We illustrated this in printing the Fibonacci sequence forwards *and* backwards. A surprising side effect of the factorial macro was the complete rendition of the factorials from 0! to 12!.

We also called attention to possible iterative, nonrecursive procedures to implement recurrence relations. Wirth (1976, p. 130) recommends using an iteration rather than a recursion whenever "there is an *obvious* solution by iteration." He suggests using a recursive procedure whenever algorithms "by their nature are recursive."

18.7

EXERCISES

1. Give a physical model for a recursion.

2. Write a program to find the g.c.d. of a pair of integers using an iteration instead of a recursive procedure. Run your program for

   (a) 65535, 7
   (b) 65535, 5
   (c) 54436, 144
   (d) 144, 65536   (change the order given in [c])

   Note: Comment on the differences between the iterative, nonrecursive procedure and an iterative procedure like the one given in Figure 18.7.

3. Write a recursive macro to implement Euclid's method so that not only is the g.c.d. obtained but also the factors for the beginning pair of integers. Run your program for the pairs of integers in Exercise 2.

4. Write a recursive macro to print the alphabet forwards and backwards.

5. Write a generalization of the macro in exercise 4 that will print the characters in a given string forwards and backwards. Allow the user to enter a string from the keyboard.

6. Write an iterative, nonrecursive procedure to compute factorials. Then write a program using this procedure to print a table of factorials from 0! to 12! Afterward, comment on the differences between your procedure and the one given in Figure 18.12.

7. Suppose we set up the sequence

   $$1, 1, 2, 4, 7, 13, 24, 44, \ldots, T(n)$$

   Call it the Tribonacci sequence, where the terms of the sequence are defined in terms of the recurrence relation

   $$T(n) = T(n-1) + T(n-2) + T(n-3)$$

and

$$T(0) = T(1) = 1 \text{ and } T(2) = 2$$

This sequence was introduced by M. Feinberg (1963, p. 71). Write a recursive procedure to print the Tribonacci sequence forwards and backwards, from T(0) to T(30).

8. Rewrite the program in Figure 18.11 so that the subroutine called LEAVES is made into an external subroutine. Also modify the main program so that

   (a) The user can select the initial values of R6 and R7. This means entering a different pair of adjacent Fibonacci numbers will produce a different part of the Fibonacci sequence.

   (b) Also allow the user to select an upper limit on the sequence, replacing #514229 with a variable (call it MAX).

   (c) Also allow the user to rerun the program for a different set of values (use the technique shown in Figure 18.10).

   Run your program for

   (d) R6 = −1, R7 = 1, MAX = 20.

   (e) R6 = −6, R7 = 5, MAX = 30.

9. Rewrite the program in Figure 18.12 so that the subroutine called LEAVES is made into an external procedure. Then, carry out the steps in (a), (b), (c), (d), (e) in exercise 8.

10. Write an assembly program with an external recursive closed routine (call it BUMP which is either a procedure or subroutine) that is called with a value of

   (a) a variable COUNT

   (b) print COUNT

   (c) increment COUNT

   (d) compare COUNT with a fixed value (a MAX) and recurse (call BUMP), if COUNT < MAX else branch to step (e)

   (e) print COUNT immediately after the recursion

   Run your program for

   (f) COUNT = 0, MAX = 5

   (g) COUNT = 0, MAX = 8

11. Write an assembly program with a recursive closed routine (call it LOP) which

   (a) Is called with a nonempty string with length L.

   (b) Prints L.

   (c) Truncates one character from the string (in effect, decrement L).

   (d) Compares L with MIN (a minimum length).

   (e) If $L >$ MIN, then calls LOP else branch to step (f).

   (f) Prints string and RTS PC.

   Run your program for

   (g) String = 'WITHYWINDLE', MIN = 4.

   (h) String = 'RIVERRUN', MIN = 5.

12. Replace the closed routine in exercise 11 with an open routine to do the same thing. Run your new program with

   (a) Values in part (g) of exercise 11.

   (b) Values in part (h) of exercise 11.

   Also

   (c) Obtain a list file copy of your program with the macro expansions shown.

18.8
LAB PROJECTS

1. Suppose we have a recursive call

       CALL LOP

   for a recursive closed routine called LOP. This routine will

   (a) Prompt for a string, a beginning ASCII code, and value MAX.

   (b) Print the string it receives in the call.

   (c) Attach the ASCII table character to the string and increment the input ASCII code by one. It will wrap around to the beginning of the table (bypass the control characters), if the next ASCII character is a lowercase z.

(d) If the number of attached characters is less than MAX, it will attach the next acceptable ASCII character.

(e) Print the new string.

Write an assembly program to do this. Run your program for

(f) String = 'Tumtytumtytumtoes', BEGIN = 164, MAX = 55.

(g) String = 'GOLDBERRY', BEGIN = 170, MAX = 200.

2. Three integers x, y, z form a Pythagorean triple, if

$$x^2 + y^2 = z^2$$

Pythagorean triples are related to right triangles, where z is the length of the hypotenuse. For example, the triple (3,4,5) gives

```
  4    5
   3
```

The Greek philosopher Plato is credited with finding that for any natural number n

$$2n, n^2 - 1, n^2 + 1$$

form a Pythagorean triple. Write a program to print a table of the first twenty-five of Plato's Pythagorean triples:

n	$2n$	$n^2 - 1$	$n^2 + 1$
1	2	0	2
2	4	3	5
3	6	3	5
$\vdots$	$\vdots$	$\vdots$	$\vdots$

3. In an unpublished paper, G. W. Leibniz (1676) gives a recurrence relation he found that produces Pythagorean triples. He noticed the importance of 1 and 2 in the production of the (3,4,5) triple:

$$2 (2(1)) = 4$$
$$2 (2(1)) - 1 = 3$$

He found that the pair (2,1) can be used to generate a new Pythagorean triple, starting with

$$a = \max (1,2) \qquad b = \min (1,2) + 2 \max (1,2)$$
$$= 2 \qquad\qquad\quad = 1 + 2(2)$$
$$= 2 \qquad\qquad\quad = 5$$

and

$$2ab = 20 \qquad 2ab + 1 = 21$$

The third number of the triple is obtained by computing

$$(2ab)^2 + (2ab+1)^2 = 20^2 + 21^2 = 29$$

and

$$20^2 + 21^2 = 29^2$$

This gives the triple (20,21,29). The numbers (2,5) generate a new triple:

$$a = \max (2,5) \qquad b = \min (2,5) + 2 \max (2,5)$$
$$a = 5 \qquad\qquad\quad b = 2 + 10 = 12$$

The new triple is (120,119,169). In general, the following recurrence relations spring from this:

$$a = \max (\text{preceding } a, \text{ preceding } b)$$
$$b = \min (\text{prec. } a, \text{ prec. } b) + 2 \max (\text{prec. } a, \text{ prec. } b)$$
$$\text{Triple} = (2ab, 2ab+1, (2ab)^2 + (2ab+1)^2)$$

Write a program to print the first twenty-six pairs of Leibniz generators. Produce a table of the form:

a	b	2ab	2ab+1
1	2	4	3
2	5	20	21
5	12	120	119
12	29	696	697
29	70	4060	4061
⋮	⋮	⋮	⋮

18.9

REVIEW QUIZ

Indicate whether the following statements are true or false:

1. A recursive routine is one that calls itself.
2. Both open and closed routines can call themselves.
3. Procedures can call themselves.
4. An iteration can be used to implement a recurrence relation.
5. It is possible to have a recursive procedure without a recurrence relation.
6. Numbers in the Fibonacci sequence can be defined in terms of a recurrence relation.
7. Factorials can be defined in terms of a recurrence relation.
8. Factorials can be computed using a recursive macro.
9. Factorials can be computed using an iterative procedure.
10. Fibonacci numbers can be computed nonrecursively.
11. Recursive procedures can be either internal or external.
12. A queue is used to save the return address during the execution of a recursive subroutine.

18.10

REFERENCES

Aho, A. V., et al., *Data Structures and Algorithms,* Reading, MA: Addison-Wesley, 1983, 65–66.

Calingaert, P. *Assemblers, Compilers, and Program Translation.* Potomac, Md.: Computer Science Press, 1979. See especially sections 4.6 and 5.3.3.

Feinberg, M. "Fibonacci-Tribonacci." *Fibonacci Quarterly* 1, no. 3 (October 1963): 71–74.

Leibniz, G. W. *Leibniz Handscriften,* 35, VIII, 30, fols. 14–15. An untitled manuscript that begins with the words "Theorema a Mariotto."

Pletcher, R. Personal communication, 1983.

Wirth, N. *Algorithms + Data Structures = Programs.* Englewood Cliffs, N.J.: Prentice-Hall, Inc., 1976.

19.
FLOATING POINT NUMBERS

In the beginning, everything was void, and J. H. W. H. Conway began to create numbers.

—D. E. Knuth, *Surreal Numbers*

19.0
AIMS

- Distinguish between fixed point and floating point numbers.
- Introduce excess-128 notation and normalized floating point numbers.
- Give steps used to convert a fixed point number to its VAX-11 F-floating point representation.
- Give steps used to convert an F-floating point bit string to a floating-to-fixed point procedure, and a floating-to-fixed point macro WRITEF.
- Illustrate the use of some of the VAX-11 floating point instructions.

19.1
INTRODUCTION

Up to now we have limited the discussion of numbers to integers and to what are known as *fixed point numbers*. A fixed point number is a number of the form

whole number . fraction part

↑
radix point

We worked with fixed point numbers in chapter 6, using a queue in Figure 6.13 to convert a fixed point number to its fractional equivalent. For example, we found the following to be true:

233/144 = 1.6180556 (base ten)

= 1.9E38E3 (base sixteen)

That is, the fixed point, hex number 1.9538E3 is interpreted as follows:

$$1.9E38E3 \text{ (hex)} = 1 + 9 \times 16^{-1} + E \times 16^{-2} + 3 \times 16^{-3} + 8 \times 16^{-4}$$
$$+ E \times 16^{-5} + 3 \times 16^{-6}$$
$$= .5625$$
$$+ .0546875$$
$$+ .0007324$$
$$+ .0001221$$
$$+ .0000134$$
$$+ .0000002$$
$$= 1.6180556 \text{ (base ten)}$$

In computers with floating point capabilities, a fixed point number would be represented as a floating point number. A number x of the form

$$x = m . B^e$$

is called a floating point number. The coefficient m is called the *mantissa*. The letter B represents the radix or *base*. The letter e represents the *exponent* or *characteristic* of the number. The number m can be a fraction like 0.35 in

$$0.35 \times 10^6$$

We can represent the fixed point number 1.9 (hex), for example, as a floating point number in binary as follows:

$$1.9 \text{ (hex)} = 1.0101 \text{ (binary)}$$
$$= .10101 \times 2^1$$

where 0.10101 (the fractional part m of the floating point number) is the mantissa. With single-precision, 32-bit floating point numbers on a VAX-11, the exponent e is in the interval

$$-2^7 \leq e < +2^7 - 1$$
$$-128 \leq e < +127$$

However, the VAX-11 does *not* store its floating exponents in this range. Instead, it uses what is known as the excess-n notation ($n = 128$) to avoid the problem of negative exponents.

19.2

EXCESS-128 NOTATION

Exponents on floating point numbers in the range

$$-128 \leq e < 127$$

can be adjusted upward so that all exponents are *represented* as positive numbers. This is necessary in a VAX-11, for example, since the sign bit of its floating point numbers is used for the mantissa. To get around the problem of using two sign bits for each floating point number, the *excess-128 notation* is used. That is, each exponent is stored as a sum, itself plus 128. This mechanism gives us the following range for stored exponents:

$$-128 \leq e < +127$$
$$-128 + 128 \leq e + 128 < 127 + 128$$
$$0 \leq e + 128 < 255$$

so that the exponent x in a VAX-11 floating point number will always be in the range

$$0 \leq x = e + 128 < 2^8 - 1$$

This is known as an *excess*-128 or *biased exponent*.

19.3

NORMALIZED FLOATING POINT NUMBERS

The hex number 5.E can be represented in binary in the following ways:

$$5.D = 101 \cdot 1101$$
$$= 10 \cdot 11101 \times 2^1$$
$$= 1 \cdot 011101 \times 2^2$$
$$= .1011101 \times 2^3 \quad \text{(normalized)}$$
$$= .01011101 \times 2^4 \quad \text{(nonnormalized)}$$

The radix point "floats" as we adjust the exponent, on successive lines. The floating point number

$$.1011101 \times 2^3$$

is *normalized*, since its most significant bit is nonzero. Floating point numbers on a VAX-11 are always normalized. Why? Since it is known that the most significant bit of a floating point fraction is 1, it does not have to be used in the representation of the number. That is, when a floating point number is stored inside a VAX-11, the leading 1 is not used. It is understood. This means a floating point number with x bits for the mantissa actually have $x + 1$ bits in their representations of floating point numbers. This adds to the accuracy of each representation, since the leading bit is understood, although it is not stored in one of the bits of a floating point number. For example, with an F-floating (single-precision) number on a VAX-11, 23 bits are used for the mantissa. Since the leading, most significant bit (a 1) is left off, 24 bits are available for fractions.

This tells us about two key features of the mantissa of every VAX-11 floating point number. First, the mantissa is always a fraction. Second, since the most significant bit is always 1, this tells about the range of the mantissa m:

$$.1_2 < m < 1$$

Since

$$.1_2 = 1 \times 2^{-1} = 1/2 = 0.5$$

which gives us

$$0.5 < m < 1$$

19.4

VAX-11 FLOATING POINT NUMBERS

On a VAX-11 computer, there are four floating point data types. The structure of two of these data types is shown in Figure 19.1.

In addition to the F-floating and D-floating types, VAX-11s have two

FIGURE 19.1
VAX-11 Single and Double Floating Point Types

Single-precision (F-floating with 32 bits):

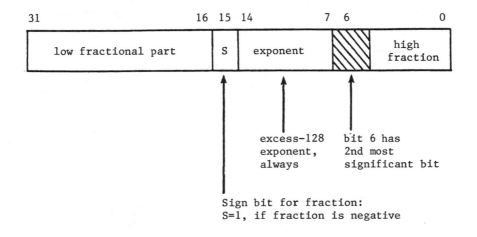

Double-precision (D-floating with 64 bits):

additional extended precision floating point types. It has a quadword G-floating point type. It has an 11-bit exponent, which contrasts with the 8-bit exponent for the D-floating type. This means 3 less bits are used for the fraction of the G-floating type. That is, the G-floating type uses 52 bits for its fractions, which contrasts with 55 bits for the mantissa of the D-floating type. Finally, there is a double quadword H-floating point data type. This type uses 15 bits for exponents, 112 bits for the mantissa. The features of these floating point data types are summarized in Table 19.1.

To get an idea of the range of the numbers, use the number of bits available for the exponent in terms of powers of 2. For example, to compute the range of numbers for the F-floating point type, use

$$2^{-128} \le number < 2^{127}$$

$$2.9387 \times 10^{-39} \le number < 1.70141 \times 10^{38}$$

Since the G-floating point numbers have 11 exponent bits, this gives us

$$2^{10} \; 2^9 \; 2^8 \; 2^7 \; \ldots \; 2^1 \; 2^0$$
$$\uparrow$$
maximum G-floating exponent

$$= 2048$$

This puts the G-floating point numbers in the following range:

$$2^{-2048} \le number < 2^{2048}$$

$$.56 \times 10^{-308} \le number < .9 \times 10^{308}$$

With the H-floating type, we have a full 15 bits for the exponent. Computing the range for these numbers is left as an exercise.

In this chapter we show how to use the F-floating data type *without* relying on a higher-level language to carry out floating-to-fixed point conversions that can be printed. This floating point data type has been fully implemented in terms of a procedure called DECIMAL written in assembly language to print out F-type numbers (this is given in IO.MAR in Appendix

TABLE 19.1
VAX-11 Floating Point Data Types

Data Type	Mantissa Bits	Exponent Bits	Significant Digits
F	23 + 1	8	7
D	55 + 1	8	16
G	52 + 1	11	15
H	112 + 1	15	33

FIGURE 19.2
Conversion of a Floating Point Number to F-floating

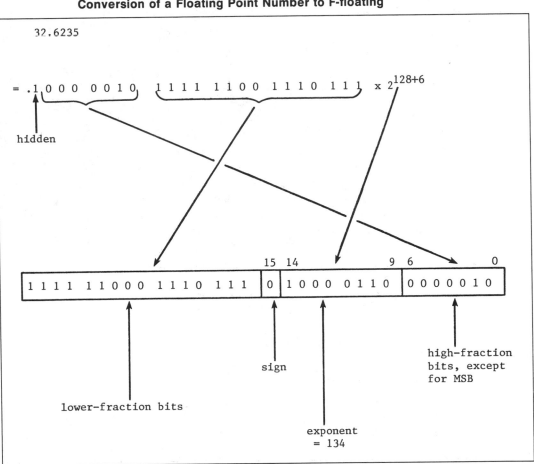

C). We have also developed a macro WRITEF to facilitate the use of the decimal procedure (this is also given in the PAS.MAR macro library in Appendix C). We explain these later. First, we look at the structure of a single-precision F-type number in two examples.

Suppose we have the following representations of 32.6235:

$$32.6235 \text{ (decimal)} = 20.FB3B8 \text{ (hex)}$$
$$= 10\ 0000\ .\ 1011\ 1111\ 0011\ 1011\ 1000_2$$
$$= .10\ 0000\ 1011\ 1111\ 0011\ 1011\ 1000 \times 2^6$$

This is a normalized floating point representation of 32.6235 (decimal). The next trick is to add excess-128 to the exponent. Then we want to split off the top 8 most significant bits of the fraction, putting all but the most significant bit into the lower 7 bits of a longword, as shown in Figure 19.2.

The VAX-11 storage directive .FLOAT sets aside a longword for a floating point number. In the above example, we could include the above fixed point number in the following scheme:

x: .float 32.6235, −2.67, 1.61764

This sets aside three longwords, one for each of the fixed point numbers shown. These fixed point numbers will be stored inside the machine in floating point form like that shown in Figure 19.2. To get at the original fixed point numbers, given the binary floating point form, takes skill. There are two things to remember before we illustrate how to "unscramble" the binary representation of a floating point number. First, we need to append the missing (hidden) most significant bit to the fraction we will *construct*. Second, we need to do what the processor does with the exponent: subtract the 128.

Suppose we have the following binary floating point number stored in a longword on a VAX-11:

0000 1111 0000 1111 0100 0000 1100 1111

Figure 19.3 shows the analysis of this bit string.

TABLE 19.2
VAX-11 Floating Point Instructions

Instruction	Interpretation
addx2 source-x, dest-x	dest-x ← (dest-x) + (source-x)
addx3 add$_1$-x, add$_2$-x, dest-x	dest-x ← add$_1$-x + add$_2$-x
clrx dest-x	Clear bits of destination
cmpx source-x, dest-x	Adjust condition codes in terms
cvtxy source-x, dest-y	Put copy of type x into destination operand of type y
divx2 divisor, dest-x	dest-x ← dest-x/divisor
divx3 divisor, dividend, quotient	
mnegx source-x, dest-x	Put twos complement of source-x into destination-x
movax source-x, dest-x	dest-x ← address of source-x
movx source-x, dest-x	Put copy of source in destination
mulx2 fac$_1$x, fac$_2$x	fac$_2$x ← fac$_2$x times fac$_1$x
mulx3 fac1x, fac2x, product-x	
pushax ele-x	address of element-x pushed
subx2 source-x, dest-x	dest-x ← (dest-x) − (source-x)
subx3 sub$_1$x, sub$_2$x, dest-x	dest-x ← (sub$_2$x) − (sub$_1$x)

Note:
x = f,d,g,h   y = f,d,g,h

FIGURE 19.3
Conversion of an F-floating to a Decimal Number

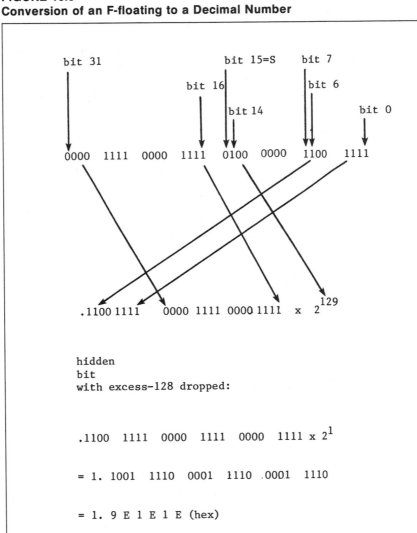

The *hidden bit* (the most significant bit) in the normalized floating point number in the above example has been put back to determine the fixed point number represented by a VAX-11 floating point number.

The VAX-11 has a complete set of floating point instructions in its repertoire, some of which are listed in Table 19.2.

19.5

FLOATING TO FIXED POINT PROCEDURE

Among the instructions in Table 19.1, one of the most useful ones is the CVTFL (ConVerT Floating point to Long) instruction, which puts a copy of the integer part of an F-floating number into a longword destination. We use this instruction to convert a floating point number to its fixed point equivalent in the procedure shown in Figure 19.4.

This procedure uses the following steps:

1. Initialize R7 with the number of places to the right of the radix point; FBASE with the radix of the fixed point number.

2. Isolate the whole number part and print it:

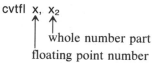

FIGURE 19.4
Floating to Fixed Point Procedure

```
        ;
        ;Ref.:   Figure 19.4 (Floating-to-fixed point procedure)

                .ENABLE GBL
        ;
FBASE:: .FLOAT                                  ;floating pt form of base
X1::    .FLOAT                                  ;convient variable
Y1::    .FLOAT                                  ;convient variable
X2::    .LONG                                   ;convient variable

                .ENTRY DECIMAL,^M<R7>
                MOVL       #5,R7                ;no. of places to rt of
                CVTLF      BASE,FBASE           ;base-value from io.mar
                MOVF       4(AP),X1             ;get floating pt operand
                CVTFL      X1,X2                ;get integer part
                WRITEVAL X2,SPACES=0            ;print it
                CVTLF      X2,Y1                ;get original floating no.
                SUBF2      Y1,X1                ;drop integer part
                BEQL       BYE                  ;if diff. zero, exit
                                                ;else
                WRITE      <.>                  ;write
LOOP1:          MULF2      FBASE,X1             ;get fraction digit
                CVTFL      X1,X2                ;get whole part=digit
                WRITEVAL X2,SPACES=0            ;print digit
                CVTLF      X2,Y1                ;get old floating no.
                SUBF2      Y1,X1                ;drop whole part
                SOBGTR     R7,LOOP1             ;do until r7=0
BYE:            RET
        ;
                .END
```

3. Convert the whole number part back to a second floating point operand (call it $y1$):

```
cvtlf x₂, y₁
```

4. Subtract to isolate the fractional part of the floating point number:

$$x_1 := x_1 - y_1 \quad (\text{now, } x_1 = \text{fraction})$$

or

```
subf2 y₁, x₁
```

5. Print a '.'

6. Isolate first digit to right of radix point:

```
mulf2   fbase, x1
cvtf1   x1, x2
```

7. Print $x2$ (the first fractional digit!).

8. Convert fractional digit back to floating point format *and* diminish size of floating point number in $x1$ (to isolate next digit *immediately* to the right of the radix point):

```
cvtlf   x2, y1
subf2   y1, x1
```

9. Repeat step 6 until count = 0.

It is possible to increase the number of significant digits printed by increasing the count in R7. In single precision, seven significant digits are available. To use this procedure, use

```
movf ⟨floating point number⟩, −(sp)
```

which will put a copy of the floating point number on the system stack. This procedure is demonstrated in Figure 19.5. In this program, which we have kept simple, we play with some of the instructions in Table 19.1. In the next section, we show an implementation of this idea in a WRITEF macro.

FIGURE 19.5
A Program with a Fixed Point Result

```
;Ref.:  Figure 19.5 (A program with a fixed point result)

;Method: To produce a fixed point result by dividing one integer
;        by another, using floating point instructions.  In doing this,
;        integers stored in longwords are first converted to floating
;        point operands, then division is carried out in terms of these
;        floating point operands stored in r6 and r7.  The floating-to-
;        fixed point procedure called decimal ( in io.mar in Appendix C)
;        is used to print the floating point result in x as a fixed point
;        number, in base 10.

;var

        x:       .float
        y:       .long 832040
        z:       .long 1346269

Begin:  .word

        writeln <----------------------------------------------->
        writeln
        writeval z
        write <  :            >
        writeval y
        write <  =            >

        cvtlf    y,r6                      ;r6 has floating pt operand
        cvtlf    z,r7                      ;r7 has floating pt operand
        divf3    r6,r7,x                   ;x <-- r7/r6
        movf     x,-(sp)                   ;push procedure argument
        calls    #1,decimal                ;print fixed point result

        $exit_s

        .end     Begin

RUN FG195

---------------------------------------------

1346269          :            832040          = 1.61803
```

19.6

A FLOATING POINT OUTPUT MACRO

A sample floating point output macro is shown in Figure 19.6.

This is included in the advanced macro library PAS.MAR in Appendix C. We bring these ideas together in the next example. The sequence of

Fibonacci numbers

$$1, 1, 2, 3, 5, 8, 13, \ldots, f(n)$$

can be used to produce approximations of the golden ratio. The ratio

$$\frac{1 + 5^{1/2}}{2} = 1.618033989$$

is called the *golden ratio*. Its reciprocal

$$\frac{2}{1 + 5^{1/2}} = 0.618033989$$

is called the *golden section*. For centuries it has been a favorite tool of architects, artists, and sculptors in deciding how to subdivide spaces. A. F. Horadam (1963, p. 41) has reported that psychologists have found that the most pleasing subdivision of space is based on the golden section.

By taking successive ratios of Fibonacci numbers, we can produce a good example of just about everything we have discussed so far about both procedures and floating point numbers (see Figure 19.7).

A natural extension to this program is to write a golden section procedure. This time, instead of using

$$f(n)/f(n-1) \qquad \text{(divide larger by smaller no.)}$$

we would use

$$f(n-1)/f(n) \qquad \text{(divide smaller by larger no.)}$$

This is left as an exercise.

In the above program, it is important to notice that the NOS array contains longwords, the members of the Fibonacci sequence. When a ratio of a pair of these numbers is to be computed, it is necessary to convert them

FIGURE 19.6
Floating to Fixed Point Macro

```
            macro writef value, spaces=1

            movf value,-(SP)

            calls #1,decimal

            space- spaces

            .endm writef
```

FIGURE 19.7
Approximating the Golden Ratio

```
;
;Ref.:   Figure 19.7 (Approximating the golden ratio)

;Method: Obtain successive approximations to the golden ratio by
;        using successive pairs of Fibonacci numbers.  We use the
;        following steps: (1)build the Fibonacci sequence:

;                         x      y       sum
;                         1 <--- 1 <---- 2 = f(2)
;                         1 <--- 2 <---- 3 = f(3)
;                         2 <--- 3 <---- 5 = f(5)

;        storing the sums in the nos-array, then (2) compute successive
;        fractions:

;                         f(3)/f(2) = 3/2 = 1.5
;                         f(5)/f(3) = 5/3 = 1.66666

;        storing these fractions in the almost-gold array and, finally,
;        (3) printing a partial copy of the two arrays.

;var

        almost_gold:    .blkl 40                ;array for fractions
        nos:            .blkl 40                ;array for Fibonacci nos
arg_list:
        place:          .long nos               ;address for nos array
        gold:           .long almost_gold       ;address for fractions
arg:
        .long    2                              ;no. of arguments
        .address place,gold                     ;argument references

Begin:  .word

        callg   arg,Fibonacci_nos               ;build Fibonacci seq.
        callg   arg,golden_ratio                ;build fraction seq.
        callg   arg,copy                        ;print results

        $exit_s

        sum:    .long 0                         ;f(n)
        x:      .long 1                         ;f(n-1)
        y:      .long 1                         ;f(n-2)

index1: .long   1

        .entry  Fibonacci_nos, ^m<r6>

        movl    @4(ap),r6                       ;assertion: this moves
                                                ;addr. of nos. array
                                                ;into r6 (verify)

do:
        addl3   x,y,sum                         ;f(n)=f(n-1)+f(n-2)
```

Figure 19.7 continued.

```
        movl    sum,(r6)+                       ;save f(n)
        movl    y,x
        movl    sum,y
        acbl    #30,#1,index1,do

        ret

index2: .long   1

        .entry  golden_ratio, ^m<r6,r7>

        movl    @4(ap),r6                       ;r6 gets nos array addr
        movl    @8(ap),r7                       ;r7 gets frac array addr

ratio:

        cvtlf   (r6),r9                         ;float for f(n-2) in r9
        cvtlf   4(r6),r10                       ;float for f(n-1) in r10
        divf3   r9,r10,r8                       ;compute f(n-1)/f(n-2)
        movf    r8,(r7)+                        ;save frac in array
        addl2   #4,r6                           ;adjust array selector
        acbl    #24,#1,index2,ratio

        ret

index3: .long   1

        .entry  copy,^m<r6,r7>

        movl    @4(ap),r6                       ;r6 gets nos array addr
        movl    @8(ap),r7                       ;r7 gets frac array addr

sequence:

        write <  >                              ;tab
        writeval 4(r6)                          ;print f(n)
        write <  :       >                      ;tab, : ,tab
        writeval (r6)                           ;print f(n-1)
        write <  =       >                      ;tab, = ,tab
        writef   (r7)                           ;print fraction
        addl2   #4,r6                           ;adjust nos selector
        addl2   #4,r7                           ;adjust frac selector
        writeln                                 ;<ret>
        acbl    #10,#1,index3,sequence

        ret

        .end Begin
```

Continued on following page.

Figure 19.7 continued.

RUN FG197

3	:	2	=	1.50000
5	:	3	=	1.66666
8	:	5	=	1.60000
13	:	8	=	1.62500
21	:	13	=	1.61538
34	:	21	=	1.61904
55	:	34	=	1.61764
89	:	55	=	1.61818
144	:	89	=	1.61797
233	:	144	=	1.61805

to floating point operands first. In the ratio loop inside the golden ratio procedure, this is the first thing we do:

cvtlf (r6), r9

cvtlf 4(r6), r10

19.7

SUMMARY

The distinction between *fixed point* and *floating point* numbers underlies what we do in this chapter. We think in terms of fixed point numbers. Computers with floating point processing capabilities represent fixed point numbers in floating point form. For the sake of efficiency, all floating point numbers are normalized inside a VAX-11. The most significant bit does *not* appear in the longword used to hold an F-floating point number. It is understood. It is always 1. This explains the interval for floating point fractions:

$$0.5 \leq m < 1$$
$$\uparrow$$
$$.1 \ (\text{binary}) = 1 \times 2^{-1} = 1/2$$

The most significant bit remains hidden in each of the other floating point types on a VAX-11. This gives us an extra bit to be used for the fractional part of a floating point number.

The mechanism used by the floating point procedure, called decimal, hinges on the use of the VAX-11 convert instructions. This is really the first time that the full power of these instructions becomes apparent. A CVTFL gives us a way to isolate the integer part of a floating point number. Once we can do this it becomes easy to isolate the digits of the fractional part of a floating point number.

The use of the excess-128 method with floating point exponents simplifies the representation of a floating point number. Without this method, we would need to maintain two sign bits, one for the fractional part and one for the exponent.

The WRITEF macro simplifies our use of the decimal procedure. Its usage hinges on the production of floating point results that can be fed to this macro. We illustrated how to do this in Figure 19.7.

Finally, it is helpful to be able to take a fixed point number and rewrite it in floating point form in base two. Then, it is necessary to separate out the 8 most significant bits of the fraction, and begin forming a longword representation of the floating point number. It is equally helpful to be able to interpret (unscramble) a floating point number contained inside longwords of a memory dump or copies in binary of floating point operands. Doing both of these things *by hand* helps. The secrets of the machine tend to reveal themselves in this way.

19.8

EXERCISES

1. Convert the following fixed point numbers to floating point form, *before* they are put into VAX-11 longwords:

   (a) 1.6

   (b) 52.3581

   (c) −7197.99999

   (d) .5

   (e) −.5917

   (f) 5917.5917

2. Give the VAX-11 F-floating representations of the floating point numbers in exercise 1.

3. Convert the following F-floating operands to their equivalent decimal, fixed point forms:

   (a) 1111 1100 1110 1000 0110 0000

   (b) 1111 1110 0111 0100 0011 0010 0010

   (c) 1110 0011 1001 0010 0000 0110 0111

   (d) 1111 0011 1101 0001 0000 0011 0011

4. Give the hex, fixed point equivalents of the floating point numbers in exercise 3.

5. Give the binary, floating point equivalent of the floating point numbers in exercise 3.

Note: Remove the excess-128.

6. Why is the excess-128 notation used?

7. What happens to the most significant bit of a floating point fraction when a floating point number is stored as a VAX-11 floating point operand?

8. With an F-floating number, how many bits are available for the fraction? Which ones?

9. Write an assembly language program to do the following:

   (a) Obtain the ages of persons in the room.

   (b) Print out the average age.

10. The number e is known as the Euler number. It is approximately equal to 2.71828. To obtain a better approximation of e we can use the following series:

$$e = 1 + 1/1 + 1/2! + 1/3! + 1/4! + \ldots$$

(The denominators are factorials, explained in chapter 18.) Write an assembly program to approximate e using this summation.

11. Write an assembly program to estimate the value of pi, using the formula

$$\text{pi}/4 = 1 - 1/3 + 1/5 - 1/7 + 1/9 - 1/11 + \ldots$$

12. Give the range for numbers for (a) D-floating point numbers on a VAX-11 and (b) H-floating point numbers on a VAX-11.

13. The following is a selection of fixed point numbers stored as floating point numbers using the .FLOAT directive:

        x: .float 2.7, 3715.199, 27.919

Write an assembly program to print out only the whole number parts of these numbers. In effect, verify that CVTFL isolates the whole number part of a floating point number.

14. In terms of the longword used to store an F-floating point number, give the bits of a longword used to store

$$1.70141 \times 10^{38}$$

15. What is printed by the following program:

```
BAIT:       .FLOAT
HOOK:       .FLOAT
FISH:       .FLOAT
DINNER:     .LONG
BEGIN:      .WORD
            MOVF        #16.1,BAIT
            MOVF        #16.9,HOOK
            ADDF3       BAIT,HOOK,FISH
            CVTFL       FISH,DINNER
            WRITEVAL    DINNER
            $EXIT_S
            .END BEGIN
```

16. What is printed by the following program:

```
NUM:        .FLOAT
SUM:        .FLOAT
ANSWER:     .LONG
BEGIN:      .WORD
            .REPT       5
            ADDF2       #0.7,NUM
            ADDF2       NUM,SUM
            .ENDR
            DIVF2       #5,SUM
            CVTFL       SUM,ANSWER
            WRITEVAL    ANSWER
            $EXIT_S
            .END BEGIN
```

19.9

LAB PROJECTS

1. Enhance the program in Figure 19.7, so that

   (a) The user can enter the beginning pair of numbers used to start building the NOS array (that is, the values of x and y).

(b) Print out the successive ratios and the difference between the preceding one and the current one.

(c) Increase the number of digits printed out to the right of the radix point.

(d) Allow the user to choose the base (radix) to use in printing out the ratios.

Run your program for

(e) $x = 144$, $y = 233$, radix $= 16$

Note: It will be necessary to modify the decimal procedure to do this.

2. Enhance the WRITEF macro to allow for the printing of floating point numbers in radices besides base ten.

3. Enhance the program in Figure 8.9 so that the following table is printed out:

1/1	1
1/1 + 1/3	1.33333
1/1 + 1/3 + 1/6	1.5
1/1 + 1/3 + 1/6 + 1/10	1.6
1 + 1/3 + 1/6 + 1/10 + 1/15	1.066667
1 + 1/3 + 1/6 + 1/10 + 1/16 + 1/21	1.114286

Run your program in terms of the first 20 triangular numbers.

19.10
REVIEW QUIZ

Indicate whether the following statements are true or false:

1. Fixed point numbers have a mantissa.

2. Every fixed point number has a fraction part.

3. The coefficient of a floating point number is called the mantissa.

4. VAX-11s use excess-128 notation to store single-precision, floating point exponents.

5. An excess-128 notation is also called a biased exponent.

6. VAX-11 floating point numbers are normalized; that is, the leading digit of the coefficient is always zero.

7. The leading digit of the coefficient of a floating point number is not stored inside a VAX-11.

8. The mantissa of a VAX-11 floating point number is always a fraction.

9. On a VAX-11, there are four floating point data types.

10. CVTFL puts a copy of the integer part of a VAX-11 F-floating point number into a longword destination.

19.11

REFERENCES

Horadam, A. F. "Further Appearance of the Fibonacci Sequence." *Fibonacci Quarterly* 1 (December 1963).

Knuth, D. E. *Surreal Numbers*. Reading, Mass.: Addison-Wesley, 1974.

Appendix A
VAX-11 INSTRUCTION SET

VAX-11 OPCODES (ALPHABETIC ORDER)

Hexadecimal Value	Mnemonic	Functional Name
9D	ACBB	Add compare and branch byte
6F	ACBD	Add compare and branch D_floating
4F	ACBF	Add compare and branch F_floating
4FFD	ACBG	Add compare and branch G_floating
6FFD	ACBH	Add compare and branch H_floating
F1	ACBL	Add compare and branch long
3D	ACBW	Add compare and branch word
58	ADAWI	Add aligned word interlocked
80	ADDB2	Add byte 2 operand
81	ADDB3	Add byte 3 operand
60	ADDD2	Add D_floating 2 operand
61	ADDD3	Add D_floating 3 operand
40	ADDF2	Add F_floating 2 operand
41	ADDF3	Add F_floating 3 operand
40FD	ADDG2	Add G_floating 2 operand
41FD	ADDG3	Add G_floating 3 operand
60FD	ADDH2	Add H_floating 2 operand
61FD	ADDH3	Add H_floating 3 operand
CO	ADDL2	Add long 2 operand
C1	ADDL3	Add long 3 operand
20	ADDP4	Add packed 4 operand
21	ADDP6	Add packed 6 operand
A0	ADDW2	Add word 2 operand
A1	ADDW3	Add word 3 operand
D8	ADWC	Add with carry
F3	AOBLEQ	Add one and branch on less or equal
F2	AOBLSS	Add one and branch on less
78	ASHL	Arithmetic shift long
F8	ASHP	Arithmetic shift and round packed
79	ASHQ	Arithmetic shift quad

Hexadecimal

Value	Mnemonic	Functional Name
E1	BBC	Branch on bit clear
E5	BBCC	Branch on bit clear and clear
E7	BBCCI	Branch on bit clear and clear interlocked
E3	BBCS	Branch on bit clear and set
E0	BBS	Branch on bit set
E4	BBSC	Branch on bit set and clear
E2	BBSS	Branch on bit set and set
E6	BBSSI	Branch on bit set and set interlocked
1E	BCC	Branch on carry clear
1F	BCS	Branch on carry set
13	BEQL	Branch on equal
13	BEQLU	Branch on equal unsigned
18	BGEQ	Branch on greater or equal
1E	BGEQU	Branch on greater or equal unsigned
14	BGTR	Branch on greqter
1A	BGTRU	Branch on greater unsigned
8A	BICB2	Bit clear byte 2 operand
8B	BICB3	Bit clear byte 3 operand
CA	BICL2	Bit clear long 2 operand
CB	BICL3	Bit clear long 3 operand
B9	BICPSW	Bit clear program status word
AA	BICW2	Bit clear word 2 operand
AB	BICW3	Bit clear word 3 operand
88	BISB2	Bit set byte 2 operand
89	BISB3	Bit set byte 3 operand
C8	BISL2	Bit set long 2 operand
C9	BISL3	Bit set long 3 operand
B8	BISPSW	Bit set program status word
A8	BISW2	Bit set word 2 operand
A9	BISW3	Bit set word 3 operand
93	BITB	Bit test byte
D3	BITL	Bit test long
B3	BITW	Bit test word
E9	BLBC	Branch on low bit clear
E8	BLBS	Branch on low bit set
15	BLEQ	Branch on less or equal
1B	BLEQU	Branch on less or equal unsigned
19	BLSS	Branch on less
1F	BLSSU	Branch on less unsigned
12	BNEQ	Branch on not equal
12	BNEQU	Branch on not equal unsigned
03	BPT	Break poiint trap
11	BRB	Branch with byte displacement
31	BRW	Branch with word displacement
10	BSBB	Branch to subroutine with byte displacement
30	BSBW	Branch to subroutine with word displacment
1C	BVC	Branch on overflow clear
1D	BVS	Branch on overflow set

Hexadecimal Value	Mnemonic	Functional Name
FA	CALLG	Call with general argument list
FB	CALLS	Call with stack
8F	CASEB	Case byte
CF	CASEL	Case long
AF	CASEW	Case word
BD	CHME	Change mode to executive
BC	CHMK	Change mode to kernel
BE	CHMS	Change mode to supervisor
BF	CHMU	Change mode to user
94	CLRB	Clear byte
7C	CLRD	Clear D_floating
DF	CLRF	Clear F_floating
7C	CLRG	Clear G_floating
7CFD	CLRH	Clear H_floating
D4	CLRL	Clear long
7CFD	CLRO	Clear octa
7C	CLRQ	Clear quad
B4	CLRW	Clear word
91	CMPB	Compare byte
29	CMPC3	Compare character 3 operand
2D	CMPC5	Compare character 5 operand
71	CMPD	Compare D_floating
51	CMPF	Compare F_floating
51FD	CMPG	Compare G_floating
71FD	CMPH	Compare H_floating
D1	CMPL	Compare long
35	CMPP3	Compare packed 3 operand
37	CMPP4	Compare packed 4 operand
EC	CMPV	Compare field
B1	CMPW	Compare word
ED	CMPZV	Compare zero-extended field
OB	CRC	Calculate cyclic redundancy check
6C	CVTBD	Convert byte to D_floating
4C	CVTBF	Convert byte to F_floating
4CFD	CVTBG	Convert byte to G_floating
6CFD	CVTBH	Convert byte to H_floating
98	CVTBL	Convert byte to long
99	CVTBW	Convert byte to word
68	CVTDB	Convert D_floating to byte
76	CVTDF	Convert D_floating to F_floating
32FD	CVTDH	Convert D_floating to H_floating
6A	CVTDL	Convert D_floating to long
69	CVTDW	Convert D_floating to word
48	CVTFB	Convert F_floating to byte
56	CVTFD	Convert F_floating to D_floating
99FD	CVTFG	Convert F_floating to G_floating
98FD	CVTFH	Convert F_floating to H_floating
4A	CVTFL	Convert F_floating to long

Hexadecimal Value	Mnemonic	Functional Name
49	CVTFW	Convert F_floating to word
48FD	CVTGB	Convert G_floating to byte
33FD	CVTGF	Convert G_floating to F_floating
56FD	CVTGH	Convert G_floating to H_floating
4AFD	CVTGL	Convert G_floating to long
49FD	CVTGW	Convert G_floating to word
68FD	CVTHB	Convert H_floating to byte
F7FD	CVTHD	Convert H_floating to D_floating
F6FD	CVTHF	Convert H_floating to F_floating
76FD	CVTHG	Convert H_floating to G_floating
6AFD	CVTHL	Convert H_floating to long
69FD	CVTHW	Convert H_floaitng to word
F6	CVTLB	Convert long to byte
6E	CVTLD	Convert long to D_floating
4E	CVTLF	Convert long to F_floating
4EFD	CVTLG	Convert long to G_floating
6EFD	CVTLH	Convert long to H_floating
F9	CVTLP	Convert long to packed
F7	CVTLW	Convert long to word
36	CVTPL	Convert packed to long
08	CVTPS	Convert packed to leading separate
24	CVTPT	Convert packed to trailing
6B	CVTRDL	Convert rounded D_floating to long
4B	CVTRFL	Convert rounded F_floating to long
4BFG	CVTRGL	Convert rounded G_floating to long
6BFD	CVTRHL	Convert rounded H_floating to long
09	CVTSP	Convert leading separate to packed
26	CVTTP	Convert trailing to packed
33	CVTWB	Convert word to byte
6D	CVTWD	Convert word to D_floating
4D	CVTWF	Convert word to F_floating
4DFD	CVTWG	Convert word to G_floating
6DFD	CVTWH	Convert word to H_floating
32	CVTWL	Convert word to long
97	DECB	Decrement byte
D7	DECL	Decrement long
B7	DECW	Decrement word
86	DIVB2	Divide byte 2 operand
87	DIVB3	Divide byte 3 operand
66	DIVD2	Divide D_floating 2 operand
67	DIVD3	Divide D_floating 3 operand
46	DIVF2	Divide F_floating 2 operand
47	DIVF3	Divide F_floating 3 operand
46FD	DIVG2	Divide G_floating 2 operand
47FD	DIVG3	Divide G_floating 3 operand
66FD	DIVH2	Divide H_floating 2 operand
67FD	DIVH3	Divide H_floating 3 operand
C6	DIVL2	Divide long 2 operand
C7	DIVL3	Divide long 3 operand

Hexadecimal Value	Mnemonic	Functional Name
27	DIVP	Divide packed
A6	DIVW2	Divide word 2 operand
A7	DIVW3	Divide word 3 operand
38	EDITPC	Edit packed to character
7B	EDIV	Extended divide
74	EMODD	Extended modulus D_floating
54	EMODF	Extended modulus F_floating
54FD	EMODG	Extended modulus G_floating
74FD	EMODH	Extended modulus H_floating
7A	EMUL	Extended multiply
EE	EXTV	Extract field
EF	EXTZV	Extract zero-extended field
EB	FFC	Find first clear bit
EA	FFS	Find first set bit
00	HALT	Halt
96	INCB	Increment byte
D6	INCL	Increment long
B6	INCW	Increment word
0A	INDEX	Index calculation
5C	INSQHI	Insert into queue at head, interlocked
5D	INSQTI	Insert into queue at tail, interlocked
0E	INSQUE	Insert into queue
F0	INSV	Insert field
17	JMP	Jump
16	JSB	Jump to subroutine
06	LDPCTX	Load program context
3A	LOCC	Locate character
39	MATCHC	Match characters
92	MCOMB	Move complemented byte
D2	MCOML	Move complemented long
B2	MCOMW	Move complemented word
DB	MFPR	Move from processor register
8E	MNEGB	Move negated byte
72	MNEGD	Move negated D_floating
52	MNEGF	Move negated F_floating
52FD	MNEGG	Move negated G_floating
72FD	MNEGH	Move negated H_floating
CE	MNEGL	Move negated long
AE	MNEGW	Move negated word
9E	MOVAB	Move address of byte
7E	MOVAD	Move address of D_floating
DE	MOVAF	Move address of F_floating
7E	MOVAG	Move address of G_floating
7EFD	MOVAH	Move address of H_floaitng
DE	MOVAL	Move address of long
7EFD	MOVAO	Moe address of octa
7E	MOVAQ	Move address of quad
3E	MOVAW	Move address of word

Hexadecimal Value	Mnemonic	Functional Name
90	MOVB	Move byte
28	MOVC3	Move character 3 operand
2C	MOVC5	Move character 5 operand
70	MOVD	Move D_floating
50	MOVF	Move F_floating
50FD	MOVG	Move G_floating
70FD	MOVH	Move H_floating
DO	MOVL	Move long
7DFD	MOVO	Move data
34	MOVP	Move packed
DC	MOVPSL	Move program status longword
7D	MOVQ	Move quad
2E	MOVTC	Move translated characters
2F	MOVTUC	Move translated until character
BO	MOVW	Move word
0A	MOVZBL	Move zero-extended byte to long
9B	MOVZBW	Move zero-extended byte to word
3C	MOVZWL	Move zero-extended word to long
DA	MTPR	Move to processor register
84	MULB2	Multiply byte 2 operand
85	MULB3	Multiply byte 3 operand
64	MULD2	Multiply D_floating 2 operand
65	MULD3	Multiply D_floating 3 operand
44	MULF2	Multiply F_floating 2 operand
45	MULF3	Multiply F_floating 3 operand
44FD	MULG2	Multiply G_floating 2 operand
45FD	MULG3	Multiply G_floating 3 operand
64FD	MULH2	Multiply H_floating 2 operand
65FD	MULH3	Multiply H_floating 3 operand
C4	MULL2	Multiply long 2 operand
C5	MULL3	Multiply long 3 operand
25	MULP	Multiply packed
A4	MULW2	Multiply word 2 operand
A5	MULW3	Multiply word 3 operand
01	NOP	No operation
75	POLYD	Evaluate polynomial D_floating
55	POLYF	Evaluate polynomial F_floating
55FD	POLYG	Evaluate polynomial G_floating
75FD	POLYH	Evaluate polynomial H_floating
BA	POPR	Pop registers
0C	PROBER	Probe read access
0D	PROBEW	Probe write access
9F	PUSHAB	Push address of byte
7F	PUSHAD	Push address of D_floating
DF	PUSHAF	Push address of F_floating
7F	PUSHAG	Push address of G_floating
7FFD	PUSHAH	Push address of H_floating
DF	PUSHAL	Push address of long
7FFD	PUSHAO	Push address of octa
7F	PUSHAQ	Push address of quad

Hexadecimal Value	Mnemonic	Functional Name
3F	PUSHAW	Push address of word
DD	PUSHL	Push long
BB	PUSHR	Push registers
02	REI	Return from exception or interrupt
5E	REMQHI	Remove from queue at head, interlocked
5F	REMQTI	Remove from queue at tail, interlocked
0F	REMQUE	Remove from queue
04	RET	Return from called procedure
9C	ROTL	Rotate long
05	RSB	Return from subroutine
D9	SBWC	Subtract with carry
2A	SCANC	Scan for character
3B	SKPC	Skip character
F4	SOBGEQ	Subtract one and branch on greater or equal
F5	SOBGTR	Subtract one and branch on greater
2B	SPANC	Span characters
82	SUBB2	Subtract byte 2 operand
83	SUBB3	Subtract byte 3 operand
62	SUBD2	Subtract D_floating 2 operand
63	SUBD3	Subtract D_floating 3 operand
42	SUBF2	Subtract F_floating 2 operand
43	SUBF3	Subtract F_floating 3 operand
42FD	SUBG2	Subtract G_floating 2 operand
43FD	SUBG3	Subtract G_floating 3 operand
62FD	SUBH2	Subtract H_floating 2 operand
63FD	SUBH3	Subtract H_floating 3 operand
C2	SUBL2	Subtract long 2 operand
C3	SUBL3	Subtract long 3 operand
22	SUBP4	Subtract packed 4 operand
23	SUBP6	Subtract packed 6 operand
A2	SUBW2	Subtract word 2 operand
A3	SUBW3	Subtract word 3 operand
07	SVPCTX	Save process context
95	TSTB	Test byte
73	TSTD	Test D_floating
53	TSTF	Test F_floating
53FD	TSTG	Test G_floating
73FD	TSTH	Test H_floating
D5	TSTL	Test long
B5	TSTW	Test word
FC	XFC	Extended function call
8C	XORB2	Exclusive-OR byte 2 operand
8D	XORB3	Exclusive-OR byte 3 operand
CC	XORL2	Exclusive-OR long 2 operand
CD	XORL3	Exclusive-OR long 3 operand
AC	XORW2	Exclusive-OR word 2 operand
AD	XORW3	Exclusive-OR word 3 operand

VAX-11 OPCODES (NUMERIC ORDER)

HEX Value	Instruction	HEX Value	Instruction	HEX Value	Instruction
00	HALT	30	BSBW	60	ADDD2
01	NOP	31	BRW	61	ADDD3
02	REI	32	CVTWL	62	SUBD2
03	BPT	33	CVTWB	63	SUBD3
04	RET	34	MOVP	64	MULD2
05	RSB	35	CMPP3	65	MULD3
06	LDPCTX	36	CVTPL	66	DIVD2
07	SVPCTX	37	CMPP4	67	DIVD3
08	CVTPS	38	EDITPC	68	CVTDB
09	CVTSP	39	MATCHC	69	CVTDW
0A	INDEX	3A	LOCC	6A	CVTDL
0B	CRC	3B	SKPC	6B	CVTRDL
0C	PROBER	3C	MOVZWL	6C	CVTBD
0D	PROBEW	3D	ACBW	6D	CVTWD
0E	INSQUE	3E	MOVAW	6E	CVTLD
0F	REMQUE	3F	PUSHAW	6F	ACBD
10	BSBB	40	ADDF2	70	MOVD
11	BRB	41	ADDF3	71	CMPD
12	BNEQ, BNEQU	42	SUBF2	72	MNEGD
13	BEQL, BEQLU	43	SUBF3	73	TSTD
14	BGTR	44	MULF2	74	EMODD
15	BLEQ	45	MULF3	75	POLYD
16	JSB	46	DIVF2	76	CVTDF
17	JMP	47	DIVF3	77	reserved
18	BGEQ	48	CVTFB	78	ASHL
19	BLSS	49	CVTFW	79	ASHQ
1A	BGTRU	4A	CVTFL	7A	EMUL
1B	BLEQU	4B	CVTRFL	7B	EDIV
1C	BVC	4C	CVTBF	7C	CLRD, CLRQ
1D	BVS	4D	CVTWF	7D	MOVQ
1E	BCC, BGEQU	4E	CVTLF	7E	MOVAD, MOVAQ
1F	BCS, BLSSU	4F	ACBF	7F	PUSHAD, PUSHAQ
20	ADDP4	50	MOVF	80	ADDB2
21	ADDP6	51	CMPF	81	ADDB3
22	SUBP4	52	MNEGF	82	SUBB2
23	SUBP6	53	TSTF	83	SUBB3
24	CVTPT	54	EMODF	84	MULB2
25	MULP	55	POLYF	85	MULB3
26	CVTTP	56	CVTFD	86	DIVB2
27	DIVP	57	reserved	87	DIVB3
28	MOVC3	58	ADAWI	88	BISB2
29	CMPC3	59	reserved	89	BISB3
2A	SCANC	5A	reserved	8A	BICB2
2B	SPANC	5B	reserved	8B	BICB3
2C	MOVC5	6C	reserved	8C	XORB2
2D	CMPC5	5D	reserved	8D	XORB3
2E	MOVTC	5E	reserved	8E	MNEGB
2F	MOVTUC	5F	reserved	8F	CASEB

HEX Value	Instruction	HEX Value	Instruction	HEX Value	Instruction
90	MOVB	C0	ADDL2	F0	INSV
91	CMPB	C1	ADDL3	F1	ACBL
92	MCOMB	C2	SUBL2	F2	AOBLSS
93	BITB	C3	SUBL3	F3	AOBLEQ
94	CLRB	C4	MULL2	F4	SOBGEQ
95	TSTB	C5	MULL3	F5	SOBGTR
96	INCB	C6	DIVL2	F6	CVTLB
97	DECB	C7	DIVL3	F7	CVTLW
98	CVTBL	C8	BISL2	F8	ASHP
99	CVTBW	C9	BISL3	F9	CVTLP
9A	MOVZBL	CA	BICL2	FA	CALLG
9B	MOVZBW	CB	BICL3	FB	CALLS
9C	ROTL	CC	XORL2	FC	XFC
9D	ACBB	CD	XORL3	FD	reserved
9E	MOVAB	CE	MNEGL	FE	reserved
9F	PUSHAB	CF	CASEL	FF	reserved
A0	ADDW2	D0	MOVL		
A1	ADDW3	D1	CMPL		
A2	SUBW2	D2	MCOML		
A3	SUBW3	D3	BITL		
A4	MULW2	D4	CLRF, CLRL		
A5	MULW3	D5	TSTL		
A6	DIVW2	D6	INCL		
A7	DIVW3	D7	DECL		
A8	BISW2	D8	ADWC		
A9	BISW3	D9	SBWC		
AA	BICW2	DA	MTPR		
AB	BICW3	DB	MFPR		
AC	XORW2	DC	MOVPSL		
AD	XORW3	DD	PUSHL		
AE	MNEGW	DE	MOVAF, MOVAL		
AF	CASEW	DF	PUSHAF, PUSHAL		
B0	MOVW	E0	BBS		
B1	CMPW	E1	BBC		
B2	MCOMW	E2	BBSS		
B3	BITW	E3	BBCS		
B4	CLRW	E4	BBSC		
B5	TSTW	E5	BBCC		
B6	INCW	E6	BBSSI		
B7	DECW	E7	BBCCI		
B8	BISPSW	E8	BLBS		
B9	BICPSW	E9	BLBC		
BA	POPR	EA	FFS		
BB	PUSHR	EB	FFC		
BC	CHMK	EC	CMPV		
BD	CHME	ED	CMPZV		
BE	CHMS	EE	EXTV		
BF	CHMU	EF	EXTZV		

Appendix B
TABLES

Table B.1 ASCII Chart with Decimal/Octal/Hexidecimal Codes

CHAR	DEC	OCT	HEX	CHAR	DEC	OCT	HEX	CHAR	DEC	OCT	HEX
NUL	0	0	0	+	43	53	2B	V	86	126	56
^A	1	1	1	,	44	54	2C	W	87	127	57
^B	2	2	2	-	45	55	2D	X	88	130	58
^C	3	3	3	.	46	56	2E	Y	89	131	59
^D	4	4	4	/	47	57	2F	Z	90	132	5A
^E	5	5	5	0	48	60	30	[	91	133	5B
^F	6	6	6	1	49	61	31	\	92	134	5C
BEL	7	7	7	2	50	62	32	]	93	135	5D
BKSP	8	10	8	3	51	63	33	^	94	136	5E
TAB	9	11	9	4	52	64	34	_	95	137	5F
LF	10	12	A	5	53	65	35	~	96	140	60
VT	11	13	B	6	54	66	36	a	97	141	61
FF	12	14	C	7	55	67	37	b	98	142	62
CR	13	15	D	8	56	70	38	c	99	143	63
SO	14	16	E	9	57	71	39	d	100	144	64
^O	15	17	F	:	58	72	3A	e	101	145	65
^P	16	20	10	;	59	73	3B	f	102	146	66
XON	17	21	11	<	60	74	3C	g	103	147	67
^R	18	22	12	=	61	75	3D	h	104	150	68
XOFF	19	23	13	>	62	76	3E	i	105	151	69
^T	20	24	14	?	63	77	3F	j	106	152	6A
^U	21	25	15	@	64	100	40	k	107	153	6B
^V	22	26	16	A	65	101	41	l	108	154	6C
^W	23	27	17	B	66	102	42	m	109	155	6D
^X	24	30	18	C	67	103	43	n	110	156	6E
^Y	25	31	19	D	68	104	44	o	111	157	6F
^Z	26	32	1A	E	69	105	45	p	112	160	70
ESC	27	33	1B	F	70	106	46	q	113	161	71
FS	28	34	1C	G	71	107	47	r	114	162	72
GS	29	35	1D	H	72	110	48	s	115	163	73
RS	30	36	1E	I	73	111	49	t	116	164	74
US	31	37	1F	J	74	112	4A	u	117	165	75
SP	32	40	20	K	75	113	4B	v	118	166	76
!	33	41	21	L	76	114	4C	w	119	167	77
"	34	42	22	M	77	115	4D	x	120	170	78
#	35	43	23	N	78	116	4E	y	121	171	79
$	36	44	24	O	79	117	4F	z	122	172	7A
%	37	45	25	P	80	120	50	{	123	173	7B
&	38	46	26	Q	81	121	51	|	124	174	7C
'	39	47	27	R	82	122	52	}	125	175	7D
(	40	50	28	S	83	123	53	~	126	176	7E
)	41	51	29	T	84	124	54	DEL	127	177	7F
*	42	52	2A	U	85	125	55				

Table B.2 Powers of Two Table

2^n	2	2^{-n}
2	1	0.500000000000000000000000000000
4	2	0.250000000000000000000000000000
8	3	0.125000000000000000000000000000
16	4	0.062500000000000000000000000000
32	5	0.031250000000000000000000000000
64	6	0.015625000000000000000000000000
128	7	0.007812500000000000000000000000
256	8	0.003906250000000000000000000000
512	9	0.001953125000000000000000000000
1,024	10	0.000976562500000000000000000000
2,048	11	0.000488281250000000000000000000
4,096	12	0.000244140625000000000000000000
8,192	13	0.000122070312500000000000000000
16,384	14	0.000061035156250000000000000000
32,768	15	0.000030517578125000000000000000
65,536	16	0.000015258789062500000000000000
131,072	17	0.000007629394531250000000000000
262,144	18	0.000003814697265625000000000000
524,288	19	0.000001907348632812500000000000
1,048,576	20	0.000000953674316406250000000000
2,097,152	21	0.000000476837158203125000000000
4,194,304	22	0.000000238418579101563000000000
8,388,608	23	0.000000119209289550781000000000
16,777,216	24	0.000000059604644775390600000000
33,554,432	25	0.000000029802322387695300000000
67,108,864	26	0.000000014901161193847700000000
134,217,728	27	0.000000007450580596923830000000
268,435,456	28	0.000000003725290298461910000000
536,870,912	29	0.000000001862645149230960000000
1,073,741,824	30	0.000000000931322574615479000000
2,147,483,648	31	0.000000000465661287307739000000
4,294,967,296	32	0.000000000232830643653869000000
8,589,934,592	33	0.000000000116415321826935000000
17,179,869,184	34	0.000000000058207660913467300000
34,359,738,368	35	0.000000000029103830456733700000
68,719,476,736	36	0.000000000014551915228366800000
137,438,953,472	37	0.000000000007275957614183420000
274,877,906,944	38	0.000000000003637978807091710000
549,755,813,888	39	0.000000000001818989403545850000
1,099,511,627,776	40	0.000000000000909494701772927000

Table B.3 Fibonacci Numbers and F(n)/Fn-1) Reciprocals

F(n)	n	F(n)/F(n-1)
1	1	
1	2	1.000000000000000
2	3	2.000000000000000
3	4	1.500000000000000
5	5	1.666666666666670
8	6	1.600000000000000
13	7	1.625000000000000
21	8	1.615384615384620
34	9	1.619047619047620
55	10	1.617647058823530
89	11	1.618181818181820
144	12	1.617977528089890
233	13	1.618055555555560
377	14	1.618025751072960
610	15	1.618037135278510
987	16	1.618032786885250
1,597	17	1.618034447821680
2,584	18	1.618033813400130
4,181	19	1.618034055727550
6,765	20	1.618033963166710
10,946	21	1.618033998521800
17,711	22	1.618033985017360
28,657	23	1.618033990175600
46,368	24	1.618033988205330
75,025	25	1.618033988957900
121,393	26	1.618033988670440
196,418	27	1.618033988780240
317,811	28	1.618033988738300
514,229	29	1.618033988754320
832,040	30	1.618033988748200
1,346,269	31	1.618033988750540
2,178,309	32	1.618033988749650
3,524,578	33	1.618033988749990
5,702,887	34	1.618033988749860
9,227,465	35	1.618033988749910
14,930,352	36	1.618033988749890
24,157,817	37	1.618033988749900
39,088,169	38	1.618033988749890
63,245,986	39	1.618033988749900
102,334,155	40	1.618033988749890
165,580,141	41	1.618033988749890
267,914,296	42	1.618033988749890
433,494,437	43	1.618033988749890
701,408,733	44	1.618033988749890
1,134,903,170	45	1.618033988749890
1,836,311,903	46	1.618033988749890
2,971,215,073	47	1.618033988749890
4,807,526,976	48	1.618033988749890
7,778,742,049	49	1.618033988749890
12,586,269,025	50	1.618033988749890

Table B.4 Hexidecimal-to-Decimal Conversion Table

Hex	0	1	2	3	4	5	6	7	8	9	10	11	12	13	14	15
00	0	1	2	3	4	5	6	7	8	9	10	11	12	13	14	15
10	16	17	18	19	20	21	22	23	24	25	26	27	28	29	30	31
20	32	33	34	35	36	37	38	39	40	41	42	43	44	45	46	47
30	48	49	50	51	52	53	54	55	56	57	58	59	60	61	62	63
40	64	65	66	67	68	69	70	71	72	73	74	75	76	77	78	79
50	80	81	82	83	84	85	86	87	88	89	90	91	92	93	94	95
60	96	97	98	99	100	101	102	103	104	105	106	107	108	109	110	111
70	112	113	114	115	116	117	118	119	120	121	122	123	124	125	126	127
80	128	129	130	131	132	133	134	135	136	137	138	139	140	141	142	143
90	144	145	146	147	148	149	150	151	152	153	154	155	156	157	158	159
A0	160	161	162	163	164	165	166	167	168	169	170	171	172	173	174	175
B0	176	177	178	179	180	181	182	183	184	185	186	187	188	189	190	191
C0	192	193	194	195	196	197	198	199	200	201	202	203	204	205	206	207
D0	208	209	210	211	212	213	214	215	216	217	218	219	220	221	222	223
E0	224	225	226	227	228	229	230	231	232	233	234	235	236	237	238	239
F0	240	241	242	243	244	245	246	247	248	249	250	251	252	253	254	255

Method: add row number to column number; sum is at the intersection of the row and column.

Example:

$$F0(row) + 6(column) = 15 \times 16^1 + 6 \times 16^0$$

$$= 240 + 6$$

$$= 246$$

Appendix C
LIBRARIES

The following libraries are used throughout this book except BEGIN-PAS.MAR in Appendix C.3 and BEGINIO.MAR in Appendix C.1. You should notice the following things:

1. Use the BEGINPAS.MAR macro library (see Appendix C.3) with the programs in the figures in chapters 16 and 17.

2. Use the PAS.MAR macro library (see Appendix C.4) with the programs in chapters 1–15 and 18–19.

3. The BEGINIO.MAR procedure library (see Appendix C.1) is used only in chapter 9.

4. The BEGINPAS.MAR and BEGINIO.MAR are libraries for beginners. They should be used to hold newly created macros or procedures which are being tried out.

5. The PAS.MAR and IO.MAR libraries are for advanced programming. These libraries should only be used for permanent macros or procedures.

6. To use PAS.MAR and IO.MAR with a new program (call it *t*), use the following steps:

   ```
   macro t + pas/lib      ;to assemble t
   link t + io/lib        ;to link t
   ```

   (Note: this assumes these libraries are in *your* account.)

7. To prepare a library for use with your programs, follow the instructions given at the beginning of each library.

8. To make a library shareable by other users in other accounts, you type, for example,

   ```
   set protection = (group:R) pas.*;*
   set protection = (group:R) io.*;*
   ```

   Then, if a user in another account wants to use these libraries, then that user must type

   ```
   macro t + [account name] pas/lib
   ```

   to assemble a source text *t*. To link an object module T.OBJ, use

   ```
   link t + [account name] io/lib
   ```

   To run *t*, type

   ```
   run t
   ```

```
;Ref.:   Appendix C.1 (Beginning I/O Procedures)
;
;BEGINNING INPUT-OUTPUT PROCEDURE LIBRARY:
;
;        TO ASSEMBLE, TYPE THE FOLLOWING:
;
;                  MACRO file_name
;                  LIBRARY/CREATE/OBJ  file_name   file_name
;
;        TO LINK WITH PROGRAM, TYPE THE FOLLOWING:
;
;                  LINK program_name + file_name/LIB
;
;
;procedure:  String input
;

instr:  .blkb 80
ttname: .ascid/sys$input:/
        .even
ttchan: .blkw 1
ttiosb: .blkw 1
ttiolen:
        .word
        .long
error:  blbs      r0,10$
        $exit_s   r0
10$:    rsb

        .entry input,0
        $assign_s               devnam = ttname       chan = ttchan
        bsbb      error

        $input    chan = ttchan     length = #80      buffer = instr       iosb = ttiosb

        cvtlb     ttiolen,@4(ap)
        movl      4(ap),r6
        incl      r6
        movc3     ttiolen,instr,(r6)

        $dassgn_s               chan = ttchan

        ret
;
;
;procedure:  String output
;

outlen: .blkl     1

        .entry output,^m<r6,r7,r8>

        $assign_s               devnam = ttname       chan = ttchan
```

```
        bsbw       error

        movzbl     @4(ap),outlen
        movl       outlen,r6
        movl       4(ap),r7
        incl       r7
        movab      instr,r8
get:
        movb       (r7)+,(r8)+
        sobgeq     r6,get

        $output    chan = ttchan     length = outlen buffer = instr        iosb = ttiosb

        $dassgn_s              chan = ttchan

        ret

;
;
;procedure:  Numeric input
;

        .entry     numeric_input,^m<r6,r7,r8,r9>

        $assign_s              devnam = ttname       chan = ttchan

        bsbw       error

        $input     chan = ttchan     length = #80     buffer = instr      iosb = ttiosb
        movzwl     ttiolen,r9
        movab      instr,r8
        clrl       r6
remove:
        subb2      #48,(r8)
        movzbl     (r8)+,r7
        mull2      #10,r6
        addl2      r7,r6
        sobgtr     r9,remove

        movl       r6,@4(ap)

        $dassgn_s              chan = ttchan

        ret

;
;
;procedure:  Numeric output
;

        .entry     numeric_output,^m<r6,r7,r9,r10,r11>

        $assign_s              devnam = ttname       chan = ttchan
        bsbw       error
```

```
                movl    4(ap),r6
                movab   instr,r9
                addl2   #80,r9
                clrl    outlen
        digit:
                clrl    r7
                ediv    #10,r6,r10,r11
                addl2   #48,r11
                cvtlb   r11,-(r9)
                incl    outlen
                movl    r10,r6
                bneq    digit
                movl    outlen,r7
                movab   instr,r6
        new_copy:
                movb    (r9)+,(r6)+
                sobgtr  r7,new_copy

                $qiow_s                 efn = #1              chan = ttchan func =
        #io$_writevblk-
                                        p1 = instr           p2 = outlen


                bsbw    error

                $dassgn_s               chan = ttchan

                ret

                .end
```

```
;
;Ref.:  Appendix C.2 (Enhanced I/O Procedures)
;
;METHOD:
;
;       MACRO IO <RET>
;       LIB/CREAT/OBJ IO IO<RET>
;       LINK IOTEST+IO/LIB
;       RUN IOTEST
;
        .ENABLE GBL
;
;DATA USED BY ALL PROCEDURES:
;
.       =. + 100                        ;storage for downwards stack
STACK:: .LONG                           ;label stack
COUNT:: .LONG                           ;counter for read routine
BASE::  .LONG 10
SET::   .BYTE 0
FBASE:: .FLOAT
X1::    .FLOAT
Y1::    .FLOAT
X2::    .LONG
```

```
INSTR:: .BLKB 80
TTNAME::            .ASCID/SYS$INPUT/          ;device name
TTCHAN::            .BLKW       1              ;channel
TTIOSB::            .BLKW       1              ;I/O Statue Block
TTIOLEN::
        .WORD
        .LONG
OUTLEN::            .BLKL       1              ;length of string

ERROR:  BLBS        R0,10$                     ;error routine for I/O
        $EXIT_S     R0
10$:    RSB

        .ENTRY      READVAL,^M<R6,R7,R8,R9>    ;reads in 1 or more values

        $ASSIGN_S -                            ;macro to specify
                DEVNAM=TTNAME, -               ;device
                CHAN=TTCHAN                    ;and channel

        BSBW        ERROR

        $INPUT -                               ;macro to read in string
                CHAN=TTCHAN, -
                LENGTH=#80, -
                BUFFER=INSTR, -
                IOSB=TTIOSB

        MOVAB       STACK,R11                  ;use R11 as pointer to stack
        MOVZWL      TTIOLEN,R9                 ;length of string read goes in R9
        MOVAB       INSTR,R8                   ;use R8 as pointer to chars of
string
        CLRL        R6                         ;clear for number
        CLRL        COUNT                      ;reset count for new subroutine
call
REMOV:  SUBB2       #48,(R8)                   ;remove ascii bias from 1st char
        CMPB        (R8),#10
        BLSS        HEX
        SUBB2       #7,(R8)
HEX:    MOVZBL      (R8)+,R7                   ;put value obtained in R7
        MULL2       BASE,R6                    ;multiply number by base desired
        ADDL2       R7,R6                      ;and add value to it
        CMPB        (R8),#48                   ;is next char a digit?
        BLSS        NEWNUM                     ;if not, it's a seperator, so a
new #
        SOBGTR      R9,REMOV                   ;else, get value of next char
NEWNUM: MOVL        R6,-(R11)                  ;store the 1st number
        INCL        COUNT                      ;we have one (more) number on the
stack
        DECL        R9                         ;we have one less char in the
string
        TSTL        R9                         ;are there more characters?
        BEQL        LEAVE                      ;if not, leave subroutine
        CLRL        R6                         ;else, clear R6 for a new number
        TSTB        (R8)+                      ;move to next char in string
        SOBGTR      R9,REMOV                   ;go to evaluate nest char
```

```
LEAVE:  $DASSGN_S -                         ;end of subroutine, deassign
                CHAN=TTCHAN                 ;the channel

        RET

        .ENTRY  WRITEVAL,^M<R6,R7,R8,R9>    ;subroutine to write numbers

        $ASSIGN_S -                         ;macro to specify
                DEVNAM=TTNAME, -            ;device
                CHAN=TTCHAN                 ;and channel

        BSBW    ERROR
        MOVAB   INSTR,R9                    ;use R9 as pointer to string
        MOVL    4(AP),R6                    ;get value of number to be printed
        ADDL2   #80,R9                      ;go to end of string, because we
                                            ;will start with 1´s place on #
        CLRL    OUTLEN                      ;clear for length of string created
UNLOAD: MOVL    R6,R7                       ;copy value in R7
        DIVL2   BASE,R6                     ;divide by base desired to get
quotient
        MOVL    R6,R8                       ;copy quotient
        MULL2   BASE,R6                     ;multiply by base
        SUBL2   R6,R7                       ;and subtract to get remainder
        ADDL2   #48,R7                      ;add ascii bias
        CMPL    #57,R7                      ;see if we need more ascii bias
        BGEQ    NEXT                        ;
        ADDL2   #7,R7                       ;provides for bases 11-36
        CMPL    #90,R7                      ;more ascii bias?
        BGEQ    NEXT

        ADDL2   #6,R7                       ;provides for bases 37-62
NEXT:   MOVB    R7,-(R9)                    ;store ascii code at end of string
        INCL    OUTLEN                      ;increment length of string
        MOVL    R8,R6                       ;restore quotient and
        BNEQ    UNLOAD                      ;get more digits, unless quotient
is
        MOVL    OUTLEN,R8                   ;zero, then prepare to print
        MOVAB   INSTR,R7                    ;prepare to put digits in beginning
LOOP:   MOVB    (R9)+,(R7)+                 :of string
        SOBGTR  R8,LOOP

        $QIOW_S -                           ;macro to queue I/O request and
wait
                EFN=#1, -                   ;for event flag
                CHAN=TTCHAN, -              ;specify channel
                FUNC=#IO$_WRITEVBLK, -      ;specify I/O function
                P1=INSTR, -                 ;1st parameter--the string
                P2=OUTLEN                   ;2nd parameter--its length

        BSBW    ERROR

        $DASSGN_S -                         ;macro to dassign
                CHAN=TTCHAN                 ;channel

        RET

        .ENTRY  WRITESTR,^M<R6,R7,R8>       ;subroutine to write strings
                                            ;to terminal
```

```
        $ASSIGN_S -                         ;macro to assign
                DEVNAM=TTNAME, -            ;device name
                CHAN=TTCHAN                 ;and channel to be used

        BSBW    ERROR

        MOVZBL  @4(AP),OUTLEN               ;get length of string to be printed
                                            ;NOTE: assumes ascic was pushed
        MOVL    OUTLEN,R6                   ;use length for counter
        MOVL    4(AP),R7                    ;get address of string
        INCL    R7                          ;bypass 1st byte of ascic
        MOVAB   INSTR,R8                    ;prepare to move string to INSTR
GET:    MOVB    (R7)+,(R8)+                 ;pop each character into INSTR
        SOBGEQ  R6,GET

        $QIOW_S -                           ;use queue and wait macro
                EFN=#1, -                   ;as explained in writeval
                CHAN=TTCHAN, -
                FUNC=#IO$_WRITEVBLK, -
                P1=INSTR, -
                P2=OUTLEN

        BSBW    ERROR

        $DASSGN_S -
                CHAN=TTCHAN

        RET

        .ENTRY  READSTR,0                   ;subroutine to read strings
                                            ;from user at terminal
        $ASSIGN_S -                         ;assign macro
                DEVNAM=TTNAME, -
                CHAN=TTCHAN

        BSBW    ERROR

        $INPUT -                            ;input macro to pull in string
                CHAN=TTCHAN, -              ;specify channel
                LENGTH=#80, -               ;specify how much to take in
                BUFFER=INSTR, -             ;specify where to put it
                IOSB=TTIOSB                 ;use I/O Status Block

        CVTLB   TTIOLEN,@4(AP)
LENGTH:
        MOVL    4(AP),R6
        INCL    R6
BYTE:
        MOVC3   TTIOLEN,INSTR,(R6)

        $DASSGN_S -                         ;that's it!
                CHAN=TTCHAN


        RET
;
        .ENTRY READNO,^M<R6,R7,R8,R9>
        $ASSIGN_S DEVNAM=TTNAME CHAN=TTCHAN
```

```
                BSBW        ERROR
                $INPUT CHAN=TTCHAN LENGTH=#80 BUFFER=INSTR IOSB=TTIOSB
                MOVZWL      TTIOLEN,R9              ;copy length of input string
                MOVAB       INSTR,R8               ;use R8 as string pointer
FETCH:
                SUBB2       #48,(R8)+              ;drop ASCII bias
                INCL        COUNT                  ;keep tally of no. of codes
                SOBGTR      R9,FETCH               ;continue until TTIOLEN = 0
                $DASSGN_S CHAN=TTCHAN
                RET
;
                .ENTRY DECIMAL,^M<R7>
                MOVL        #5,R7
                CVTLF       BASE,FBASE
                MOVF        4(AP),X1
                CVTFL       X1,X2
                WRITEVAL X2,SPACES=0
                CVTLF       X2,Y1
                SUBF2       Y1,X1
                BNEQ        FIX
                JMP         BYE
FIX:    WRITE       <.>
LOOP1:  MULF2       FBASE,X1
                CVTFL       X1,X2
                WRITEVAL X2,SPACES=0
                TSTL        X2
                BNEQ        SETTER
                TSTB        SET
                BNEQ        NOSET
                INCL        R7
                BRB         NOSET
SETTER: MOVB        #1,SET
NOSET:  CVTLF       X2,Y1
                SUBF2       Y1,X1
                SUBL2       #1,R7
                CMPL        #0,R7
                BEQL        BYE
                JMP         LOOP1
BYE:    RET
;
                .END
```

```
;Ref.:  Appendix C.3 (Beginning Macro Library)
;
;EXTERNAL MACRO LIBRARY:
;
;       TO CREATE LIBRARY IN YOUR ACCOUNT, TYPE THE FOLLOWING:
;
;
;                    LIBRARY/CREATE/MACRO PAS PAS
;
;TO ASSEMBLE & OBTAIN PAS.MLB MACRO LIBRARY MODULE.
;
```

```
        .MACRO ABS TERM WITH TYPE=L ?BYE
        TST´TYPE TERM
        BGEQ                    BYE
        MNEG´TYPE               TERM,TERM
BYE:    NOP
        .ENDM   ABS

        .MACRO TUMTY
        $EXIT_S
        .ENDM TUMTY

        .MACRO SPURT T
        PUSHAB T
        CALLS #1,WRITESTR
        .ENDM SPURT

        .MACRO TAB X ?K1 ?LAST1
        .REPEAT X
        PUSHAB   K1
        CALLS    #1,WRITESTR
        .ENDR
        BRW      LAST1
K1:     .ASCIC/  /
LAST1:  NOP
        .ENDM

        .MACRO WRITE STRING ?K ?LAST
        PUSHAB K
        CALLS #1,WRITESTR
        BRB LAST
K:      .ASCIC/STRING/
LAST:   NOP
        .ENDM WRITE
;
        .MACRO WRITELN STRING ?K1 ?LAST1
        PUSHAB K1
        CALLS #1,WRITESTR
        BRW LAST1
K1:     .ASCIC/STRING/<10><13>
LAST1:  NOP
        .ENDM WRITELN
;
        .MACRO SPACE X ?K2 ?LAST2

        .REPEAT X
        PUSHAB K2
        CALLS #1,WRITESTR
        .ENDR
        BRW LAST2
K2:     .ASCIC<32>
LAST2:  NOP
        .ENDM SPACE
;
        .MACRO WRITEVAL VAR1,VAR2,VAR3,VAR4,RADIX=10,SPACES=1
        MOVB     #RADIX,BASE
```

```
        .IF NOT_BLANK VAR1
PUSHL     VAR1
CALLS     #1,WRITEVAL
TAB       SPACES
.ENDC

        .IF NOT_BLANK VAR2
PUSHL     VAR2
CALLS     #1,WRITEVAL
TAB       SPACES
.ENDC

        .IF NOT_BLANK VAR3
PUSHL     VAR3
CALLS     #1,WRITEVAL
TAB       SPACES
.ENDC

        .IF NOT_BLANK VAR4
PUSHL     VAR4
CALLS     #1,WRITEVAL
TAB       SPACES
.ENDC

        .ENDM    WRITEVAL
;
        .MACRO READVAR VAR1, VAR2, VAR3, RADIX=10
MOVB      #RADIX,BASE
CALLS     #0,READVAL

        .IF NOT_BLANK VAR3
MOVL      (R11)+,VAR3
.ENDC

        .IF NOT_BLANK VAR2
MOVL      (R11)+,VAR2
.ENDC

        .IF NOT_BLANK VAR1
MOVL      (R11)+,VAR1
.ENDC
WRITELN

        .ENDM    READVAR
;
        .MACRO IF ARG1 CONDITION ARG2 THEN ACT1 ELSE ACT2-
            ?JUMP ?FIRST ?SECOND ?BYE
CMPL      ARG1,ARG2
.IF IDN ^"CONDITION" ^">"
BGTR JUMP
.ENDC
.IF IDN ^"CONDITION" ^">="
BGEQ JUMP
```

```
        .ENDC
        .IF IDN ^"CONDITION" ^"<"
        BLSS JUMP
        .ENDC
        .IF IDN ^"CONDITION" ^"<="
        BLEQ JUMP
        .ENDC
        .IF IDN ^"CONDITION" =
        BEQL JUMP
        .ENDC
        .IF IDN ^"CONDITION" ^"<>"
        BNEQ JUMP
        .ENDC
        JMP       SECOND
JUMP:   JMP       FIRST
SECOND: ACT2
        JMP       BYE
FIRST:  ACT1
BYE:
        .ENDM IF
;
        .MACRO FOR INDEX IS MIN TO MAX DO ACT,-
                 STEP=1 TYPE=L   ?LOOP ?BYE ?CHECK
        MOV^TYPE MIN,INDEX
CHECK:  CMP^TYPE INDEX,MAX
        BEQL      LOOP
        .IF IDN TO DOWNTO
        CMP^TYPE INDEX,MAX
        BGTR      LOOP
        .IF_FALSE
        CMP^TYPE INDEX,MAX
        BLSS      LOOP
        .ENDC
        JMP       BYE
LOOP:   ACT
        .IF IDN TO DOWNTO
        .REPEAT ^C<STEP>+1
        SUB^TYPE^2            #1,INDEX
        .ENDR
        .IF_FALSE
        .REPEAT STEP
        ADD^TYPE^2            #1,INDEX
        .ENDR
        .ENDC
        JMP       CHECK
BYE:
        .ENDM     FOR
;
        .MACRO BEGIN ACT1 ACT2 ACT3 ACT4 ACT5 ACT6 ACT7 ACT8 ACT9 ACT10 ACT11
        ACT1
        ACT2
        ACT3
        ACT4
        ACT5
```

```
            ACT6
            ACT7
            ACT8
            ACT9
            ACT10
            ACT11
            .ENDM BEGIN
;
            .MACRO END
            .ENDM
;
            .MACRO COMPUTE VAR1 IS VAR2 OP VAR3 ?QUO ?BYE
            .IF IDENTICAL DIV <OP>
DIVL3       VAR3,VAR2,VAR1
            .IF_FALSE
PUSHR       #^M<R7,R8>
MOVL        VAR2,R7
CLRL        R8
EDIV        VAR3,R7,QUO,VAR1
POPR        #^M<R7,R8>
            .ENDC
BRW         BYE
QUO:        .LONG
BYE:
            .ENDM COMPUTE
;
            .MACRO REPEAT ACT UNTIL VAR1 COND VAR2 ?DO ?BYE
DO:         ACT
CMPL        VAR1,VAR2
B'COND      BYE
JMP         DO
BYE:
            .ENDM REPEAT
;
            .MACRO WHILE VAR1 COND VAR2 DO ACT ?LOOP ?BYE ?AGAIN
AGAIN:      CMPL        VAR1,VAR2
B'COND      LOOP
JMP         BYE
LOOP:       ACT
JMP         AGAIN
BYE:
            .ENDM WHILE
;
            .MACRO SPIKE X
            FOR I := #1 TO X DO <WRITE *>
            .ENDM SPIKE
;
            .MACRO LET VAR1 EQ VAR2
MOVL        VAR2,VAR1
            .ENDM LET
;
            .MACRO CASE SELECTOR OF A ACT1 B ACT2 C ACT3 D ACT4 E ACT5 -
                    OTHERWISE=NOP ?FLAG ?A2 ?A3 ?A4 ?A5 ?NOT_DONE ?BYE
            CLRB        FLAG
```

```
          CMPL      SELECTOR,A
          BNEQ      A2
          ACT1
          MOVB      #1,FLAG
A2:       .IF NOT_BLANK B
          CMPL      SELECTOR,B
          BNEQ      A3
          ACT2
          MOVB      #1,FLAG
          .ENDC
A3:       .IF NOT_BLANK C
          CMPL      SELECTOR,C
          BNEQ      A4
          ACT3
          MOVB      #1,FLAG
          .ENDC
A4:       .IF NOT_BLANK D
          CMPL      SELECTOR,D
          BNEQ      A5
          ACT4
          MOVB      #1,FLAG
          .ENDC
A5:       .IF NOT_BLANK E
          CMPL      SELECTOR,E
          BNEQ      NOT_DONE
          ACT5
          MOVB      #1,FLAG
          .ENDC
NOT_DONE:
          CMPB      #1,FLAG
          BEQL      BYE
          OTHERWISE
          BRB       BYE
FLAG:     .BYTE
BYE:
          .ENDM CASE
;
          .MACRO WRITEF VALUE,SPACES=1
          MOVF      VALUE,-(SP)
          CALLS     #1,DECIMAL
          TAB       SPACES
          .ENDM WRITEF
```

```
;Ref.:  Appendix C.4 (Enhanced Macro Library)
;
; EXTERNAL MACRO LIBRARY.  USE
;
;                 LIBRARY/CREATE/MACRO PAS PAS
;
;TO ASSEMBLE & OBTAIN PAS.MLB MACRO LIBRARY MODULE.
;
```

```
        .MACRO ABS TERM WITH TYPE=L ?BYE
        TST´TYPE TERM
        BGEQ            BYE
        MNEG´TYPE       TERM,TERM
BYE:    NOP
        .ENDM   ABS

        .MACRO TUMTY
        $EXIT_S
        .ENDM TUMTY

        .MACRO SPURT T
        PUSHAB T
        CALLS #1,WRITESTR
        .ENDM   SPURT

        .MACRO TAB X ?K1 ?LAST1
        .REPEAT X
        PUSHAB K1
        CALLS   #1,WRITESTR
        .ENDR
        BRW     LAST1
K1:     .ASCIC/ /
LAST1:  NOP
        .ENDM

        .MACRO WRITE STRING ?K ?LAST
        PUSHAB K
        CALLS #1,WRITESTR
        BRB LAST
K:      .ASCIC/STRING/
LAST:   NOP
        .ENDM WRITE
;
        .MACRO WRITELN STRING ?K1 ?LAST1
        PUSHAB K1
        CALLS #1,WRITESTR
        BRW LAST1
K1:     .ASCIC/STRING/<10><13>
LAST1:  NOP
        .ENDM WRITELN
;
        .MACRO SPACE X ?K2 ?LAST2
        .REPEAT X
        PUSHAB K2
        CALLS #1,WRITESTR
        .ENDR
        BRW LAST2
K2:     .ASCIC<32>
LAST2:  NOP
        .ENDM SPACE
;
        .MACRO WRITEVAL VAR1,VAR2,VAR3,VAR4,RADIX=10,SPACES=1
        MOVB    #RADIX,BASE
```

```
        .IF NOT_BLANK VAR1
        IF VAR1 LSS #0 THEN <BEGIN <WRITE <->> <ABS VAR1> -
                <PUSHL VAR1> <CALLS #1,WRITEVAL> <MNEGL VAR1,VAR1>>-
                ELSE <BEGIN <PUSHL VAR1> <CALLS #1,WRITEVAL>>
        SPACE   SPACES
        .ENDC


        .IF NOT_BLANK VAR2
        IF VAR2 LSS #0 THEN <BEGIN <WRITE <->> <ABS VAR2> -
                <PUSHL VAR2> <CALLS #1,WRITEVAL> <MNEGL VAR2,VAR2>>-
                ELSE <BEGIN <PUSHL VAR2> <CALLS #1,WRITEVAL>>
        SPACE   SPACES
        .ENDC


        .IF NOT_BLANK VAR3
        IF VAR3 LSS #0 THEN <BEGIN <WRITE <->> <ABS VAR3> -
                <PUSHL VAR3> <CALLS #1,WRITEVAL> <MNEGL VAR3,VAR3>>-
                ELSE <BEGIN <PUSHL VAR3> <CALLS #1,WRITEVAL>>
        SPACE   SPACES
        .ENDC


        .IF NOT_BLANK VAR4
        IF VAR4 LSS #0 THEN <BEGIN <WRITE <->> <ABS VAR4> -
                <PUSHL VAR4> <CALLS #1,WRITEVAL> <MNEGL VAR4,VAR4>>-
                ELSE <BEGIN <PUSHL VAR4> <CALLS #1,WRITEVAL>>
        TAB     SPACES
        .ENDC


        .ENDM   WRITEVAL

;

        .MACRO READVAR VAR1, VAR2, VAR3, RADIX=10
        MOVB    #RADIX,BASE
        CALLS   #0,READVAL

        .IF NOT_BLANK VAR3
        MOVL    (R11)+,VAR3
        .ENDC

        .IF NOT_BLANK VAR2
        MOVL    (R11)+,VAR2
        .ENDC

        .IF NOT_BLANK VAR1
        MOVL    (R11)+,VAR1
        .ENDC

        WRITELN

        .ENDM   READVAR

;

        .MACRO IF ARG1 CONDITION ARG2 THEN ACT1 ELSE ACT2-
                ?JUMP ?FIRST ?SECOND ?BYE
        CMPL    ARG1,ARG2
        B'CONDITION JUMP
```

```
        JMP       SECOND
JUMP:   JMP       FIRST
SECOND: ACT2
        JMP       BYE
FIRST:  ACT1
BYE:
        .ENDM IF
;
        .MACRO FOR INDEX IS MIN TO MAX DO ACT,-
                  STEP=1 TYPE=L ?LOOP ?BYE ?CHECK
        MOV'TYPE MIN,INDEX
CHECK:  CMP'TYPE INDEX,MAX
        BEQL      LOOP
        .IF IDN TO DOWNTO
        CMP'TYPE INDEX,MAX
        BGTR      LOOP
        .IF_FALSE
        CMP'TYPE INDEX,MAX
        BLSS      LOOP
        .ENDC
        JMP       BYE
LOOP:   ACT
        .IF IDN TO DOWNTO
        .REPEAT ^C<STEP>+1
        SUB'TYPE'2            #1,INDEX
        .ENDR
        .IF_FALSE
        .REPEAT STEP
        ADD'TYPE'2            #1,INDEX
        .ENDR
        .ENDC
        JMP       CHECK
BYE:
        .ENDM     FOR
;
        .MACRO BEGIN ACT1 ACT2 ACT3 ACT4 ACT5 ACT6 ACT7 ACT8 ACT9 ACT10 ACT11
        ACT1
        ACT2
        ACT3
        ACT4
        ACT5
        ACT6
        ACT7
        ACT8
        ACT9
        ACT10
        ACT11
        .ENDM BEGIN
;
        .MACRO END
        .ENDM
;
        .MACRO COMPUTE VAR1 IS VAR2 OP VAR3 ?QUO ?BYE
        .IF IDENTICAL DIV <OP>
        DIVL3     VAR3,VAR2,VAR1
```

```
        .IF_FALSE
        PUSHR     #^M<R7,R8>
        MOVL      VAR2,R7
        CLRL      R8
        EDIV      VAR3,R7,QUO,VAR1
        POPR      #^M<R7,R8>
        .ENDC
        BRW       BYE
QUO:    .LONG
BYE:
        .ENDM COMPUTE
;
        .MACRO REPEAT ACT UNTIL VAR1 COND VAR2 ?DO ?BYE
DO:     ACT
        CMPL      VAR1,VAR2
        B'COND    BYE
        JMP       DO
BYE:
        .ENDM REPEAT
;
        .MACRO WHILE VAR1 COND VAR2 DO ACT ?LOOP ?BYE ?AGAIN
AGAIN:  CMPL      VAR1,VAR2
        B'COND    LOOP
        JMP       BYE
LOOP:   ACT
        JMP       AGAIN
BYE:
        .ENDM WHILE
;
        .MACRO SPIKE X
        FOR I := #1 TO X DO <WRITE *>
        .ENDM SPIKE
;
        .MACRO LET VAR1 EQ VAR2
        MOVL      VAR2,VAR1
        .ENDM LET
;
        .MACRO CASE SELECTOR OF A ACT1 B ACT2 C ACT3 D ACT4 E ACT5 -
                OTHERWISE=NOP ?FLAG ?A2 ?A3 ?A4 ?A5 ?NOT_DONE ?BYE
        CLRB      FLAG
        CMPL      SELECTOR,A
        BNEQ      A2
        ACT1
        MOVB      #1,FLAG
A2:     .IF NOT_BLANK B

        CMPL      SELECTOR,B
        BNEQ      A3
        ACT2
        MOVB      #1,FLAG
        .ENDC
A3:     .IF NOT_BLANK C
        CMPL      SELECTOR,C
        BNEQ      A4
        ACT3
        MOVB      #1,FLAG
```

```
                .ENDC
A4:             .IF NOT_BLANK D
                CMPL    SELECTOR,D
                BNEQ    A5
                ACT4
                MOVB    #1,FLAG
                .ENDC
A5:             .IF NOT_BLANK E
                CMPL    SELECTOR,E
                BNEQ    NOT_DONE
                ACT5
                MOVB    #1,FLAG
                .ENDC
NOT_DONE:
                CMPB    #1,FLAG
                BEQL    BYE
                OTHERWISE
                BRB     BYE
FLAG:   .BYTE
BYE:
                .ENDM CASE
;

                .MACRO READSTRING X
                PUSHAB X
                CALLS #1,READSTR
                .ENDM READSTRING
;

                .MACRO WRITESTRING X
                PUSHAB    X
                CALLS     #1,WRITESTR
                .ENDM WRITESTRING
;

                .MACRO WRITEF VALUE SPACES=1
                MOVF      VALUE,-(SP)
                CALLS     #1,DECIMAL
                TAB       SPACES
                .ENDM WRITEF
;
```

```
;Ref.:  Appendix C.5 (A writeval macro)
;
; 1. New version of writeval:
;

                .MACRO WRITEVAL VARS RADIX=10,SPACES=1
                MOVB      #RADIX,BASE
                .IRPC VAR, <VARS>
                .IF NOT_BLANK VAR
                PUSHL     VAR
                CALLS     #1,WRITEVAL
                SPACE     SPACES
                .ENDC
                .ENDR
```

```
          .ENDM    WRITEVAL
;
          .MACRO SPACE X ?K ?LAST
          .REPEAT X
          PUSHAB    K
          CALLS     #1,WRITESTR
          .ENDR
          BRW      LAST
K:        .ASCIC<32>
LAST:     NOP
          .ENDM SPACE
;
; 2. Sample program:
;
          X:        .LONG 8
          Y:        .LONG 10
          Z:        .LONG 12
BEGIN:    .WORD
          WRITEVAL <X,Y,Z,X,Y,Z>
          $EXIT_S
          .END BEGIN

;
; 3. Sample run:
;
8 10 12 8 10 12
```

SELECTED SOLUTIONS

CHAPTER 3

```
;
;Ref:    Lab project 1, Chapter 3 (A macro to draw a cube)
;
;var
        max:        .long 3
        index:      .long 0

;Definition for instruction operator:

        .macro cube
        writeln <       >
        writeln < |\    \>
        writeln < ||    |>
        writeln < \|    |>
        .endm cube

begin:  .word

statement:
        cube
        aoblss max,index,statement

        $exit_s

        .end begin
```

RUN 131

```
;
;Ref.:    Exercise 3.3
;
(c)  200  FF              (e)  200  BC
     201  FF                   201  0A
     202  00                   202  00
     203  00                   203  00


(h)  200  FF              (k)  200  10
     201  FF                   201  01
     202  FF                   202  00
     203  FF                   203  00
                               204  00
                               205  00
                               206  00
                               207  00
```

```
;
;Ref:    Exercise 3.10 (Autoincrement and AOBLSS)
;
;VAR
        X:         .BLKL  20
        BLOCK:     .LONG  20
        INDEX:     .LONG  0
        EVEN:      .LONG  2

BEGIN:  .WORD

        MOVAL    X,R6

FILL:   MOVL     EVEN,(R6)+
        ADDL2    #2,EVEN
        AOBLSS   BLOCK,INDEX,FILL

LOOP:   JMP      LOOP

        $EXIT_S

        .END BEGIN


RUN e310

^Y

$ exa 200:250

00000200:    00000002 00000004 00000006 00000008 0000000A 0000000C 0000000E
0000021C:    00000010 00000012 00000014 00000016 00000018 0000001A 0000001C
00000238:    0000001E 00000020 00000022 00000024 00000026 00000028 00000014
```

```
;
;Ref:    Exercise 3.13        (Test of CVTxy operator)
;
;VAR
        FILLBITL: .LONG ^X<F0F0F0F0>
        EMPTBITL: .LONG ^X<79F83810>
        FILLBITW: .WORD ^X<890D>
        EMPTBITW: .WORD ^X<1001>
        FILLBITB: .BYTE ^X<AB>
        EMPTBITB: .BYTE 83

BEGIN:  .WORD

        CVTBL   FILLBITB,R6
        MOVL    R6,^X<300>

        CVTBL   EMPTBITB,R6
        MOVL    R6,^X<304>

        CVTWL   FILLBITW,R6
        MOVL    R6,^X<308>

        CVTWL   EMPTBITW,R6
        MOVL    R6,^X<30C>

        CVTBW   FILLBITB,R6
        MOVL    R6,^X<310>
        CLRL    R6

        CVTLB   FILLBITL,R6
        MOVL    R6,^X<314>

        CVTLB   EMPTBITL,R6
        MOVL    R6,^X<318>

        CVTLW   FILLBITL,R6
        MOVL    R6,^X<31C>
        CLRL    R6

        CVTWB   EMPTBITW,R6
        MOVL    R6,^X<320>

LOOP:   JMP LOOP

        $EXIT_S

        .END BEGIN

RUN e313

^Y
$ exa 300:320

00000300:  FFFFFFAB 00000053 FFFF890D 00001001 0000FFAB 000000F0 00000010
0000031C:  0000F0F0 00000001
```

```
;
;Ref:    Exercise 3.15 (Average age of family members)
;
;var
        ages:      .long 17,21,26,51,51
        max:       .long 5
        index:     .long 0
        sum:       .long

begin:  .word

        moval      ages,r7
        moval      sum,r8

statement:
        addl2      (r7)+,(r8)
        aoblss     max,index,statement

        divl2      max,(r8)

        movl       (r8),^x<300>

loop:   jmp loop

        $exit_s

        .end begin


RUN e315

^Y

$ exa 300

00000300:   00000021
```

CHAPTER 4

```
;
;Ref: Lab project #2, chapter 4 (Using string lengths)
;
;var
        a: .blkb 71
        b: .blkb 71
        c: .blkb 71
        d: .blkb 71
        e: .blkb 71
        CR: .ascic <13>
```

```
begin:    .word

          writeln
          writeln
          writeln <Input 5 strings of different lengths,>
          writeln <Limit length to 70 characters, please.>

          readstring a
          readstring b
          readstring c
          readstring d
          readstring e

          writeln
          writeln
          writeln
<         string # of chars>
          writeln
<_____>

          clrl      r8

          writestring a
          writestring CR
          tab       9
          cvtbl     a,r7
          writeval r7
          addl2     r7,r8
          writeln
          writestring b
          writestring CR
          tab       9
          cvtbl     b,r7
          writeval r7
          addl2     r7,r8
          writeln
          writestring c
          writestring CR
          tab       9
          cvtbl     c,r7
          writeval r7
          addl2     r7,r8
          writeln
          writestring d
          writestring CR
          tab       9
          cvtbl     d,r7
          writeval r7
          addl2     r7,r8
          writeln
          writestring e
          writestring CR
          tab       9
          cvtbl     e,r7
```

```
          writeval  r7
          add12     r7,r8
          writeln
          writeln
          write <For a total of >
          writeval r8
          writeln <characters.>
          writeln
          $exit_s
          .end begin
```

RUN 142

```
Input 5 strings of different lengths,
Limit length to 70 characters, please.
Sue
Susu
Susan
Here's a longer string just to test out the formatting
Why not?
```

string	# of chars
Sue	3
Susu	4
Susan	5
Here's a longer string just to test out the formatting	54
Why not?	8

For a total of 74 characters.

```
;
;Ref: Exercise 4.2 (Use of I/O macros)
;
; Note: In order to input a base and use it, requires a change in the
; macro library.  In writeval, "movl #radix" must be changed to
; "movl radix" and "radix=10" to "radix=#10".
; Then to follow examples in the book, you will probably want to change
; it back.
;
;var
        number:  .long
        choice:  .long
        tiny:    .byte

begin:  .word

        writeln
        writeln
```

```
        write <Input the integer to be printed: >
        readvar number
        writeln
        write <Input the base you would like it printed in: >
        readvar choice
        cvtlb    choice,tiny
        writeln
        write <Base 10: >
        writeval number,spaces=10
        write <Your base: >
        writeval number, radix=tiny
        writeln

        $exit_s

        .end begin
```

RUN e42

Input the integer to be printed: 21

Input the base you would like it printed in: 16

Base 10: 21   Your base: 15

RUN e42

Input the integer to be printed: 65536

Input the base you would like it printed in: 16

Base 10: 65536   Your base: 10000

RUN e42

Input the integer to be printed: 65535

Input the base you would like it printed in: 16

Base 10: 65535   Your base: FFFF

RUN e42

Input the integer to be printed: 2147483647

Input the base you would like it printed in: 16

Base 10: 2147483647   Your base: 7FFFFFFF

```
;
;Ref: Exercise 4.5 (Writing bytes)
;
;var
        x:          .blkb 20
        even:       .byte 2
        max:        .long 20
        index:      .long 0

begin:  .word

        movab       x,r6

state1:
        movb        even,(r6)+
        addb2       #2,even
        aoblss      max,index,state1

        clrl        index
        movab       x,r6

state2:
        clrl        r7
        movb        (r6)+,r7
        writeval r7
        aoblss      max,index,state2

        $exit_s

        .end begin



RUN e45

2 4 6 8 10 12 14 16 18 20 22 24 26 28 30 32 34 36 38 40
```

```
;
;Ref: Exercise 4.7 (Using writestring)
;
;var:
        string:  .ascic/The Vax-11 has 16 general registers./

begin:  .word

        writeln
        writeln
        writestring string
        writeln

        $exit_s

        .end begin
```

RUN e47

The Vax-11 has 16 general registers.

```
;
;Ref: Exercise 4.9 (The location counter)
;
;var
        a = .
        b = . + 1024
        c = . + 4096

begin:  .word

        movl    #a,r6
        movl    #b,r7
        movl    #c,r7

        writeval r6,r7,r8

        $exit_s

        .end begin
```

RUN e49

512 4608 2147407216
$

```
;
;Ref: Exercise 4.11 (.Byte and .ascii)
;
;var
        x1: .byte
        .ascii/Tom              Goldberry           the/<10><13>
        x1_length = . - x1 - 1

        x2: .byte
        .ascii/   .          .            .        ./<10><13>
        x2_length = . - x2 - 1

        x3: .byte
        .ascii/   .        .          .       .      ./<10><13>
        x3_length = . - x3 - 1

        x4: .byte
        .ascii/     .      .            .     .        ./<10><13>
        x4_length = . - x4 - 1

        x5: .byte
        .ascii/     followed             down       Withywindle./<10><13>
        x5_length = . - x5 - 1
```

```
begin:  .word

        movb      #x1_length,x1
        movb      #x2_length,x2
        movb      #x3_length,x3
        movb      #x4_length,x4
        movb      #x5_length,x5

        writestring x1
        writestring x2
        writestring x3
        writestring x4
        writestring x5

        $exit_s

        .end begin
```

RUN e411

```
Tom              Goldberry           the
    .        .          .            .
       .        .            .     .       .
   followed               down          Withywindle.
```

CHAPTER 5

```
;
;Ref.:    Exercise 5.1      (Computing the branch address)
;
a & b)  dimimish =  300              operator  operand      instruction

        -8          300         C1                          add13
        -7          301                    56               R6
        -6          302                    57               R7
        -5          303                    58               R8
        -4          304         D7                           dec1
        -3          305                    56               R6
        -2          306         12                          bneq
        -1          307         F8                          displacement
                    308                                     PC-content
```

2´s complement of 8:

```
                                        0000 1000
            1´s complement of 8 = F7
                                        1111 0111
                        +1   +1
        -------------------  --
            2´s complement of 8 = F8  = 1111 1000
```

```
        so the assembler will use 12    F8

                                      ^     ^

                     bneq    2´s complement of 8
```

c) When the bneq is executed, the PC-content is at the next instruction,
which is 308 here.

```
;
;Ref.:  Exercise 5.5 (if/then/else implementation)
;
;var
        choice:  .long

Begin:  .word

again:
        writeln <  Menu:>
        writeln <--1. December, 1983 low temp. in the USA>
        writeln
        writeln <--2. December, 1983 high temp. in the USA>
        writeln
        writeln <--3. December, 1982 low temp. in the USA>
        writeln
        writeln <--4. December, 1982 high temp. in the USA>
        writeln
        write <Enter choice:  >
        readvar choice
        cmpl    #1, choice                    :was it 1?
        bneq    else1
        jmp then1
else1:
        cmpl    #2, choice
        bneq    else2
        jmp     then2
else2:
        cmpl    #3, choice
        bneq    else3
        jmp     then3
else3:
        writeln <December 1982 high temperature was >
        jmp     doorway
then1:
        writeln <December 1983 low temperature was >
        jmp     doorway
then2:
        writeln <December 1983 high temperature was >
        jmp     doorway
then3:
        writeln <December 1982 low temperature was >
doorway:
        write <Do you wish to see another record? (1=Y,0=N): >
```

```
                readvar  r7
                cmpl     #0,r7
                beql     stop
                jmp again
stop:
                $exit_s

                .end Begin
```

```
;
;Ref.: Exercise 5.7 (Find largest number in user input)
;
;var
        x: .blkl 20
        k: .long

Begin:  .word
        writeln
        writeln
        writeln <This program will find the largest number that you>
        writeln <input.  You can input up to 15 numbers.>
        write <How many do you want to check? >
        readvar k
        writeln <Now input those numbers, each on a seperate line: >
        movl     #x,r6
        movl     #x,r8
        movl     k,r7
checker:
        readvar (r6)
        cmpl     (r6),(r8)
        blss     noadjust
        movl     r6,r8
noadjust:
        tstl     (r6)+
        sobgtr   r7,checker

        movl     #x,r6
        movl     k,r7

        writeln
        write <The highest integer of >
print:  writeval (r6), spaces=0
        tstl     (r6)+
        write <, >
        sobgtr   r7,print
        write <is >
        writeval (r8)
        writeln

        $exit_s

        .end Begin
```

```
RUN e57

This program will find the largest number that you
input.  You can input up to 15 numbers.
How many do you want to check? 8

Now input those numbers, each on a seperate line:
23

456

76

19

4

234

603

3


The highest integer of 23, 456, 76, 19, 4, 234, 603, 3, is 603

Do you have another list to check? (1=Y,0=N): 1


How many do you want to check? 2

Now input those numbers, each on a seperate line:
9999

9998


The highest integer of 9999, 9998, is 9999

Do you have another list to check? (1=Y,0=N): 0
```

```
;
;Ref.: Exercise 5.12 (alphabet triangle)
;
;var
        row:      .long 1
        column:   .long 0
        count:    .long
        letter:   .ascic/a /

Begin:  .word
```

```
              writeln
              writeln
              write <How many rows do you want in your alphabet triangle? >
              readvar count
              writeln

make1:    tab 3
make2:    writestring letter
          incb     letter+1
          incl     column
          cmpl     column,row
          bneq     make2

          writeln
          writeln
          incl     row
          clrl     column
          cmpl     count,row
          blss     doorway
          jmp      make1
doorway:
          $exit_s

          .end Begin
```

RUN e512

How many rows do you want in your alphabet triangle? 5

```
                         a

                         b c

                         d e f

                         g h i j

                         k l m n o
```

CHAPTER 6

```
;
;Ref.:    Exercise 6.6  (Paper cup dispenser stack)
;
6.      A paper cup dispenser is a downward stack because the cups
    are put onto the stack below those already on the stack.
        This is an inefficient stack because all the cups are moved
    each time a new one is pushed onto the stack or an old one is
    popped off.
```

```
;
;Ref.:  Exercise 6.7 (System stack)
;
;var
        first:   .long 0
        second:  .long 1
        third:   .long
        count:   .long 0

Begin:  .word

        writeln
        writeln

replay:
        addl3    first,second,third
        pushl    third
        movl     first,second
        movl     third,first
        aoblss   #10,count,replay

        movl     SP,r6

printl: popl     r7
        writeval r7
        sobgtr   count,printl

        writeln
        writeln
        writeln <Second time around:>
        movl     r6,SP

print2: writeval (SP)
        tstl     (SP)+
        aoblss   #10,count,print2

        writeln

        $exit_s

        .end Begin


RUN e67

55 34 21 13 8 5 3 2 1 1


Second time around:

0 566231040 2147058636 2147058564 755 2147058524 1 2147407216 1 758
```

```
;
;Ref.:  Exercise 6.12 (Queue and dequeue)
;
;var
        x:          .long -1
        y:          .long 2
        z:          .long 2
        odds:       .long
        Luc_queue:          .blkl 15
        Luc_queue_head:     .long
        odd_queue:          .blkl 10
        odd_queue_head:     .long

Begin:  .word

        movab   Luc_queue_head,r6

enqueue:
        movl    z,-(r6)
        add13   x,y,z
        movl    y,x
        movl    z,y
        aoblss  #12,count,enqueue

        movab   Luc_queue_head,r6
        movab   odd_queue_head,r11

dequeue:
        movl    -(r6),r7
        clrl    r8
        ediv    #2,r7,r9,r10
        tstl    r10
        bneq    enqueue_odd
        jmp     next_Lucas_no
enqueue_odd:
        movl    r7,-(r11)
        incl    odds
next_Lucas_no:
        sobgtr  count,dequeue

        writeln
        writeln
        writeln <12 Lucas numbers:>
        movab   Luc_queue_head,r6

Lucas:
        tstl    -(r6)
        writeval (r6)
        aoblss  #12,count,Lucas

        writeln
        writeln
        writeln <Those which are odd:>
```

```
movab       odd_queue_head,r6
odd:

        tstl     -(r6)
        writeval (r6)
        sobgtr   odds,odd

        writeln

        $exit_s

        .end Begin
```

RUN e612

12 Lucas numbers:
2 1 3 4 7 11 18 29 47 76 123 199

Those which are odd:
1 3 7 11 29 47 123 199

CHAPTER 7

```
;
;Ref.:  Lab project #1, chapter 7 (coroutines)
;
;var
        rows:     .long
        char:     .blkb 3
        step:     .long 1
        index:    .long 0
        tally:    .long 1

Begin:  .word
        writeln
        writeln
        write <What character do you want to make a triangle with? >
        readstring char
        writeln
        writeln
        write <How many rows do you want in your triangle? >
        readvar rows
        writeln

        jsb      Odd

        $exit_s

Odd:
check1: cmpl     index,rows
        bgeq     out1
        add12    #1,index
```

```
        jsb      print
        jsb      even
        brw      check1
out1:   rsb

Even:
check2: cmpl     index,rows
        bgeq     out2
        addl2    #1,index
        jsb      print
        jsb      @(sp)+
        brw      check2
out2:   rsb

Print:
        movl     #1,tally
another:
        writestring char
        space    1
        acbl     index,step,tally,another
        writeln

        rsb

        .end Begin
```

RUN L71

What character do you want to make a triangle with? A

How many rows do you want in your triangle? 5

```
A
A A
A A A
A A A A
A A A A A
```

RUN L71

What character do you want to make a triangle with? t

How many rows do you want in your triangle? 8

```
t
t t
t t t
t t t t
t t t t t
t t t t t t
t t t t t t t
t t t t t t t t
```

```
;
;Ref.:   Figure 7.4 (A program with two external subroutines)
;
;var

        .global             builder,Lucas_differences

        Lucas::             .blkl 20
        x::                 .long 3
        y::                 .long -1
        max::               .long
        step::              .long 1
        index1:: .long 1
        index2:: .long 1
        diff::              .long
        answer:             .long

Begin:  .word

again:

        jsb     builder                     ;call external routine
                                            ;to build list of Lucas nos.
        moval   Lucas,r6                    ;init. r6 as list selector
        movl    #1,index1

        jsb     Lucas_differences           ;call external routine to
                                            ;compute differences
        write <Another run?--1=Y,0=N : >
        readvar answer
        cmpl    #0,answer
        beql    doorway
        movl    #3,x                        ;restore original x-value
        movl    #-1,y                       ;restore original y-value
        movl    #1,index1                   ;restore original index
        movl    #1,index2
        jmp     again

doorway:

        $exit_s

        .end Begin


;
;Ref.:   Figure 7.4 (continued)
;
;Content:        One external subroutine

        .global             builder

builder::
```

```
          write <Enter max in L(0),L(1), ... ,L(max) : >
          readvar max
          moval     Lucas,r6                    ;init. r6 as list selector

sequence:

          addl3     x,y,(r6)                     ;compute sum
          movl      y,x
          movl      (r6)+,y
          acbl      max,step,index1,sequence

          rsb

          .end
```

```
;
;Ref.:  Exercise 7.4, 2nd external subroutine (Lucas differences)
;

Lucas_differences::

          moval     Lucas,r6

print:    writeval  (r6),spaces=6
          tstl      (r6)+
          acbl      max,step,index1,print

          writeln
          movl      #1,index1
          moval     Lucas,r6
          subl2     #1,max
          write <    >

differences:
          subl3     (r6),4(r6),diff
          writeval  diff,spaces=6
          tstl      (r6)+
          acbl      index2,step,index1,differences
          writeln
          write <    >
          moval     Lucas,r6
          movl      #1,index1
          acbl      max,step,index2,differences

          writeln

          rsb

          .end

RUN e74

Enter max in L(0),L(1), ... ,L(max) : 5
```

```
2      1      3      4      7
  -1
  -1     2
  -1     2      1
  -1     2      1      3
```

Another run?--1=Y,0=N : 1

Enter max in L(0),L(1), ... ,L(max) : 10

```
2      1      3      4      7      11      18      29      47      76
  -1
  -1     2
  -1     2      1
  -1     2      1      3
  -1     2      1      3      4
  -1     2      1      3      4      7
  -1     2      1      3      4      7      11
  -1     2      1      3      4      7      11      18
  -1     2      1      3      4      7      11      18      29
```

Another run?--1=Y,0=N : 0

CHAPTER 8

```
;
;Ref.:  Lab project #2, chapter 8 (Geometric numbers with 4 external procedures)
;
;Method:
;       Use the formula
;                             i(i+1)/2, i = 1,2,3,...,n (n=natural no.)
;
;       to produce a list of triangular numbers and to use certain list
;       entries to print corresponding triangles.  Each triangular number
;       becomes the limit on the outside of three nested acbl loops.

        index::  .long 1
        nos:     .blkl 50                    ;referenced by place-arg

argument_list:

        place:   .long nos                   ;place references nos. list
        i:       .long 1                     ;used in generating nos
        a:.long 4                            ;not used
        b:.long 5                            ;not used
        c:.long ^x<aaa>                      ;not used
        resp1: .long
        resp2: .long
        resp3: .long
        arg:                                 ;ap points here!
                .long 8
                .address place,i,a,b,c,resp1,resp2,resp3
```

```
Begin:  .word
over:
        callg   arg,enquiry
        tstl    respl
        beql    bye

        callg   arg,geometric_nos          ;build list

        callg   arg,echo                   ;echo what's been done

        callg   arg,pictures               ;draw pictures

        jmp     over
bye:
        $exit_s

        .end Begin
```

```
;
;Ref.:  Lab project #2, chapter 8 (Geometric numbers with 4 external procedures)
;

        j:      .long                      ;local variable

        .entry geometric_nos,0
        movl    @4(ap),r6                  ;get address of list
        movl    @8(ap),r7                  ;get value of i (note:
                                           ;in enhanced versions of
                                           ;this pgm, this will be
                                           ;selected by the user
        addl3   #1,r7,j                    ;init. j
        movl    #1,index                   ;set up loop index

triangular_nos:

        clrl    r9                         ;set up quad for ediv
        movl    j,r8                       ;set up factor
        mull2   r7,r8                      ;i(i + 1)
        ediv    #2,r8,r10,r11              ;get quotient
        movl    r10,(r6)+                  ;save no. in list
        incl    r7                         ;new i
        incl    j                          ;new i + 1
        acbl    @28(ap),#1,index,triangular_nos    ;repeat production
                                           ;until index = 20

        ret

        .entry echo,0

        movl    @4(ap),r6                  ;get list address
        movl    #1,index                   ;init. index
        writeln
        writeln <            Triangular numbers:>
        writeln
```

```
        writeln <----------------------------------------------------->
        writeln

copy:

        writeval (r6)
        addl2   #4,r6
        acbl    @28(ap),#1,index,copy

        writeln
        writeln

        ret

local_variables:

        x:      .long 1                  ;dot-determiner
        triangle:
                .long                    ;row-determiner
        index1: .long 1                  ;innermost loop
        index2: .long 1                  ;second loop
        index3: .long 1                  ;outer loop

        .entry pictures,0

        movl    @4(ap),r6                ;get list address
        movl    #1,index3
        movl    @8(ap),triangle

        next_triangle:

                no:

                        row:

                        write < . >
                        acbl x,#1,index1,row

                movl        #1,index1
                incl        x
                writeln
                acbl        triangle,#1,index2,no

        movl    #1,index2
        writeln
        writeln
        movl    #1,x
        incl    triangle
        acbl    @32(ap),#1,index3,next_triangle

        ret

        .entry enquiry,0

        writeln
        writeln
        writeln <This program computes and prints triangular numbers>
```

```
        writeln <and then makes the triangles for these numbers.>
        write <Would you like to see a run? (1=yes,0=no) >
        readvar  @24(ap)
        tstl     @24(ap)
        bneq     continue
        jmp      doorway
continue:
        writeln
        write <Input starting place in triangular number series: >
        readvar @8(ap)
        writeln
        write <How many triangular numbers shall we make? (limit 50) >
        readvar @28(ap)
        writeln
        write <How many pictures do you want? >
        readvar @32(ap)
        writeln
doorway:
        ret

        .end

        RUN L82
```

This program computes and prints triangular numbers
and then makes the triangles for these numbers.
Would you like to see a run? (1=yes,0=no) 1

Input starting place in triangular number series: 1

How many triangular numbers shall we make? (limit 50) 10

How many pictures do you want? 10

```
            Triangular numbers:

    --------------------------------------------------

    1 3 6 10 15 21 28 36 45 55

        .


        .
        .   .


        .
        .   .
        .   .   .


        .
        .   .
        .   .   .
        .   .   .   .
```

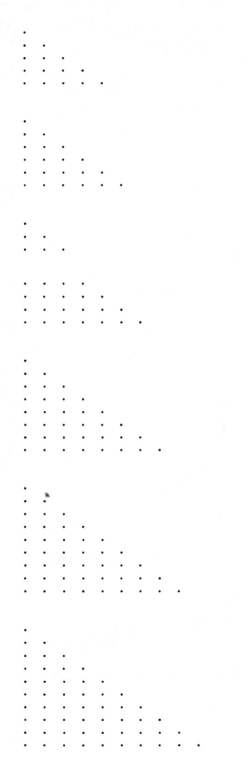

```
This program computes and prints triangular numbers
and then makes the triangles for these numbers.
Would you like to see a run? (1=yes,0=no) 1

Input starting place in triangular number series: 3

How many triangular numbers shall we make? (limit 50) 10

How many pictures do you want? 4

        Triangular numbers:

----------------------------------------------------

6  10  15  21  28  36  45  55  66  78


   .
   .   .
   .   .   .


   .
   .   .
   .   .   .
   .   .   .   .


   .
   .   .
   .   .   .
   .   .   .   .
   .   .   .   .   .


   .
   .   .
   .   .   .
   .   .   .   .
   .   .   .   .   .
   .   .   .   .   .   .




This program computes and prints triangular numbers
and then makes the triangles for these numbers.
Would you like to see a run? (1=yes,0=no) 0
```

```
;
;Ref.:  Exercise 8.6 (Using callg and exhibiting call frame)
;
;var
        a:  .long ^x<ffa>
        b:  .long ^x<999>
        c:  .long a
```

```
        d: .long b
        e: .long ^x<377>
        x: .long ^x<aabbcc>
        store: .long
        answer: .long
        list: .long 8
              .address a,b,c,d,e,x,store,answer

Begin:  .word
again:

        callg    list,sum

        callg    list,exhibit

        callg    list,enquiry

        tstl     answer
        bneq     again

        $exit_s

        .entry sum,^m<r6>
        clrl     r6
        addl2    @4(ap),r6
        addl2    @8(ap),r6
        addl2    @20(ap),r6
        addl2    @24(ap),r6
        movl     r6,@28(ap)

        ret

        index:   .long

        .entry exhibit,0

        writeln
        writeln <           Argument list:>
        writeln
        writeln <           ap    (ap)-content                    @(ap)-content>
        writeln
        writeln <----------------------------------------------------------->
        writeln

        movl     #1,index
        movl ap,r6
        write < >                             ;< > = tab
        writeval r6 (r6) radix=#16 spaces=9
        addl2    #4,r6
        writeln

loop:

        movl     @(r6),r7
        write < >                             ;< > = tab
        writeval r6 (r6) r7 radix=#16 spaces=9
```

```
        writeln
        addl2    #4,r6
        acbl     #8,#1,index,loop

        writeln
        write <The sum is >
        writeval @28(ap) radix=#16
        writeln
        writeln
        write <The addresses of a and b (contained in c and d) are >
        writeval @12(ap),@16(ap) radix=#16
        writeln
        writeln

        ret

        .entry enquiry,0
        writeln <Would you like to run this program>
        write <with your own numbers? (1=yes,0=no) >
        readvar @32(ap)
        writeln
        tstl     @32(ap)
        bneq     continue
        jmp      doorway
continue:
        write <Input 2 hex numbers: >
        readvar @4(ap),@8(ap) radix=16
        writeln
        write <2 more: >
        readvar @20(ap),@24(ap) radix=16
        writeln
doorway:
        writeln

        ret

        .end Begin
```

RUN e86

```
        Argument list:

        ap       (ap)-content     @(ap)-content

--------------------------------------------------------------
        220      8
        224      200              FFA
        228      204              999
        22C      208              200
        230      20C              204
        234      210              377
        238      214              AABBCC
        23C      218              AAD8D6
        240      21C              0
```

The sum is AAD8D6

The addresses of a and b (contained in c and d) are 200 204

Would you like to run this program
with your own numbers? (1=yes,0=no) 1

Input 2 hex numbers: 9000,25555

2 more: AB,2

        Argument list:

        ap   (ap)-content   @(ap)-content

----

        220   8
        224   200   9000
        228   204   25555
        22C   208   200
        230   20C   204
        234   210   **AB**
        238   214   2
        23C   218   2E602
        240   21C   1

The sum is 2E602

The addresses of a and b (contained in c and d) are 200 204

Would you like to run this program
with your own numbers? (1=yes,0=no) 0

CHAPTER 9

```
;
;Ref.:  Exercise 9.7 (A program with numeric and string I/O)

        prompt1:.ascic /Enter your name: /
        prompt2:.ascic /Enter your age in years: /
        cr:       .ascic<13><10><10>
        tab:      .ascic<9>
        name:     .blkb 30
        result1:.ascic /, you have lived:  /<10><10><13>
        result2:.ascic /Months    Days      Hour    Minutes    Seconds/<10><13>
        v:        .long
        w:        .long
        x:        .long
        y:        .long
        z:        .long
```

```
Begin:   .word

         pushab    cr
         calls     #1,writestr

         pushal    prompt1
         calls     #1,writestr                ;prompt for name

         pushab    name
         calls     #1,readstr

         pushab    cr
         calls     #1,writestr

         pushab    prompt2
         calls     #1,writestr

         calls     #0,readval                 ;get age
         movl      (rll)+,w

         pushab    cr
         calls     #1,writestr

         mull3     #12,w,v                     ;compute months lived
         mull2     #365,w                      ;compute days lived
         mull3     #24,w,x                     ;compute hours lived
         mull3     #60,x,y                     ;compute minutes lived
         mull3     #60,y,z                     ;compute seconds lived

         pushab    name
         calls     #1,writestr

         pushal    result1
         calls     #1,writestr                ;print explanation

         pushal    result2
         calls     #1,writestr

         pushl     v
         calls     #1,writeval                ;print months

         pushal    tab
         calls     #1,writestr

         pushl     w
         calls     #1,writeval                ;print days

         pushal    tab
         calls     #1,writestr

         pushl     x
         calls     #1,writeval                ;print hours

         pushal    tab
         calls     #1,writestr
```

```
        pushl    y
        calls    #1,writeval                      ;print minutes

        pushal   tab
        calls    #1,writestr

        pushl    z
        calls    #1,writeval                      ;print seconds

        $exit_s

        .end Begin
```

RUN e97

Enter your name: Sue

Enter your age in years: 21

Sue, you have lived:

Months	Days	Hours	Minutes	Seconds
252	7665	183960	11037600	662256000
$				

CHAPTER 11

```
;
;Ref.:    Lab project #2, chapter 11
;
;Note: use macro knuth + pas/lib
         link knuth + io/lib
;
BUF:    .LONG 0,0
K:      .LONG 0
N:      .LONG
M:      .LONG
U:      .BLKB 25                        ;U is 1st digit array
V:      .BLKB 25                        ;V is 2nd digit array
W:      .BLKB 50                        ;W is the resultant array

.ENTRY BEGIN,0
        MOVL #10,BASE
        WRITELN <Enter each factor on separate lines.>
        SPACE <6>
        CALLS #0,READNO
        MOVL COUNT,M                    ;M := # of digits in array U
        MOVC COUNT,INSTR,U+1
        WRITE <   X   >
        CLRL COUNT
        CALLS #0,READNO
        MOVL COUNT,N                    ;N := # of digits in array V
```

```
                MOVC COUNT,INSTR,V+1
                MOVL N,R6                        ;R6 is pointer for V
REPEAT:  TSTB V(R6)                              ;REPEAT
                BNEQ JUMP1                        ;IF V[R6]<>0 THEN
                JMP ELSE                          ;
JUMP1:   MOVL M,R7                               ;R7 is pointer for U
                CLRL K                           ;clear carry K
REP2:    CLRQ BUF                                 ;REPEAT
                MULB3 U(R7),V(R6),BUF            ;BUF:=U[R7]*V[R6]+W[R6+R7]+K
                MOVL R6,R10
                ADDL2 R7,R10
                ADDB2 W(R10),BUF
                ADDL2 K,BUF
                EDIV BASE,BUF,R5,R9
                MOVL R5,K                        ;K := BUF DIV BASE
                MOVB R9,W(R10)                   ;W(R10) := BUF MOD BASE
                DECL R7
                BLEQ JUMP2
                JMP REP2                          ;UNTIL R7=0
JUMP2:   MOVB K,W(R6)                            ;set W(R6) := last quotient
                BRB LOOP3
ELSE:    CLRB W(R6)                              ;ELSE set W(R6) := 0
LOOP3:   DECL R6
                BLEQ JUMP3
                JMP REPEAT                        ;UNTIL R6=0
JUMP3:   ADDL2 M,N
                MOVL #1,R6
                MOVL N,R10
                CLRL R5
                WRITELN <------------------------>
                SPACE <6>
LOOP4:   CLRL R9                                  ;print out resultant array W
                MOVB W(R6),R9                    ;get rid of first 0´s
                TSTB R9
                BNEQ PRINT
                INCB R6
                AOBLSS R10,R5,LOOP4
PRINT:   PUSHL R9                                 ;and then print the rest of the array
                CALLS #1,WRITEVAL
                INCB R6
                MOVB W(R6),R9
                AOBLSS R10,R5,PRINT
                $EXIT_S
.END BEGIN


RUN KNUTH

Enter each factor on separate lines.
     233
   x  2
------------------------
     466
```

```
;
;Ref.:  Exercise 11.5 (Enhanced bubble sort on a string of chars.)
;
;var
        buffc:   .byte
        buffl:   .long
        L:       .blkb 80
        answer:  .long
        swaps:   .byte 0
        store:   .byte 1,0
;
;
begin:  .word

again:  writeln
        writeln
        write <Input a character string to be sorted: >
        pushab   L
        calls    #1,readstr
        writeln
        writeln

        movab    L+1,r6
loop:   addl3    #1,r6,r7
        movb     #0,swaps
swap:   cmpb     (r6),(r7)
        bleq     cork
        movb     (r6),buffc
        movb     (r7),(r6)
        movb     buffc,(r7)
        movb     #1,swaps
cork:   tstb     (r7)+
        subl3    #L,r7,buffl
        cmpb     buffl,L
        bleq     swap

        tstb     swaps
        beql     sorted
        tstb     (r6)+
        subl3    #L,r6,buffl
        cmpb     buffl,L
        blss     loop
sorted:
        movl     #L,r6
        incl     r6
        movab    store+1,r7
        movb     L,buffl
ascend:
        movb     (r6)+,(r7)
        spurt    store
        sobgtr   buffl,ascend
        writeln
```

```
descend:
        movb      -(r6),(r7)
        spurt     store
        cmpl      #L,r6
        blss      descend

        writeln
        writeln
        write <Would you like to run this again? (yes=1,no=0) >
        readvar answer
        tstl      answer
        beql      doorway
        jmp       again

doorway:
        $exit_s
        .end begin
```

RUN e115

Input a character string to be sorted: computing is best in wintertime

    bceeegiiiiimmnnnoprssttttuw
wuttttsssrponnnmmiiiiigeeecb

Would you like to run this again? (yes=1,no=0) 1

Input a character string to be sorted: the PC is a sliding arrow

    CPaadeghiiiilnorrsstw
wtssrronliiihgedaaPC

Would you like to run this again? (yes=1,no=0) 0

CHAPTER 12

```
;
;Ref.:  Exercise 12.3  (Can READVAL read in a negative number?)
;
```
No. If a -233 is entered, the first character readval will discover is
the "-", for which the ascii code is 45. The test in readval is to see
if the ascii code is 48 or greater. Anything else is considered to be a
delimiter. So when the "-" is encountered, the present contents of r6
will be pushed on to the stack (this will probably be a zero) and readval
will go on to read the value 233.

```
;
;Ref.:   Exercise 12.5   (Output of value in user-specified base)
;
;var
        number:   .long
;
Begin:  .word
        writeln
        writeln
        writeln<This program will output a number input by the user>
        writeln<in a base input by the user.>
again:  writeln
        write <Input your number: >
        calls    #0,readval
        movl     (r11)+,number
        writeln
        writeln
        write <Input the base you want to see it in: >
        calls    #0,readval
        writeln
        writeln
        write <Your number:  >
        pushl    number
        calls    #1,writeval
        write < base (10), >
        movl     (r11)+,base
        pushl    number
        calls    #1,writeval
        write < base (>
        movl     base,number
        movl     #10,base
        pushl    number
        calls    #1,writeval
        writeln <)>
        writeln
        write <Would you like to run it again? (1=yes,0=no) >
        calls    #0,readval
        writeln
        movl     (r11)+,number
        beql     doorway
        jmp      again
doorway:
        $exit_s

        .end Begin


RUN e125

This program will output a number input by the user
in a base input by the user.

Input your number: 32767
```

```
Input the base you want to see it in: 16

Your number:  32767 base (10), 7FFF base (16)

Would you like to run it again? (1=yes,0=no) 1


Input your number: 1073741824

Input the base you want to see it in: 2

Your number:  1073741824 base (10), 1000000000000000000000000000000 base (2)

Would you like to run it again? (1=yes,0=no) 1


Input your number: 1073741824

Input the base you want to see it in: 16

Your number:  1073741824 base (10), 40000000 base (16)

Would you like to run it again? (1=yes,0=no) 1


Input your number: 65536

Input the base you want to see it in: 2

Your number:  65536 base (10), 10000000000000000 base (2)

Would you like to run it again? (1=yes,0=no) 0
```

CHAPTER 14

```
;
;Ref.:  Lab project #1, chapter 14 (Shift register random number generator)
;
;var
        x:          .word
        y:          .long
        rnd:        .long
        q:          .long
        product:.long
                    .long 0
        range:      .long 10
        index:      .long 0
;
begin:  .word
```

```
        $numtim_s-
                timbuf=x,-
                timadr=0
        movl    range,r7
        movw    x,r6
loop:
        ashl    #-3,r6,r6
        addw2   x,r6
        movl    r6,y
        ashl    #4,r6,r6
        addl2   y,r6
        movl    r6,product
        clrl    product+4
        ediv    r7,product,q,rnd
        abs     rnd
        writeval rnd
        cvtlw   r6,x
        acbl    #1000,#1,index,loop

        $exit_s

        .end begin
```

RUN 1141

```
0 3 2 8 7 5 2 0 4 2 0 7 1 7 8 8 8 1 4 1 9 9 8 8 0 8 6 3 3 0 1 0 6 6 3 2 0 7 0 0
7 6 3 7 4 4 1 5 2 9 6 3 0 9 2 8 1 3 8 1 1 8 1 9 7 6 7 9 0 9 0 0 8 6 0 3 8 2 0 3
5 9 5 1 7 8 4 8 2 6 6 6 4 0 2 1 2 0 8 2 7 0 4 7 6 2 8 7 5 6 3 9 3 0 0 6 3 3 9 0
3 3 0 6 8 8 5 4 2 4 1 3 5 6 2 2 9 9 5 5 8 1 8 2 5 5 3 1 4 7 0 9 4 4 2 0 3 4 5 8
3 2 2 7 8 5 2 3 5 3 3 9 5 1 5 4 8 6 8 6 8 6 5 1 6 3 1 7 9 8 6 6 9 8 9 0 0 3 7 1
6 2 3 5 6 8 1 0 1 4 6 4 1 7 3 7 8 5 7 9 5 6 9 9 6 4 7 2 0 9 6 5 0 8 3 4 1 5 5 5
3 5 8 9 5 5 9 3 3 0 2 6 6 8 3 1 1 8 2 9 6 8 6 9 0 1 6 9 7 4 0 9 8 8 9 7 7 4 2 6
2 5 9 8 1 1 4 8 6 6 5 5 5 3 4 8 2 2 5 6 9 7 4 9 5 6 2 3 2 1 7 4 3 6 2 1 4 2 7 2
4 3 8 1 9 7 9 0 3 4 5 4 4 0 2 4 2 2 6 6 4 6 0 2 1 2 2 6 7 4 0 6 3 6 9 1 5 7 9 9
0 8 7 7 7 7 0 0 6 5 3 5 3 5 4 7 0 4 0 6 0 8 9 7 4 1 6 6 5 8 6 0 4 7 1 2 1 0 4 0
8 8 8 9 0 4 1 2 9 1 2 8 3 1 2 7 5 7 4 0 2 7 2 8 9 8 8 5 6 7 3 0 9 6 9 6 0 0 9 1
2 9 6 1 0 6 2 1 1 9 5 4 0 0 2 7 0 3 1 6 7 0 6 2 3 3 3 0 3 6 1 4 9 8 5 2 9 4 5 2
9 8 8 3 0 6 0 0 9 1 5 3 4 9 1 3 7 8 7 2 4 5 3 8 6 6 3 2 6 3 6 0 2 6 6 0 2 4 8 0
8 0 8 3 0 6 8 5 3 4 7 2 0 0 8 2 6 9 9 8 2 0 7 9 8 9 6 5 2 5 2 4 0 2 4 1 0 0 7 2
2 9 1 9 1 5 5 1 2 3 6 6 1 2 2 6 0 3 3 6 6 0 4 1 5 0 5 8 2 1 0 7 9 6 4 2 7 8 7 7
8 0 4 8 7 9 6 5 7 7 7 9 5 8 2 2 8 6 1 0 3 8 7 2 2 1 6 2 2 9 1 5 7 9 3 6 2 1 6 4 3
7 6 5 4 0 1 4 9 2 7 1 6 8 8 0 7 4 4 7 0 3 8 4 4 3 7 2 7 9 2 9 8 2 1 4 5 2 9 6 6
2 5 9 4 0 7 6 9 5 7 8 5 6 6 9 9 4 5 5 6 0 1 6 9 1 3 1 1 8 6 4 8 9 2 6 8 9 0 1 9
7 1 1 4 6 7 6 4 9 8 2 9 4 6 3 9 5 6 5 0 1 8 1 8 7 8 2 4 2 3 0 1 8 0 6 8 3 0 2 3
1 9 9 5 4 8 0 2 4 7 2 2 5 6 5 7 7 3 3 7 1 6 0 0 9 0 9 2 1 0 9 4 3 7 0 6 6 4 5 4
5 5 5 7 9 7 1 5 6 7 3 1 4 6 9 5 8 4 3 8 8 2 1 0 8 3 2 0 1 0 3 9 5 9 4 4 0 1 9 5
1 8 9 4 2 0 7 2 1 4 0 6 6 8 9 9 4 1 8 0 6 2 2 8 0 0 5 2 2 6 8 1 4 2 9 0 7 5 6 8
2 3 4 4 6 4 1 1 2 5 5 2 5 0 3 4 4 6 9 5 6 1 9 8 2 3 0 2 8 6 7 8 8 9 5 7 2 4 5 8
6 6 8 5 8 9 1 4 4 0 2 6 3 2 9 4 4 5 4 1 2 5 0 1 9 2 9 7 2 5 2 9 8 0 6 6 4 8 7 0
4 2 2 5 9 8 4 9 0 2 4 4 8 4 7 4 4 1 9 1 8 2 9 2 4 2 8 2 0 4 8 8 8 6 8 2 5 4 8 9
5
```

CHAPTER 19

```
;
;REF.:  LAB project #3, chapter 19
;
CR:     .ASCIC<13>
I:      .FLOAT
J:      .FLOAT
K:      .FLOAT 1
TRINUM: .BLKL   50
RECIPS: .BLKL   50
PARSUM: .FLOAT


        .ENTRY RECIP,0

        MOVAF   TRINUM,R6
        MOVAF   RECIPS,R7

        FOR I := #1 TO #30 DO -
                <BEGIN -
                        <ADDF3          #1,I,J> -
                        <MULF3          I,J,K> -
                        <DIVF3          #2,K,(R6)+> -
                        <DIVF3          K,#2,(R7)+> -
                END> -
                TYPE=F

        MOVAF   TRINUM,R6
        MOVAF   RECIPS,R7

        WRITELN
        WRITELN <    i           i(i+1)\2        2\(i(i+1)) >
        WRITELN <-------      ----------      ------------>
        WRITELN

        FOR I := #1 TO #30 DO -
                <BEGIN -
                        <SPACE 3> -
                        <WRITEF I,SPACES=2> -
                        <WRITEF         (R6)+,SPACES=2> -
                        <WRITEF         (R7)+> -
                        <WRITELN> -
                END> -
                TYPE=F

        MOVAF   RECIPS,R7

        WRITELN

        FOR I := #1 TO #9 DO -
                <BEGIN -
                <MOVAF   TRINUM,R6> -
```

```
                  <FOR J := #1 TO I DO -
                  <BEGIN -
                  <WRITE <1\>> -
                  <WRITEF              (R6)+,SPACES=0> -
                  <IF I EQL J THEN <WRITE <    >> ELSE <WRITE < + >>> -
                  END> -
                  TYPE=F> -
        <SPURT CR> -
        <TAB 8> -
        <ADDF2    (R7)+,PARSUM> -
        <WRITEF PARSUM> -
        <WRITELN> -
        END> -
        TYPE=F

$EXIT_S

.END RECIP

RUN 1193


     i           i(i+1)\2         2\(i(i+1))
  -------       ----------       ------------

     1            1               1
     2            3               0.33333
     3            6               0.16666
     4           10               0.10000
     5           15               0.06666
     6           21               0.04761
     7           28               0.03571
     8           36               0.02777
     9           45               0.02222
    10           55               0.01818
    11           66               0.01515
    12           78               0.01282
    13           91               0.01098
    14          105               0.00952
    15          120               0.00833
    16          136               0.00735
    17          153               0.00653
    18          171               0.00584
    19          190               0.00526
    20          210               0.00476
    21          231               0.00432
    22          253               0.00395
    23          276               0.00362
    24          300               0.00333
    25          325               0.00307
    26          351               0.00284
    27          378               0.00264
    28          406               0.00246
    29          435               0.00229
    30          465               0.00215
```

```
1\1                                                                      1
1\1 + 1\3                                                                1.33333
1\1 + 1\3 + 1\6                                                          1.50000
1\1 + 1\3 + 1\6 + 1\10                                                   1.60000
1\1 + 1\3 + 1\6 + 1\10 + 1\15                                           1.66666
1\1 + 1\3 + 1\6 + 1\10 + 1\15 + 1\21                                    1.71428
1\1 + 1\3 + 1\6 + 1\10 + 1\15 + 1\21 + 1\28                             1.75000
1\1 + 1\3 + 1\6 + 1\10 + 1\15 + 1\21 + 1\28 + 1\36                      1.77777
1\1 + 1\3 + 1\6 + 1\10 + 1\15 + 1\21 + 1\28 + 1\36 + 1\45               1.80000
```

ANSWER KEY

Chapter 1 key:

1.

a	b	c	d	e	f	g	h	i	j	k	l	m	n	o	p	q
T	F	T	F	F	T	T	F	T	F	F	F	F	T	F	F	T

2.(a) F (b) 8192 (c) FFFF FFFF

Chapter 2 key:

1	2	3	4	5	6	7	8	9	10	11	12	13	14	15	16	17	18
F	T	T	F	T	F	T	T	T	F	F	F	T	F	T	F	F	T

Chapter 3 key:

1	2	3	4	5	6	7	8	9	10	11	12	13	14	15	16	17	18
F	T	T	F	F	F	T	T	T	T	F	T	T	F	T	F	F	T

Chapter 4 key:

1	2	3	4	5	6	7	8	9	10	11	12	13	14	15
T	T	F	T	T	F	F	T	T	T	T	T	F	T	F

Chapter 5 key:

1	2	3	4	5	6	7	8	9	10	11	12	13	14	15
T	F	T	F	T	F	T	T	F	F	T	F	F	F	F

Chapter 6 key:

1	2	3	4	5	6	7	8	9	10	11	12	13	14	15
F	F	F	T	T	F	T	T	T	F	F	T	F	F	F

Chapter 7 key:

1	2	3	4	5	6	7	8	9	10	11	12	13	14
T	F	T	T	F	F	T	T	F	F	F	F	T	F

Chapter 8 key:

1	2	3	4	5	6	7	8	9	10	11	12	13	14
T	F	T	T	T	T	T	F	T	T	T	T	T	F

Chapter 9 key:

1	2	3	4	5	6	7	8	9	10
T	T	F	F	T	T	T	T	F	F

Chapter 10 key:

1	2	3	4	5	6	7	8	9	10
T	F	T	F	T	F	T	F	T	T

Chapter 11 key:

1	2	3	4	5	6	7	8	9	10	11	12	13	14
F	T	F	T	T	T	T	T	F	T	T	T	T	F

Chapter 12 key:

1	2	3	4	5	6	7	8	9	10	11	12	13	14	15
F	T	T	T	F	T	T	T	T	T	F	T	T	T	T

Chapter 13 key:

1	2	3	4	5	6	7	8	9	10	11	12	13	14	15
F	T	T	T	T	T	T	F	T	T	T	T	T	F	F

Chapter 14 key:

1	2	3	4	5	6	7	8	9	10	11	12
T	T	F	F	T	T	T	T	T	T	T	F

Chapter 15 key:

1	2	3	4	5	6	7	8	9	10	11	12	13	14
T	T	F	F	T	T	T	T	T	T	T	T	T	T

Chapter 16 key:

1	2	3	4	5	6	7	8	9	10	11	12	13	14
T	T	T	F	T	F	T	F	F	T	T	F	T	T

Chapter 17 key:

1	2	3	4	5	6	7	8	9	10	11	12	13	14
F	T	T	T	T	T	T	F	F	T	T	T	T	T

Chapter 18 key:

1	2	3	4	5	6	7	8	9	10	11	12
T	T	T	T	T	T	T	T	T	T	T	F

Chapter 19 key:

1	2	3	4	5	6	7	8	9	10
F	T	T	T	T	F	T	T	T	T

INDEX